MARGARET HILLIS

UNSUNG PIONEER

MARGARET HILLIS
UNSUNG PIONEER

CHERYL FRAZES HILL

Edited by
Dr. Carroll Gonzo

GIA Publications, Inc.
Chicago

Margaret Hillis: Unsung Pioneer
Cheryl Frazes Hill

Copy edited by Bryan Gibson
Layout and Design by Martha Chlipala

G-10563
ISBN: 978-1-62277-599-6

GIA Publications, Inc.

Copyright © 2022 GIA Publications, Inc.
7404 South Mason Avenue
Chicago, IL 60638
www.giamusic.com

DEDICATION

To my parents, of blessed memory.

TABLE OF CONTENTS

PART I

PART II

──────── PART III ────────

──────── PART IV ────────

PREFACE

I wouldn't say I was close to Margaret Hillis. That circle was quite small. However, she was a part of my life for twenty-two years. During my first eight years as a member of the Chicago Symphony Chorus, my interactions with Ms. Hillis were at a distance. Only during my annual re-audition would I have any conversation with her, and it was brief. After being invited to conduct several pieces on one of the Margaret Hillis Fellowship Fund Concerts, we spoke more frequently and soon thereafter I was invited to be part of her conducting staff. In the years that followed, we would meet often, discussing music, schedules, seating charts, and Chorus business. There grew a greater familiarity between us. She was respectful, encouraging, generous, and often humorous, particularly after a long eight-hour stint of listening to Chorus auditions together. We lived in close proximity to one another and on several occasions she came to my home for lunch, insisting she could not leave before seeing my cats. During these times, I occasionally caught a glimpse of her more personal side, but never did I presume that our relationship crossed over into a friendship.

In the final few years of her life, my visits became more frequent. I would arrange to stop by on my way home from teaching at Northwestern University. Even in those final years, I made sure we had an agenda, typically in the form of score study, however the lessons often turned into lighter conversations. It was a far cry from the days when my visits were of a more pressing nature. Back then, we would meet in the second-floor office of her stately home, seated opposite one another at a massive glass-covered desk, in a sunlit room surrounded by windows overlooking

11

a tree-filled yard. The ambiance of the room took the edge off of intense, fact-filled discussions, where she would meticulously describe her expectations for music I was to rehearse for an upcoming concert series. The conversations were organized, detailed, and clearly conveyed. She always made time for my questions. I never felt rushed, but I was keenly aware of how busy she was and never overstayed my visits.

Our meetings during her final years were held at her dining room table on the main floor instead of the upstairs office. She could no longer easily manage the stairs. Despite the constant hum of oxygen tanks and yards of plastic tubing to which Margaret was connected, our meetings were less formal, though never completely relaxed. We would look at a full score of Handel's *Messiah* for a while, focusing on the analysis, transitions, hand gestures, and rehearsal approach, and then the discussion would evolve into a wonderful story from her past. I interrupted her during one of those digressions, urging her to consider writing a book about her life. She had so much to share—such a full life she had lived. Her response was that she hoped instead to write about her methods of score study and rehearsal strategies. It was never about her—she was always focused upon sharing her knowledge, believing it would best ensure the sustenance of polished choral performances— that was to be her legacy. She never digressed from that mission, even as her life was drawing to an end. I addressed her as Ms. Hillis for most of our years together. Only after she suggested I call her Margaret did I do so—and that was never really comfortable for me.

How does one write a biography such as this, knowing Margaret Hillis as I did? The answer is—with tremendous support. That support began first and foremost through my access to Margaret's vast personal collection of music and memorabilia housed in the Rosenthal Archives of the Chicago Symphony Orchestra Association. A little more than a year prior to Hillis's death, Frank Villella, then an assistant archivist for the Chicago Symphony Orchestra (CSO) and a member of the Chicago Symphony Chorus, heard through Tina Laughlin, Hillis's administrative assistant beginning in 1995 (and a former classmate of Frank's at DePaul University), that Margaret had started contemplating where her impressive private collection of music and memorabilia should ultimately reside. Frank passed this information along to Brenda Nelson-Strauss, the founding director of the archives, who in turn spoke with Martha Gilmer, then the CSO's vice president for artistic planning and a longtime friend and colleague of Hillis. Understanding the significance of Hillis's thirty-seven-year affiliation with the Chicago Symphony Orchestra and Chorus, Martha initiated the introduction of Nelson-Strauss to Hillis. Over lunch at Margaret's home, Brenda described the archives—likely unfamiliar to Hillis as it was still relatively new—and that collections held included those of founder and first music director Theodore Thomas and second music director Frederick Stock, among many others. Also, materials in the archives were routinely accessed by scholars, musicians, students, and countless other individuals researching the organization's history. Brenda encouraged Hillis to consider that her collection deserved to ultimately be a part of this impressive and historically significant repository. Soon after that meeting, Margaret looked no further and agreed to donate her collection to the CSO.

Shortly after Hillis died in February 1998, Jane Samuelson, longtime partner of Hillis, invited Brenda and her staff to come to the house and sift through thousands of bequeathed items to select what they wanted for both the archives and the music library. Over one hundred boxes were shipped to Symphony Center in May 1998, and the Margaret Hillis collection in the Rosenthal Archives was established. Several hundred unmarked scores and sets of parts were also transferred to the music library for potential future use. The collection was initially organized by several members of the Rosenthal Archives staff, including Brenda Nelson-Strauss, Alison Hinderliter, Andrea Cawelti, and Frank Villella. By the fall of 2002, Villella was the sole employee in the archives, and he soon engaged interns Andrew Lyon and Jennifer Ward to further organize and catalog Hillis's collection of marked scores and orchestral parts. In 2009, Villella reached out to James Yarbrough, a tenor of many years with the Chicago Symphony Chorus, who volunteered to further organize and catalog the enormous collection in a way that would make the items accessible for future research. Items included study charts, schedules, concert reviews, magazine and newspaper articles, interview transcripts, personal and professional correspondences, contracts, scrapbooks, awards, dissertations, financial spreadsheets, meeting minutes, photographs, repertoire lists, choral workshop materials, programs, videos, recordings, and other personal items.

Yarbrough completed his organization of the collection in 2012. It was around this time that Frank Villella invited me to a meeting. With the newly organized artifacts of the Margaret Hillis collection now available, Frank suggested I consider writing Margaret Hillis's biography, reminding me that Hillis's centennial would be celebrated in October 2021. At the time of our meeting, Frank was still a member of the Chicago Symphony Chorus—hired by Hillis in 1992—and he knew of my longtime affiliation with Hillis and the Chorus. Much credit goes to Frank Villella, whose suggestions fostered the acquisition of the Hillis collection and the idea of a book to be written about her, utilizing these newly catalogued resources.

My first step after agreeing to take on this project was to spend the next several years carefully exploring the archival collection. There were many hundreds of artifacts to read and process. It was during this time I also embarked upon a series of interviews. The first of these involved members of Hillis's family. This was a good place to start in order to gain a better understanding of Margaret Hillis from those who knew her personally. My first meeting was with Jeff Hillis, a nephew with whom Margaret was very close. Shortly thereafter, James Yarbrough joined me in a visit to Culver, Indiana, for an interview with Jeff's parents, the former United States Congressman Elwood "Bud" Hillis (one of Margaret's brothers) and his wife Carol. Jim brought along some of the family photos from the Hillis collection to share with Bud and Carol. It was a day filled with laughter, reminiscences, and a guided tour of the town where the Hillis family enjoyed their summers growing up. Upon first welcoming us into their home, Bud quipped, "I was a Republican, Margaret was a Democrat, and that is the end of the story!" We laughed but I could not help noticing his eyes briefly welling up with tears. I would come to learn that although the Hillis family was not overtly warm, it was clear how deeply Bud loved and admired his sister. My visits with Jeff, Bud, and Carol Hillis marked the beginning of many interviews to follow that would help reveal a side of Margaret Hillis I had not known but that somehow seemed familiar.

On several occasions, I traveled to Kokomo, Indiana, Margaret's hometown, where I explored materials in the Elwood Haynes Museum and the Howard County Historical Society. The Hillis/Haynes family was prominent in Kokomo, and these museums were a tremendous resource of Margaret's family history. With the generous assistance of curators in both locations and with the continuous guidance of Frank Villella and his thorough knowledge of CSO history, the puzzle pieces of Margaret's life began coming together. Through the sum total of all that was gathered in archival materials, interviews, and in Margaret's own recorded words, her story would unfold.

Margaret Hillis wanted to write her book about choral methods. Much has been written over the years about her approach to score study, rehearsal techniques, and physical gesture. There are resources at the end of this book to direct the reader to those important publications. The intention of this book is to share Margaret Hillis's story, a revealing and impressive journey to becoming the influential figure who continues to impact musicians today. There is much to be learned from Margaret's eventful life. What I know for sure is that she had a story worth telling.

ACKNOWLEDGMENTS

I am deeply indebted to so many people who supported my efforts during the research and writing of this book. A project like this is not a singular achievement. My first acknowledgment goes to a mentor of many years, Carroll Gonzo. Dr. Gonzo is a distinguished professor of music education and research and has served on a number of university faculties during his illustrious teaching career. He is the longest serving editor of the ACDA's *Choral Journal* from 1999–2013 and has served as a professional copy editor for GIA Publications. Dr. Gonzo and I first met when he was my advisor and professor during my undergraduate years at the University of Illinois, and he has been a source of constant support since that time. Through his guidance, I was able to construct the framework upon which to build this story, and most importantly he helped me find my voice. His involvement throughout this process has been indispensable.

I am deeply grateful to James Yarbrough, an important contributor to my book writing process. His detailed knowledge of the massive Margaret Hillis collection was invaluable. Jim would direct me to specific articles, interviews, recordings, and correspondences that he knew would be important to consider in the telling of Margaret's story. He also facilitated important connections for my initial interviews with Hillis family members, old friends, and even with a former member of Margaret's New York Concert Choir during the 1950s. I am so grateful for Jim's tireless work to organize the Margaret Hillis collection and in all his assistance from the beginning of my process.

The support of the Chicago Symphony Orchestra Association (CSOA) was paramount to my successful completion of this project. As mentioned, Frank Villella, director of the Rosenthal Archives, was the driving force, first inviting me to write this book and then providing me unlimited access to archival materials. Much heavy lifting, both literally and figuratively, was involved, including his frequent transporting of heavy boxes filled with archival documents, to accommodate my research. He also served as a wonderful editor. Phillip Huscher, program annotator and scholar-in-residence for the Chicago Symphony Orchestra, and colleague for over thirty years, has been a constant source of encouragement and support. As he continues working on his book, a history of the Chicago Symphony Orchestra, he has guided me by his example, providing wonderful advice and encouragement. My dear friend and colleague Dr. Donald Horisberger has been with me throughout this journey. Don and I, both associate conductors under Duain Wolfe and Margaret Hillis, have many shared experiences through the years, which we would speak of often during my writing process. His reflections and insights have been a great gift.

Chicago Symphony Chorus (CSC) Director Duain Wolfe must also be acknowledged. His decision to maintain Margaret Hillis's conducting staff when he was first appointed as her successor is what has enabled me to remain a part of the Chicago Symphony Chorus family for forty-five years. I am deeply indebted for his support of this project and for bringing the Chorus to new heights through his vision and leadership. Former CSOA president Deborah Rutter granted initial permission for this project and current CSOA president Jeff Alexander continued that support to its completion. Many of the beautiful photographs in this book were facilitated in part by the Chicago Symphony Orchestra photographer and longtime family friend Todd Rosenberg. I am so grateful for his artistry. I am very fortunate to work with so many incredible colleagues, the talented singers of the Chicago Symphony Chorus, many who have become dear friends sharing cherished memories together. The dedication of these extraordinary singers is what makes the Chicago Symphony Chorus a premier ensemble in the tradition of excellence that was established by Margaret Hillis and continues today.

Roosevelt University's Chicago College of Performing Arts (CCPA) provided tremendous support throughout this project. Thanks to the former CCPA dean Mr. Henry Fogel, the current dean Dr. Rudy Marcozzi, former associate dean Dr. Linda Berna, and my colleagues who took on some of my teaching responsibilities during my research leaves. I thank Dr. Wesley Brewer, Dr. Daniel Healy, Mr. Mark Crayton, Ms. Judy Moe, Ms. Leslie Manfredo, John Goodwin, Gabriella Klotz, and my wonderful students and colleagues at CCPA. I would be remiss if I did not mention an incredible resource on our Roosevelt University Performing Arts library staff, Ms. Anita Hwang. She became a research assistant and a detective of sorts, tracking down some of the most obscure newspaper articles based on truncated information from Margaret's scrapbooks, typically void of a specific date, author, or newspaper title. Anita's expertise contributed greatly to my acquisition of important references for the book.

Tremendous generosity was shown by so many people who knew Margaret Hillis professionally or personally and were so willing to share their recollections. Their interviews were invaluable to constructing a true picture of Margaret's life. I am particularly grateful to Margaret's brothers, Bud and Joe; nephews Jeff, Stephen, and Gregory; sister-in-law Connie; and Margaret's longtime partner, Jane Samuelson, for sharing such candid and personal memories. Dr. Elizabeth (Bettie) Buccheri was also a tremendous source of information, someone who was not only a close musical collaborator as the longtime CSC accompanist, but also one of Margaret's closest friends. Another of Margaret's friends of many years, composer and conductor Dr. Alice Parker, was extraordinarily generous in her recollections. Ms. Parker was Margaret's classmate at Juilliard, and both enjoyed a lasting friendship. Ms. Parker shed much light on Margaret's early years in New York, a time that would otherwise have been difficult to reconstruct. I am deeply indebted to Dr. Parker for her insights and advice. I am extremely grateful to all those who were interviewed for this book.

I am also grateful to the Milwaukee Symphony Orchestra and Chorus. As the conductor of the Milwaukee Symphony Chorus, I am now better able to understand Margaret Hillis's role as the director of a symphony chorus, very different than my role has been as an associate conductor. The challenges and the rewards of this position can be best understood only when one assumes this appointment. Members of the Milwaukee Symphony Chorus have generously shared their recollections of their first Milwaukee Symphony Chorus director, Margaret Hawkins, who was a close friend to Margaret Hillis. The "Margarets" referred to each other as "Margaret of the North" and "Margaret of the South." The Milwaukee Symphony Chorus and the Chicago Symphony Chorus continue very much in the likenesses both "Margarets" established. Their legacies live on through these fine symphony choruses.

I am deeply grateful to Alec Harris, president of GIA Publications. His willingness to publish this book and his patient support over a period of years, allowing me to take the time needed to complete this book, were invaluable. Alec has exhibited great enthusiasm for the importance of Margaret's story to be told. I am deeply appreciative of Alec's support throughout this process. I also wish to acknowledge GIA's excellent copy editor, Bryan Gibson, whose contributions and advice in the final stages of bringing this book to completion were incredibly valuable.

I am thankful to my friends and family who have remained supportive for all the years of this endeavor. My good friend Dr. Ramona Wis, a distinguished choral professor and author of *The Conductor as Leader*, has been encouraging from the time I embarked upon this project. Ramona's valuable advice has provided me continued guidance along the way. Other dear friends in my life, many who have nothing whatsoever to do with the music world, patiently listened as I shared my progress with a book they may have believed would never get written.

At the heart of my support system has been my incredible family. My dear sister Bobbi Frazes Goldman has been a part of this endeavor from its inception. Bobbi was a longtime member of the Chicago Symphony Chorus and was able to contribute her valuable perspective. It has been very special to share this journey with her. The sacrifices one's family makes during the writing of a book are substantial. I owe abundant thanks to my wonderful husband Dr. Gary Hill, and to our incredible children Carly and Mitchell, who all became accustomed to me being often consumed by this project. I love you and I thank you for always supporting my passions.

Finally, I am thankful to Margaret Hillis. She changed so many lives with her dedication, her talent, and her vision. I know she changed my life. She was my mentor. I am so fortunate to have worked so closely with this amazing woman. It is the honor of a lifetime to be able to tell her story, one she deserves to have told. I am deeply grateful to her and to all who have helped make this book possible.

PART I

INTRODUCTION

On the morning of November 1, 1977, *The New York Times* headline story gripped the attention of a city and the nation. Magical events of the night before, in New York City, landed Margaret Hillis squarely in the center of a journalistic feeding frenzy. The story—a *woman* saved the night at Carnegie Hall. A sold-out crowd bore witness to Margaret Hillis stepping in for an ailing Sir Georg Solti with little advance notice to conduct over three hundred musicians of the Chicago Symphony Orchestra and Chorus through Mahler's epic Symphony No. 8. Moreover, she did so *without a rehearsal*. Why would this story have made the headlines? Why such interest? Conductors have been replaced at the eleventh hour before, even in such prestigious venues as Carnegie Hall. Surely Hillis was not exceptional in that regard. Nonetheless, had any of those replacement conductors been female? The answer is NO. Margaret Hillis became an overnight sensation after twenty-five years in the music business, remaining, most of that time, in the background, despite her stellar work displayed regularly on center stage. For most of her career, Hillis was part of a supporting cast, rarely acknowledged by more than a curtain call, as audiences focused their admiration on the conductor and the musicians of the performance. On October 31, 1977, this would all change when Margaret Hillis cast her spell over a transfixed audience. She came out from the shadows and onto Carnegie Hall's center stage to lead her musical family.

Make no mistake. There was nothing overnight about Hillis's success. She came to this moment after years of preparation, and when the time arrived, Miss Hillis was ready. However, it was not her accomplishment as a conductor that was central to this headline story. It was Hillis, the *woman* that made this a newsworthy feature:

"Woman Steps in for Solti, Wins Carnegie Hall Ovation."[1] Had Margaret been a man, the story may have appeared on a different page of the paper, as it did for other conductors who stepped in as replacements in years past—not as a headline but a good story, nonetheless. Impressively accomplished on Halloween night, 1977, this concert was not conjured by "witchcraft"; it was instead made manifest by Hillis's solid performance, conducted as a seasoned pro. Years of study, struggle, and determination brought her to this moment. Approaching the podium, she was about to begin one of the most dramatic performances in Carnegie Hall history. In just over eighty minutes of conducting, Margaret Hillis had done more for women conductors than had been previously accomplished in all the years prior. Hillis became a champion of female conductors everywhere, yet for this achievement and many more she contributed to the field of music, she remains overlooked today.

There are countless legendary music figures whose vast contributions are continually lauded by generations of listeners and performers. Arturo Toscanini, Maria Callas, Ludwig van Beethoven, Leontyne Price, Leonard Bernstein, and Fritz Kreisler come to mind—still respected and admired today. Less well known, but equally worthy of remembering, are the great musicians of the choral world. In that category, the name evoking the greatest recognition is renowned conductor Robert Shaw. The one-hundredth anniversary of his birth was commemorated in a movie of his life, in choral concerts memorializing his music making, in journal articles, in books, and in many other illustrious accolades celebrating his substantial contributions to the choral art. There is no doubt that Shaw was the founder of a movement, one that changed the nature of choral ensembles from volunteer gatherings into the professional league of music making. Deservedly, in recent years, so much has been said of Shaw that his name and legacy remain current for today's generation of musicians. The same, however, cannot be said for one of Shaw's most accomplished conducting students, Margaret Hillis, who, as with Shaw, had an equally significant impact on the choral field and an even greater impact within the larger music scene. Not only did Margaret Hillis continue to carry forward Shaw's ideas, she also went on to forge her own inimitable path, establishing a teaching and conducting model for professional symphonic choruses. Consequently, she opened doors previously closed to the women who wanted a conducting career. She would also become a champion for paying singers a decent wage, particularly in choral ensembles, so they too could make a living as performers. Her conducting prowess, administrative and organizational genius, and cultural *élan* provided choruses, female conductors, and singers with a newfound level of respect, which produced increased opportunities for them all in the world of professional music. Her service work for the music profession through her workshops and institutes, choral foundation, and in her many active roles with organizations, including Chorus America and the National Endowment for the Arts, continues to impact the music industry today. Nevertheless, it is becoming harder to find those up-and-coming musicians who recognize her name, *vis-à-vis* that of Robert Shaw. Could it be that this is yet another example of gender bias? Perhaps.

Who Was Margaret Hillis?

Margaret Hillis (1921–1998) was a dreamer. From her youngest recollection, she envisioned herself becoming an orchestral conductor. However, society had other plans for her. Hillis's aspiration was not an option for women of her generation. Unable to pursue a direct route for her desired career, she was advised to find her way to the podium through the "back door"; that is, she opted to pursue *choral* conducting instead. That choice ultimately enabled her to make a name for herself as the founder and director of the Chicago Symphony Chorus, to this day one of the world's finest ensembles of its kind. Hillis's symphony chorus set a standard of excellence for choral ensembles to follow. From her early years in New York City, to her career with the Chicago Symphony Orchestra, and throughout her hundreds of guest appearances, Hillis impacted generations of musicians and set the direction of the choral scene in America and beyond. During Hillis's journey to become the conductor of this elite symphonic chorus, her many contributions to the field were born.

When Margaret Hillis first embarked upon her studies of choral conducting, the field was in a nascent stage of development compared to orchestras. Coming from almost no vocal training and having had no choral performing in her musical background, this chosen path carries even greater significance. Her life, until studying with Robert Shaw at The Juilliard School, had revolved around orchestral music. Changing her focus to a choral conducting career meant starting over. It meant learning new repertoire, new rehearsal techniques, and acquiring a thorough understanding of the vocal instrument. Shaw was helpful in setting her on the right path with his own revolutionary way of working with choruses, but he did not *teach* his methods to his conducting students directly. Even under his significant pedagogical and musical influence, Hillis found support severely lacking in her quest for choral rehearsal strategies, score study methods, and in finding quality choral literature. Hillis found herself inventing her own one-of-a-kind methods, many of them formulated out of necessity, as she began working with her own choruses. Through her experiences as a budding conductor, she developed and chronicled innovative methods for overcoming the challenges she experienced so that she could share them with others. Many were eager to know how they might replicate her consistently exquisite choral performances. She would dedicate her life to educating others, sharing all she had discovered in her career journey.

Hillis's hallmark became her precisely detailed and systematic way of organizing, preparing, and cultivating choruses in order to maintain a high level of musicianship and performance that would be viewed as equal to the professional symphony orchestras of the times. She moved choral singing, and particularly symphonic choral performance, into the professional league of music making by demanding the highest standards of those she directed. As one of her choristers reminisced, Hillis would often remark, "You are not singers; you are musicians who happen to sing."[2] This biography will provide a glimpse into the exacting methods Hillis developed that are still employed today by the most respected chorus masters.

The Margaret Hillis Effect

Of equal importance to *what* Hillis accomplished is *how* she was able to achieve all that she did, in a way that left her followers with a deep sense of gratitude and admiration for her. When one asks her colleagues, singers who performed under her direction, students who were mentored by her, instrumentalists who played in her orchestras, or conductors who trained in her conducting workshops what it was like to work with Margaret Hillis, the same wistful and heartfelt responses were conveyed: Margaret Hillis "changed our lives." What was it about her that generated such feelings of gratitude, respect, and loyalty? Can the above attributes be characterized in such a way for others to follow? As is the case with other legendary figures, Margaret Hillis was a singular presence, one that cannot be replicated. However, the formula of innovation, determination, and generosity that helped her invent new ways of doing things while influencing those around her can serve as a model for others to follow.

26

To better understand what Hillis was able to accomplish, it is important to explore her life in the context of this time and place in the country's history. Her success story is not, as some may believe, simply a matter of being in the right place at the right time. Quite the opposite. Her tireless work and devotion to raising her field can be chronicled in stories of struggle and personal sacrifice. Though one cannot recreate her life's story, one can learn from the leadership model she developed, greatly influenced early on by a rich family history. An examination of her story will reveal much about how history and personality coalesce in the most magical ways for those very special people who ultimately make a difference in the world. Margaret's story is an inimitable example of what it takes to be "one of the greats" in any field, far beyond the act of music making. The life journey Margaret Hillis undertook, as a woman of the 1940s, is an example of how insurmountable challenges can be overcome.

Margaret Hillis was able to forge a path on which few women had dared to tread. In the 1940s, women were rarely hired to play in orchestras, were given limited opportunities to serve as concert soloists, and were virtually non-existent in professional conducting—Hillis's chosen field. Added to this complexity was the fact that Margaret Hillis was pursuing choral music, a less respected genre at that time even with Shaw's improvements in choral ensembles. Choruses were viewed as an amateur "sport" in professional music circles. Fighting the good fight on two fronts, Hillis sought to break the barrier for women conductors while raising the standards of choral performance. Margaret Hillis was a pioneer, an apt description considering this same label was bestowed upon one of America's first automobiles, invented by Margaret's famous grandfather Elwood Haynes. Hillis's own indomitable spirit proved to be the force behind every goal she achieved. Hers was a life filled with great success, though at times she endured great disappointments. Her fascinating journey must be explored, simply because her legacy is one that generations of musicians and patrons continue to enjoy.

In the current age of women breaking more glass ceilings than ever before, it seems there are still some professions, including music, that remain constructed of shatter-resistant plexiglass. Not only does the struggle continue for talented women in some areas of music such as conducting, but also too does the challenge continue for those women who, despite their musical achievements, remain overlooked by history. Margaret Hillis should enjoy the same recognition alongside many other eminent musicians who have left their mark. Margaret Hillis's contributions remain a relevant part of the music world today and should not be forgotten. The secret to her success was a complex aggregate of her personality, vision, persistence, and talent. Her journey is as significant as her accomplishments. Daniel Barenboim, with whom Hillis worked during his years as ninth music director of the Chicago Symphony Orchestra, said it best in his sentimental reflection sometime after her passing: "Margaret has left a legacy that is unparalleled. She was a visionary. She saw a void and filled it with voices."[3]

ENDNOTES

1. Donal Henahan, "Woman Steps in for Solti, Wins Carnegie Hall Ovation," *The New York Times*, November 1, 1977.
2. Author's recollection.
3. John Dempsey, "Grandchildren Keep Haynes' Prolific Spirit Alive," *Kokomo Tribune*, October 14, 2007.

CHAPTER 1

THE HAYNES/HILLIS FAMILY LEGACY

To understand how Margaret Hillis was able to influence so much progress in her field, it is important to start at the beginning. One must only look to the family from whence she came. Hillis was by no means first in her family's history to achieve greatness. Notable was the Haynes/Hillis legacy containing generations of ambitious and accomplished personalities, particularly within the Haynes's heritage. The Haynes family (on Margaret's mother's side) is rich with stories of its members setting lofty goals for themselves, fulfilling their visions impressively through many generations. Glimmers of Margaret's ambition can be seen in distant relatives, some of the earliest settlers of this country, whose ability to succeed was readily apparent. Walter Haynes, his wife, and five children were among the first to settle New England's Massachusetts Bay Colony from Wiltshire England in 1638. They became a prominent family of this newly settled region. As descendants of this pre–Revolutionary War family, Margaret and her mother demonstrated their pride for family history, sustaining memberships in the exclusive National Society of the Colonial Dames of America. The Haynes family name became synonymous with careers in teaching, law, civic engagement, and in many other forms of leadership. These career choices would continue through many generations, including that of Margaret and her siblings.

ELWOOD HAYNES

Generations after the Walter Haynes family, from which Margaret's mother descended, other traits are revealed that Margaret would inherit. Haynes women were particularly remarkable in their quiet strength and accomplishment. Known for their independence, Haynes women made their mark through community service. Margaret's maternal great-grandmother, Hilinda Sophia Haynes (April 5, 1828–May 11, 1885) was one example, serving as a founder of the local Women's Christian Temperance Union. Hilinda and her husband, the highly respected Judge Jacob March Haynes (April 12, 1817–February 25, 1923) were considered some of Portland, Indiana's "most distinguished citizens"[1] (Picture 1).

Picture 1.

Judge Jacob March Haynes (1817–1923), father of Elwood Haynes, great-grandfather of Margaret Hillis. (Margaret Hillis Collection, Rosenthal Archives of the Chicago Symphony Orchestra Association)

Together, Margaret's great-grandparents, Hilinda and Jacob, often referred to by his middle name, "March," raised eight children, the fifth of whom, Elwood, would become one of America's most significant inventors. In Elwood Haynes we see so much of who Margaret Hillis was to become. Born in Portland, Indiana, on October 14, 1857, Elwood Haynes followed an extraordinary path, often worrisome to his family. Considered the "black sheep" of the Haynes family, Elwood was often the subject of conversation among his distinguished father and the Haynes children. According to Margaret's brother Elwood (named after his grandfather and nicknamed "Bud"), the Hillis family, in later years, "used to laugh because there were . . . discussions about how they [the Haynes family] would all have to take care of [Grandfather Elwood]," determining he would not amount to much.[2] Instead of studying practical subjects that would guarantee him future employment, Elwood dreamt about creating things. He loved science, often borrowing his sister's college textbooks to obtain ideas for his own scientific experiments, wreaking havoc in the process. He showed no interest in agriculture or other practical endeavors. Bud explained, "Grandfather wasn't interested in anything like that . . . metallurgy was his first love."[3] A great animal lover, Elwood spent many hours accompanied by the family dog, wandering about the heavily wooded acres of land surrounding his home, mulling over his clever ideas (Picture 2).

Picture 2.
Elwood Haynes in later years.
(Elwood Haynes Museum)

Ironically, all this curiosity in science did not translate into school success. His formal education briefly ended after grammar school. For a while, Elwood chose to focus on community and church activities. Known to have a fine tenor voice, Margaret's grandfather fortuitously joined his church choir where he became smitten by the talented church organist, Bertha Lanterman (February 28, 1858–August 31, 1933), who would eventually become Mrs. Elwood Haynes.

Before this marriage took place, Elwood returned to school, attending the Worcester Free Institute of Industrial Science in Massachusetts in 1878, where, among other things, he became active in the school glee club.[4] After graduating in 1881, Elwood came back to Portland, immediately pursuing a career in teaching. Recognized favorably among administrators for his teaching talent, Elwood was advanced to the position of principal at Portland High School. It was during this time that Elwood Haynes revealed his talent in musical composition, creating an original song for the school's graduation ceremony. The composition was displayed in the Elwood Haynes Museum with a date of 1881.[5] Haynes was considered an excellent teacher, presenting his lectures with clarity and with content so practical that students found his words to be immediately applicable and meaningful to their lives. "He endeared himself to his students both because of his devotion to the subject and his interest in teaching."[6] Elwood's love of teaching, his passion for the subject, his engaging manner of public speaking, and the clarity of his teaching style distinguished him in the classroom. These traits were later evidenced not only in Margaret's accomplishments, but also in the achievements of other Elwood Haynes's offspring.

Haynes's teaching career came to an end when natural gas was discovered in Portland, Indiana. This big news for his hometown piqued Elwood's ongoing scientific curiosities. He was a frequent visitor to the gas fields during the summer of 1885. Elwood, along with his father, became two of the initial shareholders of the Portland Natural Gas and Oil Company. By 1886, Elwood had resigned his teaching position, becoming the manager of Portland's newly formed Gas and Oil Company.[7] In this position, he was required to travel by horse and buggy throughout the state of Indiana. These challenging and often lengthy journeys motivated Elwood to ponder ideas for his first important invention. Because of his love for animals, he exhibited great empathy for his horses that routinely endured many hours of the work under harsh conditions. The solution: Haynes began his sketches for a horseless carriage.

"The great trouble [for] the horse was his lack of endurance and this became more apparent when he was driven day after day. I accordingly laid plans for the construction of a mechanically propelled vehicle for use on the highway."[8]

Elwood's position with the gas company marked the beginning of a new life. Bertha Lanterman, his sweetheart of ten years, became Mrs. Elwood Haynes on October 21, 1887. Bertha Lanterman Haynes was described as "a woman of composed and quiet spirit . . . utterly without ostentation."[9] She became well known for her generosity to those in need and she was philanthropic to a fault.[10] She supported Elwood as his career took on greater demands of his time, imposing changes upon their lives, which she graciously endured (Picture 3). In 1892, the ever-expanding gas business required Mr. and Mrs. Haynes to move away from family and friends; they settled in Kokomo, Indiana, where the Haynes/Hillis history is still celebrated today.

Picture 3.
Margaret Hillis's maternal grandmother and Elwood's wife, Bertha Lanterman Haynes.
(Elwood Haynes Museum)

It was in Kokomo that Elwood Haynes completed the plans for his "horseless carriage." Local mechanics Elmer and Edgar Apperson were hired by Elwood to build whatever he designed. The first trial run of "Haynes Original Car," later known as "The Pioneer," took place in Kokomo, Indiana, on July 4, 1894. In 1910, this vehicle, described by his daughter Bernice (Margaret's mother) as too dangerous to drive, was placed in the Smithsonian Institute.[11] As grandson Bud, Margaret's brother, explained, "The curator there told me the Smithsonian doesn't have a great number of [early automobiles]. But, he said 'we've tried to pick what are the most meaningful. . . . The reason they gave the Haynes car prominence . . . was because of its innovations"[12] (Picture 4).

Picture 4.
Elwood Haynes and his first Pioneer automobile invented in 1893, July 4, 1922.
(Elwood Haynes Museum)

"The Pioneer" took Haynes in a new direction. Elwood and the Apperson brothers formed the Haynes-Apperson Automobile Company in May 1898. Together they began manufacturing made-to-order vehicles. Though he continued his managerial work with the gas and oil company, Haynes regularly worked on design and promotion of his automobiles. It was not until his eventual split with the Appersons in 1901 that he resigned his position with the gas company, working full time for himself in the newly formed Haynes Automobile Company in 1898.[13] By 1908, the Haynes Automobile Company became one of the largest auto companies in the country.[14] Known for its luxury cars, Haynes attracted some very exclusive customers, including former United States President Theodore Roosevelt, who ordered a Haynes auto to be delivered to him personally in 1910.[15] Without the Appersons, however, Elwood Haynes was now responsible for managing the business end of his company, a duty he preferred leaving to others.[16] According to his daughter Bernice, "Father hated business, deciding who should do what. . . . He much preferred his research."[17] Margaret, as with her grandfather, preferred to immerse herself in her work, avoiding the business end of her profession whenever possible.

Tragedy struck the Haynes Automobile Company on February 28, 1911, when it burned to the ground in a massive fire. Haynes's actions reveal another character trait that would be passed down to future generations of the family, including Margaret. It was of utmost concern to Haynes that his hundreds of employees continue working despite this horrible setback. Fortunately for Haynes, just before the fire, the newly constructed cars had been stored in temporary structures outside the factory for an upcoming stock sale. That bit of luck saved many newly constructed cars from being burned in the fire. Haynes was able to modify those temporary structures into makeshift factory space so that car manufacturing could continue, thereby keeping all his workers employed. Haynes's compassion for his employees and his resilience in the face of a crisis resulted in the company's quick return to operation. Compassion and resilience would become traits of Margaret throughout her life. Elwood's business recovered and thrived until 1924, when a recession resulted in Americans no longer buying luxury cars. Sadly, the Haynes Automobile Company ultimately declared bankruptcy.

Never content with a singular focus, Elwood Haynes continually explored new ideas. All the while his automobile company flourished, he continued his developments in metallurgy. He eventually obtained a patent for his invention of Stellite, considered an indestructible metal superior to steel. First developed by Haynes in 1899, Stellite is important even today, its components used in modern jet engines and in NASA space rockets. Haynes continued his metallurgic explorations, discovering properties that improved stainless steel, with his patent in 1915, serving as the foundation of the American Stainless Steel Corporation. His Stellite Company, started in 1912, subsequently became a division of the Union Carbide Corporation, financially securing Haynes and future generations of his family. Despite the successes of Haynes's discoveries and businesses, his later years were plagued by court challenges involving his patents. He was saddled with continual financial burdens, falling victim to substantial personal debt, the result of frequent loans he generously provided to friends and business associates, of which few were ever repaid. The toll of his legal and financial challenges may have resulted in Elwood's premature death in 1925. Margaret's generosity with money as well as her willingness for others to handle her finances were traits no doubt also inherited from her equally trusting grandfather. Financial issues would also plague Margaret in her later life.

Elwood Haynes was a man of enormous vision, great wit, and charm. His interests, extending beyond the auto industry and metallurgical discoveries, included politics, community work, and the newly developing field of aviation. In an article he wrote for his October 1919 *The Haynes Pioneer*, he described his fascination with flight: "When the writer [he is speaking of himself] was invited to take a flight in a government plane . . . he accepted the invitation and entered the machine without apprehension or fear."[18] In the article he states: "There wasn't a disagreeable sensation in the whole ride."[19] As will be seen, the next generation of Haynes children and grandchildren were equally enthusiastic about flying, particularly Margaret, who no doubt inherited that adventurous side of her grandfather's personality along with a keen wit. In addition to flying, Haynes dabbled in politics with an unsuccessful bid for the United States Senate in 1916 (Picture 5).

Picture 5.
Elwood Haynes at a political rally when he ran for the United States Senate in 1916. Haynes can be seen standing in the upper left side of the photo. (Margaret Hillis Collection, Rosenthal Archives of the Chicago Symphony Orchestra Association)

He was equally philanthropic, giving of his time and financial support not only to his church, but also to local organizations, including the Kokomo Young Men's Christian Association (YMCA). Interestingly, one of Elwood's concerns in his work with the YMCA was the lack of a similar organization for girls, which prompted him to start a Young Women's Christian Association (YWCA) in town.[20] Revealed here is Elwood's interest in providing girls with equal opportunity. His dedication to this was apparent in the way he raised his only daughter, Bernice, who was to become an important part of his scientific discoveries and a role model of independence for his granddaughter. Margaret described her grandfather "as always having a smile on his face and a twinkle in his eyes."[21] He was a loyal family man remaining simple and unchanged, even as he grew in wealth and prominence. A teacher, a philanthropist, and a visionary, Elwood Haynes was undaunted by challenges he encountered along the way of building his successful path. This legendary Hoosier left a legacy of talent and drive that would reappear again and again in future Hillis/Haynes generations.

KOKOMO, INDIANA, IN THE EARLY 1920S

Margaret Hillis was born at a time of rapid change in Kokomo and in American history. World War I had just ended, giving rise to a decade of significant prosperity, followed by the stock market crash of 1929 and the Great Depression to follow. The country was changing socially, as witnessed by citizens becoming increasingly intolerant of immigrants, African Americans, Jews, and Catholics, thereby rejecting the diversity upon which America was founded. Few citizens of Kokomo were exceptions in these racist attitudes, as demonstrated by the town carrying their dubious distinction of holding the country's largest Ku Klux Klan rally in 1923. Neither Elwood Haynes nor his future son-in-law, Glen Hillis, would share these intolerant views nor did they shy away from denouncing such prejudices, despite the potential harm that could have been done to their political aspirations.

Another polarizing feature of America in the 1920s was the public consumption of alcohol. The Prohibition Era was in full force, particularly in Kokomo, where an active collection of Prohibition Party candidates, including Margaret's grandfather, would run for office against more liberal political parties. A headline in the *Kokomo Tribune* on the day of Margaret's birth, October 1, 1921, titled "Going After Arbuckle for Having Booz [sic]," exemplifies the enthusiasm of Kokomo prohibitionists for prosecuting one of their fallen citizens.[22]

Although the Roaring Twenties had found their way into the large metropolitan cities, Kokomo was still behind the political and social progressivism of the times. Margaret's grandfather and others gradually inched Kokomo forward through the growing industries of automobiles, washing machines, and other modern amenities that would make life easier than ever before. Along with the country's advancement of modern inventions, women were beginning to experience an evolution beyond their previously traditional roles, resulting in greater career opportunities. By 1920, fifty percent of all college-enrolled students were women, yet some colleges prevented them from joining campus organizations and restricted them to coursework deemed more appropriate for women, such as teaching. It was not acceptable for female college graduates to pursue a career while raising a family, which meant that college-educated women would ultimately have to choose one or the other.[23] Despite the continued efforts to limit career opportunities for educated women, there was progress in women's rights. Suffragists were finally successful after fifty years of effort in gaining the rights for women to vote when the Nineteenth Amendment was ratified in 1920. A new era was dawning for American women, even in the conservative Midwestern town of Kokomo. It is in this era, this town, and in this family that Margaret's musical interests, intellectual development, and independence were cultivated.

Endnotes

1. Ralph D. Gray, *Alloys and Automobiles: The Life of Elwood Haynes* (Indianapolis: Indianapolis Historical Society, 1979), p. 5.
2. John Dempsey, "Elwood's Innovation Known Universally: His Inventions Touch Our Everyday Lives," *Kokomo Tribune*, October 14, 2007, C6.
3. Ibid.
4. Gray, *Alloys*, p. 20.
5. The author viewed this composition on display in the Elwood Haynes Museum in 2013, however that composition has since been removed from the showcase and the current curators were unable to locate it during the return visit in 2021.
6. Gray, *Alloys*, p. 38.
7. Gray, *Alloys*, p. 42.
8. Gray, *Alloys*, p. 73.
9. "Passing Perfectly Tranquil, Example of Worthy Womanhood," Obituary, *Kokomo Tribune*, May 31, 1933.
10. Ibid.
11. Gray, *Alloys*, p. 74.
12. Dempsey, "Elwood's Innovation Known Universally," C6.
13. W. Spencer Huffman, *Elwood Haynes, 1857–1925*, Howard County Historical Society, Kokomo, Indiana.
14. Gray, *Alloys*, p. 111.
15. Ibid., p. 114.
16. Ibid., p. 110.
17. Ibid., p. 117.
18. Elwood Haynes, "The Evolution of the Aeroplane," *The Haynes Pioneer*, October 1919, p. 1.
19. Ibid., p. 16.
20. Gray, *Alloys*, p. 205.
21. Barbara Ford, "Margaret Hillis Unchanged by Fame," *Kokomo Tribune*, February 14, 1979, p. 7.
22. "Going After Arbuckle for Having Booz," *Kokomo Tribune*, October 1, 1921, p. 1.
23. Gail Collins, *America's Women: Four Hundred Years of Dolls, Drudges, Helpmates, and Heroines*, 1st ed. (New York: William Morrow, 2003), p. 294.

CHAPTER 2

THE HAYNES/HILLIS DYNASTY

Margaret Eleanor Hillis, born October 1, 1921, was the first child of the prominent Haynes/Hillis family. Margaret was the apple of her grandfather's eye. The first grandchild of Elwood Haynes, Margaret no doubt held a very special place in his heart (Picture 6). Though the Haynes family was already well known in Kokomo, thanks to Elwood's inventions, Margaret's parents were establishing themselves as impressive figures in their own right. Both well educated, Margaret's father, Glen Hillis, a successful school teacher and principal, was headed back to Indiana University in 1923 to study law, and Margaret's mother, Bernice—remarkably—had successfully earned a college degree in chemistry. As with so many other women of her generation, Bernice made the difficult choice of putting her career aside to raise her family, although it is hard to know how enthusiastically she embraced this decision. Throughout her childhood, Bernice had always been encouraged by her father to pursue her interests, participating in experiences that were not normally viewed as typical for girls. It must have been difficult for Bernice, raised to be an independent woman, to give up her career aspirations in order to support the ambitions of her husband, who was rarely home to share in the duties of the household. Here was a lady who had grown up in a life of privilege as a member of one of Kokomo's wealthiest families. She enjoyed copious and extraordinary experiences that included driving her father's horseless carriage from the time she was eight years old. She was welcomed into her father's chemistry laboratory and was nurtured to develop her own interest in science. Her active role in Elwood's discovery of Stellite is just one example of Bernice's impressive contributions. As early as 1910, thirteen-year-old Bernice was already gaining public recognition from her nationally published article describing how she first learned to drive a car and providing safety tips for future drivers.[1]

Picture 6.
Elwood Haynes with granddaughter, Margaret. This picture was taken on July 4, 1922, before a ceremony to honor Haynes. An official monument was made for the occasion: "In commemoration of Elwood Haynes of Kokomo, Indiana, the inventor, designer and builder of America's first mechanically successful automobile." Seven thousand people, including the world's leading scientists and inventors, attended the ceremony to dedicate this monument, only slightly visible in this photo, located to the left side of the car. The monument was placed at the site where the car took its first run at Pumpkinvine Pike, just outside of Kokomo. (Elwood Haynes Museum)

One of two Elwood Haynes's offspring, Bernice (December 17, 1892–June 26, 1976), was clearly the favorite. Her brother, March (January 1, 1896–January 14, 1968), named after their grandfather, Jacob March, was emotionally unstable, less capable of handling the Haynes dynasty, which may explain, in part, why Elwood invested so much support for his daughter's intellectual growth. Bernice was raised, some might say, as though she were a son. Close as she was to her father, Bernice did not share that same connection with her mother, Bertha, according to one of the Hillis grandchildren.[2] Although both Bertha and Bernice shared their common love of music, there was otherwise a lack of connection between them. Perhaps that lack of outward affection set the tone of formality that was pervasive in the Hillis household of Margaret's upbringing. Despite this absence of emotional connection from her own mother, Bernice enthusiastically nurtured the ambitions of her daughter from the time Margaret was very young. Bernice cultivated in Margaret a sense of propriety, discipline, a love for learning, and the expectation of achievement.

Margaret's father, Glen Hillis (December 9, 1891–October 19, 1965), came from a very different upbringing than his wife. He was raised on a farm, one of four boys and one girl. His parents were struggling farmers and money was scarce, requiring each member of the family to contribute financially from an early age. Glen learned early on about the value of a dollar and the meaning of hard work. After attending a small country elementary school outside of Kokomo, he entered Kokomo High School, where he first met Bernice. In one of his many summer jobs during those high school years, Glen got a taste of the good life, caddying for Kokomo's well-to-do at the local country club, located on the outer border of his family farm. Of course, Bernice was part of the society crowd that may have been an incentive for Glen's continued interest in her. They were high school sweethearts and remained "an item" during their respective college careers. Unlike Bernice, who had her father's financial support for her college education, Glen would regularly interrupt his studies at Indiana University, acquiring jobs in factories, construction, food service, and school teaching to subsidize his education. As Margaret's brother Bud explained, in those days you could teach school without a college certification, making it possible for Glen to finance his college education by teaching and administrative work.[3] Glen was driven to succeed. Margaret's youngest brother Joe described their father as having "dreams of glory" and wanting success and order in his life.[4] Glen had seen the challenges his family endured, barely able to support themselves, and was keenly observant of those who were more financially successful due in part to a college education. He wanted that success for himself, and he never faltered in his goal to become a respected member of society, pursuing a college education, becoming a successful lawyer, and eventually running for political office. The work experiences of his early life taught him empathy for the blue-collar worker and made him very popular with the average voting citizens he would eventually rely upon to advance his career. A *Kokomo Tribune* article described Glen this way,

"[N]ot afraid to get his hands dirty and the majority of his friends and acquaintances are men who are laboring men. He knows from experience the seriousness of the laboring man's problems. He has never permitted himself to become soft and can put in a day's hard labor today."[5]

This down-to-earth affability helped him along the way to his rising political career and would be passed along to his children as well.

Upon graduating in 1914, Glen returned to Kokomo, becoming a public-school principal, but only briefly in order to support his return to the university for a degree in law. His educational pursuit was again disrupted, not for financial reasons but instead by World War I. Glen enlisted and served in France with the famous Rainbow Division and was promoted to the rank of sergeant.[6] Two years after the war, he married Bernice Haynes on November 11, 1920, and once again returned to Bloomington to complete his law degree, this time with his wife and young daughter Margaret joining him. His demanding school schedule kept him in the library instead of at home with his young family. Bernice would later share with Margaret's brother Bud that their father was gone so much in those law school years, Margaret did not recognize Glen on rare days when he returned home while she was still awake. Bud mentioned a story his mother told them about Glen's law school residency when their father one day came home for lunch to a puzzled Margaret who inquired, "Who is that man in the house?"[7] (Picture 7). This pattern of absence would continue throughout the upbringings of Margaret and her brothers. Upon completion of his law degree, Glen and family returned to Kokomo, where he ambitiously pursued his career in law and in politics, while operating a 160-acre farm on the country home property they owned just outside Kokomo.

Picture 7.

Margaret Hillis at the age of three in Bloomington, Indiana, while her father was in law school, ca. 1924. (Margaret Hillis Collection, Rosenthal Archives of the Chicago Symphony Orchestra Association)

THE HILLIS FAMILY DYNASTY BEGINS

Glen's ambitions for a political career began in earnest not too long after he became an established lawyer. Describing her father as "a rock-ribbed Republican," which is another way of saying that he was uncompromising in his beliefs, Margaret would develop a more liberal political affiliation during her adult life.[8] Beginning in 1928, Glen made a successful run for Howard County's prosecuting attorney; however, his ambitious nature led to a failed bid for a United States congressional seat in 1932. Not deterred and still hungry for higher office, he was successfully nominated as the Republican candidate for Indiana governor in 1936, losing by the narrowest margin at that time in Indiana history. Throughout these early days of establishing his career and campaigning for public office, the Hillis family was growing. After Margaret in

1921 came brothers Elwood "Bud" on March 6, 1926; Robert "Bob" on June 29, 1928; and Joseph "Joe" on October 13, 1932. Bernice was often left to manage the ever-increasing duties at home.

Bernice's desire for outside intellectual stimulation eventually triumphed over these family obligations. She would leave the day-to-day child rearing and household responsibilities to hired help, enabling her to keep up with the duties of a political wife and to actively pursue her own interests, which centered around travel and the arts. Additionally, Bernice would become very involved in the family's church and in community affairs. She and Glen became active citizens of Kokomo, often featured in the socialite section of the local newspaper. Margaret would share the spotlight for her accomplishments, ranging from Girl Scout awards to musical performances. As Glen's political career grew, the Hillis children were each sent off to private schools away from home. All the Hillis children were groomed to be in the public eye and were expected to carry on the lifestyle of their civic-minded, conservative, Republican parents. During their formative years, Bud recalled his parents as "avid Republicans and anti–New Dealers," emphasizing this philosophy to the children throughout their upbringing.[9] Robert, the third of the Hillis children, spoke of many dinner conversations centering around world events.[10] Bud recalled gaining a broader understanding for opposing political views when he worked in various summer jobs during his high school years—views that did not necessarily jibe with the strong opinions of his parents. Bud explained his exposure to these opposing opinions while working on his uncle's farm and then at Continental Steel. In these jobs, he met workers who felt differently regarding what he was raised to believe about President Franklin D. Roosevelt and the politics of the day:

> That gave me a broader outlook on the world as a whole. I began to understand how things developed for many people during the Depression and how tough it was. I made the mistake one day of making an anti-Roosevelt statement to one of the workers. Instead of getting upset, he spent the rest of the summer educating me on why Roosevelt was a great man. That's when I learned there were two sides to issues and to look carefully at them.[11]

Bud's understanding of differing viewpoints would serve him well in his future as a lawyer and U.S. congressman. Bud remained respectful of his larger-than-life father but would grow to have a more moderate Republican stance. The youngest sibling, Joe, believed their father wanted a Hillis "dynasty," encouraging all his children into careers of law and business.[12] Margaret, Bud, and Robert pursued intellectually demanding careers, no doubt as a result of Glen's encouragement. Margaret later reflected that her career aspirations were attributed to her college-educated mother, a rarity in those days, and to her ambitious father, both setting the tone for what was expected of all in the Hillis household[13] (Pictures 8 and 9).

Picture 8.
Bernice Hillis with (*from left to right*) Robert "Bob" (b. 1928), Margaret (b. 1921), Elwood "Bud" (b. 1926), Joseph "Joe" (b. 1932), ca. 1937. (Margaret Hillis Collection, Rosenthal Archives of the Chicago Symphony Orchestra Association)

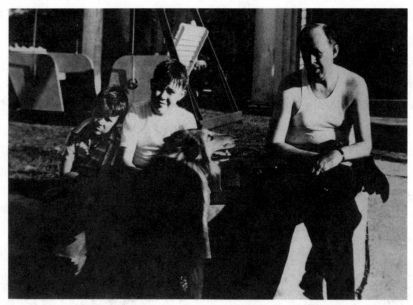

Picture 9.
Two of the Hillis sons, Joe on the left and Bob on the right, with their father and family dog.
(Margaret Hillis Collection, Rosenthal Archives of the Chicago Symphony Orchestra Association)

The Hillis family, though intellectually stimulating, was devoid of warmth and close personal connection.[14] Glen and Bernice were gone with greater frequency as the family increased in size. With both parents often away, there was little interaction with the children. If the Hillis children harbored resentment regarding their upbringing, it cannot be found in the interviews and reflections of either Margaret, Robert, or Bud. Only in the youngest, Joe, was there dismay expressed for this lack of affection.[15] Margaret described her family as eccentric by comparison to other families of that time in Kokomo.[16] Perhaps she was referring to the less conventional upbringing they experienced, with parents who left child rearing to others. Of the four children, it was the eldest Margaret who received the most attention from her mother. Bud jokingly observed: "Margaret was raised and the rest of us raised ourselves."[17] Joseph expressed frustration for what his upbringing lacked in emotional bonding. Joe described his mother and father as distant, never showing any outward expressions of affection to the children. He remembered a kiss from his mother only once, as he was getting ready to depart for college in California. He recalled "maybe ten hugs" and described his mother as rather prudish. He recounted a time they went to a Bob Hope movie when Hope kissed Dorothy Lamoure's neck below her ear, which elicited a disapproving and audible gasp from Bernice. Of his father, Joe recalled very little time spent together.

Only after Glen lost the gubernatorial election was Joe invited to spend time with his devastated father who was inconsolable by the loss. He was bedridden for months, the cause of which was an emotional breakdown. It was during this time that Joe remembered his father teaching him gin rummy, because Glen needed something to do and Joe was the only one around at the time.[18] Margaret spoke with the greatest fondness of her mother, particularly when relating the many adventures they shared. She spent more time with her mother one-on-one than did the other siblings, due in part to Margaret being fascinated, even at a young age, with music. Not only did Margaret's mother and maternal grandmother cultivate Margaret's love for music, but they also nurtured her sense of adventure, taking her on exotic trips. When Margaret was ten, she joined her mother and grandmother on a Mediterranean cruise. The cruise was scheduled to take place during Bud Hillis's fifth birthday. To make up for her absence on his birthday and just days before their departure, Bernice threw an extravagant birthday party for five-year-old "Buddy" at his school. The *Kokomo Tribune* described this party in elaborate detail, which included a beautifully decorated classroom, an Easter egg hunt for all the children, a birthday cake with ice cream, and a big Easter basket that was given to each child filled with colored eggs and candies as a souvenir of the day[19] (Pictures 10 and 11).

Picture 10.
Margaret Hillis and her mother seated on camels, enjoying an excursion to the Great Pyramid of Giza during their Mediterranean cruise in 1931. The iconic Great Sphinx of Giza can be seen in the background. Margaret was brought on this exotic trip with her mother and grandmother, Bertha, ca. 1931. (Elwood Haynes Museum)

Picture 11.
The three passport photos taken for the trip. Pictured here (*from left to right*) are Margaret,
Bernice, and Bertha. Their photos reveal the incredible resemblance of the three generations of
women. (Elwood Haynes Museum)

Margaret's mother exposed her to music from the time she was very young, encouraging her to excel as a musician. In later years, Bernice painstakingly chronicled Margaret's early concert work in New York and Chicago with incredibly detailed scrapbooks containing programs, reviews, and photographs of Margaret's early triumphs. Margaret, the favored child, was clearly a great pride and joy to Bernice. Despite this pride, affection was not openly expressed to Margaret or the boys and no doubt limited the way Margaret and her brothers would express their affection to their parents and to each other. It was easiest for Bernice to relate to Margaret since they could share their common love for music together. With the boys, who were not musically inclined despite her efforts, it would be less simple.

As will become evident later in this narrative, the lives of the Hillis children took interesting and varied paths, with each successive child choosing less and less to be in the limelight, but each became successively more emotionally accessible. Margaret's achievements as a Grammy Award–winning chorus director and as a leader in her field were followed by the equally impressive public achievements of Bud, a successful lawyer who would serve two terms as an Indiana State congressman before serving sixteen years as a United States congressman. Admired by several presidents, Bud was praised by Richard Nixon in a letter dated July 14, 1972: "You have a proven record of accomplishment and devotion to duty, one that only brings honor to the Republican Party, but also great credit to the people you serve."[20]

THE WASHINGTON POST *Friday, February 6, 1981* ··· R 1 A3

3,000 Sing 'Happy Birthday' To Reagan at Prayer Breakfast

By Marjorie Hyer
Washington Post Staff Writer

About 3,000 people, including members of Congress, the Cabinet, the Supreme Court, some state governors and many from the diplomatic corps, joined President Reagan yesterday morning at the annual presidential prayer breakfast to pray, sing hymns and offer the chief executive a rousing chorus of "Happy Birthday."

The president, who is celebrating his 70th birthday today, concluded the prayer session with a testimony of his own need for divine guidance. But first he thanked the gathering for the good wishes on the occasion of "the 31st anniversary of my 39th birthday."

Reagan said the occasion reminded him of gubernatorial prayer breakfasts he presided over in California. He said he was convinced God would sustain and help him over difficulties he will face as president. "If I did not believe that I could not face the days ahead," he said.

Evangelist Billy Graham spoke briefly to give the history of the prayer breakfast movement. The tradition, he said, dates to President Eisenhower. He recalled how Eisenhower, shortly after his election, "told a young preacher who came to call on him that he felt he was elected to help lead the nation in a spiritual renewal." The "young preacher" was Graham.

"Every president since 1954 has continued the tradition" of the massive annual prayer breakfast, Graham continued, and added that many state governors and some mayors have taken up the idea. "I believe the prayer breakfast movement has played a significant role in the revival of religious interest in America," Graham said.

The logistics of the presidential prayer breakfast are coordinated by a local, low-profile, evangelical Christian organization known as Fellowship House. One of the prime movers in that group is former U.S. senator Harold Hughes of Iowa. Prayer groups that meet weekly or monthly in both the House of Representatives and the Senate help to host the event. The breakfast is by invitation only.

Mayor Edward I. Koch of New York City worked in a quick commercial about his home town before he read the Eighth Psalm. New York, he said, is "a city of cultural and religious diversity . . . where mass is said each morning in 23 languages."

Vice President Bush read the familiar passage from the New Testament book of First Corinthians extolling a loving spirit, which begins: "If I speak with the tongue of men and of angels and have not love . . ."

In a brief message, Gov. Albert H. Quie of Minnesota gently deplored the national tendency to neglect the spiritual side of life. "We don't speak easily of spiritual matters," he said.

By Frank Johnston — The Washington Post
President, Mrs. Reagan pray. Mrs. Elwood Hillis, congressman's wife, is at right.

Picture 12.

Bud Hillis was respected by several presidents during his time as a U.S. congressman. In this photo, President and Mrs. Reagan are holding hands in prayer with Bud's wife, Carol Hillis, in Washington, D.C., on Reagan's seventieth birthday, February 6, 1981. Bud is next to Carol but not visible in this *Washington Post* picture, February 6, 1981. (Margaret Hillis Collection, Rosenthal Archives of the Chicago Symphony Orchestra Association)[21]

Bud and his wife Carol would also become close to President Ronald Reagan in later years (Picture 12). Bud was greatly respected among his peers and his constituents. The third sibling, Robert, was not interested in the fame of his father and older siblings. A more outgoing and emotionally accessible character, according to his son Rolden "Stephen," he chose instead to pursue a field much more in line with the interests of his mother and grandfather Elwood, pursuing a path in the sciences.[22] Robert worked as a chemist and as a metallurgist for Indiana companies before forming his own Hillis Engineering Company, where he designed commercial buildings in Kokomo. Robert's son spoke of his father as being warm, friendly, and forthcoming about his childhood, close to his children and openly expressive of his feelings.

It was the youngest of the Hillis siblings, Joseph, who took the most unorthodox path. A rebel child, Joe decided that unlike his brothers and sister, who all attended Indiana University, he would pursue his college experience at the liberal campus of

Stanford University. Joseph harbored great resentment for being "shipped off" to Culver Military School, as happened to both his brothers during their high school years. When it came time for college, he clearly was interested in forging a different path. To his good fortune, his first cousin Elwood "Woody" Haynes Jr., Bernice's brother March's only son, had decided to attend Stanford University, and it was on those coattails Joe was able to plead his case for a school other than Indiana University. Glen agreed to send Joseph to Stanford, where he remained after his schooling, adopting the liberal lifestyle of that time in northern California. Joe, unlike his other siblings, did not pursue a professional career. According to his first wife, Connie, Joe's life work has been teaching at a commune, the topic of which revolves around sex education. Unlike his brothers, who had long-lasting relationships, Joe has been married five times and is the father of three children from two different marriages.

Joe had a closer bond to Margaret than to his other siblings, which may be due to Margaret's role in Joe's younger years. Joe recalled Margaret as his designated babysitter, suggesting that his mother was "tired of kids" by this point, with almost ten years spanning the oldest and youngest of the children. Babysitting was not entrusted to the brothers, which turned out well for Joe who recalls having a great time with his big sister. Margaret and her best friend from high school would haul Joe around in the rumble seat of a car they drove all over Kokomo during the warm summer months. Joe referred to Margaret as his favorite of the siblings since she was his constant companion during those early years. Interestingly, Margaret and Joe would become the only Democrats in the family. Though Joe became estranged from the rest of the Hillis family, he communicated on and off exclusively with Margaret throughout their adult lives.

Margaret was the first born and, of all the children, the most obedient, restrained, and proper until she grew to an age where her adult desires and ambitions would lead to her own rebellion. Unlike Joe, Margaret was always able to keep her liberal thoughts, her personal desires, and her ambitions in balance, carefully "keeping the peace" as she moved forward with her life. She learned quickly how to navigate her life choices so that she could get what she wanted without rocking the boat unless absolutely necessary. Margaret kept her secrets, maintained her family connections, and was able to pursue her dreams with the support of her family. Her ability to keep things in check would serve her well in a profession in which women were not allowed to enjoy too much success. She was a "game changer," much to the credit of an upbringing that inspired great accomplishments.

ENDNOTES

1. Ralph D. Gray, *Alloys and Automobiles: The Life of Elwood Haynes* (Indianapolis: Indianapolis Historical Society, 1979), p. 112.
2. Interview with Rolden "Stephen" Hillis, June 5, 2014.
3. Interview with Elwood "Bud" Hillis, June 19, 2012.
4. Interview with Joseph "Joe" Hillis, April 21, 2014.
5. "G.O.P. Candidate for Governor," *Kokomo Tribune*, November 21, 1939.
6. "Glen R. Hillis," Obituary, *Kokomo Tribune*, October 20, 1965.
7. Interview with Bud Hillis.
8. Gary Panetta, "Classic by Brahms in Award-Winning Hands," *Journal Star Peoria*, September 6, 1992.
9. John Dempsey, "Elwood's Innovation Known Universally: His Inventions Touch Our Everyday Lives," *Kokomo Tribune*, October 14, 2007, C6.
10. Ibid.
11. Ibid.
12. Interview with Joe Hillis.
13. Panetta, "Classic by Brahms."
14. Interview with Connie Hillis, March 25, 2014.
15. Interview with Joe Hillis.
16. Panetta, "Classic by Brahms."
17. Interview with Bud Hillis.
18. Interview with Joe Hillis.
19. Society Page, *Kokomo Tribune*, March 6, 1931, p. 6.
20. Letter from President Richard Nixon to Elwood "Bud" Hillis (Howard County Museum).
21. Marjorie Hyer, "3,000 Sing 'Happy Birthday' to Reagan at Prayer Breakfast," *Washington Post*, February 6, 1981.
22. Interview with Rolden "Stephen" Hillis.

CHAPTER 3
THE EARLY YEARS OF MARGARET HILLIS

To whatever extent one looks at their childhood through rose-colored glasses, Margaret's earliest memories were conveyed through a series of wistful tales documented in numerous interviews she granted over the years. It may indeed be that those times in Kokomo were as blissful as she remembered, because her town—even today—feels like it could exist in a storybook, reminiscent of old television shows such as *The Andy Griffith Show* or *Lassie*. Although Margaret grew up at a time of extreme volatility in America's history, one would never know it. With the end of the Great War (World War I) in 1918, just prior to her birth, leading into the Roaring Twenties and then the Great Depression, her childhood stories were filled with music, outdoor adventure, and travel to exotic places. Margaret was able to pursue anything she pleased. The sky was her limit. Even as the country outside of her Kokomo cocoon turbulently evolved socially, politically, and economically, Margaret's hometown remained the same for just a little while longer, resisting the changes already evident in the larger urban centers surrounding it. Margaret's family enjoyed many of the modern conveniences still beyond reach of Kokomo's middle-class population. Margaret's family was elite, and with that status came the encouragement to dream big—and indeed that is what Margaret did (Pictures 13 and 14).

Picture 13.
Four-year-old Margaret sitting in her grandfather's car with Elwood's two dogs
(Elwood slightly visible behind her), ca. 1925. (Elwood Haynes Museum)

Picture 14.
Margaret seated on one of her grandfather's dogs at Elwood Haynes's home. Her love for animals
was nurtured by her grandfather who also loved animals, ca. 1923. (Elwood Haynes Museum)

Because of the family's wealth, Margaret did not suffer in the way of other Kokomo children during the Depression. Bernice instilled in her young daughter the importance of compassion and generosity, setting an example by serving those in need. Margaret recalled joining her mother on numerous occasions, delivering baskets of food and provisions to help those less fortunate during that difficult period. Bernice regularly demonstrated the traditional role as caretaker to her family and to the community, but she also revealed a fiercely independent streak, a trait that was not lost on Margaret. Such independence for a woman was less common in Kokomo but was slowly emerging throughout the United States. Women were beginning to demand greater opportunities to pursue work outside of the home. Bernice, like many other college-educated women, was caught up in the old rules of society where she was made to choose between her field of interest and her desire to marry and raise a family. It was an either/or situation in those days. But a movement was afoot in the United States to change the traditional roles for women who wanted both a family and a career. Along with opportunities in the workplace, women continued their campaign for equal rights in government representation. After many years of trying, women would finally have their voices heard, as the Nineteenth Amendment, which gave women the right to vote, was ratified just one year before Margaret's birth. This opened many doors for women, who would gradually start filling jobs that, until that time, had been available only to men. Margaret would become the beneficiary of this movement, allowing her to pursue aspirations in a way her mother could not.

Having the advantages of a wealthy few in Kokomo, Margaret was able to enjoy many of the family's assets. Among these was access to her grandparents' mansion, still standing today as the Haynes Museum located in the center of town (Picture 15). This magnificent home contained many modern amenities of the day, including a pipe organ that Elwood Haynes installed so that his wife Bertha, Margaret's grandmother, could practice for her performances in church and at various civic events. As Margaret reminisced about the Haynes family home, she shared one particular story her mother told her.

My mother tells me that when I was eight months old, I'd crawl out in the middle of that grillwork (the living room floorboards covering pipes of her grandmother's pipe organ housed in the basement) and would demand that something happen. And so Grandma would put this on [the organ] and I'd sit there [on the floorboards] and conduct [as her grandmother played the organ]. She said it was in time [to the music she was playing]. It seems a little outrageous to me but Mother said that happened, and she was a stickler for the truth.[1]

So it was that Margaret's love of music began.

Picture 15.
Home of Margaret Hillis's grandparents (Elwood and Bertha Haynes). Bernice donated it to the city of Kokomo in 1965 for the purpose of establishing it as the Elwood Haynes Museum. Located at 1915 South Webster, Kokomo, Indiana, Elwood Haynes had the house built in 1915. He lived here for ten years before he died in 1925. (Margaret Hillis Collection, Rosenthal Archives of the Chicago Symphony Orchestra Association)

Margaret's school years began at Kokomo's Washington School. She attended Wallace School, a little country schoolhouse outside of town, for the third and fourth grades, where she vividly recalled her daily rides on the school bus. When her parents moved the family back into town, she attended the much larger McKinley School, where Margaret remembered having many of the same teachers her parents had during their public-school education.[2] Margaret began piano lessons at the age of five. By the time she turned nine, Margaret added additional instruments to her music study, first learning the E-flat alto saxophone. The instrumental music teacher at McKinley recognized Margaret's talent and determined that she could help him make up for his lack of cellists in the school orchestra by having her play the cello parts on her saxophone. By the time Margaret was ten, she inherited her cousin's trumpet, which she would teach herself to play. Margaret confessed that during her music classes, she traded instruments regularly with other students when her teacher left the room, claiming this was how she learned to play the clarinet and oboe.[3] Margaret's brother Bud recalled, "[If] they needed a French horn, three weeks later she was a French horn player."[4] By the time she was in high school, Margaret could play twenty-three different instruments, often choosing to learn the ones most kids her age had no interest in playing.[5]

Margaret began a more formal study of music at a young age, taking lessons in music theory, ear-training, and composition from the Czech teacher Edward Turechek, a student of Antonín Dvořák. Margaret jokingly referred to herself as "a granddaughter of Dvořák."[6] She would take lessons every Saturday, after which Turechek formed a small orchestra of his eight students. In the summer of her eleventh year, she attended Petrie Music Camp at Lake Winona, recalling that she continued to play saxophone in the camp's band. The following summer, Bernice determined it was time for Margaret to have more rigorous training on the French horn, which Margaret had taught herself to play. Bernice arranged for Margaret to study the instrument with a professional player in the Indianapolis Symphony Orchestra. By the age of thirteen, Margaret's musical talents were regularly on public display at events hosted by her mother. Bernice routinely provided Margaret opportunities to perform in several of the clubs she hosted in their home, including the Delphian Reading Club and the Morning Musicale.[7] One event covered in the local paper advertised entertainment for the Howard County Women's Republican Club, which featured Margaret's great aunt, Mary Lanterman, a violinist, along with Margaret and her mother playing duets.[8]

Bernice diligently supported Margaret's growth as a musician, creating opportunities that only a well-to-do family could provide at a time of real financial strife for most families during the late 1920s and early 1930s (Picture 16).

Picture 16.
Margaret at age fifteen practicing piano at home.
(Margaret Hillis Collection, Rosenthal Archives of the
Chicago Symphony Orchestra Association)

Music was not the only interest Margaret pursued with gusto. She was extremely passionate about sports, including swimming, horseback riding, water skiing, ballet, tap dancing lessons, skating, and "anything that forces the body to coordinate in a rhythmic way [and is therefore] valuable to the musician."[9] She also loved playing basketball and baseball, claiming the boys in her grade school always wanted her on the team because she could hit home runs.[10] Her brother Bud admitted Margaret was by far the best athlete of all the Hillis children. He recalled Margaret hobbling around on a broken leg after falling off a horse, and yet she was able to kick a soccer ball to her brother with the other leg as powerfully as ever.[11] An avid golfer, she achieved the junior golf championship title at the age of sixteen, an event she associated with her first encounter in gender discrimination (Picture 17). In those days, she claimed women did not play golf. She recalled a man watching her drive a ball 275 yards when she knew he could only hit a drive about 150 yards, remarking, "Well, that's pretty good—for a girl. Constantly these kinds of slaps in the face."[12]

Picture 17.
Margaret was a terrific athlete, winning a championship title in the junior golf division as a teenager, ca. 1938. (Margaret Hillis Collection, Rosenthal Archives of the Chicago Symphony Orchestra Association)

It was the music that won out over her other varied interests. Even as the Hillis family was increasing in size with the births of Bud, Bob, and Joe, Margaret's mother continued cultivating her daughter's appreciation for music while pursuing her own in the process. Bernice would have Margaret join her on frequent trips to New York City, Chicago, and Indianapolis to enjoy the great performances of the day. After experiencing her first professional orchestra concert in 1930, Margaret decided she would one day become a conductor herself.[13] Margaret vividly recalled two performances during her youth that impacted her greatly. The first occurred when the Sousa Band visited Kokomo.

[John Philip] Sousa was dead by then and his assistant was conducting it. The assistant stayed in our home and my parents took me to the concert. And the sound just laid me out flat. I loved it! I just knew this was going to be my instrument, not the band but an orchestra.[14]

The other memorable experience occurred when Margaret was a teenager. Margaret and her mother attended a Chicago City Opera Company performance of Wagner's *Tristan und Isolde* at the Civic Opera House in 1937. Kirsten Flagstad was in the starring role as Isolde. Margaret would remember that performance and the rich quality of Flagstad's voice for many years to come.[15] Hillis brought her miniature score of the opera from her growing collection of orchestra and opera scores. She and her mother were seated in the front row, in close proximity to the orchestra pit, with a wonderful view of the conductor leading the orchestra. Margaret's eyes moved throughout the performance from the score, to the stage, and then into the orchestra pit, and back to the score. Her French horn teacher at that time was the bassoonist of the orchestra, and she recalled the thrill of waving to him enthusiastically before the performance began.[16] Even at this early stage in her life, Margaret Hillis was already envisioning her path—to become a conductor of orchestras. She shared her recollections with longtime WFMT program director, radio host, author, and interviewer Norman Pellegrini in the following:

> When I was about fourteen, I spent every cent of my allowance on recordings. My first one was the Stokowski transcription of the Bach *Toccata and Fugue*. Then Tchaikovsky symphonies came next. And then I began to get some good taste, [with] some Beethoven and Mozart. I had an enormous record collection, finally; [I] listened to them two to three hours a day, every day. And also practiced the piano, [but] not that much.[17]

In the fall of 1936, Margaret began her secondary education at Kokomo High School, where she busily pursued her music in both school instrumental ensembles. Playing the French horn in the orchestra and the baritone horn in the band, she became a familiar face to the instrumental music instructor. By this time, Margaret had taught herself to play the string bass, greatly needed in the orchestra, and the tuba, also needed in the band. These instruments were added to the ever-growing list Margaret had mastered. She began pestering her teacher about becoming his assistant conductor because she felt confident, having taken some conducting classes in her band camp over recent summers. When the director finally allowed Margaret a chance to conduct one of his ensembles, he recognized in her the potential that he believed he could cultivate. With Margaret's encouragement, the music director modified his weekly rehearsal schedule, instituting sectional rehearsals that he and Margaret would both lead. Margaret thrived in this teaching role.

One particular incident stood out in Margaret's mind from that time. It occurred when Margaret was put in charge of both ensembles for an entire week while her director was away at a music conference. He provided her with specific instructions for what he wanted her to rehearse while he was gone. She accomplished all the assigned music fairly quickly and decided to select an additional piece to work on with the orchestra, choosing the overture from Weber's *Der Freischütz*. Determined to polish her chosen selection, she bribed her classmates with a pool party at her home, provided they would put in some extra after-school rehearsal time on her music. When the teacher returned, he was astonished at what Margaret had accomplished. So impressed was he that he gave Margaret the opportunity to conduct her selected piece at the spring concert, which she referred to as her "first conducting job."[18] She made her second conducting appearance at the end of her sophomore year, leading the orchestra in Schubert's *Unfinished Symphony*.

Alas, schooling for Margaret and her brothers was about to drastically change. Although she was thriving in music and in academics at Kokomo High, her father's run for the governorship in Indiana would compel him to move his children to more prestigious schools. During the early years of his children's lives, Mr. Hillis had become increasingly focused on a political career, first winning the position of prosecutor for Howard County. That achievement fed his desire for higher office. Undeterred by his failed run for U.S. Congress in 1932, he decided to seek yet a higher position, organizing his run for governor beginning in 1936. In preparation for his campaign, Glen may have determined that his children should be educated in the more elite private schools for the sake of appearances. Or perhaps it was simply that he and Bernice wanted more time to pursue their own interests, which would have fewer complications if the children were away at boarding schools.

Whatever the reason, all the children were sent to private schools. The boys would attend Culver Military School, a strict environment of superb educational quality. Margaret would leave Kokomo High School in the fall of 1938, headed for Tudor Hall, an elite all-girls boarding school in Indianapolis.[19] Unlike the active music program at Kokomo High, Tudor Hall had no formal music program for Margaret to join. It did, however, present a steep challenge for Margaret with regard to academics. Comparing the schools, Margaret claimed "an 'A' in Kokomo was worth a 'C-' at her new high school."[20] "Scholastic standards were *something* [rigorous] . . . [yet] there wasn't a really ongoing music program there and I missed it very much, because [at Kokomo High] I played in the orchestra, I played in the band, and I ran around with a group of people who also did the same."[21]

Margaret was able to find several opportunities to satisfy her artistic endeavors, limited though they were at Tudor Hall. She was able to study piano privately with the head of the piano department at Indiana University, which kept her engaged in music, though not to the extent she had enjoyed back home. She was also involved in several theatrical productions at her new school, where she was featured in a prominent role in Oscar Wilde's play *The Importance of Being Earnest*. Margaret would enjoy attending Indianapolis Symphony Orchestra concerts when she was able to spare the time to do so, as she spent much of her time engaged in studying. Margaret struggled to achieve only average grades in this more rigorous school environment. There are no indications that she dwelled on the disappointment of such a dramatic shift in her daily life, particularly at a stage that would challenge most adolescents forced to adjust to such changes. She was living away from home, away from friends she had enjoyed for so many years, and away from music that had been so much a part of her life. Yet Margaret rarely complained. Her brother Bud attested to this trait in his sister. Her ability to move on when things got rough would stand her in great stead as her life progressed.

One particular instance stayed with Hillis from her Tudor Hall days. Just prior to graduation day, the headmistress called Margaret (whom she referred to as "Hecate," Margaret's nickname at the school) into her office.[22] "I thought I wasn't going to graduate."[23] Instead, the headmistress offered Margaret an apology, not realizing her high IQ (the second highest in the class) and expressing regret that they had not properly encouraged her academically. Margaret described the words that would remain with her for years to come. "The headmistress said, 'Come hell or high water, you can do anything in the world you set out to do.' I knew she was serious. The remark saw me through so many [difficult times ahead]."[24]

INDIANA UNIVERSITY AND THE WAR YEARS

Margaret had her sights set on going east for college, but that too was not possible because of her father's political aspirations. He would only support Margaret attending Indiana University (IU). "That was 1940, my father was running for governor. . . . I had to go to IU or he'd lose the election, he says. Fortunately, it had a wonderful school of music."[25] When Margaret began her studies at Indiana University, there was no undergraduate conducting major offered. She decided to enter the music school in the fall of 1940 as a piano major. Margaret was thrilled to be back in her element. "Studying music was the life I'd always wanted. I could hardly wait to get into the orchestra. At first it seemed that my schedule wouldn't permit it, but I managed—I was the principal double bass player for two and a half years."[26]

In her junior year of college, Margaret chose to pursue another one of her longtime passions: flying. It was a favorite pastime for many in the Hillis family, passed on through the generations beginning with grandfather Elwood. Margaret was convinced he would have likely pursued this avocation further had he lived long enough.[27] In an interview for a Bloomington newspaper in 1945, Margaret noted, "My whole family enjoyed flying. My oldest brother [Bud] was taking instruction from me and was about ready to take a solo flight when he went into the service.[28] Robert and Joseph also planned to complete training to qualify as pilots. Dad flew a lot . . . in the early twenties."[29] In later years, Bud Hillis would fly back and forth to Kokomo regularly from Washington, D.C., where he served in Congress. He piloted with his son Jeff serving as his copilot on those frequent jaunts, allowing Bud to remain connected with his Indiana constituents.[30]

Margaret first became intrigued with flying years earlier in 1930 during an unexpected emergency on a family vacation. Bernice ambitiously took all her children without her husband on a trip by automobile to explore Michigan, upstate New York, and Niagara Falls in Canada. During their travels, the second youngest child, Robert, became very ill. Glen Hillis engaged a private plane to retrieve his other three children while Bernice remained with Robert until he recovered. Bud described the flight home as extremely turbulent, recalling the little plane navigating through a ferocious thunderstorm. Bud recalled being terrified but he remembered Margaret enjoying the thrill ride immensely.[31]

The desire to fly remained in Margaret, but it was not until the attack on Pearl Harbor that she actively pursued her pilot training. In December 1941, Margaret, as with so many other men and women, wanted to serve her country. She enrolled in an accelerated wartime program that helped her complete her junior year by the fall of 1942 and would then take a two-and-one-half-year hiatus from her full-time studies at IU. She shifted her focus temporarily from music to becoming one of the Women's Auxiliary Service Pilots. Her father, realizing she was serious about flying, called his friend who owned an airfield in Muncie, Indiana, inquiring on her behalf. In the interview with Norman Pellegrini, Margaret described how her father first made sure there were no rules against women going to flight school with men. Glen's friend encouraged him to send Margaret to him directly. Margaret vividly recalled the nature of her meeting with Victor Kocon from the Muncie airfield:

I was wearing a dress and spectacles but "Vic" just threw me in the back of the plane and we took off. I have been flying ever since.[32]

I took all the ground school right with them [the men], and the flight instruction, got a private license, and a commercial license. And it was very funny what happened on the commercial license. I flew very well, came down, the examiner turned me down. And I went to the head of the field and I said, "What is this? I did a good test!" He said, "I know you did, but he couldn't believe a woman could fly that well, so he turned you down." Those were the days.[33]

Margaret got her license a few weeks later with another inspector, moving her one step closer to the Women's Army Service Pilots (WASP). However, by then the rules had changed. With a country now at war, the new requirement for WASP was to have 20/20 vision without glasses. Automatically disqualified from becoming a WASP under these new conditions, Margaret went to the person in charge of the airfield asking what she should do now. He suggested, "Get an instructors rating and you can teach here." So, without "missing a beat" as one path closed, she moved forward in a new direction, seemingly unaffected by the temporary obstacle in her midst. "The teaching of flying taught me how to teach and let me know that I love teaching."[34] Margaret believed that she developed her efficient skills of communicating with clarity, sequence, and precision from her experience instructing young men on matters that were truly life and death. These communication skills, later embedded into her exemplary rehearsal methods, became hallmarks of her work as a conductor. Teaching her young, inexperienced flight students was no easy matter. Bud noted that she was given the weakest candidates, courtesy of the men charged with assigning students to their flight instructors. They figured since Margaret was a "girl" there was no sense in giving her any but the seemingly least capable students. They would likely be rejected from the program and therefore would not require good instruction that only men could deliver. As was typical in Margaret's life experience, she was continually underestimated. This time was no exception. As Margaret explained, "My job was to rescue the guys ready to wash out of pilot training."[35] These boys were from Brooklyn and the Bronx . . . had never driven a car . . . a few of them had never even ridden a bicycle . . . they were terrified. Well, that experience taught me how to teach. It taught me how to focus, because the lives of those boys were in my hands"[36] (Picture 18).

In one harrowing flying lesson, Margaret had a close call with one of her students.

> I was demonstrating spins to a student in a Piper Cub, and before he made his attempt to repeat the maneuver, something told me to take the plane back up to 4,000 feet, although students routinely practiced spins from 3,000 feet. We did two spins and then, I think, two more, and I said, 'Ok, now take us out.' His elbow hit the lever that held his lap belt tight and it started playing out. At that time, we were upside down and his head went through the fabric roof of the airplane. The belt held with a few inches to spare— otherwise he would have gone right out through the roof. I took control until he had regained his composure, and we landed safely. I was calm, but when I stepped out onto the ground, my knees gave way.[37]

That is the story she shared publicly. Her brother Bud supplemented the ending of the story years later, explaining that when the young man was far enough away where she could no longer be seen by him, she vomited. However, she was grace under fire, and this too would sustain her in years to come.[38]

Picture 18.
Margaret Hillis, a Navy flight instructor at the Muncie Airport during World War II, 1942.
(Margaret Hillis Collection, Rosenthal Archives of the Chicago Symphony Orchestra Association)

The Navy finally had enough pilots before the war ended, and the program in which she taught had closed. Margaret remained on as a private instructor, only one of three persons out of twenty-six who were kept on.[39]

Margaret joined many other students returning to campus under the G.I. Bill. Hoping to graduate in a timely manner, she discovered certain courses were currently unavailable if she wanted to complete her piano performance degree. Still harboring a desire to become a conductor, she decided to switch her major to musical composition, surmising that this major would help her gain a better understanding of a composer's intentions, so necessary for a conductor, which she hoped to become. "I worked my fool tail off. . . . The dean [her counterpoint teacher and a student of Ottorino Respighi] kept giving me C's in counterpoint. And I went in and talked to him about it, and he said, 'It's always correct but it's not very musical.'"[40]

In her final year at Indiana University, Margaret had her first experience conducting a chorus. She was an active member of Sigma Alpha Iota (SAI), a women's music sorority with the purpose of raising standards for music and promoting American music. As part of the organization, she sang in the IU Chapter SAI chorus. A fellow choir member with one semester of conducting class under her belt was appointed to lead the group, preparing them for an upcoming performance. According to Margaret, the young woman was not at all enthusiastic about her conducting role and became continually flustered during rehearsals. She finally asked if someone else wanted to take over. Hillis volunteered, thinking to herself, "I know nothing about choruses. . . . I haven't conducted a chorus in my life. I've never liked choruses. But I do know a little about conducting, so I'll try." The choir, consisting mostly of piano and instrumental majors, had less experience vocally than Margaret, which provided an added layer of comfort to Hillis who knew little about singing technique herself. However, in Margaret's ear remained the sound of Kirsten Flagstad, whom her mother had taken her to see as a teenager. She claimed that even though there were only a few voice majors in the choir, she was able to get color, phrasing, in-tune singing, good line, and excitement using Flagstad's sound as her guide.[41] As she conducted rehearsals, Margaret also discovered that she could focus upon the same musical elements she would with an orchestra, stating, "That was the first time that I realized a chorus was . . . a decent musical instrument."[42]

Margaret's counterpoint teacher, who had been giving her C's on her compositions, attended the SAI performance and must have been very impressed, as Margaret attributed the straight A's she received after that concert to her success directing the group. Also in attendance to the concert was Margaret's beloved composition teacher Bernhard Heiden. Heiden, a former student of the composer Paul Hindemith, was greatly admired by Margaret, who trusted his advice not only in compositional techniques but also in matters of her future career planning. At first, Heiden suggested Margaret pursue graduate composition studies at Yale and work with Hindemith. When Margaret insisted she wanted to become an orchestral conductor, Heiden explained that though he was impressed by her conducting (having also seen her choral concert), she would be wasting her time.[43] Describing the challenges for a man pursuing orchestral conducting, it would be almost impossible for a woman to have any chance of succeeding. Heiden's wife was a cousin of William Steinberg, a prominent conductor of that time, and they knew firsthand how difficult it was for a *man* in the field.[44] In Margaret's words, "That had been my big dream since I was [a] small child. I nearly had a nervous breakdown over that."[45] "I wanted to be a conductor. I was told there was no way—that I, as a woman—could possibly break into the orchestral field, at which point I decided I might as well go home and knit."[46] Heiden suggested that she pursue the choral field, advising her to consider going to

Juilliard to study choral conducting with Robert Shaw. "I'd played in orchestras all my life and loved the orchestra and the repertory. I didn't know anything about choruses or choral repertory."[47] Besides, "there were no master conductors at that time who would take on a woman conductor as their student."[48] "That's the way it was in 1947."[49] Upon graduating from IU, another one of her professors approached Margaret's parents, saying, "Your daughter is a fine conductor . . . too bad she doesn't wear pants."[50] Margaret realized Heiden was right and accepted his guidance, acknowledging this to be the best suggestion she had ever received. Margaret would heed her beloved professor's advice, heading to New York to study with the renowned chorus master and newly appointed head of choral conducting at the Juilliard School, Robert Shaw.

ENDNOTES

1. Anna Madrzyk, "Margaret Hillis, Maker of Music: The Road to Success Has Not Been Easy," *The Sunday Herald Tribune*, December 14, 1980, p. 5.
2. From the Helen Lilley Estate Collection in the Howard County Historical Society. Helen Lilley was a reporter for the *Kenosha News* in the 1960s when Margaret Hillis conducted the Kenosha Symphony Orchestra. She was well acquainted with Margaret Hillis and wrote about her on a number of occasions. These were notes by Ms. Lilley, from an interview with Margaret Hillis, no date given on the notes as to when this interview took place.
3. John Dempsey, "Grandchildren Keep Haynes' Prolific Spirit Alive," *Kokomo Tribune*, October 14, 2007.
4. Interview with Elwood "Bud" Hillis.
5. John Dempsey, "Elwood's Innovation Known Universally: His Inventions Touch Our Everyday Lives," *Kokomo Tribune*, October 14, 2007, p. 1.
6. Margaret Hillis, interview by Norman Pellegrini (transcribed by Stanley G. Livengood), October 6, 1997, p. 1.
7. "Delphians Enjoy Guest Day Party at Hillis Home," *Kokomo Tribune*, April 30, 1934.
8. "Mrs. Purdum To Head County's G.O.P. Women: Club Officers are Elected Thursday in Meeting at Hillis Home," *Kokomo Tribune*, February 2, 1934, p. 9.
9. Sue Bradle and Tom Wilson, "Music Is My Life," *Accent* 6, no. 1 (September/October 1980): p. 12.
10. Margaret Hillis, interview by Pellegrini, p. 3.
11. Interview with Elwood "Bud" Hillis.
12. Margaret Hillis, interview by Pellegrini, p. 3.
13. Rogert P. Riger, "Margaret Hillis, Admired Conductor, Spends a Holiday at Oak Bluffs," *Vineyard Gazette*, July 17, 1979.
14. Margaret Hillis, interview by Pellegrini, p. 2.
15. The performance attended by Margaret and her mother was Kirsten Flagstad's staged operatic debut in Chicago, taking place on November 24, 1937. It was sensationally reviewed. Flagstad's voice left a lasting impression upon Margaret. She would often refer to Flagstad's vocal color when she encouraged her choruses to produce a rich, full vocal tone.
16. Margaret Hillis, interview by Pellegrini, p. 3.
17. Ibid., p. 3.
18. From Helen Lilley Estate Collection.

19. In 1970, Tudor Hall for girls merged with the Park School for boys and became Park Tudor, which the school is known as today.

20. Margaret Hillis, interview by Pellegrini, p. 2.

21. Ibid.

22. Hekate (Hecate), a goddess in Greek Mythology, was known for her powers of witchcraft, often feared by others. Hecate has become a symbol for feminist figures due, in part, to her fierce independence. Margaret Hillis earned the nickname "Hecate" while attending Park Tudor School. Friends and faculty members would refer to her by this name, and she was addressed this way in later years in letters written to her by former classmates. *Hecate* is the title of an internationally circulated journal, featuring articles relating to women with feminist views. Margaret's independent spirit likely earned her that name.

23. "Maestro: P.E.O. Profile," *The P.E.O. Record* (May 1983): pp. 12–13.

24. Ibid.

25. Jon Bentz, "Interview of Margaret Hillis Director Chicago Symphony Orchestra, September 19, 1989, Archives Committee, Oral History Project, 1992," p. 4 (Margaret Hillis Collection, Rosenthal Archives of the Chicago Symphony Orchestra Association).

26. Jane Samuelson, "For the Love of Music," *Chicago Magazine* (April 1980): p. 230.

27. Harriet Weaver, "Grandpa Haynes Invented Auto but Margaret Hillis Prefers 'Plane," *The World Telephone*, September 22, 1945, p. 1.

28. Bud's son Jeff shared that Margaret and Bud had an agreement. She would teach him how to fly if he would keep the apartment they briefly shared in Bloomington clean. Margaret was known to make such arrangements with others when sharing living arrangements, particularly when it came to cleaning and laundry, both tasks she clearly did not enjoy. Jeff Hillis described this arrangement during an interview on May 3, 2012.

29. Weaver, "Grandpa Haynes."

30. Interview with Jeff Hillis, May 3, 2012.

31. Interview with Elwood "Bud" Hillis.

32. Weaver, "Grandpa Haynes."

33. Margaret Hillis, interview by Pellegrini, p. 4.

34. Ibid., p. 5.

35. "Maestro: P.E.O. Profile," p. 12.

36. Margaret Hillis, interview by Pellegrini, p. 2.

37. Samuelson, "For the Love of Music," p. 230.

38. Interview with Elwood "Bud" Hillis.

39. Bentz, "Interview of Margaret Hillis," p. 2.

40. Margaret Hillis, interview by Pellegrini, p. 5.

41. Ibid.

42. William Barry Furlong, *Season with Solti: A Year in the Life of the Chicago Symphony* (New York: Macmillan Publishing, 1974), p. 223.

43. Madrzyk, "Margaret Hillis, Maker of Music," p. 4.

44. Bentz, "Interview of Margaret Hillis," p. 3.

45. Margaret Hillis, interview by Pellegrini, p. 6.

46. John Kraglund, "From Choral Triumphs to Orchestral Mastery," *The Globe and Mail*, July 21, 1982, p. 15.

47. Karen Campbell, "A Choired Excellence," *Symphony Magazine* (November/December 1992): p. 65.

48. Ulla Colgrass, "Conductor Hillis Reversed the Odds," *Music Management Magazine* (November/December 1981): p. 15.

49. Madrzyk, "Margaret Hillis, Maker of Music," p. 4.

50. Karen Monson, "Musician of the Month: Margaret Hillis," *High Fidelity and Musical America* (October 1978): MA6–MA7.

CHAPTER 4
AN HISTORICAL PERSPECTIVE

To fully appreciate Margaret Hillis's challenge when embarking upon a conducting career in the late 1940s, it is important to have the historical perspective from which to view this daunting aspiration. Her ultimate triumphs as a conductor become all the more impressive when understanding how female musicians were viewed when Margaret's professional journey began. Equally important to consider is the status of choral ensembles at the time Hillis pursued her studies in choral conducting. Attitudes about choruses and women as professional musicians look very different when viewed through a 1940s lens.

CHRONOLOGY OF ORCHESTRA, OPERA, AND PROFESSIONAL CHOIRS IN AMERICA

Orchestras, opera companies, and choruses in America emerged in the early 1800s, but it was not until the turn of the nineteenth century that these evolved into professional endeavors. By that time, music ensembles in Europe had already been supported by aristocrats or churches for many years; however, America did not have an established wealthy class nor the support of church institutions to sustain professional music making. "With no aristocracy and few leisured rich before 1870, America had no resources or time to support anything but the most modest and amateur musical activity.... Consequently ... American music ensembles at all levels served as a pastime rather than an art."[1] More sophisticated orchestras emerged in the mid to late 1800s, and by the turn of the nineteenth century a handful of symphony orchestras were forming, beginning with the New York Philharmonic in 1842, the Boston Symphony Orchestra in 1881, the Chicago Symphony Orchestra in

1891, the Cincinnati Symphony Orchestra in 1895, and the Philadelphia Orchestra in 1900.[2]

Opera arrived onto the American music scene in the early 1800s with performances in New York's Park Theater in 1817. Mozart's *Don Giovanni*, Rossini's *The Barber of Seville*, and other operas, well known in Europe, had come to America, performed with English translations. Interestingly, Lorenzo da Ponte, librettist of Mozart's "da Ponte" operas, *The Marriage of Figaro, Don Giovanni,* and *Così fan tutte*, had moved to New York in the early 1800s to escape creditors, and while teaching Italian at Columbia University he authored several English translations of his original librettos. Da Ponte was influential in establishing the first opera house in America, the Italian Opera House, in 1833.[3] Though the venture ultimately failed, other opera theaters would follow. The Metropolitan Opera Company was founded in 1883, and the house opened with its first production on October 22, 1883.

The earliest choruses emerged in the form of American choral societies beginning in the early 1800s. These societies attracted untrained singers who wanted to experience music making at a higher level than they could attain in their small church choirs. An additional benefit of these larger choral groups was the camaraderie they offered to those who shared a common interest in musical performance. The Handel and Haydn Society of Boston, established in 1815, is the oldest choral organization remaining today. This ensemble was the first in America to perform many of the great choral symphonic masterpieces, including Handel's *Messiah*, Haydn's *The Creation*, Mozart's Requiem, and Beethoven's Symphony No. 9. The rich history of this organization included their participation in memorial services for Presidents Thomas Jefferson and Abraham Lincoln.[4] This chorus greatly influenced the development of amateur singing societies throughout the United States.

An influence on the growth of singing societies was the influx of German immigrants who brought their choral society tradition to America and, with it, "a strong sense of duty, community participation, broad religious sentiment, rising nationalism and enthusiasm."[5] Festivals like the Sängerfests brought together singers from all parts of the country to perform large-scale classical choral-orchestral works. These Sängerfests gave rise to the first established American festival, Cincinnati's May Festival, founded in 1873 by Theodore Thomas, who would later serve as the founder and first music director of the Chicago Symphony Orchestra. The May Festival often featured symphonic choral performances. By the mid-1870s, choral societies and festivals of mixed choruses emerged in many of the large cities, with memberships numbering in the hundreds.

One of the best known of these societies was the Oratorio Society of New York, established in 1873 by Leopold Damrosch, a German orchestral conductor who had moved to America, bringing with him the great choral traditions of his native country. During his career in New York, he was appointed the conductor of the New York Philharmonic. Eventually, he would conduct at the Metropolitan Opera, and on some occasions he would involve his Oratorio Society of New York to serve as the chorus for his opera productions. For the most part, however, America's choral societies were stand-alone organizations, not affiliated with professional opera companies or with orchestras in their region.

In the early part of the twentieth century, a more polished artistry was beginning to emerge in choral organizations with groups such as the MacDowell Chorus of New York City, established in 1909. The MacDowell Chorus regularly performed works with a professional orchestra and therefore had higher standards for its members, selecting those with more formal training in voice and a higher level of musicianship. Composer Gustav Mahler scrutinized this chorus, inviting them to perform with the New York Philharmonic, first in 1910 and continuing in subsequent seasons.[6] Singers were not paid, but the audition and performance standards for members were raised to a higher level than that of its amateur predecessors.

Professional choruses began to appear first in New York City, with the earliest ones established in 1925. Professional choruses, for the purpose of this conversation, are defined as those providing regular pay to a significant number of chorus members, excluding church, opera, or musical theater choruses. Among America's oldest professional choirs was the Eva Jessye Choir, established in 1927 and directed by Eva Jessye. She was the first black woman to become an internationally known professional choral conductor.[7] Her choir was known for its rendition of music from the Black oral tradition. They performed in the original production of Gershwin's *Porgy and Bess*, giving them national and international recognition. Another professional choir of the early 1900s, the Hall Johnson Choir, established in New York in 1925, first performed professionally in 1928. Known for their superb performances on Broadway and on motion picture soundtracks, they were also known for their outstanding performances of spirituals, many of which were arranged by the choir's founder and director Hall Johnson. These fine spiritual arrangements have remained standard choral repertoire to this day. Other professional choirs established in the early years of the choral movement in America included: Fred Waring and the Pennsylvanians, Roger Wagner Chorale, Du Paur Infantry Chorus, Norman Luboff Choir, Robert Shaw Chorale, Margaret Hillis's American Concert Choir, the Chicago Symphony Chorus, Robert DeCormier Singers, and Michael Korn's Philadelphia Singers.[8]

Beginning in the early 1930s, choirs were more accessible to larger populations throughout the country thanks to radio broadcasts. Fred Waring created a vocal ensemble for the purpose of performing a radio program airing five nights a week. Waring's Pennsylvanians—paid professional vocalists—became popular for their refined singing that was instantly embraced by the public due to the vocal and musical maturity of these well-trained singers. Moreover, the Pennsylvanians performed superb arrangements of popular music, often joined in performance by the most recognized singers of the day, including Bing Crosby and Frank Sinatra. Waring hired Robert Shaw, a young conductor at the time, who subsequently learned by working with Waring's chorus and by studying his compositional techniques. Shortly after Shaw and Waring parted ways, Margaret Hillis would arrive at Juilliard to study with Shaw. It was Shaw's techniques, in part influenced by Waring and carried forward by Margaret Hillis, that served as the foundation for the high level of choral singing heard today.

College and university choirs were also contributing to the choral scene, creating their own singular philosophies for choral tone. Two major American choral traditions became influential. First was the St. Olaf Choir tradition, founded by F. Melius Christiansen in 1912, encouraging a more homogenous tonal blend of limited vibrato. The second was the Westminster Choir tradition of John Finley Williamson in 1923, promoting a more soloistic sound, containing a fuller vibrato and rich vocal production. Other styles of choral singing emerged, including a brighter and livelier approach to singing heard in the glee clubs of such places as Yale University, performing student songs written by composer Marshall Bartholomew. College glee clubs, including the Harvard Glee Club, directed by Archibald T. Davison, would eventually tackle the more traditional repertoire. All of these styles, repertory, and approaches to choral singing became more readily accessible to the public once they were heard on radio broadcasts. High schools, colleges, and church choirs nationwide were using these as models to emulate. Choral programs became popular in schools throughout the country, attracting students without the prerequisite of formal training. All were welcome to participate in the art form. On the other hand, instrumental ensemble directors had the expectations for their students to read music and to have some training in playing their instruments in order to participate. In its earliest stages, choral music was predominantly an amateur endeavor, and that would be a difficult reputation to overcome. Unlike orchestras and opera companies, which would gain respect in the field of music, choruses were looked upon as untrained ensemble experiences. It would be many years of struggle, championed by Margaret Hillis, to bring choruses into the professional ranks. This was the state of choral music in the 1940s when Margaret arrived in New York.

History of Women Pursuing Professional Music Careers

Another important contextual piece to consider at the time of Margaret's arrival in New York is the way in which women were viewed in all areas of professional music making. Negative stereotypes were placed upon women playing instruments, making it even more challenging for women aspiring to become conductors. It was an uphill battle at the time Hillis was just beginning to pursue her professional training as a conductor. Margaret and those few women who bravely persevered conducting had to be innovative and undeterred if they hoped for a fighting chance of fulfilling their musical passion.

Acceptance of women as professional musicians would take many years to be fully realized, but their initial breakthrough into the professional music scene can be attributed, in part, to the women's movement, gathering momentum as the twentieth century began. Women were demanding more equality in the workplace and in many other walks of life. As Susan B. Anthony aptly expressed, "We have got the new woman in everything except counting of her vote at the ballot box . . . and it's coming sooner than most people think."[9] Twenty-five years after Anthony expressed those sentiments, women finally gained the right to vote and, along with it, increased opportunities in the workplace. For women desirous of a music career, however, those workplace opportunities were slower to be realized.

In order for women to gain acceptance as professional musicians, another factor had even greater impact than their right to work and to vote: the availability of formal music training, heretofore only available abroad. Music conservatories and outstanding teachers for those schools were emerging in greater numbers in America by the early twentieth century. Prior to the twentieth century, men and women who wanted to study music at the highest level found it necessary to train in Europe, because few options existed of equal quality at home. Only a small number of women pursued formal study abroad, specifically those considered child prodigies, since it was a tremendous commitment for a family to undertake. A young woman studying far from home would have to be accompanied by at least one parent. There was the added financial burden that came with a family split between two locations, and then there was the added expense of the training itself. The obvious sacrifices that an entire family would be required to make for a female with limited chances of a future successful music career resulted in few girls studying abroad.

As music schools increased in number and locations throughout America, women's opportunities to train in the music field grew exponentially. Once American music conservatories emerged, aspiring musicians could finally acquire professional music training at home. These conservatories were open to men and women, leading to an increased number of females now pursuing music, but there remained an elitist profile of those women who attended. Young ladies enrolled in American conservatories were, by and large, from wealthy families. Additionally, the focus of their training was based upon the premise that most of these female music students intended to become music teachers. Unlike their male counterparts, women were discouraged from having professional performance aspirations because it was deemed unladylike behavior. Even Margaret was reticent to publicly admit her intention of becoming a performance-oriented musician. When interviewed by Bloomington Indiana's local newspaper, *The World Telephone*, for a feature story about her, Hillis discussed her future plans after graduating from Indiana University. She stated her intention to pursue a master's degree, after which she planned to teach music in a college or university.[10] Margaret Hillis never expressed this desire to teach in any other interviews throughout the years. As she became more experienced in conducting, she viewed her role on the podium as being educative and very much enjoyed teaching, but only within the context of conducting and rehearsing. The only time she stated that her music training was in preparation for becoming a teacher was in that very public feature story in a Bloomington Indiana newspaper. No doubt, the negative view of women intending to pursue performance careers, along with the prominence of her father throughout the state of Indiana, contributed to Margaret's hesitancy in stating her true aspirations in music.

This negative view of women as performers was not exclusively an American phenomenon. Such attitudes were equally prominent in Europe. Talented female instrumentalists, both in America and abroad, grew increasingly frustrated by male-dominated symphony orchestra members denying them the chance to audition, even if they had comparable talent with their male counterparts. Taking matters into their own hands, European women formed all-female orchestras—the first being The Vienna Ladies Orchestra of 1867. This trend grew in Europe, and eventually professional all-women orchestras appeared in the United States. The establishment of the Fadette Women's Orchestra of Boston, founded in 1888, was followed by the creation of the Philadelphia Women's Orchestra in 1921 and the Woman's Symphony Orchestra of Chicago in 1925. These orchestras eventually opened doors not only for female instrumentalists who had longed to play the music they were so capable of, but also provided an *entrée* for women conductors who had equal passion for leading these ensembles.

The all-female orchestras paved a path for women to be seen as professional performers despite the pervasive stereotypes and biases against women performing in public. Instead of giving in to prejudiced viewpoints, women in these orchestras took advantage of their gender, promoting the unique aspect of being part of an all-female ensemble. It turned out that this became a draw for audiences by virtue of the extraordinary and unique nature of their membership. People would attend concerts to see what an orchestra comprised only of women looked like. This aspect cut both ways, however, because it helped attract audiences for the spectacle while at the same time perpetuating the very mindset that kept women out of the more established male-populated symphony orchestras. "One reviewer seemed more impressed by the attractiveness of the women than by the fact that they were accomplished musicians."[11]

In a 1998 article published in the *College Symposium,* Shelley M. Jagow cited the astonishing comments made by conductor Sir Thomas Beecham in the 1940s related to women playing in professional orchestras. Made around the same time Margaret was beginning her conducting studies in New York, Beecham stated, "I do not like, and never will, the association of men and women in orchestras and other instrumental combinations. . . . As a member of the orchestra once said to me, 'If she is attractive, I can't play with her and if she is not I won't.'"[12] Imagine how Beecham would have reacted to a female on the podium? Remarkably, Leopold

Stokowski, conductor of the Philadelphia Orchestra from 1912–1935, was one of a very few conductors who did not share Beecham's sentiments. He described the idea of excluding women in the orchestra as an "incomprehensible blunder."[13] Though Stokowski defended the idea of women in the orchestra, he only admitted three women into his Philadelphia Orchestra, and that occurred during his final season as the conductor. Later, in the 1960s, his American Symphony Orchestra admitted many women, including female members of minorities.[14]

Unlike Stokowski, many conductors, instrumentalists, and others shared the sexist views of Beecham, directed first against female instrumentalists and eventually against female conductors. Eve Queler, an accomplished conductor and contemporary of Margaret Hillis, recalled, "One of our leading artist managers stated at a meeting that women with good figures have a problem on the podium because they are sex symbols."[15] Antonia Brico, just one generation ahead of Margaret Hillis, and the first woman to conduct the New York Philharmonic, received increased opportunities in her career as she aged. "It is worth noting that Antonia Brico . . . whose extremely promising career foundered when she was thirty and sexually attractive, is now flourishing when she is seventy-two, craggy-faced and sensible shoe'd."[16] It is presumed that Sarah Caldwell, another contemporary of Margaret and the first female conductor at the Metropolitan Opera, was considered to have an advantage due to her large size and her deep voice. Stated one of the musicians who worked with her, "If she'd been a babe we'd have walked right over her."[17]

An interesting side note is that when Margaret was fourteen years old, she observed Antonia Brico conduct. Margaret's mother had taken her to see a woman conductor at New York's Carnegie Hall. As Hillis explained in a 1995 WFMT radio interview, Brico was working then with a volunteer orchestra and through the years had very little experience working with professionals. Only after the pop singing artist and composer Judy Collins, a former piano student of Brico, made the 1974 documentary movie *Antonia: A Portrait of a Woman* did people become interested in watching her conduct. After that film was released, invitations increased for Brico to conduct major orchestras. She was, by then, at the "right age" to be more acceptable for this position. Hillis conveyed that Brico had conducted the Chicago Symphony Orchestra in her latter years, but only once and she was never asked back.[18] Hillis explained that Brico's weakness was not having enough experience working with professional orchestras and therefore she did not understand the nuances of working with professional players when she was on the podium. Hillis emphasized that it is important to treat players as colleagues and to offer them the respect they deserve. Brico instead adopted a more authoritarian role, which contributed to her struggles as a professional orchestral conductor. In another interview, when discussing the rise of female conductors, Hillis remarked, "Despite the false starts with media-hyped conductors such as Antonia Brico, whose modest accomplishments were taken by many as proof that women just didn't have the knack . . . there are now several women of outstanding talent whose contributions are genuine and meaningful."[19]

Added to the aforementioned challenges for female musicians was the scrutiny of how a woman should move while performing. Her use of facial expression and body movement, so important to conveying the expressive qualities of music, needed to be contained within the acceptable limits of what was deemed ladylike. The role model for following the unspoken rules of femininity was the great opera singer Jenny Lind. Among the first professional female musicians to enjoy fame in America, Lind's success was attributed not only to her beautiful voice but also to her stage decorum. "Her unqualified popularity was her ability to project on stage the qualities considered appropriate in the perfect woman—beauty, grace, generosity, modesty, and humility."[20] These very qualities that worked for Jenny Lind were less easily manageable for female instrumentalists wanting to display their full spectrum of artistry. Men and child performers had the advantage over women of being able to publicly display unrestrained motion while performing.[21] Women who used excessive movement in performance were often reviewed negatively. Pianist Fannie Bloomfield-Zeisler, in her 1925 performance with the Chicago Symphony Orchestra, was criticized by a reviewer for "superficial and annoying manifestations. . . . There were the tossings [sic] of arms aloft; there was facial italicizing of deep-seated emotions."[22]

As difficult as it was to comply with a modest amount of movement while playing an instrument, imagine how limiting these restrictions were for female conductors of that era. In order for any conductor to elicit emotion and excitement, it is sometimes necessary to move in a very animated way, requiring more extreme body motions and facial expressions. Such behavior was deemed inappropriate for a woman. Female conductors who dared to perform in this way often encountered harsh criticism. A prime example was a circumstance regarding Ethel Leginska, a prominent female pianist who turned to composing and then to conducting in the 1920s. Leginska had a larger-than-life personality and was not afraid to express herself, which she did through her body movements on the podium and in her manner of dress. She embraced her own singular style despite the criticism she received. Being the first woman to appear on the podium at Carnegie Hall, Leginska was highly scrutinized in her manner, her dress, and in her on-the-podium gestures, all of which were central topics of newspaper concert reviews. Members of the orchestra and critics were known to give Leginska a hard time, as exemplified in a scathing 1915 review in which she was accused of trying to dress like a man.[23] Leginska *did*, in fact, try to dress in that way to give herself every advantage with the orchestra and the audience. In one of her many interviews in 1915 she stated, "The only way a woman could succeed . . . was to emulate a man in dress and hairstyle."[24]

It was Leginska's movement on the podium that invited the harshest criticism. Leginska's strong personality was embodied in her use of large animated conducting gestures, labeled by one critic as a fiasco, claiming she lacked "conductorial technique."[25] These reviews no doubt damaged her credibility with members of the orchestra who unwittingly became collateral damage in the criticisms that were lodged against Leginska's alleged eccentricities. For her Carnegie Hall conducting debut on January 9, 1925, one reviewer commented, "At least to her credit . . . nothing very serious occurred to mar the performance for which she so energetically beat time."[26] It is said that when the performance ended and Leginska gestured the orchestra to stand and share a bow acknowledging the thunderous applause of the audience, the players remained seated. This refusal to rise could be viewed as a gesture of respect to credit Leginska, but more likely it was the orchestra's way of distancing themselves from the audience's enthusiasm for the female conductor. It was, in fact, an undermining of Leginska's success that night. Some years later, a very unflattering cartoon mocking Leginska's conducting gestures was published in *Musical America* with a caption that read, "Leginska, the Country's Most Noted Skirted Conductor, in Her Arduous and Versatile Duties with the New Boston Philharmonic"[27] (Picture 19).

City of Cabots Views Its Dynamic New Leader

"Our Foolish Correspondent" Gives Impressions of Ethel Leginska, the Country's Most Noted Skirted Conductor, in Her Arduous and Versatile Duties With the New Boston Philharmonic

Picture 19.

This extremely unflattering caricature of Ethel Leginska's movement and expression while conducting appeared in a *Musical America* publication, 1927.[28]

Margaret Hillis would later express similar sentiments regarding the need for restraint as a female conductor. In an interview she gave in the late 1970s, she reflected about her formative years as a young conductor. "I was very self-conscious—the audience expected a man to walk out and instead they saw a woman. I think it affected my style. I learned to use very small movements, so I wouldn't come between the chorus and the audience, wouldn't be too conspicuous."[29] This restricted style would later be criticized, with Hillis often reviewed as being less expressive and that her performances were void of emotion. It was difficult for female conductors to win approval, given the climate that limited how they could move on a podium.

The optics of women conductors were magnified exponentially as they became more prominent on the podium. Intense scrutiny over a woman's appearance, often focusing on her choice of attire, remained central in documented conversations for many years following comments about Ethel Leginska's choices. Other women on the podium have endured similar criticism. Professor/conductor Beverly Taylor, featured in Joan Catoni Conlon's book, *Wisdom, Wit, and Will: Women Choral Conductors on Their Art*, spoke of an experience that she described as reminiscent of "old battles" when she was approached by a woman after conducting a performance in 1979. The woman expressed to Taylor that "she had never seen a woman conductor before and that she had never thought women would make good conductors because they looked funny from behind."[30] JoAnn Falletta, music director of the Buffalo Philharmonic since 1998, explained her struggle to choose appropriate conducting attire in Beth Abelson Macleod's book *Women Performing Music*. When conducting in Long Beach, Falletta "experimented with tails or skirts or black-and-white outfits. And when conducting in the South, she stuck with dresses 'to avoid appearing masculine.'"[31] Despite her efforts, the dress code was a discussion in a 1990 concert review, in which a critic inquired about what kind of "psychosexual message" Falletta's attire was intending to convey.[32] If women looked too feminine, they were accused of being too sexual on the podium, but if they dressed in slacks instead of the more feminine-looking dresses, they were accused of looking too masculine. They could not win.

Margaret Hillis weighed in on the challenges of appearance and appropriate dress for a female conductor. "Hillis said she . . . had to cope with a lot of little practical problems—problems that men conductors never have to think about."[33] This topic was the focus of a 1983 interview for a local Columbus, Ohio, newspaper promoting the upcoming Beethoven *Missa solemnis* performances Hillis would be conducting. The reporter based a good deal of the interview on what Hillis planned to wear while conducting the performance, focusing in part on her shoes. Hillis brought up her continuing issues with foot problems, which she claimed were developed over years of conducting in improper footwear. She acknowledged that even the male conductors developed these problems, citing a case in point with Leopold Stokowski, with whom she shared the same podiatrist. Their doctor identified similar foot issues in both conductors. Hillis explained to the reporter that in addition to her family history of foot problems and considering how much she had to be on her feet as a conductor, she had to take great care in selecting the right shoes for the podium.

Hillis further explained that the equivalent of a man's dress shoe for a woman was a pair of dress black patent leather high heels. Conducting a *Missa solemnis* or *Messiah* in heels was extremely difficult, resulting in Hillis's eventual foot problems.

She often chose to wear black athletic shoes under her fancy brocade gowns, but she did not reveal this detail in the interview. When the reporter questioned how Hillis resolved the challenge of selecting proper footwear, Hillis simply stated, "You will see."[34] In that same interview, Hillis reflected upon the many other challenges she encountered breaking into the field as a female conductor. Hillis explained: "There were no role models when I was coming up—no one to ask for advice about things like, what does a woman wear? What kind of shoes do you wear?"[35] Her point in this article was as it had always been, that she was there to make music for listeners, not lookers, and that getting an orchestra and an audience to see beyond her gender had been the challenge central to her entire career.

One event in the early 1900s gave women hope for countering the practice of excluding them from professional orchestras. Local music unions were absorbed by the American Federation of Labor in 1903, which made it necessary for orchestras to give fair consideration to women wanting professional orchestral positions.[36] The merger forced the union to accept qualified women, which of course put pressure on theaters to hire women instrumentalists. As these pressures mounted, some of the old arguments that prevented women from being admitted early on were no longer sufficient. That is, concerns about a woman's looks, how she moved and dressed were no longer appropriate means for denying them employment. As a result, a new tactic emerged to keep women out of these positions. Music directors and male instrumentalists determined that by challenging a woman's skill level and stamina, it would be harder for a union to defend them, even with the new union labor laws. One music director, Gustave Kerker, was furious with the idea of women joining the ranks, particularly if they were players of specific instruments that he thought only men had the strength to play. He critically remarked,

> Nature never intended the fair sex to become cornetists, trombonists, and players of wind instruments. In the first place they are not strong enough to play them as well as men; they lack the lip and lung power to hold notes, which deficiency makes them always play out of tune. One discordant musician might not be noticed in an orchestra, but if you have several women members or a whole band composed of them, the playing verges on the excruciating![37]

He also complained that women could not be relied upon to work as hard as men, nor were they able to rehearse as regularly as men could.[38] The conductor of the 1916 New York Symphony, Josef Stransky, said that he would accept women in his orchestra but only if they were better players than the men applying for the same positions.[39] Similarly, others justified the denial of women their rightful place in professional orchestras because they lacked the stamina of male instrumentalists. In Macleod's book, *Women Performing Music*, she cites an article published as far back as 1895 about a woman's lack of stamina: "Her physical incapacity to endure the strain of four or five hours a day of rehearsal, followed by the prolonged tax of public performances, will bar her against possible competition with male performers."[40] Despite male efforts to discourage female instrumentalists, the new union rules gradually began to open doors of opportunity.

FEMALE CONDUCTORS FIND A WAY

Female conductors unfortunately did not share in the modest gains of female instrumentalists who benefitted from the new union supports. The barriers for women wishing to lead orchestras continued with fervor. The only recourse for early trailblazers such as Hillis and other aspiring women conductors in need of experience to hone their skill was to create their own opportunities. One option involved forming their own ensembles. Caroline Nichols, who established the aforementioned Fadette Women's Orchestra of Boston in 1888, provided herself conducting opportunities with the ensemble. Bertha Roth Walburn Clark and Grace Kleinhenn Thompson both founded urban orchestras in the early 1930s that they would conduct.[41] Other female conductors followed this trend, allowing themselves the experience and podium time they so greatly desired. Margaret Hillis would form her own ensemble in years to come, a mixed chorus she established following one summer at Tanglewood.

Another option for women conductors was to sacrifice deserved compensation in exchange for conducting established orchestras. Women understood that if they wanted to gain conducting experience it would often be without compensation. Ethel Leginska willingly sacrificed income for the opportunity to refine her craft by taking conducting positions offered to her, whether paid or not. "I don't want to make any money of art. . . . I won't starve and physical things mean very little to me."[42] In 1925–1926, Leginska accepted an arrangement to work without pay, guest conducting the People's Orchestra in Boston, which consisted of former Boston Symphony Orchestra (BSO) members who left their positions when the BSO was not permitted to unionize. Through her five appearances with them, Leginska gained experience conducting professional players. Under normal circumstances, Leginska would have been denied that same opportunity. Leginska took advantage of this unique situation and, as a result of her diligent work, the People's Orchestra was quite successful. The People's Orchestra of Boston could not afford to pay any conductor given the financial challenges it faced in paying their instrumentalists. Leginska justified her financial sacrifice in service of becoming a better conductor. Despite her willingness to work at no fee, she was passed up when the People's Orchestra named their permanent conductor, Stuart Mason. Leginska's successful reviews and the well-received concerts were not sufficient for the board to offer her the position over a male candidate. Her conducting appearances that followed were mostly comprised of opportunities she created for herself. She would establish several orchestras in the years ahead, most often working without pay. Leginska would eventually leave the conducting profession. In 1940, at the age of fifty-four, Leginska moved to Los Angeles, pursuing a piano teaching career. For the next thirty years, she would continue teaching, never performing publicly as a conductor nor as a pianist again.

In the 1930s, Antonia Brico approached the challenge of gaining podium time in much the same way as had Caroline Nichols during the late 1800s. Antonia Brico, the first woman to conduct the Berlin Philharmonic in 1930, received very positive reviews from that performance in Europe. However, when she came to America, she received minimal invitations to conduct professional orchestras. Although she was the first woman to conduct the New York Philharmonic in 1938, she had already been fired at the Metropolitan Opera in 1933 when a baritone refused to work with a woman on the podium.[43] By the mid-1940s, with few offers coming in, Brico took matters into her own hands, forming the New York Women's Orchestra. This orchestra provided her the podium time she desired while gaining great public support. The enthusiasm for this orchestra and its conductor occurred despite a lack of press coverage that would have generated greater financial stability. The New York Women's Orchestra secured much of their support from wealthy society women who were not taken seriously by the press, and therefore the orchestra was not treated with the publicity it so richly deserved.[44]

Margaret Hillis would also make great financial sacrifices over the years, often taking little or no fee for conducting opportunities. When bringing her New York Concert Choir to appear several times with the Chicago Symphony Orchestra, prior to the formation of the Chicago Symphony Chorus, Hillis did not take a fee for her services. She wanted the collaborations to work and tried to keep expenses down by excluding herself from the total budget she submitted to the Orchestral Association that hired them. In later years, it would become clear that Margaret was underpaid, as compared to other conductors, all of them males, doing the same work with choruses and orchestras. This inequity of payment would come up frequently both with her Chicago Symphony Orchestra negotiations and in many guest appearances, which became a source of increased frustration in her later years.

The path forged by female conductors and instrumentalists preceding Margaret made her pursuit just a little easier. It took many years for women to gain admission into professional orchestras based upon their playing ability. Their brave efforts to perform were further supported by historic events of the day, including World War II. Opportunities for women were created, borne of necessity, while many of the male instrumentalists were off to the war and players were in demand. Although after the war most of those temporary orchestral positions were returned to the men who initially held them, the situation gradually changed people's perceptions about female instrumentalists, eventually opening professional orchestral slots for women. Ironically, one of the first permanent orchestral positions given to a woman was awarded in 1944 to Doriot Anthony Dwyer, the great-grandniece of Susan B. Anthony![45]

For women conductors, it would be a much longer wait. At the time Hillis first aspired to become a conductor, only a few women, including Antonia Brico, Ethel Leginska, and Nadia Boulanger, led major professional orchestras in America and abroad, even on a sporadic guest-appearance basis. That glass ceiling would take much longer to break. In similar fashion to another female conductor, Margarete Dessoff, Hillis made the difficult choice to pursue the choral conducting path instead of her original plan. Dessoff was the first woman to conduct a major choral concert in New York City, leading the Schola Cantorum. She founded the well-known Dessoff Choirs in 1924, which still thrives today. Hillis was in good company with these distinguished women who made numerous sacrifices throughout their conducting journey.

Hillis encountered similar challenges with her female conducting contemporaries and resolved them like the others, sacrificing income for conducting opportunities and often financing her performances at great personal expense. However, Hillis claimed that her greatest challenge in pursuit of a conducting career was lacking a mentor. She summarized that despite her studies with eminent conductors, including Robert Shaw, what she needed most she was prevented from attaining, largely due to her gender. In Hillis's words, expressed in an interview for a master's degree thesis by author Kay Lawson, she stated her feelings of inadequacy, having no one to guide her.

I was able myself to finance a series in Town Hall with the help of my family, got a good bit of the experience I needed, but the thing at that point was that no master conducting teacher would take a woman as a student . . . because she had no hope for a career. He wanted to spend his time with the . . . talented men who had a chance for a career and not, no matter how talented, with a woman. So I couldn't get a master teacher. It wasn't until a good many years later (that) I did get to a master teacher . . . Otto-Werner Mueller. I learned enormously from him. It was a great liberation. Since then, I'm not scared of orchestras any more.[46]

As with the women before her, Margaret would follow any path that would give her the experience she needed to build a conducting career. The women before her led the way. It was Hillis who would move the goal further along. Inheriting her ability to "dream big" from her grandfather and her father, along with the belief she could do whatever she set out to accomplish, instilled in her by her mother and the headmistress at Tudor Hall School, Hillis felt empowered to succeed. The added support of plentiful resources from her family's fortune enabled Margaret to make her conducting aspirations more than just a fantasy. Her fine musical training at Indiana University and the disciplined strategic teaching methods she developed while training pilots to fly in World War II, combined with her staunch work ethic and an adventurous spirit, which she inherited from generations of Haynes and Hillis predecessors, would prove the winning combination for the future she set forth to pursue. Although this journey began differently than she originally envisioned, she was ultimately able to find her way to the top of the conducting field. She wisely chose to listen to the guidance of her beloved Indiana University professor Bernhard Heiden, studying with Robert Shaw at Juilliard. It was in New York City that Margaret Hillis would begin to carve the path she most desired.

ENDNOTES

1. John Ogasapian and Lee N. Orr, *Music of the Gilded Age* (Westport: Greenwood Press, 2007), p. 9.
2. Kate Hevner Mueller, *Twenty-Seven Major American Symphony Orchestras: A History and Analysis of Their Repertoires Seasons 1842–43 through 1969–70* (Bloomington: Indiana University Press, 1973).
3. Joan Acocella, "Nights at the Opera," *The New Yorker*, January 8, 2007.
4. William Robert Bucker, "A History of Chorus America: Association of Professional Vocal Ensembles," DMA dissertation (University of Missouri–Kansas City, 1991), p. 33.
5. Ibid., p. 112.
6. Gustav Stickley, "The MacDowell Chorus: A New Music Development in New York," *The Craftsman* 19 (October 1910–March 1911): p. 316.
7. Paul Hill, "The Professional Choir in America: A History and a Report on Present Activity," *Choral Journal* (April 1980): p. 10.
8. Ibid.
9. Gail Collins, *America's Women: Four Hundred Years of Dolls, Drudges, Helpmates, and Heroines*, 1st ed. (New York: William Morrow, 2003), p. 304.
10. Harriet Weaver, "Grandpa Haynes Invented Auto but Margaret Hillis Prefers 'Plane," *The World Telephone*, September 22, 1945, front page.
11. Christine Ammer, *Unsung: A History of Women in American Music* (Westport, Connecticut: Greenwood Press, 1980), p. 102.
12. Mary Brown Hinley, "The Uphill Climb of Women in American Music: Performer and Teachers," *Music Educators Journal* LXX/8 (April 1984), p. 201.
13. Sidney Lanier, *Music and Poetry* (New York: C. Scribner's Sons, 1914), p. 39; Frédérique Joanne Petrides, "Women in Orchestras," *Etude* 56 (July 1938): pp. 420–430.
14. Jan Bell Groh, *Evening the Score: Women in Music and the Legacy of Frédérique Petrides* (Fayetteville: University of Arkansas Press, 1991), p. 60.
15. Shirley M. Jagow, "Women Orchestral Conductors in America: The Struggle for Acceptance—An Historical View from the Nineteenth Century to the Present," *Chicago Music Symposium* 38 (October 1, 1998), 6 of 22.
16. Robert Jones, "Walking into the Fire," *Opera News* XL/14 (February14, 1976), p. 11.
17. Ibid.
18. It turns out that Hillis's recollection of Antonia Brico's Chicago appearance was not entirely accurate. Brico led members of the Chicago Symphony Orchestra (a reduced roster with nearly one third of the musicians not being contracted CSO members) on only one occasion, on January 12, 1976, at the Auditorium Theatre. The concert was organized as a benefit for the Business and Professional People for the Public Interest and was not presented under the auspices of the Orchestral Association. Hillis likely was not aware of this, incorrectly stating that Brico was "never asked back" when she had not been hired by the Orchestral Association in the first place. Ann Feldman interviewed Margaret Hillis in 1995. Feldman has an MA in piano from The American University and a PhD in History of Culture from the University of Chicago. She is also a Visiting Scholar in Gender Studies at Northwestern University. She was the host of *Noteworthy Women,* a radio series of ten-programs celebrating Women's History Month. The first four programs were syndicated by WFMT Fine Arts network in 1995. A recording of this program is part of the Margaret Hillis Collection in the Rosenthal Archives of the Chicago Symphony Orchestra Association.

19. Nancy Malitz, "For Hillis, Chorus Era Is Here," *The Cincinnati Enquirer*, March 30, 1980, p. I-2.
20. Beth Abelson Macleod, *Women Performing Music: The Emergence of American Women as Classical Instrumentalists and Conductors* (Jefferson, North Carolina: McFarland and Company, 1945), p. 26.
21. Ibid., p. 27.
22. Ibid., p. 29.
23. Ibid., p. 101.
24. Ammer, *Unsung*, p. 109.
25. Kay D. Lawson, "Women Orchestral Conductors: Factors Affecting Career Development," Master's thesis (Michigan State University, 1983), p. 33; citing Richard Schickel, *The World of Carnegie Hall* (New York: Julian Messner, 1960), p. 226; thesis in the Margaret Hillis Collection, Rosenthal Archives of the Chicago Symphony Orchestra Association.
26. Macleod, *Women Performing Music*, p. 110.
27. Macleod, *Women Performing Music*, p. 118.
28. "City of Cabots Views Its Dynamic New Leader," *Musical America* 45, January 22, 1927, p. 4.
29. Karen Monson, "Sweet 'Brava!' for an Old Pro," *Chicago Daily News,* November 1, 1977.
30. Joan Catoni Conlon, *Wisdom, Wit, and Will: Women Choral Conductors on Their Art* (Chicago: GIA Publications, 2009), p. 137.
31. Macleod, *Women Performing Music*, p. 147.
32. Ibid.
33. Ibid.
34. Barbara Zuck, "Hillis Conducts for Listeners, Not Lookers." *Columbus Dispatch Weekender*, January 21, 1982, p. 3.
35. Ibid.
36. Jagow, "Women Orchestral Conductors," p. 5; citing Ammer's *Unsung*.
37. Jagow, "Women Orchestral Conductors," p. 5; citing Adrienne Fried Block and Carol Neuls-Bates's *Women in American Music: A Bibliography of Music and Literature* (Westport, Connecticut: Greenwood Press, 1979), pp. 202–203.
38. Ammer, *Unsung*, p. 205.
39. Jagow, "Women Orchestral Conductors," p. 4 of 15.
40. Ibid., p. 15.
41. Ammer, *Unsung*, p. 212.
42. Macleod, *Women Performing Music*, p. 116.
43. Blair Tindall, "Call Me Madame Maestro," *New York Times*, January 14, 2005, p. E.1.
44. Macleod, *Women Performing Music*, p. 131.
45. Ammer, *Unsung*, p. 202.
46. Lawson, "Women Orchestral Conductors," pp. 60–61.

Part II

CHAPTER 5

NEW YORK: THE JUILLIARD YEARS

hat was it like for Margaret Hillis to leave the safe, tranquil, and rather sheltered environments of Kokomo and Bloomington for the brazen atmosphere of Manhattan in the late 1940s? Margaret arrived in New York City in 1947, a time she referred to as New York's golden age.[1] In Dan Wakefield's book, *New York in the '50s*, one can view New York City from the perspective Margaret would have likely held. Wakefield, of similar background to hers (i.e., born and raised in Indiana), spent some of his college years at Indiana University and then, like Margaret, moved to New York City to pursue his life's work. In his book, Wakefield documented these coming-of-age adventures in the big city, studying at Columbia University in 1952, and remaining there for his young professional life as a budding writer. He described in vivid detail the cultural contrasts between his experiences growing up in conservative midwestern Indianapolis with the richly diverse and artistically creative environment of this burgeoning international city. His family expressed their concerns about his attending the "liberal stronghold of Columbia in alien New York City" as a true threat to the morality of his upbringing. Wakefield, as with Hillis, was similarly inspired by one of his IU professors, who suggested he continue his education in the place that could truly help him expand his craft. New York City for Wakefield "bore no resemblance to the idyllic, pastoral campuses of the movies, or the ones [he] knew in the Midwest, where ivy-clad buildings were set on rolling hills with ancient elms and [where] chapel bells tolled the slow passage of time."[2] Wakefield acknowledged a much more stimulating artistic environment in his new home, including the rich music life he encountered.

"New York was not just our laboratory but our theater, our art museum, our opera house. It was one thing to take a music appreciation course . . . but quite another to have the music of great professionals performed live."[3]

> Our chosen place of exile from middle America was not Europe but New York. . . . There was a cross-pollination of music, painting, writing, an incredible world of painters, sculptors, writers, and actors, enough so we could be each other's fans. . . . I threw all-night parties with new friends who, like myself, had come from the hinterlands to make their fame and fortune and "find themselves" in the pulsing heart of the hip new world's hot center.[4]
>
> I debated politics and books with James Baldwin and Michael Harrington . . . saw Jason Robards in *The Iceman Cometh* and Geraldine Page in *Summer and Smoke* . . . went with buddies and dates to the Amato Opera, a converted movie house with a single piano as orchestra, where music students carried cardboard elephants in the grand march of *Aida*.[5]

Indeed, Margaret herself would come to know nascent luminaries across the arts, eventually befriending famous writers, including Langston Hughes, Thornton Wilder, and William Stanley Merwin, along with many brilliant musicians, including Igor Stravinsky, Leontyne Price, Alice Parker, Aaron Copland, Lukas Foss, Ned Rorem, Samuel Barber, Leonard Bernstein, Elliott Carter, Edgard Varèse, and many others. Skyscrapers replaced the greenery of Indiana's flatlands. Noisy subways, buses, and taxis bombarded the senses for these Hoosiers, both hailing from far more tranquil surroundings. More people could be seen in one square block of Manhattan than perhaps would have been encountered in one full day of walking an entire Indiana town. So many colors, ethnic food aromas permeating the streets, so many languages, so many people. Margaret, as with Dan Wakefield a few years after, was filled with aspiration of achieving the seemingly impossible and found the very place where this was most likely to happen. Margaret's path began at Juilliard in the fall of 1947 (Picture 20).

Picture 20.
Margaret Hillis Juilliard School photo, ca. 1947. (Margaret Hillis Collection, Rosenthal Archives of the Chicago Symphony Orchestra Association)

STUDYING WITH ROBERT SHAW

At the start of Hillis's advanced studies in choral conducting at Juilliard, she knew it would be in some ways as if starting over. Her background in orchestral music provided her little familiarity with choral repertoire, choral rehearsal strategies, or singing technique for that matter. At the time she matriculated at Juilliard, she claimed, "I didn't know Bach's B Minor Mass from a hole in the ground. . . . There was one [choral] piece I loved, and that was the Fauré Requiem. But I hadn't heard any others."[6]

Adding to the complexity of embarking upon this new field of study was Hillis's bias about the chorus as a musical ensemble.

I didn't have much respect for choruses at that point, [because] most of them sounded as if they ought to go home and knit. Most of them should have. But Bob Shaw had a very beautiful chorus . . . so I sang in the chorus under him. . . . I observed him . . . we had some lessons . . . but he was very busy at this time with his own career . . . so the best that the students could do was analyze his scores along with him and observe him and try to analyze what it was that he had in his ear and how he went about getting the things that he did.[7]

Margaret enrolled in Juilliard's Extension Division in the fall of 1947. Many of the classes she took were taught by Robert Shaw. However, Shaw's classes seemed more like an apprenticeship than traditional classes. The conducting classes were less helpful than expected. Only fleetingly would Shaw give Hillis, or any of his other students, direct guidance. Hillis conveyed in her 1997 interview with Norman Pellegrini, "[Shaw] wasn't much of a teacher. But you did learn from observing him and trying to figure out what was happening in his ear."[8] Hillis went on to describe a story about Shaw's astonishment after observing Hillis in a final conducting exam.

It was the first one of the five pieces, Op. 104 of Brahms, which I just adore still, all five of them. And we [Shaw and Hillis] went walking down the hall afterwards, and Bob [Shaw] said to me, "Where did you learn to handle the cadences like that?" I said, "What do you mean?" He said, "I was sure you were ritarding, but you weren't, and they were so elegantly . . ." I said, "Well I learned it from" . . . chuckles . . . [she indicated Shaw]. He said, "Ah, it comes down through talent."[9]

This experience was corroborated by Margaret's classmate, future renowned composer and conductor Alice Parker. Both women, the only females in Juilliard's conducting program, shared similar opinions regarding Shaw's lack of direct input regarding their growth as conductors.

Parker relayed her impressions of taking coursework with Shaw, stating:

We never did anything intellectually challenging in the conducting class. In fact, the only time he gave me any hand gesture indication was at Tanglewood when I was an active conducting student, and I was doing one of the Hindemith pieces that was in 7/8 or something like that and he was there trying to get me to focus my hands so that someone else could see that I was doing 7/8 and not something else.[10]

Laying aside this circumstance, both women expressed that the benefits of being a student of Shaw were great despite his teaching limitations. Though both Hillis and Parker considered Shaw a mediocre teacher, they both admired him greatly and benefited tremendously from their work with him. They were watching a master at work, and this alone reaped great rewards for both women.

To better understand why Robert Shaw taught the way that he did at the point when Alice Parker and Margaret Hillis were his students, it is worth exploring where he was in his own career progression. Shaw had been appointed the director of choral music at Juilliard only two years before Margaret's arrival and he was, in many ways, a novice himself. He was twenty-nine years old and came into this position as he had so many other musical opportunities to that point, with modest experience and limited musical background. Though enormously talented, Shaw was well aware that his students were coming to Juilliard with more formal musical training than he had as their teacher. After all, Margaret Hillis had just graduated with a music degree from Indiana University, played many instruments, and had performed in orchestras since her youth. She also possessed a solid background in music theory and composition. Shaw had never formally studied theory, composition, or conducting, nor did he play any instruments, and he was now to be her master teacher. Being in a position to teach when he himself believed he had much to learn explains why he may have been hesitant to teach in the formal ways of most professors. His hope was that his students could learn by watching him as he had learned from his mentor, Fred Waring.

Shaw began his work in choral music with no intention of becoming a professional musician. He wanted some extra money as he pursued studies in religion and literature at Pomona College in Claremont, California. He did so by directing the Pomona Glee Club, where he was discovered by Fred Waring, the well-known bandleader and radio personality, who had come to Pomona's campus for the filming of a movie. Waring was so impressed with the choral sound Shaw was eliciting from his untrained glee club singers that he immediately offered him a job. Shaw would eventually agree to accept this offer, moving to New York City to form a glee club that Waring could conduct for his national radio show. It was the first professional radio choir in the United States, broadcasting two performances a day, five days a week. Shaw's role was to audition and rehearse the singers that Waring would direct on the radio. Waring saw in Shaw the natural musical intuitions, his enormous talent, and a charisma that could motivate people. From 1938–1945, Shaw worked closely with Waring and learned by his example how to rehearse a choir efficiently, how to arrange popular music for choirs, and how to guide a choir to communicate the meaning of the text. Waring helped his singers convey words more effectively through a hyper-focused attention to articulating every syllable. This tone-syllable approach was a method Waring had devised "in which his singers would perform with 'all the beauty, in all the sounds, of all the syllables, in all the words' [Shaw's definition], which were sounded phonetically."[11] In this way, attention was given to sound out each syllable so that words would be clearly understandable to an audience. Shaw determined that this careful attention to text worked well for performing popular music, but as Shaw's interests grew in the direction of classical music, he realized that this technique would need to be modified to fulfill the true intentions of classical composers. Shaw believed that text in classical composition should be subservient to the musical line. He never completely departed from the tone-syllable approach, but he learned to balance it in service of the vocal line. In a sense, Shaw took Waring's approach to the next level by applying the tone-syllable concept to the musical line.[12]

Another benefit of Shaw's work with Waring on the radio shows they would produce together was Shaw's development of a keen sense of timing. Time became almost an obsession for Shaw. He would calculate to the minute how his time would be spent in rehearsals. He was equally careful with tempos he would conduct, continually alert to any variations. This sensitivity to time would also emerge in his approach to rhythm. Shaw became extremely demanding for rhythmic precision and vitality in the ensembles he conducted. In a 1996 *Choral Journal* interview to commemorate his eightieth birthday, Shaw stated:

> All problems with enunciation were cured by an attention to metric precision and most intonation problems were vastly improved by having people arrive at the same moment of music simultaneously. Matters of articulation and accentuation depended completely on time. Therefore, the rehearsal techniques [that Shaw developed] were simply practical devices used to establish an absolute integrity of metric utterance.[13]

Just four years prior to his Juilliard appointment and while he continued to work for Waring, Shaw was determined to pursue the more classical side of musical performance. To that end, he developed the Collegiate Chorale, first formed in 1941. Shaw was initially invited to guest conduct the group, and shortly thereafter he would become the conductor. This large chorus of mixed voices, consisting of both amateur and professional singers, was not paid but nonetheless created a professional sound through Shaw's insistence on precision and accuracy. Shaw's intentions for this chorus were to showcase the immense talent pool of singers inhabiting New York as a platform for promoting classical choral music while espousing his views of humanity. The group performed serious choral literature, largely a cappella, but also included some of the more contemporary music of the day. Shaw auditioned hundreds of singers, inviting the most talented and musically adept into the chorus. He welcomed a diverse ensemble, referring to his chorus as a "melting pot that sings."[14] As one who was keenly sensitive to the injustices put upon diverse races and ethnicities at this time in America, Shaw chose to use the influence of his ensemble to represent his rejection of such prejudices.

As Shaw expanded his choral background through his work with the Collegiate Chorale, he was gaining notice by prominent figures in New York's music scene, including William Schuman, who had just become the president of Julliard. Schuman wrote, "The sounds of [Shaw's] chorus were as magnificent as the musical innocence and scholarly ineptitude of its leader."[15] Schuman would become an important mentor for Shaw, recognizing in him the pure artistry he possessed even though he lacked the scholarship. Schuman had found in this novice that the shortcomings could be easily overcome, knowing Shaw's ability to work tirelessly along with his knack for absorbing what he learned with great speed. Schuman offered Shaw the position at Julliard, which prompted him to leave Waring's employ. Shaw explained to Waring that moving into an academic position was a decision that would provide him the opportunity to learn by working with the school's outstanding school orchestra and through his association with other conductors and composers who could teach him in the areas where he felt such profound inadequacy as a musician. Shaw shared his reasoning for leaving Waring upon entering the Julliard position. Aware of his shortcomings, Shaw revealed his frustrations about himself:

Now that discontent was . . . due to the limitations of my own musicianship; for at no time during those years [of working with Waring] was I ready—nor am I now ready—to step into the symphonic and concert field as a schooled and authoritative musician. But while my study the past few months has been only enough to show how much is to be learned and how great is my lack, I feel I know the way I must go and the music with which I must work. It is a hard decision, for with the music I love and believe in most, I am the greater child and novice. My going to Juilliard then is largely a "musical" decision.[16]

At this same time, circa 1946, Shaw met the other powerful influence in his early career, Julius Herford, a well-known pianist and choral conductor. A refugee of Nazi Germany, Herford had immigrated to New York and began teaching at Columbia University. Lukas Foss introduced Herford, with whom he was studying, to Robert Shaw while they were collaborating on Foss's new work, *The Prairie*. Herford would become a major teacher for Shaw, helping him develop techniques he sorely lacked in score analysis. These techniques would guide Shaw's approach to discovering a composer's intent through the structure of a piece. Herford became a colleague of Shaw's, teaching at Juilliard from 1946–1949. Shaw relied upon Herford for regular counsel, guiding him in learning harmony, counterpoint, and even providing him lessons in piano, an instrument Shaw would never master. In a memorial resolution written by Professor Jan Harrington and published in Bloomington Faculty Council Minutes of Indiana University on October 5, 1982, Herford's talent as a teacher was described in glowing terms: "Anyone encountering Julius Herford in a score study seminar remembers the almost mystical vision flowing from his minute observation of the simple details of the score, the gentle humor, and the startling insight revealing new truths in masterworks long familiar."[17] Shaw was able to count on Herford's extraordinary teaching prowess, preparing Shaw for music he was about to rehearse and conduct, thereby enabling him to learn scores more thoroughly than ever before. Though Shaw had hoped to take a sabbatical to study with Nadia Boulanger in Europe for further expansion of his score preparation, it never happened. Shaw's lack of formal musical training would haunt him throughout his career. He never believed he was completely worthy of the opportunities that came his way, and no amount of hard work would compensate for the feeling of ineptitude that followed him throughout his career.

One year after beginning his position at Juilliard, Shaw began to record professionally as chorus master of the Broadway show *Carmen Jones*, and then in 1945 he recorded *Six Chansons* by Paul Hindemith. In 1946, he recorded Bach's

Magnificat and other Bach compositions, and by 1947, he recorded his first Bach Mass in B Minor and Brahms *Ein deutsches Requiem*. Shaw was beginning to work with important conductors in New York, preparing his chorus for Leonard Bernstein's recording of *On the Town* in 1945. It was also in 1945 that Shaw began to work with Arturo Toscanini. Shaw was hired to prepare the Collegiate Chorale in the final movement of Beethoven's Symphony No. 9 for Toscanini. When Toscanini witnessed Shaw in rehearsal and heard the chorus, he embraced Shaw, praising the beauty of the chorus under Shaw's direction. Shaw would regularly prepare choruses for Toscanini with the NBC Orchestra, thereafter becoming Shaw's greatest mentor.

By 1947, Shaw had his own radio program with his chorus. His career and his frenetic schedule were featured in *Time* magazine in December 1947, describing him as the "busiest musician in town." The article highlighted his schedule at Christmas time. Shaw's first stop included his conducting of the RCA Victor Chorale for the NBC RCA Victor Show, followed by a commute four blocks away to the CBS Studios to conduct Beethoven's Mass in C Major, and two days later to conduct his Collegiate Chorale at Carnegie Hall in Bach's *Christmas Oratorio*, followed the next night with conducting Christmas carols for CBS's annual holiday program and finally conducting Juilliard's Christmas concert. This grueling schedule was not unusual for Shaw, who was also married and had a young family eagerly awaiting him at home.[18]

In the summer of 1948, Shaw became director of choral music for the Berkshire Music Center in Tanglewood, Massachusetts. At the same time Shaw was to be in Tanglewood, he was also directing a summer radio program in New York City. Shaw would commute between New York City, recording the radio show on the weekends, and the Berkshires, teaching at Tanglewood during the week. The Robert Shaw Chorale was formed in 1948 primarily for this radio show. The forty-voice professional ensemble, drawn from the larger Collegiate Chorale, became well known and well respected, performing a wide range of repertoire from popular to classical, recording regularly, and touring nationally and internationally.

It is not a wonder with the schedule and personal career aspirations Shaw possessed that he was less attentive to his teaching responsibilities at Juilliard. It was one of many hats he wore, likely making teaching the lowest of his priorities as he began his meteoric rise in conducting. Nevertheless, there is no doubt that students such as Margaret Hillis took note of the exhaustive schedule Shaw endured and would come to follow in those footsteps not long after studying with him.

Picture 21.
Robert Shaw conducting in Salt Lake, 1981.
(Estate of Robert Shaw)

ALICE PARKER, MARGARET HILLIS, AND THE JUILLIARD EXPERIENCE

Alice Parker began her studies with Shaw at Juilliard one year prior to Hillis's arrival. Parker was one of seven students and the only woman in the choral conducting program until Hillis arrived to join her. Parker described Hillis as being very serious, focused, and reserved in the beginning. Parker explained that Margaret was hard to get to know, but as time went on she gradually opened up to Alice and they would become lifelong friends. Parker described how she and Margaret basically followed Shaw around. He required his students to attend and participate in his Juilliard chorus. Hillis and Parker sang in the alto section of the chorus. During Hillis's first year, in May 1948, Shaw prepared the choir for a performance of Beethoven's Symphony No. 9, which was conducted by Serge Koussevitzky. In Hillis's second year, she performed under Shaw's direction a Haydn symphony and the New York premiere of Bernard Rogers's choral-orchestral work *The Passion*.

As part of their degree studies under Shaw, Hillis and Parker were required to observe rehearsals of the Collegiate Chorale. They would sit on the side and carefully take in Shaw's rehearsal techniques. Hillis often sang in the Collegiate Chorale. Parker, describing herself as an "eager beaver," would take detailed notes throughout Shaw's rehearsals, meticulously tracking his choice of warm-ups, rehearsal strategies, and masterful timing of everything he did in each rehearsal. She explained that by recording on index cards every moment of his rehearsals, she developed the ability to predict what he would do next, enabling her to incorporate some of these skills as her own rehearsal techniques. Often after a Collegiate Chorale rehearsal, Shaw and students would go out to the local pub and talk for hours about the rehearsal that had just taken place. This was where Parker said she was able to ask questions and gain the most insight into Shaw's approach. The "pub experiences" were where the real teaching and learning from Shaw occurred.[19]

One of the requirements Shaw had for his conducting students was that each of them must have their own chorus to conduct. He would never come out to observe any of their rehearsals or performances, but he insisted that his young conductors had a chorus of their own to practice the techniques they were learning from him. Hillis was able to find a chorus to work with, explaining, "I had to be very enterprising. I finally found one in Brooklyn, a Black chorus sponsored by the NAACP [Metropolitan Youth Chorale] and only three out of the sixty singers could read music!"[20] Margaret described this choir when she began her work with them in 1948 as a group of "wonderful people." There were no auditions. Anyone who wished to join could do so, which led to a very unbalanced membership of voices. The Metropolitan Youth Chorale was comprised of six tenors, twelve basses, and "thousands of women [including] lots of altos who were just lazy sopranos."[21] Though she claimed Shaw only taught her technique and not the practical side of rehearsing, it was clear that his influence in structuring a rehearsal filtered into her inventive ways of building a chorus up from the most basic skill level. The statement below reflects Shaw's influence on Hillis's rehearsal efficiency through extreme attention to detailed planning and time management, two traits for which she would become well known as her career progressed.

So, first thing I did was to set up sight-reading exams. . . . I had to plan my rehearsals so that in a rehearsal everybody sang the tenor line first . . .

then the bass and then we put the two together and when I was pretty well convinced that the tenors thought that they were singing a tune . . . then I would add the alto part and finally add the soprano, otherwise the tenors would be singing the soprano line an octave below all the way through. I planned every rehearsal in detail—if you would have asked me what I was doing at three minutes after eight I could have told you what note was being sung.[22]

Hillis learned quickly to "stick to her guns" when it came to repertoire choices for her chorus. The singers wanted to sing music they were more familiar with. "They wanted Victor Herbert, things like that. I said, I love Victor Herbert, but that is not my repertory."[23] When she suggested a conductor who might be more to their liking, because he specialized in the music they were requesting, they insisted they only wanted her as their conductor. Her response, "Well, love me, love my dog."[24] Her first concert with them was Schubert's Mass in G Major along with some other smaller pieces, including several solos. In subsequent concerts, she would perform music of Bach, Schütz, and even Brahms's *Nänie* with orchestra. She said that her singers were initially concerned their families and friends would not enjoy this music, but it turned out the opposite was true. Hillis had this chorus for three years and credits this experience as the starting point of her rehearsal techniques. Applying what she had learned from watching Shaw, whose methods she described as "marvelous," she shaped the singers into a refined ensemble.[25]

Reflecting upon classes she experienced while at Juilliard, including several she shared with future opera superstar Leontyne Price, Hillis recalled accompanying her in a vocal literature class. As Hillis told Norman Pellegrini in a 1997 interview, both classmates reconnected during the 1977 performances and recording of Verdi's Requiem with the Chicago Symphony Orchestra and Chorus, which won Hillis her first Grammy Award in 1978 for best choral performance. Hillis recalled how she and Price reminisced about their Juilliard days, sitting next to one another in an Italian diction class where they told "dirty jokes" instead of paying attention to their boring instructor. Hillis recalled that during one of the recording sessions of the Requiem, as Hillis approached conductor Sir Georg Solti about a balance problem, Price leaned over to Margaret and commented, "This is sure different from Juilliard, isn't it?" to which Margaret replied, "It sure is!"[26]

During her Juilliard years, Hillis continued to hone her craft, observing Shaw in rehearsals, applying those lessons with her Metropolitan Youth Chorale of Brooklyn, and increasing her studies even further as she began working with Shaw's mentor, Julius Herford, as well. Herford, by then on the faculty at Juilliard, taught Hillis the needed score analysis techniques that Shaw had also experienced with him. Hillis would study with Herford from 1947–1950, after which they maintained a professional and personal connection for years to come. Together, Herford and Hillis would eventually become peers, teaching choral seminars together throughout the country. They remained in correspondence until Herford's death at the age of eighty in 1981.

Hillis chose to cut her work at Juilliard short due to the departure of Robert Shaw in 1949. Unlike Alice Parker, who completed her graduate work a year earlier, Hillis would end her Juilliard training without completing a terminal degree. Since Shaw was the reason for Hillis being at Juilliard, she likely saw no compelling reason to remain once he was gone. After all, she had come to Juilliard not so much to earn another degree but instead to study with the master of her field. Having no intention of teaching, a graduate degree was of less value to her than the practical training she would gain by continuing to work with Shaw. The fall of 1949 was the beginning of Hillis's journey toward a professional conducting career. As with her female conductor predecessors, she would create opportunities for herself, often at great personal and financial sacrifice, but all in service of fostering her growth to build a career in the field of conducting, which she so greatly desired.

ENDNOTES

1. Jane Samuelson, "For the Love of Music," *Chicago Magazine* (April 1980): p. 230.
2. Dan Wakefield, *New York in the '50s* (New York: Open Road Integrated Media, 2016), Kindle, p. 427 of 7627.
3. Wakefield, *New York*, p. 755 of 7627.
4. Wakefield, *New York*, Introduction.
5. Wakefield, *New York*, p. 121 of 7627.
6. Margaret Hillis, interview by Norman Pellegrini (transcribed by Stanley G. Livengood), October 6, 1997, p. 6.
7. Jon Bentz, "Interview of Margaret Hillis Director Chicago Symphony Orchestra, September 19, 1989, Archives Committee, Oral History Project, 1992," p. 2 (Margaret Hillis Collection, Rosenthal Archives of the Chicago Symphony Orchestra Association).
8. Margaret Hillis, interview by Pellegrini, p. 6.
9. Ibid.
10. Interview with Alice Parker at Chorus America, Washington, D.C., June 12, 2014.
11. Keith C. Burris, *Deep River* (Chicago: GIA Publications, 2013), p. 63.
12. Ibid.

13. Jeffrey Baxter, "An Interview with Robert Shaw: Reflections at Eighty," *Choral Journal* (April 1996): p. 9.

14. Burris, *Deep River*, p. 108.

15. Ibid., p. 70.

16. Ibid., p. 75.

17. Jan Harrington, "Memorial Resolution, Julius Herford," *Bloomington Faculty Council Minutes*, October 5, 1982, accessed September 11, 2021, http://webapp1.dlib.indiana.edu/bfc/view?docId=B07-1983.

18. Burris, *Deep River*, p. 105.

19. Interview with Alice Parker at Chorus America, Washington, D.C., June 12, 2014.

20. Ulla Colgrass, "Conductor Hillis Reversed the Odds," *Music Management Magazine* (November/December 1981): p. 15.

21. Bentz, "Interview of Margaret Hillis," p. 3.

22. Ibid.

23. Margaret Hillis, interview by Pellegrini, p. 6.

24. Margaret Hillis, interview by Pellegrini, p. 4.

25. George McElroy and Jane W. Stedman, "The Chorus Lady," *Opera News*, February 16, 1974, p. 11.

26. Margaret Hillis, interview by Pellegrini, p. 23.

CHAPTER 6
A CAREER IS LAUNCHED

By 1949, Margaret Hillis had only been training as a conductor in the choral field for a few years, yet she was determined to step out into the real world of music making. Remarkably, she made this vision a reality in a short period of time. How she was able to launch her career so quickly was a combination of hard work, courage, sheer determination, and the backing of her generous, wealthy family. Before tracking Hillis's meteoric rise, it is worth taking stock of her strengths and weaknesses as she was about to step into the big leagues.

Hillis would leave Juilliard at the end of her spring semester in 1949 with a basic knowledge of choral rehearsal techniques and repertoire. Fortunately, she could not have had a better training ground than her work with Robert Shaw, who filled in the learning gaps between her instrumental and choral background. Hillis had come into Juilliard a complete novice with regard to choral repertoire, but that would all change when she became a member of Shaw's Juilliard chorus and his Collegiate Chorale. In those ensembles, she would perform high-quality choral literature under the guidance of a true master of the craft. Exposure to Shaw's musical selections was significant in that finding quality choral music in the late 1940s was difficult. Shaw's programming became the example by which Hillis developed her taste in repertoire. In addition to providing Hillis a model for programming and repertoire, Shaw taught his methods of making music come alive by example. He applied rehearsal strategies he had learned from *his* mentor, Fred Waring, and developed them even further into his own. Through the techniques of Shaw and Waring, Hillis would learn the importance of efficiency in rehearsing, managing time masterfully, and problem solving in the most practical and straightforward manner. Shaw's obsession with time and how he organized a rehearsal, dividing segments into carefully timed fragments of focus, was not lost on Hillis, who would adapt this into her own methodology.

Lacking prior singing experience, Hillis was able to learn how to approach text from her work with Shaw. She observed his techniques for unifying sound through careful management of the diverse languages in his choral selections. Having only the modest training of Juilliard's diction classes, such as the one she shared with Leontyne Price described earlier, Hillis was able to benefit from Shaw's detailed approach to pronunciation of text for ensemble singing, which varied significantly from the basic pronunciation of languages she was taught in those diction classes. Shaw's corporate approach to pronunciation enabled an audience to understand the words being sung. Shaw had learned how to manage diction from Fred Waring, but he would adapt those methods, believing that Waring's extreme approach disrupted the musicality. Shaw believed, "In choral music, the musical line is predominant . . . the words must be subservient to the music and the musical line cannot be bent or broken. Musicality cannot be compromised."[1] Designing this modified approach, Shaw insisted his singers listen and line things up with extreme attention to rhythmic precision. His use of count singing—along with rhythmic placement of syllables, consonants, and vowels—would become part of Hillis's rehearsal techniques.

The most important lesson Hillis learned that can be attributed to her years working with Robert Shaw was choral tone. The rich, warm, unified, flexible, and unforced vocal sound was one she first encountered in Shaw's choruses. That sound was continually reinforced in Margaret's ear through many hours of observing Shaw and singing under his direction. He would focus his singers on creating shimmering tone without allowing the sound to become broken in service of the text. Shaw instilled in his singers the importance of listening to one another while singing. In her own choirs, Margaret would refer to this phenomenon as "a listened-to sound," created when singers align themselves perfectly to the sound around them. For Shaw "words were not king—sound was," and the way he built this singular tone quality of his choruses was the most important lesson Hillis and her fellow students would take from their observation of and participation in his rigorous rehearsals.[2]

Shaw's methods became Hillis's foundation, upon which she would build her own style. Added to the lessons learned in recent years at Juilliard, she would apply her own strengths as she began to develop her rehearsal methods. One significant strength she possessed was her ability to communicate. When rehearsing, she kept her talking to a minimum and chose her words carefully to keep an efficient and tightly run rehearsal. It was the clarity of the words she chose that distinguished her beyond the level of her mentor, who would sometimes digress in rehearsals with embellishments to enhance the singers' experiences. Hillis's meticulous word choice can be attributed to her natural ability as a teacher, which she developed while teaching the Muncie pilots to fly during World War II. Hillis conveyed her sentiments about the role conductors play as teachers, remarking in an interview, "Of course, [teaching] that's a conductor's function, whether it be choruses, orchestra—whatever. They're teachers."[3] The strategic and straightforward manner in which Hillis communicated information, injecting just the right amount of humor at precisely the right moments, would become a signature strength of her rehearsal methods.

As Hillis was about to go out on her own, she had already benefited from several years working with her Metropolitan Youth Chorale in Brooklyn. When she first began her work with this group, the singers had no sight-singing ability, were of modest vocal talent, and had almost no experience part-singing. Hillis learned how to shape a chorus from the most basic level by first instilling the fundamentals. These rehearsal techniques were not taught by Shaw, which forced Hillis to develop methods of her own for working with choral beginners. Her growing accumulation of rehearsal strategies would become extremely valuable to her as she built her own choruses from the ground up. These methods served her well going forward with every level of choruses she would direct.

Applying all she had learned from Shaw and in her earliest conducting experiences, Hillis began to develop her methodology. As she encountered a problem in her ensemble work, she would find a way to resolve it. Once she found the solution, she would add it to her growing list of rehearsal techniques. Hillis chronicled all she had learned and would soon begin to share her pedagogical discoveries in choral workshops, supporting other young choral conductors interested in acquiring her methods.

As any other novice leaving the safety net of academia, Margaret would confront challenges as she moved into the professional world. Some of these difficulties would be due to external forces, and others were based upon her own personal limitations. Margaret was not easily deterred by roadblocks. Ever resourceful in solving problems, Margaret relied upon her Juilliard training and would then experiment with her own ideas. Her resourcefulness was a strength that would distinguish her for years to come.

One challenge Hillis initially encountered was finding choral music of substance for her ensembles to perform. She greatly appreciated the music she was exposed to at Juilliard and in the Collegiate Chorale, and she became determined to share these acquisitions with other conductors in the field facing similar difficulties. At the time, there were no choral journal publications to peruse for suggestions of quality choral literature. There was no Internet to consult for newly published material. Only limited choral recordings had been produced to gather ideas for programming. There were very few places where one could go to explore and purchase choral music, and there was no centralized way to exchange ideas and repertoire with other colleagues. Hillis would ultimately resolve this issue for herself and others by forming a choral foundation, which not only provided her and other conductors access to quality literature but also provided educative support. Hillis's future establishment of her American Choral Foundation was the first organization of its kind for the exchange of choral pedagogy and literature to support the growing choral scene in America.

In addition to the limitations of external forces, such as resources, Hillis faced internal challenges as she stepped out on her own. She would continually struggle with her inability to inspire her ensembles in the way she had experienced with her mentor. A key asset for any conductor is being able to elicit expressive performances. Through gesture, inspirational words, and by showing an emotional connection with the music, conductors are able to inspire their musicians. Hillis did not acquire Shaw's knack for emotionally connecting with his singers. He did this naturally with his huge personality. Admittedly, Shaw's charisma was a mixed bag, often turning into aggressive and even angry moments in his quest to inspire a desired sound or effect. Shaw had a temper that would more than occasionally rear its ugly head in the midst of an intense rehearsal. Alice Parker referred to some rehearsals as being "very inflammatory" in which she described "much yelling and book throwing" to have taken place.[4]

Hillis would develop the opposite style, knowing Shaw's fiery approach could never work for a woman, nor was it in any way part of her personality. Hillis had learned from a young age the importance of comporting herself with complete control and dignity, which suited her well in the way she would eventually be received as a conductor. Being a member of the most elite Kokomo family, she was accustomed to being on display, learning from early on what acceptable behavior looked like as well as the consequences of being too aggressive, which would deem her less feminine than what was expected of her. She saw how the consequences played out for other women in the conducting field, who were viewed as less appropriate due to their strong personalities and gestures. Negative press and mocking cartoon illustrations were often the consequence for Hillis's predecessors, such as those Ethel Leginska encountered. Though Hillis's extreme control of her behavior served her well as a woman in a man's field, it caused her rehearsals to be viewed as dry and formulaic, uninspiring for some who would sing under her direction.

Unlike Shaw, who could be said to have worn his heart on his sleeve, Margaret's way of making music was much more prescriptive. Alice Parker recalled Hillis as being precise but lacking emotionality. Parker attributed this to Hillis not being an "intuitive musician," yet Parker respected Hillis greatly for her incredible precision and for her many other contributions to the choral field.[5] Unlike Parker's first impression of Margaret when they met at Juilliard, in which Parker described Hillis as reserved and serious, she later recognized Margaret's warm and humorous personality. But this lighter side of Margaret was revealed only to the closest of her friends and colleagues, which included Alice and her husband, Tom Pyle. The reserved side of Margaret's personality was what she most often conveyed publicly, both in her interactions with professional colleagues and in her music making.

Hillis's inability to reveal the warmth she possessed caused limitations in what she could elicit from her singers emotionally. Because she held herself back, her choirs could only go so far in their attempt to be expressive. Instead, Hillis would take an almost scientific approach to make the more intimate aspects of music come alive. Margaret compensated for her inability to inspire her ensembles emotionally by prescribing just the right amount of dynamics, articulations, word stress, and other expressive techniques in order to help her ensemble bring forth the expressive dimension of a work. Through her concise instruction, the emotional elements would ultimately be achieved. Occasionally, Hillis would reveal her inner connections with the music through a facial expression or a physical gesture that provided a glimpse into her feelings. However, if she sensed the chorus "getting ahead of themselves" by becoming too emotional at the expense of precision, she would remark, "You are not ready to be enjoying this music yet." This limitation in Hillis's rehearsal process would plague her throughout her career and would often find its way into reviews of her performances.

Though Margaret was not an overtly demonstrative personality, such as her role model Robert Shaw, she had a quiet charisma that became every bit as impactful but in a completely different way. The feelings she had for the music were there, but she could not show them. The reasons for Margaret's circumspection were complicated. First, the limits placed upon women in music, including what they could say and do, described previously, can account for a part of Margaret's restrained approach. Added to the complexity of limitations thrust upon women, there was yet another interference preventing Margaret from being a more emotionally available conductor. Hillis acknowledged years later that she experienced a tremendous level of fear that was always present at this early point in her career. While still at a novice level, she was in one way very brave, willing to put her talent on public display. Yet to do so she would have to compartmentalize yet another emotional layer, further contributing to the somewhat distant approach to her performing. In journalist Jane Samuelson's 1980 interview with Margaret for *Chicago Magazine,* Margaret conveyed that her level of fear was due to a true lack of self-confidence early on.

> The real terror was that I couldn't meet myself—myself as a human being, myself as a talent. And you have to see the terror through, somehow. I see young musicians today in similar situations. They don't often express it, but you sense it now and then . . . [You] have to have the guts to carry it through. And "guts" is the right word, because that's where you feel the terror. . . . When I first started out in the professional field, I didn't know very much, and I knew I didn't. . . . I took on a public image that was not my true self. I think my image gave out the message: Don't undermine me. I was scared. . . . It was the realization that most people didn't believe that a woman belonged there on the podium. But I did! And I had a certain self-consciousness also about being looked upon as a woman conductor rather than as a conductor. . . . So, I stood up there and said, "By God I am going to be a conductor and the hell with them!"[6]

Margaret hid behind a façade of confidence, conveying the most acceptable feminine behavior she could muster.

MARGARET'S PRIVATE WORLD

There was another layer of restraint that Margaret placed upon herself that prevented her from revealing her authentic self on the podium. She carefully hid a secret life she would fully explore in New York. Margaret Hillis was a lesbian. Because of her sexual orientation, she would make every effort to control her manner of behavior and appearance, so as not to reveal her more natural inclinations. Often keeping to herself, Hillis was viewed as a very private person. Alice Parker initially viewed Hillis this way when they first met. However, unlike Alice who was eventually allowed to access Margaret's true personality, most would only see her as illusive, private, and independent. She avoided opening herself up emotionally for fear her secret may be discovered.

Hillis had earned the nickname "Hecate" during her high school days. Hecate was a mythological character associated with magic and witchcraft, and she was also considered a goddess of outcast women. The ability to overcome rejection through a strength of character became emblematic of the name Hecate. This label was eventually associated with the women's liberation movement, as demonstrated by a publication in Queensland, Australia, with the same name. Having the nickname Hecate suggests that Margaret may have conveyed her private side and her independence during her time at Tudor Hall. She would continue to be addressed as Hecate by her former Tudor classmates, as can be seen in letters she kept over the years in her personal files.[7]

Whether or not she pursued intimate relationships at Tudor Hall is not clear. By the time she reached New York City, she would more actively engage in these relationships. The prevailing attitude in the country at this time in history was in no way accepting of gay and lesbian relationships and would have caused grave consequences for Margaret's career. The 1950s in America was a time of extreme conservatism, extending even to a person's sexuality. During this time period, the well-known composer Gian Carlo Menotti wrote *The Unicorn, the Gorgon, and the Manticore* to express his own personal struggles with the condemnation he believed he would have received by others had they known he was a gay man. Instead of going public with his feelings, Menotti found his voice through composition, using the poetry of homosexual French novelist Marcel Proust to help him more aptly express sentiments deeply felt. Menotti conveyed his desire to write an opera on this subject, expressing these thoughts to his student Ned

Rorem ten years before writing the work.[8] When he had finally completed the composition, the allegorical story represented the disapproval of others for his personal relationships. He in fact kept the relationship with his partner, composer Samuel Barber, private during his lifetime, fearing retribution. This fear was real to anyone who shared Menotti's sexuality.

Margaret would have to scrutinize every moment of her life to keep this private. Were this fact ever to be revealed, Margaret's career and possibly the status of her entire family in conservative Kokomo could be at risk. She had to be ever vigilant about how she carried herself and how she behaved, compelling her to hide the most natural part of her being from everyone she encountered. Interviewers would often inquire about her marital status, curious if she had any future plans to marry. Margaret would find a way to respond to her single status, blaming her busy schedule or the fact that she had not ruled out marriage in her future.

This cover-up of her true self worked against her as a conductor. A conductor, as with any artist, must be able to authentically open themselves up emotionally in order to be expressive and to inspire emotion in others. With so much of Margaret's life restricted, in terms of how she must move, how she must dress, and how she must behave as a woman, and having to hide her most natural instincts, all of this, no doubt, interfered with her ability to honestly express herself as a musical artist and limited her ability to inspire others as a consequence. Margaret's secrets would remain her own, as she stepped into the public realm as a young female conductor.

BUILDING HER NETWORK

The challenge for Hillis was to plot a path for what came next after the safety net of college life ended. Any future opportunities would need to be offered or created. In the case of women conductors at Juilliard, there were no substantial offers for conducting positions after graduating from the most prestigious choral program in the country. Alice Parker spoke of her frustration after visiting Juilliard's job placement office hoping for assistance. Unlike her male classmates, there was nothing in the way of advanced conducting nor collegiate teaching positions available for a woman. "No colleges wanted us," Parker explained, not even with her undergraduate degree from Smith College and a graduate degree from Juilliard. The only job Juilliard's placement office could find for Ms. Parker was the position of music teacher for grades 7–12 at North Shore Country Day School, a private school in Winnetka, Illinois. It was a difficult position to step into for many reasons, not the least of which was that Parker had no training in working with junior high and high school students. She claims to have made "every mistake in the teaching book" and called the experience "trial by fire," but she committed herself to remain for two years so she could save every penny and return to New York to study piano with Julius Herford and to return to the dynamic music life and further her career.[9]

Margaret was more fortunate than Alice Parker. Her wealthy family was willing and able to support her through this transition from school to career, financing experiences more on the level of the training she had just completed. The financial backing of her family freed her up to find conducting opportunities without worrying about having to afford the rent. With little support from Juilliard's placement office, Margaret's conducting jobs would be up to her to cultivate. She used her extensive network of brilliant musicians whom she'd met at Juilliard, along with those she met through Robert Shaw and his Collegiate Chorale, to begin her conducting pursuits.

Some of those in Hillis's network would also become personal friends, though Hillis exercised great caution in determining whom she could trust, for reasons of privacy described above. Juilliard friends, including Alice Parker and her husband Tom, were cultivated through their many shared experiences together at school and in Collegiate Choir activities. In the years ahead, both Alice and Tom would collaborate regularly with Margaret. Hillis would come to rely on both of them personally and professionally as her career began to take flight.

There was one select group of friends with whom Margaret connected, sharing a deeper commonality. Hillis met these friends in much the same way she did her other New York acquaintances, through professional connections, but with these friends she was free to be herself. She had no fear of being judged. This group of friends included Ned Rorem, a well-respected young composer, and Nell Tangeman, a renowned mezzo-soprano of the 1950s in New York. Ned Rorem and Margaret first met when both were beginning their graduate work in 1947. They shared the common bond of an upbringing in the Midwest, which may have initially gravitated them to each other. Equally inviting to Margaret was the bold personality Rorem possessed, readily apparent from his writing in published memoirs and diaries. Rorem's honesty about himself, his homosexuality, and his gregarious persona made him a likely candidate for Hillis's friendship and trust, as she was drawn to people who, unlike herself, were unapologetically authentic. Rorem was already becoming a respected young composer, having worked closely with the well-known composers Virgil Thomson and Aaron Copland, whom Rorem referred to as "the father and mother of American music."[10] When Rorem met Hillis, he had already been an assistant to Thomson and had studied composition with Copland at Tanglewood. Tanglewood Summer Festival was a superb training program for serious young musicians to work alongside renowned composers, conductors, and other musical artists to hone their craft. During the summers of 1946 and 1947, Rorem was able to work with conductors Leonard Bernstein and Serge Koussevitzky, whom Rorem referred to as "Koussie," along with other giants of composition present at Tanglewood, including Benjamin Britten and Lukas Foss.

By the time Rorem and Hillis met in the fall of 1947, he was already becoming well connected with important American musical figures and was making a name for himself as a composer. No doubt, Rorem's talent and connections would have piqued Hillis's interest as she began to branch out, building a network amongst her peers. Rorem showed support for his friend Margaret, attending her conducting performances as she was getting her start. In one of his memoirs, he spoke of attending one of her Metropolitan Youth Chorale concerts. "Last night, we penetrated deep into the Negro section of Brooklyn to hear Margaret (Hillis's) choral program and once again the perfect Schubert Mass."[11] Though Rorem admired the results of her performances, he was less flattering when it came to her as a conductor, describing her as "not exciting, not inspiring, but nice, appreciative, patient, and not blaming others."[12] He found Hillis to be always "correct" but "hesitant" in her musicianship, which filtered down to her as a performer.

Rorem had a close friendship with Nell Tangeman around the same time that he and Hillis became friends. Nell, a recognized young singer in New York by the late 1940s, first met Rorem when she contacted him in 1947, asking him to be her accompanist. She had recently divorced her husband Robert Tangeman, who had served as her accompanist until they separated. Rorem was coincidentally a student of Robert Tangeman's at Juilliard when Nell invited Ned for the job. It is likely Margaret and Nell first met either through their mutual friend, Ned Rorem, or perhaps through Margaret's work with Nell and the Collegiate Chorale. Nell premiered the solo role in Aaron Copland's *In the Beginning*, which she would perform with the Chorale under the direction of Robert Shaw. Margaret, at that point, was assisting Shaw with the Chorale. Margaret may have first encountered

Robert Tangeman at Juilliard. Hillis clearly knew him, as they would reconnect after she established her choral foundation, inviting him to join her advisory board. Nell and Robert Tangeman interestingly first met in Bloomington, Indiana, at the same time that Margaret was a music student there. Robert was teaching musicology at Indiana University when he and Nell first got together. It is entirely possible Margaret first met Nell and Robert in Bloomington during that time. In whatever way Margaret first met Nell, Hillis, Nell, and Ned were often together enjoying each other's company.

According to Ned Rorem, Margaret and Nell became roommates shortly after Nell and Robert divorced. In a letter sent to Ned while he was living in Paris, dated May 26, 1949, Nell wrote, "Maggie and I, [Rorem noted: "Margaret Hillis, choir director, Nell's roommate"] . . . went wandering for a place to eat and I remembered the Sevilla."[13] The personalities of Margaret and Nell could not have been more different. Margaret, reserved and very private, was living with a person whom Rorem described as "a free soul."[14] Rorem also described Nell in this way:

> Nell Tangeman liked to give the impression of being bisexual (lesbianism had a certain naughty cachet in those days, while male inversion was simply a stigma). She could drink as much as I could and behaved worse at parties. The drunker she got, the hornier, making passes at everyone . . . while growing ever less comely . . . her social comportment was cheap, messy, dangerous, oral quite literally . . . though I loved Nell, I never really liked her.[15]

There is no evidence to support nor deny whether Nell and Margaret were lovers, but the mere fact that Margaret and Nell lived together raises that possibility. On the surface, this would be the odd couple, but in fact there remained a consistency about the choices Margaret made in friends who would be welcomed into her private world, and Nell certainly fit the pattern. Additionally, Nell was an extraordinary talent, which was something that must have drawn Margaret to her as well. Rorem wrote,

> [Nell] was the most formative singer of my life: everything vocal that I composed over the next six years [from the time they met in 1948] (until I began to be commissioned by other singers of other sexes and other timbres)

was composed for her specific capabilities . . . and why even today sopranos and basses say that my inclinations seem to sway around the mezzo tessitura.[16] [Nell demonstrated] "a brand of vocalism that no longer exists: a true contralto that passes from a velvet growl to a clarion purr, or descends from a heady altitude to a golden chest-tone, all in the space of a breath."[17]

Nell met with a very tragic death in 1965, perhaps attributable to her somewhat reckless lifestyle. She was thought to have invited a stranger into her apartment, where she was left for dead, having been beaten to death. She died at the young age of fifty. This private circle of friends allowed Margaret to be herself, and though she was not completely free in the way she presented herself, she was surrounded by friends who were. Friends such as Ned Rorem would remain close to Margaret throughout both of their careers, as they collaborated personally and professionally in the years ahead. Margaret's New York years were truly her coming of age.

SETTING THE STAGE FOR A CONDUCTING CAREER: 1949–1951

In the fall of 1949, Margaret began to chart her course as a freelance conductor. Continuing to conduct the Metropolitan Youth Chorale, she also remained active with Shaw's Collegiate Chorale. While keeping some of her current musical activities, she began to formulate her next steps for conducting opportunities to build her résumé and to gain exposure in New York's music scene. Her years of performing with Robert Shaw both at Juilliard and in the Collegiate Chorale made her hungry for a chorus of her own that could handle the challenging repertoire she desired to conduct. She believed she was prepared to step into the professional conducting field but needed a better chorus than her Brooklyn singers, a chorus that had the potential to succeed in professional circles. She would set her sights upon finding an ensemble worthy of providing her the platform to launch her career. Her first move in that direction came in the summer of 1950. Following in the footsteps of many Shaw students and her friend Ned Rorem, Hillis pursued further conducting study at Tanglewood Summer Institute, where Shaw had been the choral director just two years earlier. The Tanglewood experience provided Margaret guidance with master conductors who coached her as she conducted singers possessing good vocal technique and some musical background. These singers would become Hillis's conduit for the chorus she needed to launch her career. After that summer, Margaret remained in touch with many of the Tanglewood singers. As Hillis recalled, it was over a spaghetti dinner at one of their frequent social gatherings that the idea was launched to establish a chorus in New York comprised of Tanglewood chorus alumni.[18] The plan was for Hillis to lead this newly formed group, which fit nicely into her stratagem for working with singers of a higher caliber than she had thus far conducted. This Tanglewood chorus would fulfill the perfect next step for Margaret's career plan.

In the fall of 1950, the Tanglewood Alumni Chorus modestly commenced. With her newly formed ensemble, Hillis arranged performances in venues that would expose her to the discerning critics of New York's major newspapers. Risky business though it was, she was willing to take her chances. This chorus was described by Margaret as a semi-professional group, but initially all the participants paid dues and sang for the love of it. The chorus began with a membership of forty people. Margaret envisioned that this group would eventually become fully professional and perform their own concert series in a major New York venue. Wisely, Hillis understood that in order for the choir to succeed, she would have to carve out a singular niche for them. She carefully chose repertoire that would not likely be performed by the larger orchestras and choruses in town. By programming less frequently performed works, she realized she could offer something atypical of the choral scene. The choir started out performing repertoire such as Bach's *Magnificat*, Renaissance madrigals, Debussy's chansons, and newly written works that would not likely have been heard outside of music schools such as Juilliard. Margaret explained her concept for her newly formed alumni choir:

When I first started out as a conductor, I felt I had to have a particular niche. At the time, New York City had the Philadelphia and Boston orchestras visit regularly and the New York Philharmonic had its own concert series. There were several little orchestra societies, but there was a certain repertory that these groups avoided: Bach cantatas, the Mass in B Minor, *St. John's Passion*, *St. Matthew's Passion*, contemporary works, or any piece that didn't use the horns, trombones, clarinets, etc. I formed my own chorus and orchestra to perform these kinds of works. I did a lot of world premieres of composers, plus a lot of contemporary music. New York is still the place to go if you want to make a name for yourself as a conductor."[19]

In their first year, 1951, the Tanglewood Alumni Chorus would perform wherever she could arrange engagements, with appearances in hospitals and at the William Taft High School Community Center. They were also featured on a WNYC radio broadcast of the Festival of American Music, recorded from the Brooklyn Museum. Margaret "wore all the hats" as she launched her choir. She sought out the performance opportunities, acquired all the music, conducted all the rehearsals, hired the instrumentalists, and managed all communications for this chorus from its inception. Rehearsals were held at Margaret's home, 121 West 79th Street, a large apartment that could accommodate the choir of forty in her living room, thereby saving the rental fee for rehearsal space in New York. Her family generously supported her in this apartment, a clever design that was actually two apartments combined into one, containing a double living room in the front and Margaret's living quarters in the back (Picture 22).

The choir's final performance of that first year was held at Times Hall, an intimate 300-seat theater later known as The Little Theatre and then the Helen Hayes Theatre. Though these performances were not officially reviewed, critics were present, aware of the new chorus in town, as indicated by future reviews referring back to these early performances. No official reviews of these first performances were published, however Hillis was able to learn from the feedback she received directly or otherwise. She revealed in an interview years later that she was prompted to change the name of the chorus from the Tanglewood Alumni Chorus to the New York Concert Choir, apparently after hearing of a critic who was keenly aware that Margaret had added several singers to the group who were not Tanglewood alumni. Perhaps those singers were from the Collegiate Chorale, added to improve the sound. Hillis alluded to this "calling out" by a New York critic prompting the name change. Additionally, a reviewer, hearing this chorus at their official 1952 Carnegie Recital Hall debut, wrote about the noticeable improvement, saying, "Miss Hillis had left a fairly unfavorable impression on this listener with her choral conducting for last year's WNYC Festival of American Music. Last night's performance served to erase this impression."[20]

THE NEW YORK TIMES, SUNDAY, MARCH 6, 1955.

DVORAK'S "RUSSALKA" IN CONCERT FORM AT TOWN HALL FRIDAY

Peter Herman Adler, right, rehearses the New York Concert Choir and soloists. The latter, in front row, are Virginia Haskins, Lorna Sydney, Leon Lishner and Robert Holland.

Picture 22.

Photo of a rehearsal in one of Hillis's apartments where rehearsals of the Alumni Chorus were held. This rehearsal was for Dvořák's *Rusalka* several years after the Tanglewood Chorus began, with the conductor Arthur Gamson rehearsing the singers and Hillis looking on (*far right upper corner*). This photo appeared in *The New York Times*, March 6, 1953. Hillis rehearsed her choir in her apartment for all the years of its existence, which saved her from having to pay for rehearsal space (Scrapbook #2, 1954–56). (Margaret Hillis Collection, Rosenthal Archives of the Chicago Symphony Orchestra Association)

In addition to running her newly formed chorus in the 1950–1951 season and working with her Metropolitan Youth Chorale, Hillis accepted a faculty position at Juilliard, assisting Shaw's replacement, Robert Hufstader. As Hufstader's conducting assistant from the fall of 1950 to spring of 1953, Margaret was exposed to a greater array of choral repertoire. Hufstader's programming of Renaissance repertoire of Vittoria and di Lasso, along with Bach motets such as *Der Geist hilft unsrer Schwachheit auf*, Ravel's *Trois Chansons*, Brahms's *Neue Liebeslieder Walzer*, Op. 65, together with Elliott Carter's *Musician's Wrestle Everywhere* would prove inspirational models for future programs Hillis would formulate for her chorus. She learned from both Hufstader and Shaw not only the standard repertoire of the past but also the adventurous repertoire of contemporary composers.

Additional to her assistance with the Juilliard chorus, Hillis was assigned to teach sight-singing classes at Juilliard, which were not as much to her liking as her conducting duties. She described one such class:

> I had these huge choruses that were supposed to be used to teach sight-singing, which was a stupid idea. But I did as best as I could. No way to check up on them to find out whether they learned anything or not. There'd be 150 in each chorus. I had three of 'em. And I always got a headache before I went in there, because I thought I'm really betraying these kids, but there's nothing I can do about it.[21]

Added to all of these conducting and teaching responsibilities was yet another added appointment during the 1950–1951 season. Margaret's role with Robert Shaw would change as he was becoming busier with his Robert Shaw Chorale. Needing assistance with his Collegiate Chorale, Shaw would appoint Hillis his assistant conductor of the ensemble. She not only filled in for him at rehearsals, but she would also assist him as he worked on other projects. Hillis conveyed an amazing story of one such incident in an interview with Helen Lilley, a staff writer who covered the arts for the *Kenosha News* and wrote frequently about Margaret Hillis in the 1960s when Margaret was conductor of the Kenosha Symphony Orchestra. In transcribed notes from one of those interviews, Margaret described what had once occurred with Shaw:

> The telephone rang one morning. I picked it up. It was Robert Shaw. "Maggie," he said, "I need some children." "Sir," I replied, "This is very short notice!" It turned out the Shaw Chorale was making a recording of *Carmen* with Fritz Reiner conducting and he needed a children's chorus. Because the language was so much more difficult than the music especially for American youngsters, I went to a small French school on Fifth Avenue, in the 1990s in N.Y.C. and asked if they would be interested in having some of their children sing in a chorus for this recording. They had no music program in the school at all and were delighted to have the children do some music.

I auditioned, to make sure that the youngsters could carry a tune. . . . So, we had fifteen little girls. The rehearsals were absolute chaos. Over half the children did not speak English, and my own French was not fluent enough to give directions quickly in that language, so I gave directions in English, which the English-speaking portion of the class would translate to the portion that did not speak English. These translations went on at such supersonic speed that it was often difficult for me to tell whether or not the chatter going on legitimately had to do with the business of the moment. However, we got the music learned in plenty of time for the first rehearsal with the Shaw Chorale.

We arrived at the studio, and Mr. Shaw promptly put the children every other one among his chorus and got the whole bunch to march around the room as they sang. (First rehearsal was at the Metropolitan Opera House.) After the first hour of this rehearsal, Mr. Fritz Reiner arrived and seemed to be very pleased with the whole proceedings.

The following day was our first recording session. Although the children were singing very well the words were not quite clear, so I told the youngsters the words were not coming through. At the recording session we made one take. . . . It was just about time for the youngsters to come in, and I realized he (Reiner) was not going to give them a cue. They had been instructed to count to thirty-two and then come in, so when it was time they started, but it was rather tentative because they had not been given a positive cue. Once they got started it was very lusty singing indeed. As usually happens at any recording session, the first take was played back to check for balances.

The fifteen children gathered around an enormous speaker in the corner of the room. . . . When the play-back occurred, they turned toward me with big eyes and said, "The words aren't clear enough!" . . . This time knowing they would not get a cue from Mr. Reiner, I began to give them cues from across the room to help them. The result was that all of their entrances were firm and assured.

On the third and final take, Mr. Shaw was standing about ten feet behind Mr. Reiner conducting the Shaw Chorale and I was about ten feet behind Mr. Shaw conducting the children, and Mr. Reiner was hardly moving at all surveying the whole scene and with a pleased and amused look in his eyes. This was the take that became the RCA Victor recording of the last act of

Carmen. [Recording made in 1951 with Risë Stevens, Licia Albanese, Jan Peerce, and Robert Merrill].[22]

Margaret Hillis was dedicated to Robert Shaw, and this heroic effort is just one example of many instances of her role as his very able assistant. Interestingly, Margaret was not credited for any of her work with the children on this recording. The children were acknowledged with the notation on the album credits "Children's Chorus From The Lyçee Français," but no mention was made of Hillis's preparation. As it happened, this would be the first of many times in years to come that Margaret would prepare a chorus for her future boss, conductor Fritz Reiner. He would become a great mentor for her, playing a major role in Hillis's future conducting career.

By the fall of 1951, while continuing the management and direction of her newly formed chorus, teaching at Juilliard, working with the Collegiate Chorale, and continuing her work with the Metropolitan Youth Chorale (a job she would keep for this one final season), she was also invited to join the faculty of the Union Theological Seminary, teaching ministers of music the techniques of score study and musical analysis. Julius Herford had recently given up his lecturer position there, and Alice Parker recalled that both he and Robert Shaw recommended Hillis for the position. Margaret remained in this position for ten years, teaching and also conducting their amateur string orchestra. She started a small chorus there as well. Occasionally, she was able to engage wind players, which when added to the string ensemble allowed her the opportunity to conduct bigger works for chorus and orchestra. The American premiere of Britten's *St. Nicholas* was among those larger works she conducted at Union Seminary.

In Hillis's 1989 interview with Jon Bentz, she made a point of paying tribute to some of her players in the Union Theological Seminary Orchestra who had been refugees escaping Nazi Germany.[23] She described them as taking her under their collective wing. Though some were better players than others, she spoke of her first violinist who was teaching theological German at Union Theological Seminary. Although he was not much of an instrumentalist, he was passionate about music, having been good friends with the famous German conductor and composer Wilhelm Furtwängler. Hillis described how this violinist would invite everyone back to his home after a Seminary rehearsal, where they would listen to recordings he loved. He had grown up in the German tradition of gathering with friends in their homes to play string quartets and piano compositions for four hands. He generously gave many of his Mozart scores to Margaret, and as she explained, he was just one of many refugees who generously shared their music with her. Through her experience at Union Theological Seminary, Margaret was able to return to her first love: conducting an orchestra.

Margaret's first years after leaving Juilliard proved to be eventful, with many conducting opportunities and the beginning of a promising conducting career. Though her family provided the financial support, Hillis owed her start to her own ambitious and resourceful attitude, finding ways to practice her craft. She forged ahead, relying upon her personal strengths while bravely working to overcome weaknesses, wisely building her network of support along the way. Hillis's work was already becoming recognized and rewarded, which would make up for the times she would work for no pay at all, assisting her mentor Robert Shaw and in the launching of her New York Concert Choir. All her jobs combined did not likely add up to very much money, which was why her family's fortune was a critical component for the launching of her career. Margaret was ready to embark upon the world of professional music making, and though she was inexperienced and somewhat disadvantaged by personal and professional challenges, she promoted herself by accepting opportunities wherever they became available. Hillis was singularly minded when it came to succeeding as a conductor. She was determined to make this work!

ENDNOTES

1. Keith C. Burris, *Dee
   p River* (Chicago: GIA Publications, 2013), p. 63.
2. Ibid.
3. Margaret Hillis, interview by Norman Pellegrini (transcribed by Stanley G. Livengood), October 6, 1997, p. 5.
4. Interview with Alice Parker at Chorus America, Washington, D.C., June 12, 2014.
5. Ibid.
6. Jane Samuelson, "For the Love of Music," *Chicago Magazine* (April 1980): p. 233.
7. Letters from former Tudor classmates found in correspondences (Margaret Hillis Collection, Rosenthal Archives of the Chicago Symphony Orchestra Association, Box 12).
8. Jonathan Ledger, "Menotti's The Unicorn, The Gorgon and the Manticore A Study in Artistic Integrity and Sexual Identity," *Choral Journal* 60, no. 10 (May 2020): p. 38.
9. Interview with Alice Parker.
10. Ned Rorem, *Knowing When to Stop: A Memoir* (New York: Simon and Schuster, 1994) p. 207.
11. Rorem, "Knowing," p. 376.
12. Interview with Ned Rorem, November 22, 2013.
13. Rorem, "Knowing," p. 394.
14. Ibid., p. 345.

15. Ibid., p. 347.

16. Ibid., p. 345.

17. Ibid., p. 344.

18. Lillian McLaughlin, "Miss Hillis Busy with Choir Here," *Des Moines Tribune*, July 8, 1957.

19. Sue Bradle and Tom Wilson, "Music is My Life," *Accent* 6, no. 1 (Sept/Oct 1980): p. 13.

20. In Hillis Scrapbook #1, 1952–54. Newspaper clipping without a date, nor citation of what paper it was from. Title of article: "Margaret Hillis Choir" (Margaret Hillis Collection, Rosenthal Archives of the Chicago Symphony Orchestra Association).

21. Ibid., 6.

22. Interview of Margaret Hillis, labeled "Anecdote in the Life of Margaret Hillis," as transcribed by D. Zerk, on a conversation that took place November 1, 1962, between Margaret Hillis and Helen C. Lilley. The transcription was labeled "Anecdote 1." It was passed on to me by Dave Broman, who at the time was Director of the Howard County Historical Society. The Historical Society received this transcription and other items from the Helen Lilley estate that related to Margaret Hillis, as Helen Lilley, a reporter for the Kenosha News, often wrote about Hillis in the when she conducted the orchestra.

23. Jon Bentz, "Interview of Margaret Hillis Director Chicago Symphony Orchestra, September 19, 1989, Archives Committee, Oral History Project, 1992" (Margaret Hillis Collection, Rosenthal Archives of the Chicago Symphony Orchestra Association).

CHAPTER 7

MARGARET HILLIS
AND THE NEW YORK CONCERT CHOIR: 1951–1953

Margaret could not have scripted a more extraordinary and rapid rise to success in New York's music scene just a short time after leaving Juilliard. She was establishing herself as a working musician in New York. By 1951, her multiple jobs included an instructorship at Juilliard, an assistant conductor position for Robert Shaw, and an additional faculty appointment conducting an orchestra and teaching courses at Union Theological Seminary. Added to these duties was the directing of her two choruses: her Metropolitan Youth Chorale and her newly formed concert choir. However, she was not yet content with this impressive array of employment. She would only be satisfied when her newly formed New York Concert Choir (formerly the Tanglewood Alumni Chorus) could begin to perform in prestigious venues around town, thereby enabling her to promote herself and her chorus in the way of other respectable musicians of the day. It was Margaret's intention to have a chorus she could showcase. Bringing her Concert Choir up to New York's lofty artistic standards would take time, and only once she believed the choir was ready for public scrutiny would she be willing to make her move. How she molded this group of singers into a finely polished ensemble worthy of prestigious New York City venues is a process worth closer exploration.

Hillis made modifications after the inaugural 1950–1951 Concert Choir season, beyond the name change, which included personnel adjustments to improve the group's sound. Beginning in the fall of 1951, Hillis added a paid core of singers, officially making it a semi-professional chorus. The funding came from her family money. Having a small paid group of singers within the larger ensemble gave them a more refined tone quality. Hillis established a focused mission for the choir: "to promote choral performance in order to give choral repertoire its rightful place as a major musical force."[1] This mission statement bore great resemblance to Shaw's mission for his Collegiate Chorale, which included his promotion of the choral art "by performance of the distinguished musical literature."[2]

Hillis continued to have her Concert Choir perform in high schools, community centers, and again for the American Music Festival, as was done the previous year, but the final concerts of this second season would take place at Carnegie Recital Hall. Hillis considered this to be her official professional conducting debut. The Carnegie performances, just two weeks apart, required Hillis to program her repertoire carefully so as to attract audiences for both performances. For the first Carnegie concert on May 12, 1952, Hillis programmed Haydn's *Theresienmesse*; *Three Psalms* by Eliot Greenberg; Brahms's *Liebeslieder Waltzes*, Op. 52; and Debussy's *Trois Chansons*. Her choice of repertoire for the second Carnegie concert on May 26 included Vivaldi's *Gloria*, Bach's *Jesu meine freude*, Robert Witt's *Te Deum*, Hindemith's *Six Chansons*, Winslow's *Huswifery*, and Billings's *Consonance* and *Modern Music*. The program notes for both concerts were authored by her friend and former Juilliard classmate, Alice Parker. The common thread in Hillis's programming was the inclusion of less frequently performed choral works than those heard in New York's standard symphonic choral concerts. A typical Hillis program included a multi-movement work, such as Haydn's mass, followed by more challenging unaccompanied choral works, such as those of Debussy and Hindemith, and then a newly composed work, often in a debut performance. Some of the works Hillis would program were those she had first come to know through her work at Juilliard. The Robert Witt piece from her May 26 concert, for example, was given its debut two months earlier at a Juilliard composition symposium. Having been on faculty during that symposium, Hillis would likely have heard it there first. Margaret hired a chamber orchestra to accompany portions of both Carnegie concerts. The May concerts were performed with a chorus of thirty-two singers and sixteen instrumentalists. Payments for the hall rental, her professional core singers, and the instrumentalists were underwritten by Hillis's generous family. Margaret's proud mother would be in attendance for one of the two Carnegie performances to observe the rewards of their investment.

Reviews of these first professional Concert Choir appearances were mostly positive, revealing the advancements Hillis had made since their inaugural season.

Hillis collected all of her reviews, both good and bad, keeping them in a scrapbook. She wisely considered the critical comments; taking in feedback paid off, as she eventually won those critics over. Being a woman, her presence on stage was a novelty, an unusual occurrence in such an impressive venue as Carnegie Recital Hall. The focus of critics was on Hillis, the *female* conductor, a point they made very apparent in reviews she collected. There were often descriptors such as "this young woman" or "her modest demeanor." Many of her reviews were positive, in contrast with commentary written about her female conductor predecessors. It was a fine line Hillis walked as a female conductor, and she knew it. Non-musical observations over her manner of dress and contained gestures were sometimes given more coverage than the quality of her music making. Critics and the public were curious about a woman in this male-dominated profession and therefore they focused less upon Hillis's technical prowess. Any criticism that was registered about Hillis's conducting would often be followed by a complimentary remark. Perhaps the preoccupation over Hillis's appearance and gesture afforded her the uncharacteristic kindness shown by her reviewers. As a result, less attention may have been given to any weaknesses in her performance. It is possible that being female finally worked to her advantage for a change!

When reviewers did address her conducting, they often picked up on signature traits in Hillis's gestures. First, they noticed that her gestures were precise, delivered without ostentation. She minimized her conducting movements to avoid criticisms like those received by her predecessors. However, critics did not overlook Hillis's lack of expressiveness, borne of her efforts to call as little attention to herself as possible while still remaining clear to her performers. "Miss Hillis is an unassuming young woman who uses a long baton and conducts with no evident signs of emotion or rapture. Yet she gets beautiful effects in what appears to be the most businesslike manner. She is clearly a very talented conductor."[3] Critics could not help but notice her ability to elicit sensitive phrasing, balance, and beauty in her performers despite little outward showing of emotion. They often found the orchestral ensemble less polished than the chorus.[4] This is ironic in that orchestral music had previously been Margaret's comfort zone when she first arrived at Juilliard. On the other hand, Juilliard had made her an expert in the choral field, and her lack of orchestral conducting experience was beginning to appear as a deficit in comparison to her work in choral conducting. Hillis would accept the criticism as a launching point for her planning of the next concert season.

After the success of Margaret Hillis and the Concert Choir's professional debut with two Carnegie Recital Hall concerts, she set her sights upon featuring her choir with its own concert series for the 1952–1953 season. She determined that by making the chorus a fully paid ensemble she would have a group she could confidently display on the professional New York concert scene. Her family would underwrite a four-concert series at the prestigious Town Hall, an ideal venue for Hillis's Concert Choir. Musicians from all over the world flocked to this site, taking advantage of the wonderful acoustics in the intimate 500-seat theater. How ironic that Margaret, a woman breaking ground in a male field, would launch her career in the very hall that thirty-one years earlier was founded as a gathering place for suffragists advocating for the Nineteenth Amendment, giving women the right to vote! Hillis waged her own feminist battle for acceptance when she chose to display her choral artistry in this hall. Hillis knew that featuring her group in a Town Hall series would no doubt bring them to even greater visibility.

Paying her full chorus of singers a union wage enabled Hillis to attract some of the finest choral musicians in town. With the assistance of Alice Parker's husband, Tom Pyle, a contractor of professional singers in New York, Hillis auditioned hundreds of singers for her thirty-six available slots in the chorus. A critic reviewing one of the New York Concert Choir Town Hall performances noted a significant overlap of members between Hillis's chorus and Robert Shaw's touring Chorale. The implication was that Margaret was only able to attract this professional pool of singers by paying them a respectable fee.[5] Otherwise, how would a woman be able to find singers willing to work with her? No such comments were made about her mentor, who also paid his Chorale singers a respectable fee. In fact, some of the finest singers in New York depended upon Tom Pyle to find them work with choruses such as those of Hillis and Shaw in order to earn a living as singers.

One of those professional singers in Hillis's Concert Choir was Charlotte Carlson, also known as Charlotte Boehm and Charlotte DeWindt. Charlotte's name appears in several forms, having been advised by her agent to change her name from "Boehm," which was deemed too Germanic for the post-war anti-German sentiment prevailing in the early 1950s. Charlotte decided initially to adopt her mother's maiden name, "Carlson," for her stage work, which she then changed again, upon marrying, to "DeWindt." One of these three names would appear in programs and reviews during Charlotte's time with the New York Concert Choir. Charlotte was often a featured soloist in Hillis's concerts. Having just come out of Tanglewood in the summer of 1952, Charlotte heard about auditions for Margaret Hillis's new chorus. She said the word around town was that Margaret paid her musicians generously because Hillis was "an heiress and had lots of money."[6] Charlotte recalled the audition consisting of sight-reading and singing a solo. Rehearsals were held regularly from 5:30–7:30 p.m., enabling those singers to participate who needed to work a day job in order to supplement their income. Then, as now, it was difficult to earn a living wage working solely as a singer, and for a choral singer it was all the more challenging to support oneself. This issue would become a motivation for Hillis's soon-to-be-established choral foundation, with one objective being financial support for choral singers.

Rehearsals, Charlotte recalled, took place in Hillis's generously sized apartment on 21st Street, reminiscent, she claimed, of apartments in Amsterdam. According to Charlotte, the apartment was up one flight of stairs and the room, long and narrow, was set up tightly with folding chairs and a grand piano in the front of the room. Charlotte described how she and her colleagues always remarked about the incredible artwork surrounding the "rehearsal space," otherwise known as Hillis's living room. One art piece that stood out to Charlotte was "a gigantic wood carving of Don Quixote."[7] The rehearsals were very intense. Charlotte had memories of Margaret's respectful and organized methods. Though Charlotte admired Hillis's strength as a teacher, she confessed that it was sometimes hard to get excited about rehearsing with her. Charlotte marveled at Hillis's keen ear and the magnificent results she achieved in the three years she worked with Hillis's Concert Choir.

Charlotte was able to offer some insight into Margaret's more casual personality, mostly hidden from the chorus, when Hillis directed her musicians. Unlike the serious professional demeanor Hillis conveyed to her Concert Choir, Charlotte was able to experience another side of Margaret in a rare social encounter. When Charlotte got married during her time with the chorus, she invited Margaret to her wedding. Unable to attend the event, Margaret generously gifted the couple one dozen sets of sheets from Bloomingdale's. To thank her, Charlotte and her husband invited Margaret to their apartment for dinner, where Charlotte saw a different side to her conductor. During the dinner party, Charlotte observed a very down-to-earth, humorous, and accessible Margaret Hillis, who was enjoying deep conversations with Charlotte's new husband as they debated the beauty of Stravinsky's compositions. Hillis was championing the contemporary writing of Stravinsky which Charlotte's husband did not quite understand. Their conversations were relaxed and animated as Hillis smoked her cigarettes, enjoying a lovely meal. Looking back on this event, Charlotte described herself as so young and naïve, finding it hard to believe she actually had the nerve to invite a conductor to her home but grateful to have experienced the more casual side of Hillis that few of her colleagues would ever see (Picture 23).

Picture 23.

From Charlotte Carlson's personal photographs. Margaret Hillis is enjoying a casual evening with Charlotte and her husband in their Brooklyn apartment. (Margaret Hillis Collection, Rosenthal Archives of the Chicago Symphony Orchestra Association)

To ready her chorus for the season's Town Hall concert series, Hillis needed a solid plan. She knew the stakes were getting higher as her chorus would soon be making regular appearances in this respected concert venue. The way to best ensure a polished chorus for this new level of scrutiny would be to work with them throughout the season to keep them in top form. However, increasing the number of rehearsals would greatly increase the expense. Supporting this concert series was already a tremendous investment for Margaret's family, with chorus members paid for rehearsals at union rates. Added to this were the costs of a chamber orchestra and concert hall rental fees. If Margaret was to keep her choir singing throughout the season, she would need to find an additional funding source. The situation required resourcefulness—Margaret's specialty. She cleverly managed to find a solution without breaking the "Hillis bank" by affiliating herself with other musical organizations in town that would "lease" her ensemble for their own productions. In doing so, she got someone else to pay for her group's additional rehearsals and performances during the concert season, enabling her to keep her chorus in prime condition. It was a brilliant solution.

One such underwriter for the Concert Choir was the American Opera Society. Margaret obtained a position as chorus director for the opera company. In that position, Hillis was expected to provide vocal ensembles for operas and any other concerts the company performed. The opera company was very active in New York during the 1950s and 1960s, where many well-known opera singers appeared. According to Hillis, Elisabeth Schwarzkopf and Joan Sutherland were two of many fine singers appearing with this company.[8] Hillis prepared 120 different operas during her years with the company, working with such brilliant artists as soprano Maria Callas. As the New York Concert Choir prepared for these opera productions, along with their Town Hall concerts, they would rehearse regularly several nights per week. These additional rehearsals enabled Hillis to keep her Concert Choir in top form while at the same time making the ensemble into a lucrative part-time job for the singers she hired. Thanks to Margaret's resourcefulness, her Concert Choir performed throughout the season, building their quality and their reputation along the way—but there was an additional bonus in this collaboration. All American Opera Society performances were held in Town Hall, providing the Concert Choir the added advantage of growing comfortable in the same venue where their own concert series would occur. The Concert Choir's first appearance at Town Hall took place on November 9, 1952, in a performance of Purcell's *Saul and the Witch of Endor* and Rousseau's *Le devin du village*. The performance was conducted by Arnold Gamson, and the stage director was Friedelind Wagner, granddaughter of Richard Wagner. Though the opera performances were not favorably reviewed, "the choral sections were effectively rendered."[9]

The second appearance of the choir was particularly fortuitous. One of the opera company's regular collaborations was with the New Friends of Music Concert Series, featuring well-known musical artists in New York, including Igor Stravinsky. The Concert Choir was conducted by Igor Stravinsky, premiering his *Cantata on Elizabethan Songs*. This event on December 21, 1952, sparked a long and successful musical relationship between the composer and Hillis. Their first performance

135

together featured mezzo-soprano Jennie Tourel and tenor Hugues Cuénod with a four-part women's chorus. Margaret recalled a specific challenge of the piece: "The lower you go in the voices, the less real intensity there is in the sound. You need another voice or two. Instead of using the sixteen [Stravinsky] had asked for, I used seventeen and hoped he wouldn't object. So, I went to him and I said, 'Before you get excited, I want to tell you something.' So, I told him about it. He said, 'Genius, absolute genius!' I thought, well, we're going to go a long way, brother!"[10] She was right. There were many Stravinsky/Hillis collaborations to follow, including recordings and concert work, launching the Concert Choir into higher visibility in the arts community thanks, in part, to the endorsement of the renowned composer.

Margaret took on an additional affiliation that added visibility for her Concert Choir. In her new position on the editorial staff of the publication *Choral and Organ Guide*, she developed a conducting workshop series that would eventually involve her chorus as part of her lecture demonstrations. In Carl Fischer Hall, down the street from Carnegie Hall, Hillis would instruct conductors and organists in her rehearsal methods, providing her Concert Choir as the demonstration ensemble. Cleverly, she determined that if she scheduled these events just prior to her Town Hall concerts, her choir could gain valuable performance experience with their repertoire. It is always desirable to perform repertoire more than once, enabling the ensemble to grow more comfortable with the music. These workshops, sponsored by Chorus and Organ Enterprises, gave Hillis and her chorus such an opportunity. A few days before her first Town Hall concert, Hillis provided a conducting workshop on Tuesday, January 13, 1953. The pieces upon which she would demonstrate her choral techniques included Bach's *Magnificat* and Poulenc's motets *Exultate Deo* and *Salve Regina*. All three works were performed just three days later in the Town Hall series debut. Conductors who attended these clinics were clearly enthusiastic for her guidance, as was apparent by comments appearing in the February *Choral and Organ Guide* publication following this first of three clinics she gave that season. In "Letters to the Reader," there were such comments as, "I found this clinic very instructive" and "Illustrations of structural rehearsal [were] very enlightening," along with suggestions, including, "Would you discuss soft singing on very high pitches for girls' voices at your next clinic?" and "How do you audition new members?"[11] These clinics provided yet another way for Hillis to keep her ensemble prepared for their Town Hall appearances. Her affiliation on the editorial staff of the *Choral and Organ Guide* was additionally beneficial, connecting her with other respected musicians in the choral field, including Howard Swan, Robert Fountain, and Peter Wilhousky, all of whom were involved with this publication. This affiliation was worth the added workload for Margaret and her chorus, providing Hillis continuous opportunities to refine her choral workshops while enabling her New York Concert Choir to be showcased on a regular basis. The added bonus for Hillis herself was the opportunity to increase her network of choral colleagues.

Town Hall's only professional choral concert series began with Hillis's New York Concert Choir on January 16, 1953. Thirty singers and thirty instrumentalists performed a program consisting of Monteverdi, Bach, Poulenc, and Schubert. Program notes were written by Alice Parker. *The New York Times* reviewed the concert in a positive way, observing Hillis's conducting as "efficient, clean-cut, vigorous, almost masculine" and further characterizing it as "honest straight-forward music making."[12] *The Musical Courier* review characterized the program as "difficult, interesting, and delightful," but suggested that the orchestra somewhat overbalanced the chorus. The review implied that the chorus was somewhat restrained, stating, "One wondered if greater freedom of emission might not have been encouraged in the singers, with a more uniform instrumental and vocal balance resulting."[13] *Musical America* reviewed the concert similarly, stating that not only were there balance issues between orchestra and chorus, but [also] the men's section overbalanced the women's section as well.[14] All three reviews concurred that the a cappella pieces, particularly the Poulenc, were the most successful.

The second Town Hall program of the choral series on February 12, 1953, was equally varied, with music representative of a cross-section of styles from Italian madrigals and Mozart's Requiem to a new work by her beloved professor from Indiana University days, composer Bernhard Heiden. Also included in the program were Poulenc's *Sept Chansons*. This variety of literature provided Hillis the opportunity to display her chorus's versatility. Reviews again favored the a cappella performances over the choral-orchestral works, with the madrigals and Poulenc's chansons gleaning the highest praise. Less favorably reviewed was Hillis's conducting of Mozart's Requiem, for which Hillis embellished the number of choristers from her typical group of thirty to a larger chorus of thirty-nine singers to create a better balance between orchestra and chorus. "Miss Hillis, conducting a competent but sometimes pedestrian performance by the chorus and orchestra in the Requiem, provided freer and more inspiring direction when leading the chorus alone."[15] The chorus and orchestral balances were again criticized. More favorable commentary was given to the soloists, who came from the chorus, including contralto Charlotte Carlson and her good friend soprano Suzanne der Derian.[16] Despite some critical comments on aspects of the second Town Hall concert, each reviewer found favor with Margaret and this newly established chorus. The *New York Herald Tribune*'s review provided a strong endorsement of Hillis's artistry, stating, "Thanks to superb control and unerring sense of artistic values, Miss Hillis has already moved to the forefront of America's younger choir leaders"[17] (Picture 24).

Picture 24.
Margaret Hillis conducting the New York Concert Choir and Orchestra with soloists at Town Hall, ca. 1954. (Margaret Hillis Collection, Rosenthal Archives of the Chicago Symphony Orchestra Association)

As Hillis prepared for her third Town Hall program, she was interviewed by *The New York Times,* as interest in Margaret and her chorus was growing. The writer began his article by referencing "the familiar caricature of a woman choral conductor," stating that unlike those unflattering renderings, Margaret was an exception: " . . . masterfully and gracefully in command of conducting techniques."[18] Hillis responded in that interview, "That hilarious cartoon has got fixed in people's minds and I hope I can blot it out, if I do nothing else."[19] This third program was reviewed as "delectable" and reminiscent of the previous two Town Hall programs in its quality and entertainment. With similar construct to the previous two concerts, this one opened with Bach's *Lobet den Herrn,* followed by Carissimi's oratorio *Jephte,* a seventeenth-century masterwork rarely heard in performance by New York concertgoers. Also included in this third of her Town Hall series was a contemporary work, *From an Unknown Past,* by her good friend Ned Rorem. Additionally, Hillis programmed Brahms's *Fünf Gesänge,* Op. 104, the same set that had so impressed Robert Shaw during her Juilliard days. The program concluded with sixteenth-century French chansons. Innovative programming was fast becoming a signature of Hillis, as she continued to program rarely heard selections along with newly composed works. She made sure to include several works of more recognizable composers along with other lesser-known selections, all to the delight of her New York audiences and critics.

Reviewers remained consistent regarding several aspects of Hillis's concerts. She was continually criticized when the chorus was accompanied by instrumental forces. The *Lobet den Herrn* accompanied by a string quartet was reviewed as a "foggy performance." Diction was another criticism that often appeared in reviews, as one critic stated that although the Brahms *Fünf Gesänge* were sung beautifully, "scarcely a word of German was distinguishable." In stark contrast were more favorable comments about the performances of unaccompanied works.[20] Continual scrutiny appeared in reviews regarding how Hillis moved as a conductor. "Miss Hillis is an excellent conductor, and can achieve any degree of sensitivity, any dynamic level, with no fuss or bother, by some method all her own of understatement and economy of movement."[21] The less she moved, the better, according to critics. It was rare to see similar comments made about male conductors of that time, regarding their economy of gesture as being considered an asset.

In the final Town Hall performance of the 1952–1953 concert series, Hillis took a bold step forward, presenting the chorus in a complete performance of Bach's Mass in B Minor. The April 21, 1953, concert, accompanied by a chamber orchestra, was well received, but the critical comments remained consistent with those of her previous Town Hall concert reviews. Although critics were complimentary of the performance in statements such as "careful preparation" and "generally praise worthy," some found the performance "curiously heavy-handed," suggesting a rigid and controlled performance that needed a freer spirit.[22] Equally noticeable in these latest reviews were signs that Margaret was beginning to improve. Where previous criticism was made of her work with instrumentalists, these concert reviews offered several compliments regarding her work with the orchestra. "The orchestra was in good form in a well-coordinated performance." Though some concerns remained, such as "the orchestra managed to find its own way quite nicely while Miss Hillis directed herself mostly to her singers," there were glimpses of increasing improvement in her management of all forces on the stage. There was also praise extended to her soloists, Suzanne der Derian and Charlotte Carlson.[23] Despite any criticism, there was clearly enthusiastic support for what Hillis was accomplishing. "The excellent musicianship of Miss Hillis was in large part responsible for the outstanding qualities of the performance, for its human warmth and strength. Despite an occasional rough spot, a rare freshness, depth, breadth, and mobility usually prevailed"[24] (Picture 25).

Picture 25.
Promotional material for the New York Concert Choir and Orchestra Town Hall performance of Bach's Mass in B Minor appearing in Sunday's *New York Times*, April 19, 1953 (Scrapbook #1, 1952–1954). (Margaret Hillis Collection, Rosenthal Archives of the Chicago Symphony Orchestra Association)

During the 1952–1953 season, Hillis was balancing her time carefully, "wearing many additional hats." As music director of multiple ensembles, her concert schedule grew noticeably more extensive. Performances would often take place in close proximity, such as the Union Seminary Orchestra on January 28, 1953, just twelve days after her inaugural choral series at Town Hall. Using a similar template of programming to that of her Town Hall concerts, the Union Seminary program included Handel's Concerto No. 4 in F Major for organ and orchestra; Bach's Brandenburg Concerto No. 4 in G Major for solo violin, two flutes, and orchestra; and Poulenc's Concerto in G Minor for organ, string orchestra, and timpani.

Adding to an already busy teaching load at Juilliard, along with her conducting and editorial duties, Hillis was in her fourth year with the Collegiate Chorale, now serving as a substitute for Shaw while he toured his fully professional Robert Shaw Chorale. In the 1952–1953 season, Hillis would be completely in charge of the Collegiate Chorale. Her debut appearance with them came in late October 1952 as the group made their ninth consecutive appearance for the *Herald Tribune* Forum, but for the first time it was led by Margaret Hillis. Naturally, the newspaper hosting the event gave it good coverage with a keen interest in the new young female conductor filling in for Shaw. A focus of the feature article about Hillis was her work ethic with Shaw's chorus. Attention was given to her one-hour rehearsal prior to their performance and how she insisted upon clear diction in Billings's *Modern Music*, a comedic setting that would be lost on an audience if the words were unclear. Hillis explained, "I had to insist that they get their words out . . . it is the fun of the piece."[25] In the article, mention was also made of a last-minute warm-up session in the foyer of the ballroom in which they were to sing because Hillis was concerned that "voices would get cold and lose flexibility, thereby singing out of tune."[26] Hillis was attentive to every detail of the Chorale's preparation for this, her debut performance with them as their conductor. The program was right out of the Shaw playbook, consisting of American music, with the *Battle Hymn of the Republic*, Billings's *Modern Music*, several William Dawson spirituals, and closing with the *Star-Spangled Banner*.

It is here that one can see Shaw's influence in Margaret's work, as she juggled many roles in similar fashion to her mentor. Not only in her work ethic and her attention to detail, but also in one particular form of communication with the Chorale, she was channeling her mentor's method to inspire the group. Shaw regularly wrote letters to his choristers, providing thoughtful ideas about their responsibility as singers and giving his insights into repertoire that was being rehearsed. He would use this opportunity to share his philosophy of music or give his singers technical suggestions about their singing. Most importantly, these letters were a way of spreading motivational messages, a carry-over of his youth as he trained to become a minister. Using Shaw's same salutation, "Dear People," Margaret wrote to the members of the Collegiate Chorale, connecting with them in similar fashion to that of Robert Shaw. In a letter dated October 30, 1952, Hillis shared her thoughts about the mission of the group in the absence of Shaw.

Dear People,

The Collegiate Chorale has this year a very great musical potentiality, one that if it is realized, can lead to three of the most exciting concerts the Chorale has ever given. Because of this, you and I have a tremendous responsibility. My responsibility is to help you wherever I can to learn to sing phrases, to make musical line, and to understand the spirit of the music we are performing. Perhaps this all boils down to the fact that a conductor's greatest responsibility is to keep a chorus thinking . . . you as the performers of the Poulenc, the Beethoven, the Meyerowitz, the Hindemith, and the Janáček are the important people. You are the thinking people. It is only through the contribution of the best in yourself that the Chorale can achieve its great music potentiality. . . . It is my job to make it possible for you to achieve this involvement, and it is your job to meet the challenge of it. See you Monday night at 7:20—the rehearsal will begin at 7:30.[27]

The second Collegiate Chorale program Hillis would direct was their Christmas concert at Hunter College on December 15, 1952. Two hundred singers along with a full orchestra would perform at this annual event. The program, as alluded to in her October "Dear People" letter, consisted of four Poulenc Christmas motets (the American premiere), Beethoven's Mass in C Major, *Music for Christmas* by Meyerowitz (a world premiere), and traditional Christmas carols. A favorable review in the *Musical Courier* took issue only with the balance between chorus and orchestra in Beethoven's Mass in C Major. However, other works with orchestra and chorus were more favorably reviewed.[28] *Choral and Organ Guide*, on which she remained an editorial staff member, went further in their criticism of the Beethoven mass, claiming it "appeared to be the weakest spot in the concert, not because of the music but because the conductor did not seem to have a complete grasp of it. We learned later that this was the first time she had conducted it, and that but a few short weeks were allowed for preparation. Beethoven to be Beethoven cannot be thrown together in such a manner."[29]

The New York Times concurred with these two reviews, also taking issue with the Beethoven mass performance, going into greater detail as to what may have gone wrong.

> In the Beethoven Mass [Hillis] had some trouble. For one thing, her soloists drawn from the Chorale were simply not up to this music. [Hillis used soloists from her Concert Choir in her Town Hall performances. When doing works like the Beethoven Mass, however, those singers, unlike Shaw's members who she used for this performance, were professional soloists in their own right and could more easily provide solo support when needed.] For another, the orchestral ensemble, while a good one, had evidently not enough time together. The performance seemed to move under restraints. Miss Hillis however kept her large company of performers together and there was some choral singing of color and impact.[30]

All three reviews had positive things to say despite these criticisms, using adjectives such as "highly dignified" and "top flight" to describe Hillis and the Collegiate Chorale's performance. In Howard Taubman's opening remarks of *The New York Times* review, he described Hillis as "a slim young woman in black" and further remarked, "There have been women conductors in New York before, but they are still rare enough to warrant special attention . . . and Miss Hillis has talent for the job."[31]

Hillis penned another "Dear People" letter following the Hunter College Christmas performance in which she took the opportunity to thank the Chorale and the support staff for their work.

Dear People,

In your singing last Monday night, the Christmas spirit and the spirit of music spoke eloquently. Even though I couldn't hear much of the performance, the acoustics being what they were in the hall, I could feel it, and that feeling is an experience that I know I shall never forget. You have yourselves to thank for that concert, because it was only for the love of music, for the love of singing that it was given, and there is no purer motivation. The experience of our working together has been for me one of tremendous growth, and I know that my contribution to you could not have been as great as yours was to the music.[32]

MARGARET'S LIFE OUTSIDE OF MUSIC

Considering all that Hillis was doing between teaching and conducting, there must have been little respite for her, which may explain why there is little documentation of Hillis's social life during these early career years in New York. She was very careful to keep her private life out of the limelight with what little socializing there may have been. There is some indication, however, that she did enjoy down time with friends. She kept two lovely telegrams in a scrapbook that read in a way good friends might communicate with one another. Margaret must have valued them because she kept these telegrams alongside her many reviews and programs she collected in her early years of professional work. The messages in the telegrams conveyed wishes of good luck for her upcoming Collegiate Chorale Christmas concert.

One of these messages came from Tom Pyle, husband of Alice Parker. According to Alice, Tom would often sing with the groups for whom he contracted. Pyle had a fine baritone voice and sang for his good friend Robert Shaw for all of the years the Robert Shaw Chorale was in existence. He was on tour with the Chorale during Hillis's Hunter College program and sent a telegram wishing her well for the upcoming performance. Parker claimed that her husband would also sing with Margaret's Concert Choir whenever he was available. He enjoyed working with Margaret due to her incredibly organized, straightforward, and thorough rehearsal preparation.[33] Tom and Alice would often socialize with Margaret. Alice remembered spending time at Margaret's home, enjoying her well-known weekend gatherings of friends, which involved guests reading from Shakespeare plays or playing games and music. Margaret would remain close to Alice Parker and her husband, Tom

Pyle, for years to come. When Hillis began her commute to and from Chicago, Tom sublet her apartment on 79th Street, using it for office space he needed in New York City. Alice recollected Hillis leaving behind a closet full of magnificent custom-made conducting gowns that she generously gave to Alice's young daughters. Alice recalled, with a smile, how her three daughters wore those one-of-a-kind garments to many a school dance and dress up party on the upper west side![34]

Picture 26.
Alice Parker with her husband, Tom Pyle, and their five children, taken in 1963. Parker and Pyle were dear friends to Margaret. Sadly, Tom Pyle would die suddenly of a heart attack twelve years after this photo was taken at the age of fifty-seven, leaving Parker to raise her five children alone while supporting her family. Alice Parker would become internationally known as a composer, conductor, and she remains an inspirational teacher. She and Margaret Hillis remained close friends throughout Margaret's lifetime. (Elisabeth Deane, photographer)

A second telegram came from someone else in the Collegiate Chorale. They did not sign their name but instead used a code of sorts, signing it "92." This may have been the number this chorister was assigned in the Chorale. (Hillis adapted a similar numbering system years later when conducting the Chicago Symphony Chorus. It was an efficient way to provide ranking and seating of singers and avoided the time-consuming writing of everyone's names for all such administrative tasks.) The person sending the telegram may have preferred to use code to avoid signing their name and betraying any privacy issues the two may have shared around their friendship. The wording of this telegram in fact had a familiarity and somewhat flirtatious connotation about it, using wording similar to what could be found in Chaucer or Shakespeare, both of whom Hillis was a connoisseur. The telegram stated: "It is Thy day Sweet" with the signature "Best wishes." Perhaps the person sending the cryptically signed telegram was an attendee to one such event. When Margaret was asked about her social life in *The New York Times* feature article prior to the third Town Hall appearance, she discussed with the reporter what she enjoyed doing in her spare time. "Extra-curricular life finds her dancing ('Takes my mind off Bach'), cooking ('Cooking chicken every way possible'), exercising daily ('To keep the body in good tone') and on weekends having friends in to join her in reading Shakespeare aloud or to play trios ('They play, I relax').[35]

Margaret Hillis had become well established as one of the elite young professional conductors in New York City after only a short time out of Juilliard. As in all things Margaret tackled in her life, she approached the launching of her career with a vision of what it was to be and then carefully strategized every step along the way. Like her mentor Robert Shaw, she formed a choir consisting of professional singers. Hillis understood that they would need a niche identity in order to stand out in the competitive music scene of New York, and she came up with a formula that set her ensemble apart, programming music rarely performed by the other orchestras and choruses in town. Using her expert training, she disciplined this ensemble, and once they were ready, she featured them in prestigious venues that gained them instant attention in the arts community. Margaret wisely kept her ensemble in prime form by continually rehearsing and performing with them, and she was able to finance them beyond the support of her family through extended affiliations, such as the American Opera Society, that could pay their way. As Margaret's reputation as a conductor grew, she wisely considered critical commentary about her work, enabling her to continually improve her craft. It was clear that Margaret's attention to feedback was paying off. Her chorus was becoming distinguished for its clarity, accuracy, and beauty. From Stravinsky, to critics, to audiences, Margaret Hillis was acquiring a reputation as a master of her craft. She quickly gained the respect of critics and colleagues in New York, no easy task for a woman. There were no shortcuts in Margaret's upward climb. Yes, she had the great advantage of her family's fortune to help her acquire the forces she needed to give her a respectable head start, but there was no shortage of hard work and commitment she would demonstrate as she set her sights upon a burgeoning conducting career. Resourceful, disciplined, open to criticism, and willing to work tirelessly to improve herself, she would soon move to the next level in her rapid rise to the top of her game.

ENDNOTES

1. Early Press Book for The New York Concert Choir, by David W. Rubin Artists Management, 1954, author's personal collection.
2. Joseph A. Mussulman, *Dear People . . . Robert Shaw* (Chapel Hill: Hinshaw Music, 1979), p. 29.
3. R. P., "Margaret Hillis Directs Concert Choir Here," *The New York Times*, May 13, 1952 (Scrapbook #1 of the Margaret Hillis Collection, Rosenthal Archives of the Chicago Symphony Orchestra Association).
4. P. G. H., "Concert Choir," *Herald Tribune*, May 27, 1952 (Scrapbook #1 of Margaret Hillis Collection, Rosenthal Archives of the Chicago Symphony Orchestra Association).
5. Lillian McLaughlin, "Miss Hillis Busy with Choir Here," *Des Moines Tribune*, July 8, 1957.
6. Interview with Charlotte Carlson (Boehm/DeWindt), June 29, 2012.
7. Ibid.
8. Allan Kozin, "Allen Sven Oxenburg, 64, Dead; American Opera Society Founder," from obituary of Allen Sven Oxenburg, *The New York Times*, late edition, July 7, 1992: B.7. Oxenberg, according to Kozin, is credited with engaging many up-and-coming opera stars to perform with the American Opera Society.
9. Harriett Johnson, "Rousseau Opera by New Friends," from Words and Music section, *New York Post*, November 10, 1952.
10. Margaret Hillis, interview by Norman Pellegrini (transcribed by Stanley G. Livengood), October 6, 1997, p. 9.
11. "Letter to the Readers," *Choral and Organ Guide*, February 1953 (Scrapbook #1 of Margaret Hillis Collection, Rosenthal Archives of the Chicago Symphony Orchestra Association).
12. Howard Taubman, "Religion is Theme of Concert Choir: Poulenc's *Exultate Deo*, Bach's *Magnificat in D*, Schubert *Mass*, Sung in Town Hall," *The New York Times*, January 17, 1953.
13. L. C., "The Concert Choir," *Musical Courier*, February 1, 1953 (Scrapbook #1 of Margaret Hillis Collection, Rosenthal Archives of the Chicago Symphony Orchestra Association).
14. C. B., "Concert Choir Town Hall January 16," *Musical America*, February 1953 (Scrapbook #1 of Margaret Hillis Collection, Rosenthal Archives of the Chicago Symphony Orchestra Association).
15. Francis D. Perkins, "Concert and Recital Choral Music," *New York Herald Tribune*, January 17, 1953.
16. A. B., "Concert Choir Town Hall February 12," *Musical America*, February 1953. (Scrapbook #1 of Margaret Hillis Collection, Rosenthal Archives of the Chicago Symphony Orchestra Association).
17. "Concert Choir Sings at Town Hall," *New York Herald Review*, February 1953. (Scrapbook #1 of Margaret Hillis Collection, Rosenthal Archives of the Chicago Symphony Orchestra Association).
18. Albert J. Elias, "From Kokomo to Town Hall—Margaret Hillis Started as a Conductor at 14," *The New York Times,* March 1, 1953.
19. Ibid.
20. R. S., "Concert Choir Town Hall March 12," *Musical America*, March 1953. (Scrapbook #1 of Margaret Hillis Collection, Rosenthal Archives of the Chicago Symphony Orchestra Association).
21. P. G. H., "Concert and Recital Margaret Hillis and Choir," *New York Herald Tribune*, March 13, 1953 (Scrapbook #1 of Margaret Hillis Collection, Rosenthal Archives of the Chicago Symphony Orchestra Association).
22. J. B., "Bach's B minor Mass Heard at Town Hall," *The New York Times*, April 22, 1953 (Scrapbook #1 of Margaret Hillis Collection, Rosenthal Archives of the Chicago Symphony Orchestra Association).

23. "Concert Choir, Margaret Hillis Town Hall April 21," *Musical Courier*, May 15, 1954 (Scrapbook #1 of Margaret Hillis Collection, Rosenthal Archives of the Chicago Symphony Orchestra Association).

24. Ibid.

25. "A Tradition Observed Collegiate Chorale Sings at Forum in Ninth Consecutive Appearance," *Herald Tribune*, October 26, 1952 (Scrapbook #1 of Margaret Hillis Collection, Rosenthal Archives of the Chicago Symphony Orchestra Association).

26. Ibid.

27. Letter found in Scrapbook #1 of the Margaret Hillis Collection, Rosenthal Archives of the Chicago Symphony Orchestra Association.

28. "Collegiate Chorale Premieres," *Musical Courier*, January 1, 1953 (Scrapbook #1 of Margaret Hillis Collection, Rosenthal Archives of the Chicago Symphony Orchestra Association).

29. *Choral and Organ Guide*, January 1953 (truncated clipping in Scrapbook #1 of Margaret Hillis Collection, Rosenthal Archives of the Chicago Symphony Orchestra Association).

30. Howard Taubman, "Margaret Hillis Leads Collegiate Chorale in Its Annual Christmas Festival Concert," *The New York Times*, December 16, 1952.

31. Ibid.

32. "Dear People" letter in Scrapbook #1 of the Margaret Hillis Collection, Rosenthal Archives of the Chicago Symphony Orchestra Association.

33. Interview with Alice Parker, June 12, 2014.

34. Ibid.

35. Albert J. Elias, "From Kokomo to Town Hall—Margaret Hillis Started as a Conductor at 14," *The New York Times*, March 1, 1953.

CHAPTER 8

A PIVOTAL SEASON: 1953–1954

For the first time since departing the Juilliard School, Margaret would end work affiliations acquired early on that she determined were no longer needed. The conducting work she chose to retain going forward had a direct connection to the advancement and promotion of her New York Concert Choir or to her growth as a conductor. By the fall of 1953, Hillis had ended her teaching at Juilliard, and this would also be her final season serving as assistant conductor for Robert Shaw's Collegiate Chorale. Shaw was gone most of the time touring with his professional Robert Shaw Chorale and in his new position as music director of the San Diego Symphony, leaving Hillis solely in charge. From her perspective, the point of retaining this position was to learn by watching her mentor. With Shaw away, the position was of less value to her. Hillis had more than enough conducting duties to attend to and needed sufficient time to prepare her Concert Choir for their upcoming performances of the 1953–1954 season. She remained in her position with the American Opera Society, which continued to provide supplemental income for the Concert Choir while offsetting costs for the Hillis family. Margaret also retained her position at the Union Theological Seminary, which provided her regular practice in conducting an orchestra.

These days, Hillis was more selective when it came to accepting conducting invitations. One she accepted in the fall of 1953 was an appearance for the Sigma Alpha Iota Golden Anniversary Concert in Chicago. This internationally renowned music fraternity was established to support and promote music making of the highest standards, which was consistent with Hillis's own priorities as a musician. This engagement also allowed her an opportunity to return to her beloved Midwestern roots, something she was able to do less frequently these days given her busy life in New York. For the event, Margaret directed an all-female chorus comprised of SAI chapter choirs from Drury College, Illinois Wesleyan, and Drake and Susquehanna universities. Among the works on the program was a composition awarded the SAI American Modern Music Award. The winning choral score, *Remember* by Richard Willis, was one of several contemporary works Hillis directed.[1] She accepted very few additional guest appearances that fall, protecting time for the major preparations she'd be making for the coming season.

Hillis would devote most of the fall to her preparation for an ambitious opening Town Hall concert consisting entirely of Igor Stravinsky's choral works. By this time, Hillis was one of the most experienced conductors of Stravinsky's choral compositions, having often prepared her Concert Choir for his New York choral concerts and eventually for his recordings. Their work together provided Hillis the inimitable opportunity to learn Stravinsky's music in the way he wanted it performed. Their frequent collaborations also made the difficult technical challenges in Stravinsky's music a bit easier for Hillis to manage. Stravinsky found Hillis's work utterly meticulous, and through their work together, she gained great admiration for the composer and he for her as well. It was a logical, albeit risky, choice for her to program an entire concert of his complex compositions, as it provided her an added niche to further distinguish her chorus and herself.

Hillis knew that in order to prepare her singers and the accompanying instrumentalists adequately—not to mention preparing herself to conduct these difficult pieces—she would need to devote extra time to the Stravinsky program. This circumstance required master planning since she had to balance the study and practice of Stravinsky's music with all of the other programs she was preparing for the 1953–1954 concert season. Hillis designed an intricate rehearsal schedule to accommodate the learning process. Taking into consideration all the chorus needed to accomplish between the Town Hall series and the American Opera Society programs coming up, she had much to juggle. Beginning in January 1954, concerts would be occurring in close proximity, making the fall an important period of preparation for her and the choir. Just three days after the January Stravinsky performance, for example, the Concert Choir was scheduled to perform Gluck's opera *Paride ed Elena* with the American Opera Society. Additionally, the entire 1954 season was scheduled with sometimes only days between major performances. Planning carefully would be an important component for success in this and future seasons.

When Margaret reflected upon preparing to conduct the Stravinsky program, she stated that it was "like riding a wild horse."[2] In her efforts to secure herself for conducting the most demanding piece on the program, *Les noces*, she scheduled hours of rehearsal time with the four pianists, who carried the major responsibility for the instrumental accompaniment. She worked with them frequently before combining them with her chorus. One of those four pianists was John Wustman, who would become an internationally renowned piano coach and accompanist. At the time they were working together for Hillis's Stravinsky concert, they had only recently met. Wustman attributed his career being launched, in part, to Margaret's support.

John Wustman first met Margaret Hillis just after moving to New York City from Michigan, where he grew up. He had hopes of gaining admission into Juilliard's prestigious piano program. While auditioning for the faculty, he was tested in sight-singing by Hillis, who was in her final year on Juilliard's faculty. Wustman sailed right through the sight-singing exam with the aid, he claimed, of his perfect pitch. Recognizing his sight-reading skill, Hillis knew John could be a valuable asset to the Collegiate Chorale, and as a consequence, she encouraged him to audition for the choir. He had never sung in a chorus before, but intrigued by the invitation, he auditioned and gained immediate entry into the group. The very first night of attending rehearsal, he was asked to replace the accompanist of the ensemble, who had just announced he was leaving to take a position in Los Angeles. Hillis, knowing John's piano skills and impeccable musicianship, recommended him to Robert Shaw. That recommendation resulted in Wustman becoming the Collegiate Chorale's new accompanist. From that fateful appointment, Wustman would meet Nancy Murchie, his future wife who was then a member of the ensemble. Moreover, he acquired many dear friends, including Margaret Hillis, Robert Shaw, Tom Pyle, and Alice Parker. Wustman fondly reminisced about being a part of the Shaw and Parker/Pyle entourage, traveling together each summer to accompany Shaw for his San Diego choral workshops. Through their travels the families grew close, with Wustman serving as the best man at *Tommy* Pyle (as John called him) and Alice Parker's wedding. John recalled a time, many years after he and Shaw had lost touch, when Shaw phoned him, having heard that John's wife was critically ill. Shaw made nightly calls to John throughout that week with one exception, on January 25, 1999, which turned out to be the night Shaw passed away from a sudden illness.[3] Myriad bonds made by Wustman through his work in the Collegiate Chorale remained treasured memories. He attributed a significant support at the onset of his career to Margaret Hillis, who secured not only the Collegiate Chorale position for him but also numerous additional jobs, helping Wustman establish himself in New York City. His work in those early years provided him the networking and experience that eventually blossomed into a brilliant career of teaching and accompanying the great opera stars from the mid-1900s on. Some of those stars included Jan Peerce, Luciano Pavarotti, Birgit Nilsson, Renata Scotto, Mirella Freni, Elisabeth Schwarzkopf, and Nicolai Gedda, along with many others. Wustman would often appear with these famous artists in recitals all over the world, and he often joined them on late night television shows, including *The Tonight Show* with Johnny Carson, where these renowned singers presented their classical artistry to a wide television-viewing audience.

It is no surprise that Margaret would hire Wustman for the New York Concert Choir's Stravinsky program as one of the four top-flight pianists she needed for *Les noces*. Wustman recalled being in rehearsals with Hillis for hours and hours, repeating the same passages of *Les noces* as she conducted them. He considered the rehearsals serving as more of an assist for her learning process rather than in service of the pianists who managed their technical challenges of the piece after only a few rehearsals. Hillis needed significant rehearsal time to master the difficult conducting gestures necessary for keeping the chorus, pianists, and percussionists together. Though Wustman believed they rehearsed the piece more than was necessary, he nevertheless valued his work with Margaret greatly. He appreciated the professionalism he first encountered with both her and Shaw when working with the Collegiate Chorale. He was particularly struck by the way this volunteer chorus was treated with the same expectations as a professional group. Those same standards, Wustman observed, were continued by Hillis with her Concert Choir. As Wustman recalled, the rehearsals in both groups would begin and end precisely, and rehearsal time was spent constructively and efficiently. He admired the detailed preparation Margaret would apply to her rehearsals and he remembered how greatly Robert Shaw respected Margaret, which Wustman witnessed firsthand when observing Shaw's interaction with his valued assistant of the Chorale.[4]

The Stravinsky concert, Margaret openly admitted, made her "scared to death" because she was preparing the most challenging concert she had ever conducted. Priding herself on precision and accuracy, she took painstaking efforts to be as exacting with Stravinsky's markings as she could possibly be. The rigors of her rehearsals with her four pianists in *Les noces*, along with all the other instrumentalists and vocalists, eventually paid off. The full program, which included Stravinsky's *Pater noster, Ave Maria, Mass, Symphony of Psalms,* and *Les noces,* was a huge critical success. Even Stravinsky himself, who attended the concert, was impressed. As Hillis humorously recalled, Stravinsky's comment to Margaret after the performance was that she should not take him so literally.[5] She noted that Stravinsky often followed that philosophy simply because he was not quite so meticulous regarding the conducting of his music.

The reviews for Hillis's herculean efforts were impressive. Although most critics gave some attention to the "female conductor" aspect, she was gaining admiration for her skill as a musician, as a conductor, and as an artist. The ten vocal soloists, along with her orchestral forces, four pianists, six percussionists, and her Concert Choir performed the difficult *Les noces* "with an exactitude of musical detail and authenticity of style [exceptional] in this listener's experience of the works." The reviewer, Virgil Thomson, a well-respected composer and critic, went on to say, "There is no question about it. Miss Hillis knows her Stravinsky scores . . . far better, indeed, than most of the name conductors, including Stravinsky. . . . Hers is a first-class musical temperament, powerful, relentless, and thorough. . . . Her aim seems to be the performance of the music in hand, nothing else. . . . Such an approach inspires respect . . . by its innate nobility but also by its effectiveness."[6]

In one particular review, found in Hillis's scrapbook collection 1952–1954, the writer stated, "Miss Hillis . . . avoids Robert Shaw's occasional tendency to overdramatize this kind of writing that is meant to excite by its very austerity."[7] Ironically, the less emotive nature of Stravinsky's music may well have worked in Margaret's favor. As a rather stolid woman, she would frequently shy away from the more emotional aspects of music she conducted. Early reviews of Hillis recognized how controlled and contained she kept her gestures, resulting in a more straightforward and less emotional performance. This detail was frequently stated as an observation, though there was often a hint of criticism in early reviews, implying that perhaps there should be more musicality in her performance. Nonetheless, conducting gesture was something Hillis worked hard to contain, knowing that overly expressive movements could result in criticism, particularly for a female conductor. It was also not part of Hillis's personality to be so extroverted in public. Stravinsky's music was the perfect choice of repertoire to avoid overly flamboyant performance, and at the same time it allowed Hillis to display the commanding precision she had worked so hard to achieve. Hillis was very good at self-restraint, keeping her emotions tucked carefully away at all times. In contrast, those dramatic tendencies would have been difficult for her teacher Robert Shaw to avoid; he was known to bring out the most dramatic elements of music he conducted. As Hillis tells it, [Stravinsky] "was very much against these interpretive conductors. Do what's on the page! So, I did what was on the page! And there were certain places where I wanted to let the piece [*Les noces*] . . . breathe a little bit more. . . . I didn't allow myself to do it because of what he had said [on his score markings]."[8] Stravinsky's music was compatible with the careful, contained approach Margaret would gravitate to in all of her music making. Keeping her guard up in so many other aspects of her personal and professional life, Stravinsky's music was a good choice for her preference of precision over emotional display. It was the perfect formula for a successful opening of the Town Hall season!

Following the achievement of that first Town Hall concert, Margaret wisely arranged for a recording to be made of the entire Stravinsky program. Hillis tells of one rehearsal for that upcoming recording project where she had an unexpected Stravinsky encounter.

> So, we were doing it again [rehearsing *Les noces*] . . . [so] that we could record it. I called the Chorus together in order for us to hear a tape-back of that first performance . . . and we gathered together in this room on 57th Street in New York City and a friend of mine arrived . . . he is also a friend of Stravinsky and guess who was with him—STRAVINSKY—! I thought 'Oh God! This is terrible!' So, what could I do? I had to go ahead and run it—so I did and when it was over Stravinsky said . . . 'Very good, very good . . . you keep doing my music, but let it breathe a little more!"
>
> . . . So, that performance came out cleanly and we made the recording— and even though Stravinsky had recorded it in Europe maybe five or six years earlier and it was just a mess . . . this one was clean, and it was [a] really good performance recording of *Les noces*.[9]

The reviews of Margaret's recording [Vox PL 8630] confirmed her impressions about the quality she had achieved in the pieces, particularly of *Les noces*. "The performance [of *Les noces*] is expert with a kind of jangled, metallic brilliance about it . . . the full English text is printed in the album though a surprising amount of it is understandable."[10] "Vox is certainly to be congratulated for making this available on disk, particularly since Margaret Hillis's performances were hailed at the time as being as good as anyone could hope to hear, including the composer's"[11] (Pictures 27 and 28). In a monthly *Gramophone* review, the critic heaped praise upon the recording: "enthusiastically [performed] by a group of unfamiliar artists," describing Hillis's control of the musicians and her grasp of the music.[12]

Although the recording was successful, it was important for the records to sell if she had hopes of being sponsored for future recordings with her Concert Choir. It is likely the Hillis family had financially secured the making of her first record. Therefore, it is not surprising that she elicited the support of her youngest brother Joe and sister-in-law Connie, who would purchase a sizeable quantity of the records in order to push the statistics of its popularity. Joe Hillis and his recent bride Connie would soon be more involved with the promotion of Margaret's enterprises.

Picture 27.

The New York Times, Sunday, June 20, 1954. Margaret conducting a recording session of her Stravinsky album (Scrapbook #1, 1952–1954). (Margaret Hillis Collection, Rosenthal Archives of the Chicago Symphony Orchestra Association)

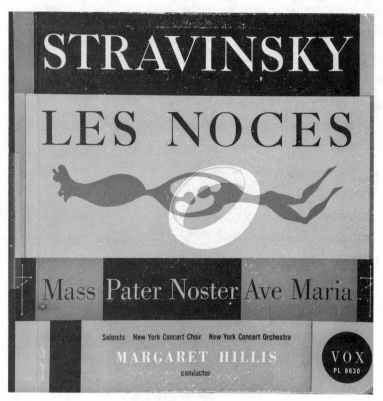

Picture 28.
Album of Stravinsky's music conducted by Margaret Hillis, recorded shortly after the Town Hall performance. (Margaret Hillis Collection, Rosenthal Archives of the Chicago Symphony Orchestra Association)

The Stravinsky concert of January 1954 proved a wonderful launching point of Hillis's most successful Town Hall season to come, from the standpoint of reviewers and audiences. Stravinsky's music became a hallmark for Hillis, especially because she was rapidly becoming known for her expertise—specifically of Stravinsky's *Les noces*—leading to future performances and recordings of the work. Five years after her own recording, Hillis was invited to participate in Stravinsky's recording of his *Les noces*, engaging her New York Concert Choir.

The choir was joined by a prestigious ensemble of well-known composers who served as the pianists for the project—Lukas Foss, Samuel Barber, Aaron Copland, and Roger Sessions. Hillis claimed Foss was "the only [true] pianist among them."[13] In preparation for the recording session, Stravinsky arranged for a performance of the piece. Hillis talked about several humorous episodes that took place during that concert and in the recording session thereafter. The first incident involved Aaron Copland, who had been a friend of Margaret's, most likely through her affiliation with Juilliard where he was often present, collaborating with the school's president, William Schuman. With Copland's contemporary choral works becoming more well known, it is likely Hillis and Copland would have first met while she was a student or a faculty member at the school. At the rehearsal of *Les noces*, Copland asked Hillis to turn his pages during the performance. Hillis explained, "He kept getting lost [in the rehearsal] and I'd start counting for him. So, we were ready to go on stage for the performance. I said, 'Aaron, what about this counting business? I know it's very annoying if you don't need it.' He said, 'If I grunt, you count.' . . . So, he'd grunt, and I'd count, and I'd see he was back on and I'd quit counting."[14]

Directly after that performance, all the performers headed to Columbia Studios to make a recording of the piece. Starting with the first tableau, Hillis claimed that with each repetition things got slower and slower because Stravinsky was becoming more and more tired. As Hillis tells it,

> Finally, Lukas Foss came up to me and said, "You'd better conduct this, or we will not have a recording." Hillis responded, "I just can't conduct behind the old man's back . . . I just can't. It's such disrespect." Lukas responded, "It's either that or [no] recording."

Hillis then agreed. She positioned herself behind Stravinsky, conducting off her miniature score that she was using to coach her chorus, but it was too small to be as useful as a full-sized score from which to conduct. "So, we were on our last take of the first tableau and I stood behind Stravinsky and conducted it from memory, and it was together, and it was clean, and the tempi held. You know to this day I have not had the courage to listen to that record."[15]

Following the January 1954 Town Hall concert success, Hillis and her chorus moved full throttle into the rest of a busy concert season. Rehearsals were held four nights a week, providing her singers a decent wage to support themselves in New York. As Hillis explained, "Half a dozen choruses were operating [in New York at this time] or rather, the same singers were darting from one conductor's rehearsals to another's. . . . For once it was almost possible for choristers outside the Metropolitan Opera to earn a living, and they developed incredible versatility and readiness."[16]

As the Town Hall season progressed, Margaret herself was becoming more the central focus of public interest than her chorus. In a *New York World Telegram and Sun* article, "Smart Girls Tell How to Hit Jackpot," Hillis along with an actress, a chemist, and a television personality were featured as accomplished New York women in their chosen fields.[17] With the exception of the actress, the other ladies were highlighted for the distinct nature of their professions, often thought of as being for men only. Hillis would make herself available for any publicity coverage, knowing that although her priority was to promote her chorus and her conducting work, the articles would likely focus on her clothing or her hairstyle choices instead. Nonetheless, any publicity would give some attention to her chorus, thereby creating interest and hopefully encouraging attendance to a future performance. One article featuring Margaret was all about the rarity of female conductors but focused mostly upon how Hillis selected her concert wear, a less complicated task for men who did not have the style dilemmas women encountered. Of particular note was the final paragraph of this feature article. The writer, obviously curious about Hillis's marital status inquired, "What? No husband?" to which Hillis replied, "I am not married . . . not yet."[18] Truly, these intrusive questions about her personal life, her dress code, her hair style, and other subjects unrelated to the incredible accomplishments she had achieved so far demonstrated how women in professional fields at this time still had a long way to go. The public was not yet ready for accomplished, independent, professional women. Margaret simply worked with whatever opportunities were available to promote her Concert Choir and tolerated the distractions of the curious public along the way.

FRITZ REINER COMES TO TOWN

Hillis's 1953–1954 Town Hall season continued to impress audiences and critics. Margaret's second Town Hall concert, with typical programming for Hillis, included works of old masters interspersed with premieres. The day after her second very successful Town Hall performance, Hillis and her chorus hosted an important guest. Fritz Reiner was in his first season as sixth music director of the Chicago Symphony Orchestra, and he was on a mission to find a chorus to perform with his orchestra. Hillis's manager, knowing why Reiner was coming to town, wisely arranged his visit to a Concert Choir rehearsal to audition her group. Unaware that he had indirectly worked with Hillis once before when she prepared the children's chorus for his

Carmen recording, he had heard about her excellent work and wanted to see if her chorus would fit the bill. Reiner was concerned about using local Chicago amateur choruses, particularly because he was considering more challenging choral repertoire for the following season.

There had been a long-standing tradition in Chicago to use local amateur choral groups, including the Apollo Chorus as well as local university and high school choirs for the CSO's choral symphonic performances. Reiner attempted to carry on this tradition, engaging one of the local university choruses to perform with the Orchestra during his first season. It was arranged for Northwestern University to provide a men's chorus for Brahms's *Alto Rhapsody*, to be performed on a subscription series Thanksgiving Day and the day after the holiday, November 26 and 27, 1953. There was an additional university collaboration, perhaps also with Northwestern University, for a women's chorus to sing Debussy's *La Damoiselle élue* with the Chicago Symphony Orchestra, scheduled December 24 and 26, 1953. Both concerts were scheduled over what would have been the students' holiday breaks. According to Hillis, there had been a miscommunication with some of the students, resulting in a number of them missing a conductor piano rehearsal with Reiner. As Hillis described it, "Suddenly about two days before the rehearsal was to take place, somebody [at the school] caught on . . . they sent [students] telegrams, made long distance calls. . . . About a third of the chorus was in attendance when Reiner got there." He canceled the Debussy program on the spot. There is no verification that the women's chorus was also from Northwestern University, however it is a possibility that such an arrangement was made. Perhaps while Reiner was on campus working with the men's chorus on the *Alto Rhapsody*, he wanted also to work with the women. Those women living out of town had likely gone home for their Thanksgiving break, unaware that this was also to be their rehearsal time with Reiner. Whichever university was involved in the misunderstanding, the timeline supports that a conductor piano rehearsal (CPR) for the Debussy most likely took place during the Thanksgiving holiday break. This is corroborated by a newspaper article by Seymour Raven appearing in the *Chicago Daily Tribune* on November 22, 1953, where the Debussy program is included in listings of upcoming concerts with the CSO.[19] However, by December 10, 1953, the Debussy program had been replaced by another concert. The only school break that would have taken place between November 22 and December 10 would have been Thanksgiving. It is logical to assume that the women's conductor piano rehearsal had been poorly attended, leading Reiner to cancel it. The men's chorus of Northwestern University performed the *Alto Rhapsody* in November as planned. Whatever the cause of the unfortunate situation leading to the cancellation of the Debussy program, Reiner was unhappy with what had transpired, according to Hillis, and he was determined to explore better options for a chorus.

Hillis recalled, "[Reiner] came stomping into New York, looking for a professional chorus that would be reliable!"[20] She vividly described the events that followed, taking place on February 13, 1954.

[Reiner] came about fifteen minutes late, and I motioned him in and had him sit down and we continued rehearsing a little Mozart piece, [likely to use this for the audition, in that there was no "little Mozart piece" scheduled for their final two concerts of the season] . . . and I stopped the basses who had made an entrance that wasn't very good, and he said to me, "How do you do?" It was the first time I had [officially] met the man . . . and he said the same thing to the chorus and in unison they said back—"How do you do?"

"Do you have the Verdi Requiem?" Well, immediately I figured that my manager had gotten something upside down . . . he had it in my repertory list and not the chorus's repertory list, and I said, "We don't have enough copies to go around." . . . So, he said, "Well do you have the *Missa solemnis*?" I again said, "Sorry, but we don't have enough copies to go around." Then he got very impatient and said in a gruff voice, "Well what do you have?" I said, "Well we have the Bach *Magnificat*." He said, "So you have the Mass in B Minor?" I said, "Yes, we do." So, we handed it out.

Now I had done this work with this chorus maybe two years before [actually it was in the previous season] so I looked around and noticed that the personnel had changed enormously . . . and I did not know how many of them had done it, and I just hoped he would not ask for the Gloria but here I was—you know like sometimes when I was in the air with a student and he'd freeze at the controls and I wondered what I should do next—but you keep your head . . . so, I just said, "Which movement would you like to hear?" He said, "The first Kyrie will be fine."

I breathed a sigh of relief, but it is a deceptively difficult movement and we started it, and, after the first four measures, I looked at him and I saw his hand moving so I took his tempo and they sang it absolutely beautifully, and when we came to the end of it, he said, "Fine, fine." I then saw him over to the door and he said, "Tell me, do they sight-read?" I said "Yes, of course, they do very well." There was silence, thank God, behind me in the room. Then he said, "You will hear from me" and the door closed behind him, and when I turned around to the chorus, they just went bonkers. I said to them, "How many of you have ever done this piece before?" There were about four hands raised out of forty-four people—all the rest did it by sight-reading.[21]

Indeed, the New York Concert Choir did hear from Maestro Reiner, and rather quickly at that. Impressed by what he heard during his visit, the chorus was invited to join the Chicago Symphony Orchestra the following season to perform Samuel Barber's recently composed *Prayers of Kierkegaard* and Orff's *Carmina Burana*, both new pieces for the orchestra and considered much more challenging for choruses than Beethoven's Ninth Symphony, which he begrudgingly gave to a local Chicago chorus, the Swedish Choral Club. Just one month after his visit to New York, the Chicago papers were carrying the news about the New York Concert Choir that would be appearing with the symphony next season. Writer Irving Sablosky weighed in about the choice of these "newcomers" whom he had heard when he was in New York, remarking [the Concert Choir] "has much the same makeup as Shaw's touring chorus."[22] In what appeared to be somewhat of an endorsement, he must have felt compelled to connect Hillis with Shaw and his touring singers to justify this invitation to his readers. Yes, in fact, Hillis and Shaw did share some of the same singers. Hillis used Tom Pyle, the same contractor as Shaw, to hire her singers. However, this alone did not justify Reiner's choice of the New York Concert Choir. Reiner knew of Hillis's recent successes with this chorus. Her achievements were of her own merit as a conductor and the critic should not have needed her or her chorus to be connected with anyone else to justify their worth. Unfortunately, it was Margaret's connection to a more well-known male conductor that gained Sablosky's initial support.

Extending Her Reach—Opera Conducting

A busy winter season continued with the Concert Choir performing in Rossini's *La gazza ladra* with Arnold Gamson conducting Hillis's chorus for the American Opera Society production. Just one night later, twenty-three singers in the Concert Choir were back on the Town Hall stage for their third program of the season, which was reviewed as being sung with "more spirit than one ordinarily encounters in comparable groups . . . maintaining a commendable high standard of style and vocal delivery."[23] It appeared Hillis had found the perfect balance of choral masterworks alongside contemporary and newly composed works, all of which were lesser known to the New York audiences who welcomed these refreshing choices. The Concert Choir continued their successful season, receiving laudatory reviews praising the chorus and Hillis's exceptional programming.

Trusting her judgement for innovative programming, Hillis decided to digress from her typical formula for her final concert of the season. She chose to present a concert version of Rameau's opera *Hippolyte et Aricie*. Additionally, Hillis would also direct this American premiere for the opening of a new concert hall in the Metropolitan Museum of Art. Featuring soloists from the Metropolitan Opera and New York City Opera rather than selecting soloists from her chorus, Hillis sought to attract audiences who would expect nothing less when attending other operas in New York City. Margaret went all out with her planning of this program, taking special steps to promote the event by inviting well-known New York concertgoers and artists. She sent out engraved invitations to her specially selected guests for the Town Hall concert, to be followed by a black-tie reception at the Waldorf Astoria Hotel, courtesy of the Hillis family (Picture 29). Margaret received telegrams from Robert Shaw as well as numerous other well-known dignitaries, which showed the extent to which Hillis reached out to her artist community for support of this special performance.

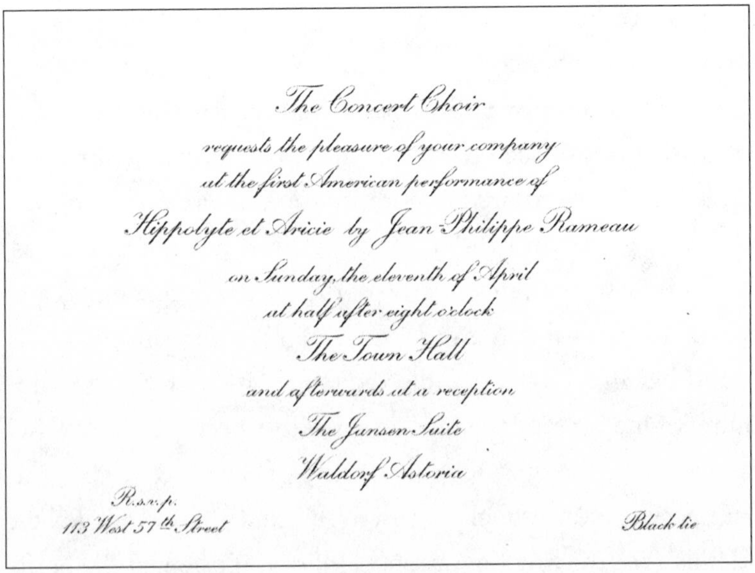

The Concert Choir
requests the pleasure of your company
at the first American performance of
Hippolyte et Aricie by Jean Philippe Rameau
on Sunday, the eleventh of April
at half after eight o'clock
The Town Hall
and afterwards at a reception
The Jansen Suite
Waldorf Astoria

R.s.v.p.
113 West 57th Street   *Black tie*

Picture 29.

Invitation Hillis sent out to elite concertgoers and New York artists to attend Rameau's *Hippolyte et Aricie*. Hillis would be conducting at Town Hall and a black-tie reception she and her family hosted following the performance (Scrapbook #1, 1952–1954). (Margaret Hillis Collection, Rosenthal Archives of the Chicago Symphony Orchestra Association)

Picture 30.

First performance at Grace Rainey Rogers Auditorium, Metropolitan Museum of Art, opening the Baroque Music Festival. Margaret Hillis conducting the New York Concert Choir and Orchestra in a performance of Rameau's *Hippolyte et Aricie*, May 11, 1954. (Margaret Hillis Collection, Rosenthal Archives of the Chicago Symphony Orchestra Association)

Conducting opera turned out to be a stretch for Hillis, as it highlighted established weaknesses in her conducting. The critics immediately seized upon those weaknesses in their reviews of Hillis's performance. Apparently, she managed the more boisterous sections of the opera, but she was unable to shift in more sensitive scenes, which would have required a more emotionally nuanced approach. Said one critic, "[Hillis] was good with the 'tumult' . . . but her tendency was to lead the whole work as if they were raging nearly all the time. . . . It came as a positive relief when the chorus of Fates finally sang softly."[24] The criticism for Hillis's approach centered around her inability to handle the tender moments of the opera with the subtlety required. One writer called it "an inflexible performance."[25] Whereas some criticism was saved for the questionable quality of the piece itself, "the reasons for the work's neglect are not difficult to discover," and the brunt of the criticism fell squarely on Hillis's conducting limitations. Hillis would repeat the performance two more times, May 11 and 14, to open the new Grace Rainey Rogers Auditorium at the Metropolitan Museum of Art (Picture 30). For this performance, she brought fifteen fewer choristers and five fewer instrumentalists to accommodate the smaller stage. The critic for those performances alluded to the criticism of her earlier performances, attributing the negative comments to the "novelty and unconventional treatment of forms of Rameau's day." Instead, he complimented Hillis's performance at the new auditorium, which he described as "formal and ceremonious," thereby contradicting the harsh criticism of previous reviewers.[26]

Margaret Hillis continued to collect all her reviews, including the ones that pointed out her weaknesses, and these *Hippolyte* reviews were no exception. Margaret knew how to learn from critical commentary and took full advantage of what must have been a disappointing final concert of an otherwise successful season. She used negative reviews as a starting point for her future steps to develop as a conductor. Where criticism in such a public forum would devastate some, Hillis wisely kept things balanced. These critical remarks would become her agendum. As she often said, "You either get better or you get worse as you move forward. One can never remain the same."[27]

The 1953–1954 concert season was a pivotal time in Margaret Hillis's development. During this period, Hillis demonstrated her incredible planning ability, enabling her sufficient time for learning and teaching the music during a particularly packed concert season. Her innate understanding of time became one of the most important assets Hillis would demonstrate. Additionally, Hillis's willingness to take risks as a conductor and her ability to handle both the successes and the failures she would encounter when going out of her comfort zone strengthened her. She remained open to criticism, willing to learn from the positive and negative feedback she would encounter. Added to these assets was her growing reputation of generosity as a colleague. She did not hesitate to help other young musicians getting their start, though she was not much further along in her own career. John Wustman was one of many examples of artists whom she positioned to succeed in the competitive music scene of New York City.

Margaret would also acquire a reputation of reliability. Particularly impressive was her ability to remain calm in the most intensely challenging of circumstances. Whether in front of an audience conducting music she was not completely comfortable with or while encountering a world-famous conductor putting her New York Concert Choir through their paces, Hillis demonstrated her complete control in stressful situations, which made her particularly valuable in the profession. These traits would auger well for the next level of her career, particularly as her network expanded nationally and internationally. So much of what Hillis accomplished in this 1953–1954 season was the culmination of all that she had learned so far and would help her carve a path for her future growth. The season to come would mark new, exciting advancements for Margaret Hillis's conducting career.

ENDNOTES

1. "Sigma Alpha Iota Golden Anniversary Marked at Convention," *Musical Courier*, October 1, 1953 (Scrapbook #1 of Margaret Hillis Collection, Rosenthal Archives of the Chicago Symphony Orchestra Association).
2. Ulla Colgrass, "Conductor Hillis Reversed the Odds," *Music Management Magazine* (November/December 1981): p. 15.
3. Interview with John Wustman, March 19, 2014
4. Ibid.
5. Colgrass, "Conductor Hillis Reversed the Odds," p. 15.
6. Virgil Thomson, "Music: Concert Choir," *New York Herald Tribune*, January 13, 1954.
7. Nat, "The Concert Choir Town Hall." No information about the publication nor the date. Date would be between January and February 1954 (Scrapbook #1 of Margaret Hillis Collection, Rosenthal Archives of the Chicago Symphony Orchestra Association).
8. Jon Bentz, "Interview of Margaret Hillis Director Chicago Symphony Orchestra, September 19, 1989, Archives Committee, Oral History Project, 1992," p. 42 (Margaret Hillis Collection, Rosenthal Archives of the Chicago Symphony Orchestra Association).
9. Ibid.
10. "Stravinsky: 'Les Noces,' Mass, and Two Motets," *Chicago Sun Times*, June 27, 1954 (Scrapbook #1 of Margaret Hillis Collection, Rosenthal Archives of the Chicago Symphony Orchestra Association).

11. C. B., "Russian Wedding," *Musical America*, February 1954 (Scrapbook #1 of Margaret Hillis Collection, Rosenthal Archives of the Chicago Symphony Orchestra Association).

12. "Stravinsky Les Noces: Mass; Two Motets—Pater Noster and Ave Maria." *Critique: A Monthly Review of Gramophone Records* 6, no. 9 (February 1955) (Scrapbook #2 of Margaret Hillis Collection, Rosenthal Archives of the Chicago Symphony Orchestra Association).

13. Bentz, "Interview of Margaret Hillis," p. 43.

14. Margaret Hillis, interview by Norman Pellegrini (transcribed by Stanley G. Livengood), October 6, 1997, p. 9.

15. Bentz, "Interview of Margaret Hillis," p. 43. The album is a Columbia Masterworks recording MS 6372 entitled *Stravinsky Conducts Stravinsky*, with *Les Noces* recorded in December 1959 and the rest of the album recorded and released in 1962. By 1959 the New York Concert Choir would undergo another change to their name, now called the American Concert Choir, to align with the American Choral Foundation.

16. George McElroy and Jane W. Stedman, "The Chorus Lady," *Opera News*, February 16, 1974, pp. 10–13.

17. Hope Johnson, "Smart Girls Tell How to Hit Jackpot," *New York World Telegram and Sun*, February 4, 1954.

18. W. G. Rogers, "Miss Margaret Hillis Conducts Concert Choir; Also Instructs Navy Fliers," *[Newspaper title not available]*, July 7, 1954 (Scrapbook #1 of Margaret Hillis Collection, Rosenthal Archives of the Chicago Symphony Orchestra Association).

19. Seymour Raven, "Symphony to Carry Most of Schedule," *Chicago Daily Tribune*, November 22, 1953, p. D1.

20. Margaret Hillis, interview by Pellegrini, p. 10.

21. Bentz, "Interview of Margaret Hillis," pp. 8–9.

22. Irving Sablosky, "Reiner's Plans for Next Season," *Chicago Daily News*, March 11, 1954.

23. H. C. S., "Concert Choir Sings in Unusual Program," *The New York Times*, March 12, 1954 (Scrapbook #1 of Margaret Hillis Collection, Rosenthal Archives of the Chicago Symphony Orchestra Association).

24. R. P., "Miss Hillis Leads Opera by Rameau: Concert Choir Ends Season With 'Hippolyte et Aricie,' Said to Be U.S. Premiere," *The New York Times*, April 12, 1954 (Scrapbook #1 of Margaret Hillis Collection, Rosenthal Archives of the Chicago Symphony Orchestra Association).

25. Miles Kastendieck, "Town Hall: Rameau Opera," *New York Journal America*, April 12, 1954.

26. Olin Downes, "Music Finds a Place in Metropolitan Museum as New Auditorium is Opened," *The New York Times*, May 16, 1954.

27. This was a saying she would share often with the Chicago Symphony Chorus during rehearsals to motivate them, encouraging them to avoid complacency or resting on previous success.

CHAPTER 9

THE 1954–1955 SEASON: NEW BEGINNINGS

The 1954–1955 concert season would prove to be the most ambitious yet for Margaret Hillis, requiring a major shift in her standard routine. In recent years, Hillis dedicated the fall months to studying music and rehearsing her chorus for their upcoming fall appearances with the American Opera Society and for their Town Hall series that would begin in January. Once the Town Hall series commenced, concerts were spaced in close proximity through the month of May, making it necessary for most of the heavy lifting in musical preparation be done during the fall. That plan would be dramatically altered for the 1954–1955 season due to an incredible opportunity given to Margaret and her chorus.

New York's DuMont television network executives approached Hillis about doing a television series featuring her New York Concert Choir and Orchestra. It would be hosted by Mitch Miller, a popular musical entertainer of the day. The series was scheduled to run in the fall of 1954. Knowing it was too good to pass up, Hillis accepted the offer. She then set about the task of reorganizing the already packed rehearsal schedule, now allotting extra time to prepare her chorus for their exciting television debut. Before this television offer had been made, the upcoming concert season was already busier than in past years. Two programs had been added to their Town Hall series, now for a total of six concerts. Concert touring had also been added this season with two tours scheduled. The most important addition to the season was the Concert Choir's debut with the Chicago Symphony Orchestra. With so many concerts scheduled and such high stakes in these events, how she managed it all is worth a closer look. The 1954–1955 season was off to a dramatic start as the Concert Choir prepared for their televised performances. Charlotte Carlson shared, "It was a big deal for everyone."[1] None of them had ever before appeared on television and there was great excitement within the chorus for the coming event. Such an opportunity would expose Hillis and her musicians to a much wider audience, far exceeding the audiences attending their Town Hall concerts.

Television broadcasting of the mid-1950s was in its early stages, particularly when it came to live musical performance. Programs dedicated to classical music were just beginning to appear. The first televised orchestra concerts began in 1948. On March 20, 1948, Arturo Toscanini conducted the NBC Orchestra (NBC) and Eugene Ormandy conducted the Philadelphia Orchestra (CBS). The NBC Opera Theatre began its first televised production in 1949, broadcasting opera scenes and single acts of operas. With the broadcast of Gian Carlo Menotti's made-for-television opera *Amahl and the Night Visitors* on December 24, 1951, televised opera began its popularity among television viewers.[2] Leonard Bernstein's televised orchestra programs were among the first broadcasts of classical orchestral music to gain widespread popularity among viewers. Beginning on January 18, 1958, the Young People's Concerts with the New York Philharmonic made classical music more accessible, with Leonard Bernstein acting as commentator and conductor. Margaret's television series was the first choral broadcast of its kind when it aired in the fall of 1954. Unlike orchestral music and opera, classical choral music was less familiar to the listening public, making Hillis's series a greater challenge for winning viewership. Added to this was the technical aspect of effectively filming classical vocal music for television. Hillis and her chorus had their work cut out for them to make this a successful venture.

The Concert Choir series, "Concert Tonight," was taped live at the Adelphi Theater in New York City. Tickets were distributed among friends of the performers, who witnessed the live broadcasts (Pictures 31 and 32). The first broadcast took place on September 15, 1954, the second on September 22, and the third on September 29. Hillis wisely programmed music that her choir had recently performed, allowing spare rehearsal time for other upcoming programs. Included in the television series were pieces from last season's Stravinsky concert along with Bach's *Lobet den Herrn*, Brahms's *Liebeslieder Waltzes*, and other works by Mozart and Haydn.

A Special Invitation To

"CONCERT TONIGHT"

DUMONT TELEVISION NETWORK
SEPT. 15, 22, 29, OCT. 6

THE NEW YORK
CONCERT CHOIR

THE NEW YORK
CONCERT ORCHESTRA
MARGARET HILLIS, Conductor

Presenting a series of four Wednesday evening concerts of choral and orchestral music.   Consult your local paper for time and programs.

B A C H   ✦   M O Z A R T

S T R A V I N S K Y

BRAHMS   ✦   HAYDN   ✦   BARBER

Picture 31.

Ticket to the DuMont television live broadcast of the New York Concert Choir and Orchestra series "Concert Tonight" (Scrapbook #2, 1954–1956). (Margaret Hillis Collection, Rosenthal Archives of the Chicago Symphony Orchestra Association)

Picture 32.

One of several photographs Charlotte Carlson donated to the Rosenthal Archives. This photograph was taken from someone's home during one of the television broadcasts, ca. 1954. (Margaret Hillis Collection, Rosenthal Archives of the Chicago Symphony Orchestra Association)

Reviews were modestly complimentary, describing Hillis as doing a "competent job."[3] However, a review of the show itself was a different matter. As one critic put it, the program was "fine for heavier music fans . . . fascinating music for music enthusiasts but absolutely nothing for anyone else."[4] Camera work was criticized, described as "a chair-hopping spree not still for more than thirty seconds—to the point of distraction" and moving too rapidly for viewers to properly take in the music.[5] Additionally, the host of the series, Mitch Miller, garnered rather negative reviews. Although he was praised for avoiding the usual stuffiness of others who might narrate this high-brow music, Miller was said to have added little to the viewer's enjoyment.[6] One critic claimed Miller "talked into his beard between the excellent chamber exercises."[7] By the third show on September 29, the fate of the series was sealed: "It's a pity the network is killing it [the television series] instead of devoting some thought and imagination to making the picture and talk as good as the music."[8] The fourth program scheduled for October 6 did not take place—the series was canceled.

STRATEGIC PLANNING: A HILLIS HALLMARK

Without missing a beat, Hillis moved forward, continuing on with the demanding work ahead. The fall season officially began with the chorus joining the American Opera Society's production of Gluck's *Paride ed Elena* at Harvard University on Sunday, October 31, 1954. The Concert Choir had done this opera during the previous season, making it easy to resurrect. The choir's familiarity with the opera also enabled Hillis to devote some of that allotted opera rehearsal time to other music coming up. Her double-duty strategy for rehearsing the choir on multiple programs, funded in part by outside sources like the Opera Society, provided some welcome relief from expenses already building up for the Hillis family in this busy season.

Margaret also took advantage of the fact that her choir would be in Boston performing at the Opera Society's expense by adding a choral concert on their way back to New York. She booked a performance at Cornell University, knowing that the added concert would increase her Choir's exposure while giving them a chance to sing some of the music that would be performed on their upcoming spring concert tour. Hillis booked the spring tour to coincide with their performances in Chicago, also taking full advantage of the Chicago Symphony Orchestra covering travel expenses for her chorus's CSO appearance. Such clever strategy allowed Hillis to expose her choir to audiences who would not otherwise have an opportunity to hear them. By wisely coordinating these tours around concerts paid for by other organizations, like the Opera Society or the Chicago Symphony Orchestra, Hillis saved excessive travel expenses while promoting her choir.

The first Town Hall concert of the 1954–1955 season took place in December 1954, earlier than their typical start in January, as in previous seasons. Margaret cleverly programmed music of recent past performances to accommodate the early timing of this season's first concert. This December program included music the Concert Choir performed in their fall television series, including Haydn's *Theresienmesse,* Mozart's *Te Deum,* and compositions from the previous year's repertoire. Also included were Christmas works Hillis had conducted several years earlier with the Collegiate Chorale.

Hillis was repurposing repertoire not just for the sake of helping her singers prepare more quickly. Hillis also needed to account for her own readiness to conduct these programs. Consideration for learning scores was very much a part of her concert planning. With barely a month transpiring between Town Hall concerts, Hillis had little time to study and prepare herself and her choir with new music. Perhaps Hillis considered these time constraints when selecting repertoire for the second Town Hall concert of 1955. The all-Beethoven program of January 20 included music already familiar to Hillis as well. Hillis programmed Beethoven's *Egmont* Overture, a work Serge Koussevitzky guest conducted at Juilliard on May 9, 1948, when Margaret was first a student there. She may have observed those rehearsals as a conducting student, motivated to learn by observing a great conductor, or perhaps she had played that work herself as a member of the Indiana University Orchestra. Also included on that January program, Hillis chose Beethoven's Mass in C Major, a work she had first conducted with the Collegiate Chorale two years prior. Hillis was realistic about her ability to learn scores in a given amount of time, taking into consideration all that was on her schedule.

Just one month after the January concert was the next on February 20, 1955. The program was Bach's Mass in B Minor. Although some members of the choir had performed the Mass in B Minor two years earlier (April 1953), it was nonetheless a courageous undertaking to prepare this ambitious program while readying them for the difficult new material in their upcoming Chicago Symphony Orchestra appearances. Charlotte Carlson recalled rehearsing for this season's multiple performances four to five nights a week. Although this rehearsal regimen was monetarily lucrative for the singers, she claimed that it was not enjoyable. Charlotte did not particularly look forward to rehearsals with Margaret. She appreciated the thoroughness of Margaret's preparation, but she never became artistically moved by working with Margaret. Charlotte described how Margaret would carefully and meticulously go through the music to the point of tedium. "We went over every measure of the "Hosanna" [from the Bach Mass in B Minor], in every rehearsal . . . but the passion was always missing." Charlotte blamed some of the issues on the music itself but felt that Margaret's approach was equally to blame. Charlotte contrasted the experience of working with Hillis to that of her work with Roger Wagner and Robert Shaw. Those conductors, according to Carlson, would get the singers "fired up . . . they were emotionally involved" and they helped engage that emotion in their singers through their own connection to the music.[9] Charlotte mentioned how Wagner would from time to time criticize his singers, saying, "You look like a bunch of Anglo-Saxon statues," hoping to encourage more expressive singing. Charlotte never experienced those stimulating rehearsal techniques of other directors when working with Margaret. Hillis used a dryer, more technical approach, void of any emotional expression. A review of Bach's Mass in B Minor performance corroborates Charlotte's recollection:

> Miss Hillis herself was at the top of her form, which is high level indeed. Her clear beat that is both fluent and emphatic brought forth eloquent results from her assembled resources. . . . Her tempi were perfection. . . . Not a shred of this young conductor's own personality is allowed to project itself unduly upon the interpretation.[10]

Though the review showed much improvement over Hillis's previous go at this piece several years earlier, it is the last line of the review that confirms Charlotte's frustration. Hillis did not allow her personality nor emotional investment to find its way into the music. As a result, Charlotte and a number of her colleagues made this season in the New York Concert Choir their last. The challenge of keeping singers motivated, particularly with the pressure of such a demanding schedule, made it difficult for Hillis to retain some singers for multiple seasons, even at the guaranteed union wage she was paying them.

Without question, Margaret's ability to plan was particularly impressive; however, as her choir got busier, it would become more apparent that she must reconsider some of her scheduling. This season's rigors revealed several errors in judgement that Hillis would correct in future seasons. After the February performance of Bach's Mass in B Minor at Town Hall, Hillis decided to schedule one more concert to secure their preparation for the upcoming Midwest concert tour. Hillis chose a smaller tour ensemble from within the sixty-voice group she was bringing to Chicago. That smaller group would be touring before and after the Chicago Symphony Orchestra appearances. Hillis decided to schedule a "run-out" concert on March 4, 1955, in Washington, D.C., for the small group within her twenty-four-voice touring group. It became apparent that Hillis's demanding rehearsal and performance schedule was beginning to take its toll on her singers. The strain caught up with one of the octet singers, who became ill just prior to the Washington, D.C., concert, leaving her unable to sing. This left only one alto for two quartets, performing movements of Brahms's Liebeslieder Waltzes. Reviews indicated that just one alto performed in both quartets. Though critics were complimentary about this alto's heroic efforts, the concert was described as "long and strenuous."[11] The concert, criticized for being "ordinarily sterile," would leave a similar impression on audiences during their tour. The singers were being stretched physically and emotionally by Hillis's rigorous demands. They were getting tired before the tour had even begun.

Added to the overscheduling was the challenge of performing in so many differing styles of music at one time. After having just completed Bach's Mass in B Minor in a Baroque style of singing, Hillis was now rehearsing the full chorus for Carmina Burana and Prayers of Kierkegaard, requiring a much fuller vocal production. She would then rehearse her touring choir in the lighter Poulenc motets and madrigals. So many shifts and styles of singing could have added to the singers' vocal fatigue.

Perhaps finances dictated some of Hillis's overscheduling. For example, just prior to the Chicago tour, Hillis added one more commitment on March 11, 1955. The choir would perform in Dvořák's Rusalka, a collaboration with the well-known conductor of the NBC television opera series, Herman Adler. A likely rationale for Hillis cramming this performance into an already packed schedule might have been money. Television appearances were lucrative. Adding extra concert appearances, such as the one in Washington, D.C., and this television performance increased the choir's bottom line. The Hillis family was supporting the chorus, but recent increased expenses with added rehearsals for a heavy concert season would only be offset by taking on extra work. Performance opportunities and television appearances were the best options for increasing income. Could this chorus do it all? It remained to be seen. Hillis and her singers would just need to figure out how to keep up this pace!

Directly following the March 11 *Rusalka* performance, it was time for the chorus to depart for Chicago. Charlotte recalled the excitement in the Concert Choir as they were flown to Chicago and compensated well for their rehearsals and performances. Margaret did not take a fee for this project. "I wanted this thing to work and I didn't want to burden them [the Orchestral Association] with further financial obligations."[12] This would be the first of many times Hillis would forgo her fee for the good of a performance. Hillis would sacrifice her fees repeatedly in years to come, shortchanging her value for the sake of keeping the work.

The chamber chorus of the New York Concert Choir began the Midwest tour before the Chicago Symphony Orchestra series began. Their first stop was the University of Illinois in Urbana, Illinois, for a performance on March 15, 1955. A new work in the choir's repertoire, *Canti di Prigionia*, by Luigi Dallapiccola, was programmed for the U of I appearance and would again be performed later that season for an upcoming Town Hall performance. Hillis cleverly engaged the university's student orchestra for the Dallapiccola work. A review of the concert in the local newspaper the next day was mixed. In their performance of Bartók's folk songs, the critic claimed the performance "unfortunately suffered from an un-folk-like musical rigidity . . . lacking both the lyric lilt and rhythmic vitality." However, the Dallapiccola piece was "more successful, rising to moments of 'ecstatic fervor.'"[13] Similar mixed reviews would appear throughout the tour with the notable exception of their most important appearance with the Chicago Symphony Orchestra. The success of that performance would ultimately change the trajectory of Margaret Hillis's career in the very near future.

CHICAGO: THAT TODDLIN' TOWN

The New York Concert Choir's debut with Chicago's world-class orchestra in a subscription concert series took the city by storm. What must it have been like for New York's choir members to step onto the stage of the Chicago Symphony's grand Orchestra Hall for the first time? Orchestra Hall, built in 1904, was almost twice the size of Town Hall, with over 2,500 seats, a venue no doubt larger than any other hall the Concert Choir had ever experienced. Yes, they had enjoyed frequent appearances in New York concert halls, including many performances in Town Hall that Charlotte referred to as "a nice little venue." Yet taking that first glimpse of the magnificent Chicago hall, with its three balconies above the main floor, each level ornamented in decorative lights, amid white and gold filigreed décors housed under an enormous dome, must have been a breathtaking sight, even for these seasoned New York veteran performers.

Charlotte explained that it was not the hall nor their singing with this renowned symphony that intimidated them. It was working with Fritz Reiner that made Charlotte and other members of the chorus "scared to death."[14] Reiner was known by outsiders to be a tyrant, but as Charlotte explained, the New York Concert Choir encountered a very different conductor than they anticipated. Charlotte, as with the other singers, feared the worst as they began their first rehearsal with Chicago's orchestra. The singers anticipated a maestro who would lose his temper at their slightest error. Just as things seemed to be going along smoothly, Charlotte's roommate, Diane Griffith, became panicked, having developed a serious nosebleed. As this was happening right in the middle of the rehearsal, Charlotte decided to help her distraught friend. Flagging down Hillis as inconspicuously as possible, Charlotte hoped not to interrupt Reiner. Once Hillis assessed the situation, she immediately approached the maestro to explain the problem. Reiner abruptly stopped the rehearsal. As the chorus fearfully awaited what would come next, Reiner patiently and kindly instructed Diane to go across the street where she could purchase supplies to assist with her problem. He then explained that he had endured the very same problem just a week earlier. Greatly relieved, Diane promptly departed per the maestro's instructions and the rehearsal went on as if nothing at all had taken place. Reiner's empathetic response immediately diffused any tension and fear the chorus may have had of Reiner, endearing him to the chorus going forward.

Hillis admitted that Reiner could be extremely intimidating, and she likely put that fear into her chorus to guarantee they would come prepared. However, Hillis soon learned about the warmer side of Reiner and would encourage friends and colleagues who were concerned about working with him, reassuring them with words of support. One such instance was a conversation Hillis had with her friend Adele Addison, who was about to work with Reiner for the first time, in part thanks to Hillis's recommendation. Addison, a well-known soprano in New York, often recruited by Margaret for her New York concerts, expressed fear of Reiner, to which Margaret replied, "Look, Adele . . . he'll love you like his favorite granddaughter because you're musical and you're intelligent."[15] Adele discovered that Hillis was right, telling her after working with him that he was wonderful to her. Hillis explained, "If somebody was gifted and bright, Reiner just had a ball with him [or her] and just loved him [or her]. But if he [or she] wasn't good . . . Reiner could be inhumanely cruel."[16]

One of the challenges the chorus would have to overcome in working with Reiner was to follow the very tiny beat pattern he was known to use. Charlotte remarked how difficult this was for the chorus, in particular given the distance they were from the conductor's podium. However, this turned out not to be an issue. It helped that the chorus was able to work with Reiner once before they made their trip to Chicago, giving the Concert Choir a chance to become accustomed to his small beat in closer proximity. When Reiner attended a New York Concert Choir rehearsal a month or so before they arrived in Chicago, he told Margaret, "I came in to spy. I want to see your bag of tricks."[17] His main intention for the visit was to introduce some of his expectations for the upcoming performance series, but he was also satisfying his curiosity about Hillis's rehearsal methods, which he had revealed in the humorous "spy" comment he made upon his arrival. Hillis told Pellegrini how she too learned by watching Reiner as he worked with her singers.

> So, I was conducting away, and there's one place in the *Carmina Burana* where the chorus gets on a fermata, and then after . . . [she sings the line]— immediately after [the chorus continues the line] with no break [Likely the *Swaz hie gat umbe* movement]. And, I never could get them off the fermata right. . . . And so, he got to the fermata [when he conducted it], and he just flipped his baton and they moved all together. I said, "How did you do that?" He said, "I have my bag of tricks too."[18]

The Chicago Symphony Orchestra concerts were a great success for the New York Concert Choir, praised in reviews following opening night. Both pieces, new to Chicago's orchestra and audiences, were successful, but *Carmina Burana* was the clear favorite according to *Chicago Daily News* critic Irving Sablosky, who stated, "Barber's music [*Prayers of Kierkegaard*] was received cordially enough, but Orff's was a real hit. . . . The Concert Choir (a professional group from New York) has exceptionally pretty voices to begin with and its director Margaret Hillis has blended and polished them in a unified luster. We're not used to hearing choral singing of such refinement. I hope we'll hear more."[19]

Upon completion of the three Chicago performances, the Concert Choir tour continued with their next appearance on March 24, 1955, at Indiana University. This being Hillis's alma mater, she, no doubt, hoped to score a big impression. With faculty and friends present, Hillis's singers performed their standard tour material that by now was more comfortable and refined. The performance should have been a great success. Instead, this concert was panned. The cause was the venue, a much larger hall than should have been chosen for such an intimate group of twenty-four singers. Charlotte Carlson, one of those singers, described the harrowing experience, explaining that they were too spread out on a massive stage, unable to hear each other. It caused them to be preoccupied with the technical aspects of their singing, leaving little room for an inspiring performance. The review the next day was most unflattering and must have been a great disappointment to Margaret. Critic Robert Lee Stilwell claimed,

The New York Concert Choir's performance was almost unquestionably the least successful of this season's Auditorium musical programs. . . . The works they chose to perform were difficult to listen to and often tiresome . . . [The] *Liebeslieder Waltzes*—are crabbed and dull . . . and the madrigals . . . were hardly the most outstanding of their kind. . . . The Rorem selection [*From an Unknown Past*] was of no great importance. Only the Bartók's *Four Slovak Folk Songs* was liked.[20]

A letter to the editor, written by Donald Williams several days later, challenged this negative review, stating, "If the concert is to be branded 'unsuccessful' by your reviewers, perhaps the following may account for this lack of its intimate appeal to some of the audience."[21] Williams then listed three causes for the audience's difficulties with this fine performance, including the fact that the audience was not prepared for a twenty-four-voice choir, claiming Midwest audiences were more prone to welcome large festival choruses that they were accustomed to seeing. Second, he commented on the ill-chosen venue as being another disadvantage for this smaller ensemble. What he objected to most was the criticism of Hillis's repertoire choices. Unlike many choirs that specialized in what the writer labeled "warhorses," Hillis's choir specialized in music that was extremely sophisticated in a different way. What he most appreciated was Hillis not playing down to this crowd but instead presenting music that challenged and inspired listeners. "The concert was for many of us one of the finest, musically and artistically, of the current series. . . . Let us only hope that the 'unsuccessful' label doesn't frighten the committee out of scheduling such worthwhile and unusual programs in the future."[22]

The Concert Choir's Midwest tour wrapped up with appearances at Purdue University on March 25, 1955, and then one final concert on March 26, held in Hillis's hometown at her family's Grace Methodist Church. Kokomo's proud residents sponsored this event, a festive homecoming for their very own celebrity Margaret Hillis. Kokomo welcomed the singers with a magnificent dinner before the performance and an elegant reception for invited guests directly following the concert. The highly anticipated event did not disappoint. Kokomo residents showed their enthusiastic appreciation repeatedly throughout the concert.

> The first ovation for Margaret and her singers was stupendous, and applause for every number was enthusiastic. But when she returned for the second part of the program and the entire audience arose and burst into applause, followed by the chorus members themselves, the former Kokomo girl was intensely moved.[23]

This performance, underwritten by Hillis's parents and the Morning Musicale, an organization in which Margaret's mother had been active for many years, provided a fitting end to the first large-scale tour of the New York Concert Choir. It was time to head back to New York and the next Town Hall concert, only a few days later.

Allowing little time to recover from the action-packed Midwestern tour, Hillis featured her twenty-four-voice touring ensemble for the Town Hall concert. The repertoire, not surprisingly, was the same as what had been performed during the Midwestern tour, requiring no extra rehearsal time, as it was still fresh from multiple performances. Reviews of this concert were somewhat consistent with the lukewarm reviews during the Midwestern tour stops. Reviewers described the performance as "laudable [with] unity . . . balance . . . and clarity of musical detail . . . [however] lack[ing] something of the essential spirit of the music," which was consistent with the reviews from their tour.[24] Close on the heels of this concert was the final Town Hall performance of the season, April 15, 1955. The Concert Choir and orchestra would perform contemporary works including a premiere of Robert Moevs's *Cantata sacra*. Hillis also programmed another premiere for New York audiences, the Dallapiccola work they had performed at the University of Illinois while on tour. Also included on this program were two works that had been programmed in previous Town Hall concerts, Janáček's *Kinderreime* and Stravinsky's *Les noces*. The final concert of the season was enthusiastically received by New York critics who were particularly impressed with the challenging twelve-tone Dallapiccola work, stating, "Margaret Hillis did nothing short of an astonishing job in preparing this significant work."[25]

Margaret's tremendous strengths in planning and programming concerts would prove to be an important formula for the continued success of the New York Concert Choir, although this season revealed that Hillis would need some work to modify ambitious scheduling so as not to exhaust her singers. Her talent for long-range planning was impressive, nonetheless. Though the season was a great success in many respects, Margaret would struggle to keep her singers motivated during her arduous rehearsal process. Her emotional restraint impacted the musicians with whom she worked, impeding their enjoyment of the rehearsal process along with their ability to perform expressively. This issue of restraint would plague Hillis throughout her career, sometimes leaving her audiences uninspired. Nevertheless, there was no getting around the extraordinary precision and clarity of this superb vocal ensemble. Their exquisite tone production was consistent in all styles of music, as showcased by Hillis's innovative concert programs. These Hillis hallmarks were the reason for audiences returning time and time again to witness this female conductor's impressive work. Margaret was quickly approaching a crossroad in her career where her strengths and weaknesses would become even more consequential as she was about to step into an even higher visibility position. Change was on the horizon.

ENDNOTES

1. Charlotte Carlson interview.
2. Danielle Ward-Griffin, "As Seen on TV: Putting the NBC Opera on Stage," *Journal of the American Musicological Society* 71, no. 3 (2018): p. 595, accessed April 3, 2021, https://link.gale.com/apps/doc/A568118601/ITOF?u=scha51546&sid=ITOF&xid=dedde978.
3. Rose, "'Concert Tonight,' with New York Concert Orchestra, Margaret Hillis, Conducting, Mitch Miller, Commentator," *Variety*, September 22, 1954 (Scrapbook #2 of the Margaret Hillis Collection, Rosenthal Archives of the Chicago Symphony Orchestra Association).
4. Jack O'Brian, "Serious Music," *New York Journal America*, September 16, 1954.
5. Rose, "Concert Tonight."
6. Ibid.
7. Jack O'Brian, "Serious Music."
8. Jay Nelson Tuck, "On the Air, DuMont's Concert Tonight," *New York Post*, September 29, 1954.
9. Charlotte Carlson interview.
10. P. G. H., "Margaret Hillis," *New York Herald Tribune*, February 21, 1955.
11. Day Thorpe, "New York Choir's Concert Bridges Loss of 8th Voice," *The Evening Star*, March 5, 1955.
12. Steven Hillyer, "Podium Interview with Margaret Hillis," November 20, 1982, p. 9 (transcription of the interview in the Margaret Hillis Collection, Rosenthal Archives of the Chicago Symphony Orchestra Association).
13. Imanuel Wilhelm, "Margaret Hillis Directs Group in Contemporary Arts Program," *Daily Illini*, March 15, 1955.
14. Charlotte Carlson interview
15. Hillyer, "Podium Interview," p. 8.
16. Ibid.
17. Margaret Hillis, interview by Norman Pellegrini (transcribed by Stanley G. Livengood), October 6, 1997, p. 10.
18. Ibid.
19. Irving Sablosky, "Two Word Review, 'It's Fun' Sums Up Sprightly Orff Music," *Chicago Daily News*, March 18, 1955.
20. Robert Lee Stilwell, "Concert Choir Program Described as 'Unsuccessful,'" no name of the paper in which it appears, nor the date. Concert took place at Indiana University, and this review is covering that concert (Scrapbook #2 of Margaret Hillis Collection, Rosenthal Archives of the Chicago Symphony Orchestra Association).
21. Donald Williams, "As You See It; Margaret Hillis's Choir Deserves Praise," editorial written by a graduate opera assistant, School of Music, Indiana University. No name of the paper in which it appears, nor the date. Concert took place at Indiana University, and this is the contradictory viewpoint of Robert Stilwell's negative review of that concert (Scrapbook #2 of Margaret Hillis Collection, Rosenthal Archives of the Chicago Symphony Orchestra Association).
22. Ibid.
23. Lena Shannon, "Margaret Hillis Concert Well Received Here Saturday," no date or name of the paper indicated from the clipping (Scrapbook #2 of Margaret Hillis Collection, Rosenthal Archives of the Chicago Symphony Orchestra Association).
24. Francis D. Perkins, "Concert Choir at Town Hall with 'Vocal Chamber Music,'" *New York Herald Tribune*, April 2, 1955.
25. M. D. L, "Hillis conducts All-Contemporary Concert," no newspaper title or date in this clipping (Scrapbook #2 of Margaret Hillis Collection, Rosenthal Archives of the Chicago Symphony Orchestra Association).

CHAPTER 10

A NEW FOUNDATION: THE 1955–1956 SEASON

D emands were growing for Margaret Hillis's Concert Choir. For the upcoming 1955–1956 concert season, Margaret ambitiously extended their reach, again adding a choir tour to their second Chicago Symphony Orchestra appearance. This season, like the last, would begin with obligations in the early fall, as her choir and orchestra would make their first appearance in Pittsburgh's Carnegie Hall for the city's 1955–1956 Music Guild concert series. The Town Hall series would begin shortly thereafter, requiring Hillis to carefully program this season as she did the last. She chose her ensemble's signature piece, Stravinsky's *Les noces*, along with other recently performed works for the Pittsburgh concert, enabling her chorus and orchestra ample time to brush up on familiar material while devoting the rest of their rehearsal time to learning new music for the busy season ahead.

Hillis's appearance in Pittsburgh elicited great excitement, as could be seen in newspaper coverage promoting the event. The focus was centered upon Hillis, *the woman*, who would be conducting. One article, titled "Woman to Direct Guild Concert Here," remarked, "A tall attractive brunette will celebrate her thirty-fourth birthday tomorrow in a most unusual manner, at least for a woman."[1] Another newspaper expressed similar fascination with a female at the helm, stating, "[Margaret Hills] is the only woman conductor of orchestra and choir in the United States."[2] Hillis and her ensemble received rave reviews in Pittsburgh, however there was little time to dwell upon this success. Hillis and company headed home, immediately focused upon their upcoming Town Hall series. Her programming again proved impressive with engaging repertoire, very much in keeping with the ensemble's growing reputation as a champion of music seldom heard elsewhere. At this point in her career, Hillis was competing only with herself to provide the innovative programming her audiences had come to expect.

One member of the chorus during that demanding 1955–1956 season was Robert Page, who had recently joined the group. Page arrived in New York in the fall of 1955 to complete a residency for his doctorate at New York University. As he tells it, he auditioned for everything musical in town that he could find.[3] After a successful audition with Tommy Pyle, as Page referred to him, he was accepted into the Concert Choir. Tom Pyle was now working regularly with Margaret, hiring some of the top New York choral singers for her group. Page recalled his first encounter with Margaret Hillis as being quite different than any other conductor he had experienced up to that point. He remarked about Hillis's consistently solid approach when preparing her singers. Despite the constant demands of closely scheduled concerts, Hillis was never shy about insisting upon absolute precision. Page explained that his choral work up to this point had been limited to what he referred to as the "Westminster approach," which he defined as "having to do with a great deal of emotion and empathetic response but not a hell of a lot of musicianship."[4] Page continued, "Margaret taught me immediately the sanctity of the right notes in the right place at the right time. PERIOD!"[5] Mr. Page would go on to have an incredible conducting career in his own right, becoming the future director of the Cleveland Orchestra Chorus and Pittsburgh's Mendelssohn Choir. Moreover, he was an esteemed choral conducting professor at Carnegie Mellon University, a beloved teacher, and the winner of two Grammy Awards and several nominations. Page insisted that much of his ultimate success in his professional life was due to his work with Margaret Hillis. He lovingly considered her one of his greatest mentors and one of his very dearest friends.

Page described the rigors of that 1955–1956 Concert Choir season, recalling Hillis's determination to keep the chorus from becoming too lax. The Town Hall season opened in November with Stravinsky's challenging *Oedipus Rex* and a premiere of Jan Meyerowitz's mass, *Missa Rachel Plorans*. Close on the heels of that concert was the December Town Hall performance, which he remembered as also having difficult repertoire for the chorus to master. Page discussed Hillis's preparation of the chorus under this constant pressure of a rather quick turnaround time. He claimed that one of Margaret's favored methods for motivating professional singers when things were not going well was her not-so-subtle art of persuasion. She would often repeat a story that was a favorite for both to tell. In an interview with Norman Pellegrini, Hillis jokingly described how Page often reminded her about a particular rehearsal in which she placed the responsibility of the choristers' vocalism squarely upon their shoulders. She was rehearsing a spot in Schoenberg's *Friede auf Erden*. "The tenor line goes up to a high B-flat. And it must be a ringing one . . . [the high B-flat] wasn't very good in that rehearsal. . . . I stopped, and I said, 'Tenors, if you have vocal problems in this piece, you better get over them by tomorrow! And by golly, they did!"[6] Page appreciated the rigor, the wisdom, and, occasionally, the humor of Margaret's methods for getting the best out of her choirs, which he would emulate in his own choirs in the years to come (Picture 33).

Margaret Hillis and Robert Page in the Chicago Orchestra Hall Ballroom, 1979

Picture 33.
Margaret Hillis and Robert Page, 1979.[7]

DEDICATION TO PAYING CHORISTERS A RESPECTABLE WAGE

Hillis's singers were in demand thanks to her tireless efforts to keep them regularly employed. With ever-increasing passion, Hillis was championing the cause for choral singers to earn a decent wage in the same way as their orchestral counterparts. She had initially shouldered this responsibility herself with the assistance of her family's support of the Town Hall concert series. However, she and her family could not sustain the six concerts that had taken place last season and decided to revert back to a four-concert series for this current season. By cutting back the Town Hall programs, Hillis felt compelled to supplement her singers' income in other ways. The best way she managed this was by affiliating with additional organizations, such as the American Opera Society. Hillis added another position this season to help her singers financially, becoming the chorus director of the Little Opera Society. She further supplemented the choristers' incomes by booking run-out tours with a small contingent of her Concert Choir. She was dedicated to keeping her choristers working.

Margaret's efforts to provide her singers more pay meant an increased workload for her and for her chorus. For Hillis, the added musical preparation was just one facet of the added duties she would be required to handle. Since the earliest days of the New York Concert Choir, Margaret was responsible for all the details of running a professional choir, including the logistics. As the number of concerts increased each season, so too did Hillis's managerial duties, such as acquiring the music, arranging payment for her artists, coordinating complex rehearsal schedules, and handling all the other details connected with upcoming performances. These responsibilities would have to be worked around her score study for current programs along with time to examine new works for programming of future concerts. Something had to go. Hillis soon recognized the need to leave the day-to-day management of non-musical affairs to others if she was to keep up with the increased volume of work coming their way.

> I was in a position where I had to be an administrator, a fundraiser, a conductor, a musician. I even had to order the music and be the librarian and the wardrobe mistress. Well . . . I finally made a decision. . . . I said, "Look I can be either a darn good administrator . . . or I can be a musician. . . . I have a choice, because I cannot do them both and be first class." So, I gave up all the administrative things.[8]

Despite paring down her responsibilities related to the daily running of her chorus and orchestra, there was one task she could not pass off to someone else. She still needed to manage the raising of money for her musicians. If that was not done properly, there would be no chorus to conduct. Knowing her family could not support her artistic endeavors indefinitely, Margaret began considering an idea that would become a reality during the current 1955–1956 season. Hillis decided to form a choral foundation to help her fundraise for the chorus but at the same time would provide a service to her fellow choral conducting colleagues. The seeds of this idea were planted when she ran those choral workshops through Choral and Organ Enterprises. She knew how important they were to the profession. A foundation would allow her to continue this important work and at the same time offset the growing expense of keeping her chorus employed. When Hillis was interviewed years later as to why she began her foundation, she explained,

> There wasn't anything out there to help professional choruses or professional singers. And I think at the time that I started, there were only three professional choruses in the United States—me, Bob Shaw, and Roger Wagner. And I didn't realize it until just fairly recently—mine was the first resident professional chorus. Bob and Roger toured. And we did a couple of little tours, but mainly it was in New York. We began to run out of money. . . . That's the name of the game, especially long before the National Endowment came in. I needed a non-profit institution to help, so that I could raise funds . . . my family helped me a great deal [up to that point but she explained that the Concert Choir needed more support than her family could continue to provide].[9]

Margaret cleverly combined her need for chorus funding with a need of her fellow choral conductors. Understanding the continual challenges her colleagues faced in finding repertoire and scholarly resources, she knew her idea "had legs." For a fee to members who joined her Foundation, she would share her recently acquired experience and knowledge. These members became a revenue source to help keep her chorus afloat.

Margaret Hillis established the American Choral Foundation, incorporating it as a non-profit organization in December 1954. In its founding statement, Hillis demonstrated her understanding of what the choral profession needed to further advance:

> After careful investigation, the American Concert Choir [which she renamed her New York Concert Choir to reflect the foundation's title] and Choral Foundation finds that the necessary tools for study of performance techniques

and for the selection of repertoire are woefully inadequate. There has been no central agency from which advice on the organization and administration of choral groups could be obtained.[10]

The American Choral Foundation became a catalyst for professionalizing the choral field in America. Hillis's first priority was to create a mission statement for the organization "to further the cultivation of choral conductors and to foster the development of choral groups in the United States." Hillis segmented the Foundation into three divisions: musical activities, services, and research and publications. The Musical Activities Division served to showcase exemplary choral ensembles, performing choral repertoire at the highest of standards. The newly renamed American Concert Choir was the mainstay of this division. The Services Division of the Foundation was initially designed to maintain a rental library of choral works, also providing an advisory service to answer inquiries about the repertoire or to address administrative and organizational challenges related to choirs. Finally, the Research and Publications Division would provide information gathered from scholars in the field that would be disseminated in Foundation publications.

The Foundation was established, in part, with the guidance and encouragement of Margaret's father, far more savvy in financial matters than Margaret herself. Glen Hillis, aware of his own failing health, likely encouraged her to explore other means for funding her chorus and her own income, as the family reserve was deep but not limitless. According to Margaret's former sister-in-law, Connie Hillis, Margaret was provided a large sum of money to get her chorus started.[11] Equally generous sums were given to each of Margaret's brothers to help them as they started their families. Connie explained that the New York chorus was viewed by Margaret's parents as her substitute family. Margaret was given an equitable sum to fund her life's endeavor, as her family understood that Margaret would likely never have a family of her own. Music was her life, and her ensemble members were her family.

The Foundation, as will be seen, would endure a troubled financial history once it was supervised by Margaret instead of family members. After her father's passing in 1965, Margaret would only sporadically attend to monetary matters, leaving the details to others. The Foundation was the first of several financial challenges Margaret would face during her lifetime. Her focus on music left her little time to be attentive to money matters. Money would become a recurrent stress for her as the years went on. Problems would crop up initially as mere inconveniences but would grow into major impediments. Because of the way she was raised, money had never been an object of Hillis's concern. She relied upon others to "mind the store," spending money freely and paying little attention to the balance of funds. She left the details to her father and her brother Bud. However, as time went on, Margaret's father would pass away and her brother Bud would become busier with his life as a United States congressman, with little time to oversee her financial situation. Without concern for her income and spending, she would hastily assign the duties to those she trusted. Several errors in judgement put her Foundation at great risk, forcing her to resolve the challenges herself. When forced to deal with impending disaster, Margaret was actually quite good at managing the bottom line. It simply did not interest her, nor did she have the time for it. She was busy making music.

The launching of her American Choral Foundation came about gradually, going public during the 1955–1956 season. Margaret enlisted the support of such renowned figures as composers Milton Babbitt and Aaron Copland; esteemed professors Alfred Mann and Archibald Davidson; savvy politicians, including New York's United States Senator Jacob Javits; and generous philanthropists, including Mrs. E. S. Heller. During this season of 1955–1956, the American Concert Choir was now officially functioning as the performing arm of the Foundation. All appearances of the chorus going forward, including concerts, touring, and choral workshops, acknowledged the American Choral Foundation as their sponsor.

Hillis continued to dedicate herself to the growth of the choral profession through her Foundation and eventually through other organizations that her Foundation helped create. To this, she was deeply dedicated. Perhaps Margaret's decision to pursue her *second* choice, going the choral conducting route, compelled her to become a pioneer for the profession. Hillis was honest in her interviews throughout her career, stating what little respect she had for choruses when she first pursued the field. Deeming choruses to be below the level of orchestras in musicianship and discipline, she set out to change that status. Even after being superbly trained as a choral conductor, she felt ill-equipped to raise her choruses to a professional level. Having asked and answered her own questions about choral techniques through trial and error, she created her own choral pedagogy. Those methods were the result of her own ingenuity and downright hard work. During her frequent travels around the country presenting conducting demonstrations and workshops, she received multitudinous inquiries from other choral conductors about how she was able to achieve such incredible results with her choir. It was then that Margaret realized there was, in fact, a real need for her techniques to be codified and disseminated. All these experiences contributed to the founding of her American Choral Foundation.

Concomitant with this time frame of Hillis promoting her own choral pedagogy, professors of choral music throughout the country were on a similar quest. While Hillis was establishing her Foundation, Russell Mathis, a choral conductor and professor of music, was collaborating with other professors about the state of choral music education, prompting several leaders of university choral programs to create an organization just one year after the Foundation was established with a similar mission to Hillis's own. Mathis would become a charter member of the new American Choral Directors Association, and eventually he would be a president of the organization. Reflecting back to the state of choral affairs in the mid-1950s, Mathis contextualized the time period.

> Imagine if you can when choral conductors had infrequent opportunities to hear choral performances, a time when there was no television, no compact discs, limited occasions to talk to others in their profession, and the most accessible choral performances were radio broadcasts of Fred Waring's Pennsylvanians on the *Chesterfield Hour*. There was the rare symphony broadcast of Beethoven's *Ninth Symphony* or Verdi's Requiem, as well as a few excellent touring college choirs, so one might occasionally hear an inspiring choral performance. However, the local civic, high school and church choirs were generally all that was available. Choral recordings were limited in number and fidelity, fragile, and by today's standards, clumsy. A few professional organizations were offering some help: The Music Educators National Conference gave some attention to in-service training, but these sessions often lacked the specialization that was needed. If conductors taught in a rural area, they were isolated. . . . Choral conductors did not have access to choral models, so they limped along doing the best they could, with little help or understanding as to why they were unable to do better . . . these conductors continued to make the same mistakes, employing the same hackneyed literature, knowing in their hearts something was not right.[12]

Mathis went on to explain how the American Choral Directors Association took form, with initial discussions that led to the forming of a national choral organization in 1957. The committee identified choral directors who were respected leaders of choruses in education, in churches, and in other areas of choral music making and formulated a list of fifty-eight choral conductors who would become charter members of this new organization. The new ACDA drew up by-laws based upon those already extant for band directors through the American Bandmasters Association and the College Band Directors National Association. Charter choral conducting members identified the weaknesses of the profession and sought to raise the standards in similar fashion to predecessor organizations in related fields. "The early planners identified and isolated the musical and pedagogical problems endemic in American choral music education: poorly trained choral conductors. They recommended the development and adoption of a new music teacher preparation curriculum for those who desired to work primarily with choral groups."[13]

The founders also realized that it was imperative to receive the endorsement of prestigious conductors of this time period, identifying Roger Wagner, Robert Shaw, and Margaret Hillis as leaders in the field. All three were invited to attend early ACDA conferences. The focus of this new endeavor centered upon collegiate training of future choral conductors and a general raising of the standards of choral music. Though this organization may have, in theory, conflicted with Margaret's Foundation membership, one thing was clear: Hillis was unselfishly dedicated to improving the profession with little concern about any competition with her own organization. Instead, she chose to support anyone on a similar path. Her constant focus was set on raising the level of choral performance so that singers could earn an equal respect as orchestral players. Hillis put the generosity of supporting her profession above any personal stake she may have had in raising her own stature in the field. As always, this was never about Margaret Hillis. She selflessly supported the people with whom she had shared interests over and above anything that would directly reward her personally.

Hillis's American Choral Foundation remained a Hillis family affair, at least in its early stage of existence. Margaret's father and brother Bud "minded the financial store," enabling Margaret to focus completely on her music making, blissfully unaware of how the finances of the Foundation worked on a day-to-day basis. She left the financial well-being of the organization to her trusted family members who took care of the fiscal end of things as they had done for her and the Concert Choir up to this point in her career. It was therefore not a surprise when Margaret extended an invitation to her youngest brother, Joe, to bring his new bride Connie to New York to help promote the American Choral Foundation.

Along with Hillis's efforts to develop her Foundation, the busy 1955–1956 concert season required most of her attention. With the newly added affiliation of the Little Orchestra Society, Hillis's chorus performed Berlioz's *L'enfance du Christ* under the baton of the society's founder, Thomas Scherman, for an audience of 2,700 people at Carnegie Hall on December 14, 1955. Scherman would play a role in helping Hillis increase her choir's income, hiring them to perform for massive audiences at Carnegie Hall and in a new summer performance venue, thereby expanding the chorus's visibility. The substantial touring season began with their second Chicago Symphony appearance on January 19 and 20, 1956. The concert series included Mozart's Mass in C Minor (*The Great*) and Bruckner's *Te Deum*, conducted by Fritz Reiner. Although the chorus was again well reviewed in Chicago, Reiner's conducting was called "boring" by one reviewer, who preferred the fiery Bruckner performance to Reiner's lesser Mozart mass interpretation. Hillis's chorus was hailed by Roger Dettmer, stating, "Margaret Hillis's magnificent [choir], easily the finest professional chorus in this country today, [performed] with uncommon brilliance."[14]

As she had done in their first Chicago appearance, Margaret planned another concert tour in the Midwest, this time heading up to Minnesota. They were hosted by concert series organizations and universities throughout the state in a tour lasting several weeks. The Concert Choir then returned to New York for an American Opera Society performance in mid-February. Just two weeks after the opera, the Concert Choir returned to Town Hall, performing compositions they had just done with the Chicago Symphony Orchestra, this time with Margaret Hillis on the podium. Hillis was praised for her bold programming of such substantial works as the Mozart and Bruckner pieces, with critic Howard Taubman stating, "Give Margaret Hillis credit for bravery and high intentions. . . . It was not an interpretation that scaled the heights of religious feeling . . . but it provided a grateful audience with a faithful traversal of a stirring and exalted work."[15]

The Concert Choir was then off on another tour, this time traveling throughout upstate New York and then making an appearance on a Canadian television network. Upon their return to New York City, Margaret's conducting of Bach's *St.*

Matthew Passion for the final Town Hall performance of the season garnered reviews revealing a new level of respect she was earning from the critics. Reviewers were not only impressed by her growth as an artist but also by her willingness to undertake a Bach Passion just one month after her Town Hall Mozart and Bruckner program. As Hillis revisited masterworks like Bach's Passions for repeat performances, she was beginning to acquire a refinement that can only come with experience. Critics observed as much. "Miss Hillis achieved an outstanding success in her 'musicianly' direction of the oratorio, bringing the music, voices, and orchestra up to a well-balanced high level of drama."[16]

Hillis and her chorus achieved more consistent critical acclaim this season than ever before. Nonetheless, money remained a constant challenge to keep the Concert Choir in business. Although her primary focus was on continued exposure for her chorus, including all their many tours and concerts, Hillis found time to continue developing her Foundation. She knew this organization would have to succeed in order for her to continue her conducting career with the American Concert Choir and Orchestra.

A Glimpse into Margaret's Social World

Joe Hillis's arrival in New York to help with the Foundation provided Margaret some welcome relief. Considering how the Hillis family had helped Margaret launch this project, it is no surprise that she was now entrusting the promotional work to her newly graduated and newly wedded brother. Margaret first met her new sister-in-law when Joe brought Connie to New York in 1956. The young Hillis couple discovered there was much to be learned as they pivoted from the peaceful campus life at Stanford University to the intensity of bustling New York City. Connie explained that she and Joe were quite naïve when they first moved to the big city, enduring inconveniences such as hundreds of dollars in parking tickets within their first few weeks of arrival.[17] They did not understand how leaving their shiny red Thunderbird parked overnight in front of Hillis's apartment violated the strictly enforced laws for parked cars on New York's side streets. This was a concept foreign to both, coming from the comparatively less rigid parking policies of Palo Alto.

Connie described Margaret's apartment on 21st Street as "tremendously big" with a front façade that looked more like a warehouse than an apartment. Overlooking a Jewish Portuguese cemetery, as Connie recalled, Hillis's residence was the size of two apartments with a large living room on one end and a smaller cozy apartment, complete with a kitchen, another bedroom, and living room space, on the other end. Margaret inhabited the cozy unit and enjoyed having a kitchen to cook in. Though Hillis fashioned herself to be a great cook, Connie vehemently disputed it. The rear-end quarters provided to Connie and Joe amounted to a single room that served as both their living room and bedroom. Connie recalled being awakened many a morning, sometimes as early as 8:00 a.m., by rehearsals Margaret was conducting in the room directly adjacent to Joe and Connie's space. It is from Connie's perspective that we get another glimpse of Margaret's life.

Connie marveled at an endless stream of fascinating people who frequented Margaret's apartment. When she wasn't rehearsing, Margaret entertained poets, composers, writers, and artists of every kind, cooking dinners, enjoying cocktails, or engaging in spirited readings of poetry and plays by Shakespeare. Connie was somewhat intimidated by the accomplished, colorful cast of characters frequently convening in the Hillis residence. Between the rehearsals by day and a steady flow of visitors by night, life was never dull at Margaret's place. Connie and Joe were kept busy with many opportunities to attend rehearsals and concerts Margaret directed, most often at Town Hall, and they were both amazed by Hillis's ability to maintain a balance between the incredible demands of her professional life and a robust social life, both seamlessly interwoven. According to Connie, one constant presence in the apartment was Fran, Margaret's secretary. Connie recalled Fran being around all the time, though she did not live at the residence. Fran was responsible for all the details Margaret no longer cared to handle. However, Fran was also a companion to Margaret, whom Connie assumed was also her partner, though this was all kept very private and was not ever discussed between Margaret and Connie.

After some time living with Margaret, Joe and Connie moved into their own apartment and would soon welcome a new baby, Gregory, into their lives. Margaret was excited about this newest Hillis family member and was determined to help out, insisting that Joe and Connie needed time to themselves. She offered up herself and Fran to babysit young Gregory. Thrilled to have this opportunity, Connie described one particular evening the couple left Margaret and Fran in charge. After some brief instructions, Joe and Connie departed for an evening free of changing diapers and bottle feeding. Connie described their utter shock upon returning home several hours later to find Gregory asleep, and deeply asleep at that. When Connie inquired about how Margaret and Fran had done such a wonderful job of getting the baby to bed, Margaret simply stated that she put some of her favorite Ballantine whiskey into Gregory's evening bottle. Whiskey was the secret to Margaret's babysitting success! Stunned though they were, Connie recalled that her obstetrician was not opposed to such measures in those days, but nonetheless she was surprised to hear that this bold move was taken without the prior consultation of Connie and Joe.

The young parents enjoyed a lively year, becoming closer to Margaret. A special bond was formed between Margaret and Connie, one that would last longer than Connie and Joe's marriage. Connie looked back at this time of her life as being very special, meeting so many exciting people. Connie specifically recalled meeting one of her idols, Leonard Bernstein, who had flagged Margaret down with an enthusiastic "Maggie" shouted from the other side of an airport terminal, where Connie, Joe, little Gregory, and Margaret were awaiting their flight. The New York experience was short-lived for Connie and Joe since he ultimately had little success assisting Margaret with the Foundation, prompting him and his family to return to California in pursuit of other endeavors.

Margaret continued to balance the demands of score study, programming, performances, exploration of new repertoire, appearances in workshops, and coordination of her Foundation along with her stimulating and colorful social life. She was dedicated to doing her best musical work while advocating for singers and choral conductors whom she guided to a new level of expertise in choral music. Though she was extremely busy, her routine seemed to be hitting a manageable stride. Little did she know that just around the corner a new opportunity would change her routine, her destiny, and the history of American symphonic choruses.

Endnotes

1. "Concert Choir and Orchestra: Woman to Direct Guild Concert Here," *Pittsburgh Sun Telegraph*, September 30, 1955.
2. "Woman Leader Opens Season for Music Guild: Margaret Hillis Brings Choir, Orchestra for Carnegie Hall Charter Concert," *Pittsburgh Post-Gazette*, October 1, 1955.
3. Interview with Robert Page, June 11, 2014.
4. It should be noted that Westminster Choir College is a well-respected choral program with a long tradition of excellence.
5. Interview with Robert Page.
6. Margaret Hillis, interview by Norman Pellegrini (transcribed by Stanley G. Livengood), October 6, 1997, p. 8.
7. Photograph from *The Voice of Chorus America* 20, no. 4, 1997.

8. Jon Bentz, "Interview of Margaret Hillis Director Chicago Symphony Orchestra, September 19, 1989, Archives Committee, Oral History Project, 1992," p. 6 (Margaret Hillis Collection, Rosenthal Archives of the Chicago Symphony Orchestra Association).

9. Ibid., p. 4.

10. Alfred Mann, "In Memoriam Margaret Hillis 1921–1998," *American Choral Review* XL, no. 2 (Summer-Fall 1998): p. 1.

11. Interview with Connie Hillis, March 25, 2014.

12. Russell Mathis, "ACDA's Forty-Year Journey," *The Choral Journal* 40, no. 4 (1999): pp. 9–25.

13. Ibid.

14. Roger Dettmer, "Extravaganza at Orchestra Hall," *Chicago American*, January 20, 1956.

15. Howard Taubman, "Music: Mass by Mozart, Margaret Hillis Leads Choir in C-Minor Work." *The New York Times*, March 6, 1956.

16. L. C., "New York Concert Choir," *Musical Courier*, April 6, 1956.

17. Interview with Connie Hillis.

CHAPTER 11
CHANGE IS ON THE HORIZON: 1956–1958

The 1956–1957 concert season began as previous seasons had for Margaret Hillis and her Concert Choir with one notable exception. The summer of 1956 was their first opportunity to participate in summer work thanks to a budding relationship Hillis had recently established with the Little Orchestra Society's founder and conductor, Thomas Scherman. Scherman was pleased with Hillis and her choir when they joined him for the performance of Berlioz's *L'enfance du Christ* in December 1955 at Carnegie Hall and subsequently invited them to join him again for his upcoming summer production of Mussorgsky's *Boris Godunov* at Lewisohn Stadium on July 16, 1956. Lewisohn Stadium was a popular music venue, attracting large audiences of diverse socio-economic backgrounds.[1] The amphitheater, seating 8,000 people, was larger than the choir had ever before experienced in a live venue. These concerts were also broadcast over the radio, extending their audience base even further. The American Concert Choir appearance at Lewisohn Stadium gave them not only wonderful exposure but also a welcome summer wage.

In Hillis's continued quest for increasing income for her singers, she added another appointment to her ever-growing list of conducting positions. Hillis accepted an invitation to be the chorus master of the New York City Opera for the 1956–1957 season. This coveted position was extended to Margaret by the newly appointed general director and conductor of the company, Erich Leinsdorf. By this time, Leinsdorf had already made a name for himself at the Metropolitan Opera. Margaret's affiliation with him and the well-respected opera company would raise her stature all the more in the classical music community. Leinsdorf's plan for the current New York City Opera Chorus was to integrate them into Hillis's Concert Choir for his productions.

As the American Concert Choir and Orchestra prepared for their fifth Town Hall season, scheduled to begin December 10, 1956, the choir was also preparing for their full schedule of fall performances. The first concert of their season was a return engagement for Pittsburgh's Music Guild series. Following their well-received *Les noces* performance the previous season, they were invited back. They were also preparing for upcoming opera performances with Thomas Scherman, including Enrique Granados's *Goyescas* and Luigi Cherubini's *Medea*, scheduled in both Philadelphia and New York. Shortly thereafter, the choir would make their first appearance with Erich Leinsdorf in the New York City Opera's production of Offenbach's *Orpheus in the Underworld*. That debut appearance would unfortunately also be her chorus's last appearance with Leinsdorf. The production was poorly received by critics, adding stress to an already financially challenged opera company. Blame was cast upon Leinsdorf for his rather unusual programming of lesser-known works, which ultimately resulted in his dismissal by November 1956. The opera company then abruptly canceled the rest of their season. Hillis and her chorus would not return to the New York City Opera thereafter.

Luckily, Hillis had a steady stream of additional bookings to keep them solvent despite the loss of their New York City Opera affiliation. One very lucrative opportunity was an upcoming NBC televised production of Prokofiev's opera *War and Peace,* conducted by Herman Adler. In an interview about the production, Hillis stated that television work paid her singers very generously and therefore she would accept television offers over others that might be considered. Noticeable improvements had been made in the broadcasting industry since the early days of their DuMont television shows. Now that the television medium was becoming more accurate in capturing the beauty of vocal performance, it was considered the best means of promotion, along with being a more lucrative venture for Hillis's Concert Choir.

Amid all these American Concert Choir performances, Hillis was expanding her visibility as a conductor in her own right. She accepted numerous guest-conducting appearances and workshops during this season, sponsored by her American Choral Foundation. A good friend, Melvin Kaplan, would be instrumental in helping her acquire conducting work beyond her American Concert Choir engagements.

Kaplan, a superb New York oboist, met Margaret in 1948 when he was an eighteen-year-old freshman at Juilliard and she was in her final year at the school. Their friendship would continue through the early years of both careers and Margaret eventually called upon Melvin to serve as her contractor, hiring instrumentalists for her New York Concert Choir and Orchestra performances. According to Kaplan, he would also play for Hillis any time she needed an oboist for an ensemble. During the summer of 1956, Kaplan said that Hillis asked him to "mind the store," watching over the American Choral Foundation office while she was gone for the summer. In Melvin's words, Hillis also asked him to see what he could "cook up" in the way of conducting work for her when she returned in the fall.[2] Kaplan explained that he developed the idea of establishing a chamber ensemble featuring first-chair players from the instrumentalists he had hired for her American Concert Orchestra. Together, they decided to be called the New York Chamber Soloists. Hillis funded this endeavor at the outset to get them up and running. Her investment included the rental of Carnegie Recital Hall for a "Twilight Series" they established. The investment paid off because concerts were enthusiastically reviewed from the start. Hillis conducted this small chamber ensemble of select instrumentalists and three superb vocalists, beginning in the fall of 1956. Soon, the ensemble was receiving requests to appear outside of New York. As Hillis became consumed by other conducting appearances, she eventually stepped away from this chamber group. In turn, they decided to carry on without a conductor. Into his nineties, Melvin Kaplan has continued his leadership of this concert series.

Respect for Margaret's professional prowess continued to increase, in part through her branching out as a conductor in areas beyond her choral concert work. As her reputation grew, people were taking notice of her as an instrumental conductor. Growing interest in Hillis earned her a spot as a featured guest on the popular Saturday matinee broadcast of the Metropolitan Opera intermission program. Her desire to expand her reputation as a conductor was finally taking hold in New York City and beyond.

Despite all of Hillis's concert work, guest conducting, and speaking engagements, she always protected time to continue developing her American Choral Foundation. As part of the Foundation's mission, Hillis would seek out newly written works to perform with her American Concert Choir and Orchestra, including compositions by her friend Ned Rorem. His works were regularly given world premieres on Hillis's

American Concert Choir and Orchestra programs. This season was no exception as she prepared her choir for another new Rorem work, *The Poets' Requiem*, to be premiered in an upcoming Town Hall performance. Ned Rorem, years later, claimed to have dedicated this composition to her as a gesture of his deep appreciation for her generosity in promoting his music.[3] She always seemed to find time for an opportunity to advance musicians whose work she admired (Picture 34).

Rehearsal for world premiere of Ned Rorem's *"The Poets' Requiem" by The American Concert Choir and Orchestra on Feb. 15 under the direction of* Margaret Hillis *(right), with* Ellen Faull *(center) as soloist. The composer is at the piano. (See review below.)*

Picture 34.
Ned Rorem and Margaret Hillis collaborating on a new work, one of many times she promoted his work in her concerts, February 10, 1957 (Scrapbook #3, 1956–1958). (Margaret Hillis Collection, Rosenthal Archives of the Chicago Symphony Orchestra Association)[4]

Noticeably absent in the choir's schedule this season was another appearance with the Chicago Symphony Orchestra (CSO). At the point the CSO approached Hillis about returning to Chicago for the 1956–1957 season, her choir had only very limited availability. Given their commitments with three different opera companies, four Town Hall concerts, touring, television bookings, and other run-out concerts already scheduled, there was not much flexibility. The Chicago Symphony Orchestra had only one symphonic choral concert scheduled for that season, and they were not able to agree upon a date. Ironically, this schedule conflict may have inadvertently played a part in the creation of the Chicago Symphony Chorus.

The Orchestral Association programmed Brahms's *A German Requiem* for the 1956–1957 season. Given that Hillis's chorus was unavailable for any dates that were offered, the CSO was again made to rely upon a local chorus to fill the bill. Northwestern University, sometimes providing choruses for the orchestra, was called upon for the Brahms performances. Professor William Ballard began rehearsing his university choirs in the autumn of 1956. Knowing one university chorus alone would be insufficient to balance the CSO, he decided to prepare multiple choirs from the university, which he could then combine into one large chorus for the event. Frank Conlon, husband of Joan Catoni Conlon (the well-known choral conductor, scholar, and author of *Wisdom, Wit, and Will,* a superb book about women in the choral conducting field), was one of the singers who took part in this university performance. Conlon, a freshman in Northwestern's Men's Glee Club in 1956–1957, was not a music major. However, as with many of his fellow glee club singers, he enjoyed participating in choral singing at the university. According to Frank Conlon, Ballard combined Frank's men's chorus with the other campus choirs to form a massed choir, which was called the Northwestern University Choral Union.

Conlon recalled that the first time all the choirs were brought together to rehearse the Requiem was the very day CSO guest conductor Bruno Walter was scheduled to work with them. According to Conlon's recollection, after hearing them, Maestro Walter recognized the hard work ahead of him to make this disparate group of singers into a more cohesive ensemble. Since it was the first time the choirs were joined together, there was a lack of unified sound within each section, the result of not ever having sung together before this rehearsal. Additionally, many of the singers were hearing all four parts of the piece for the very first time. Women's Glee Club singers had not ever heard the men's harmonies, nor had the Men's Glee Club heard the women's harmonies before that day. There were some mixed voiced choruses participating, putting them at the greatest advantage for having heard all four parts during their rehearsals. The challenges were plentiful for this diverse group of singers to become a balanced and blended ensemble.

Adding to the challenge of tone, Conlon thought that the weakest part of their preparation was their German diction, which he attributed to there being no language coach present at their preparatory rehearsals to help them through the pronunciations. In addition to these issues, the choristers were packed into Scott Hall for this rehearsal. Scott Hall, the school's student union in those days, was the only space on campus large enough to hold this massed choir. The space was not designed for singing, nor had the students ever sung in that hall prior to this first rehearsal with Bruno Walter. To top things off, this was the first rehearsal after the students had returned from their winter break, which meant they were a bit rusty vocally and musically. Nevertheless, Bruno Walter faced the task head on, working quickly to ready these students for the performance of Brahms's *magnum opus.*

The *Chicago Tribune*'s acerbic critic Claudia Cassidy described the Requiem performances as "scattered," attributing the results—in part—to "the lack of mature voices in the chorus . . . [and only] now and then [creating a sound] . . . with the radiance of youth."[5] She described herself witnessing "a complicated score, tackled so bravely by a student chorus."[6] According to Frank Conlon, Bruno Walter was quoted as remarking of Cassidy's review, "How could anyone be so keen in discouraging young people from singing?"[7] Whether this was the final straw for Fritz Reiner, who was advocating for his own symphony chorus for Chicago, can be debated, but the timing is certainly compelling for what was to follow.

Fritz Reiner had insisted on increasing the choral repertory at the time he was hired to lead the Chicago Symphony Orchestra. After trying to work with local choirs and being less than satisfied with the results, Reiner persuaded the CSO's board of trustees to utilize Hillis's choir, justifying his need for a more experienced group of singers to tackle difficult works, such as *Prayers of Kierkegaard* and *Carmina Burana*.[8] Hillis's New York chorus had already proven themselves worthy in their two previous appearances with the CSO. Reiner had every confidence in Hillis's ability to consistently provide unequivocal artistic results. Although Hillis's chorus was unavailable for the 1956–1957 season, Reiner was already hoping they would return in 1957–1958 for his performances and a recording of Verdi's Requiem. He was certain he could not use a university nor a community chorus for this project.

The Orchestral Association had other ideas for Reiner's chorus, suggesting he invite the Lyric Opera's chorus for his upcoming Verdi project. After an agreement had been finalized to engage Lyric's chorus, Reiner had a change of heart, perhaps in part influenced by Claudia Cassidy's less-than-flattering review of the chorus in Walter's Brahms's Requiem performances. Without first consulting with the general manager of the Chicago Symphony Orchestra, George Kuyper, Reiner took it upon himself to dissolve the agreement with Lyric's general manager, Carol Fox.[9] Determined to reengage Margaret Hillis and her chorus for his Requiem, Reiner instructed George Kuyper to contact Hillis for the Verdi project. Hillis described the conversation with Kuyper regarding this matter:

I had brought sixty voices [to Chicago], which worked in the previous repertory, but the Verdi I didn't want to do with sixty [singers] I wanted 120. . . . I told George Kuyper . . . that the amount of money going out of Chicago [to bring in a chorus of 120 from New York] would be absolutely ridiculous. . . . I told him, "$18,000." [She explained to the interviewer that would have amounted to what would today be $180,000.] He gasped and said, "We were thinking about $14,000." I said, "The $18,000 is bare-bones cost, with no fee for me. If you were thinking of $14,000 . . . then start your own chorus."[10]

Kuyper agreed to consider the idea. Hillis fully anticipated what would follow, knowing Kuyper would likely pitch the idea to Reiner and that she would then be hearing from Reiner himself. Hillis wisely prepared for that conversation, heading to a local New York hotel to find a *Chicago Yellow Pages* book in order to look up all the singing organizations in the area that she could recommend to him. "Sure enough there was a Harvard Club, a Yale Club, and I thought they could sing more than the *Whiffenpoof* song, and there were also thousands of churches and temples all of which would have choruses. So, I was all prepared the next day when Reiner called."[11] "And the next morning the phone rang, 9:00 a.m. 'Margarette?' 'Yes?' 'Reiner,' as if I didn't know. And he said, 'Vere ve get de singers?'"[12] Hillis replied that with so many singers in Chicago, this would not be difficult.

She shared some of her findings and then dictated a schedule of how to organize the process, including the scheduling of auditions, a rehearsal plan, and other details of creating a chorus based upon the concert dates for the upcoming season. She then offered to come out to Chicago and help George Kuyper get the project underway. To that, Reiner replied, "No, ve don't have it unless you conduct."[13] Margaret recalled being stunned by his statement. It had never dawned on her that Reiner would make such an offer. She hastily replied that she would call him back the next morning with her answer. She searched her datebook for bookings already lined up for the next year-and-a-half and was surprised to discover that she had nearly every Monday night free in that time span. She also happened to have Verdi's Requiem dates for Chicago's performances available as well. She checked airline schedules and discovered that she could fly out to Chicago on Sunday nights and return on midnight flights back to New York after the Monday rehearsals in time to teach her

Tuesday morning 11:00 a.m. class at Union Theological Seminary. She called Reiner the next day, agreeing to accept the position. She planned to stay three or four years at most.[14]

Reiner, who longed for a chorus he could rely upon to perform the major choral works at a level akin to his orchestra, was able to persuade Eric Oldberg, the Orchestral Association board president, along with the trustees to create a chorus Hillis would direct, one that would be a permanent ensemble available to the orchestra for symphonic choral works.[15] By May 1957, the Association was actively working to finalize the founding of a new Chicago Symphony Chorus. On Hillis's advice, the Chicago Symphony Chorus would begin as a completely amateur organization but with the promise to the American Guild of Musical Artists, the union for vocal musicians, that in time this group would become professionalized.[16]

Before going further with Hillis's process of beginning the Chicago Symphony Chorus, it is important to clarify the history of this prestigious ensemble. Margaret Hillis's chorus is often thought of as the first chorus formally affiliated with the Orchestral Association's history. It was actually the second chorus with this distinction. The first chorus in the Chicago Orchestra's history was initiated in 1896 by Theodore Thomas, the founder and first music director of the Chicago Orchestra. (This was the name of the orchestra until 1905.) Thomas engaged his friend and colleague Arthur Mees, with whom he had worked years earlier when Mees directed the Cincinnati Festival Chorus. It was Thomas's hope that Mees would serve as his assistant conductor of the orchestra while also serving as the chorus master of a newly formed Chicago chorus. Auditions for the chorus of the Association were announced in September 1896, but little interest was shown among the public to participate. Even with the meager turnout, a chorus was formed, with ninety-five singers participating. They made their first appearance with the orchestra, leading the audience in a rousing rendition of the *Star-Spangled Banner* on October 31, 1896, which served as the encore for the orchestra's concert. The chorus made their official debut on December 18, 1896, in an all-Beethoven program, performing the *Choral Fantasy* and the chorus from *The Ruins of Athens* (Picture 35). The chorus made several more appearances that first season, performing in Grieg's *Olav Trygvason*; Nicolai's Festival Overture on *Ein' feste Burg*; and selections from Wagner's *The Flying Dutchman*, *Tannhäuser*, and *Parsifal*. They appeared in five concerts the following season, performing Bach's *Reformation Cantata* (no. 80), Beethoven's

Ninth Symphony, Brahms's *A German Requiem*, and Mendelssohn's *Psalm 114* and selections from *A Midsummer Night's Dream*. Just two years after their debut, the chorus was disbanded. By that seventh season, the orchestra was operating at a deficit and Arthur Mees, who had led the chorus, returned to New York to conduct the more well-established Mendelssohn Glee Club.

BEETHOVEN CONCERT.

LUDWIG VAN BEETHOVEN, born December 16, 1770; died March 26, 1827.

FRIDAY AFTERNOON, DECEMBER 18, 2:30.
SATURDAY EVENING, DECEMBER 19, 8:15.

CHICAGO ORCHESTRA,
ASSISTED BY THE
ORCHESTRAL CHORUS
AND
MR. HANS BRUENING, PIANIST.

PROGRAM.

OVERTURE, King Stephen, - -	*Opus 117*
SYMPHONY No. 4, B flat, - - -	*Opus 60*
ADAGIO—ALLEGRO VIVACE. ADAGIO. MENUETTO. ALLEGRO MA NON TROPPO.	
FANTASIA for Piano, Orchestra and Chorus, -	*Opus 80*
SYMPHONY No. 8, F major, - - -	*Opus 93*
ALLEGRO VIVACE E CON BRIO. ALLEGRETTO SCHERZANDO. TEMPO DI MENUETTO. ALLEGRO VIVACE.	
MARCH AND CHORUS, The Ruins of Athens, -	*Opus 114*

Programs Nos. 10 (Request) and 11, pages 39 and 40.

Chicago String Quartette (Theodore Thomas, Director,) page 28.

Steinway Piano used.

Picture 35.
The Chorus of the Association's first program, given on December 18 and 19, 1896.
(Rosenthal Archives of the Chicago Symphony Orchestra Association)

A NEW CHICAGO SYMPHONY CHORUS: 1957–1958

Hillis began to plan for her new routine involving a weekly commute from New York City to Chicago beginning in the fall of 1957–1958 season. Hillis reminded author Jeannine Wager in an interview for her book *Conductors in Conversation* that flying from New York to Chicago before the jet age was a lengthier and sometimes more harrowing process than it is today. Explained Hillis, "I remember one flight on an old four-engine propeller Constellation. The stewardess told us, 'The head wind is a hundred and fifty miles an hour, and it's going to take us six hours to get to Chicago. Fasten your lap straps and westward ho!'"[17]

Margaret's first impression of Chicago was formed, in part, by characterizations presented to her through the eyes of friends currently living in the city. Based upon conversations with those friends, Margaret determined that "Chicago had a terrible second-city complex."[18] They warned her that she might have trouble finding anyone to audition for her new chorus. They cautioned her further, saying that "if people with good voices audition for you, they won't be able to read [music]. Or, if they read, they won't have a good voice . . . and if they read and have a good voice, they'll [sic] never come to rehearsals."[19] Hillis determined that in order for her to gain the singers' respect for her new chorus, she would design auditions to test their professional skills, including sight-reading and vocal technique. Hillis believed high vocal standards for choristers were somewhat lacking in Chicago at the time she began her quest to populate her chorus. Hillis also needed to make a decision that would impact the way she would ultimately proceed. "Do I take bodies and have a big chorus, or do I take a small number and stick by quality? I took a small number and stuck by quality."[20] Hillis knew that in doing so she would attract singers who, over time, would help her establish a chorus worthy of the Chicago Symphony Orchestra.

The work of starting a symphony chorus was added to Hillis's myriad musical activities in New York, which she had no intention of reducing; she believed she would return to her full-time musical life in New York after a few years of commuting to Chicago and did not want to disrupt the work she had so diligently cultivated over recent years. After finalizing negotiations with the Orchestral Association in the spring of 1957, she returned her focus to fulfilling the remaining commitments of the 1956–1957 season in New York, including her final Town Hall concert of Bach's *St. John Passion*. That concert resulted in some of the most glowing reviews to date for Hillis. New summer work followed with an invitation to perform in the Empire Festival, which was added to return appearances for her chorus at Lewisohn Stadium. The Empire Festival in Ellenville, New York, not only added increased pay and exposure for her New York chorus but also added important connections for Hillis, which she would cultivate in the years ahead. The Empire Festival provided Hillis her first opportunity to work with the renowned conductor Leopold Stokowski on July 18 and 20, 1957, in a program of Stravinsky's choral music and Orff's *Carmina*

Burana. Stokowski was impressed by Margaret's preparation, sending her a note of thanks at the end of the summer season (Picture 36). The Empire Festival also made possible Hillis's connection with the Honorable Jacob Javits, a United States representative and then senator for the state of New York, who served as honorary chair of the music festival. He was a great supporter of the arts, eventually helping to create the National Endowment for the Arts, of which Hillis would become an active participant. Javits would also become an advisory member of Hillis's Choral Foundation in future years, which gave even greater credibility to her organization.

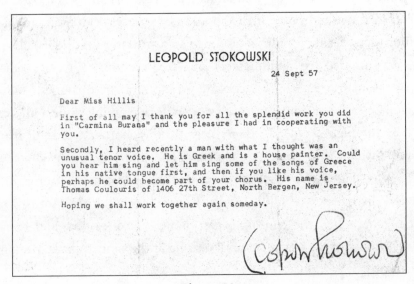

Picture 36.
A thank you note from Leopold Stokowski to Margaret Hillis, September 24, 1957 (Scrapbook #3, 1956–1958). (Margaret Hillis Collection, Rosenthal Archives of the Chicago Symphony Orchestra Association)

With the end of a busy summer, Margaret became completely focused on the work of finding singers for her new Chicago chorus. Local papers announced the formation of a new symphony chorus with auditions that would be held on October 5, 1957. Rehearsals would begin in early November. Singers were expected to attend Monday evening rehearsals, and once a month on Tuesday evenings they were to attend a sectional rehearsal. One auditionee from that first audition cycle was Jane Scharf. Jane, a conductor of a church choir at that time, received the letter announcing auditions for a new symphony orchestra chorus. The letter, signed by Fritz Reiner, requested choir directors to encourage any of their interested singers to audition for the new symphony chorus. Jane decided to sign herself up for an appointment to audition.

When she arrived at Orchestra Hall, Jane very much wanted to be in this new group but was realistic regarding the limited possibility of her being selected. Though she was an accomplished musician, she was not a trained vocalist. Nervously, Scharf introduced herself to Ms. Hillis and began with one of the two songs required, a selection in English and one in a foreign language. After completing the first number, Jane confessed that she did not consider herself a singer, nor had she ever before sung in front of anyone. She assured Hillis, however, that she was a good musician. She apologetically asked Hillis if she should leave rather than continuing on with the audition. Jane recalled Hillis's response as warm and kind. She told Jane that everyone was allotted ten minutes and suggested moving on to the sight-reading portion of the audition. Scharf successfully sang straight through a 6/8 diatonic melody with absolute certainty and accuracy. With a beaming smile, Hillis explained to Jane that although she needed big voices for the chorus, it did not matter how big the voice was if they couldn't sight-read. She told Jane, "I need a few people like you." What Jane's voice lacked in size and training it made up for in accuracy of pitch and rhythm, which Hillis needed in order to build her chorus. Thrilled to be chosen, Jane joined the chorus, began taking voice lessons, and remained an important member of the ensemble until retiring at the same time as Margaret Hillis in 1994 (Picture 37).

Picture 37.
Jane Scharf and Margaret Hillis during the Chicago Symphony Chorus's twentieth anniversary reception in Orchestra Hall's ballroom on May 19, 1977. (Terry's Photography) (Rosenthal Archives of the Chicago Symphony Orchestra Association)

The October auditions had gone very well, better than Hillis's friends initially predicted. The *Chicago Tribune* announced that very productive auditions yielded "an exceptionally high rate of successful applicants . . . [producing singers with] skill in sight-reading, interpretative ability, and voice quality [which] were the main prerequisites for success. Voices with a tremolo or breathless quality were automatically rejected."[21] Where the auditions fell short was in the men's section. In an effort to encourage a few more men to audition, a newspaper ad announced a second audition date on Sunday, October 13, 1957. A total of three hundred singers auditioned, from which Margaret selected one hundred and six members. Although she had hoped for 120 singers, particularly with the Verdi's Requiem project in mind, she stuck by her plan to choose quality over quantity. New members included church choir directors (like Jane), teachers, lawyers, music professors, secretaries, clerks, housewives, and, of course, a few trained singers. There were several outstanding musicians, but the rest would need careful training in order for the ensemble to be worthy of the great orchestra with which they would collaborate.

Hillis's mission was to establish "professionalism" in the chorus straight away. "Professionalism does not mean [nor] even mention 'money.' What it means is 'commitment—a sense of calling, almost like a religious calling. I was looking for people who had this sense . . . that they were in music because they couldn't live without it."[22] Hillis would create a professional environment, starting with the structure of the chorus. Selected members would take attendance, which included Jane Scharf, who was appointed to sign in the singers for her soprano section. All the general mechanics of the chorus, including communications and week-to-week non-musical details, were overseen by the chorus's first manager, George Hinners. Hillis knew she would need to emphasize a high level of discipline, starting with singers arriving to rehearsals on time. In an interview, Hillis conveyed that in her first year of the chorus, getting singers to arrive promptly was "like pulling teeth."[23] She was determined to begin every rehearsal on time and chose to make an example of one tenor who believed his strong voice and musicianship made him an exception to the rule. "There was one tenor who was pretty darn good, [but] who was consistently 15 minutes late, so I fired him. All of a sudden, the people began to come 15 minutes early."[24]

The other critical challenge Hillis faced was making a chorus of amateur singers sound like a polished ensemble. "I had to work my head off to get them to articulate clearly, to feel things together, to phrase, to sing in tune, to listen, and so on."[25] Jane Scharf recalled doing much clapping, marching around the room, and so forth. Hillis described this as a way of engaging the body to get everyone feeling the same thing at the same time, for a sense of togetherness within the whole group . . . becoming of one mind."[26] Over the years, this rehearsal stratagem would not be necessary, but it was imperative when the choir was in its nascent stage. At this juncture in her career, Hillis had copious experiences of building a chorus in its formative state, and she put those self-taught methods to good effect.

The Chicago Symphony Chorus and Margaret Hillis had their multiple challenges, even before the first downbeat. Immediately on the agenda there would be three performances she needed to prepare. The first performance was scheduled just one month away on November 30, 1957, a private concert with the orchestra, for a gathering of the Annual Sustaining Members for the Chicago Symphony Orchestra. Their second appearance would be the official debut of the Chorus for the December subscription concerts of Handel's *Messiah*, conducted by Fritz Reiner. The final concert of the season would be Verdi's Requiem, to be performed in early April 1958. Hillis was asked to add yet another concert to this premiere season. The Orchestral Association wanted Mozart's Requiem added, which was to be scheduled just three weeks before the Verdi performances. Hillis knew she could not add anything more in this first season of her new Symphony Chorus and would likely have to give up the *Messiah* to make the Mozart Requiem plan possible. However, in doing so, it would mean that her chorus would be making their official debut with Bruno Walter instead of with Fritz Reiner, as Walter was slated to conduct the Mozart concerts. Hillis was put in a very uncomfortable situation, caught between the Orchestral Association and Fritz Reiner.

> Well, how it happened is that Eric Oldberg was the chairman of the board at that point, and he was a particular friend of [Bruno] Walter's. It was Oldberg who called me first, saying that he wanted very much that the Chorus do the Mozart Requiem during Walter's scheduled appearance that season, [which was to be his final concert series in Chicago]. I said that the Verdi comes three weeks later, that this is really Reiner's chorus, that Reiner is the one

who has to say yes or no. "I can get both pieces," I said, "but I don't want Reiner to feel uncomfortable. First, it's his Chorus and he should have the right to introduce it. And secondly, he might feel uncomfortable and afraid that the two dates are too close together." Well, Oldberg called me then three or four times, so I finally called Reiner to get his permission. He was the music director. And he said yes. In a way—and I don't remember whether I said this to Reiner—the Verdi was better, just because they'd had a crack at a performance [before the Verdi], because they were mighty scared when they went out there for the Mozart.[27]

The Chorus's first appearance, for sustaining members on November 30, 1957, was deemed a success. Reiner conducted the first half of the concert. Margaret Hillis shared that concert with him, conducting the Chorus in two a cappella works, Thompson's *Alleluia* and Billings's *Modern Music,* and then she would conduct two pieces with the Chorus and Orchestra: Purcell's *Ode for St. Cecilia's Day* and the "Servants' Chorus" from Donizetti's *Don Pasquale.* One review of the private concert published in the *Chicago Tribune,* December 1, 1957, entitled "Woman Takes Reiner's Baton—For a While—First of Her Sex on Chicago Podium" demonstrated the novelty of a woman conducting the Orchestra, something that had not been seen in Chicago until now.[28] The reviews had very positive predictions for this new Chicago Symphony Chorus, occasioned by this first performance, one critic describing it as "fresh voiced, musically sensitive, already balanced internally."[29]

Most surprising was Reiner's willingness to share the conducting podium with Margaret Hillis. Though it was patently clear that he admired and respected her preparatory work with choruses, he made no secret of his feelings about most women conductors. In the early years of Reiner's position with the Orchestra, he rejected the suggestion of a certain female conductor who he claimed had been "pestering him for some years" to guest conduct in Chicago. Reiner's justifications for rejecting this unnamed female conductor's request were: "(1) Chicago is not ready for this sort of experimentation. (2) It might create the impression of a sideshow. (3) There is no future for a female conductor with a male orchestra. (4) She wants to use my invitation to get other engagements. (5) The lady is obnoxious and (6) she is no Lollobrigida [stunningly beautiful actress of that time, Gina Lollobrigida].[30] Reiner clearly had a different impression of Hillis's capabilities and would showcase her conducting skill, as this was the first of many times Ms. Hillis was welcomed to the podium with the Chicago Symphony Orchestra and Chorus, thanks to Reiner's support.

The performances that followed the Chorus's November appearance were no less enthusiastically received. On March 13 and 14, 1958, Hillis's Chorus bravely took the stage for their official debut with Bruno Walter in Mozart's Requiem (Picture 38). The very toughest of Chicago critics, Claudia Cassidy, could not deny the incredible results Margaret had achieved in such a short time with her newly formed ensemble, stating:

> The evening's card up the Mozartean sleeve was the new Chicago Symphony Orchestra Chorus of about 100 voices, expertly chosen and admirably trained by Margaret Hillis. It had balance and hints of brilliance, it was adroit in attack and it had moments of reassuringly imaginative song. The *Confutatis* in particular caught the haunted terror that was Mozart's when the mysterious commission for the *Requiem* convinced him that the death knell he wrote was his own.[31]

Only mild criticism was expressed in another critic's review, suggesting that the soprano section was forcing the sound in their approach to high notes, but also stating, "The whole group [was] finely drilled."[32]

CHICAGO SYMPHONY ORCHESTRA
FRITZ REINER, Music Director

TWENTY-SECOND PROGRAM

THURSDAY EVENING, MARCH 13, 1958, AT 8:15

FRIDAY AFTERNOON, MARCH 14, 1958, AT 2:00

BRUNO WALTER, *Guest Conductor*

MARIA STADER, MAUREEN FORRESTER,
DAVID LLOYD and OTTO EDELMANN, *Soloists*
CHICAGO SYMPHONY ORCHESTRA CHORUS
MARGARET HILLIS, *Director*

SYMPHONY No. 8, B Minor, ("UNFINISHED"),
(D. 759) . . . . SCHUBERT
ALLEGRO MODERATO.
ANDANTE CON MOTO.
INTERMISSION

REQUIEM, D Minor (K. 626) . . . . MOZART
REQUIEM.
DIES IRAE.
TUBA MIRUM.
REX TREMENDAE.
RECORDARE.
CONFUTATIS.
LACRIMOSA.
DOMINE JESU.
HOSTIAS.
SANCTUS.
BENEDICTUS.
AGNUS DEI.

The Chicago Symphony Orchestra uses the BALDWIN Piano

Patrons are not admitted during the playing of a composition. Considerate persons will not leave while the orchestra is playing. Ladies will please remove large hats. The performance of the final composition on this program will require about fifty-eight minutes.

Advance Program on Pages 33-35-36.

3

CHICAGO SYMPHONY ORCHESTRA CHORUS
Margaret Hillis, *Director*

Sopranos

JOAN LOUISE ANDERSON	BARBARA GILBERT	JOAN R. LUSK
DORIS A. ARCHER	GERALDINE C. GLOVER	MARY LOU MURPHY
JANIS A. BARRINGTON	FORD GOODLETTE	GLORIA GLENN PUGH
MARCIA BASS	ALICE HOOFT	JANE SCHARF
ANITA BURNS	CAROL N. HYMAN	ROBERTA L. SCHUTTLOFFEL
SOPHIA VERA CANTU	ROBERTA KILANOWSKI	ELIZABETH A. SWANSON
LOUISE CHAMBERLAIN	STEPHANIE KOMANISZYN	JOYCE M. WELLS
ANADA COSGROVE	CAROLYNE L. LARSON	HELEN ROBINS WHITE

Altos

LEONA E. AUSLAND	JEAN K. HURST	MARTHA SABRANSKY
BARBARA M. BARNES	ALLETTA KOVALCHIK	BETTY ANN SCHMELLING
DOROTHY BYRD	PATRICIA KREUTZER	MARLENE H. STAHL
MRS. ROBERT L. FARWELL	ELAINE LAVIERI	MARIE STRAHL
LEONA S. FIFE	VALERIE R. NIZICH	ELLEN THRO
RAE JANE GIBBONS	NANCY OSBORN	MARIA B. VANDERHAAR
MARY R. GILKEY	GRACE ORR OSBORNE	CORNELIA VAN DER KLOOT
JUNE C. GILSON	HELEN S. POLLAK	HELEN V. WARNER
JOAN HORVATH	ANNE PORAYKO	SUSAN B. WIEGAND

Tenors

HORST F. ABRAHAM	JOHN E. HOELM	ROBERT J. O'MARA
VERNON BOYSEN	BILLY D. HOPKINS	WALLACE R. OSTLUND
ALONZO D. CHANCELLOR	JOSEPH KREINES	ED QUISTDORFF
WILLIAM H. CUNNINGHAM	EDWARD LIEBERMAN	JEROME ROTHENBERG
ADOLPH R. ERST	JOHN W. LOBSINGER	RICHARD H. SNOW
MITCHELL GAGALSKI	RONALD E. LOCKE	KENNETH D. WESTERDAHL
JOSEPH P. GIDLOW	TERENCE H. NOBLE	JAMES WILSON
NATHANIEL B. GREEN		MANFRED F. ZIEMER

Basses

CHARLES BRIDGES	SOLON A. HUNT	RAYMOND PALUCH
HOWARD DONALDSON	THOMAS B. JOHNS	TOM PECK
ROBERT W. FRAZIER	CLIFFORD H. JOHNSON	JONATHAN PUGH
JOSEPH GARDNER	NORMAN E. KANGAS	EDWARD W. ROTHE
HARRY E. GUDMUNDSON	KARL J. LOHRMAN	JERRY SEYER
RONALD C. HARM	JERRY McLAIN	ALFRED SCHOEPKO
GEORGE O. HINNERS	FRANK NOWAKOWSKI	ROBERT P. THOMPSON
FREDERIC HOUGHTELING	JOHN R. OLIVO	JOHN L. VOLLBRECHT

32

Picture 38.

Program and roster for the Chicago Symphony Chorus's debut subscription concerts with Bruno Walter on March 13 and 14, 1958 (Scrapbook #3, 1956–1958). (Margaret Hillis Collection, Rosenthal Archives of the Chicago Symphony Orchestra Association)

Three weeks later, on April 3 and 4, 1958, Reiner finally had the opportunity to conduct *his* Chorus in the long-awaited Verdi's Requiem. With more familiarity of the concert hall, the orchestra, and with the confidence that followed recent successful performances, the Chorus approached this concert more courageously. *Chicago Sun-Times* reviewer Robert Marsh alluded to the earlier successes of the Chorus when writing his review for the Verdi performances. "Miss Hillis's chorus proved its virtues earlier this season. Again, its excellent enunciation, reliable intonation and intelligent response were praiseworthy."[33] The Chorus was off to a tremendous start with the first season under its belt, beginning a pattern of what would be a long history of artistic triumphs for this ensemble.

BALANCING CHICAGO AND NEW YORK

With all that was going on in Chicago, it is important to remember that Margaret was keeping her work going in New York as she launched this new symphonic chorus in the Midwest. Though she reduced the number of Town Hall concerts in the sixth season from four concerts of the prior season to only one concert this current season, she was able to keep her singers employed by other means. She did so through her affiliations with opera companies, summer festivals, and by organizing concert tours. Reducing Town Hall appearances provided Hillis more time for score study. She needed to protect time for herself in order to learn music for her Chicago Symphony Chorus position, in addition to other concert work with her American Concert Choir and conducting appearances she was doing on her own. In some ways, her schedule appeared less busy than in previous seasons; however, looks are deceiving. The pressure of creating a symphonic chorus for this great orchestra was not a simple matter and would demand much of Hillis's careful thought and attention if it was going to fly.

Here was the schedule Hillis was balancing as she traveled weekly between two cities during the 1957–1958 concert season.

CONCERT SEASON SCHEDULE: 1957–1958

October 5 and 13, 1957, Chicago
Auditions for the Chicago Symphony Chorus

October 8, 1957, New York
American Opera Society, Donizetti *Anna Bolena*, Town Hall, Arnold Gamson, conducting

November 5, 1957, New York
American Opera Society, Gluck *Paride ed Elena*, Arnold Gamson, conducting

November 30, 1957, Chicago
First appearance of the Chicago Symphony Chorus with the Orchestra
Purcell *Ode for St. Cecilia's Day*, Thompson *Alleluia*, Billings *Modern Music*, and Donizetti "Servants' Chorus" from *Don Pasquale*, Margaret Hillis, conducting

December 20, 1957, New York
Little Orchestra Society, Berlioz *L'enfance du Christ*, Little Orchestra
Society, Brooklyn Academy of Music, Thomas Scherman, conducting

December 22, 1957, New York
Little Orchestra Society, Berlioz *L'enfance du Christ*, Carnegie Hall,
Thomas Scherman, conducting

January 1958, New York
New York Chamber Soloists, Margaret Hillis, conducting

February 19, 1958, New York
The American Concert Choir and Orchestra Town Hall Concert, Purcell
Ode for St. Cecilia's Day (1692), Kohn *Rhapsodie Hassidique*, *Vocalise*,
and *Three Madrigals* (world premieres), Stravinsky *Renard*, Margaret
Hillis, conducting

February 25, 1958, New York
Union Theological Seminary, Bach *Brandenburg* Concerto No. 1 in F
Major and No. 4 in G Major, Cantata No. 51 (*Jauchzet Gott in allen
Landen*), Margaret Hillis, conducting

February 25, 1958, New York
American Opera Society, Monteverdi *Coronation of Poppea* with Leontyne
Price, Arnold Gamson, conducting

March 5, 1958, New York
American Opera Society, Purcell *Saul* and *The Witch of Endor*, Harvard
University, Arnold Gamson, conducting

March 6, 1958, New York
American Opera Society, Purcell *Dido and Aeneas*, Harvard University,
Arnold Gamson, conducting

March 13 and 14, 1958, Chicago
Chicago Symphony Chorus, Mozart's Requiem, Bruno Walter, conducting,
Orchestra Hall, Chicago

April 3 and 4, 1958, Chicago
Chicago Symphony Chorus, Verdi's Requiem, Fritz Reiner, conducting,
Orchestra Hall, Chicago

April 12, 1958, Chicago
The Chorus as a Musical Instrument Workshop for Secondary and College
Level teachers, sponsored by Chicago Public Schools and Music Educators
Club, Margaret Hillis, conducting

May 4, 1958, New York
American Concert Choir, Marvin David Levy one-act opera *Escuria* (world
premiere), Kaufman Auditorium, New York, Margaret Hillis, conducting

May 14 and 15, 1958, New York
American Concert Choir, members of the Collegiate Chorale, American
Concert Orchestra Contemporary Music Concert, Hindemith *Lehrstück*,
Wolpe Quintet with Voice for the Rothschild Foundation, New York,
Margaret Hillis, conducting

July 7–11, 1958, College Park, Maryland
High School Choral Workshop, University of Maryland, Margaret Hillis,
conducting

As Hillis kept track of her numerous musical responsibilities and during her
weekly travels to Chicago, she was also carefully crafting ideas to foster the growth
of her American Choral Foundation. In the fall of 1957, Hillis distributed surveys
to three thousand college, community, professional, and religious chorus leaders,
inquiring about their repertoire and asking other questions about their programs.
The intention was to gather information and then share it with choral conductors
nationally through her American Choral Foundation publication. This survey was
also intended to inform Hillis about the type of materials her Foundation might
provide its members to further support their growth and development.

Hillis came up with another idea to advance her Choral Foundation by honoring
important people in the music field and in political circles. In doing so, she could
add greater distinction to her organization through their affiliation. Margaret
established the Tripos Award, based upon a third-century B.C. honor given in
ancient Athens to the "Choragus" or conductor of the choir who won the festival

of Dionysius. Hillis awarded this to recipients demonstrating exceptional vision, musical accomplishment, or significant support for the choral music field. In fall of 1957, the first year of this award, Hillis chose two recipients for this honor. She wisely chose Dr. Archibald T. Davidson, a professor emeritus of Harvard University. Well-regarded for his choral work at Harvard University, he was greatly admired in the field for his scholarship and choral accomplishments. The other awardee was Senator Jacob Javits, whom Hillis had recently met through her work in the Empire Music Festival the previous summer. Hillis knew that having the support of this powerful figure provided her an all-important political connection that could greatly benefit the Foundation in the future. During a lavish dinner at the Waldorf Astoria in December 1957, Hillis served as the master of ceremonies, welcoming speakers who provided laudatory remarks to honor the awardees. Among the speakers honoring his former Harvard professor Dr. Davidson was Dr. Robert Tangeman, Hillis's former Juilliard professor, ex-husband of Nell Tangeman, and now her colleague at the Union Theological Seminary. Hillis had the foresight to understand how important it was to gather distinguished members of the artistic and political communities to bring greater credibility to her Foundation.

The 1957–1958 season was filled with many firsts for Margaret Hillis. Recently acquired affiliations with the New York City Opera and the Chicago Symphony Orchestra, national television and radio broadcasts, and a very active performance schedule brought greater attention to the Hillis brand. The New York Chamber Soloists, along with continued teaching and conducting at the Union Theological Seminary, provided her further opportunities for growth as an instrumental conductor. Conducting workshops and continued expansion of her American Choral Foundation helped Hillis build her reputation as an expert pedagogue in the choral field. While keeping her current connections with the American Opera Society and the Little Orchestra Society, she was able to keep her American Concert Choir actively employed while reducing her family's financial investments supporting the choir and the Town Hall series. Instead, she obtained her artists' salaries from the opera companies eager to hire Hillis and her chorus for their own opera productions.

It would soon be time for Margaret to make some major decisions. Was her musical future in New York or in Chicago? In the early days of the Chicago Symphony Chorus, this was not a question Margaret considered. She was fairly certain her work in Chicago would be temporary. However, the New York opportunities for her chorus began to diminish once she reduced her family's contributions to the Town Hall concert series. The other unanticipated factor was that her love for Chicago would grow during those initial years of building the Chicago Symphony Chorus. In the next five years of Hillis's life, while making music in two cities, her career direction would become abundantly clear.

ENDNOTES

1. Jonathan Stern, "Music for the (American) People: The Concerts at Lewisohn Stadium, Volume 1, 1922-1964," PhD dissertation (The City University of New York, 2009), https://academicworks.cuny.edu/cgi/viewcontent.cgi?article=3282&context=gc_etds

2. Interview with Melvin Kaplan, May 3, 2020.

3. Rorem dedicated *The Poet's Requiem* to Margaret Hillis, who gave the piece its premiere in 1957. He communicated this to her in a handwritten message (see Chapter 18).

4. Picture from a newspaper clipping advertising *The Poet's Requiem* (clipping found in Scrapbook #3, 1956–1958, from Margaret Hillis Collection, Rosenthal Archives of the Chicago Symphony Orchestra Association). Picture from *New York Herald Tribune*, February 10, 1957.

5. Claudia Cassidy, "On the Aisle: 'Tusch' Standing Tribute Honor Walter in Orchestra Hall," *Chicago Tribune*, January 25, 1957, part 3, p. 1.

6. Ibid.

7. Interview of Frank Conlon, December 15, 2019.

8. Philip Hart, *Fritz Reiner: A Biography* (Evanston: Northwestern University Press, 1994), p. 163.

9. From the dissertation of Stanley G. Livengood, "A History of the Chicago Symphony Chorus, 1957-2000," University of Oklahoma, 2001; he cites this information from George Kuyper, in a memo to Dr. Eric Oldberg, May 20, 1957 (Rosenthal Archives of Chicago Symphony Orchestra Association).

10. Steven Hillyer, "Podium Interview with Margaret Hillis," November 20, 1982, p. 3 (transcription of the interview in the Margaret Hillis Collection, Rosenthal Archives of the Chicago Symphony Orchestra Association).

11. Jon Bentz, "Interview of Margaret Hillis Director Chicago Symphony Orchestra, September 19, 1989, Archives Committee, Oral History Project, 1992," p. 10 (Margaret Hillis Collection, Rosenthal Archives of the Chicago Symphony Orchestra Association).

12. Ibid.

13. Ibid.

14. Margaret Hillis, interview by Norman Pellegrini (transcribed by Stanley G. Livengood), October 6, 1997, p. 11.

15. Hart, *Fritz Reiner*, p. 163.

16. Ibid.

17. Jeannine Wagar, *Conductors in Conversation: Fifteen Contemporary Conductors Discuss Their Lives and Profession* (Boston: G.K. Hall & Co., 1991), p. 110.

18. Hillyer, "Podium Interview," p. 6.

19. Ibid.

20. Ibid.

21. "Chorus Auditions Pay Off," *Chicago Sun-Times*, October 5, 1957.

22. Bentz, "Interview of Margaret Hillis," p. 12.

23. Ann Feldman radio interview, February 15, 1995.

24. Bentz, "Interview of Margaret Hillis," p. 12.

25. Ibid., p. 6.

26. Feldman interview, February 15, 1995.

27. Hillyer, "Podium Interview," p. 9.

28. Frank Villella, "The Founding of the Chicago Symphony Chorus: 'A New Factor in the City's Musical Life,'" featured in Chicago Symphony Presents, March 2018, p. 13.

29. Robert Marsh, "Symphony's Chorus Excellent in Concert," *Chicago Sun-Times*, December 2, 1957.

30. Hart, *Fritz Reiner*, p. 161.

31. Claudia Cassidy, "Bruno Walter and the Chicago Symphony in a Memorable Mozart Requiem," *Chicago Tribune*, March 14, 1958.

32. Roger Dettmer, "Spontaneous Ovation Greets Beloved Bruno Walter 81," *Chicago American*, March 14, 1958.

33. Robert C. Marsh, "Verdi Work Nobly Performed by Chicago Symphony, Soloists," *Chicago Sun-Times*, April 4, 1958.

CHAPTER 12

SUCCESS IN A MUSIC CAREER
REQUIRES MORE THAN MUSICAL TALENT

With the first season of the Chicago Symphony Chorus successfully completed, Hillis could enjoy the satisfaction in knowing that her choral pedagogy had yet again yielded superb results. She was accustomed to consistent successes these days, with her American Concert Choir often glowingly reviewed in New York and beyond. Hillis's challenge would be to produce similar results in Chicago with singers, mostly untrained, who would be reviewed with similar metrics as those of the symphony orchestra with whom they collaborated. Hillis's formula proved successful again with her selection process for singers that included a well-thought-out audition along with her regimented training of the Chorus. What Hillis could not anticipate with this new appointment was a series of additional challenges she would encounter. These challenges were of a non-musical nature and therefore nothing she could have prepared for during her formal musical training; yet these hurdles were just as important to navigate. Hillis was quick to realize that her interactions with Chicago colleagues, including conductors, administrators, and trustees, would require an extreme measure of diplomacy, yet another Margaret Hillis strength.

She had actually been practicing her people skills throughout her life without realizing how important they would become in her music career. During her earliest days in New York, she gained a reputation for the professional manner in which she treated people. Although much of the time she worked with people whom she personally employed, which may have made them more deferential toward her, she did not take advantage of the situation, always treating colleagues with respect.

219

Hillis had witnessed conductors along the way who were less considerate of their musicians, and she determined that was not her way. In Chicago, as a newly hired conductor joining a large staff of a major orchestra, she observed interactions that could sometimes be destructive, nested primarily in the power structure. Hillis was able to quickly assess each situation and, when confronted, would apply her circumspective personality style, refined over years of maneuvering in a man's world as a conductor. Entering the highly charged political climate of the Orchestral Association, Hillis employed her dignified and diplomatic style with people, which guided her in navigating the turbulent waters of strong-willed conductors, administrators, and musicians. Her *savoir faire* in dealing with people sustained her through abstruse encounters that required thoughtful and sensitive responses.

HILLIS AND REINER

Fortunately, Hillis had a good working relationship with her immediate superior, Fritz Reiner, who was clearly Hillis's champion. However, that is not to say that he always made their interactions easy. Reiner was ever demanding but, as Hillis saw it, always fair. As Hillis recalled, "Most people were terrified of him. A lot of people hated him. I thought he was a 'puddycat.' He had respect for people who had the goods . . . that's the starting point. . . . But if you didn't do well, look out! I think he was unnecessarily cruel, but he had an incredible sense of humor, and I regarded him sort of as my grandpa."[1] Reiner respected Hillis from their very first collaboration, and this admiration continued throughout their time working together in Chicago. Despite Reiner's comfort level with Margaret, at no point did he allow their collegial relationship to spill over into a friendship. Hillis was happy to keep their interactions on a strictly professional level. She believed Reiner had an affection for her. However, even when lunching in Rambleside, the Reiner's Connecticut home, as Hillis did numerous times, Reiner rarely showed Margaret a lighter cordiality, as did his wife, Carlotta. Hillis knew just how to mollify Reiner, and it served her well throughout their collaborations (Picture 39).

Picture 39.
Fritz Reiner, music director of the Chicago Symphony Orchestra 1953–1962. (Oscar Chicago)
(Rosenthal Archives of the Chicago Symphony Orchestra Association)

Hillis developed a great loyalty to Reiner since he supported her from the very beginning. She sensed his support through many of their interactions. During the early years of the Chorus's existence, he often attended Chicago Symphony Chorus rehearsals to be helpful, providing encouragement and advice when it was warranted. He always relegated the conducting of the Chorus to Margaret whenever he was in attendance, including the final conductor piano rehearsal (known as the CPR, the rehearsal with the performance conductor, taking place just prior to the first orchestra and chorus rehearsal; most often conducted by the performance maestros). While Reiner would sit in a chair beside her, Hillis would conduct the Chorus through the piece, and he would occasionally interject a directive along the way. Trying her best to mimic his tempos, she would glance over to watch his hand motion, indicating his preferences. Reiner showed deference to Margaret, even during his orchestra rehearsals. In several rehearsals for Verdi's Requiem, Hillis explained how he subtly collaborated with her, seeking her aural perceptions of balance issues between the chorus and orchestra.

I remember one place—the *Tuba Mirum*, where the brass is carrying on like crazy—[and there is] supposed to be just the basses singing [in the choral part that join the brass at that point in the music]. I had added the tenors to [the basses]. The chorus didn't come through, and Reiner turned [to Hillis] in the rehearsal and I said, "Hmm." So, I added the altos [at the] next rehearsal. And then [after the first] performance, Reiner called me backstage, and he said, "That was a very beautiful job you did." I said, "Thank you." He says, "But on the *Tuba Mirum*, you—you 'Schvindled!' I said, "Yes I did." He said, "Keep on schvindling." [They laughed.][2]

Hillis said she was often summoned to Reiner's dressing room post-performance because he would want to thank her for her wonderful preparation of the Chorus.

Of course, Reiner's most ringing endorsement of Hillis was his invitation for her to conduct his Orchestra on subscription concerts. This arrangement provided her the opportunity to conduct one choral/orchestral work every season. To help Margaret succeed in these concerts, Reiner sometimes acted as her assistant conductor during her orchestral rehearsals. In preparation for her debut subscription appearance in December 1958, Hillis was rehearsing Honegger's *Christmas Cantata*, programmed for the second half of a concert she would share with Reiner. "He sat out front and helped me as an assistant conductor would. He'd come up and say, 'We're getting a little too much trombone here,' or 'Here the strings need to bite a little bit more.' He was just wonderful."[3] Reiner showed his respect for Hillis in other ways as well. He would occasionally consult with her when choosing vocal soloists, knowing her extensive work with outstanding singers in New York even though he himself had conducted at the Metropolitan Opera. Soprano Adele Addison and contralto Florence Kopleff were two examples of singers Reiner hired through Hillis's recommendations. When asked in an interview if Reiner ever sought Hillis's approval about repertoire, Hillis replied that he made most of those decisions and she would agree with his ideas, as it was always best to do so with Reiner. Applying her good judgement, she explained, "Well, occasionally I would advise him when he asked me about something. But only when it was very apparent that he wanted my advice."[4]

Margaret was one of only a few who were allowed to witness Reiner's wonderful sense of humor. She recalled an incident early on in her Chicago years.

I remember once I was waiting for a taxi on the corner of Goethe and the inner drive. I kept trying. Then this [taxi] came along. There was a little figure in the back seat. I thought, on a Sunday morning, a pick-up?—I was young enough then. And the door opened, and it was Reiner. He said, "Where you go?" I said, "To the Hall, to rehearse the tenors and basses." He said, "Good. I go to the Palmer House to do a recording, get in." We were going along, he said, "Do you know the latest thing on Maria Callas?" I said, "No." [He said], "She's been fired from every place except Cape Canaveral!" [Now the Kennedy Space Center.][5]

Though he was often respectful and generous to Hillis, Reiner's relationship among the musicians and administrators was very different. He could be quite difficult with the Orchestra, making unilateral decisions sometimes resulting in players having a reduction in their salaries, which contributed to orchestra members organizing a player's committee.[6] The increasingly contentious relationship between players, conductor, and administration was blamed squarely on Reiner, though this may not completely have been the case. Reiner's desire for privacy further impaired his relationship with the Chicago Symphony Orchestra (CSO) administrators. The initial excitement of Reiner's appointment with the Chicago Symphony Orchestra in 1952 was not to last long because he continually avoided opportunities to be an ambassador for the Orchestra. He rarely interacted with the public and showed little interest in activities related to the CSO, including the Civic Orchestra, Children's Concerts, or any type of community outreach. Reiner would arrive in Chicago just in time for rehearsals to start for the season and would leave promptly at the onset of the post-season, investing no extra time before, during, or after the season to make connections that would build the Orchestra's relationship with the public. Reiner regularly declined social invitations for post-concert receptions, denying donors a chance to get "up close and personal" with the conductor. He and his wife turned down most every "human interest" interview, refusing to allow the public any opportunity to know them better. This behavior became a constant source of strain between Reiner, administrators, and trustees, who thought it hampered their efforts to fundraise for the Orchestra. Reiner disagreed, saying, "They have my music; they cannot have my body."[7] By the time Hillis had joined the Chicago Symphony Orchestra family, sentiments for Reiner were beginning to deteriorate.

Reiner made one exception when it came to his limited social life in Chicago, and that was with the *Chicago Tribune* critic Claudia Cassidy and her husband, William Crawford. Cassidy, known about town as "Acidy Cassidy," wielded a great deal of influence when it came to the Chicago Symphony Orchestra. Her opinions were weighed heavily when conductors were selected and dismissed, which had less to do with her musical expertise than it did her convincing and pointed writing, often swaying readers and Orchestral Association administrators. Cassidy was very vocal in her disapproval of Désiré Defauw, the first conductor to replace the legendary Frederick Stock, who had led the Orchestra for almost forty years. Scathing reviews of Defauw included one Cassidy wrote describing his conducting of Debussy's *Nuages* in the most unflattering of terms: "[H]is treatment of the winds turned that Debussy fog into a far less lovely frog." Many such reviews contributed to Defauw's departure after a brief tenure with the CSO. The conductor following Defauw, Artur Rodzinski, though strongly endorsed by Cassidy, lasted less than one year due to his temperamental behavior, causing much trouble for the Orchestral Association.[8] Cassidy, unhappy with Rodzinski's dismissal, took her frustrations out on the next conductor to lead the CSO, Rafael Kubelík. With more harsh reviews thrust upon Kubelík's performances, she helped persuade trustees, already on the fence about him, to find yet another music director. Fritz Reiner's agent, a friend of Cassidy, wisely arranged a meeting between the two in Chicago in the hopes Cassidy would endorse a Reiner appointment. The meeting succeeded in helping Reiner's cause, and a friendship emerged between Reiner, Cassidy, and their spouses. According to Reiner's diaries, they socialized with the Cassidys more frequently than with anyone else.[9] Claudia Cassidy became an enthusiastic campaigner for Reiner's appointment to the CSO. As a powerful critic, such an alliance with Cassidy worked favorably. Unfortunately for Reiner, the tide eventually turned, resulting in negative reviews for his work that would ultimately end his tenure in Chicago.

Reiner began butting heads with administrators at the time of Hillis's hiring. Margaret's first inkling that something was going on came about directly in her first season, when Orchestral Association board chair Dr. Eric Oldberg suggested that the first appearance of the Chicago Symphony Chorus be with Bruno Walter in Mozart's Requiem instead of with Reiner for his Verdi Requiem performances. Hillis, taking matters into her own hands, secured Reiner's approval for the opening concert to be with someone other than himself. In doing so, she kept the peace with Reiner while helping Dr. Oldberg get his way, on behalf of his good friend Bruno Walter. Her finesse in resolving this dicey matter won her favor from everyone involved.

In Margaret's first few seasons with the Chicago Symphony Chorus, she benefited from Claudia Cassidy's good reviews of both the Chorus and Reiner, a result of that positive Reiner/Cassidy alliance. However, as things changed between Reiner and Cassidy, so did the reviews, turning more critical and negative. Hillis and her Chorus became collateral damage of the failed friendship. The fallout of Cassidy and Reiner stemmed from a proposed European tour planned for the Orchestra in 1959. Cassidy heavily endorsed this tour. However, Reiner voiced many concerns over the tour during its planning. One of the sticking points was the number of concerts per week that Reiner would be expected to conduct. Reiner wanted to limit himself and his Orchestra to five concerts within a seven-day period. The Orchestral Association was pushing beyond that number, which Reiner knew he would have trouble handling due to his age and current health. He was equally concerned about how his Orchestra would manage playing so many days in a row without rest. After much debate, Reiner decided to cancel the tour. That gesture was the beginning of a contentious falling out with Cassidy, Oldberg, the trustees, and the players, all angered regarding Reiner's decision. As comity continued to deteriorate between Reiner, Cassidy, and the Orchestral Association, Hillis wisely exercised a careful balance, maintaining her loyalty to Reiner while being mindful of those at the helm who no longer shared her enthusiasm for the maestro. Hillis, acutely perceiving a social and political "brouhaha," kept her distance, understanding she could not get herself embroiled in this unfortunate turn of events she was powerless to repair. Margaret was clearly angered by Cassidy's treatment of Reiner, but she remained neutral—a stance she would exhibit many times in the future—often removing herself from complicated entanglements. Hillis's resentment of Cassidy is apparent in an interview years later. Hillis explained how Cassidy's hostility stemmed from her role in raising money for the tour that Reiner canceled. Hillis reflected:

Of course, Claudia . . . didn't know anything about music—she was on an ego trip. And if you really read her reviews, you don't know what she's talking about. She doesn't know anything about music. . . . She was in love with her word and the purple prose. I don't know what Chicago did to deserve her. She wrecked many a career and she was out to wreck Reiner's.

He might have lived longer if it hadn't been for Claudia. As soon as that cancellation came [the European tour], she turned against me. Nothing I did could be right, nothing that Reiner did could be right. I don't think she could even read music. I always thought she'd be wonderful at writing a travel column. That she could do very well. But she should stay away from music. . . . She was a dilettante.[10]

As the tide turned against Reiner, he began to exhibit mistrust toward everyone involved with the CSO. It was here that Margaret's wise handling of people was on full display. Right after the cancellation of the tour, Reiner suspected everyone he worked with was against him, including Hillis and her Chorus. In rehearsals, he would accuse the Chorus of doing things that they were not doing, as if they were purposely going against him. Hillis knew what was going on and found a way to reassure him that she and the Chorus were in his corner without making a public spectacle of the matter. Hillis described his first rehearsal with the Chorus following the canceled tour. The Chorus was rehearsing Handel's *Judas Maccabeus* for a performance series in April 1959. During the CPR rehearsal, Reiner stopped Hillis in one spot while she was conducting the piece, accusing the basses of taking the lower octave of a chord instead of what was written in the score. Instead of Hillis becoming defensive, she calmly responded, "Well, let's do it again." When they repeated the passage, Hillis purposely stopped on the chord in question, without saying a word, and Reiner heard right away that they had been singing correctly, as they had the first time. As Hillis tells it, "So we got on the chord and I stopped them . . . I looked at him and he looked at me and then we went on and did the middle section. And this opening came back to the same cadence. I stopped on it [again] . . . and a little light began to flicker in his eye. He knew what I was doing. I wasn't about to let him alienate the chorus."[11] She claimed that at this moment, Reiner realized that she was still loyal to him and was making her point without shaming him. As she tells it, "He was terrified of somebody calling him down or shaming him about something."[12] Hillis remained loyal to Reiner, maintaining their good working relationship until he departed Chicago.

Reiner left the CSO partially because his health had deteriorated following a heart attack in October 1960. He died on November 15, 1963. The Chorus performed in a concert series two weeks later on November 28 and 29, 1963, with music Jean

Martinon originally programmed for those dates. Stravinsky's *Symphony of Psalms* and Mozart's Requiem were conveniently fitting choices for what would now be a memorial concert series to honor the memory of Fritz Reiner. However, the traumatic event of President John F. Kennedy's assassination on November 22, 1963, just one week prior to the concert series, changed the focus of the program which instead became a memorial to the fallen president. With scarcely any acknowledgment of Reiner, he was not given the dignified closure worthy of this important music director. As Hillis saw it, Reiner was never fully appreciated during his tenure with the CSO. "Chicago didn't know what it had in Reiner."[13]

HILLIS AND MARTINON

The stage was set for an even more turbulent time ahead following Reiner's resignation from the CSO. This was another circumstance requiring Hillis to call upon her superb interpersonal skills, the byproduct of her exceptional IQ and EQ—intelligence and emotional quotients—and her reasoning prowess. With a change in directors, so too would Margaret's role evolve, giving her increased responsibility with the new conductor and the Orchestral Association. This evolution came about because of Hillis's ability to win over the trust of the new music director, Jean Martinon, who conducted the Chicago Symphony Orchestra from 1963–1968. Hillis described Martinon as "a peculiar guy," explaining that he did not trust anyone, including her, when he first began with the CSO.[14] Hillis was able to overcome the barriers Martinon put forth, eventually winning his confidence. An additional contributing factor to Hillis's increased role was the result of managerial dysfunction within the Association. "Martinon came at a particularly difficult time in the history of this orchestra. We had a poor management—in fact not just poor but a destructive management—and here was this 'poor little lamb being led to the slaughter.'"[15] Hillis described the years following Reiner as "those AWFUL years," not because of Martinon but because of the dysfunctional inner workings of the Association at the time of his appointment.[16] As Hillis saw it, Martinon was the right man at the wrong time[17] (Picture 40).

Picture 40.
Jean Martinon, music director of the Chicago Symphony Orchestra 1963–1968.
(Rosenthal Archives of the Chicago Symphony Orchestra Association)

George Kupyer, who had managed the CSO beginning in 1944, had abruptly resigned in November 1959, partly due to his extreme disappointment with Reiner's cancellation of the European tour. Dr. Oldberg was equally dismayed with Reiner's action. Of course, both were as culpable as Reiner for the tour's cancellation. Though Reiner was chosen as the scapegoat, all three had equal parts in the demise of the project. Oldberg, who was already plotting Reiner's replacement, now needed to arrange to fill Kupyer's position. He calculated the ideal choice for Kupyer's replacement to be Seymour Raven, Claudia Cassidy's close associate at the *Tribune*. Oldberg assumed he could guarantee Cassidy's future support of a Reiner replacement by hiring her longtime friend. Oldberg miscalculated. Jean Martinon, Oldberg's choice for the new music director, was ultimately unsupported by Cassidy who would have preferred Maestro Karl Böhm. Additionally, Seymour Raven was inexperienced as an orchestra manager, which led to many challenges going forward between the Orchestra and the Association, some of which Hillis would step in to help manage. The die was cast for the tumultuous years ahead, and it was Margaret Hillis who would play a major role in keeping the whole operation afloat, using her ability to safely maneuver through the dense political climate.

Primarily blaming the Association for Martinon's difficulties, Hillis described the atmosphere as being akin to living in a Kafka novel. She described Martinon as an honest man, just trying to do a good job, but that was made impossible with the untrustworthy atmosphere Hillis accused the new manager, Seymour Raven, of creating at the Hall.

> The musicians would make outgoing calls. We used to think that the telephones were bugged. It turned out they were. . . . The phones were bugged in order that Raven could get things on them when the union negotiations came up, or blackmail them into backing down. . . . When I was doing special classes for the chorus on my own time, for no extra pay at all, he accused me of trying to earn extra money and of using the chorus improperly. He was paranoiac. It was just a mad time."[18]

Martinon was persuaded by one of the very few people he trusted, his sister-in-law Myrtha, to speak with Margaret Hillis, believing she could be trusted to help him figure out what was going on at the Hall.

> And Myrtha kept pleading with him to talk to me, because these were the years of that Seymour Raven nightmare. And I knew what was going on, and I kept my mouth shut. And she kept pleading with him to speak to me, because I had talked to her a little about it. And he didn't trust anybody. So, finally he had to trust somebody. So, we had a Verdi Requiem rehearsal. I was conducting when he came [in]. When the rehearsal was over, for once Seymour Raven was not there . . . usually . . . you know, I'd run into Martinon in the hallway, and immediately [Raven] was right at our elbows, and this was the first time, really, I'd seem [Martinon] alone. And he said, "You know what's going on at the Hall?"
>
> And I said, "Yes, I do." He said, "Whose side are you on?" I said, "I'm on the side of music!" And he said, "Can you help me? Is there anybody on the Board?" . . . [Hillis responded that she did not know who was on the board that he should contact but told him], "I know where to find out." So, Phil Hart . . . I called him up.[19]
>
> We talked; I think from midnight until about 4:00 in the morning. And he ran down the background of each member of the Board. And he said,

"McDonald is the one he should go to." . . .And so I told Martinon . . . So, he went to him and the following week, Seymour [Raven] was out of there . . . after that, Claudia [Cassidy] then really got after [Martinon].[20]

Hillis made it a policy to recuse herself from the politics, up to this point, but she was not afraid to confront controversy when the greater good could be served. Having the good judgment to know when and how to intervene in situations such as this reveals her talent for such matters. She was guided by principles of fairness and professionalism; she was unwilling to compromise her standards even when challenged by a difficult choice. Putting the music ahead of herself and her job security, she demonstrated her support for Martinon and for the Chicago Symphony Orchestra, an organization she had grown to love. All these attributes were paramount in her consideration to enter the fray of this politically charged situation. She believed the risk was worth taking.

After going out on this limb for Martinon, he appointed her as his musical assistant from 1966–1968. It was a post she kept for the remainder of his term but relinquished upon his departure. For whatever reason, she insisted upon keeping this position private. Hillis confided in trusted family and friends, revealing this new title but insisting it not be shared publicly. She was clearly pleased to have this appointment, in part because it also meant an increase in her salary. Margaret described this job as "a lot of dirty work. I did . . . research for [Martinon] regarding Haydn symphonies. . . . There were political problems among the players that I was to help iron out. I didn't like that role very well but because I said I'd do this job, I did it."[21] Martinon had Hillis ameliorate these personnel situations within the Orchestra as part of her duties. Hillis explained that the Orchestra was divided so badly that they hardly spoke to each other. Yet "knowing all this nonsense and bitterness was going on—I would marvel that it never affected their playing."[22]

Hillis was also asked to intervene in matters involving the hiring of soloists or arranging for extra instrumentalists needed for upcoming performances. Hillis explains:

Of course, at that point, we had a management that didn't know how to hire soloists. There were many soloists who came during those years without having gotten a contract. They came on my word, on my personal word.

It's a good thing I was around, because [the soloists] could trust me. A harpsichordist was hired to do a piano concerto, things like that. Idiotic. Or you'd suddenly find out that with *Les noces* coming up a few weeks later, no pianists had been engaged for it. So, I'd have to scramble around and find pianists.[23]

So, they came and they sang, or came and they played. I called them and/or management and I said, "Look, they are expected here, and I know that they don't have a contract"—then the contract would be signed *after* the performance, and of course, that is totally unheard of. But, because I was well known around New York, they took my word. Otherwise, things would have just fallen apart.[24]

Hillis was, of course, aware that Martinon was not completely faultless in the challenges that befell him during his CSO years. She described him as being a very stubborn man, sometimes to his peril. Describing one particular instance, Hillis tried to advise him in his performance of *Les noces*, which, of course, was a work she knew very well. From her conducting experience with the piece, she advised him to distribute the pianists evenly, making sure there was at least one very strong pianist on either side of the stage distributed between the four pianists who would be playing with the Orchestra. Martinon had two very strong pianists and two who were less so. Instead of heeding Hillis's advice, he decided to do just the opposite. The result: one of the performances nearly fell apart in one section, but as Hillis described it, "The Chorus kept it together and Martinon was able to get through the difficult passage. I thought, 'Damn you! If you would just listen now and then—I do have your best interests at heart—I have the best interest of this orchestra at heart—and these performances at heart.' Well, now and then he would go against any advice and nearly always he was wrong."[25]

In looking back at the Martinon years, Hillis reflected upon all the good he had done for the CSO. Working yet again for a maestro she believed was underappreciated, she thought he deserved greater support and respect than he was ultimately given. First and foremost, Margaret considered him a very gifted conductor whose strengths included a talent for contemporary music, a master of Schumann symphonies and of the French repertoire. Hillis was aware these featured performances were not properly promoted through CSO recording projects done at the time of his tenure.

Hillis averred there was no greater conductor of Ravel's *Daphnis and Chloe* than Martinon.[26]

Hillis credited Martinon for his continued support of the CSO's phenomenal music library. The CSO library was first established by founder and first music director Theodore Thomas, whose vast personal music collection became the foundation of the CSO's music library. Second music director Frederick Stock continued to expand the scope of the library during his years with the Orchestra. Martinon supported the library's ongoing development, which continued to rival many other symphony orchestra libraries in the world. Martinon also reconfigured the structure of the orchestra librarian position. Though it is unclear whether this was a part-time or full-time position prior to Martinon's arrival at the CSO, Hillis claimed it was with Martinon's encouragement that this became a full-time position going forward. Hillis recalled how Lionel Sayers, the librarian during the Martinon era, was often required to take home scores and mark them until four o'clock in the morning instead of working on music during regular business hours. According to Hillis, Martinon changed that practice, restructuring the job as full-time employment with more reasonable working hours.

Hillis also credited Martinon with taking interest in the Civic Orchestra, which had not been overseen by a CSO music director since the days of Frederick Stock. It was Stock who created the Civic Orchestra and served as its first music director during the 1919–1920 season. Known then as the Civic Music Student Orchestra, Stock originally conceived of this orchestra as a way of providing young talented players with the experience of being in a symphony orchestra, training players under the leadership of fine conductors. After years of neglect by music directors who followed Stock, Martinon took an interest in rebuilding the orchestra, shaping it into a fine training orchestra just in the way it was originally intended. This circumstance saved it from some of the politics that were beginning to fester regarding the sustenance of this orchestra within the Orchestral Association. Hillis was somewhat instrumental in dictating the way the Civic Orchestra would evolve. When Martinon asked her opinion of who the next conductor of that orchestra should be, she responded: "Gordon Peters [principal percussion of the CSO at the time] . . . and [Martinon] said, 'Why?' . . . I said, 'He's had conducting experience, and he's an *honest* man and there will be no political footballs and nonsense going on' . . . Gordon assumed the position [in 1966], a transition that began the evolution of the Civic Orchestra as we know it today—namely—a first-class training institution of its kind and those kids play very well . . . and, of course, we owe that to Martinon."[27] Margaret Hillis would be invited to join Peters as a resident conductor for the Civic Orchestra one year later.

Most important, Hillis believed that Martinon sustained the discipline that Reiner had established within the Orchestra and continued that level during his time with the CSO. Though Hillis believed Claudia Cassidy's harsh reviews and the mistreatment he had endured with CSO manager Seymour Raven accelerated Martinon's departure, Martinon reassured her that he left only a year or two before he ultimately had intended to depart. Martinon left by choice, having accomplished all he could in Chicago.

Margaret Hillis handled the "people side" of her CSO position with the same professionalism she applied to her musical preparation. What began as a musical appointment quickly evolved into a role she had mastered in her early years of developing the New York Concert Choir: the administrative requirements of the job. She knew how to manage people. Hillis became an integral part of the inner workings of the Chicago Symphony Orchestra, not because she sought it out but because she was good at it, stepping in when she was needed to keep the organization together during challenging times. Margaret Hillis's diplomatic and nuanced style of working with people allowed her and her Chorus to thrive despite the turbulent working environment of Orchestra Hall at that time. Not only was Hillis a vital force during the tenures of Fritz Reiner and Jean Martinon, but her presence helped influence positive changes within the Association during her early history with the Chicago Symphony Orchestra.

ENDNOTES

1. Margaret Hillis, interview by Norman Pellegrini (transcribed by Stanley G. Livengood), October 6, 1997, p. 27.
2. Ibid., p. 12.
3. Steven Hillyer, "Podium Interview with Margaret Hillis," November 20, 1982, p. 9 (transcription of the interview in the Margaret Hillis Collection, Rosenthal Archives of the Chicago Symphony Orchestra Association).
4. Ibid., p. 7.
5. Margaret Hillis, interview by Pellegrini, p. 27.
6. Andrew Patner, *A Portrait in Four Movements: The Chicago Symphony Under Barenboim, Boulez, Haitink, and Muti* (Chicago: University of Chicago Press, 2019).
7. Philip Hart, *Fritz Reiner: A Biography* (Evanston: Northwestern University Press, 1994), p. 168.
8. Patner, *A Portrait*, p. 14.

9. Hart, *Fritz Reiner*, p. 200.
10. Hillyer, "Podium Interview," p. 16.
11. Margaret Hillis, interview by Pellegrini, p. 27.
12. William Barry Furlong, *Season with Solti: A Year in the Life of the Chicago Symphony* (New York: Macmillan Publishing, 1974), p. 225.
13. Hillyer, "Podium Interview," p. 13.
14. Margaret Hillis, interview by Pellegrini, p. 28.
15. Jon Bentz, "Interview of Margaret Hillis Director Chicago Symphony Orchestra, September 19, 1989, Archives Committee, Oral History Project, 1992," p. 32 (Margaret Hillis Collection, Rosenthal Archives of the Chicago Symphony Orchestra Association).
16. Ibid., 50
17. Hillyer, "Podium Interview," p. 13.
18. Ibid., pp. 14–15.
19. Hart was the author of the Fritz Reiner biography, amongst other books, and was then the assistant manager of the CSO, where he remained for five years. He departed in 1961 to join the administrative staff at Juilliard. Hillis knew she could trust Hart.
20. Margaret Hillis, interview by Pellegrini, pp. 28–29.
21. Hillyer, "Podium Interview," p. 17.
22. Bentz, "Interview of Margaret Hillis," p. 50.
23. Hillyer, "Podium Interview," p. 17.
24. Bentz, "Interview of Margaret Hillis," pp. 32–33.
25. Ibid., p. 34.
26. Ibid., p. 34.
27. Ibid., p. 33.

CHAPTER 13
A TALE BETWEEN TWO CITIES: 1958–1968

Admittedly, Margaret's mindset upon accepting the Chicago Symphony Chorus position was to stay for only a few years. Her long-term goal was to return to New York, continuing her conducting career where it had its inception. However, as time passed, Margaret's plans would change. While Hillis's performance opportunities were expanding in Chicago, they were diminishing in New York. There would be other factors compelling Margaret to reconsider her return to New York. Circumstances of the next few years would help Hillis determine the direction her career would take.

By 1959, Margaret's conducting appearances in New York were greatly reduced. The American Concert Choir's Town Hall series, until now, had provided Hillis her most frequent conducting opportunities. Once Hillis decided to reduce her family's contributions to the series, there was a drastic reduction in her conducting appearances. Only one Town Hall concert was scheduled during the 1958–1959 season. Even with the recent support of the American Choral Foundation to help subsidize the Concert Choir, the expenses remained substantial, exceeding what her family could continue to provide. Without Hillis's family money to underwrite performances, the Concert Choir was slowly edging toward insolvency. "There was no way that I could really sustain the Town Hall series, because there was just so much difficulty in raising the funds for it."[1] Hillis continued marketing her Concert Choir for stand-alone performances, but without the Town Hall series, they were most often booked to serve as a chorus for opera companies in town. Hillis's New York work now centered on preparing her Concert Choir for others to conduct.

Even as outside invitations continued to be offered to the Concert Choir, money remained the problem. One important invitation Margaret was saddened to decline was a request from the State Department for the Concert Choir to represent the United States at the 1958 World's Fair in Brussels. The cost would have exceeded $30,000. Hillis realized she could not possibly provide nor raise the funds necessary for this prestigious event. It became evident to Hillis that she would need to move beyond the American Concert Choir if she planned to continue advancing her conducting career.

Under the circumstances, the timing of her Chicago Symphony Chorus appointment could not have been more auspicious. Not only did Hillis have the opportunity to prepare a symphony chorus for performances with one of the world's great orchestras, but she was also given the opportunity to conduct this orchestra and chorus in one concert series every season. Chicago was offering her greater conducting visibility than she was currently able to duplicate in New York. Even more desirable was that this conducting opportunity came without the added stress of fundraising or contributing personal funds, as was the case in New York. The Second City was becoming even more enticing as Margaret's conducting activity there increased. Hillis would soon begin to seriously consider making a change to her permanent residence. Would she finally return to her Midwestern roots? It would not take her long to decide.

By the summer of 1959, Hillis was no longer pursuing prospects for summer work in New York as she had done for her Concert Choir in recent years. She chose instead to cultivate guest conducting summer appearances for herself. Eliminating her Concert Choir's summer work also provided her additional time to learn the less familiar repertoire she was now encountering with the Chicago Symphony Chorus. Using her masterful planning, Hillis designed a schedule to accommodate the rehearsals and performances in Chicago along with her New York commitments with the American Concert Choir, the Union Theological Seminary Orchestra, the New York Chamber Soloists, and any additional guest conducting and speaking engagements she accepted. Commuting time back and forth between cities was carefully considered while also protecting time to continue working on her American Choral Foundation. In the most adroit manner, Hillis created a seamless plan to make everything coalesce.

There was no sacrificing quality in all the work Hillis was balancing, as was confirmed by numerous glowing reviews of performances in both cities. Even great artists, including Maria Callas, expressed their admiration for Hillis's pristine choral preparations. Hillis described an encounter when both she and Callas were involved in a Carnegie Hall production of Bellini's *Il Pirata* in January of 1959. Because Hillis was regularly commuting to Chicago during final rehearsals of the opera, she and Callas did not have the opportunity to meet one another until after one of the performances. Approaching Hillis, Callas remarked, "You prepared the chorus didn't you! It is exquisite and I thank you!"[2] Callas was, as Hillis saw it, a generous colleague. Despite Callas's reputation for being difficult, Hillis saw Callas as an artist who expressed appreciation to those who practiced the same high standards of excellence as her own. Hillis must have been honored by Callas's remarks, sharing them often in future interviews.

Despite her keen skill of balancing work in two cities, Margaret was occasionally challenged by her singers who questioned her ability to be equally attentive to all of them. In one such case, Hillis was preparing part of her American Concert Choir for Berlioz's *Les Troyens* with one opera company and was also preparing another part of her Concert Choir for *The Gypsy Baron* by Johann Strauss II with a different company. Aware of Margaret's multiple obligations, one of her tenors approached her, stating, "Now we'll find out where your loyalties lie . . . which chorus are you going to be with [for the upcoming performances]—to which Margaret answered, 'I am going to be in Chicago, doing a sectional rehearsal with the men of the Chicago Symphony Chorus.'"[3] Despite her involvement in multiple rehearsals and performances in two cities, Hillis's superb organizational skills and work ethic would be on full display as she managed to keep it all in balance.

Hillis's American Choral Foundation was gaining national exposure by the late 1950s. Funds were gradually increasing, enabling Hillis to use this Foundation in the way she had conceived it, to further the development of the choral profession in the United States. Hillis wisely kept the Foundation office in New York, taking full advantage of the many scholars and conductors who lived there and with whom she had cultivated professional relationships over the years. Objectives for the Foundation were formulated by 1958, further focusing on three divisions that had been originally established. The Services Division of the organization was now engaged in two important projects. The first project, undertaken in 1957, coincided with the establishment of the Chicago Symphony Chorus. There was, in fact, a collaboration between the Chicago Symphony Orchestra and the American Choral Foundation that supported the establishment of the Chicago Symphony Chorus. Hillis and her Foundation played a strategic role in engineering the creation of the ensemble with the Foundation providing significant financial contributions toward its formation.

The other important project, begun by the American Choral Foundation, was the establishment of the Association of Choral Conductors (ACC). By-laws for this new arm of the Foundation were completed in January 1959. Members would pay an annual fee of $15.00, enabling them to access a substantial loan library of music Hillis had acquired from American Concert Choir performances of recent years. By this point, Hillis had collected 12,000 scores of 300 works, with a minimum of forty copies per work that would be made available on loan to paid members.[4] There were perusal scores of contemporary works as well as lesser-known works of established composers, including Haydn, Brahms, Bartók, Hindemith, and others. Members would also receive the *American Choral Review*, a publication of the American Choral Foundation, as well as the informative *Research Memos*. In addition, the Services Division of the Foundation provided members direct access to experts in the choral field for advice and guidance. A detailed survey disseminated in 1958 by the Foundation to choral conductors throughout the country provided helpful feedback to guide the mission of the Association of Choral Conductors. Two hundred and seventy choruses provided input for the survey.[5] In 1959, the first meeting of the new ACC was held in Chicago.

CHICAGO: THE BUILDING BLOCKS FOR A SYMPHONIC CHORUS

Hillis's mission in the early years of the Chicago Symphony Chorus (CSC) was to build a quality chorus with the intention of eventually creating paid positions. This would only happen once she believed the Chorus was at a level where members would qualify for this status. She had been working with singers of a professional level in New York for a number of years now, and she had similar parameters in mind for singers who she would eventually pay in Chicago. Hillis reflected, "I simply was not ready to go professionally [in her first three years as director of the CSC], because they did not understand how to place a sixteenth note after a dotted eighth and [they] could not sub-divide"[6] (Picture 41).

Picture 41.
Margaret Hillis (chorus director), Fritz Reiner (music director), and Walter Hendl (associate conductor) with the Chicago Symphony Orchestra and Chorus in March 1959. (Oscar Chicago) (Rosenthal Archives of the Chicago Symphony Orchestra Association)

From the start, Hillis established discipline in her Chicago singers, starting first with her insistence on their timely arrival to rehearsals, as previously described. She ran a tight ship with carefully planned rehearsals that instilled musical discipline throughout the learning process of each concert series. She knew how to build a choir from the ground up, having done so for many years, starting with her Metropolitan Youth Chorale in New York. The level of her Chicago singers required her to continually drill discipline of rhythm, intonation, vocal quality, color, style, and diction. Her pedagogical skills had been well developed by this point, but she now needed to adjust them for a much larger ensemble. Though new challenges arose with a larger choir than she was used to shaping, she would not forfeit nor compromise the precision she expected of any chorus, no matter the size. She was quickly becoming an expert of *symphonic* choral pedagogy as she found ways to modify her rehearsal techniques for her massive symphonic group.

Hillis started the building process by first setting up an infrastructure to help her manage the large number of singers in the CSC. Hillis instilled a rigorous selection process for new members but soon required annual re-auditions for returning members. Through the audition process, Hillis would record each singer's results on a carefully detailed audition form, which would remain on file and would be referenced when a singer returned each year for their re-audition. Attendance records and any other important information were also kept in the files. There was no guarantee of being readmitted into the Chorus. Hillis would monitor each singer's vocal progress and attendance records, providing them individual feedback and holding each singer personally accountable for their contributions to the ensemble.

After three years of an all-volunteer chorus, Hillis recognized that the skill level had grown to such a point that she was ready to professionalize the ensemble. She started this gradually by first offering sixteen paid positions for a core of singers who qualified for this status. One of the ways she would select this paid core was based upon their musicianship, which would be evaluated during the audition. If a singer requested consideration for a paid position, they were given a more challenging excerpt to read. If a singer passed the rigorous audition, they were then required to take a written music theory and music history exam.

Audition results were carefully evaluated, after which Hillis would rate singers using an intricate ranking system she had formulated. Each singer was assigned a number, which would be used for seating charts and for attendance purposes. Each section (soprano, alto, tenor, and bass) was numbered specifically, with sopranos in the 100s, altos in the 200s, tenors in the 300s, and basses in the 400s. Therefore, Singer 101 would be her top soprano singer, and so on. In later years, when she increased the number of paid singers, non-paid singers were ranked with the number 1 added to their number, so that the top volunteer soprano would be 1101, and so forth. Second sopranos, altos, tenors, and basses were indicated using the number 50, making the top paid second soprano 151 (or 1150 if they were a non-paid soprano). A singer's number would change from year to year based upon changing personnel. A singer's yearly improvement or decline, as evaluated in the annual audition, also impacted their numerical ranking. The first rehearsal of each season was highly anticipated, as singers obtained their new number for the year. Hillis would consult this number system when selecting singers for smaller elite choruses. She would also refer to her ranking system when selecting singers for understudy roles.

One singer who recalled Hillis's ranking process was the internationally renowned opera baritone Sherrill Milnes. Milnes was the first of a number of Chicago Symphony

Chorus alumni to achieve a successful opera career after leaving the Chorus. Milnes credited Margaret Hillis for playing an important role in preparing him for his career by her insistence upon accuracy and precision and through the invaluable experiences the Chorus provided. Hillis first met Milnes while he was completing a graduate degree in music education at Drake University. She was a guest conductor for Drake's high school summer music camp in July 1957 when she met Milnes, who was in his last summer of coursework. As Milnes explained it, Hillis was given occasion to hear him sing while she was on the campus.[7] Recognizing his potential, Hillis encouraged Milnes to audition for the Chorus when he returned to Chicago at the end of that summer. Flattered by the invitation, Milnes auditioned and was accepted for the CSC's second season of 1958–1959. Milnes spoke respectfully of Hillis's highly organized and disciplined way of working, including her use of the numerical ranking system. He recalled receiving the coveted number 401, her top singer in the bass section. Milnes admired the cleverness of this system, which allowed Hillis to select preferred singers for special assignments without calling out names in the middle of a rehearsal. As Milnes saw it, the use of numbers instead of names mitigated any resentment that could build among members.

Milnes recalled, with admiration, Hillis's ability to technically discipline her singers, something he had never before encountered to that degree in a chorus. He described rhythm as Hillis's primary focus when working with the Chorus, explaining that this was particularly necessary with Fritz Reiner's conducting, because Reiner would rarely support the Chorus with important cues the Chorus needed, such as cut-offs and entrances. The Chorus was so well-prepared from a rhythmic standpoint that they could manage independently, not reliant upon Reiner's gestures. They were trained to count in much the same way as an instrumentalist is trained. Milnes had a significant instrumental background, which made him all the more appreciative of the Chorus's rhythmic accuracy. "We were dead on. She was so precise about rhythm that there was never a question about the Chorus's accuracy."[8]

After Milnes's first season with the Chorus, she encouraged him to join her in 1959 at the Santa Fe Opera, where she was on the staff as a conductor and principally charged with providing an apprentice group. Milnes and other select CSC members participated in this, the third Santa Fe Opera summer season, where they all sang in the opera choruses and performed in Benjamin Britten's cantata, *Saint Nicholas*, conducted by Hillis. Milnes recalled performing on several sacred music choral concerts she directed there as well. He remembered participating in an opera Hillis conducted that summer, Marc Blitzstein's *Regina*, the only staged opera she ever conducted in her career. Hillis's work both in this difficult experimental opera she was assigned to conduct and in all the choral work she prepared that summer elicited favorable reviews. For Sherrill Milnes, this opportunity provided him important exposure early in his career, in which he too received positive reviews for his minor role in Puccini's *Madama Butterfly*.[9]

Hillis provided Milnes numerous solo opportunities during his four years with the Chorus; he often appeared as a soloist with the Chicago Symphony Orchestra when she was conducting the concerts. She also chose Milnes to join her when she guest conducted in other cities and needed a baritone soloist. Even after Milnes's career blossomed and he was no longer a regular member of the Chorus, Hillis encouraged him to return to sing in the CSC any time he was in Chicago. Her only requirement was that he attend the last two preparatory weeks before a concert series. Milnes enjoyed doing this whenever he was available, emphasizing his love for choral singing and his enjoyment of working with Margaret.

Milnes marveled at Hillis's conducting career, remarking how much more difficult it was for a female to achieve all she had accomplished during that time in the music field. He described situations when he spoke of Margaret Hillis to others in the music world. When someone did not recognize her name, he would refer to her as "the female Robert Shaw," which he said was a frustration to him, having to qualify Hillis's work by using a male figure like Shaw to distinguish her value.[10] He firmly believed she should have been recognized on her own merit for her incredible contributions to the choral art. Milnes described Hillis as "a great musician who taught me the deeper truths of music making and an incomparable education in symphonic literature."[11] He enjoyed a long and successful opera career and returned to Chicago many times over the years to solo with the Chicago Symphony Orchestra and Chorus.

As each year progressed in the first decade of the Chicago Symphony Chorus, Hillis would provide additional resources for her singers, including class offerings in musicianship, International Phonetic Alphabet, score analysis, and others to increase the knowledge of singers who may not have had formal music training. These classes were voluntary, taking place one hour before rehearsals would begin. Hillis also designed a home study chart for every work the Chorus prepared, providing singers information about the difficulty of each movement within a piece and listing movements covered in every rehearsal leading up to the performances. In this way, singers were encouraged to work on their music independently between rehearsals, either to review previous material or to prepare for what would be covered in the next rehearsal.

Hillis also instituted sectional rehearsals, initially scheduled on Tuesday nights but moved to select weekends in later years, with sopranos meeting on Saturdays from 2:00–5:00 p.m. and altos from 4:00–7:00 p.m., allowing a one-hour overlap, 4:00–5:00 p.m., for combined work with both sections. Tenors and basses would have the same schedule on Sundays. Margaret conducted those sectionals, which for her amounted to ten hours of rehearsal on a given weekend. It was a grueling schedule to maintain, but it reaped great rewards because she was able to focus on each section exclusively without other sections sitting idle. Hillis would provide written feedback to the ensemble on a regular basis, sending them periodic "Dear People" letters, using the same salutation as did her mentor, Robert Shaw, with his Collegiate Chorale. Hillis used these messages to provide praise, concern, suggestions, and encouragement.

All these measures of discipline, training, and communication provided the means for continual growth within the Chicago Symphony Chorus. As Hillis observed years later, "The chorus was not an overnight success."[12] As a matter of fact, subscription ticket holders would often turn back their tickets during the earliest years of the Chorus. But as Hillis explained, the Chorus gradually came into its own without her noticing.[13] As the Chicago Symphony Chorus's reputation grew, so too did Hillis's reputation as an expert in the field of symphonic choral conducting. With each passing year, Hillis would increase the number of paid singers in her ensemble, attracting well-trained singers in ever-increasing numbers, thereby improving the quality of the ensemble all the more.

The Chorus was improving, not only through Hillis's carefully crafted rehearsals but also as a result of the exciting projects in which they participated. As early as in their second season, Reiner conducted the Chorus's first recording with the Orchestra in Prokofiev's *Alexander Nevsky*. By the fourth season, the Chorus would make their second recording with Reiner, Beethoven's Symphony No. 9, which included contralto Florence Kopleff as a soloist, a good friend of Margaret from their work together in New York where they first met in the Collegiate

Chorale. The Chorus would soon begin their long-standing relationship with the Ravinia Festival in the summer of season three, performing Mahler's Symphony No. 2 on July 9, 1960, with Walter Hendl, CSO associate conductor and Ravinia's artistic director. All these added experiences contributed to the steady growth of the Chicago Symphony Chorus.

Hillis particularly enjoyed conducting the Chicago Symphony Orchestra and Chorus in at least one concert series per season. Though most of her appearances were non-subscription concerts, she did appear occasionally on the subscription series, making her not only the first woman to conduct the Chicago Symphony Orchestra in concert but also the first woman to conduct on a subscription series. Hillis was often chosen to conduct on the CSO Popular Concert series, which gave her the opportunity to perform more recognizable symphonic choral works that she had often prepared as a chorus master but rarely had the chance to conduct in performance. Even for those concerts, her choices were subject to approval by the music director. "I would not ask for a *Missa solemnis* or Brahms Requiem or something of that kind. I do those pieces elsewhere . . . repertory of that kind I do when I'm a guest conductor away from Chicago or when I conduct my own orchestra."[14]

Conducting the Chicago Symphony Orchestra and Chorus was a spectacular opportunity for her no matter the repertoire limitations. This experience truly challenged Hillis. Conducting symphonic choral works with a professional symphony orchestra was beyond anything Hillis had experienced in her New York days. However, these performances would sometimes reveal her weaknesses. The criticisms, occasionally appearing in reviews, were similar to those she had encountered in New York concerning her lack of expressivity, no doubt magnified by the added dimension of working with a professional symphony orchestra. Yet there was always respect and admiration conveyed for what she was accomplishing as a woman in this very singular role.

Kenosha and Kokomo

There was no question that Hillis had the potential to grow as an orchestra conductor; however, the fact remained that she lacked the formal training of other orchestra conductors invited to conduct the Chicago Symphony Orchestra. Having little consistent rehearsal time with a large symphony orchestra and with no conducting mentor, Margaret needed the opportunity to develop orchestral techniques in the same way she had developed her choral techniques. She needed regular podium time with a symphony orchestra to prepare her for the annual concerts she was conducting with the CSO. Up to this point, she had only worked with her small amateur Union Theological Seminary Orchestra and periodically with professional instrumentalists of her slightly larger American Concert Orchestra, a pick-up ensemble of hired players with whom she rehearsed briefly in final dress rehearsals for her Town Hall concert series. Both orchestras were nothing like what she was encountering with the CSO. It would be important for her to find a symphony orchestra of her own to provide her the experience she needed to gain a greater sense of confidence when conducting a world-class orchestra.

The opportunity presented itself in the form of an invitation to become the music director of the Kenosha Symphony Orchestra. Kenosha, Wisconsin, located ninety minutes north of Chicago, would be rather easy to get to from her Illinois residence. Hillis, now in her fifth season with the Chicago Symphony Chorus, embraced the opportunity to work with this Wisconsin orchestra beginning in the fall of 1961. She was warmly welcomed to this new position, and she made herself regularly available for community outreach, including speaking engagements at women's club luncheons and other forms of community engagement on behalf of the Kenosha Symphonic Society (Picture 42).

Picture 42.
Margaret Hillis and the Kenosha Symphony Orchestra. (Howard County Historical Society)

One of the advantages Hillis was able to enjoy in leading her own orchestra was the opportunity to perform repertoire with the Kenosha Symphony Orchestra that she would then take to bigger venues in New York and Chicago. An example of this occurred in December 1962, as Hillis was slated to conduct the Symphony of the Air at New York's Lincoln Center for the Great Names in Music concert series. Hillis cleverly programmed Weber's Overture to *Der Freischütz*, Stravinsky's *Circus Polka*, and Hindemith's symphony *Mathis der Maler* on two Kenosha Symphony Orchestra programs (October 17 and December 5) before making her December 12 conducting debut with those pieces at Lincoln Center. Having the opportunity to first conduct these orchestral pieces in Kenosha before doing them at Lincoln Center provided Hillis a greater sense of security. Hillis had engaged in a similar practice with her Concert Choir in New York and would cleverly continue this again with her Kenosha orchestra. The Kenosha Symphony performed six concert programs in a typical season. Occasionally, Hillis was able to bring major artists from New York to perform in Kenosha for her concerts. One example was a guest appearance Hillis arranged with the popular opera singer Shirley Verrett, who Margaret engaged to perform Brahms's *Alto Rhapsody*. Hillis's connections with such New York artists provided Kenosha's audiences these special performances.

Hillis continued a tradition she had established in recent years, bringing her ensembles to Kokomo whenever possible. Her family would assist with funding these appearances, proudly showcasing their daughter for the hometown crowd. In May 1966, Hillis arranged for her Kenosha Symphony Orchestra to perform Honegger's *King David* in Kokomo. The performance was a major draw in town. The Haven Auditorium of Indiana University's Kokomo campus had an unprecedented turnout for the event, historic in this auditorium's history, with nine hundred people in attendance, flanked by two hundred others who stood or sat on the floor for the performance.[15] The Kenosha Symphony Orchestra was joined by a chorus from Kokomo, which may have contributed to the spectacular turnout. This chorus became a contributing factor in Margaret's mission for stimulating the arts community of Kokomo (Picture 43).

Picture 43.

Margaret Hillis conducting a chorus in Kokomo, Indiana, in preparation for Honegger's *King David* with the Kenosha Symphony Orchestra in May 1966. (Howard County Historical Society)

Hillis remained with the Kenosha Symphony Orchestra until 1968. As Hillis described in an interview for the book *Conductors in Conversation*, "At that time, Kenosha was entirely American Motors oriented, which gave it a Depression mentality. I just could not get it moving. It's changed since American Motors moved out of there. . . . It's a better orchestra now."[16]

As Hillis increased her time in the Midwest with duties in Chicago and Kenosha, she would make more frequent visits to Kokomo. Her father, Glen Hillis, had retired in 1954 and was beginning to experience health issues by the time Margaret was hired by the Chicago Symphony Orchestra. This circumstance made her visits home more important to her than ever before. With Hillis returning to Kokomo more frequently, she began to entertain new ideas for bringing performances to her hometown. Bernice Hillis, Margaret's mother, was a helpful agent in providing support for whatever ideas her daughter would conjure up. As an active member of Kokomo's federated music club, the Morning Musicale, Bernice and other club members would promote Margaret's guest appearances when she performed in town. Kathryn Connor, another member of Morning Musicale and music director of Hillis's family church, the First Presbyterian

Church of Kokomo, would also play an important role in supporting Margaret's efforts to bring her music back to Kokomo.

Kathryn, a fine vocalist, was once offered a contract with Columbia Management in New York to establish herself as a solo performing artist, but she chose instead to live in Kokomo with her husband, Ted, whom she had met when they were both studying music in college. In a June 2012 interview with Kathryn and Ted Connor, Kathryn shared that she preferred to raise her three children with her husband in their Kokomo home, making music the way she wanted to make it rather than "having to answer to people she did not want to answer to," as she put it.[17] Kathryn explained that she knew about Margaret Hillis's career and asked Bernice if she thought Margaret might consider conducting a choir for the dedication ceremony of the new church building in town.[18] Margaret agreed to come for this event, and Kathryn spent the next year working with her church choir on "How Lovely is Thy Dwelling Place" from Brahms's *A German Requiem*. When Hillis conducted this choir for the dedication ceremony, she was impressed with the quality of Kathryn's preparatory work, encouraging her to consider starting a community chorus in Kokomo. Hillis promised that if Kathryn would organize and prepare the choir, Margaret would direct them in concerts. Kathryn, familiar with other church choir directors in town and knowing many of the singers in the area, was able to attract a respectable number of volunteers for this new venture. Her own excellent training as a singer and as an experienced choir director resulted in a well-prepared chorus for Margaret to conduct.

Thus began the Community Chorus of Kokomo, which Margaret would actively support beginning in the late 1950s. Kathryn prepared the chorus with Margaret's specific instructions provided to her in a marked score that she dutifully followed. Recalling the excitement of her choristers every time Margaret would rehearse the Kokomo chorus, Kathryn explained that these visits occurred not only in the final rehearsals before a concert but also during Hillis's occasional weekend visits to town. Hillis would come to a rehearsal at the early stage of their preparation to instill the important performance details she expected of them. The Community Chorus combined with the Kokomo Symphony Orchestra for one symphonic choral performance per season. Kathryn prepared the chorus and sometimes stepped in to rehearse the orchestra as well. Hillis and Kathryn would also collaborate on smaller choral projects that would surface for various other occasions during the year.

Hillis brought in her finest Chicago Symphony Chorus singers as featured soloists for the Kokomo performances; this was one of many ways Hillis supported her CSC singers with budding solo careers. Sherill Milnes was among those soloists Hillis brought to Kokomo. Kathryn Connor recalled with great fondness being part of a solo ensemble with Milnes in Mendelsohn's *Elijah*, performed in May 1961. It was one of many times Kathryn was selected by Hillis to solo while also serving as chorus master for the performance. Kathryn and Ted admired the way Hillis was able to transform the sound of the amateur chorus into a refined ensemble. As Kathryn explained it, Hillis knew the voice and no matter the level of the singers, she made them into a polished ensemble. Kathryn's work of preparing the notes and rhythms was the blueprint upon which Hillis would put her artistic stamp. Kokomo choristers, well aware of Hillis's stature in the music world, were always eager to do their best for her. It is no wonder that Ted and Kathryn described Margaret as always being relaxed when she was in Kokomo. She enjoyed working with the singers and the orchestra and was truly approachable and down-to-earth in this environment. She enjoyed socializing with friends and family after a concert with a drink in one hand and a cigarette in the other.[19] In Kokomo, she could drop her guard in a way she could do in no other place. It was different in Kokomo; she was home.

Hillis was a regular guest conductor in Kokomo until the late 1970s when her schedule became too busy for annual performances, though she would return thereafter any time her schedule permitted. Kathryn recalled preparing the community chorus for Margaret's performances of Vivaldi's *Gloria*, Fauré's Requiem, Mendelssohn's *Elijah*, and Brahms's *A German Requiem,* among others. Kokomo's community chorus, formed with Hillis's encouragement and Kathryn Connor's able guidance, became a staple of the town's cultural community. Kathryn and Ted Connor eventually retired to Arizona, with Kathryn's final concert taking place in 1994, but the ensemble remained active even after her departure. Hillis's ingenuity and vision for performance opportunities in Kokomo resulted in a treasured gift she bequeathed to her beloved hometown.

Seasons of Change

By 1962, it was becoming clear to Margaret that her future was in Chicago. Her work was becoming plentiful in the Midwest. By now, instead of commuting to Chicago, she claimed to have settled down in Chicago and was commuting to New York. She kept a presence in New York, maintaining two apartments there. One apartment was for her to stay in when she was in town (sublet to Tom Pyle). The other served as an office for her staff, the music library, and storage for research bulletins of the American Choral Foundation. By 1960, she had relinquished her conducting duties with the New York Chamber Soloists and had ended her teaching/conducting work at the Union Theological Seminary. She would continue with the American Opera Society until the late 1960s, after which the American Concert Choir was disbanded. By 1961, Hillis had acquired a teaching position in Chicago at the Chicago Musical College (now Roosevelt University's Chicago College of Performing Arts) as director of choral activities, a job she held for one year. She also began a relationship with Elizabeth Burton, who had joined the Chicago Symphony Chorus in the second season and would become Hillis's personal secretary and longtime partner (Picture 44). With all these changes, Hillis found herself commuting to New York less and less. Her decision was made in 1962. Chicago became her new home.

Picture 44.
Margaret Hillis with Elizabeth Burton at the twentieth anniversary reception of the Chicago Symphony Chorus, May 19, 1977. (Terry's Photography)

In 1965, Hillis's world was abruptly altered with the passing of her father, Glen Hillis, who died unexpectedly on October 19. Glen Hillis had been the stabilizing force when it came to Margaret's finances, overseeing the expenditures that supported her career. As the president of Margaret's American Choral Foundation (ACF), he carefully managed the organization's bottom line, allowing Margaret to focus on the artistic side. With Glen's passing, the Foundation's financial state began to unravel. The organization had operated at close margins in the past, but without Glen's careful scrutiny the Foundation became a challenge to maintain.

One month prior to Glen Hillis's passing, Margaret began to acquaint herself with the financial arrangements of the ACF for the first time. In a message dated September 19, 1965, to Jacob ("Jack") Schwartz, a lawyer by trade and comptroller for the ACF, she stated, "For about a year, I have become increasingly uncomfortable concerning my lack of a clear grasp of exactly what is happening [with the finances of the Foundation] so I decided the only thing I can do is ask questions."[20] Hillis was perfectly capable of understanding the finances of the ACF, which she demonstrated repeatedly in years to come, stepping in to keep the Foundation afloat. However, these matters and all her financial transactions, until now, had been handled by her father, which was a typical arrangement for women prior to the mid-1970s. Back in the day, women could not have their own bank accounts or charge cards, nor could they apply for loans without the signature of the husband or, if single, as in Margaret's case, the father. Margaret never needed to understand finances. They were always managed for her by others.

Margaret admitted to Jack Schwartz that her sense of urgency on fiscal matters had increased recently due to the surgery her father had undergone a month before to remove his right eye. His deteriorating health prevented him from taking part in any ACF activities.[21] She was therefore turning to Schwartz to explain how everything worked. Up until this time, all of Hillis's earnings and investments were deposited into the Foundation, upon which she would draw funds to cover her living expenses, including apartments in New York and Chicago. Hillis was well aware that her expenses in Chicago had increased recently after moving from a North Sheridan Road apartment to one on East Chestnut Street, a very expensive part of town. Hillis was also aware that the Foundation was not bringing in as much money as was anticipated through memberships of the Association for Choral Conductors. These circumstances must have contributed to her concern about access to funds, heretofore approved by her father. Once he would pass away, that arrangement could be altered. Hillis requested a meeting with Jack Schwartz, which he enthusiastically welcomed.²² He was less enthusiastic, however, with another idea Hillis shared. She informed him, "One of the results of my intensive and careful examination of the American Choral Foundation during the course of this fall has been the realization that a development director, who is acquainted with the musical field and who is creative, is mandatory if the ACF is to survive."²³

Determined to bring someone else onto the ACF staff in order to increase the membership of the ACC, she had just the person in mind. Sheldon Soffer, a colorful character she had recently befriended, seemed the ideal person to bring the ACC to higher visibility.²⁴ The two had met through mutual acquaintances, one of whom was composer Marvin David Levy. Hillis had conducted one of Levy's compositions on a recent Concert Choir program. Levy and Soffer were roommates. Hillis also gained familiarity with Soffer during her collaborations with the Little Opera Society, where Soffer served as the associate manager. Through these mutual associations, a good friendship was formed.

Soffer started in the music business as a conductor but soon realized he would be more successful as a manager, promoter, and artist representative. He claimed that it was Hillis who gave him his first opportunity to represent her and her Foundation, claiming that he won her confidence when she saw him in action through the opera company he managed.²⁵ Margaret became the first client of what would eventually become the Sheldon Soffer Management Agency in New York. Hillis determined that with Soffer's managerial experience and with his understanding of the music business, he could be a good fit for the position she was creating for the Foundation. Anxious to get him started, Hillis included Soffer in the meeting with Jack Schwartz regarding the inner workings of the Foundation. Schwartz's reaction to Hillis's invited guest was less than enthusiastic. "At this moment, I do not understand where Sheldon fits into the picture, but if you desire a meeting with Sheldon, then let me know so I can make the necessary arrangements."²⁶

Sheldon proved to be a valuable addition to the Foundation, in no small part through many important people he introduced to Margaret. The most valuable connection Hillis made through Soffer was that of Ernest ("Pick") and Rose ("Red") Heller, well-known philanthropists of the New York arts scene. The Hellers had known Soffer for a number of years and they treated him as part of their family.

Soffer first met Mrs. Heller while he was the music director of an off-Broadway opera company called Lemonade Opera. "Red" (Mrs. Heller) was on the board of the opera company. "Pick" (Mr. Heller) had made his fortune in the jewelry business, specifically in pearls. He and his wife had no children, devoting a great deal of their time and money to supporting art, music, and theater. The Hellers would become very close to Margaret, avid champions of her work, providing generous financial support and counsel to her Foundation. They treated Margaret as though she was their daughter, proudly attending her performances throughout the country and celebrating her conducting achievements. Margaret was even provided a room in their luxurious apartment any time she was in New York, which she particularly appreciated once she relinquished her New York residence. The Hellers would prove to be incredibly supportive of Margaret, helping her navigate the turbulent times ahead for the Foundation.

One month after the initial written exchange between Margaret and Jack Schwartz, Glen Hillis died. In early November 1965, Schwartz and Hillis finally met in New York, where Hillis quickly got up to speed on the financial problems arising within the Foundation. After that meeting, Hillis conferred with Soffer and the Hellers, and they came to agree that Schwartz had been ineffective in his role with the ACF. In a letter to "Pick" Heller, Hillis conveyed, "As you have already seen, Jack Schwartz did not act as a comptroller but only as a kind of clerk to pay bills."[27] By the end of March, Schwartz was sending out alarms about the financial state of the Foundation. He claimed the organization had been self-sufficient as of January 1965, but due to Hillis's mounting expenditures, the Foundation was now "at a crisis situation."[28] Hillis sent a pointed response, detailing all of the funding that she had personally contributed to the Foundation and that in fact she could be much wealthier at this stage of her career had she not been so devoted to the financial well-being of the organization.[29]

Hillis approached the Foundation crisis in the same meticulous manner as she had all her other endeavors, giving the matter careful thought and strategic planning and then consulting with those who could advise her properly. By January of 1966, she began to take action. First, Soffer was brought into the organization officially and was given clear instructions to begin downsizing the Foundation. His first directive was to find options for storing the massive music collection Hillis had accumulated. He was also instructed to find alternative options for the printing and distribution of the *American Choral Review* and *Research Memorandum* series.[30]

Unbeknownst to Jacob Schwartz, Hillis had secured a new lawyer, John Taylor III, who would guide her. She appointed Ernest Heller as treasurer for the Foundation, and Rose Heller was appointed the Foundation's first vice-president. Hillis also sought her brother Bud Hillis's counsel, but he was preparing to make a run for the state congressional seat in March 1966 and declined her offer to take over their father's role of overseeing the Foundation.[31] Bud would actually be listed on future ACF letterhead as the co-president of the organization, alongside Margaret, helping her monitor expenditures through the rest of her life, though she now had others to manage the Foundation budget, replacing the role her father played as Foundation president.[32]

By December of 1966, Hillis had completed the reorganization of the American Choral Foundation. She requested Schwartz's resignation, effective May 1, 1966.[33] Sheldon arranged for the *American Choral Review* to now be published by the University of Missouri Press and for the Foundation's music to be relocated to the Free Library of Philadelphia.[34] Through significant financial contributions of Margaret and the Hellers and with Sheldon's assistance in rearranging the Foundation holdings, Hillis was able to "right the ship." Sheldon claimed Hillis was grateful to him for watching over the finances of the organization.[35] He remained with the American Choral Foundation until 1984. The Foundation would continue to pose financial challenges for Hillis, but for now, things were under control and Hillis could return to focusing on her art, leaving the finances and management of the organization to Sheldon Soffer.

A New Decade for Hillis and the Chicago Symphony Chorus

Led by two music directors in their first decade, the Chicago Symphony Chorus treasured the champion they had in Fritz Reiner, whose confidence they had earned by fulfilling his vision of a chorus worthy of performing with his Chicago Symphony Orchestra. In their second music director, the Chorus found in Jean Martinon a personality very different in style and manner than that of Reiner's, whose they much preferred. However, despite their resistance to Martinon, they continued to grow in both tone quality and musicianship. Such growth could be attributable, in part, to Martinon's challenging repertoire choices, some of which the Chorus did not enjoy. Nonetheless, Martinon's selections cultivated an increased level of musical discipline. As he became more acquainted with the Chorus, Martinon gradually increased his programming of choral works in a concert season. This would further impact their workload, already growing through their increased collaborations with the CSO at Ravinia's summer festival. Both venues gave the Chorus greater visibility, establishing them as an integral part of the Chicago music scene. The ultimate stamp of Martinon's approval came on November 12, 1967, when the Chorus joined the Orchestra for their first appearance at Carnegie Hall. The performance was met with great enthusiasm, as demonstrated in Donal Henahan's *New York Times* review of the concert, stating, "Margaret Hillis's delicately tuned professional chorus, which was making its first New York appearance . . . presented the first performance here of Hans Werner Henze's *Muses of Sicily* as well as orchestral and vocal fragments from Ravel's two *Daphnis and Chloe* suites."[36]

The Chorus had a very different relationship with Martinon than they had enjoyed with Reiner. As longtime member Jane Scharf shared in an interview, [Martinon's] "different accent seemed exotic and he didn't have the timing down in rehearsals with both the Chorus and Orchestra. The Chorus would often sit for extended periods while Martinon worked exclusively with the Orchestra."[37] Despite the Chorus's misgivings with Martinon, they were challenged by his singular repertoire choices. As with Reiner, Martinon proved to be an equally enthusiastic supporter of Hillis, continuing to endorse her annual conducting appearances with the CSO, going even further with her appointment as his assistant music director. Though Martinon in many ways was equal to Reiner in his support of the Chorus and Hillis, Martinon's departure after five years was less traumatic than Reiner's. The person to follow would usher in a new age for the Chicago Symphony Orchestra and Chorus.

By the end of the Chicago Symphony Chorus's tenth season, 1966–1967, so many things had changed for Margaret Hillis. In that time, she made the monumental decision to move her home base from New York to Chicago, closer to the substantial work she was acquiring in the Midwest. During these early years in Chicago, her Chorus was transforming into an elite ensemble. Given her additional roles with the Chicago Symphony Orchestra, both on the podium and behind the scenes, she was fast becoming an indispensable part of the Orchestral Association. Other factors contributed to Hillis's move to Chicago, including her relationship with partner Elizabeth Burton and her growing desire to be closer to family, particularly as her parents were aging. Margaret was being drawn to this Second City in many unexpected ways.

These first ten years of the Chicago Symphony Chorus were a time of tremendous growth. Out of one hundred volunteer choristers in 1957 emerged a finely chiseled ensemble of over 130 voices, many professionally trained. This Chorus would now set the standard for symphony choruses as more were gradually emerging throughout the country. By 1967, the Chorus had participated in four recordings, providing them increased exposure. Their appearances at Carnegie Hall and at the Ravinia Festival would also begin during this first decade in their history. Two music directors, numerous guest conductors, challenging concert programs, and new venues all contributed to the growth and polish of the Chicago Symphony Chorus, now coming into its own.

Hillis's intention to create an ensemble as professional as any fine symphony orchestra kept her constantly driven. She was as demanding of herself as she was of her singers, always seeking innovative ways to improve upon her rehearsal and conducting methods. Though she continually strove to expand her conducting career, always top-of-her-mind was dedication to the choral profession. Throughout these ten years, Hillis continually devoted herself to her singers and to her Choral Foundation. She would seek new ways to "spread the gospel," inspiring choral directors of all levels to join her in refining their craft. The decade ahead would bring Hillis and her chorus to even greater heights. Soon, two giants would align in what would become a golden era for the Chicago Symphony Orchestra and Chorus.

ENDNOTES

1. Jon Bentz, "Interview of Margaret Hillis Director Chicago Symphony Orchestra, September 19, 1989, Archives Committee, Oral History Project, 1992," p. 6 (Margaret Hillis Collection, Rosenthal Archives of the Chicago Symphony Orchestra Association).
2. Ibid., p. 7.
3. Ibid., p. 9.
4. Typewritten report about the Association of Choral Conductors. No date nor author (Margaret Hillis Collection, Rosenthal Archives of the Chicago Symphony Orchestra Association, Box 9).
5. Milton Goldin, "The Foundation's Survey of Choral Groups," *Bulletin of the American Concert Choir and Choral Foundation, Inc.* 1, no. 1 (June 1958): p. 1.
6. Bentz, "Interview of Margaret Hillis," p. 12.
7. Interview with Sherrill Milnes, May 26, 2020.
8. Ibid.
9. Eleanor Scott, *The First Twenty Years of the Santa Fe Opera* (Santa Fe: Sunstone Press, 1976), p. 22.
10. Milnes interview.
11. Jane Weiner Lepage, *Women Composers, Conductors, and Musicians of the Twentieth Century: Selected Biographies* (N.J. and London: The Scarecrow Press, 1980), p. 78.
12. Margaret Carroll, "Hillis's Artful Compromise for a Passion," *Chicago Tribune*, April 11, 1976, ProQuest Historical Newspapers, p. D3.

13. Ibid.

14. Steven Hillyer, "Podium Interview with Margaret Hillis," November 20, 1982, p. 25 (transcription of the interview in the Margaret Hillis Collection, Rosenthal Archives of the Chicago Symphony Orchestra Association).

15. Proof of an article submitted to the *Kokomo Tribune* with edits by Helen Lily; from the Helen Lily Estate collection of the Howard County Museum of Kokomo, Indiana.

16. Jeannine Wagar, *Conductors in Conversation: Fifteen Contemporary Conductors Discuss Their Lives and Profession* (Boston: G.K. Hall & Co., 1991), pp. 111–112.

17. Interview with Kathryn and Ted Connor, June 4, 2012.

18. Ibid.

19. Ibid.

20. Letter from Margaret Hillis to Jacob Schwartz, September 19, 1965 (Margaret Hillis Collection, Rosenthal Archives of the Chicago Symphony Orchestra Association, Box 9).

21. Ibid.

22. Letter from Jacob Schwartz to Margaret Hillis, September 23, 1965 (Margaret Hillis Collection, Rosenthal Archives of the Chicago Symphony Orchestra Association, Box 9).

23. Letter from Margaret Hillis to Jacob Schwartz, January 5, 1966 (Margaret Hillis Collection, Rosenthal Archives of the Chicago Symphony Orchestra Association, Box 9).

24. Interview with Sheldon Soffer, August 10, 2019.

25. Ibid.

26. Letter from Jacob Schwartz to Margaret Hillis, September 23, 1965 (Margaret Hillis Collection, Rosenthal Archives of the Chicago Symphony Orchestra Association, Box 9).

27. Letter from Margaret Hillis to Ernest Heller, May 6, 1966 (Margaret Hillis Collection, Rosenthal Archives of the Chicago Symphony Orchestra Association, Box 9).

28. Letter from Jacob Schwartz to Margaret Hillis, March 29, 1966 (Margaret Hillis Collection, Rosenthal Archives of the Chicago Symphony Orchestra Association, Box 9).

29. Letter to Jacob (Jack) Schwartz, April 20, 1966 (Margaret Hillis Collection, Rosenthal Archives of the Chicago Symphony Orchestra Association, Box 9).

30. Letter from Margaret Hillis to Sheldon Soffer, January 5, 1966 (Margaret Hillis Collection, Rosenthal Archives of the Chicago Symphony Orchestra Association, Box 9).

31. Letter from Elwood Hillis to Margaret Hillis, March 14, 1966, (Margaret Hillis Collection, Rosenthal Archives of the Chicago Symphony Orchestra Association, Box 9).

32. Letter from Dave Volner to Sheldon Soffer, April 29, 1966 (Margaret Hillis Collection, Rosenthal Archives of the Chicago Symphony Orchestra Association, Box 9).

33. Letter from Margaret Hillis to Jacob Schwartz, April 20, 1966 (Margaret Hillis Collection, Rosenthal Archives of the Chicago Symphony Orchestra Association, Box 9).

34. Letter dated December 15, 1966, from Sheldon Soffer to Members of the Association of Choral Conductors on American Choral Foundation stationery, announcing the reorganization of the Foundation (Margaret Hillis Collection, Rosenthal Archives of the Chicago Symphony Orchestra Association, Box 9).

35. Interview with Sheldon Soffer.

36. Donal Henahan, "Chicagoans Play at Carnegie Hall," *The New York Times,* November 13, 1967.

37. Stanley G. Livengood, "A History of the Chicago Symphony Chorus, 1957-2000," DMA dissertation (University of Oklahoma, 2001), p. 36.

PART III

CHAPTER 14
Everything Comes Together: 1968–1975

A new era was about to start for the Chicago Symphony Orchestra and Chorus. The Chorus's twelfth season would be noteworthy for Jean Martinon's final alliance with them, after which a new music director would enter the scene. Georg Solti was appointed to lead the Chicago Symphony Orchestra (CSO) in December 1968 and would begin with the 1969–1970 season. The adjustment following Martinon would be swift. Solti had been considered for the position in 1961 but was not agreeable to the conditions at that time, which included conducting sixteen weeks of concerts and residency in Chicago.[1] He was particularly hesitant, as he had recently accepted the post of music director for London's Royal Opera at Covent Garden. Now, eight years later, Solti's arrival was timely. Many dissensions among orchestra players and the administration were at their peak when Solti arrived. His appointment would be the catalyst for change in the dysfunction that was pervasive at Orchestra Hall. Solti's intensity paired well with the gentler personality of the Orchestra's first principal guest conductor, Carlo Maria Giulini, who would share conducting duties, making them the perfect team to settle the contentious atmosphere at the CSO in the late 1960s. In April 1969, the Chorus would have their first collaboration with Solti, performing Maher's Symphony No. 2, the *Resurrection Symphony*. In many ways this selection was apt, as in one sense there was a return to life for the Orchestra. Solti had a charisma about him that the Chorus had missed after Reiner's departure and was never replaced by Martinon. From the moment Solti entered the rehearsal room, the Chorus recognized they were in the hands of someone special. Instantly embraced by the singers, Solti brought his fiery spirit and brilliant vision to Orchestra Hall. In a very short time, Maestro Georg Solti would catapult the Chicago Symphony Orchestra and Chorus to the very top of their field (Picture 45).

Picture 45.
Sir Georg Solti. (Rosenthal Archives of the Chicago Symphony Orchestra Association)

According to Hillis, she was included in the decision-making process to bring Solti to Chicago. During the first decade of the Chicago Symphony Chorus (CSC), Margaret had gained the trust not only of the two music directors she had worked under but also of those who ran the Orchestral Association. One who would consult Hillis's opinions was Louis Sudler, president of the Orchestral Association from 1966 until 1971 and then chairman of the Association from 1971 until 1976. Sudler was a man whose generosity, wisdom, guidance, and love for the CSO during his time on the Association's board greatly contributed to the Chicago Symphony Orchestra's international success. Sudler was a man of great wealth, founding the respected real estate firm Sudler and Company along with his brother, Carroll. Together they managed some of the most prestigious properties in Chicago, including the iconic John Hancock Building. With his beautiful baritone voice, Sudler initially pursued music, studying voice at Yale. In his early years as a performer, he appeared with such prestigious companies as the Chicago Opera Company and the Chicago Symphony

Orchestra. When the Chicago Opera Company closed in 1946, Sudler had the choice to continue his singing career, which would have required him to relocate, or remain in Chicago with his burgeoning real estate business. He ultimately chose the latter but maintained his connection with the arts, joining the Board of the CSO in 1964. Sudler's superb business acumen became an invaluable asset to the board and to the future success of the Chicago Symphony Orchestra. Equally important to the Orchestra was Sudler's generosity. He contributed millions of dollars, which paved the way for the CSO to attract John Edwards. Edwards would become one of the finest general managers in the Orchestra's history. Together, Sudler and Edwards were responsible for bringing together the inimitable team of Georg Solti and Carlo Maria Giulini, thereby changing the entire artistic and administrative landscape of the CSO. As Hillis expressed, "If any statue should go up for anyone—it should be for Louis Sudler—he cared deeply about the Orchestra."[2]

Hillis claimed that the CSO had been trying for many years to attract John Edwards to Chicago, but he would only do so if the Orchestral Association would raise one million dollars. According to Hillis, Sudler succeeded in raising the money, much of which came out of his own pocket.[3] Edwards was a well-respected figure in the music field, admired by musicians including Henry Mazer, associate conductor of the CSO from 1970–1986, who stated that Edwards was not only a good musician himself but also, "He knows all music and all levels of performance."[4] Edwards was well connected in the music business and, more importantly, he knew how to deal with musicians. He spent thirty years managing orchestras and turned down the Chicago Symphony Orchestra on two previous occasions when offered the managerial position. Hillis knew Edwards from her guest conducting appearances with the Pittsburgh Symphony Orchestra when he was managing it, and she greatly respected him. Fortunately, Edwards accepted the CSO managerial position when it was offered to him a third time in 1967. He immediately thereafter embarked upon the task of finding a new music director for the CSO (Picture 46).

Picture 46.
Margaret Hillis and John Edwards clinking glasses at the Chorus's twentieth anniversary reception, May 19, 1977. (Terry's Photography) (Rosenthal Archives of the Chicago Symphony Orchestra Association)

Edwards and Sudler originally considered bringing in three conductors: one to serve as music director, the other two sharing principal guest conductor duties. The three under consideration were Herbert von Karajan, Carlo Maria Giulini, and Georg Solti. After numerous meetings and conversations with all three, it appeared the best pairing would be Solti and Giulini, both of whom were good friends of Edwards.[5] One of the noteworthy components of the selection process was gathering input from musicians of the Orchestra who were "astounded and gratified" to be asked their opinions, though no commitment was made to adhere to any suggestions that were offered.[6] Margaret Hillis was included among those who were consulted, explaining the scenario in which she was approached by Louis Sudler. According to Hillis,

> One night Louis Sudler called me, and he said, "For the new music director—what do you think of von Karajan?" And I said, "I think that would be a great mistake because there are still pictures of him standing with Goering . . .

patting him on the back. . . . I think it would be a GREAT MISTAKE! About a week later he called me up and said, "What do you think about Solti?" And I said, "I think that is brilliant!" . . . And he said, "Giulini as the principal guest conductor?" I said, "Marvelous!"[7]

Regarding the various reasons Martinon came at exactly the wrong time in the Chicago Symphony Orchestra history, Solti would come at precisely the right time. Solti brought a fresh approach to the Chicago Symphony Orchestra, filled with confidence—a byproduct of more than twenty-five years of his international conducting achievements. Martinon, according to Donald Peck, principal flutist in the Chicago Symphony Orchestra from 1958–1999, had approached the orchestra as a nice man who wanted to be liked by the players. By asking this strong orchestra for acceptance, "they absolutely clobbered him."[8] Peck explained that Solti took a different approach. "Solti . . . [He] would never ask for acceptance; he commanded respect. . . . The result: Chicago fell completely and rapturously in love with him."[9] Solti reminisced in his autobiography, *Memoirs*, that being in charge of the Chicago Symphony Orchestra was a fulfillment of his dreams. Reflecting upon his term as music director of the Chicago Symphony Orchestra, Solti describes this as being "the happiest time in [his] professional life."[10] Solti referred to the city of Chicago, when he first arrived as the new music director in November 1969, as a "sleeping beauty. . . . There was a wind of change in the air, however within a few months of my arrival, Chicago began to awake from her sleep."[11] He saw this evolution in the impressively massive new buildings being erected downtown, which he likened to the way he was building his orchestra. He understood his mission as bringing a greater and venerable visibility, nationally and internationally, to this fine orchestra, noting that of the "Big Five Orchestras" (Boston, Cleveland, New York, Philadelphia, and Chicago), only Chicago had not toured as much in America nor had they toured in Europe.[12] All of this would change under Solti, whose vision for his Orchestra would also extend to the Chorus once he became more fully confident in their quality.

Initially, Hillis found Solti to be "a bearable skeptic" when it came to the chorus. She explained, "He had been told what a beautiful chorus it was, but he had no idea how true it was."[13] Solti also did not know anything about Margaret Hillis, or so he thought. Hillis had actually demonstrated her ability to deliver a good chorus to him, but he would only later be made aware of the circumstances that resulted in her saving one of his performances. In the summer of 1957, just before the Chicago Symphony Chorus was to begin rehearsals that fall, Hillis had been engaged by Northwestern University to give a three-day summer conducting workshop. She was living in New York at the time, coming to town specifically for this event. She was met at the airport by an anxious choral assistant from the school who was carrying a score under his arm. He explained to Hillis that the university summer chorus was to perform Haydn's *The Seasons* at Ravinia under Georg Solti's direction two weeks later, on July 27, 1957, and they had not yet gotten through the piece. He anxiously handed her the score, asking if she would cover this piece in her workshop and rehearse it with their chorus instead of covering the music she had originally planned. Hillis recalled:

> I didn't know it [*The Seasons*], so that night I studied it. . . . [During the rehearsals with the chorus] I worked backwards since they hadn't seen the back part of the work. I had hoped to get back [to the beginning of the work] that they had already done but there wasn't time in just three days. I had just an hour and a half or maybe two hours in each day and I got a clean, rhythmically, sparkling energy [from the chorus in the movements she covered].[14]

Hillis explained that she was able to get through all but the first three choruses before her workshop ended. She returned to New York without knowing how the performance turned out. Some years later, Hillis ran into one of the choristers from that workshop who shared the results of her efforts. According to what Hillis was told, Solti started at the beginning of the work and the chorus was "just awful."[15] Hillis was told that Solti was in despair over what he was hearing. Once he arrived at the fourth chorus, where she had worked with them, everything began to go beautifully, and he became very pleased. Twelve years later, when Solti began his work with Hillis in Chicago, she informed him that in fact it was she who had prepared that university chorus for him, and as she describes, it was at that point their friendship began.[16]

As Solti grew more confident with Hillis and the Chorus, his demands grew significantly greater. At the beginning, according to Hillis, Solti scrutinized her preparatory work, often questioning her about various details and carefully checking her score markings.[17] After conducting the Chorus in Mahler's Symphony No. 2 and Haydn's *The Creation*, she claimed Solti's attitude toward her "changed dramatically."[18] He conveyed his trust in her, evidenced by his request that she prepare the works that followed with little preliminary consultation. By the 1970–1971 season, Solti increased the Chorus's presence, engaging them in one of their busiest seasons thus far, including eight concert preparations between Giulini, Solti, Hillis, and Claudio Abbado. Works included Beethoven's Mass in C, Beethoven's Symphony No. 9, Mahler's Symphony No. 3, Denniston's *Sun Song*, Verdi's Requiem, Bach's *St. Matthew Passion*, a challenging world premiere of Alan Stout's Symphony No. 4, and the season-ending blockbuster, Mahler's Symphony No. 8. In the season that followed, an even greater challenge was handed to the Chorus, beginning with their opening appearance.

Solti chose to open the 1971–1972 season with Schoenberg's *Moses and Aaron*, putting Hillis and her Chorus to the greatest test of their fifteen-year history. Solti determined this work to be the perfect showpiece in which he could proudly feature the Chorus's return engagement to Carnegie Hall. This choice would prove to Solti, Hillis, and her singers their true potential and expertise. In terms of the choral-orchestral symphonic repertoire, few works are more difficult to master than Schoenberg's *Moses and Aaron*. Hillis was accustomed to preparing difficult contemporary works, but only with her completely professional American Concert Choir of forty singers. She had yet to manage the challenge with a large-scale semi-professional symphonic chorus, particularly in a work of such complexity. Moreover, the musical stakes were never higher. Tremendous financial investment would be made to bring the Chorus and a children's choir to New York. Added to finances were the extra rehearsals Hillis would require in order to have her Chorus performance-ready. Hillis wisely began her planning for this epic project months in advance. The concert was to be performed in early November, giving Hillis just six weeks of rehearsal time to prepare the Chorus. Her first step was to call upon one of her well-cultivated resources. In early July 1971, Margaret reached out to composer and theorist Milton Babbitt. Babbitt had written an essay, recently published in *Perspectives on Schoenberg and Stravinsky*. The topic was the composition *Moses and Aaron*. In her letter to Babbitt, Hillis explained that she did not need an analysis for theoretical insight into the piece as much as she needed guidance for an approach to help her teach the music to a "basically non-professional and tonally-oriented chorus."[19] Obtaining the information she needed, Hillis sent out the first in a series of "Dear People" letters to her choristers. Her first message to them in mid-summer of 1971 included the tone row and the inversions from *Moses and Aaron*, likely supplied by Babbitt, which she wrote out for her singers to practice (Picture 47).

Picture 47.

A tone row and inversion, written out by Hillis, were sent to Chorus members with a message encouraging them to learn these themes before their first *Moses and Aaron* rehearsal, July 26, 1971. This tone row was later used by Hillis at Chorus auditions to test sight-reading for singers requesting professional status in the Chorus.[20] (Margaret Hillis Collection, Rosenthal Archives of the Chicago Symphony Orchestra Association)

In her message, Hillis encouraged the singers to learn and practice the challenging intervals of the tone row and inversions in preparation for their first rehearsal in September. Her message, dated July 26, 1971, stated, "If you get these intervals into your ear before the first rehearsal, our progress in learning the piece will be accelerated considerably."[21] In the meantime, Hillis was conferring with John Edwards regarding the impending arrival of music that was being loaned to the CSC from the Royal Opera House in London, where Solti had recently performed the work. As early as June 4, 1971, Hillis began meeting with John Edwards about the music situation. By June 29, Hillis wrote to Edwards, telling him, "I hope by now the music from London is on its way. If it has not arrived by July 12, we are going to be in an ungodly mess, and I see no way that we can perform the piece."[22] By July 17, 1971, Hillis's tone in her next message to Edwards sounded even more dire.

> The fact that the music for the vocal forces involved is not yet available is deeply distressing. At this point, with the month of August hard upon us, getting any cooperation from anyone in Europe is quickly becoming impossible. The telephone strike only compounds the difficulties. The first choral rehearsal is Saturday, September 11. Obviously, the first of September is too late to finalize any arrangements for text clearance, or performance rights. We are now at red alert, and I suggest that if these matters have not been cleared up within the next week, you call Mr. Solti and suggest that he change his program.[23]

Understandably, Hillis was under enormous pressure, but the fact that she was expected to track the music delivery in addition to her other responsibilities highlights an equally striking situation. Hillis was wearing too many hats in addition to being the chorus director. Fortunately, the music arrived shortly after her July 17 correspondence to Edwards, and the rehearsal process was able to commence as planned on September 11, 1971. Shortly before the first rehearsal, Hillis sent another "Dear People" letter, mentally preparing the singers for the project, knowing the extent of the grueling rehearsal process ahead.

> Before Mr. Solti left last May, he told me that when the Covent Garden chorus started work on *Moses and Aaron*, he had a rebellion on his hands. Not only did they hate the piece, but they were sure they could not learn it. Once they had mastered it, they loved it, and it became their favorite opera. That you will learn it, I have not doubt. Whether you love it is up to you. Be grateful that you don't have to perform it without music, while slipping about on a ketchup-filled stage in the orgy scene, as our Covent Garden friends did.[24]

As the performance deadline approached, Hillis's messages revealed some of the strain she was experiencing as she drove her singers to the finish line. Stressing the importance for the singers to attend rehearsals and to study their music at home, Hillis's emphatic tone is unmistakable.

We have only three full rehearsals left before Solti's first piano rehearsal. Please make every effort to attend all of those rehearsals. . . . There are five people who have missed three rehearsals. One more missed [disqualifying them to perform] and you would make the burden on your colleagues even more severe. . . . NO other chorus in the world could learn this piece in such a short time, and we can't either without your individual study and practice at home—twenty minutes a day.[25]

The sectionals this weekend are crucial to our final mastery of this fiendishly difficult work. . . . There are still a few people in the chorus who do not understand the absolute necessity of keeping vibratos under control. No music can be learned by substituting brawn for brains. When you give in to the impulse to belt things out, you not only make it impossible for you yourself to hear, but you interfere with the hearing of everyone sitting near you. One reason the CSC is a great chorus is because it sings its rehearsals thoughtfully. If you cannot control your impulse to belt, you do not belong in this chorus. . . . There are just a few people who have been leaving early without submitting an excuse. If you are one of those people . . . the CSC does not need you.[26]

Also contained in the October 17, 1971, letter was an invitation for singers to arrive early for the rehearsal on November 3 if they wished to hear a recording of Solti's London performance of *Moses and Aaron*. The recording would be played at 6:00 p.m. prior to the 7:00 p.m. rehearsal. It is worth taking a moment to contextualize the limitations of technology in those days, requiring a concert recording to be shared only through a collective listening event. These limitations are hard to imagine in today's world, where accessibility and mass distribution are the common practice.

Added to Hillis's stress of readying the Chorus was a distressing letter she received from management just weeks before the performance series was to open.

The letter requested Hillis to reduce the size of the Chorus from 170 singers to 120 for the New York performance. Hillis was rightfully upset about the negative impact this could have on the upcoming performance after giving meticulous attention to every chorister's function throughout the heavily divided voicings of the work. Any reduction of forces could impact the balance, accuracy, and security of her ensemble. She also feared disappointing her singers, all of whom had worked diligently to learn this difficult piece in a short period of time, and now some may be denied the opportunity to perform at Carnegie Hall. Hillis called upon the support of Solti, wisely crafting a letter to him just two weeks before opening night.

> I understand that there is some consideration on the part of management for cutting the full stage chorus to one hundred twenty singers for the New York performance. I strongly feel that a decision of this kind is in the musical realm and that the decision about the size of the chorus should be yours and yours alone.[27]

Her strategy in taking the matter directly to Solti instead of engaging with management proved to be the correct move. Hillis knew she could count on Solti's good judgement and support and that he alone had the power to insist upon the entire Chorus performing in New York, which is exactly what happened.

Though the efforts were great, with frustrations often running high, the results were magnificent, both in Chicago and New York. Glowing reviews like that of Robert Marsh in the *Chicago Sun-Times* stated, "The real active force in this opera is the Chosen people, and here the Chicago Symphony Chorus after two months of intensive study with Margaret Hillis not only sang some of the most difficult choral music ever written with extraordinary beauty and skill, but acted their various roles in a manner that turned the choral ranks into a dynamic part of the drama."[28] As Harold Schonberg stated in his *New York Times* review of the Carnegie Hall performance, "Mr. Solti's performance provided an opportunity, in effect, of hearing the opera as it should be heard . . . [shedding] all kinds of new light on the score. . . . Mention must be made of the fine work of the Chicago Symphony Chorus and the Glen Ellyn Children's Choir."[29] Fifty-one hours of rehearsals crammed into six weeks convinced Hillis and the CSC that they could accomplish great things once they set their minds to it. In Hillis's final letter to the Chorus on the topic of *Moses and Aaron,* she expressed her gratitude for their first three performances in Chicago, conveying her excitement for their upcoming performance on November 20, 1971, in New York.[30] Solti also sent his appreciation in a letter, affirming his pride and gratitude for their monumental achievement (Pictures 48 and 49).

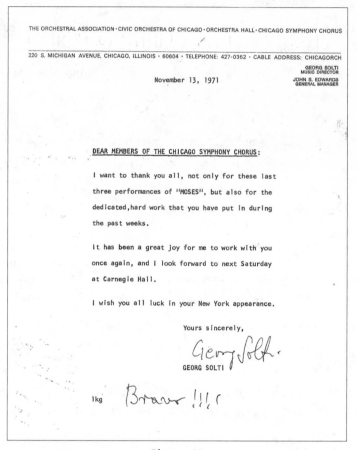

THE ORCHESTRAL ASSOCIATION · CIVIC ORCHESTRA OF CHICAGO · ORCHESTRA HALL · CHICAGO SYMPHONY CHORUS

220 S. MICHIGAN AVENUE, CHICAGO, ILLINOIS · 60604 · TELEPHONE: 427-0362 · CABLE ADDRESS: CHICAGORCH

GEORG SOLTI
MUSIC DIRECTOR

November 13, 1971

JOHN S. EDWARDS
GENERAL MANAGER

DEAR MEMBERS OF THE CHICAGO SYMPHONY CHORUS:

I want to thank you all, not only for these last three performances of "MOSES", but also for the dedicated, hard work that you have put in during the past weeks.

It has been a great joy for me to work with you once again, and I look forward to next Saturday at Carnegie Hall.

I wish you all luck in your New York appearance.

Yours sincerely,

Georg Solti

GEORG SOLTI

Bravo !!!

Picture 48.
Letter from Sir Georg Solti to the Chorus thanking them for their wonderful work on Schoenberg's *Moses and Aaron,* November 13, 1971. (Margaret Hillis Collection, Rosenthal Archives of the Chicago Symphony Orchestra Association)

Picture 49.

Schoenberg's *Moses and Aaron*, Orchestra Hall, November 13, 1971. (Robert M. Lightfoot III, photographer) (Rosenthal Archives of the Chicago Symphony Orchestra Association)

When Solti performed *Moses and Aaron* at the Royal Opera House several years earlier, "he'd accepted that the singers could only approximate the score of Schoenberg," while, according to Solti, the Chicago Symphony Chorus had the opposite issue, which he referred to as "extreme precision."[31] As Solti explained it, such precision took the passion out of the piece, which he needed to ignite once he took over. As he confessed, "Even *I* don't know every note!"[32] Despite the issue of superb accuracy, a good problem for any conductor to have, Hillis handed Solti a pristinely prepared canvas upon which he could impose the color and texture for his dramatic rendition.

THE HILLIS-SOLTI DUO

That Hillis and Solti were a dynamic duo was now a proven fact. Additionally, Hillis provided yet another dimension to their relationship, one that endeared her to Solti all the more. Hillis provided the calm in many storms that arose during Solti's tenure. One such storm would brew in the fall of 1973. As William Barry Furlong, author of *Season with Solti*, surmised, "In moments of professional tension, [Solti was] always . . . able to rely on a particular kind of professional woman—self-sufficient, self-confident, able to anticipate his needs and wishes without stepping on his prerogatives. Margaret Hillis . . . is such a woman: she would play an enormously important part in resolving the tensions [at the CSO]."[33] When Solti programmed Beethoven's *Missa solemnis* during two particularly heavy concert weeks of the 1973–1974 season, Hillis would demonstrate her unshakeable calm and utter reliability, which Solti would come to rely upon. Added to an already demanding schedule the week prior to *Missa solemnis* was a runout CSO performance in Milwaukee, all while Solti was fighting a bad cold. An already fatigued maestro was none too pleased upon receiving unfortunate news from one member of his carefully chosen quartet just days before *Missa* rehearsals were to begin. The renowned tenor, Peter Schreier, informed Solti he was canceling his appearance in Chicago due to a case of laryngitis. Fortunately, John Edwards was able to swiftly find his replacement, George Shirley, after which Edwards thought he had mitigated a close call. Unfortunately, it was only the beginning of a series of cancellations that would plague Solti, who ended up with numerous solo changes during the three-concert series run. First, the bass, Karl Ridderbusch, struggled through the orchestra rehearsals only to cancel the night before the opening, having what was often referred to as "Chicago throat," a frequent malady of guest soloists encountering the ever-changing Chicago weather at that time of year. Solti was able to find a bass replacement, calling Carol Fox, impresario at Lyric Opera of Chicago, who kindly assisted in the matter with her recommendation of Theo Adam. However, Adam was only available for the first two concerts because he was needed back at the Lyric Opera for a performance, requiring yet another bass replacement, Thomas Paul, for the third CSO performance: When things finally seemed to settle down, the soprano, Wendy Fine, began to show signs of vocal struggle on opening night, forcing her to cancel her next two appearances. This circumstance was the most concerning with only three-and-a-half hours of notice she gave to Solti before the matinee performance. There was no time to find her replacement before the concert, creating a true crisis situation that could have caused a cancellation of the performance. With so little time to spare, Solti called upon Margaret to find a solution. Hillis looked to her "bullpen" of understudy soloists, whom she regularly chose from her Chorus, allowing up-and-coming solo singers an opportunity to learn the repertoire. Understudies would coach with Hillis and were often called upon to sing their understudy roles during Chorus rehearsals and occasionally for the conductor during the conductor piano rehearsals (CPR). Fortunately, Solti had heard Hillis's chosen soprano understudy for the *Missa solemnis* during his CPR earlier that week.

Sarah Beatty, a soprano in her second season with the Chorus, impressed Solti enough that he asked Hillis if she thought Sarah was ready to step in as a soloist for the performance that afternoon. Hillis assured him Sarah could do it. Hillis then carefully strategized the way she would break the news to her singer, determining it would be best to inform Sarah when she arrived for the 2:00 p.m. chorus warm-up, giving her less time to become nervous with anticipation of the performance. Upon Sarah's arrival, Hillis pulled her aside, calmly asking how she was feeling after the previous evening's strenuous singing of the piece. Sarah replied that she felt just fine, in good voice for today's performance. Margaret then informed Sarah that Wendy Fine was ill, and Solti requested Sarah to sing that afternoon's performance in Ms. Fine's place, to which Sarah replied, "You're kidding!" Hillis assured Sarah that she was not kidding, promptly instructing her to go to Solti, who was in his dressing room waiting to meet with her before the concert. As Hillis predicted, Sarah performed beautifully and would also sing the Saturday evening concert. Beatty chose to wear her Chorus attire for both performances rather than a fancy gown she could have selected. This gesture gave honor to Hillis and her fellow choral colleagues on stage. A grateful maestro, Solti promptly reengaged Beatty the following season to perform roles in *St. Matthew Passion* and *Salome*.[34] It was Hillis's keen foresight into having several sets of carefully rehearsed understudies at the ready for just such emergency situations, providing Solti an extra layer of security he could rely upon when necessary. These emergencies would occur periodically over the years, launching opera careers for several of the CSC's most talented choristers. Such events distinguished the Chorus, as clearly demonstrated by singers among their ranks, who were capable of stepping into the solo spot when the occasion arose. Solti depended upon Hillis's calm demeanor in a crisis, her keen preparation of her singers, and her impeccable judgement as to whether a singer was ready for the experience of a lifetime. He knew he could rely upon Margaret in these challenging situations.

Despite the wonderful relationship between Hillis and Solti, there were occasions through their years together when his actions would be disappointing and occasionally hurtful to her. Though his intentions were always focused upon what was best for the performance, his choices were sometimes insensitive. These situations required a nuanced response from Hillis, who would call upon her lifelong practice of circumspective behavior, seldom letting on how she felt when hurtful events occurred. Sometimes she would bury these feelings, never revealing her sentiments. Other times, she would control her reaction until the timing was right.

When she did respond, she expressed herself in a measured, direct, and professional manner, never revealing a hint of anger nor frustration in her response.

One such case occurred early on, involving Mahler's Symphony No. 8, a piece that in later years would provide Hillis some of her greatest moments with the CSO. However, in Hillis and Solti's first collaboration with the piece, the opposite was true. Hillis put together a superb cast for Solti's Mahler Symphony No. 8 for the spring of 1971. She prepared all the choral forces, including the Chicago Symphony Chorus, the Northwestern University Chorus, the North Park College Chorus, and the Glen Ellyn Children's Theater Chorus. Hillis took an active role in uniformly training these singers, ensuring a precisely unified ensemble for this massive production. The performances, held at Chicago's Civic Opera House on May 7 and 8, 1971, were superb. On August 30, 31, and September 1 of that year, Solti had arranged for the Chicago Symphony Orchestra to record the piece in Vienna's Sofiensaal as part of the Orchestra's first European tour. The choruses chosen for this recording included the Vienna Singverein, the Vienna State Opera Chorus, and the Vienna Boys' Choir. Solti later regretted this decision. Reflecting upon the choral forces on the recording, Solti remarked, "They were singing sloppy, like an opera chorus. . . . I told them I am bringing you an orchestra that can play Mahler for twenty minutes and never make the smallest mistake. Will we have to stop the recording session because the chorus makes mistakes?"[35] He had come to expect the precision that Margaret Hillis consistently delivered and was disappointed with a chorus quite different from what he had just conducted in Chicago. Margaret too was disappointed in his decision to record this epic work with another chorus. Publicly, she stated that she completely understood his choice, which she explained away as a financial decision, whereby bringing the Chorus to Europe would have been too costly. She made no mention of what would have been a logical option: to record the work in Chicago with the forces that Hillis had so carefully prepared.

The soonest Hillis revealed any discontent on the matter was at a point she believed she could affect real change. Soon after the recording of Mahler's Symphony No. 8 was released, Cathy Weingart-Ryan, in her first season of many with the CSC, vividly recalled Margaret reading a letter to the Chorus, one she had already sent to John Edwards. The letter stated Hillis's position on the CSC being replaced for the Mahler CSO recording. According to Weingart-Ryan, a particular phrase stood out in her recollection. Hillis stated that her position would become "untenable" if the

Orchestra were to ever again record a choral work with any other chorus but theirs.[36] The timing of this declamation made sense, in that the recording had recently won Best Classical Album and Best Choral Performance, Classical (other than opera) at the 1972 Grammy Awards, likely adding to the humiliation of Hillis and the Chorus for not taking part in this project. The letter to Edwards made Hillis's stance on the matter clear, as she advocated on behalf of her Chorus. Hillis's carefully timed action was intended as much for the sake of her Chorus's morale as it was for her own. Margaret's words must have impacted Solti, because never again did he record the CSO with any chorus other than the CSC.

Hillis's interactions with Solti were always positive and professional despite any resentment she may have harbored. Martha Gilmer, longtime Vice President for Artistic Planning and Audience Development of the CSO believed, "[Solti] really loved [Margaret]," and it is likely that the admiration between them extended to the Chorus.[37] Solti's pride for the Chorus was apparent. He could often be heard saying, "*My* Orchestra, *my* 'Chor' [Choir]." Whether Margaret's nuanced handling of difficult situations influenced Solti's good feelings toward the Chorus cannot be known, but Hillis's wise judgement in her handling of difficult situations can be added to the many intellectual and emotional strengths she demonstrated in this demanding position.

Her Chicago Symphony Chorus was realizing its fullest potential and so too was Hillis. During this time, her skills in building, shaping, and refining the Chorus were nothing less than remarkable. The Solti-Hillis duo were setting a standard unmatched in the industry. Hillis would remain a respected colleague of the Chicago Symphony Orchestra family, one they could rely upon not only as a music director but also as a trusted colleague. Her talent as an unmatched chorus master all but guaranteed her long-lasting position with the CSO. Yet it was her stolid ability to navigate the complexities of symphony politics, particularly as a woman in this man's world, that provided her the greatest assurance of longevity with the Orchestral Association.

ENDNOTES

1. Sir Georg Solti, *Memoirs* (New York: Alfred A. Knopf, 1997), p. 147.
2. Jon Bentz, "Interview of Margaret Hillis Director Chicago Symphony Orchestra, September 19, 1989, Archives Committee, Oral History Project, 1992," p. 34 (Margaret Hillis Collection, Rosenthal Archives of the Chicago Symphony Orchestra Association).
3. Ibid., 35.
4. William Barry Furlong, *Season with Solti: A Year in the Life of the Chicago Symphony* (New York: Macmillan Publishing, 1974), p. 67.

5. Ibid., p. 74.
6. Ibid., p. 72.
7. Bentz, "Interview of Margaret Hillis," p. 35. In his autobiography, *Memoirs,* Solti explained that he and Giulini had come to an agreement about the arrangement of Solti serving as music director and Giulini serving as principal guest conductor. Solti had initially suggested a shared arrangement, fearing he was still quite busy with Covent Garden. Giulini preferred Solti, whom he described as more organized, and would be a better music director. Giulini was happy to serve as principal guest conductor.
8. Furlong, *Season with Solti,* p. 98.
9. Ibid.
10. Solti, *Memoirs,* p. 157.
11. Ibid., p. 164.
12. Ibid., p. 165.
13. Furlong, *Season with Solti,* p. 225.
14. Bentz, "Interview of Margaret Hillis," pp. 14–15.
15. *Georg Solti, A City Remembers, The Chicago Years, 1969–1997,* Remarks of Margaret Hillis, booklet by the Chicago Symphony Orchestra Association, p. 13.
16. Ibid.
17. Furlong, *Season with Solti,* p. 225.
18. Ibid.
19. Letter from Murata to Milton Babbitt on behalf of Margaret Hillis, July 1, 1971 (Margaret Hillis Collection, Rosenthal Archives of the Chicago Symphony Orchestra Association, Box 3).
20. Tone Row and Inversions of *Moses and Aaron,* handwritten out by Margaret Hillis (Margaret Hillis Collection, Box 5).
21. Letter from Margaret Hillis to the Chorus, July 26, 1971 (Margaret Hillis Collection, Rosenthal Archives of the Chicago Symphony Orchestra Association, Box 3).
22. Letter from Margaret Hillis to John Edwards, June 29, 1971 (Margaret Hillis Collection, Rosenthal Archives of the Chicago Symphony Orchestra Association, Box 3).
23. Letter from Margaret Hillis to John Edwards, July 17, 1971 (Margaret Hillis Collection, Rosenthal Archives of the Chicago Symphony Orchestra Association, Box 3).
24. Letter to the Chorus from Margaret Hillis, September 7, 1971 (Margaret Hillis Collection, Rosenthal Archives of the Chicago Symphony Orchestra Association, Box 3).
25. Letter to the Chorus from Margaret Hillis, October 14, 1971 (Margaret Hillis Collection, Rosenthal Archives of the Chicago Symphony Orchestra Association, Box 3).
26. Letter to the Chorus from Margaret Hillis, October 17, 1971 (Margaret Hillis Collection, Rosenthal Archives of the Chicago Symphony Orchestra Association, Box 3).
27. Letter to Solti from Margaret Hillis, October 15, 1971 (Margaret Hillis Collection, Rosenthal Archives of the Chicago Symphony Orchestra Association, Box 3).
28. Robert Marsh, "'Moses and Aaron' a Triumph for Solti," *Chicago Sun-Times,* November 12, 1971.
29. Harold C. Schonberg, "Opera: 'Moses and Aaron' in Concert," *The New York Times,* November 22, 1971.
30. Letter to the Chorus from Margaret Hills, November 13, 1971 (Margaret Hillis Collection, Rosenthal Archives of the Chicago Symphony Orchestra Association, Box 3).
31. Furlong, *Season with Solti,* p. 226.
32. Ibid., p. 226.
33. Ibid., p. 204.
34. Ibid., p. 230.
35. Ibid., p. 211.
36. Interview of Cathy Weingart-Ryan with the author, July 28, 2020.
37. Interview of Martha Gilmer with the author, October 13, 2012.

CHAPTER 15

A Balancing Act

Solti was enthusiastic about collaborating with the Chicago Symphony Chorus (CSC), which created an impressive workload for Hillis. Despite all she was doing with the Chorus, Hillis continued to pursue outside opportunities to cultivate her conducting career. She had not yet relinquished her ambition as a performance conductor. During the period of the late 1960s to the late 1970s, Hillis maintained the heavy schedule with the Chicago Symphony Orchestra (CSO) while taking on outside conducting work, including several conducting appointments. Somehow, she managed to keep it all in balance. She was driven to a goal she had yet to fulfill—to be a conductor, not just in rehearsal settings, but in performance.

The Chicago Symphony Orchestra provided Margaret some satisfaction in her quest, offering her an annual concert series with the Orchestra and Chorus. Additionally, she enjoyed her position as a resident conductor of the CSO's training orchestra, the Civic Orchestra of Chicago, a post she began during the Martinon era. Sharing her Civic post with CSO principal percussionist Gordon Peters, they conducted concerts with the Civic Orchestra at Orchestra Hall. The CSO showed growing confidence in Hillis's work, inviting her to substitute for the ailing Rafael Kubelík in performances of Handel's *Jephtha* on March 30, 31, and April 1, 1972. Yet despite these gestures by the CSO, Hillis understood that she needed more regularity as a performance conductor in order to gain true consistency and confidence on the podium.

Hillis was aware of her strengths in conducting, but she was equally aware of her weaknesses. Beyond her own self-awareness, the Chicago critics were there to remind her of those weaknesses, lest she forget. Civic Orchestra concerts were often reviewed by the same critics who covered CSO performances, and those reviews were sometimes less than flattering. Despite any criticism, Hillis remained undeterred, willing to place herself in these vulnerable circumstances. It was a means to an end, as she took full advantage of these prestigious opportunities to conduct on the stage at Orchestra Hall, knowing her work would be constantly scrutinized. Never one to delude herself, Hillis remained self-aware and determined to improve, seeking out any opportunities to hone her craft. It was the only way to master the art of conducting.

Hillis knew that only through greater frequency of working with orchestras could she hope to improve her orchestral conducting technique. No longer conducting the Kenosha Symphony Orchestra, Hillis was pleased to acquire a new conducting appointment that would provide her more consistency as an instrumental conductor. In 1971, she was appointed music director of the Elgin Symphony Orchestra. Elgin, a western suburb of Chicago, was an easier commute than her previous Kenosha Symphony Orchestra position, which she had relinquished by 1968. With Elgin, Margaret would again have an orchestra of her own upon which to further shape her conducting technique. Eager to build an orchestra of outstanding caliber, Hillis was able to transform this amateur orchestra into a professional one during her tenure as Elgin's music director. Similar to her reviews with Civic, Hillis's Elgin reviews were also variable. Not to be discouraged by critics, she kept her focus on the task at hand, gaining increased comfort conducting orchestras.

Prior to being offered the Elgin appointment, which gave Hillis weekly experience conducting an orchestra, she acquired a position much more in line with her CSO appointment. In 1969, Hillis accepted the position of chorus director with the Cleveland Orchestra Chorus. Cleveland held an appeal for Margaret for many reasons, not the least of which was this outstanding orchestra's affiliation with her former teacher, Robert Shaw. Shaw was brought in by music director George Szell in 1956 to become the chorus director and the associate conductor of the orchestra. Shaw would remain in Cleveland for ten years, building a first-class symphony chorus before leaving to become music director of the Atlanta Symphony Orchestra. He would return to Cleveland for a guest appearance in 1969, assisted once again by his former student and Collegiate Chorale assistant, Margaret Hillis. It was a reunion both would enjoy. The establishment of the Cleveland Orchestra Chorus in 1952 predated Chicago's and was a well-respected ensemble, greatly due to the combined forces of Shaw and Szell.

This appointment took on a second and more enticing appeal for Hillis. The job included an opportunity to conduct Cleveland's outstanding symphony orchestra in concert at least once per season. This made the appointment irresistible. During her time with Cleveland, Hillis collaborated with principal guest conductor Pierre Boulez, whom she would eventually work with in Chicago, and also with a young James Levine, then the assistant conductor of the orchestra. In the future, Hillis and Levine would enjoy many collaborations in Chicago at the Ravinia Festival. Hillis masterfully kept her work and travel schedule in balance, as she had done when she commuted between Chicago and New York during the early days of the CSC, keeping an efficiency apartment in Cleveland and carefully configuring this additional new position around her other commitments.

Though hard to believe, Hillis's scheduling contortions would continue to increase with yet another appointment she would accept in the fall of 1968. Hillis took the position of professor and director of choral activities at Northwestern University. Located in Evanston just north of Chicago, Hillis accepted what began as a one-year appointment to fill in for the director of choral activities on a sabbatical leave. It would evolve into nine years of a university teaching career, a role she would treasure. The position included several days per week of conducting classes and directing the university's top choir. The appointment appealed to her on several levels. First, it allowed her to pass along her knowledge of choral methods to the next generation of artists. This mission was never far from her heart. The other appeal was her opportunity to conduct the university's choruses and orchestra in concerts during the school year, providing her increased podium time to further advance her technique.

Hillis was able to balance this added teaching commitment with an already demanding schedule due to classes meeting during the day, and therefore not in conflict with the many conducting duties she maintained in the evenings. She took full advantage of the talented singers she directed, adding the Northwestern University Chorus to her Chicago Symphony Chorus for Mahler's Symphony No. 8 in 1971. Northwestern University became somewhat of a training ground for her future CSC singers. Sarah Beatty, who had substituted for the soprano in the 1973 *Missa solemnis* performances, was first known to Hillis through their work together at Northwestern. Many other fine singers would come to the Chicago Symphony Chorus through Hillis's affiliation with Northwestern.

Assembling Her "A" Team

In addition to the fine singers Hillis was able to attract into her Chicago Symphony Chorus, two of her most important connections were made through her work at Northwestern. The first was Dr. Gertrude Grisham, who first met Margaret Hillis when both were teaching at the university. Gertrude was fulfilling her teaching obligations, assigned to her as a doctoral student in German literature. The fortuitous meeting of both women was made through a shared student, who invited both to participate in his upcoming graduate conducting recital. Gertrude, who had grown up in Vienna, was particularly proficient in languages, speaking French, Italian, German, and English. A student of art history, stage diction, and music at the University of Vienna, she eventually came to America on a fellowship to study drama at the University of Washington, where she met her husband, William. Upon moving to Chicago, Grisham continued her scholarly pursuits at Northwestern University. The collaboration of both women on a student project resulted in Grisham becoming the most treasured language and diction coach of the Chicago Symphony Chorus for over forty years. Her expertise in later years would continue through her work with Ravinia's Steans Music Institute, where she guided young professional singers with her linguistic expertise. Renowned conductors, including James Conlon and James Levine, would come to rely upon Grisham's prowess in literature and language for deeper insights into the repertoire they were conducting.

Frau Grisham, as she was called by students and choristers, told the story of a graduate student in conducting who was auditing her class in preparation for passing a rigorous German reading exam, one of several language requirements for the doctoral degree. In the spring quarter of 1974, while preparing to conduct one of his three required doctoral concerts, he requested her assistance narrating John Tavener's composition *Nomine Jesu*. The cantata contained parts for chorus, instrumentalists, a soprano soloist, and several narrators, each speaking in a different language. Gertrude was asked by her student to read the German narration, joining composer and Northwestern professor Alan Stout who would read the Latin, along with several additional speakers brought in for the other languages. Margaret Hillis agreed to narrate the English portion of the work. Standing next to one another, Margaret and Gertrude became acquainted while participating in the rehearsals and two performances of the piece. For the second performance, all except the French narrator returned to participate, leaving Gertrude to step in as a last-minute replacement. Hillis noticed Grisham's facility with languages, as Gertrude quickly adapted to the French along with her German narration. Several days after that second performance, Hillis wisely sent her university choral assistant, Cory Winter, to contact Gertrude on her behalf, asking if she would be available to assist Hillis with German diction in preparation of a university performance of Brahms's *A German Requiem*. Although Grisham was ambivalent about taking on an added commitment given her teaching load, two small children at home, and a doctoral degree yet to complete, she felt compelled to support this respected colleague she had come to know. Much to her surprise and delight, Grisham found herself enjoying the experience, claiming she had "an absolute ball" coaching such magnificent texts that Brahms had arranged using "Luther's gorgeous biblical language."[1]

Gertrude recalled Hillis's chorus having no clue how the German was supposed to be pronounced. Hillis must have known that also, for she, along with many choral conductors of that era, had limited facility in foreign languages, particularly when it came to coaching the modifications singers needed to employ. Hillis was already encountering diction obstacles with greater frequency, but fortunately she had just enough experience with languages to know what questions to ask. One such encounter had occurred in preparation of the 1973 *Missa solemnis*. When Hillis consulted Solti prior to beginning her preparation of the work, she asked him if there was anything special she needed to do with the piece, to which he assured her that she knew him well and should prepare it as she saw fit. Wisely, Hillis followed up his response, inquiring, "Do you want Beethoven's Latin or the Pope's Latin?"[2] Solti promptly answered that he wanted Beethoven's Latin. This would be the first time Hillis was ever asked to prepare this dialect of Latin, containing significant differences within the pronunciation of vowels and consonants, such as in the word "pacem"—pronounced "paCHem" in the Pope's Latin, but pronounced "PaTSem" in Beethoven's Latin. Though Hillis met the challenge for Solti with modest success, she was very much aware that she needed an expert to achieve the precision required of her premier Chorus. Gertrude demonstrated this expertise from their very first collaboration at Northwestern University in 1974.

Gertrude believed that the whole idea of having a diction coach for a chorus, now a common practice of most symphonic choruses, was first created by Hillis. Gertrude reflected that such a practice had not been done in Europe to her knowledge at the time she began this kind of work with Margaret.[3] Vance George explained that when he was serving as music assistant for Bob Page with the Cleveland Orchestra Chorus in the early 1970s, he helped Page with the chorus's diction, having a greater facility for languages, though not a specialist of diction by any means.[4] The practice of a dedicated diction coach was new and proved effective with choruses when Hillis implemented the practice.

During the intermission of Hillis's university Brahms performance, she invited Grisham to coach her Chicago Symphony Chorus for their upcoming Ravinia performance of Mahler's Symphony No. 8. This was to be the first time the piece was performed at Ravinia. Grisham had only heard recordings of this Mahler symphony and would need to learn the entire score in a short period of time. Excited by the prospect of working with this prestigious ensemble, and given her great love of music, she recalled being stimulated by this new challenge. Following the success of the Ravinia Mahler performance, conducted by James Levine on June 27, 1974, Hillis invited Gertrude to return again to coach the CSC the following season. There was no formal announcement of Grisham's new role as official diction coach for the Chicago Symphony Chorus. It just evolved. In the years ahead, Grisham's expertise in diction and in her incredible lectures to the CSC, particularly when they worked on music containing texts of Schiller, Goethe, or other such literary giants, Grisham was able to add a rich dimension to the singer's experience. Dr. Gertrude Grisham became part of a first-rate team Margaret Hillis constructed in support of her work with the Chicago Symphony Chorus (Pictures 50, 51, and 52).

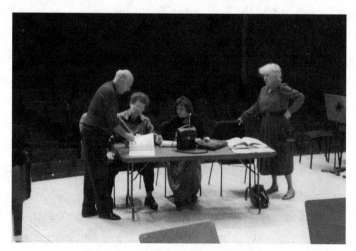

Picture 50.
Sir Georg Solti, Margaret Hillis, Cheryl Frazes Hill, and Gertrude Grisham in rehearsal at Orchestra Hall, late 1980s. (Author's collection)

Picture 51.
Gertrude Grisham at the side of Margaret Hillis backstage during a recording session of Wagner's *The Flying Dutchman* at Medinah Temple, May 1976. (Robert M. Lightfoot III, photographer) (Rosenthal Archives of the Chicago Symphony Orchestra Association)

Picture 52.
Dr. Gertrude Grisham.
(Margaret Hillis Collection, Rosenthal Archives of the Chicago Symphony Orchestra Association)

Another member of Hillis's "A" team during this period was the sensational pianist Dr. Elizabeth "Bettie" Buccheri (Picture 53). A connection was made between Buccheri and Hillis thanks to Walter Hendl, the dean of Eastman School at the time Buccheri was a student there. Bettie impressed Hendl when they collaborated on numerous performances. Hillis knew Hendl from his days serving as Fritz Reiner's associate conductor of the Chicago Symphony Orchestra when Hillis had first begun the Chicago Symphony Chorus. When Buccheri informed Hendl of her plans to move to Chicago, he was anxious to help her find work. He called upon several important musicians he had come to know during his Chicago sojourn to audition Bettie for a job. One of those connections was Margaret Hillis. She agreed to have Bettie audition for her rehearsal accompanist position at the university. As Bettie explained, Hillis met Buccheri for a preliminary interview at the school, advising her to prepare two works that would be rehearsed: an unaccompanied piece by Victoria (Bettie would play parts when needed) and Stravinsky's *Symphony of Psalms*. Bettie practiced both diligently and on the day of the audition, Hillis announced to the choir that Bettie was auditioning so that Margaret "could determine if their chemistries matched."[5] Hillis began the rehearsal by instructing Bettie to give the starting pitches of the Victoria piece. Bettie gave those pitches and then, appropriately, did not play as the chorus sang. Hillis stopped, gave the chorus several corrections, and Bettie recalled knowing intuitively where Hillis would start next. When Hillis asked for pitches of the next entrance, Bettie quickly and accurately responded. This scenario continued for quite a while, with Bettie barely playing a note in the rehearsal. Upon concluding the Victoria work, Hillis announced, "She's hired."[6] Bettie said she could hardly believe it. "I hadn't played a note! But because I was quick knowing where she was going to start—one real plus of Margaret's—she was always clear about where she was going to start—I would know where she was going next."[7] Bettie then continued the rehearsal, accompanying the Stravinsky composition, which went fine, after which Hillis marched Bettie into the dean, explaining she needed a professional accompanist and insisting Bettie be immediately hired. Many years later, Bettie reflected upon that fateful audition in a letter she wrote to Margaret in 1988. Bettie shared, "That day in 1968, when you accepted me as an accompanist, remains one of the significant milestones in my musical life. I still don't know how you knew the potential of our working relationship after a single, three-minute a cappella piece!"[8]

After a time in this position, Bettie determined that she was not able to continue the Northwestern job, in part because she had been hired for a full-time teaching position at North Park College. In the meantime, Hillis invited Bettie to periodically substitute for Mary Sauer at Chicago Symphony Chorus rehearsals. Sauer was the rehearsal accompanist for the Chorus and a pianist for the Chicago Symphony Orchestra. As Bettie tells it, when Solti decided to program *Moses and Aaron* in 1971, Sauer was unwilling to play the CSC rehearsals of the piece. Sauer took Bettie up to Solti's office at Orchestra Hall and introduced her to him, explaining that Bettie would replace her for this preparation. Solti looked at Bettie with an intense stare, as she recalled, asking, "Can you play this?"[9] Bettie responded that she could. Having played a good amount of contemporary music at Eastman, much of which Bettie deemed to be well beyond the difficulty of Schoenberg's work, she had no hesitation accepting this assignment. Buccheri would become the principal accompanist of the Chicago Symphony Chorus for the next twenty years. Additionally, she and her husband John would become very close friends of Margaret and Elizabeth, regularly socializing, enjoying dinners together, and becoming a part of Hillis's exclusive "inner circle." The dynamic trio of Grisham, Buccheri, and Hillis, combined with the genius of Solti, brought the Chorus into the next dimension of symphonic choral music makers.

Picture 53.
Bettie Buccheri, longtime accompanist of the Chicago Symphony Chorus, with Margaret Hillis. (Elizabeth Buccheri's collection)

Establishing the Choral Institute:
A Workshop for Choral Conductors

With all that Hillis was managing, she somehow found time to continue her commitment with the American Choral Foundation. Sheldon Soffer had been instructed early on in his work with the Foundation that part of his job description included creating projects to foster growth and development of the choral field, which in turn would perpetuate her foundation. In typical form, Hillis was always generating new ideas to fulfill the mission of educating conductors in the field. One of her ideas came to fruition during this very busy period of the mid-1960s to the mid-1970s. In July 1966, when Soffer and Hillis were first reconfiguring the Foundation, she suggested creating a workshop for conductors. This workshop would be different from the others she had presented in the past. Possibly inspired after a very successful month-long guest conducting appointment at Stanford University, where she taught classes and conducted performances, she wrote Soffer regarding her idea:

> While at Stanford, I thought up a wonderful summer project that I will outline in detail and get off to you in the next few weeks. . . . I wanted to see what you thought about Ford or Rockefeller [Foundation] support . . . to get a real professional training grant for conductors, choristers, as well as instrumentalists under way (July 19, 1966).[10]

Her idea became a reality in 1968 with the creation of the Choral Institute, a workshop for conductors oriented toward chorus and orchestral conducting techniques. In addition to addressing conducting gestures and dealing with matters of choral tone, she provided choral conductors with the fundamentals for working with an orchestra. Hillis would teach conductors her methods for score analysis, providing guidance in her historical and analytical process of score preparation. She used a practical approach, demonstrating these methods and techniques through the study of select masterworks (i.e., the Renaissance, Baroque, Classical, Romantic, and contemporary eras of music). All sessions would be taught by her and by other leading experts in the disciplines of musicology, performance practice, and conducting. In Hillis's original proposal, she stated, "Unfortunately the education of choral conductors is generally oriented toward the superficial aspects of choral techniques, with almost no recognition of the fact that choral directors must be primarily musicians." Therefore:

> The course here outlined will stress performance practice in the particular style of each area. All lectures on historical period analysis will be oriented to the music being performed. Special aural training (normally called solfège—an area which has been neglected in the training of nearly all musicians) will be presented in terms of phrasing and articulation, rather than with the usual emphasis on pitch and the rigid metrical treatment of rhythm.
>
> As part of his practical training, the choral conductor will be expected to deal with instrumentalists as well as with voices, the objective being a profound grasp of the total score. Most choral conductors, because of lack of experience, almost always leave the orchestra to fend for itself and conduct only the chorus, with no recognition of the total responsibilities which they are expected to undertake.[11]

Students would attend lectures in various topics relevant to the era, including information on editions, performance practice, instrumentation, ornamentation, stylistic considerations, and such, after which they would be given podium time with the professional ensemble in residence. Hillis invited colleagues of the highest caliber to lecture and coach the student conductors of her institute, including such luminaries as Julius Herford, Alfred Mann, Paul Henry Lang, and Otto-Werner Mueller. She also invited talented friends and colleagues along to participate, often renting a luxurious home with a pool, which she paid for and shared generously with friends, including Bettie Buccheri; Harriet Wingreen, a pianist, colleague, and friend from her New York days; Elizabeth Burton; and others whose company she enjoyed.

Hillis's timing for her workshop idea was fortuitous. Just one year before Hillis had finalized this concept, the passage of the National Foundation on the Arts and Humanities Act of 1965 prompted the formation of the National Endowment for the Arts. This new endowment could serve as a resource for artists to obtain government funding. In the National Endowment and the National Council on the Arts' fiscal report, published in June of 1967, Chairman Roger Stevens's opening statement reiterated the mission of the organization, stating, "If the arts are to flourish in the

United States . . . we believe that the time has come for our society to give not merely ceremonial honor to the arts, but genuine attention and substantive support."[12] Hillis was able to take full advantage of this newly available funding source in large measure due to the assistance of Sheldon Soffer. Sheldon, who was very well connected in those days, used his influence to persuade a member of the newly formed NEA committee to consider Hillis's project for funding. According to Soffer, in the early days of the National Endowment for the Arts, they had money to spend, but they did not have any projects in which to invest. Soffer explained there was a gentleman from the NEA who liked him very much and would call him periodically, asking, "What project do you have for us?"[13] Soffer naturally recommended the Choral Institute, which became the first choral project ever funded by the NEA. The American Choral Foundation received a per-dollar matching grant of $50,000 three years consecutively for a total of $150,000 of support. This funding enabled Hillis to fulfill every detail of her wish list for her institute.

Hillis and Soffer worked tirelessly to construct a summer schedule rich in substance, designed to expose choral conductors to conducting and score study more akin to instrumental conductor training. After hundreds of communications between Hillis and respected colleagues, the shared ideas came together for this summer workshop. The final design was comprised of two four-week sessions, the first of which was held at the University of Wisconsin in Madison, focusing on the Renaissance and Baroque eras. The second four weeks took place at State University of New York, focusing on the Classical and Romantic eras and contemporary music. Both universities contributed funding for the workshops, which offset the matching portion of the grant, making this endeavor affordable for the Foundation. Participants would spend their days, nights, and weekends immersed in lectures, conducting workshops, and performances, surrounded by some of the most accomplished figures in the music profession. The *Choral Journal* reviewed this institute with great enthusiasm.

> History was made . . . when for the first time on an organized basis, conductors of choral background and training were offered an unprecedented opportunity to work with a professional orchestra. . . . The concept of choral conductors practicing on a professional orchestra was revolutionary and expensive . . . but when the National Foundation on the Arts and Humanities, the American Choral Foundation, and two participating schools agreed to

underwrite the cost of the institute, Miss Hillis . . . without guidelines or models of any kind to follow, drew up what came to be known as Choral Institute '68.[14]

The article went on to describe the cohesive role of the faculty, all of whom would attend one another's lectures and would collaborate to provide a rich experience for the students who moved from lectures in history and analysis to applying those concepts for their interpretation on the podium.

Margaret served as director of the Choral Institute. She would teach during each session but also observed her colleagues in action. One colleague who got her immediate attention was the orchestra conductor on faculty at the University of Wisconsin, Otto-Werner Mueller. After hearing Mueller speak to one of his classes, Hillis determined, "I've got a few things to learn from this man!"[15] She instantly recognized that Otto-Werner Mueller could finally be the mentor she had been seeking. Mueller showed his occasional "ire" for choral conductors in these sessions, saying things such as, "The second violinist can read his one line of music better than you can the full score. This must not be!"[16] He would constantly criticize the student conductors, insisting they not "interfere" with the players, emphasizing, "Let them play!" and "Don't make the beat more important than the music. . . . Conductors should not be seen more than the music is heard." He also stated, "It is the conductor's fault if at least half the orchestra hates him," and "The worst fakes are conductors, auto mechanics, and politicians!"[17] Hillis approached Mueller after one of his classes, asking if he would work with her, and he agreed to do so.

Otto began to work with me. I went to him . . . sort of behind the scenes. I was head of the Institute but I knew I wanted to learn from this man, and I learned a great deal! We'd use cameras on the kids so I got him to use a camera on me in private sessions; he got my arm working properly. I also finally got my head together on score analysis by working with him. I'd always worked like crazy before, but he showed me an orderly fashion to go about score study. It changed the way I listened, and it changed the way I conducted.[18]

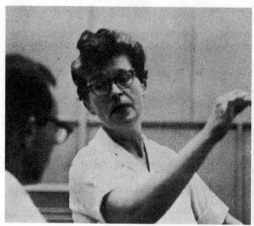

Picture 54.
Hillis and Otto-Werner Mueller working with conducting students at Choral Institute '68.
(*Choral Journal* IX, no. 5, March–April 1969, p. 20)

By the age of forty-seven, Hillis had long practiced conducting gestures, many of which would be difficult to change, but she allowed herself to be open to this professor's methods, believing he would help her overcome bad habits. Otto-Werner Mueller was a strong personality, displaying little compassion for the Institute choral conductors who clearly lacked the instrumental conductor training he emphasized with his own university conducting students. Perhaps that tough approach was what Hillis thought she needed; his style was blatantly honest with little tolerance for errors. Working with Mueller set Margaret up for the same harsh criticism she witnessed in his daily institute sessions. Not concerned about what might be revealed about her conducting skill, she was willing to leave herself open to change. Bettie Buccheri and Harriet Wingreen both commiserated about Mueller's feckless remarks to them privately about Hillis's conducting, which were less than kind. His attitude could not have been lost on Hillis during their lessons. Hillis bravely accepted his feedback, which she claims resulted in a complete transformation in her use of the baton, her approach to bar line analysis, and her entire attitude *apropos* to learning music.[19] "I'd learned [score study technique] *sort of* from Julius Herford, but not the way I learned it from Otto."[20] To learn at her august stage of musical acumen meant being completely vulnerable. Though this mentor would not ever become Hillis's champion, she relied upon his guidance, which ultimately gave her a new level of confidence on the podium, particularly when she faced the intimidating members of the Chicago Symphony Orchestra.

Bob Page was less enamored by the newfound techniques Margaret would enthusiastically share with him whenever they were together. Showing Page what she had learned from her newly acquired mentor, he lovingly quipped, "Maggie, what in the hell are you doing?"[21] Critical of her minimalistic style, he insisted her new gestures were tendentious and "boring." Good friends that they were, she enjoyed sparring with her colleague, and their debates often ended in a chuckle. Hillis trusted that Page's criticism was done with love and respect. Despite Page's concerns about Mueller's influence on Hillis, he recognized the many strengths of Mueller's teaching, inviting both him and Hillis to similar workshops he sponsored when organizing Temple University's Ambler University Festival Institute. Mueller went on from the University of Wisconsin to teach and conduct at Juilliard, Yale, and Curtis Institutes, hailed everywhere as a superb teacher and conductor. Hillis had found in Otto-Werner Mueller someone who would give her guidance, feedback, criticism, and ultimately the confidence she craved and heretofore lacked. She would always be grateful to him.

The Choral Institutes would continue in one form or another over the next ten years, eventually inspiring the creation of many more that still flourish today. Funding for Hillis's institutes was acquired elsewhere after 1971, since the NEA had already subsidized three years of these sessions and would go on to support other endeavors. Hillis found other sources to keep these programs afloat, believing that this instruction was what choral conductors needed to equal the playing field with their instrumental conductor colleagues. Hillis extended her support of choral conductors in other ways as she began to engage in government advocacy. From 1968–1971, Hillis served on the Advisory Panel of the Illinois Arts Council, and by the mid-1970s she was invited on to the Music Panel of the National Endowment for the Arts. These appointments would become a central focus of Hillis's service to the profession, extending her impact upon the choral art through her acquisition of a powerful national platform.

Margaret Hillis was coming into her own during the period beginning in the late 1960s. Her role with the Chicago Symphony Orchestra would have been sufficient for many conductors, but Hillis was unsettled. She longed for a comfort level on the podium she had yet to conquer. She yearned for the choral field to be elevated in status, which remained an elusive achievement. During this time period, Hillis would make great strides in both arenas. Putting herself through an exhaustive series of conducting and teaching positions, Hillis finally acquired a mentor, helping her to gain greater confidence in her work. It would take extreme bravery for her to transform her conducting, but the risks paid off as she grew more comfortable, no longer plagued with self-doubt. Her innovations for raising the status of the choral field took form in her Choral Institutes, providing a model that would continue for years to come. Driven by Hillis's deep love and commitment for her work, she remained tireless in her efforts to realize all that she had dreamed of for herself and her profession. A lifetime of learning and practice was soon to come together in an event that would gain worldwide attention. She could never have imagined how important these years of preparation would be for what was about to take place.

ENDNOTES

1. Interview of Gertrude Grisham with the author, April 10, 2013.
2. Jon Bentz, "Interview of Margaret Hillis Director Chicago Symphony Orchestra, September 19, 1989, Archives Committee, Oral History Project, 1992," p. 13 (Margaret Hillis Collection, Rosenthal Archives of the Chicago Symphony Orchestra Association).
3. Ibid.
4. Interview of Vance George with the author, December 12, 2012.
5. Interview of Bettie Buccheri with the author, October 27, 2012.
6. Ibid.
7. Ibid.
8. Letter written by Bettie Buccheri to Margaret Hillis, March 8, 1988 (Box 16).
9. Ibid.
10. Letter from Margaret Hillis to Sheldon Soffer, July 19, 1966 (Rosenthal Archives of the Chicago Symphony Orchestra Association, Box 9, Hillis American Choral Foundation 1956–1968).
11. A proposal for an Institute for Choral Conductors, divided into quarterly sections, oriented to work with Chorus and Orchestra, by Margaret Hillis. Proposing the Choral Institutes, begun in 1968. This document was likely part of an application for funds that was submitted to the Rockefeller or Ford Foundations, or perhaps to the newly formed National Endowment for the Arts. (No date.) (Margaret Hillis Collection, Rosenthal Archives of the Chicago Symphony Orchestra Association, Box 9).
12. National Endowment for the Arts, National Council on the Arts, "Annual Report," U.S. Government Printing Office, 1967.
13. Interview of Sheldon Soffer with author, August 14, 2019.
14. Paul E. Paige, "Choral Institute '68," *Choral Journal* IX, no. 5 (March–April 1969): pp. 20–21.
15. Margaret Hillis, interview by Norman Pellegrini (transcribed by Stanley G. Livengood), October 6, 1997, p. 31.
16. Paige, "Choral Institute," p. 21.
17. Ibid.
18. Jeannine Wagar, *Conductors in Conversation: Fifteen Contemporary Conductors Discuss Their Lives and Profession* (Boston: G.K. Hall & Co., 1991), pp. 111–112.
19. Interviews of Bettie Buccheri, October 27, 2012, and Harriet Wingreen, March 18, 2014.
20. Margaret Hillis, interview by Pellegrini, p. 31.
21. Interview of Robert Page, November 17, 2012.

CHAPTER 16

THE CROSSROAD: 1976–1977

argaret Hillis was at a crossroad by the fall of 1976. Despite the incrementally growing number of accolades for her Chicago Symphony Chorus and her own accomplishments on podiums with the Chicago Symphony Orchestra (CSO) and beyond, Margaret seemed to be searching for an elusive achievement that would quell her restless ambition. Recognition of Hillis's stellar work, appearing in press reviews, awards, and in other acknowledgements, including honorary doctoral degrees from Temple University, Indiana University, and the University of Notre Dame, would satisfy most conductors. However, for Margaret, there was no sign of any such personal fulfillment. She continued to drive herself inevitably toward a destination still unknown, perhaps even to herself. At the onset of her twentieth season with the Chicago Symphony Chorus in the fall of 1976, she received continuous critical acclaim for their performances and recordings, which were accumulating in ever-increasing numbers. Nevertheless, despite so many celebratory moments, Hillis's attention would be drawn instead to conflicts within the CSO family and beyond. These subtle contretemps manifested as a deleterious effect regarding the good feelings Hillis should have been experiencing from myriad extraordinary achievements she and the Chorus were amassing. Perhaps these periodic irritations fueled her to drive herself all the more. However, during this period of great success, she rarely revealed any personal acknowledgement of how far she had come. Only the most extraordinary confluence of events would allow Margaret a momentary pause to reflect upon where her journey had taken her.

By 1976, the Chorus was well known and greatly appreciated in Chicago, New York, and beyond. Two Carnegie Hall programs were scheduled for the 1976–1977 season, along with three major recording projects. In the fall of 1976, the Chorus would perform an extremely challenging program, including Verdi's *Four Sacred Pieces* on the first half of the concert and Walton's *Belshazzar's Feast* on the second half. The Orchestral Association's management enacted a money-saving measure whereby the Chorus departed for New York on a very early morning flight, attended a late-morning dress rehearsal at Carnegie Hall, performed the concert, and returned to Chicago at 2:00 a.m. the next morning. The entire trip amounted to less than twenty-four hours. Hillis had cause for concern about this exhausting schedule, which had every possibility of impacting a concert demanding extraordinary vocal stamina. Choristers were up in arms about what they considered a draconian itinerary. Objections, made by Hillis on behalf of her Chorus, must have been heard, because the spring 1977 Carnegie Hall trip arrangements were much more reasonably scheduled, including hotel arrangements for the Chorus following their May 13, 1977, performance of Beethoven's *Missa solemnis*. Hillis was painfully aware of the continual cost-cutting measures imposed at her Chorus's expense. These small infractions became increasingly frustrating to Hillis at a point when her Chorus was receiving greater appreciation and approbation than ever before.

The Chorus was emerging as a popular feature in CSO concerts. By the mid-1970s, subscribers attended more reliably and enthusiastically than they had in the early years of CSC appearances. By 1975, Ravinia performances with the Chorus had increased, with as many as six appearances during a summer season. They were a draw for Ravinia audiences, particularly when popular classical concerts such as Mozart's Requiem were programmed. Impressive crowds would gather outside the front festival gates, awaiting their opportunity to claim premier picnic space. With the blare of CSO brass signaling the park's opening, legions of music lovers raced in, converting the massive festival lawn into a colorful palette of blankets, revealing none but a few blades of grass. In their Carnegie Hall appearances, the Chorus experienced similar popularity with New Yorkers who treated the singers as though they were "rock stars." As Chorus members arrived and departed the Carnegie Hall stage door, fans awaited, cheering them on, sometimes requesting autographs.[1] New York audiences were effusive in their approval of the Chorus, as would be demonstrated by thunderous ovations at the conclusion of concerts, the most extraordinary decibels reserved for Solti's reentry to the stage with Margaret Hillis at his side. Such popularity the Chorus was receiving made it even harder for Hillis to justify having to advocate for her singers when actions were taken by the Orchestral Association that did not have their best interests in mind.

Beginning in 1972, recordings that included the Chorus were produced with greater frequency, significantly increasing their public profile. Solti's confidence in the Chorus's ability was demonstrated in his approval of these recording projects, beginning with Beethoven's Symphony No. 9 in 1972 (Picture 55). By the 1976–1977 season, the Chorus had completed five recordings conducted by Solti and two recordings with guest conductors. Within that time span, the Chorus's Verdi Requiem had won them their first Grammy Award on February 23, 1978, for Best Classical Choral Performance (other than opera). An accomplishment of this magnitude could have perhaps been more greatly relished by Hillis had it not been for events surrounding the project that diminished her satisfaction of the achievement. Verdi's Requiem was performed only once at Orchestra Hall, featuring soloists Leontyne Price, Dame Janet Baker, Veriano Luchetti, and José van Dam, on May 31, 1977. Tickets were in great demand for this spectacular event, a benefit concert for the Musicians' Pension Fund, which Solti wisely chose to record thereafter, featuring his all-star soloists, his wonderful Orchestra, and his outstanding Chorus. Members of the Chorus were justifiably thrilled to be part of this special recording project. Much to Hillis's surprise, however, she was informed only days before the recording sessions were to begin that only 110 of the 180 singers involved in the performance would be allowed to participate in the recording. The RCA recording label, to which Leontyne Price was exclusively bound, imposed these restrictions upon the Chorus. As a result, Hillis was forced to eliminate some of her singers from this experience. Once again, Hillis was put into a situation that impacted the morale of her singers, who had dedicated themselves to the preparatory rehearsals and the performance of this piece. She must have also been concerned about the impact a significantly reduced chorus would have on the quality of the recording. Though the results of the recording were successful, it was, nonetheless, an artistic price to be paid at the Chorus's expense.

Picture 55.

Margaret Hillis receives notes from Sir Georg Solti during playbacks for Beethoven's Symphony No. 9 at the Krannert Center at the University of Illinois in May 1972. (Robert M. Lightfoot III, photographer) (Rosenthal Archives of the Chicago Symphony Orchestra Association)

In addition to monitoring the actions of the Orchestral Association, Hillis felt compelled to monitor the actions of her singers. As with any successful ensemble of some longevity, maintaining excellence, and in Hillis's case, continuing their musical development, was a constant challenge. Even this chorus, with so many paid singers, required regular supervision, a job that often fell to Hillis. One indicator of Hillis's management style was demonstrated by her scrutiny over singers' attendance records, which were carefully reviewed at re-auditions. If Hillis saw that a singer was accumulating an excessive amount of absences, it would be addressed at the singer's most vulnerable time, while they were re-auditioning for the Chorus. Hillis would not hesitate to address concerning behaviors in the form of "Dear People" letters when the situation warranted the full Chorus's attention. Beginning as early as 1972, Hillis took a more aggressive stance in matters that otherwise could have negatively impacted the integrity of her singers and challenged all the good work she had done to build the Chicago Symphony Chorus.

One such matter took place in January 1972, resulting in Hillis removing a significant number of Chorus members from an upcoming concert program. Though this action impacted the Chorus's balance, particularly due to Hillis removing several strong singers, she was committed to keeping the policies of the Chorus firmly intact despite potential consequences. Her actions demonstrated her adherence to the policy that no singer was above the rules, no matter how valuable they were to the Chorus. In her "Dear People" letter of January 17, 1972, she stated,

> We lost fourteen choristers prior to the Bach (B Minor Mass) performances due to absence from one of the two mandatory piano rehearsals conducted by Mr. Giulini. They were disappointed to find they could not sing the performances, and I was disappointed to lose them. However, there are some exceptions that cannot be made, for the sake of both the chorus and the performance. I cannot emphasize strongly enough the importance of checking your rehearsal schedule to ascertain performance requirements. . . . Attendance at Conductor Piano Rehearsals and at orchestra rehearsals is essential . . . exceptions to these . . . have not been made in the past, nor will they be in the future, barring extraordinary circumstances.[2]

Hillis did not hesitate to communicate with individual choristers directly if her action to remove a chorister from a performance series needed further explanation. In 1972, Isola Jones, one of the Chorus's strongest vocal talents, would receive just such a notification. Hillis was greatly supportive of Jones and would continue to be even after an incident resulting in her removal from an upcoming concert. Jones arrived late to a mandatory conductor piano rehearsal. Hillis corresponded with Jones in a letter, explaining that she held "no personal animosity" towards Isola, but that Jones was dismissed from the rehearsal because she had arrived ten minutes before it ended, thereby disqualifying her from singing the performances. Two other singers were also dismissed under similar circumstances. The closing paragraph of the letter reminded all three singers receiving similar letters to understand that Hillis's actions were not a personal vendetta, as such actions can often be misconstrued. "As a professional member of the Chorus for several years, surely you realize that certain responsibilities are solely those of the chorister. Fulfilling contractual obligations and meeting the requirements necessary for performance are among them."[3]

Isola Jones, a member of the CSC from 1968–1977, and also a student of Hillis at Northwestern University, was not immune to such disciplinary action despite her immense talent and familiarity with Hillis. Though Hillis was strict with her singers, she did not hold a grudge, particularly when singers demonstrated their ability to improve. Such was the case when providing Ms. Jones with her "big break" in 1975. Ms. Jones acknowledged that Hillis did indeed play an important role in positioning her for what would become a substantial opera career.[4] As Jones explained it, her luck first began with Hillis appointing her as the mezzo-soprano understudy for an upcoming performance series of Verdi's Requiem, conducted by Solti, in April 1975. When Jones arrived at the final orchestral rehearsal of the Requiem, she was informed that soloist Yvonne Minton was ill, and Jones was asked to sing in her place for that rehearsal. After a brief meeting with Solti, he brought Jones to the stage, introducing her to the other soloists with whom she would perform. To Isola's right was superstar soprano Leontyne Price, who had been Isola's inspiration for her singing career. To her left was world-class tenor Luciano Pavarotti, and next to him was the outstanding bass Gwynne Howell. Jones recalled singing her first solo entrance, *Liber scriptus*, after which Pavarotti and Price, on either side of her, each took her hand, conveying their approval.[5] It was a surreal moment for Isola. Upon returning home that evening, she received a call from CSO Artistic Administrator Peter Jonas, stating that Solti had been impressed with her performance and would like to contract her for a part in Wagner's *The Flying Dutchman* performances and recording, scheduled for the following CSO season. From that understudy opportunity given to Isola by Hillis, several more "breaks" followed, including a recording contract with Leonard Slatkin conducting Gershwin's *Porgy and Bess* and a performance of Stravinsky's *Les noces* at Ravinia, conducted by James Levine. Levine, then music director of the Metropolitan Opera, subsequently offered Jones a contract with the Met beginning in the spring of 1977. Jones remained at the Met for fourteen years before moving on to a teaching career in Arizona. Hillis had no hesitation promoting wonderful singers in her Chorus, such as Isola, sometimes overlooking prior transgressions of her singers which Hillis attributed to youthful errors. She chose instead to serve the greater good in supporting these promising young artists.

In addition to monitoring her choristers' attendance, Hillis would also need to step in to correct Chorus misbehavior. An incident in May 1972 occurred during a trip to the University of Illinois in Urbana for a recording session of Beethoven's Symphony No. 9 at the acoustically superb Krannert Center's Great Hall. This was, in fact, the Chorus's first recording project with Solti. Hillis was dismayed to learn of behavior unbecoming of several Chorus members during their return trip. Responding to these reports, Hillis wrote a "Dear People" letter:

> After such a successful day, it is disappointing to learn that the homeward trip was spoiled for some of you by the irresponsible behavior of a few. It is natural to look forward to the change of scenery and also to a good time. To this there is no objection. However, whether in a restaurant, hotel, concert hall, or on the street, you are representing the CSC and you should conduct yourselves accordingly. It is also expected that you treat your colleagues with consideration and respect. If such things are not important to you, you do not belong in this chorus. It is regrettable that this has to be said. It should not be necessary and I hope it will not happen again.[6]

Hillis found herself monitoring on-stage decorum as well. An audience member had reported in a letter to Hillis and CSO management of a male singer in the top row of the choral risers blowing a kiss to a young man seated near the front row of the audience.[7] This event in 1971 occurred just before the maestro was to enter the stage, when the hall becomes quiet and the lighting changes to focus the audience directly onto the stage. It made this singer's inappropriate behavior even more noticeable. Hillis appointed her CSC associate director and Chorus manager Ronald Schweitzer to respond to the matter, however she was well aware of the situation and carefully directed how the matter should be handled.[8]

Language coach Gertrude Grisham recalled that in her first several years with the Chorus, beginning in 1974, she observed a change in Margaret's interactions with her choristers. During Grisham's first year or two, she observed Hillis as very approachable, but she saw this change shortly thereafter. Gertrude claimed that Hillis came to regret her less formal relationship with the singers, realizing that there were a few untrustworthy characters in the Chorus trying to take advantage of her kind nature. Grisham observed a steady withdrawal of Hillis's congenial interactions with her singers one-on-one, though she always remained respectful of the Chorus at large. Gertrude believed Hillis enjoyed the new "formidable" persona she adapted, allowing her to more easily distance herself from Chorus members, particularly when it came to those who required disciplining.[9]

Hillis's vigilance in overseeing matters between the Chicago Symphony Chorus and the Orchestral Association was not the only distraction from her good work. Added to this was the continual criticism appearing in newspaper reviews of her conducting in CSO concerts, Civic Orchestra concerts, and in her guest conducting appearances. Stinging commentaries written as early as 1968 continually served as constant reminders of what Hillis had yet to achieve. In a review of an Allied Arts choral series concert Hillis conducted on December 15, 1968, with the Chorus and members of the Chicago Symphony Orchestra, a reviewer made an assessment of her talent that must have been hurtful for her to read. The program included several a cappella pieces, Stravinsky's Mass, and Britten's *St. Nicholas*. The reviewer stated, "[Hillis's] talents are *more* remarkable in the sphere of choral training than in that of actual conducting. For this reason, the group tends to be at its best when Miss Hillis does her exceptionally rigorous groundwork and someone else comes in to lead the concert itself."[10] Reviews of her Civic Orchestra performances stated additional shortcomings, with one reviewer describing Hillis's interpretation of the music as "eminently sound and adequately majestic," however "if . . . telltale pauses . . . had been allowed a little more time, this would have been an even more powerful reading."[11] Even when making guest appearances, as she did in four Handel *Messiah* concerts with the National Symphony Orchestra at the Kennedy Center in December 1976, one reviewer defined Hillis's performances as rather sterile despite her clear conducting strengths. Irving Lowens wrote, "Margaret Hillis is a technician of awesome excellence, but very little more. . . . The piece came out with every 'i' dotted and every 't' crossed but without heart. . . . What I missed in the performance was something to love."[12] These critical comments would recur despite many good reviews written about her conducting and choral preparations. It must have been discouraging for her to read these criticisms, which are often remembered far longer and taken more to heart than good reviews. However, Hillis continued to take risks during this period. Her repertoire with the CSO and the CSC included premieres of challenging contemporary works, including Roberto Gerhard's *The Plague* in 1972, and a world premiere of Alan Stout's *Passion* in 1976. She would also perform pieces she had conducted during her New York years, which she had done with much smaller forces, but she would now conduct with the full complement of the CSO and CSC. Concerts included such works as Bach's Mass in B Minor, Dallapiccola's *Canti di prigionia*, and Stravinsky's *Les noces* and *Symphony of Psalms*. It seemed that the more critical the reviews, the more ambitious Hillis became to prove them wrong.

Margaret would endure further disappointment in her career when in 1977 she was not rehired at Northwestern University after eight years of building the choral program. Teaching had always been an important part of her professional life from early on when she first provided workshops and demonstrations in New York to share her newly acquired choral pedagogy. The Northwestern position was her opportunity to pass along the wisdom attained in her experiences of more than twenty-five years to the next generation of choral conductors. She treasured her work with young singers and young conductors, shaping a very respectable university conducting program in the way she believed would elevate the profession.

Although there was no clear reason stated for Hillis being released, several who knew her in that capacity had opinions as to why she was being replaced. Professor Paul Aliapoulios, who began his Northwestern University career as an associate dean of undergraduate studies during Hillis's final year at Northwestern, believed that she had modeled her choral program more like a symphonic chorus, often performing works like Bach's *St. Matthew Passion*, Brahms's *A German Requiem*, and the like. Aliapoulios surmised that the university administration may have been interested in a more diversified choral program, such as those trending universities at this time, whereby choirs performed a wider variety of musical styles and genres. Aliapoulios recalled students and faculty liking Hillis very much, and her university choir was excellent. In his mind, it was a matter of conflicting visions between Hillis and the university administration.[13] Gertrude Grisham had a different explanation for Hillis's release. Calling it "typical academic horseplay," Grisham claimed Hillis was denied tenure "because she would not get involved in the administrative hassles. She did not have spare time to spend in committee meetings where they were debating [unimportant things]."[14] According to Grisham, Hillis was upset with Northwestern administrators who suddenly began to make these new demands of her. She did not have the time to add any more to an already packed schedule and therefore was not agreeable to these abrupt changes in their expectations. Grisham claimed that when Hillis was denied tenure, "it hurt her very much, her pride, her professionalism."[15] Hillis's public explanation for leaving Northwestern was consistent with her always professional demeanor, as she stated that her increasingly demanding conducting schedule no longer allowed her to maintain this role at the university.

It is an understatement to describe the loss this was for Northwestern University. Dr. Don Horisberger, a superb conductor and organist, who would become one of her assistant conductors with the Chicago Symphony Chorus, expressed how deeply he valued his studies with Ms. Hillis, as she was called. A graduate student in 1973, Horisberger first began his conducting studies with Hillis to fulfill a requirement of his master's degree in organ performance. Horisberger had a reasonable background in choral conducting before coming to Northwestern and sought out Hillis for permission to take her higher-level conducting course instead of the more basic conducting class offered to the organ majors. Through his master's and doctoral studies, Horisberger remained a regular participant in Hillis's conducting seminars and her university concert choir.

What thrilled and amazed Horisberger most was the depth with which Hillis approached every aspect of her musical preparation, from the music-learning stage, through the rehearsal preparations, to the final performance of a work. As Horisberger explained, he was familiar with methods of the music study process, but he was struck by how much more thoroughly Hillis approached the task.[16] Several major choral works were studied each semester with repertoire often concurrent with what was being rehearsed at Orchestra Hall. When beginning a new piece, Hillis would first provide the students with background information, giving them directives to engage in further study of the history, the style, and the composer of the piece. Hillis would then provide an overview of the work, giving her students an initial sense of the piece and calling their attention to things they should focus on as they embarked upon their exploration. She would caution them to pay attention to the interactions between instrumental and vocal parts, advising them of such things as how pairings of certain instruments and voices required the conductor to guide both singers and players to adjust their approach to the color of their sound or to the balance, stating such things as, "Be careful here, or the trumpets will overwhelm your soprano voices."

Hillis would teach her intricate score marking system using an array of colored pencils and highlighters to mark everything from entrances of specific vocal and instrumental parts to the bar line divisions of phrasing, as well as marking the dynamics, articulations, and, when applicable, the primary and secondary themes in the music. Specific colors and symbols were used to represent volume, articulation, phrase direction, tempo changes, beat patterns, motives, and so forth.[17] When students returned for the next class, Hillis would have them compare their score markings with one another and then she would reveal her fully marked score, a meticulously detailed and colorfully marked visual rendering of the sound that would ultimately be heard. Much attention and discussion were given to issues of text treatment, vocal color, balance, and style, which varied greatly from piece to piece. Most importantly, Hillis would spend class time instructing her students on *how* to guide a chorus to achieve the technical details revealed in their score study. Only after such carefully marked scores were completed would there be discussion of physical conducting gestures. Hillis would encourage a curvy rather than angular conducting motion, sometimes having her students place their arm on hers to allow them to feel the motion she was encouraging.

Another of Hillis's former students recalled the Northwestern conducting classes as being "stimulating and exhilarating in a way that transcends words."[18] As Francis Fowler Slade described, "In conducting class, everything revolved around studying scores . . . which she taught as a step-by-step process." Slade listed Hillis's steps:

1. Create a general chart of the work, which showed each movement or section of the work, including key areas, tempos, instrumentation, and voicing;
2. Next, mark the smaller sections of each movement, first through harmonic analysis, identifying changes in key, tempo, texture, and text;
3. Next, do a bar-line analysis, identifying single ideas, motives, or phrases;
4. After these preliminary steps, an intricate color-coding process is applied to the score, marking important entrances of voices and instruments, dynamics, articulations, and other details.

Hillis advised her students embarking upon a new piece to always start with the general aspects of the music, moving to the more specific elements as study continues, and then return to the larger picture of the work. When presenting the piece to the chorus, Hillis stressed the importance of first providing the ensemble with an overall understanding of the work before diving into the details. She emphasized the paramount importance of knowing the score thoroughly, which she deemed to be the conductor's main job, enabling him or her to earn the respect of the ensemble beyond anything else. Other advice Slade gleaned from the class was of a *practical* nature, a trademark of Margaret Hillis's teaching:

- Rehearse slow movements fast.
- Rehearse fast sections slowly.
- Rehearse without text first.
- Emphasize short notes so as not to lose them.
- Help your singers internalize rhythms by doing something physical.
- Rehearse polyphonic pieces [with the singers seated] in quartets.
- Speak texts in rhythm.
- Sing *legato* texts *staccato* and vice versa.
- Crescendo on sustained notes.
- Principal and subordinate material may be highlighted by singing one or the other with text while the other is done without text or by varying the articulation of each to help the singers hear both.
- If a work is in French, double the rehearsal time (she would also apply the same strategy to other languages singers less frequently encountered).
- Match vibrato.
- Keep still and listen like crazy![19]

Don Horisberger distinctly remembered one particular class when he became overwhelmed by the amount of detail Hillis expected her students to incorporate when rehearsing their own choirs. He recalled inquiring that this level of detail would work well when dealing with a professional or a university level ensemble, but he wondered how she changed her approach when working with choirs of a more limited background. Hillis's response was simple: "You don't." She continued, "Well sung music is well sung music" no matter what level choir one is working with, and though the results may not be the same with a less experienced choir, she never lowered her standards, always working towards the same goals with every chorus she encountered.[20] This was one of many lessons Hillis was able to pass along to a new generation of conductors.

Losing the Northwestern position, though disappointing, was only a short-term loss, which Margaret swiftly replaced with a new endeavor. Never dwelling on disappointment, she resolved a setback by changing course. This coping mechanism was not new. Margaret's brother Bud was always impressed by his sister's resilience when faced with adversity, a trait he observed in her throughout her life. As one of the most recognized choral conductors by 1975, Hillis had plenty of options to move forward. An invitation to join the Advisory Panel of the National Endowment for the Arts (NEA) in 1972 developed into her appointment to serve as director of the choral section of the Advisory Panel in 1976. This prestigious appointment provided her a national platform for advocacy of the choral field and became one way she refocused her energy in a positive direction. In 1977, Hillis would be invited to join a second organization that, in combination with her NEA position, would provide her greater opportunities to impact the choral profession than she had heretofore been able to achieve through her teaching and her American Choral Foundation (ACF).

Since 1955, when Hillis first began her Foundation and administered the initial ACF survey to choral conductors throughout the country, it was clear what challenges confronted the choral industry. Yet now, almost twenty years later, Hillis believed the choral field was still fighting old battles, continuing to be viewed as "less than" other fields of musical performance. This was due, in large measure, to the majority of choral singers being amateur musicians in contrast with orchestra and opera musicians who were almost always professionally trained. Although choral conductors were predominantly trained professionals, their ensemble members were not. Two central questions Hillis posited from that original survey were: "Why haven't [choral] professional groups been developed?" and "What can be done to develop such groups?"[21] To resolve these situations, Hillis originally shaped the focus for her foundation. Her Choral Institutes, beginning in 1968, were one step in the right direction, providing choral conductors with quality methodology, repertoire, research, and organizational support to infuse greater professionalism in their choirs. But Hillis had a second solution in mind: to establish permanent professional ensembles throughout various locations in the country. She delineated a three-step process to meet this goal:

1. Selecting communities that over a period of ten years had shown interest in choral music, as reflected by the number and quality of concert and opera performances.
2. Forming a group in each of these select communities "comprised of the best elements of all the choral groups in the community."
3. Subsidizing the groups [including payment of singers and conductors] until they establish a strong base of community support so as to become financially self-sufficient.

Though this plan for launching professional choral groups nationally was never realized through her Foundation, Hillis never gave up on the idea.

Almost twenty years later, with Margaret's appointment to the NEA's Music Advisory Panel, she became energized anew, hoping that this position might allow her to finally fulfill the unrealized goals of her Foundation. Her friend Bob Page, now director of the Mendelssohn Choir of Philadelphia, preparing choruses for Eugene Ormandy and the Philadelphia Orchestra, was also asked to the Panel. Page recalled his shared experiences on the Panel with his friend "Maggie," stating that while attending the Music Advisory Panel meetings, "We would sit in the corner like second cousins [of the Music Advisory Panel]," waiting for any opportunity to represent choruses [to the Panel].[22] Hillis and Page were soon appointed to chair a newly formed Choral Panel where they, along with other esteemed choral experts, would review applications and make recommendations for choruses requesting funding. The Panel's recommendations were then sent to the National Council, a committee of presidential appointees, who would almost always approve the Panel's choices. The Choral Panel functioned as a pilot program to explore the possibility of creating a permanent Choral Program of the NEA Music Advisory Panel. Under co-chairs Hillis and Page, the Choral Panelists determined that NEA funding should be directed to artists trying to make a living as musicians, including professional singers and choral music composers. The majority of grants were therefore initially given to those choruses considered "professional."

THE ASSOCIATION OF PROFESSIONAL VOCAL ENSEMBLES

In the meantime, Philadelphia Singers conductor Michael Korn and Gregg Smith, of the Gregg Smith Singers, expressed concern that their choirs were not receiving sufficient NEA funding due to there being no clear definition for what constituted a "professional" choir. In a letter sent by Gregg Smith to several of his conducting colleagues, he stated,

> A professional chorus by definition is a vocal ensemble in which the singing members are paid for their services on a consistent basis. . . . At this moment the whole question of professional choral music is being argued (and quite heatedly) on the highest level of government support, namely the NEA. Unfortunately, I think those of us who have given of our time, blood, and

money do not have a good voice at present, even though the NEA has limited
its support primarily to the professional choirs.[23]

Smith offered a way of resolving this dilemma by forming a new organization
representative of professional choruses, in part to help their cause for attaining NEA
funds to advance professional choral work in the United States.[24] Thanks to the vision
and efforts of Michael Korn and Gregg Smith, the Association of Professional Vocal
Ensembles (APVE) was officially incorporated in December 1977. Hillis was invited,
along with several other distinguished American professional choral conductors, to
become a charter member of the APVE's board of directors. (Other charter board
members included Walter Gould, Michael Korn, Hugh Ross, Gregg Smith, Roger
Wagner, and Janice Kestler.) No longer teaching, Hillis had time in her schedule to
become actively involved in APVE while still maintaining her NEA position. As a
charter board member, Hillis took a leading role in formulating the organization's
objectives, which bore great resemblance to the ideals Margaret had developed years
earlier for her Foundation:

- to promote the growth and expansion of professional vocal ensembles;
- to create greater appreciation for vocal ensembles by all segments of
  American society;
- to improve quality and quantity of choral music presentations;
- to promote the establishment, development, and improvement of
  professional vocal ensembles.

A top priority for APVE was to develop language the NEA could use for selecting
choruses to fund. APVE board members believed there was an indirect request
made of them by the NEA to create such guidelines. APVE board members were
particularly invested in doing so, as there were concerns that if parameters were not
drafted soon the NEA might do away with the pilot Choral Panel altogether.[25] Hillis
played an integral role in developing that language and then became the conduit
between APVE and the NEA to make sure it was applied to the process. By June
1978, Hillis, serving both as an APVE board member and as a newly appointed co-
chair of the NEA Choral Panel, became the staunch advocate for protecting NEA
funds for professional choirs.

When the word first got out that such funding was available, there were increasing numbers of inquiries as to how the Panel determined which choirs were considered professional and therefore eligible for this support. As early as July 1976, a statement from the American Choral Director's Association to the NEA conveyed, "The Choral Art in America is in need of more substantial support from the National Endowment for the Arts. Conductors of both non-professional and professional choral organizations are deserving of consideration for financial assistance. . . . The level of funding . . . should be increased at least 100%."[26] By September 1978, the president of ACDA, Walter Collins, was rallying ACDA members to contact their senators, congressmen, and the director of the NEA Music Program, Walter Anderson. The message Collins encouraged them to convey was that amateur choruses should receive a "seat at the [NEA] table," and they should receive an increase in funding, but most importantly that monies should not be going only to *professional* choruses. Instructing his ACDA members to advocate for this, he stated in an open letter, published in the September 1978 *Choral Journal*:

> ACDA has long attempted through persuasion to encourage the Endowment to devote a commensurate share of its resources to the amateur choral movement. . . . [He then instructs:] You should emphasize the importance and the strength of the amateur choral movement and the size and potential resource value of ACDA in that movement. It should also be made clear that ACDA, as the largest American choral organization by far, should have at least two representatives on the Panel.[27]

Walter Collins's open letter was responded to in an APVE newsletter by Paul Hill, director of the Paul Hill Chorale, and a charter member of APVE. First, Hill stated that professional singers make a significant improvement in the sound of a chorus. Second, he stated that though choral ensembles have been traditionally amateur, "[if it remains so] we have no hope of justifying our university departments of choral studies, our conservatory training for singing musicians, and all the training of which we good ACDA members are so proud." He goes on to say,

> Are we to tell our most talented choral students, "Here's your degree in choral music; Now you know there's no work?" Why are we teaching if the

end product is total amateurism? Do we send exceptional people to school to become amateur violinists, amateur dentists? I am an ACDA Life Member. I'm gung-ho . . . As a university choral director, I feel I am a wanted part of ACDA. As a professional choral director, however, I find that ACDA is embarrassed about me. It helps me if I teach, but not if I practice.[28]

The battles for funding, particularly with regard to the "professional" *vis-à-vis* "amateur" choirs, were just beginning. APVE was formed in part to represent professional choruses and to help the NEA resolve these challenges. Advocates like Margaret Hillis and members of the APVE were positioning themselves to raise the choral profession through NEA funding in order to support establishment of increased numbers of professional choruses throughout America.

It was clear to the APVE board of directors that nothing could be permanently resolved by the piloted Choral Panel until it became a permanent *program* of the NEA. This opinion was officially stated during the first Annual APVE Conference in June 1978, where the APVE board of directors crafted a letter urging the NEA to change the piloted Choral *Panel* into an official Choral *Program* as part of the Endowment. The letter stated,

> WE, THE BOARD OF DIRECTORS, have met and identified the immediate goal toward this end, as: . . . the development and proliferation of fully professional regional choruses throughout America which perform regular seasons and provide full-time employment for professionally-trained singers. . . . FURTHER, we would ask the immediate attention of the NEA in convening a panel of representatives of the choral field in order that guidelines may be adopted for a *Choral Program* of the Endowment and that appropriate funding for such a program be initiated. . . . Much time was spent discussing the possible criteria for [a Choral Program]. We have a draft copy of these suggestions.[29]

In this letter, it became clear that APVE was directing the NEA to dedicate their funding to develop and sustain regional *professional* choirs. Hillis and her APVE colleagues understood that only when professional singers could count on choral work as a means to make a living would the choral field ascend to a comparable level of their compensated colleagues in the orchestra and opera fields. Funding was the key requirement to establishing professional choruses. The NEA officially changed the pilot Choral *Panel* to a permanent Choral *Program* of the NEA's Music Advisory beginning in 1980. One of the people with whom Hillis worked closely from 1978–1981 was Carleen Hardesty (now Carleen Dixon Webb), who was then NEA Choral Program specialist. Hardesty was effusive in her praise and respect for Hillis during their work together.[30] When Hillis was eventually rotated off the NEA's Choral Program, Hardesty included in her official notification to Hillis, ". . . thanks in part to your guidance, the Choral Program is now firmly established."[31] Handwritten on that official letter, Hardesty added, "It has been one of the greatest pleasures of my job to have had the opportunity to work with you."[32] Hillis was in fact the driving force to make this Choral Program possible. After many years of unsuccessful efforts by Hillis to provide such funding through her Foundation, she was finally in a position to support professional choruses in a way that could substantively change the field of choral music. It was Hillis's hope that through her service work with the APVE and NEA she would carry forward the goals where her Foundation left off.

PERSONAL SACRIFICES FOR A CONDUCTING CAREER

Hillis's exciting work with APVE and NEA would carry her through the disappointments she encountered professionally. She was less successful in her ability to compartmentalize the personal challenges that arose, particularly during this time period. Hillis's sentiments, though rarely revealed, were briefly accessible during a television interview when the host asked Margaret about her personal sacrifices made throughout her conducting career. Hillis conveyed that early on in her New York days she struggled with her feelings about this chosen profession. "I resented the amount of time and the enormous demands. . . . It was like a monkey on my back, but I couldn't shake it." She shared that she had so many other things in life she enjoyed, but because of the time constraints of her work, she could not pursue them. "I wanted to travel, I love to read, I adore poetry, literature . . . but there was no time for it." She then shared a story about leaving the stage after successfully conducting Bach's *St. Matthew Passion* [April 1956 with the New York Concert Choir], completely drained from the lengthy and demanding performance, "but when I walked off the stage, a little voice said to me inside my head, 'Margaret, who do you think you are that you resent being part of such beautiful music?' And after that there was no further resentment." As she described, it was all a matter of disciplining herself. "A discipline means getting rid of things that are extraneous, and I had to just rule some things out."[33] As the years went on, those other interests, which may have been what she referred to as extraneous to her career, remained important in her life.

A glimpse into Hillis's desires beyond her musical life could be gleaned from letters she had written over the years. With finances tied up in her Foundation, Hillis would periodically express her frustrations for things she desired to have and to do, which were made impossible due to her substantial investments of family money going towards the support of the ACF. As fundraising remained elusive, it was predominantly Hillis's personal funding of the Foundation that provided support for such things as the founding of the Chicago Symphony Chorus. Additionally, Hillis would continue to support other worthy causes through her Foundation as well, but all at great personal expense. Hillis voiced her frustrations for what she was denying herself in a letter drafted to her lawyer, Jacob Schwartz. This letter, never sent, revealed some of her sentiments, just the same. In it, Hillis stated, "There are a great many things I have continued to deny myself for the sake of the growth of the Foundation."[34] In the letter ultimately sent to her lawyer, she wrote of things she wished to have but could not because of her expenditures for the Foundation. Among her wishes she stated her "intense desire to own land . . . I've wanted this for many years but have never spoken of it, because it seemed too remote."[35] When Hillis wrote another letter to Schwartz seven months later, she was already thinking about how she could reorganize the Foundation to lessen her financial obligation, stating, "In light of how hard I have to work to maintain this enormous structure, the Foundation as it is constituted makes no sense."[36] Even after undergoing a complete reorganization with Sheldon Soffer at the helm, the Foundation continued to endure financial hardship, as indicated by a letter written to Margaret by the ACF office manager, Mary Lou Tuffin, on July 16, 1975. "Here is the horrible news I have been promising you, and it is pretty grim. I have divided it into three parts: Where We Are, Where We Will Be in the Immediate Future, and How We Got That Way." Ms. Tuffin then proceeded to list the debts accrued by the Foundation, which Hillis would again bail out using her own money.[37] Though Hillis lived a very comfortable life, the Foundation added continuous financial strain, committing her to put some of her personal desires aside while keeping the Foundation solvent.

The mid-1970s proved additionally challenging with the passing of Margaret's mother. In the years just prior to her death, Bernice Hillis's health was deteriorating, but Margaret's schedule prevented her from spending much time with her mother, whose memories of her daughter were slowly fading away. On June 26, 1976, Margaret's most avid supporter, who had cultivated her love of music from the start, was gone. Though Margaret would rarely express regret for time she could not spend with her mother, other family members, and friends, there are hints throughout her career that this missing piece was one that stayed with her, particularly when she allowed herself time to reconnect with the people who meant so much to her. When Margaret was able to make the time, she spent it with her partner, Elizabeth Burton, and a few choice friends. Hillis found time to travel, and even when that travel was connected to work, she allowed herself time for fine dining, touring, and relaxation. One of the highlights of her work travels came about when Hillis was invited to teach and conduct at Stanford University in Palo Alto, California, providing her the opportunity to become reacquainted with relatives who thereafter would feel close to Margaret for the rest of her life.

Margaret had not seen her sister-in-law, Connie Hillis, since she, Joe, and their baby Gregory had left New York, returning to California once it became clear that Joe could not succeed in raising money for her Foundation. It had been years since they were together, and Connie, now divorced from Joe, was raising son Gregory alone. When Margaret told Connie she was coming to town, Connie insisted she stay with them. At that point, Gregory was nine years old. Connie, with her effervescent and loving personality, welcomed Margaret with great enthusiasm. As Connie recalled, "There was a mutual fondness between us both."[38] With many hours of "down time" during the four weeks of that first Palo Alto summer in the late 1960s, Margaret found herself cooking, interacting with Gregory, creating a garden for Connie, and greatly enjoying the connection with family again. Connie recalled Margaret's generosity to all of them, citing many nice things in her home which were "courtesy of Margaret."[39]

Also living in that part of California was Margaret's Aunt Esther, second wife of Margaret's Uncle March, Bernice's brother. Margaret referred to Aunt Esther as her "second mother," and she was thrilled to see her aunt again.[40] During one of their get-togethers, Aunt Esther recommended to Margaret a favorite activity she enjoyed sharing with nephew Gregory—pro wrestling! On Esther's recommendation,

Margaret agreed to take Gregory and some of his friends to a professional wrestling tournament in town. Margaret decided it was worth a try since her Aunt Esther seemed so enthusiastic about it. This particular wrestling match was going to be a big event at Cow Palace, an enormous arena often hosting rodeos. As soon as the match began, Gregory recalled Aunt Margaret becoming "instantly mortified at how vulgar and violent it was."[41] Particularly upsetting to her was all the abhorrent head banging. Though she did not enjoy the experience, she remained for the entire match, determined not to ruin her nephew's good time with his friends. Gregory chuckled as he reminisced about that evening, explaining that it meant so much to him that she had made this grand effort to share in something he enjoyed.

Margaret would return several times to Palo Alto over the years, sometimes bringing Elizabeth along to join her. In a letter to Bud following that first visit, she updated him on Joe, whom she described as lacking direction. Margaret surmised Connie to be reasonably happy and functioning well despite her circumstances, and she was doing a fine job of raising Gregory whom she described as a remarkable young man."[42] Margaret expressed her hopes for seeing her brother Bud, his wife Carol, and their boys in the not-so-distant future "to just get reacquainted with all." The Hillis family, according to Connie, was not close, rarely together for holidays or reunions, but it seemed Margaret longed for these family connections and would express these wishes in letters and invitations she sent out for family members to attend her concerts. When time permitted, she continued making efforts to bring her family together.

By the fall of 1977, as Hillis was approaching fifty-six years of age and in her twenty-first season of the Chicago Symphony Chorus, her future seemed predictable. Work was her life. So much had been sacrificed through her years of dedication to the profession, including missed opportunities with family and friends, and substantial financial sacrifices made to keep the Foundation afloat. No longer considering a return to New York, Hillis made a permanent commitment to the Midwest with the purchase of a magnificent home on a tree-lined street in a beautiful northern Chicago suburb. Perhaps one consideration for this location was to be closer to Northwestern University, where she was teaching at the time she purchased the home. She left Northwestern the following fall. The large, six-bedroom Georgian-style home resembled the stately residences of her childhood in Kokomo. An avid animal lover, Hillis was finally in a position to acquire several four-legged companions.

O'Banshee, the enormous 170-pound Irish wolfhound, would become her constant companion (Picture 56). Any opportunity to walk her majestic pal would garner instant attention during their beloved neighborhood jaunts. Hillis would even have O'Banshee present for Ravinia orchestra rehearsals, much to the delight of animal-loving musicians, although less embraced by Ravinia's executive director, Edward Gordon. O'Banshee shared the Hillis residence with three cats, keeping him company while Margaret was away.

Jane Samuelson

Hillis and her best friend, O'Banshee, a 170-pound Irish wolfhound. They're a good pair—both are even-tempered, highly disciplined, and fun-loving.

Picture 56.
Margaret Hillis and her beloved Irish wolfhound, O'Banshee, in the backyard of her home.
(Jane Samuelson, photographer) (*Chicago Magazine*, April 1980, p. 234)

These pets became a family of sorts for Margaret, particularly once her longtime partner Elizabeth Burton moved to the West Coast. Bettie Buccheri observed some unpleasant interactions between Elizabeth and Margaret when she joined them in a shared ride home after rehearsals that Bettie had played and Elizabeth had sung. Bettie recalled Elizabeth harshly criticizing Margaret over various aspects of the rehearsal that had just taken place. Bettie was surprised that anyone would speak to Margaret in such a manner, offering uninvited critiques, particularly in front of Bettie. Buccheri contextualized their relationship, likening Margaret's occasional treatment of Elizabeth to that of a "handmaiden."[43] Hillis expected Elizabeth to manage Margaret's every need as she carried on her full schedule of work. Perhaps this ultimately built resentment within Elizabeth when her role as Margaret's secretarial assistant began to lose its luster. That may have been what prompted Elizabeth to consider her options. After one of their pleasure trips to Seattle, Elizabeth determined it was time to make a new life for herself in that picturesque, distant region of the country. Though there was a break-up of sorts in the relationship, Margaret remained in close contact with Elizabeth after her move, continuing to pay some of Elizabeth's living expenses that had been part of their arrangement for many years prior. Margaret would continue her generosity towards Elizabeth, sending extravagant gifts for holidays and special occasions, including a new television that arrived for Elizabeth's first Christmas in her new residence. Despite the long-distance connection, this change left Hillis living a more solitary life. With a schedule devoted to study, teaching, rehearsing, performing, and committee work for the APVE and the NEA, Hillis was looking at a career with fewer years ahead than had already passed. Was this to be the extent of her life's work, conducting the CSO once a year, making periodic appearances with other choruses and orchestras, and with her primary role as preparatory conductor for the Chicago Symphony Chorus? Was she fulfilled with what many would describe as very respectable accomplishments despite the challenges and disappointments this career had wrought? Whether or not she was asking these questions of herself, she could not have imagined how dramatically her future was about to change.

Following a busy summer of 1977 with six Ravinia concerts, the twenty-first season of the Chicago Symphony Chorus opened with Mahler's Symphony No. 8. The program commenced on Thursday, October 27, 1977, with three concerts scheduled in Chicago, followed by a fourth performance scheduled on Monday, October 31, in New York's Carnegie Hall. Margaret was juggling her time that final rehearsal week between Chicago and Elgin, where she was to conduct her Elgin Symphony on Sunday afternoon, October 30, before flying out to New York for the Mahler performance at Carnegie Hall. As always, Hillis had masterfully planned every minute of that week to accommodate the demands of both concert programs. The CSO Mahler concert series in Chicago opened with great success, enabling Hillis to focus on Elgin, conducting her final orchestra rehearsal on Saturday afternoon. When that rehearsal ended, Hillis promptly departed for Orchestra Hall, where she arrived at 5:30 p.m., to prepare her warm-up for the CSC's third Mahler performance. Upon Hillis's arrival, she was immediately summoned to general manager John Edwards's office, where she was greeted by Edwards and Peter Jonas, artistic administrator of the CSO. As Hillis recalled, "I went up [to Edwards's office] thinking that one of the [solo] singers who had been having a little bit of throat trouble [needed] her understudy [from the Chorus] to step in or something to that effect."[44] Instead, and much to her surprise, Hillis was informed that Solti had fallen while exiting an elevator at the Ritz-Carlton Hotel that afternoon. The manual elevator had not been properly aligned with the floor before Solti exited it. He took a severe fall, badly straining his arm and shoulder. He was unable to conduct the concert that evening. John Edwards asked Hillis, "Can you conduct the performance tonight?"[45] Hillis did not feel confident with Part II of the symphony, which has many complex solo lead-ins and passages she did not feel prepared to conduct. She explained to Edwards that Part I was not a problem for her, as that is almost completely choral and Hillis knew it very well. She was not ready to step in on short notice to manage Part II with the same confidence. Hillis responded to Edwards, "I can do the first movement . . . but I refuse to touch the second movement because those quick changes in tempo . . . have to be prepared way ahead of time to work. I'll fall on my face. . . . However, if on Monday night you need me, I will be ready. I will know Part II."[46]

Hillis's next duty was to apprise the Chorus of the situation. In Orchestra Hall's ballroom, where the Chorus was to warm-up, several singers had already heard the announcement made on the classical radio station, informing anyone holding tickets to that evening's CSO performance that the concert was canceled. The rehearsal room was buzzing with choristers anxious to know what was going on.[47] Hillis calmly entered the room and announced the news that everyone feared—Solti was injured and would be unable to conduct the concert that evening. The question on everyone's mind was what would happen to the Carnegie Hall performance. In her typically controlled manner, Hillis explained that Solti's status for Monday night in New York was yet to be determined. She assured the Chorus that if Solti was unable to conduct on Monday night, she would be up to the task. She then swiftly departed, leaving behind a stunned symphony chorus with no idea what to expect for their upcoming New York appearance.

Hillis's next stop was to the recording booth at Orchestra Hall. Most concerts were recorded for potential future radio broadcasts, and Hillis decided she would obtain the recordings of Solti's Thursday night Mahler performance, hoping she could get a better idea of how he managed the intricate details of the symphony's second part. Arriving home that evening, she phoned her assistant conductor of the Elgin Symphony, Robert Hanson, informing him that he would now be conducting the Sunday matinee, as Hillis needed to prepare Mahler's symphony for a possible Carnegie Hall appearance. She then opened an unmarked score and began to listen to Solti's recorded performance. "I listened to it for five minutes and I thought, 'Phooey,' this does me no good at all. . . . That's one of the things I will not let a conducting student of mine do and that is to listen to a tape in order to 'learn a piece'—you can't do it. Because then it becomes entirely external and you've got to do an internal [study]."[48]

Hillis studied until midnight and realized she had better get some sleep. She arose the next morning at 7:00 a.m. and continued her study process. She phoned CSC accompanist Bettie Buccheri that morning, inviting her to go through the score. Bettie had played all the soloist rehearsals for Solti and she knew where the singers breathed, how Solti managed the frequent tempo changes, and other important details. Upon arriving at Hillis's home, Bettie recalled how they went through the piece page by page. Among the details discussed, Bettie advised Margaret of Solti's beat patterns in places that needed further clarification.[49] As Hillis tells it, ten minutes after Bettie departed, her phone rang. It was Solti's wife, Valerie, telling her that the maestro was offering to go over the score with Hillis if she would like. Hillis, thrilled to have this meeting, quickly changed her plane reservation to the latest flight she could get out of Chicago for New York and raced to the downtown hotel where Solti was recuperating.

He was lying in bed and in considerable pain, but we began to go over the score and he said, "Now at this point the soprano takes a deep breath . . . just take the sound out and then go on." Well, I needed to know that. Then he said, "This phrase over here is a long one for the tenor—you have to make a very slight accelerando—otherwise he's not going to be able to make it on one breath." Phew! I marked that into the score . . . things of that sort that the soloists did.[50]

As Hillis departed their meeting, Solti said to her, "My dear, this takes a great deal of courage on your part."[51] Hillis returned home to continue her study, then gathered her things and departed for the airport. She finished her analysis of Part II on the airplane. Even after arriving in New York, she had yet to be informed as to whether or not she would conduct on Monday night, however after meeting with Solti, it was clear she must be up to the task.

On Monday morning, she was officially notified that she would indeed conduct that evening. Unfortunately, she was not granted any rehearsal time with the orchestra. She would first see them when she stepped on the podium that evening. However, Margaret was granted rehearsal time with the soloists, the organist, the off-stage brass, and the chorus. The chorus had yet to be informed about the conductor for that evening's performance. Upon seeing Hillis approaching the podium, they immediately realized the magnitude of her responsibility for the evening to come. Hillis calmly and carefully took the performers through the most treacherous spots in the symphony, clarifying how she would lead them, with only keyboard accompaniment of the rehearsal. Before everyone departed the hour-long rehearsal, Hillis provided these words, "Look, don't try to help me do my job. Your job is to sing and play. Mine is to keep the whole shooting match together."[52] Hillis's confidence was the *sine qua non* for the task ahead, providing comfort to all who had attended her only rehearsal for that evening's performance. The orchestra, to Hillis's recollection, was not made aware of the conductor change until it was announced to the audience, immediately before she took her place on the podium to conduct them.[53]

A sold-out crowd at Carnegie Hall had no idea what was about to happen. Only choristers and a few close friends Hillis had invited for this historic night knew the situation and all were instructed to keep it quiet. Hillis recalled thinking about the last time she had conducted on the stage of Carnegie Hall, on December 7, 1957, the same year she founded the Chicago Symphony Chorus.[54] Her experience of previous performances on that stage provided an extra layer of security, as she knew the sound and balance she would hear from the podium was consistent with what would be heard in the hall. She "trusted the hall," which she believed was a worry she would not need to contend with.[55] What happened next is shared in Hillis's words.

They say that fans are fickle. Well, they were not. I still had an enormous following in New York City. So Julius Bloom went out to make the announcement . . . Julius said—"Mr. Solti has had an accident." Well, of course, that was a terrible shock on the part of the audience—He said,

"However he is fine and will be conducting tomorrow night's concert, but the doctor said he cannot perform tonight." . . . And he then said, "He has put this performance in the hands of the distinguished conductor of the Chicago Symphony Chorus," and he didn't even get my name out when there was yelling, and screaming, and clapping.[56]

Not only was that a moment Hillis would long remember, but also it would become an indelible memory for members of the Chicago Symphony Chorus. It was indeed a very emotional moment for choristers, witnessing their director acknowledged so supportively for her talent after many years of behind-the-scenes contributions to magnificent concerts Chicago and New York audiences had come to expect. Now she was in the spotlight. Hillis recalled saying a short prayer before entering the stage. "Mr. Mahler, you have conducted here before. Please come down and help me tonight."[57]

The overwhelming applause welcoming Hillis to the stage provided added adrenaline to an already highly charged moment. As the concert began, the opening invocation, "Veni," required chorus members to summon their strength, overcoming tightened throats from pent-up emotions of this singular moment, allowing the powerful opening statement to resound throughout the massive hall.[58] "Veni creator spiritus"—"Come, creator spirit!"—was a sentiment shared by the performers and Hillis alike, as all embarked upon this spiritual journey. Hillis recalled never having concentrated harder on any project in her life as she did while preparing and conducting this concert. She shared that she was hardly aware of an audience behind her once the concert began, only sensing their profound silence in those moments when they too were fully engaged in the music. Having the piece almost memorized, Hillis claimed she would need to remind herself to turn the pages as she performed. Speaking about the performers she was conducting, Hillis recalled, "I have never felt so many eyes on me in my life. . . . I was aware of [hundreds of] people looking at [me] . . . with great intensity . . . [210 in the adult chorus and 60 in the children's choir plus over 100 instrumentalists in the orchestra] . . . and I thought, 'Oh boy, I had better move right—or the whole building is going to come tumbling down.'"[59] There were many more pairs of eyes watching Hillis's every move from the audience in a fully packed Carnegie Hall. Hillis insisted that she was not nervous for this performance, claiming she was so focused on what she had to do that she could not pay any attention to herself nor her feelings.[60] That composure in the midst of challenging circumstances was ingrained in her and fully accessible when it counted.

The moment the concert ended Hillis experienced great relief. "My God, WE DID IT."[61] The ovation that followed this performance was beyond anything the Chorus had experienced in their recent Carnegie Hall performances. A ten-minute ovation was given to the Orchestra, the Glen Ellyn Children's Choir, and the Chicago Symphony Chorus, many tearful for their director's success. The most resounding cheers of the evening were reserved for New York's very own Margaret Hillis, who had never been forgotten for her many accomplishments in that city all those years ago (Picture 57).

Picture 57.
Margaret Hillis takes her first bow following Mahler's Symphony No. 8 in Carnegie Hall on October 31, 1977. (Cheryl Frazes Hill collection)

A small reception followed that evening's performance. Along with soloists and management, Hillis invited several longtime friends who had supported her career aspirations from the beginning.

Some of my wonderful friends who in a way had shepherded me along—I had known them since 1952 and they are now quite elderly—but they had been at the performance and they just sat both of them and the tears were welling up—they were so proud—just as if I was their "child" since they didn't have any children . . . but they sort of brought me up and listened to all my problems about management—about raising money—and they tried to be helpful and indeed they had been very helpful—on a practical level as well as morale—anyway they were at this little reception, and I was so pleased that THEY were able to come.[62]

The dear friends Hillis referred to were "Pick" (Ernest) and "Red" (Rose) Heller. The Hellers supported Hillis in so many ways from her early days in New York, through her trials and tribulations with the American Choral Foundation, and to the present, sharing with her in this most significant moment of her professional life. The Hellers, who had no children, treated Margaret like one of their own. They would have been in their late seventies at the time of this concert, and no doubt they were thrilled to witness Margaret's impressive accomplishment.

It was not until the next morning, as she awakened at the Heller home, that Margaret became fully aware of the impact her performance had made upon the music world. "I did not dream that it was to be a personal success for me. What I felt was [the Orchestral Association] put all this money and effort into the performance in New York City and I had to save my family . . . I was doing it for US."[63] Hillis described a regular stream of phone calls and interviews, *The New York Times*, the BBC, NBC's *Today Show*, reporters from Canada, and many additional national and international news outlets. Headlines filled the New York papers, touting the success of a woman replacing Georg Solti at iconic Carnegie Hall. "Happily, Miss Hillis's performance proved worthy of the occasion. She did not attempt to imitate Mr. Solti's tempestuous Mahler, but her professionalism was evident in the fact that her Eighth Symphony ran within a minute or two of the one recorded by the [CSO] Orchestra . . . in Vienna a few years ago."[64]

Of all the attention thrust upon Margaret, the most meaningful messages were those coming from friends and colleagues. Leonard Bernstein, or "Lenny" as she called him, was one of many who sent telegrams conveying pride and excitement for Hillis's success. Bernstein, who related to this experience as a last-minute replacement, had

323

been in a similar circumstance thirty-four years earlier when, as a twenty-five-year-old assistant conductor, he stepped in for Bruno Walter, conducting the New York Philharmonic at Carnegie Hall. Bernstein's message to Hillis—"Congratulations. I know what it feels like. More power to you."[65] But possibly the most meaningful exchange occurred while speaking with Eve Queler, a contemporary of Margaret's, experiencing similar challenges of building a conducting career as a female. In their conversation together, Hillis recalled, "When Eve Queler called me the day after the concert to congratulate me, I said, 'Eve, I hope that what I've done will help us all.'"[66] Not lost on Hillis was what this achievement meant for her present and future female conducting colleagues.

Reflecting upon what she had achieved, Hillis recalled the times when she was teaching those young men to fly during World War II, and her beginner students would freeze at the controls of the airplane while they were in the air. "It takes that kind of nerve and when you perform—somehow you have a life [situation] that you're dealing with and you're responsible for [it]."[67] Hillis felt that same intensity when it came to this performance, and she was able to manage it as effectively as she did with those young men she taught so many years before.

Despite the challenges and personal sacrifices of recent years distracting Hillis from all she had achieved, the accomplishment of October 31, 1977, forced Hillis to momentarily pause and reflect upon how far she had come. A return to the city where it all began, in the concert hall that had borne witness to so much history, there was now a new historic date to enter, chronicling the stellar performance of a female conductor, Margaret Hillis. In the days and weeks following her Mahler performance, Hillis was asked to tell her story many times over. Finally, her career journey was gaining national and international interest. Explaining her success, she humbly stated, "All I did was my job."[68] However, that job was no ordinary one, particularly for a woman. Her "overnight success" entailed many years of struggle, study, preparation, disappointment, and sacrifice. When the opportunity finally presented itself, Hillis was ready to take the mantle. As Raymond Ericson stated in the second article run by *The New York Times*, in as many days, he concluded, "The recognition given Miss Hillis on Monday night is not likely to affect her personally, although it might well inspire other orchestras to engage her for guest appearances."[69] To this, Hillis responded, "There's something that has to do with staying power. . . . I've never been discouraged. I love music, and I get back from it more than I ever gave to it."[70] Ericson's prediction was correct. Hillis would now be in demand. The question was how she would handle this "newfound fame." Her future was suddenly less predictable, filled with unanticipated possibilities. Just for this moment, however, Margaret Hillis was satisfied.

ENDNOTES

1. Recollection of the author during the mid-1970s Carnegie Hall appearances.
2. "Dear People" letter, January 17, 1962 (Margaret Hillis Collection, Rosenthal Archives of the Chicago Symphony Orchestra Association, Box 3).
3. Letter to Isola Jones from Margaret Hillis, February 9, 1972 (Margaret Hillis Collection, Rosenthal Archives of the Chicago Symphony Orchestra Association, Box 3).
4. Interview with Isola Jones, August 11, 2020.
5. Ibid.
6. "Dear People" letter, May 22, 1972 (Margaret Hillis Collection, Rosenthal Archives of the Chicago Symphony Orchestra Association, Box 3).
7. Letter to Margaret Hillis, March 29, 1971 (Margaret Hillis Collection, Rosenthal Archives of the Chicago Symphony Orchestra Association, Box 3).
8. Letter to Margaret Hillis from Ronald Schweitzer, April 6, 1971 (Margaret Hillis Collection, Rosenthal Archives of the Chicago Symphony Orchestra Association, Box 3).
9. Interview with Gertrude Grisham.
10. Bernard Jacobson, "Symphony Chorus Gives Soft, Subtle Performance," *Chicago Daily News*, December 16, 1968.
11. Bernard Jacobson, "Civic Scores in Demanding Test," *Chicago Daily News*, May 8, 1972.
12. Irving Lowens, "Messiah Makes Season Official," *Washington Star*, December 10, 1976.
13. Interview with Paul Aliapoulios, April 23, 2014.
14. Interview with Gertrude Grisham.
15. Ibid.
16. Interview with Don Horisberger, May 6, 2014.
17. A list of resources for a more detailed explanation of Hillis's score study is available in Appendices.
18. Francis Fowler Slade, "The Hillis Conducting Seminar: An Appreciation," *The Voice of Chorus America* 20, no. 4 (1997): pp. 8–9.
19. Ibid.
20. Interview with Don Horisberger, May 6, 2014.
21. William Robert Bucker, "A History of Chorus America: Association of Professional Vocal Ensembles," DMA dissertation (University of Missouri–Kansas City, 1991), p. 261.
22. Interview with Robert Page, June 11, 2014.
23. Letter from Gregg Smith to Margaret Hillis and twenty-one other choral conductors to become charter members of a new APVE organization, September 10, 1975 (Margaret Hillis Collection, Rosenthal Archives of the Chicago Symphony Orchestra Association, Box 8).
24. Bucker, "A History," p. 142.
25. Bucker, "A History," p. 36.
26. A position statement directed to the advisory NEA Choral Panel (not signed but likely sent by the president of ACDA), dated July 1976 (Margaret Hillis Collection, Rosenthal Archives of the Chicago Symphony Orchestra Association, Box 8).
27. Walter S. Collins, "Presidents' Open Letter to the Membership," *The Choral Journal* (September 1978): p. 7.

28. Paul Hill, "Paul Hill Letter," *Association of Professional Vocal Ensembles Newsletter* 1, no.1 (October 1978): pp. 8–9.

29. Letter from APVE Charter Board of Directors, including Walter Gould, Margaret Hillis, Michael Korn, Hugh Ross, Gregg Smith, and Roger Wagner, sent to Dr. Walter F. Anderson, Chairman of the NEA Music Program, June 26, 1978 (Margaret Hillis Collection, Rosenthal Archives of the Chicago Symphony Orchestra Association, Box 8).

30. Interview with Carleen Dixon Webb (Hardesty), August 31, 2019.

31. Letter from Carleen Hardesty to Margaret Hillis, October 8, 1981 (Margaret Hillis Collection, Rosenthal Archives of the Chicago Symphony Orchestra Association, Box 8).

32. Ibid.

33. Margaret Hillis, interview with Pat Cheffer, *Lifestyle with Pat Cheffer*, Continental Cablevision program, March 1989.

34. Draft of a letter to Jacob "Jack" Schwartz from Margaret Hillis (Margaret Hillis Collection, Rosenthal Archives of the Chicago Symphony Orchestra Association, Box 9/14).

35. Letter to Jacob "Jack" Schwartz from Margaret Hillis, September 19, 1965 (Margaret Hillis Collection, Rosenthal Archives of the Chicago Symphony Orchestra Association, Box 9/14).

36. Letter to Jacob "Jack" Schwartz from Margaret Hillis, April 20, 1966 (Margaret Hillis Collection, Rosenthal Archives of the Chicago Symphony Orchestra Association, Box 9/14).

37. Letter to Margaret Hillis from Mary Lou Tuffin, office manager of the American Choral Foundation, July 16, 1975 (Margaret Hillis Collection, Rosenthal Archives of the Chicago Symphony Orchestra Association, Box 10).

38. Interview with Connie Hillis and Gregory Hillis, March 25, 2014.

39. Ibid.

40. Jane Samuelson, "For the Love of Music," *Chicago Magazine* (April 1980): p. 193.

41. Interview with Gregory Hillis, March 17, 2014.

42. Letter to Elwood Hillis, July 19, 1966.

43. Interview with Bettie Buccheri, October 27, 2012.

44. Jon Bentz, "Interview of Margaret Hillis Director Chicago Symphony Orchestra, September 19, 1989, Archives Committee, Oral History Project, 1992," p. 25 (Margaret Hillis Collection, Rosenthal Archives of the Chicago Symphony Orchestra Association).

45. Ibid.

46. Bentz, "Interview of Margaret Hillis," p. 26.

47. Personal recollection of the author.

48. Bentz, "Interview of Margaret Hillis," p. 26.

49. Interview with Bettie Buccheri, October 27, 2012.

50. Bentz, "Interview of Margaret Hillis," p. 28.

51. John von Rhein, "Hillis Stands on Her Own as a Stand-in for Solti," *Chicago Tribune*, November 3, 1977, p. 3.

52. Ibid.

53. Bentz, "Interview of Margaret Hillis," p. 28.

54. Karen Monson, "Sweet 'Brava!' for an Old Pro," *Chicago Daily News*, November 1, 1977, p. 4.

55. Jeannine Wagar, *Conductors in Conversation: Fifteen Contemporary Conductors Discuss Their Lives and Profession* (Boston: G.K. Hall & Co., 1991), p. 117.

56. Bentz, "Interview of Margaret Hillis," p. 29.

57. von Rhein, "Hillis Stands on Her Own," p. 3.

58. Author's recollection of the performance.

59. Bentz, "Interview of Margaret Hillis," p. 30.

60. Ibid., p. 32.

61. Ibid., p. 30.

62. Ibid., p. 31.
63. Ibid., p. 29.
64. Donal Henahan, "Woman Steps in for Solti, Wins Carnegie Hall Ovation," *The New York Times,* November 1, 1977, p. 1.
65. Giovanna Breu and Sally Moore, "For Margaret Hillis the Night to Remember Involved 395 Musicians, Mahler, and No Rehearsal," *People,* November 28, 1977, p. 84.
66. von Rhein, "Hillis Stands on Her Own," p. 3.
67. Bentz, "Interview of Margaret Hillis," p. 30.
68. Raymond Ericson, "Miss Hillis Carries Her Baton Lightly," *The New York Times,* November 2, 1977.
69. Ibid.
70. Ibid.

CHAPTER 17

FINDING HER PATH: 1977–1986

M argaret Hillis's Carnegie Hall success story continued to reverberate beyond the days and weeks following that fateful Halloween night of 1977. Her magical scenario caused the plexiglass shield keeping women off the conductor's podium to crack just enough that female conductors might finally see their way through the seemingly impenetrable barrier. Sensational coverage in the media following Margaret's Carnegie Hall success gave way to a plethora of overwhelming performance opportunities that she would accept, carefully configuring them around an already demanding array of commitments. Orchestras across the country and beyond were extending invitations no longer limited to choral symphonic works. She was now receiving invitations to conduct purely orchestral programs. The career opportunities Hillis had envisioned from the time she embarked upon a conducting career had finally arrived. The question was: Would she seize upon them, and, if so, at what cost? The next nine years of Margaret's life became a performance roller coaster from the moment she stepped off the Carnegie Hall stage. The highs would be sensational—the lows equally breathtaking. This unanticipated period would put Margaret's ambitions to the test—those she had been preparing for her entire life. In the fall of 1977, Hillis was suffused in a rehearsal/performance schedule, including one of the busiest Chicago Symphony Chorus (CSC) seasons to date. Her increasing outside engagements were manifold albeit manageable in her current schedule. Nonetheless, with so much outside interest in Margaret Hillis as a conductor these days, her balanced scale could easily be tipped.

Further complicating an already packed calendar was Hillis's service work—for example, her role in the new Association of Professional Vocal Ensembles (APVE)—added to her responsibilities with the National Endowment for the Arts (NEA) and her American Choral Foundation. Initially, Margaret could not resist accepting the multitudinous offers coming her way. At some point, however, she would pay the price for taking on as much as she did. Amazingly, for several years, she was actually able to make it all work, but eventually the consequence of not being able to be in two places at once would become problematic. Understanding what Hillis was balancing, it is difficult to fathom all that she was able to fulfill during this time of her career. As her star was rising, she learned to choose wisely.

Upon Hillis's return to Chicago after the New York triumph, her schedule for the remainder of the season was already planned. Coordinating her time in the intricate way for which she was best known, Hillis was able to add the numerous requests for television, radio, and magazine interviews, as well as additional conducting and speaking invitations she was receiving. She even made time to accept new awards coming her way. Each of these opportunities required time out of Margaret's already set calendar. However, Margaret understood the value of making time for these appearances in what might amount to a once-in-a-lifetime opportunity. Such visibility was good for her career, no doubt, but even more important, she was keenly aware of what this could mean in raising visibility for the choral profession and for women conductors.

With Carlo Maria Giulini due to arrive in only a few short weeks for the upcoming performances of Mozart's Requiem in November 1977, there was no time to bask in the recent Mahler success. The Chorus returned to their normal rehearsal routine on the Monday night following their Carnegie Hall appearance. Every month of this busiest 1977–1978 season involved a Chorus appearance. During this heavily scheduled period, Margaret would make a special trip to Washington, D.C., in April 1978, to plan for a coveted invitation she would fulfill in April 1979, when she and select Chorus members would perform at the annual White House Correspondents' Dinner for President Jimmy Carter and distinguished guests (Picture 58). The Chicago Symphony Chorus 1977–1978 season culminated in the spring with the full chorus making a return trip to Carnegie Hall performing their signature piece, Brahms's *A German Requiem*, which Solti chose to record when they returned to Chicago. This decision by Solti was prescient because it was a sensational performance series for which critics and performers could not offer enough superlatives. Solti was so moved by the audience's response at Carnegie Hall that he gave Hillis a solo bow.

Margaret's demanding schedule was carefully managed around her top priority: keeping the Chorus at peak performance level. The Chorus's first Grammy Award for Verdi's Requiem in 1978 brought an even brighter spotlight on the ensemble, now suddenly experiencing their own "overnight success" in their twenty-first season. Hillis understood that with greater attention comes greater scrutiny, and she was not about to let her singers "rest on their laurels" despite recent exemplary press coverage. Whatever additional obligations Hillis was accepting, she understood that her first priority was maintaining the excellence of the Chorus she had worked for so many years to establish.

Picture 58.
Jimmy Carter, Margaret Hillis, and the CSC at the White House Correspondents' Dinner following their performance at the White House, April 28, 1979. (Official White House photograph)

Hillis acquired two new appointments during her busy years of the mid-1970s. These new positions would further complicate her scheduling of newly acquired work that was continually being added as a result of her Mahler success. At the suggestion of Norman Pellegrini, a well-known radio producer and program director of WFMT, one of Chicago's classical music stations, Margaret was encouraged to meet with Al Booth, a successful real estate executive and great supporter of the arts.

During a 1975 meeting, Booth pitched his idea for Margaret to assist him with a Do-It-Yourself *Messiah* concert series that he first witnessed while living in London. He explained that he had participated in this concert experience at a London parish church, enjoying it so much that he pledged he would bring it to Chicago. The production involved the audience participating as members of the chorus during a performance of Handel's *Messiah*. A full orchestra would accompany four soloists for all of the solo movements, and then the audience would perform the choral movements with the orchestra. Booth invited Hillis to consider becoming the artistic director for this event, coordinating all the musical details, including the hiring of the soloists, harpsichordist, organist, and conducting the orchestra for the performances. Hillis listened carefully to the idea, recalling at the time how she thought it could work but wondering if she should attempt it. Hillis stated that having heard so many "stuffy" performances of *Messiah*—"scholarly versions with tiny choruses and authentic out-of-tune instruments," as she put it —she believed she could do Handel a service by providing a more uplifting version of the piece, one "filled with vitality . . . designed to drive musicologists 'right up the wall.'"[1] Once she agreed to this ambitious undertaking, the production was launched in December 1976, gaining immediate popularity and eventually inspiring this performance concept in other parts of the country.

The challenges of the Do-It-Yourself *Messiah*, as it came to be known, were immense. Hillis was tasked with keeping together the forces of an amateur orchestra and thousands in the chorus, mostly untrained singers, packed into Orchestra Hall. The only professionally trained musicians in the production were Hillis, the harpsichordist, the organist, and four soloists she selected from her symphony chorus. Tickets to the event were free and quickly became the most in-demand acquisition of the holiday season. National television talk show personality Phil Donahue added further excitement to the event when he was quoted in a *Wall Street Journal* headline story covering Chicago's singular *Messiah* production. He stated that he was a regular chorus participant every year in Chicago, claiming, "These are the hottest tickets in town."[2] The *Wall Street* journalist described the event in detail. "To join this mighty chorus, all you have to do is pick up a free ticket, show up the night of the performance, make your way to the right section . . . for your voice [part], and sing when the conductor tells you"[3] (Picture 59).

CHICAGO — Margaret Hillis, conducting at Chicago's fourth "Do-It-Yourself Messiah," turns from the 40 amateur musicians to give direction to the novice chorus in the unrehearsed production at Orchestra Hall. Photo was taken Dec. 17, 1979. (UPI)

The Do-It-Yourself Messiah:
A Musical Feast For Amateurs

CHICAGO (UPI) — More than 200 years ago, the Church of England was up in arms over George Frederic Handel's "Messiah" being performed in a playhouse.

But how times change. Now, thousands of people are packing music halls around Chicago to sing in "do-it-yourself Messiahs." Handel would be delighted.

T Handel would be delighted.

The allure is that anyone can participate. Although some soloists are professional, many of the thousands of singers are the "bathroom shower" variety. Many musicians also are amateurs.

This year, 10 sing-alongs for the three-hour symphony celebrating the birth of Christ were listed in Chicago Magazine, including one at Chicago Temple-First Methodist Church, billed as the city's first, and a spectacular production con-

ducted at Orchestra Hall.

The "Messiah" was warmly received at its premiere performance in Dublin, Ireland, in 1742. But the reception in London a year later provoked the ire of some members of the Church of England who said any work about God should never be performed in a playhouse.

That belief, however, was not embraced by King George II, who was so moved by the fervor of the "Hallelujah Chorus" that he jumped to his feet and remained standing until the last note had sounded.

The king's enthusiasm began the custom of standing during the "Hallelujah Chorus" — other members in the audience could not stay seated while the king stood.

Margaret Hillis, director of the Chicago Symphony Chorus, said the popularity of the sing-along is simple:

"The 'Messiah' is the most beloved piece of music ever written.

"And it has to do with the season and getting oneself sort of geared to it," Mrs. Hillis said. "And in Chicago, no one has to pay ... it's a human thing."

This year, Mrs. Hillis conducted two performances of the "do-it-yourself Messiah" at Orchestra Hall, which seats 2,500, ecause some 5,000 people were turned away from last year's one performance.

The hall was packed both nights. Tickets are free, but must be obtained in advance. They are snatched up quickly.

Ricardo Schwarz, a physicist and violinist for the West Suburban Orchestra said the music itself draws the crowds.

"It's something the masses can perform," Schwarz said standing onstage. The sounds of

Christmas carols and musicians tuning their instruments almost overpowered his voice. "Handel created it for the masses. There is nothing elite about it."

Several seats away, Robbie Janov flipped through his score for the last time. For Robbie, just 12 years old, it was his first performance and he was "a little nervous."

Mrs. Hillis has conducted the public Messiah since 1976, when Chicago real estate executive Al Booth patterned its debut after a production he had seen in a parish church outside of London.

But the city's first version was the brainstorm of the late senior pastor at Chicago Temple-Methodist Church, Dr. Robert Bruce Pierce.

Pierce, explained choir director Norma Lee Barnhart, got the idea from an elderly man.

Picture 59.

Do-It-Yourself *Messiah* in Orchestra Hall, Margaret Hillis conducting the audience that served as the chorus, December 17, 1979. Article entitled "Do-It-Yourself Messiah: A Musical Feat for Amateurs." (Margaret Hillis Collection, Rosenthal Archives of the Chicago Symphony Orchestra Association)

Shortly after launching the first Do-It-Yourself *Messiah*, Booth discussed another concept with Hillis, inspired by another musical experience he enjoyed while living in England. He explained, "I had a real estate office in London. . . . Every Thursday, they had a lunchtime concert in the [Bishopsgate] Library, near my office and I attended."[4] Booth went on to say that he did not understand why there was such a lack of federal support for American artists, and perhaps by establishing a similar program in Chicago, young artists in this city could be promoted. Booth was hoping Hillis would administrate this series, serving as the point person to collect and read résumés, listen to recordings of applicants, and decide who should be featured in the weekly noon-time programs. Hillis shared Booth's passion for promoting young talent and agreed to be involved.

The Chicago Public Library offered space for the recital series in Preston Bradley Hall, a large room with a magnificent Tiffany-domed ceiling and splendid acoustics. A local savings and loan bank underwrote the costs of this weekly event, which Booth named in memory of Dame Myra Hess, a British pianist who had arranged hundreds of lunchtime concerts free of charge to Londoners during World War II. Hillis was paid a fee to select performers who would benefit not only from a live performance opportunity but also from the extended exposure of the simultaneous radio broadcast on WFMT. Hillis began organizing this program, which began in October 1977.

During this busy time period of the mid-1970s, Margaret began her role as the artistic director for these two new projects, soon to become long-standing traditions in Chicago. Hillis's name would become synonymous with holiday *Messiah* performances, resulting in invitations throughout the country to conduct both the Do-It-Yourself style and the traditional version. Coverage of Hillis's Do-It-Yourself concerts in Chicago gained national interest, providing her publicity not only in the Chicago newspapers but also in popular nationally circulated magazines, touting the production among the nation's most popular ways to celebrate the holiday season.[5] As a result of this national publicity, Hillis's popularity continued to grow exponentially, first with national attention she was gaining through her numerous *Messiah* performances beginning in 1976 and then shortly thereafter from her 1977 triumph in New York. Hillis's latest ventures in collaboration with Al Booth were added to an already weighty workload she would now be tasked to manage.

In the midst of an increasingly busy Chicago Symphony Chorus schedule, her additional conducting duties, and her added work with the Dame Myra Hess concerts and Do-It-Yourself *Messiah* performances, Margaret accepted yet another position in 1981, becoming music director of the Liberty Fremont Society Orchestra in Libertyville, Illinois. Since this was a local orchestra, she would not need to travel far to keep her orchestra "conducting chops" sharp. Because her study time was at a premium, she cleverly programmed the same concerts for Liberty Fremont as she had planned for the Elgin Symphony located several suburbs away. By duplicating these programs, Hillis wisely managed preparation time, making this added orchestra a somewhat doable feat.

By the time Hillis had added another orchestra conducting position to her schedule, she had already replaced her university appointment at Northwestern with another teaching position, beginning in 1978. Invited to be a visiting professor at Indiana University, she could not turn it down. Her teaching schedule consisted of conducting classes and included an invitation to conduct one concert performance each school year. Her first performance at Indiana University was a massive production of Mahler's Symphony No. 8, performed October 31, 1979, exactly two years to the date from when she had conducted it at Carnegie Hall. As Hillis often quipped, "*This* time I was able to rehearse it first!" Replacing the teaching she had greatly loved at Northwestern University, she was eager to continue cultivating the next generation of choral conductors. Hillis would fly to Bloomington, Indiana, every Tuesday morning (after conducting her CSC rehearsals on Monday nights), teach all day Wednesday and Thursday, return to Chicago on Thursday afternoon, and head out to conduct her Elgin Symphony Orchestra on Thursday evening. Liberty Fremont Orchestra rehearsals would be fit into the schedule as time permitted. The calendar was breathtaking, but Hillis seemed able to keep it all in balance.

Around all of her weekly standing commitments, Hillis accepted an ever-accumulating list of guest-conducting appearances, no longer limited to university performances that had once accounted for the majority of her outside work. By 1981, Hillis was guest conducting major symphony orchestras and national festivals around the country, including the Basically Bach Festival at Avery Fisher Hall, the National Symphony Orchestra at the Kennedy Center in Washington, D.C., and Roger Wagner's Los Angeles Master Chorale with the Los Angeles Philharmonic. It was clear that audiences were eager to see the woman who had made such a "splash" at Carnegie Hall.

CONTINUING HER SERVICE TO THE INDUSTRY

It would seem under the recent constraints of her weekly routine Margaret would have sought ways to reduce her workload, perhaps suspending involvement on the NEA and APVE committees. However, Hillis was keenly aware of significant progress being made on behalf of professional choruses due, in part, to her efforts. Perhaps the other draw for Hillis was the bond she was forming with colleagues in these organizations, who shared her vision and passion for the profession. They were becoming more than colleagues; they were now trusted companions, akin to extended family. Considering the tangible progress finally being made through Hillis's work on the NEA and APVE and these treasured friendships she was developing, she may have surmised this was not an appropriate time to step back from her service commitments despite the relief it would have provided to her exhaustive schedule.

As fate would have it, Hillis played critical roles on both the NEA panel and the APVE board of directors during this time period. Not only was she significantly responsible for crafting the goals and objectives of these organizations, she also became critically important in enabling those ideas to materialize. She did so by calling upon her incredible connections to people in the highest governmental positions. By this time in her career, Hillis was well-connected with United States congressmen, which started in her earliest days of working with Senator Jacob Javits on her own Foundation. From then to this current time, with her brother now serving as a member of the United States Congress, Hillis had many whom she could call upon to enlist support. Margaret Hillis's reach was vast. She knew how to work the system and was singularly focused on doing so.

During the first year of APVE in 1977, Margaret joined forces with APVE's executive director, Michael Korn, cleverly organizing a letter-writing campaign to influence the pending replacement of NEA's first chairperson, Nancy Hanks, who was stepping down. Hanks had been a true champion for choruses, wisely selecting Margaret and Bob Page to lead the original Choral Panel in 1975. Hillis understood the importance of Hanks's replacement towards guaranteeing future advocacy on behalf of the choral field. Having an insider's perspective, Hillis advised Michael Korn to enlist APVE support for Livingston Biddle. In Korn's first annual executive director report to APVE's membership, he acknowledged the successful results of the letter-writing campaign, which he believed contributed to President Jimmy Carter's appointment of Livingston Biddle as the new chairman of the NEA[6] (Picture 60).

The choice proved successful almost immediately after Biddle took office, because he loosened financial restrictions previously imposed on NEA panelists, thereby increasing funding for worthy ensembles and projects. Biddle was also instrumental in ratifying NEA language defining "professional" choirs, which the APVE had crafted. Such clarification was critical, considering the ongoing challenges the Choral Panel faced when choosing choruses to fund. (They would acquire greater influence once the Panel became the Choral *Program* in 1980.) The definition of "professional" was a center of controversy at this time and would continue to be contested for years to come. The statement approved by Biddle in November 1978 read:

> The word "professional" as it appears in the statement reflects the extent to which artists evidence an intense and demonstrable commitment to their arts. Whether or not they earn their total livelihood from the arts, or endeavor to do so, their art is a central feature of their lives. Hobbyist, as such, is not.[7]

Picture 60.
Margaret Hillis, Michael Korn, Walter Gould, and Robert DeCormier of the APVE attending a reception in Orchestra Hall's ballroom following a June 2, 1979, open rehearsal for the APVE. (Terry's Photography) (Rosenthal Archives of the Chicago Symphony Orchestra Association)

Biddle also supported Margaret's most important goal while she served as chairperson of the Choral Panel: the formation of a permanent Choral *Program* in 1980. Margaret knew this was a necessary step in order to protect the Choral Program from potential elimination within the NEA. There is no doubt that with Margaret Hillis seated at both the NEA and APVE "tables," the communications were streamlined in a way that allowed progress to be made more swiftly than would have otherwise been possible. Even as she served out her tenure as chair of the Choral Program, the NEA made it clear that they wanted Hillis to remain involved in an advisory capacity, as was stated in Carleen Hardesty's letter informing Margaret that she was being rotated off the panel.[8] Hillis's continued involvement in the NEA and APVE provided tremendous influence on future challenges within the choral field.

Just prior to November 1981, when Margaret officially stepped down from her role with the NEA, disruptive changes were on the horizon. In January 1981, Ronald Reagan had taken office as president, and very soon thereafter he proposed a dramatic reduction in public funding for the arts to fulfill a promise he had given to his conservative base. Hillis stated, "We are scared to death the National Endowment is going to go under. . . . What Reagan did in California [while he was governor] was to wipe out the Arts Council and get a lot of wealthy people together instead to support the arts. When it is in the hands of a bunch of wealthy people, it will become a matter of 'who knows who' [to get funding], instead of decisions made by professional people who care deeply about the arts."[9] Hillis predicted that Reagan was positioning himself to do this on a national scale. Reagan's attitude toward government funding of the arts amounted to an about-face from President Carter's enthusiastic NEA support. Reagan's position drove Hillis to use her vast network to run interference against his potentially catastrophic policy shift.

Reagan positioned himself to succeed in this aggressive defunding campaign by first replacing Livingston Biddle with Frank Hodsoll, a man with no background in the inner workings of the NEA. Reagan's intention was for Hodsoll to do his bidding. By May 1981, Margaret was using any press coverage at her disposal to expose what was happening with Reagan and the NEA. In one interview featuring Hillis in a St. Louis paper promoting her upcoming St. Louis Symphony Bach Mass in B Minor performance, Hillis made an overt endorsement for continued national funding of the arts. Reiterating the importance for professional singers to support themselves financially, she explained that it would be harder for them to do so given Reagan's current intentions. She explained, "The Reagan Administration's proposed slashing of the budget for the arts . . . [would mean that] funds for the nine-year-old Choral Program . . . may be cut up to fifty percent."[10] Such a move would threaten support that the NEA could give to choruses, providing needed income for professional singers. Hillis contacted congressmen she could rely upon, including her brother, urging their efforts for overturning Reagan's proposal to cut 32 million dollars from the NEA budget.

Despite Margaret's heroic efforts to minimize NEA cutbacks, some did occur, directly impacting Hillis's Chicago Symphony Chorus back home. Meanwhile, the intense disagreements continued between NEA panelists and presidential appointees on the NEA's National Council, who were the final decision makers when it came to allocating funds for NEA awards. One notable National Council member who engaged in the debate over funding of choruses was Robert Shaw. Shaw was invited to attend a Choral Program meeting to discuss allocations of support for professional versus amateur choruses. Carleen Hardesty described the memorable meeting in full detail, which was later corroborated by Gregg Smith, his wife Rosalind Reese, and Bob Page.[11] Hardesty conveyed the meeting was "seared into her memory," as she felt responsible for having extended the invitation to Shaw, whom she hoped could be persuaded to support their cause.[12] Hardesty and the Choral Program were campaigning to protect the "professional" choir from losing funding, some of which was being allocated to "amateur" choirs. This was even more critical now that federal funds were being reduced. The contentious subject was brought to a climax when Shaw gave an impassioned speech before the Choral Program in a meeting that was open to the public. With many nationally prominent choral conductors present, Hardesty characterized Shaw as having gone on "a tirade," vehemently defending volunteer choirs, whose participants he claimed were in it for the love of singing rather than the compensation, and for that alone they should be supported with equivalent funding to that of professional choirs. As Gregg Smith's wife Rosalind remembered it, Shaw stated that his heart went out to his volunteer singers who go from their 9:00 to 5:00 jobs, grab a quick dinner, and then rehearse for three hours each week, preparing for performances.[13] Shaw believed that this dedication warranted better attention (and funding) by the NEA. Rosalind Rees recalled that Bob Page and Paul Hill seated behind Gregg Smith "poked" him, encouraging him to challenge Shaw's remarks.[14] Smith spoke up, challenging Shaw's position, stating that he too had loyalty to his wonderful volunteer Long Island Community Chorus, however it was his professional singers who had much more "on the line," often sacrificing reasonable livelihoods to earn a living as singers.

The hypocrisy of Shaw's position was missed by no one in attendance, as all were keenly aware that it was with Shaw's professional chorale that he ultimately made a name for himself. Yet he was advocating for professional choir funding to be reduced in support of amateur ensembles. Shaw's stance became a source of great resentment among many of his choral colleagues who had fought long and hard to promote their professional ensembles. Shaw's presence at the Choral Program meeting ultimately resulted, as Hardesty predicted, in Shaw having a change of heart, at least temporarily. He listened to the other side of the matter, as Choral Program panelists including Gregg Smith and others expressed their struggles with finances to sustain their professional choirs. When it came time for Shaw to state his position to the National Council, he ultimately supported the Choral Program's recommendation to protect funding for professional choirs. Though Hillis was no longer on the Choral Program panel when this meeting took place, she was well aware of what had transpired and came to realize the powerful position of NEA National Council members.

Despite continuous efforts to protect NEA funding for professional ensembles, cutbacks ensued, leaving Hillis's symphony chorus and orchestral ensembles, like many others, in challenging financial straits. Hillis was notified in June 1983 that she would need to remove forty professional singers from her Chicago Symphony Chorus roster as a cost-cutting measure. This stance on the part of the Orchestral Association was beyond discouraging for Hillis, whose Chorus had recently experienced some of the greatest achievements in their history. By February 1983, they had acquired four Grammy Awards. They had also made numerous triumphant appearances at Carnegie Hall between 1977–1980. Now, Hillis was being asked to remove some of the very singers who brought them to this place in their history. It would be a difficult time for Hillis.

Margaret's first obligation was to inform her singers of the impending challenges ahead. In a "Dear People" letter sent out on June 16, 1983, Hillis put her Chicago Symphony Chorus singers on notice:

Because of the economy and cut-backs in government support, the Orchestral Association faces a substantial deficit. The Executive Committee of the Board of Directors has made mandatory a budget cut in all departments not under continuing contractual obligations. I was notified yesterday that no more than 105 paid positions will be available in the Chorus for at least the coming two seasons. Painful as it is, I have the burden of making the choices. The choices will be based on: Good singing, Musicality, Reading ability, Attendance record and General reliability and Availability. Should you not be one of the 105, you will be invited pending successful re-audition to participate as a volunteer. If you cannot afford volunteer status, you will be put on leave of absence with reauditioning privileges for at least one season. Good luck. I love and respect the ideals of each and every one of you.[15]

In her usual fashion, Margaret took charge of the situation. She immediately embarked upon a letter-writing campaign, using her vast network to resolve this budgetary crisis. She realized that other professional choruses around the country must also be enduring the same challenges. The day after sending out her notice to her choristers, Hillis contacted NEA chairman Frank Hodsoll, sending out a signal for help, stating, "Forty people [will be] losing a substantial part of their income . . . the quality of this Grammy-winning chorus is in danger of being impaired. We are not the only organization suffering. If the Chicago Symphony is faced with these kinds of problems, then all the arts institutions of the United States are endangered. The cutbacks in government support have been damaging to all concerned . . . I plead with you to appeal to Congress for as much support as is prudently possible."[16] Hillis's next message was to Solti, communicating the urgency of this situation and the potential impact on their work together. Solti responded promptly to Hillis's message with a letter sent to her from Bayreuth.

Dear Margaret, (handwritten above his typed message)

Just a few lines to thank you for your note of June 17. You can imagine how serious I find the situation and I therefore hope your letter to Mr. Hodsoll might prove a practical step. In the meantime, please rest assured that I shall place the matter high on the agenda for my discussions with John Edwards when he is here in August.

Yours as ever,
Georg (handwritten)[17]

Hillis would then enlist her brother's support in making her plea to Congress, in the hopes of blocking further cutbacks President Reagan was recommending. By the end of June, Margaret was already seeing progress. A letter sent to Margaret from her brother on congressional stationery provided her the first glimpse of victory. In a letter dated June 29, 1983, Bud stated, "As you may have learned, the Interior Appropriation Bill passed the House yesterday. That bill provides for 34.5 million dollars more for the NEA than what the President requested. There was an attempt to cut the funds to the President's level, but that amendment failed. It is still too early to predict what the Senate will do or if the President will sign the bill. However, I will try to help in whatever way possible to keep the funding at the House passed level," signing off, "Love, Bud."[18] In October 1983, Hillis received the long-awaited news she had hoped for: "Art supporters have scored an impressive victory on Capitol Hill. . . . For the first time during [Reagan's] administration . . . members of both houses approved major increases in next year's funding for federal arts and humanities programs."[19]

Hillis understood that without an official role on the NEA, she had less power to monitor important legislation and arts allocations. After experiencing the consequences of the NEA financial crisis firsthand, Hillis decided it was time for her to return to the NEA. However, this time she would seek the more powerful position on the National Council on the Arts. This position was far more complex to attain than was her Choral Program appointment. The National Arts Council position required a presidential appointment from President Reagan—no easy task!

Undeterred, Hillis began her pursuit of this coveted spot, embarking yet again upon a letter-writing campaign. First and foremost, Hillis enlisted the support of numerous colleagues, including current and past NEA Choral Program members. Frank Hodsoll was flooded with recommendations for Hillis to be considered for this prestigious National Arts Council appointment. Next, Hillis enlisted the support of her brother to recommend her directly to the president. Bud immediately cooperated, using his good relationship with Reagan to curry favor for his sister. On June 24, 1983, Bud sent the following message to President Reagan. After stating several other issues he had been dealing with in Congress on the president's behalf, Bud wrote:

The real purpose of my letter is to lobby for you on behalf of a close personal relative, my sister. It is my understanding that she is being considered for an appointment to the National Arts Council to take the place of Mr. Robert Shaw when his term expires, which will be soon. This is a Presidential appointment and I would like to say a word on her behalf.[20]

Bud went on to describe Margaret's accomplishments with the Chicago Symphony Chorus and in the choral field. He concluded his letter stating, "The point I am trying to make is Margaret is well-regarded in her field and would be eminently qualified in my opinion to serve on the National Arts Council. . . . I certainly hope you will give her favorable consideration."[21] Bud then enlisted support of fellow congressmen, including Senator Dick Lugar and Representatives John Porter and George O'Brien. By August 1984, Margaret was officially notified of her appointment to the National Council on the Arts. She would return to a position of influence at a time when her presence would be needed most. During the mid to late 1980s, additional challenges would befall the NEA, requiring Margaret's intervention on behalf of choruses and singers who have her to thank for the support they received at a critical time, enabling many of these professional choral ensembles to survive and continue flourishing today.

During the period just prior to joining the National Arts Council, Hillis focused her advocacy efforts back home, trying to increase financial support for her Chicago Symphony Chorus members. She decided to reinstate a fund that had been gifted to her at the end of the Chicago Symphony Chorus's inaugural season. The Margaret Hillis Fellowship Fund (HFF), established in May 1958 under the auspices of the Orchestral Association, was intended to be managed by the chorus director. Hillis never developed this fund at the time it was established, but she remembered its existence and, given the current financial climate, she determined it would be good to pursue. Hillis wanted to ease the burden for her singers, who were paying for voice lessons and musical study. In March 1981, Hillis formed a committee to launch the Margaret Hillis Fellowship Fund. This committee would review applications and make recommendations, awarding funds to deserving members. With these funds, Hillis also arranged events benefiting all Chorus members, including a lecture series on various theoretical or historical topics, as well as vocal master classes with such luminary artists as Elly Ameling and Sherrill Milnes.

Given her already intense schedule of responsibilities, Hillis would come to rely upon committee members to do the heavy lifting for this fund, including the oversight of finances. One of the HFF committee members who enthusiastically volunteered to oversee the entire operation would later become a sinister character in Hillis's life. At this busy point in her career, Margaret was susceptible to others willing to "mind the store," and she welcomed assistance. Hillis eventually entrusted the leadership position of the fund to Christopher Graves, a person with bad intentions, portraying himself as a competent administrator. A tenor in the symphony chorus, Graves initially *volunteered* his time to take charge of the Fund. Not long after he began managing the Fund, he gained Hillis's trust and was given complete access to the Fund finances and eventually to all of Hillis's personal finances. His unlimited access to her money proved disastrous for Hillis and for the Fellowship Fund. This was not the first time Margaret had abdicated her financial responsibilities, becoming all too trusting of people who claimed they could "fill the bill" in her absence.

During the first year of launching the Hillis Fellowship Fund, Margaret was persuaded by Graves to provide him a stipend for his efforts. She convinced the other committee members who volunteered their time to lobby on behalf of Graves, proposing he deserved remuneration for his time-consuming efforts. The proposal submitted to the Orchestral Association stated:

> Mr. Graves currently logs between fifty to sixty hours per month in service to the Fund. He is paid by being granted an additional ten hours per month in hourly rehearsal fees at the rate of $6.00 per hour. Obviously . . . the allocation to administer the fund is inadequate to do justice to the task. We urge that funds be provided to compensate Mr. Graves for the exact amount of time expended at a rate more appropriate for the task. The members of the committee desire to remain volunteers.[22]

Graves would organize development meetings taking place every month or two. These meetings began with lavish dinners, paid for by Hillis. As part of his duties, Graves would arrange the dinner locations and menus. Mary Ann Beatty, a member of the committee, representing the soprano section of the Chorus, recalled these dinners that had little expense spared. Marsha Waxman Link remembered these dinner meetings to have taken place in various upscale restaurants around town or they would be catered in Hillis's suburban Wilmette home. Graves used Classic Chorale Catering, a company owned by his good friend David Logan, another member of the Chorus. Graves worked for David in this company and together they arranged extravagant menus for Hillis. Meals included cocktails, elegant *hors d'oeuvres*, wine with dinner, and delectable desserts, all coming at a hefty fee paid to the catering company. Hillis would also use this caterer to occasionally provide food and drink for gatherings of the entire Chicago Symphony Chorus and guests at her home for parties, also coordinated by Graves. Solti would even sometimes be in attendance.

Beatty recalled meetings run with a very organized agenda. Agendum included brainstorming sessions, planning of upcoming fundraising events, and grant-writing activities. One of the fundraising ideas implemented was Vocal Valentines. Bobbi Frazes Goldman, one of several choristers who coordinated the event, recalled how these valentine serenades were not only a fairly lucrative venture for the Fellowship Fund, but equally helpful in promoting the Chorus. For a fee, quartets of choristers would serenade people by phone or in person throughout downtown Chicago office buildings. This event became quite popular, advertised on radio and television, promoting the Chorus in a popular genre of singing.

The most lucrative fundraiser was a series of Hillis Fellowship Concerts. Once a year, beginning on December 19, 1981, choristers donated their services, performing annual concerts at Orchestra Hall. These concerts were performed without the Chicago Symphony Orchestra, accompanied instead by piano or organ with occasional services of a harpist or a percussion section. Concerts were typically scheduled during the holiday season, in the hopes that audiences would be motivated to hear the Chicago Symphony Chorus performing their favorite holiday music.

Mary Ann Beatty recalled other fundraising methods, including those requiring committee members to attend cocktail parties underwritten by Hillis, hosted in homes of wealthy donors where committee members would mingle with attendees to elicit donations for the Fund. As Beatty conveyed, it was not an easy nor comfortable task for many of the committee members to be raising money in this way, but it was necessary to keep the Fund growing.[23] Hillis had been challenged by fundraising before, first with her American Choral Foundation and now with this new effort to support singers. In typical fashion, despite the difficulties of raising money, Hillis was determined to try. The results of her efforts provided welcome support for many CSC members during the 1980s and 1990s.

CALIFORNIA: HERE SHE COMES!

Hillis continued to rely upon Chris Graves and the committee to manage the Hillis Fellowship Fund due to a steady stream of incoming conducting requests she was receiving. One particularly enticing offer she accepted for the 1982–1983 concert season was the directorship of the San Francisco Symphony Chorus. In the spring of 1982, Hillis was invited to California by administrators of the San Francisco Symphony to hear the chorus, hoping for her honest assessment of the group. She recalled her first impression. "When it was loud, it was loud, and when it was soft, it was soft. There was no color. Nothing."[24] She was made aware that they were considering changes in a future season, including the possibility of new leadership. Hillis came to realize that in fact they were hoping *she* would consider accepting the position, but as she stated in an interview, she told her hosts, "There is no way I am leaving Chicago. . . . You need somebody who is a resident [of San Francisco]. . . . However, I would be very happy to be an advisor to you."[25]

Shortly after Hillis's visit, she received an urgent phone call from San Francisco, informing her that their current chorus master, Lou Magor, had abruptly resigned, and they would need a temporary replacement until a permanent one could be found.[26] They asked if she could do it. With the San Francisco Symphony's entire 1982–1983 season finalized and publicized, this was a crisis situation that needed rapid resolution. Hillis indicated that she would assist them with this situation. But how? Her schedule for 1982–1983 was already filled to the brim.

Looking over her commitments, Margaret knew she could direct the chorus for part of the season, but she would need someone to share the position with her. Her calendar allowed some flexibility, excluding her guest conducting schedule already locked in. Hillis immediately called upon her dear friend Bob Page, realizing that he may know someone qualified to share duties with her in San Francisco. Page trained many fine choral conductors over the years as director of choral activities at Temple University and then as head of music at Carnegie Mellon University, and Hillis knew his recommendation could be trusted. As she recalled telling Bob, "Look, I've got to find somebody who's ready, who can be out there [in San Francisco]" to which Bob replied, "Take Vance George. He's been my assistant [with the Cleveland Orchestra Chorus] for six years."[27]

Hillis was already familiar with Vance, dating back to when they first met in 1965. Vance had traveled to New York City's Lincoln Center to observe Margaret

Hillis's preparation of *Les noces*, a piece in which he knew she had much expertise. He was preparing to conduct the work shortly thereafter and hoped to ask her for guidance. Recalling his first introduction to Margaret, courtesy of Tom Pyle, he remembered his "utter shock" upon hearing her say, "I've heard a lot about you" in her signature deep baritone voice. Recalled Vance, "My jaw dropped. . . . In fact, her low register was something she good-naturedly fostered. I think she found the deception delicious."[28] Vance said they would have a good laugh about this for years to come.

Vance asked Hillis if she would work with him to prepare *Les noces*, and Hillis agreed. They would meet in Oshkosh, Wisconsin, midway between Madison, where Vance was commuting from, and Kenosha, where Hillis was directing the orchestra. For the price of a duck-à-l'orange dinner, Vance was treated to "sage advice and superb score study."[29] Vance continued his collaborations with Margaret, subsequently hosting the first of her Choral Institutes at the University of Wisconsin, where he taught at that time. For Hillis's Choral Institutes, Vance would teach beginner conducting courses. It was from these Institute classes that he acquired Hillis's nickname for him, "ballet master," due to the intricate choreography he used when teaching gestures to conducting participants.

Vance George left the University of Wisconsin in 1971, becoming the head of choral activities at Kent State University. He chose Kent State, in large measure, due to the school's affiliation with the Blossom Music Festival, which hosted many of the country's leading musicians. Vance would collaborate with well-known conductors, preparing Kent State music students to sing with the Cleveland Orchestra at the orchestra's summer residence. A frequent guest conductor of the festival was Robert Shaw, providing yet further enticement for Vance, who was anxious to know him better. Among Vance's faculty assignments as head of the vocal music division, he would invite conductors for the festival. Vance decided to invite Bob Page to conduct one of the summer symphonic choral concerts, which proved to be a fortuitous choice. While dining together one evening, Page surprised Vance, asking him to become his assistant conductor with his Cleveland Orchestra Chorus. Thrilled to accept, he immediately joined Page, and he would be guided by this master in the world of symphonic chorus preparation. Vance recalled Page's extreme generosity, showing by example how he prepared and rehearsed many of the great symphonic choral works, which Vance was learning for the first time. Page modeled meticulous rehearsal techniques and then provided Vance podium time to apply all he had learned from regularly observing him. Vance learned what it meant to prepare a symphony chorus for the level of performance expected of any ensemble working with a major symphony orchestra. The Cleveland Orchestra Chorus had a longstanding tradition of excellence, first begun under Robert Shaw who was there from 1956–1967, followed briefly by Clayton Krehbiel (1967–1969), and then directed by Margaret Hillis (1969–1971). She passed it on to Robert Page who continued its growth. Vance George became the beneficiary of this incredible legacy, learning from a master of choral conducting, Bob Page.

Of course, Page attributed much of his knowledge about leading a chorus to Margaret Hillis, one of his great mentors. It was no surprise that Page offered up Vance, his treasured assistant whom he had mentored for seven years, to further the advancement of the San Francisco Chorus. Hillis immediately approved of Page's choice. Vance recalled his excitement when he received the call from Hillis and subsequently wasted no time informing Kent State that they would need to approve a four-month leave of absence for him in the fall of 1982, lest he be forced to resign.[30] Though he had no guarantees of becoming the next director of the San Francisco Symphony Chorus, he believed it was worth the experience, no matter the outcome. As it happened, he had enthusiastic support from his university department chairman, Dr. Walter Watson, who stated he would be very agreeable to this arrangement, particularly if Margaret Hillis would come to the Blossom Festival for one week the following summer.[31]

The San Francisco Symphony's music director, Edo de Waart, knew of Hillis's tremendous success in Chicago and he was eager for Hillis to work her magic in San Francisco. The idea of mentoring another symphony chorus in the CSC's image added to her grooming of a chorus master, and the invitation to conduct one concert series that season was enough to convince Hillis she must accept this mammoth undertaking. Before finalizing her agreement with San Francisco, Hillis wisely chose to meet with John Edwards. She urged his support, understanding it would impact her presence in Chicago for the upcoming season. Fortunately, the CSC concert schedule for 1982–1983 was unusually light compared with past seasons, conveniently concluding in early March 1983. This circumstance allowed Hillis to be in San Francisco with greater regularity from March until the end of San Francisco's season, concluding in late June. In that Vance was able to cover

Hillis from August through December 1982, she would simply need to arrange for her associate conductor, James Winfield, to cover her CSC rehearsals in January and February. Assuring John Edwards she would be present for all rehearsals just prior to and including concert openings, Edwards agreed to this arrangement. Hillis next informed Solti of her plans, reassuring him that accepting this San Francisco work would in no way impact her obligations with the Chicago Symphony Chorus. Promising this to be a one-year appointment, she characterized this as her sabbatical, the first she had taken in over twenty-five years with the CSO. Her letter to Solti made it clear that this arrangement had been approved by John Edwards, stating, "As it turns out, I am doing over twice as much with the Chicago Chorus [for the upcoming season] as John and I had [previously] discussed."[32]

Hillis was named the director of choral activities for the San Francisco Symphony for one year with the stipulation she must spend a minimum of fifty days between August 1, 1982, and July 31, 1983, working with the San Francisco Symphony Chorus. Her first step was to meet with Vance George to explain exactly how she wanted the chorus operation run. Deborah Borda, San Francisco's music administrator at that time, flew out to Chicago, joining Hillis and Vance in a marathon session of planning. Hillis recalled writing up an entire infrastructure, including membership rules, policies, and, as Hillis described it, "getting the whole thing hammered out."[33] The plan was for Hillis to oversee the entire operation, advising Vance every step of the way. She would start things off in August, running an intensive four-day rehearsal session with the chorus to set the standards. She would then leave things in Vance's hands, conferring with him regularly by phone to monitor his progress during her time away. Only during the intensive four-day rehearsal series were Vance and Hillis together. After their brief collaborative effort, Margaret did not return to San Francisco until January 1983, when she began preparations for Britten's *War Requiem*. She was particularly pleased to be readying this work for Edo de Waart in March, as she herself would be conducting it with the Spokane Symphony one month later. By December, Vance had completed his work in San Francisco and returned to Kent State (Picture 61).

Picture 61.
Vance George sitting on the stairway in the lobby of Davies Symphony Hall, 1993.
(Terrence McCarthy, photographer)

Margaret Hillis and Vance George proved a formidable duo for San Francisco. From the first "Dear People" letter Margaret wrote to her San Francisco choristers in July 1982, she set the tone, explaining her goals for the ensemble. "The most important single element that makes a chorus great [is] an established core of loyal, hardworking members, namely, you. My interest in you is not only that you master the choral craft, but that you continue growing musically as an individual, as well."[34] Her letter went on to introduce Vance George as her associate director, claiming his standard of excellence to be equal to her own.

Vance was able to maintain Hillis's standards, adding his own flare. He had clearly left his mark. In December 1982, shortly after returning to Kent State, Vance received a phone call from Edo de Waart in Holland, offering Vance a one-year contract to return to San Francisco for the 1983–1984 concert season. Elated with the invitation, Vance took a leap of faith, knowing that a one-year contract was no guarantee for his future. However, after thirteen years at Kent State, Vance was up for this adventure, recalling that he just wanted to know "if this was all going to work." Well, it did! That one-year appointment turned into twenty-three years of remarkable accomplishments, including two Grammy Awards and an Emmy Award involving his San Francisco Symphony Chorus. Vance produced one of the finest symphony choruses in America. He stated many times over of Margaret's incredible generosity through the years, believing Hillis to have played a significant role in his ultimate career success.[35] He, like many others whose talent she recognized, cultivated, and fostered, became part of the next generation to carry forward the Hillis legacy of choral excellence.

Margaret always made time to mentor conducting talent, no matter the schedule she maintained. From her early days as a mentor to Bob Page and then her support of Vance George, and through her university teaching and summer workshops, she was always happy to generously share what she had learned with conductors of potential who sought her counsel. Another of Margaret's mentored conductors to become a success story was Doreen Rao. Rao, an internationally recognized and award-winning conductor, educator, and scholar, attributes Margaret's encouragement, generosity, and mentorship to her ultimate success. Doreen began her career in Chicago, teaching music in a public school, singing professionally, and serving on the teaching staff of an all-city high school chorus. Shortly after graduating college, she auditioned for the Chicago Symphony Chorus and was given a professional spot in the early 1970s. At the time Doreen began with the Chorus, Margaret was collaborating with Barbara Born, founder and director of the Glen Ellyn Children's Choir, the chorus of choice when children's choirs were programmed with the CSO.

Hillis had begun collaborating with Born during Solti's first CSO production of Mahler's Symphony No. 8 in 1971, and the collaborative relationship continued thereafter. When Born was planning to step down from her Glen Ellyn Children's Choir, she wisely sought Hillis's advice for her replacement. Born was familiar with Doreen's work as a singer and as a teacher and asked Margaret if she might consider Doreen as a possible replacement.[36] Margaret agreed to attend a rehearsal to watch how Doreen worked. Liking what she saw, Hillis approved of Born's choice, subsequently inviting Doreen to take over the Glen Ellyn Children's Choir. Doreen confessed that at the time she was asked to this position she felt inadequately prepared to direct a children's chorus, particularly for such high-level performances. She would come to rely upon Hillis's guidance as she embarked upon this professional advancement of her conducting career, and Hillis provided Doreen every support, no matter how busy she was. Doreen emphasized Hillis's support of her early conducting career.

Margaret was indeed my mentor. . . . I knew nothing about working with children. . . . I was a singer and a [junior high school music teacher]. I would sing with Margaret and the symphony chorus on Monday nights, and I would go to my Glen Ellyn rehearsals on Thursday afternoons, replicating whatever Margaret [had done in her CSC rehearsals] with the Glen Ellyn Children's Chorus. I didn't know children were not expected to work at that standard. I simply used different literature and the same rehearsal techniques [as Hillis used] along with some of my own teaching expertise, teaching them to sing, teaching them to read. Whatever Margaret did on Monday nights with the symphony chorus, I did with the children's chorus.[37]

Hillis was very "hands on" in the beginning, attending Doreen's rehearsals in Glen Ellyn, sometimes working with the children for a portion of those rehearsals. Hillis provided Doreen with marked scores detailing every expectation and would sometimes go through the music with her to ensure Doreen's consistency with Margaret's preparations. As time went on, she completely trusted Doreen to bring a fully prepared children's chorus to symphony rehearsals. Calling Margaret "the quintessential teacher," Doreen was supported until the point when Margaret withdrew as the children's choir representative, encouraging Doreen to interact directly with maestros Solti, Levine, or whomever was conducting, instead of Margaret speaking on Doreen's behalf. As Doreen explained, Hillis encouraged these world-famous conductors to rely upon Doreen as the expert, a status she had earned by then.

In the years to follow, Doreen stated that Hillis continued to support her in multifarious ways and on many levels of her career. Doreen continued her formal training as a graduate voice student at Northwestern University while Margaret was on the faculty. Well aware of Doreen's desire to continue her growth as a conductor, Hillis would welcome Doreen to visit her conducting classes and choral rehearsals. Margaret then wisely guided Doreen to expand her conducting background, introducing her to the orchestral side of conducting. Doreen had a vocal background steeped in choral and solo vocal repertoire, but she had little orchestral experience. Knowing this, Margaret invited Doreen to join her at Elgin Symphony Orchestra rehearsals, where Hillis exposed Doreen to the inner workings of orchestral conducting. Hillis would seat Doreen on the stage next to the podium, and while rehearsing, Hillis would mutter various instructive details for Doreen to listen for, such as: Did you hear the string *pizzicato,* or did you notice this balance between sections? These experiences helped Doreen learn orchestral rehearsing and conducting techniques in a one-to-one mentorship within the context of a live rehearsal situation. It was shortly thereafter that Hillis recommended Doreen to take over her Liberty Fremont position in 1983, which aided Hillis in reducing her increasingly heavy schedule. At the same time, it gave Doreen an opportunity to work with an orchestra. Doreen became the standard bearer for excellence in children's choir directing and went on to develop an illustrious career, providing impressive scholarly contributions in the conducting field. In addition to teaching and publishing, she became an award-winning conductor of choruses and orchestras nationally and internationally. She humbly acknowledged that it was Margaret who created a path for her to follow (Picture 62). Margaret loved to mentor talent. She was good at it and realized it was important for her to continue, no matter how busy her life had become.

Picture 62.

Margaret Hillis and Doreen Rao following the Margaret Hillis Fellowship Fund holiday concert, December 14, 1985. (Jim Steere, photographer) (Rosenthal Archives of the Chicago Symphony Orchestra Association)

A Rude Awakening

With so many obligations in this busy period of the early 1980s, Margaret would find ways to make it all work. She relied heavily upon her assistant conductors both with her CSC and with her Elgin Symphony Orchestra. Hillis also chose to reduce her teaching schedule at Indiana University, now returning from Bloomington one day earlier each week, which provided her additional study time. Unable to downsize her previously scheduled performance commitments for the 1982–1983 season to accommodate San Francisco, she worked around them as best she could. Those commitments included performances with the Atlanta Choral Guild, Indianapolis Symphony Orchestra, New Mexico Symphony Orchestra, St. Paul Chamber Orchestra, Chicago Symphony Orchestra, Civic Orchestra of Chicago, New York Choral Society, Spokane Symphony Orchestra, Toronto's Royal Conservatory of Music, the Adirondack Music Festival, Indiana University Symphony Orchestra, and the Kokomo Symphony Orchestra. Added to guest conducting were her ongoing commitments with the San Francisco Symphony Chorus, her American Choral Foundation, the Association of Professional Vocal Ensembles, and the Hillis Fellowship Fund. It is impossible to imagine how she was able to make it all work. Yet, she did. Performances throughout this busiest of seasons were favorably reviewed, with no hint of all she was balancing.

Despite Hillis's efforts and heroic scheduling, problems did arise. Her ambition would come at a cost. One consequence arose during her salary negotiations when her loyalties to the Chicago Symphony Orchestra would be questioned. Hillis's heavy schedule would also cost her two orchestra appointments, one by choice (Liberty Fremont) and the other by force (Elgin Symphony). During this period, Hillis would also relinquish a portion of her American Choral Foundation, a product of leaving her finances to be overseen by someone else. The challenges before Hillis caused her to rethink the offers coming her way. She was beginning to realize she just could not do it all.

During Hillis's many guest appearances between the late 1970s to the mid-1980s, she became aware of inequities between her Chicago Symphony Chorus salary and that of other symphony chorus directors (all others being male). In 1983, during Hillis's collaboration with San Francisco, she was surprised to discover that Vance George had been offered payment equal to her earnings with the Chicago Symphony Chorus. Adding insult to injury, his salary offer for a one-year appointment was equal to what she was being offered in her twenty-seventh year on the job. The realization that she was being grossly underpaid set Hillis on a path to finally demand equitable compensation to that of men in the same line of work.

Salary inequities were not new for Hillis. Similar to women then and now responding to such inequities, Hillis was hesitant to confront issues of payment. She had set an acquiescent tone early on with the CSO, beginning by never requesting to be reimbursed for her weekly commutes to and from New York City. Back then, she paid all travel expenses herself. She also paid a substantial portion of the salary for her administrative assistants, necessary to help her manage the many duties she held with the CSO along with her other work. There were several occasions in her early years with the CSO when Hillis stood up for more compensation only to back down when she encountered resistance. One issue was her representation in these negotiations. After initially representing herself, she turned things over to her inexperienced, trustworthy friend Sheldon Soffer. Neither Soffer nor Hillis were any match for the sophisticated management of the Ravinia Festival and the Orchestral Association. One example of ineffective negotiation occurred in 1972 between Soffer and Ravinia's Ed Gordon. Soffer was asking, on behalf of Hillis, for a more appropriate fee for her work at Ravinia. Gordon's response to Sheldon's hardball tactics was met with indignation. Gordon stated that he did not appreciate the tone of Sheldon's letter. He went on to state:

> I had hoped that on the basis of my close association with Margaret and our long friendship, she would be willing to cooperate [for a lesser fee]. . . . You know, Sheldon, there is very little need to point out to me time and again the amount of work Margaret puts in and her value to me and to Ravinia. I am perfectly cognizant of it, and wish I were in a position to be able to say YES [to her requested fee].[38]

Margaret then intervened, sending Gordon a response, stating she believed she was requesting an appropriate fee for her work and that she hoped the situation could be revisited. Stating that though she appreciated Gordon's monumental expenses, particularly when the Chicago Symphony Chorus was involved, she believed her professional services should not be used to compensate for Ravinia's financial challenges. Her compromise was to offer a substantial personal donation to Ravinia for the coming season, provided she would have Gordon's word that she would receive her requested fee that year and in future years. Gordon agreed to these terms, but only after Hillis's personal donation was offered.

Hillis became much more insistent for an equitable salary upon returning from her San Francisco guest directorship. She was no longer willing to settle for the salary she had been earning with the Chicago Symphony Orchestra. According to Vance George, Hillis was using the San Francisco position, in part, as a bargaining chip in her negotiations with the CSO, perhaps even considering a move to San Francisco.[39] In any case, when it came time for Hillis to negotiate her next CSC multi-year contract beginning with the 1984–1985 season, she became much more emphatic about her expectations than ever before. In Soffer's letter, initiating contract discussions with John Edwards, dated December 7, 1983, Hillis instructed Soffer to add numerous clauses to the contract, including a healthy pay raise, health insurance, retirement benefits, payment for her administrative assistant, and deadlines for her to receive CSC dates for the following season so she could book herself for outside work in a timely fashion. She also insisted upon a minimum number of professional singers for the CSC, trying to bring that number back to where it had been before the Chorus size was reduced.

Edwards's response, one month later, did not address the salary request, instead challenging the numerous other conditions stated in the proposal. Most noteworthy was Edwards's statement questioning Margaret's loyalty. "I think it is up to her to establish some priorities for her personal career as an orchestra conductor. Her career up to the present time has been outstanding as a choral director and founder of the Chicago Symphony Chorus."[40] This statement must have been somewhat of a wake-up call to Hillis, implying that she was putting her guest conducting appearances ahead of her work with the Chicago Symphony Chorus. She insisted that Soffer's response clarify this matter. Soffer rebutted, "The over-all priority that Margaret has had and will always have is that the CHICAGO SYMPHONY CHORUS COMES FIRST."[41] In this same letter, Soffer brought back the salary issue by informing Edwards of the discrepancy in Hillis's pay as compared with others in her position around the country. "I would like to bring to your attention the fact that the San Francisco Symphony recently engaged Vance George (a veritable newcomer to the profession) for a sum [that was comparable to Margaret's current earnings]."[42] There was no response from John Edwards to this letter, nor did Soffer attempt to follow up with him after that February communication.

John Edwards passed away unexpectedly in August 1984, leaving Hillis without a contract to begin the 1984–1985 season. Hillis did not keep track of Sheldon's progress with her contract prior to Edwards's passing. She trusted that Sheldon would continue negotiating on her behalf, however Sheldon clearly "dropped the ball." As a result of Soffer's negligence, Hillis worked for most of the 1984–1985 season without a contract. He eventually took up negotiations with Paul Chummers, interim CSO manager, finalizing Hillis's contract for the 1984–1985 season in May 1985. It would be the last negotiation Sheldon Soffer would do on Hillis's behalf. Wisely, she secured new representation and better contracts followed thereafter. Regardless of her improved representation, Hillis was aware that her heavy schedule was causing the CSO, and perhaps others, to question her priorities.

Hillis's schedule would have other consequences as well. Leaving her Elgin Symphony Orchestra in the able hands of her assistant, Robert Hanson, in her absence proved a mixed blessing. By that busy fall of 1982, Margaret was beginning her eleventh season in Elgin but would often be gone with so many performances and commitments during that year. Hillis had made impressive strides with the orchestra during her tenure. Her process included establishing a board of directors, a women's league to engage community support, fundraising, and organizing activities connected with the orchestra. She initiated a youth symphony orchestra, a youth string orchestra, a children's choir, a youth concert series, and she forged a close alliance with the Elgin Choral Union. Adding promenade concerts and a pops series further increased the orchestra's popularity. Most importantly, she increased the number of paid positions in the orchestra. She implemented yearly auditions for her orchestra members in similar fashion to what she had done with her Chicago Symphony Chorus. The quality of the orchestra improved greatly under Hillis's leadership. The orchestra that barely attracted one hundred patrons when Hillis first began was now so popular that second concerts were added to each symphony orchestra program. Describing the orchestra as "the last step before a major orchestra," Hillis's players were frequently moving directly from Elgin to top-flight symphony orchestra appointments. With a tremendous talent pool to choose from being in close proximity to Chicago, Margaret described those who auditioned for the orchestra as being "the cream of the crop." Hillis claimed that she would conduct works with them that she had never conducted before, making this a wonderful opportunity for her to learn new repertoire with Elgin before conducting these pieces elsewhere. As she observed, "I'm very lucky with this orchestra in many ways."[43]

Having built the orchestra, she had high expectations for them to play at a level commensurate with other orchestras she was conducting around the country.[44] However, Hillis's increased time away from Elgin caused her to encounter greater resistance when she would return to them. Having heard meticulous playing from other orchestras she conducted, Hillis expected that same attention to detail from her now mostly professional Elgin orchestra. However, players were becoming more comfortable with Hanson, a consistent and qualified presence, who had earned their trust, particularly when he pushed them to higher levels of playing. As the discomfort between players and Hillis grew, Hanson recalled one particular rehearsal when Hillis's impatience for getting them to play with greater precision erupted with her making an uncharacteristically negative remark. In a moment of frustration, she told the players that she conducts wonderful orchestras all over the country and that they are *not* a wonderful orchestra.[45] Hanson described that to be a turning point in which players rebelled.

It was shortly thereafter that Hillis's contract as the music director was not renewed. Instead, she was invited to conduct several concerts for the 1985–1986 season. She would resign. In her resignation letter to John Gerlach, president of the Elgin Symphony Orchestra, dated July 24, 1985, she expressed that she was sorry to hear of the enormous financial difficulties facing the orchestra, which suggested they used this as an excuse to bring her back only as a guest conductor. She explained that though she was invited to conduct several performances, she had not received a contract and therefore she would be unavailable for the dates offered. Under the circumstances, she would no longer conduct their Do-It-Yourself *Messiah* programs, which had become a very popular event in Elgin. "It is with sadness and regret that I tender my resignation effective as of your receipt of this letter."[46] It seemed that Hillis's demanding schedule had contributed to her ending a thirteen-season relationship with Elgin.

Yet another matter arose due to Margaret's busy schedule. As she was devoting her time to the APVE and the Hillis Fellowship Fund, her own American Choral Foundation would suffer. With less time to spare for the Foundation she had built and supported for over twenty years, the ACF remained a continuous financial drain. When problems arose initially for the Foundation in 1965, Hillis entertained an option to resolve the finances, one that she never enacted. When problems arose again in the mid-1980s, Hillis would revisit that idea. Prior to hiring Sheldon

Soffer to manage the Foundation, Hillis proposed incorporating her ACF with the American Choral Directors Association. During ACDA's biennial board meeting held in March 1966, this idea was discussed, and an executive committee was appointed to investigate the ramifications of such an arrangement. Hillis, anxious for a more rapid resolution, instead hired Soffer as part of the ACF's first reorganization in 1966. Initially, Soffer would do good work for the Foundation, but this proved only a temporary fix. Though Soffer was effective in some aspects of ACF development, the finances continued to be a challenge. By 1975, serious concerns were mounting regarding accumulating debt, but by then Hillis was busily involved in NEA matters and in her numerous conducting commitments. She entrusted Soffer to manage the organization properly. Hillis would neglect to attend to the growing ACF debt as her conducting schedule continued to increase.

Other people who were working for the ACF were aware of the financial problems and began contributing ideas for the Foundation's sustenance. In a letter from Alfred Mann to Mary Lou Tuffin, Mann mentioned a meeting he had with former president of ACDA, Dr. Walter Collins. While Mann remained the editor of the ACF's *American Choral Review*, he was also contributing to the ACDA's research and publication committee and was working with Collins, who was now chairing the research committee. According to Mann, Collins had mentioned that ACDA was considering a new quarterly research publication, which in addition to the existing *Choral Journal* would provide scholarly content. Mann conveyed to Tuffin, "In order to avoid duplication and unavoidable mutual disserve, Dr. Collins had raised the interesting question whether our *American Choral Review* (ACR) might not serve for this purpose. . . . It was understood that our and above all Margaret's interest would be in preserving the identity of the ACR and Dr. Collins saw no problem in this point. . . . The *Review* [ACR] would become an official journal of the ACDA."[47] This did not come to pass, however there were other arrangements made at some point whereby ACDA members would receive a sizeable discount if they chose to join the American Choral Foundation. This discount proved to be costly for the ACF's bottom line. When the financial situation of the ACF grew dire, Hillis was finally forced to step in, and she decided in 1984 to take decisive action. She called a meeting of APVE and ACF board members and offered a proposal that would greatly reduce the ACF debt. Her solution was one spawned from her original idea back in 1966 to merge with another organization.

However, instead of forging an alliance with ACDA, she chose instead to merge with her trusted colleagues of APVE.

On October 26, 1984, the APVE executive committee gathered with the ACF's board of directors to discuss "the possible merging and/or cooperation of the two organizations."[48] During that meeting, it was decided that the first step would be to focus upon transferring over the Services Division, including the research journals, which had been a costly expenditure for the ACF. At this meeting, there were discussions about canceling the agreement with the ACDA, whose members were given a sizeable discount if they joined ACF. If that agreement could not be canceled, there should at least be a fee increase to benefit ACF.

In a report to the ACF board of directors covering the history of ACF, it was implied that Sheldon Soffer had mismanaged the oversight of the Foundation. The report stated, "In recent years, *due to poor management* [under Soffer's watch], activities dwindled." Explaining the necessity of the merger, the report went on to state,

> The Foundation *was in such disarray* and [since] the original goals for the Foundation's activities were similar to those sought by the Association of Professional Vocal Ensembles, Margaret Hillis began dialogue with Michael Korn . . . to investigate the possibility of the APVE's administering the Services Division of the Foundation. Such a step would improve the management of the Foundation. . . . APVE agreed to administer the Services Division as of March 1, 1985, and the Performance Division was moved to Miss Hillis's offices in Chicago.[49]

The official announcement that the ACF publications [*American Choral Review* and *Research Memorandum*] would be administered by APVE was made on January 23, 1985. Hillis arranged for all back issues of both publications to be moved out of the expensive rental space in New York and would be taken over by the choral library of Temple University. The transfer of the Services Division to APVE provided stability Hillis needed for her Foundation to remain intact. She would take further action in the years that followed but wisely remained somewhat more attentive to the Foundation for the remainder of its existence.

Hillis would pay a price for doing it all. The challenges that arose from her mounting popularity in the years following her Carnegie Hall success would cause significant disruption, particularly in relation to the long-standing commitments she had enjoyed. The consequences of this period in Hillis's career would cause her to reconsider her priorities. She was beginning to see that there was no substitute for her presence when it came to her Foundation and to her ensembles. Margaret had always been aware of the importance of her physical presence at rehearsals for ensembles she directed and in overseeing her Foundation. In an interview in 1979, as demands for Hillis were growing, she stated how much she enjoyed guest conducting. But she interjected, "If Mama isn't around, [her ensembles] feel a little bit deserted. I think some of them feel that way about me."[50] Despite her awareness that leaving her responsibilities to others was risky, she could not resist the opportunity to accept offers coming her way. Her star had risen astronomically after her 1977 Carnegie Hall performance, resulting in the most active period of Hillis's conducting career, but it would come at a price. What became abundantly clear to Hillis, after a time, was her need to set some limits upon herself or pay the consequences. In order to do so, she would first need to determine what was most important to her going forward. The temporary excitement of guest conducting, guest speaking, and accepting awards would need to be tempered, lest it threaten those things that fulfilled her most. She would need to think twice before accepting concerts and conducting positions that caused her to be away for extended periods of time.

After Edwards questioned Hillis's priorities during the contract negotiations in 1984, she realized what may be at risk if she continued along the same path. She knew for a fact that her Chicago Symphony Chorus work was a continual source of fulfillment and pride. Equally rewarding was her service work, now even more so with the added excitement of a presidential appointment to the National Council on the Arts in 1984. She was also greatly fulfilled by her teaching and mentoring, understanding that these efforts would best ensure her life's work would continue for future generations. The fleeting joy of applause and adulation for a concert well done, along with the artistic largesse she received during this time period, provided only temporary satisfaction.

By 1986, Hillis had acquired many prestigious awards, including a total of six Grammy Awards, a Grand Prix du Disque, the *Ladies Home Journal* "Woman of the Year in Classical Music" award, and numerous honorary doctoral degrees. Her impressive guest conducting appearances included a performance in Iceland along with many other outstanding performances with major American orchestras. She enjoyed countless guest speaking engagements and interviews for radio, television, newspapers, and magazines. She even participated in a television documentary entitled *For the Love of Music*, based on her career. Even with all she had achieved, she realized that returning home she could not simply pick up where she left off. Going forward, Hillis would continue to accept outside work but only at a more manageable pace that allowed her a regular presence with her ensembles. This realization would be her bottom line regarding any new offers coming in after 1986. The period between 1977–1986 was a time of tremendous artistic visibility and with it would come greater self-awareness. For the first time, Margaret had come to realize her limits and the consequences of exceeding them. Even *she* could not do it all. Focused on what mattered most, she would be able to survive and thrive amid the "slings and arrows of outrageous fortune" about to manifest themselves in the decade to come.

ENDNOTES

1. Robert Marsh, "'Do-It-Yourself Messiah' Wonderful, Naturally," *Chicago Sun-Times*, December 11, 1980, p. 107.
2. Meg Cox, "Big Chicago Chorus is Set to Show How It Handles 'Messiah,'" *Wall Street Journal*, December 17, 1979.
3. Ibid.
4. Lillian Williams, "Realty Exec Orchestrates Free Concerts," *Chicago Sun-Times*, October 25, 1982, p. 26.
5. Britton Hadden and Henry Robinson, "Joyful Christmas Sounds and Sites," *Time*, December 29, 1980, p. 6.
6. Michael Korn's Report of Executive Director, June 3, 1978 (Margaret Hillis Collection, Rosenthal Archives of the Chicago Symphony Orchestra Association, Box 11).
7. National Endowment of the Arts Statement of Goals sent by Livingston Biddle to all NEA Panel Members, November 3, 1978. (Margaret Hillis Collection, Box NEA).
8. Letter from Carleen Hardesty to Margaret Hillis, October 8, 1981 (Margaret Hillis Collection, Rosenthal Archives of the Chicago Symphony Orchestra Association, Box 8).
9. Ulla Colgrass, "Conductor Hillis Reversed the Odds," *Music Management Magazine* (November/December 1981): p. 17.
10. Patricia Rice, "Big Voice in Choral Singing," *St. Louis Post-Dispatch*, May 19, 1981, p. 5D.
11. Interviews with Carleen Hardesty, April 29, 2014, and Gregg and Rosalind Rees Smith, April 28, 2014.
12. Interview with Carleen Hardesty, April 29, 2014.
13. Interview with Gregg Smith and his wife, Rosalind Rees, April 28, 2014.
14. Ibid.
15. "Dear People" letter sent to members of the Chicago Symphony Chorus, June 16, 1983 (Margaret Hillis Collection, Rosenthal Archives of the Chicago Symphony Orchestra Association, Box 8).
16. Letter to Frank Hodsoll from Margaret Hillis, June 17, 1983 (Margaret Hillis Collection, Rosenthal Archives of the Chicago Symphony Orchestra Association, Box 8).
17. Letter from Sir Georg Solti to Margaret Hillis, June 23, 1983 (Margaret Hillis Collection, Box 4).
18. Letter to Margaret from her brother Elwood ("Bud") Hillis, June 29, 1983 (Margaret Hillis Collection, Rosenthal Archives of the Chicago Symphony Orchestra Association, Box 8).

19. "Special Arts Update from Congressman Tom Downey." A flyer sent to Margaret Hillis at Orchestra Hall, Chicago, October 1983 (Margaret Hillis Collection, Rosenthal Archives of the Chicago Symphony Orchestra Association, Box 8).

20. Letter from Elwood ("Bud") Hillis to President Ronald Reagan, June 24, 1983 (Margaret Hillis Collection, Rosenthal Archives of the Chicago Symphony Orchestra Association, Box 11).

21. Ibid.

22. A proposal by Margaret Hillis from the Hillis Fellowship Fund Committee, sent to the Orchestra Association March 5, 1981 (Margaret Hillis Collection, Rosenthal Archives of the Chicago Symphony Orchestra Association, Box 14).

23. Interview with Mary Ann Beatty, Chicago Symphony Chorus member, June 16, 2016.

24. Margaret Hillis, interview by Norman Pellegrini (transcribed by Stanley G. Livengood), October 6, 1997, p. 14.

25. Jon Bentz, "Interview of Margaret Hillis Director Chicago Symphony Orchestra, September 19, 1989, Archives Committee, Oral History Project, 1992," p. 25 (Margaret Hillis Collection, Rosenthal Archives of the Chicago Symphony Orchestra Association).

26. An interesting side note is that Margaret Hillis recommended Lou Magor for the San Francisco position. He had been her conducting student when she taught at Northwestern University, and when music director Seiji Ozawa first initiated the establishment of the San Francisco Symphony Chorus in 1973, he contacted Hillis for her guidance. At her recommendation, Magor became the first director of the San Francisco Symphony Chorus. Former chorister James Sampson recalled Magor as being a dynamic, charismatic conductor, very well-liked by members of the Chorus. It was at the request of Ozawa's successor, Edo de Waart, that Magor be replaced. The process was set into motion with Margaret Hillis's visit to assess the chorus under Magor's direction. Shortly after Hillis's visit, Magor abruptly resigned.

27. Bentz, "Interview of Margaret Hillis," p. 26.

28. Vance George, "View from the Podium," *Cadenza* VI, no. 4, p. 2.

29. Ibid.

30. Ibid.

31. Letter from Vance George to Margaret Hillis, July 7, 1982 (Margaret Hillis Collection, Rosenthal Archives of the Chicago Symphony Orchestra Association, Box 3).

32. Letter from Margaret to Solti, September 15, 1982 (Margaret Hillis Collection, Rosenthal Archives of the Chicago Symphony Orchestra Association, Box 4).

33. Bentz, "Interview of Margaret Hillis," p. 26.

34. "Dear People" letter to members of the San Francisco Symphony Chorus, July 7, 1982 (Margaret Hillis Collection, Rosenthal Archives of the Chicago Symphony Orchestra Association, Box 3).

35. Interview with Vance George, December 21, 2012.

36. Interview with Doreen Rao, July 5, 2012.

37. Ibid.

38. Letter to Sheldon Soffer from Edward Gordon, February 28, 1972 (Margaret Hillis Collection, Rosenthal Archives of the Chicago Symphony Orchestra Association, Box 3).

39. Interview with Vance George, December 21, 2012.

40. Letter to Sheldon Soffer from John Edwards, January 30, 1984 (Margaret Hillis Collection, Rosenthal Archives of the Chicago Symphony Orchestra Association, Box 5).

41. Letter to John Edwards from Sheldon Soffer, February 15, 1984 (Margaret Hillis Collection, Rosenthal Archives of the Chicago Symphony Orchestra Association, Box 5).

42. Ibid.

43. Transcription of Margaret Hillis interview with Steven Hillyer, November 20, 1982 (Margaret Hillis Collection, Rosenthal Archives of the Chicago Symphony Orchestra Association).

44. Interview with Robert Hanson, April 17, 2012.

45. Ibid.

46. Resignation letter, July 24, 1985, from Margaret Hillis to John Gerlach of the Elgin Symphony Orchestra (Margaret Hillis Collection, Rosenthal Archives of the Chicago Symphony Orchestra Association, Box 1).

47. Letter from Alfred Mann to Mary Lou Tuffin, November 28, 1980 (Margaret Hillis Collection, Rosenthal Archives of the Chicago Symphony Orchestra Association, Box 10).

48. Notes of Meeting of APVE Executive Committee with Board of Directors of the American Choral Foundation (Margaret Hillis Collection, Rosenthal Archives of the Chicago Symphony Orchestra Association, Box 10).

49. "Brief History, American Choral Foundation" (Margaret Hillis Collection, Rosenthal Archives of the Chicago Symphony Orchestra Association, Box 11).

50. Staff Writer, "Margaret Hillis Unchanged by Fame," *Kokomo Tribune*, February 1, 1979.

CHAPTER 18

MAKING THE BEST OF THE WORST OF TIMES: 1986–1989

With Margaret's Chicago Symphony Chorus (CSC) three-year contract for 1985–1988 finally settled at the end of the 1985–1986 season, Hillis was careful about the future scheduling of her extra commitments, knowing how they impacted her regular responsibilities. The upcoming Chicago Symphony Chorus season would be active, including six concert series programs. Hillis returned to the podium this season, conducting the Civic Orchestra and the Chicago Symphony Orchestra (CSO) in a subscription concert series. Hillis would also conduct the Fellowship Holiday Concert to raise funds for her Hillis Fellowship Fund. Also added to her duties this season, Hillis would serve as assistant conductor, covering Michael Tilson Thomas for his performances of works by Ives and Bartók, with the Chicago Symphony Orchestra and Chorus. Following a busy downtown concert season, the summer of 1986 proved equally active, including the concert version of Strauss's *Elektra*, followed by Berlioz's *Damnation of Faust*, Poulenc's *Gloria*, Mozart's Requiem, Liszt's *Eine Faust-Symphonie*, and several Ravinia "Pops" programs, occupying the Chorus through the month of August.

Active CSC seasons such as this became more manageable now that Hillis was setting limits on outside work. Cutting back on her guest conducting appearances seemed less of a sacrifice given so many exciting projects she was acquiring at home with the CSO. Rather than accepting conducting invitations, she increased the number of conducting workshop appearances she was accepting, as these would require the least amount of time away from home. Workshops could be contained to a day or two and were more easily scheduled around her extant Chicago Symphony

Orchestra commitments. Unlike workshops, symphony guest conducting often required her to commit to a date several years in advance, well before Hillis had access to her complete CSC schedule. Limiting her bookings to one year ahead and keeping them contained to one- or two-day commitments, this careful selection of outside engagements prevented conflicts with the CSO that had bedeviled Margaret in previous years.

Hillis enjoyed directing workshops, which allowed her to educate the next generation of conductors. She was active in this role throughout the year, including the summer months (e.g., working at APVE-sponsored workshops such as Saranac Lake and the Berkshire Music Festival). As for her outside conducting during the 1985–1986 season, she fulfilled the obligatory commitments made several years earlier, making this the last season she would be taking on this type of schedule. Hillis's upcoming season, conducting Handel's *Israel in Egypt*, Bach's Mass in B Minor, Handel's *Dettingen Te Deum*, Beethoven's Symphony No. 5, and Verdi's Requiem, in addition to conducting the Chicago Symphony Orchestra and Civic Orchestra concerts, would be considered enormously demanding by most standards. However, this season was actually less arduous when compared to recent years of Hillis's outside commitments. She learned her lesson the hard way and would take steps to avoid over-scheduling herself this way in the future.

The 1985–1986 season proved particularly enjoyable for Hillis when she was reunited with two old friends. In February 1986, Leonard Slatkin was scheduled to conduct Britten's *War Requiem*. In April 1986, composer Ned Rorem, her friend from the New York days, would be in Chicago to watch Hillis conduct his *An American Oratorio*. Working closely with both Slatkin and Rorem undoubtedly added special excitement for Hillis in the season ahead. Leonard Slatkin, then the music director of the St. Louis Symphony Orchestra, initially met Margaret through John Edwards, one of Slatkin's mentors. Slatkin would be a regular visitor to Chicago, serving as a guest conductor for the CSO and the Civic Orchestra. He also enjoyed any opportunity to observe Solti conducting the Chicago Symphony Orchestra.[1] Edwards often hosted dinner parties following those concerts and would extend an invitation to Slatkin when he was in town. Slatkin recalled that on numerous occasions Hillis would also attend Edwards's gatherings, and it was there that she and Slatkin first formed their friendship.[2] In the years to follow, Margaret and Leonard would get together periodically, discussing music for an upcoming program they were preparing. Often, the piece was a contemporary work. Slatkin shared Margaret's enthusiasm for contemporary music, describing her as extremely curious, particularly when it came to discussions about contemporary orchestral repertoire. He recalled her expressing frustration with the lack of significant American contemporary choral/orchestral works and was particularly pleased whenever they collaborated on such pieces.[3]

Another interesting connection between Margaret and Leonard was his mother, Eleanor Aller Slatkin, a renowned musician herself, who became a good friend to Margaret when Eleanor moved from the West Coast to serve as chairwoman of the string department at DePaul University in Chicago (1968–1970). Leonard Slatkin had come from a family of fine musicians. His father, Felix Slatkin, was an outstanding violinist who coincidentally played under Fritz Reiner while a student at the Curtis Institute of Music. Though both parents were superb classical musicians, they gravitated to the steady and lucrative work of the Los Angeles movie studios. Not unusual for Leonard growing up was the constant stream of celebrities in and out of his home, including luminaries: "Igor Stravinsky to Danny Kaye, and Arnold Schoenberg . . . to Nat King Cole."[4] Another frequent guest was Frank Sinatra, whom Leonard called "Uncle Frank." When visiting their home, Sinatra would occasionally sing Leonard and his brother to sleep. Sinatra relied heavily upon the talents of Leonard's parents for his recordings. In the predominantly male studio orchestra, Eleanor, a superb cellist, was the first woman to hold a titled position as a musician at Warner Brothers Studio. She quickly developed a strong sense of self. She and Hillis shared that same pioneering spirit, both sharing singular vantage points as lone women in their line of work. They became fast friends. Leonard humorously recalled occasionally joining them for dinner, claiming he could not get a word in edgewise as these two ladies, "smoking up a storm," would talk shop in the most colorful language imaginable.[5]

Another friend who would be reunited with Hillis during this symphony season was Ned Rorem. The longtime friendship of Ned Rorem and Margaret Hillis, described earlier, continued on as both blossomed impressively in their respective fields since the time they first met in the late 1940s. Margaret enjoyed performing Rorem's works, dating as far back as their New York days. He never forgot those times. A card Hillis received from Rorem years later demonstrated his continued fondness for her. Referring to *A Poet's Requiem*, a piece Hillis's New York Concert Choir premiered in 1957, Rorem reminded Margaret that it was to her the work was dedicated. Signing off his message, "I love you," his affection and admiration was evident (Picture 63). Understandably, Hillis would want to feature a work of her dear friend. She chose to conduct *An American Oratorio* for her April 1986 subscription series with the Chicago Symphony Orchestra and Chorus. Rorem attended the final preparatory rehearsals and all performances of the series, during which the interactions between both made evident the admiration mutually shared.[6] The satisfaction of fine performances and treasured friendships that filled the 1985–1986 season would become fleeting memories in the season ahead.

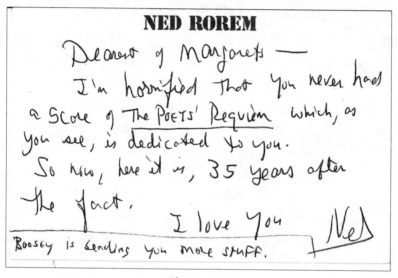

Picture 63.

Note from Ned Rorem to Margaret Hillis, 1990. The message reads: "Dearest of Margarets—I'm horrified that you never had a score of *The Poet's Requiem* which, as you see, is dedicated to you. So now, here it is, 35 years after the fact. I love you, Ned. Boosey [and Hawkes—publisher of the piece] is sending you more stuff." (Margaret Hillis Collection, Rosenthal Archives of the Chicago Symphony Orchestra Association)

FALL 1986: TROUBLING TIMES AHEAD

At the onset of fall 1986, Margaret seemed to have her commitments and responsibilities under control. The coming CSC season included a lighter-than-average schedule, ending early in March 1987. Though 1986 was technically the thirtieth-anniversary season of the Chicago Symphony Chorus, the official celebration would be completed the following year. For the first season in many years, Hillis was not invited to conduct the Chicago Symphony Orchestra. This obvious slight must have stung, particularly in light of this being her thirtieth year with the CSO.

However, this significant disappointment would pale by comparison to the personal and professional disappointments that were soon to come.

Though Hillis was scheduled to conduct the Civic Orchestra again this season, her role with them was also reduced to a single concert performance. The majority of the 1986–1987 season was instead given to the two newly appointed CSO conductors, associate conductor Kenneth Jean and assistant conductor Michael Morgan, who would conduct four of the six scheduled concerts, leaving Hillis and Gordon Peters with one concert each. Times were about to change for Peters and Hillis with regard to their Civic Orchestra duties. Newly appointed CSO Executive Director Henry Fogel, replacing John Edwards, would have very different ideas than his predecessor regarding the future of this training orchestra of the Chicago Symphony Orchestra. Fogel notified both Peters and Hillis that he would be canceling their entire summer season of 1987 with the Civic Orchestra, claiming the reason to be a cost-cutting measure. Peters was able to convince Fogel to allow both Hillis and himself to run several sight-reading sessions, covering repertoire with Civic that was already in the Orchestra's library. At a greatly reduced fee for both Hillis and Peters of $100 per rehearsal, Fogel agreed to this offer. As Fogel recalled, Solti was not happy with his decision to take these assignments from Margaret and Gordon. Fogel explained how Solti hated confrontation and he feared that Gordon, the principal percussionist with the CSO, and Margaret, his chorus master, would both harbor resentment as a byproduct of this demotion.[7] The Civic Orchestra was now the only orchestra Hillis was regularly conducting since her recent resignation with the Elgin Symphony Orchestra. Therefore, this demotion presented new challenges for Hillis—i.e., keeping her orchestral rehearsal techniques sharp.

An additional issue was brewing at Orchestra Hall for Hillis. As part of the planning for the concerts and recording of the upcoming Bach's *St. Matthew Passion* in the spring of 1987, Solti determined it necessary to audition every singer Hillis had already selected for this reduced Bach chorus. It was the first time Solti had ever made such a request. The audition involved choristers individually singing for Solti, a very intimidating prospect. Each singer would wait off stage, unable to hear the previous singer. When their name was called, they would enter the backstage area and proceed onto center stage of the concert hall with only the accompanist occupying the massive stage. Solti and Hillis were seated three quarters of the way back in the main floor seating area, almost completely out of view. Solti would instruct each chorister to sight-read a specific passage from the *Passion*, not previously announced to the singer and not necessarily the same as the passage that was given to the previous singer. Added to the challenge of singing a piece that had not yet been rehearsed (and for some had never been previously learned), Solti would interject "auf Deutsch" (in German) if the singer mistakenly chose to sing on a neutral syllable or in English rather than German. One by one, singers would step out of their comfort zone to perform for one of the most famous conductors in the world. As each singer completed their performance, Solti would simply remark "*Sank* you" in his heavy Hungarian accent and the singer would exit the stage, unaware of their status until several weeks later.[8] Solti ultimately approved all of the singers Hillis had originally chosen, but the process was one that must have been embarrassing to Hillis, whose judgement seemed to be in question. Solti would do this audition process again in three years when he decided to record Bach's Mass in B Minor with the CSC.

Added to the distractions at Orchestra Hall, Margaret was encountering another problem in the fall of 1986 involving her long-standing collaboration with Al Booth. By this time, Margaret and Al Booth had worked together for over ten years, continuing the successful Do-It-Yourself *Messiah* concerts and Dame Myra Hess recital programs, both now treasured Chicago traditions. However, problems between Booth and Hillis had been brewing since 1984, shortly after they returned from a trip to Israel together, and by 1986, things were coming to a head. Both Hillis and Booth had traveled to the Holy Land to pursue Booth's dream of producing a Do-It-Yourself *Messiah* in Jerusalem at Christmastime. This event was to be part of a "musical peace conference," as Booth described it for a 1982 interview in *Chicago Magazine*.[9] Both Booth and Hillis traveled to Israel to meet Stanley Sperber, a prominent conductor there, in the hopes of gaining his assistance for producing the Do-It-Yourself event in Jerusalem. Sperber was a logical person for Booth to pursue, as he was the conductor of three fine choirs—the Jerusalem Academy Choir, the National Choir of Israel, and the Israel Philharmonic Choir—all of which could potentially participate in the DIY event. During their meeting, Sperber recalled promising Booth and Hillis he would engage his singers (to serve as audience choristers) for this event, "to help get this thing off the ground."[10] However, Booth and Hillis wanted many more than the two hundred singers Sperber could guarantee. Sperber explained that this could be difficult in that Israelis were not as familiar with Handel's *Messiah* as were people in the States, and he was concerned that he would not be able to gather as many singers as they were requesting to fill the large hall that was being considered for the concert. Sperber suggested that a DIY program of Handel's *Judas Maccabeus* might be more feasible, as it was a more familiar work to singers in Israel. Though Hillis and Booth liked the idea, it never materialized (Picture 64).

In the meantime, Booth was being pressed to increase the number of DIY programs per season in Chicago. Executives at Talman Federal Savings and Loan sponsoring the series were receiving many complaints after turning thousands of people away each year due to tickets almost instantly selling out after being released.[11] In a letter to Hillis dated August 13, 1984, Booth pitched the idea to Hillis of adding a third concert for their upcoming 1984 season. However, he had already selected a third concert date and he had already been in touch with Stanley Sperber to conduct that third concert in place of Hillis, whom he assumed was unavailable. Apparently, at some earlier point, Hillis had communicated with Booth regarding her limited availability in December.[12] No doubt, Booth was motivated to satisfy their sponsor by swiftly adding a third concert date and conductor. He was equally motivated to have Sperber conduct this event to further entice his support of a Jerusalem DIY, still under consideration.

Hillis would respond to Booth's August letter two months later, conveying a subtle tone of disapproval for his handling of the situation. In Margaret's October 3, 1984, response, she shared his enthusiasm for adding a third date for a Do-It-Yourself *Messiah,* but she had concerns about arrangements Booth had already made in selecting the specific date and a conductor without contacting her first. Identifying the challenges such an arrangement may create, Hillis stated, "Before a third date is added, it is only fair to the public that it be announced that Stanley Sperber will conduct in my stead . . . since many of the people who attend these performances do so expecting to see me on the podium as I always have been in the past."[13] Hillis went on to explain that Sperber, whom she referred to as a "wonderful conductor," would be required to conduct the concert using her markings and her interpretation, in that the orchestra is at "a very low artistic level, and he'll have a rough time of it [if he attempts to make changes]." Al Booth had likely not considered the difficulties of adding a new conductor to take over a concert series already prepared and in progress. Choosing a date and a conductor without first consulting with Hillis was not favorably received by Margaret.

Margaret Hillis, Conductor of the Chicago Symphony Chorus, visits Jerusalem
in advance of the December 25 presentation of the "Do It Yourself Messiah"

Picture 64.
Margaret Hillis visiting the Holy Land, traveling with Al Booth in the hopes of developing a
Do-It-Yourself *Messiah* program in Jerusalem, ca. 1984. (Margaret Hillis Collection, Rosenthal
Archives of the Chicago Symphony Orchestra Association)

The Stanley Sperber drama did not end in 1984. There was a second mishap in
1985 that would cause further resentment between Booth and Hillis. With a third
concert added to the schedule in 1984, the plan was to continue the three-concert
schedule for 1985. Hillis apparently had told Booth she would only be available for
one of the three concerts in 1985 despite the fact that this was the tenth anniversary
performance series for the Do-It-Yourself programs. Booth hired Sperber to return
again in 1985, however two complications made it necessary for Booth to cancel
Sperber's appearance. First, Booth was able to secure a larger performance venue,
Medinah Temple, which held an audience of 4,500 instead of the 2,600 capacity of
Orchestra Hall. This would mean that Booth could return to a two-concert series,

which was preferable to him and to his sponsor. The other complicating factor was Margaret Hillis, who apparently changed her mind once she realized that this was a tenth-year celebration of the Do-It-Yourself concerts, and she decided to conduct both programs.[14] This decision forced Booth to retract his offer to Sperber now that Hillis would be conducting both concerts. Booth was clearly upset by this situation, which came out in a letter to Hillis in 1986.

In his September 1986 letter to Hillis, Booth urged her to consider giving up one of her two upcoming December 1986 concerts to Sperber since his contract had been canceled in 1985. In Booth's letter to Hillis, he stated, "I'm sure you recall last year when you decided that you would only be able to do one *Messiah* performance, I engaged Stanley Sperber to do the other one. Then, when you decided you wanted to perform both, I called Stanley and he willingly agreed to take a rain check. I promised him I would make it up to him this year if at all possible. . . . So, if you will let me know which of the two dates you prefer, I'll drop him a note confirming his date."[15] When he received no response from Hillis, he sent a second more aggressive message, just five days later, further pressing her on the matter.

> I'm sure you can't expect me to treat Stanley like an office boy at this stage of the game and cancel him again. I assume if your management firm is worth its salt, they shouldn't have any difficulty finding Margaret Hillis one more engagement by Christmas. . . . As to the money you may have lost, try to remember the years that I got you more money than you asked for and that the Do-It-Yourself *Messiah* has also brought you other engagements during the past ten years. Let's really transact our business professionally next year.[16]

On September 18, 1986, Margaret was swift to reply to the disrespectful tone of Booth's second letter.

> Somewhere wires have become seriously crossed. . . . I have no memory of your having discussed Stanley Sperber's participation in this year's Do-It-Yourself *Messiah*. I have two performances on my calendar, which had come from your office. In addition, I am listed on your letterhead as the Artistic Director of the Dame Myra Hess Memorial Concert series and unless I am

mistaken I was designated Conductor of the Do-It-Yourself *Messiah* "1976 to Infinity." This being the case, any invitation to another conductor should be issued from me and not you.

I consider Stanley Sperber a respected colleague, and since you managed to get yourself bolloxed up in this matter, I will invite him to conduct one of the two dates with the clear understanding that in the future, all artistic control will remain in my hands if I am to be associated with you in any of your enterprises. This means that you do not engage anyone without my prior knowledge and consent in writing. Since it was through me that you were able to get yourself established in Chicago, I consider your actions disloyal to me and to the public.[17]

There was no mistaking the anger in Margaret's communication with Al Booth. Hillis also copied her response to the president and the senior executive vice-president of their benefactor Talman Federal Savings and Loan, along with Stanley Sperber, and Hillis's management representatives.

Margaret followed up with Stanley Sperber shortly after the contentious September 1986 exchange, reiterating that Booth had created confusion, requiring her to intervene. In her letter to Sperber, Hillis wrote, "As you can see from the enclosed correspondences, the right hand did not know what the left was doing. . . . It had been my intention to invite you back in the future, however Al jumped the gun."[18] She went on to explain that despite the challenges, she will help him work things out to best ensure a good performance. "It is utter insanity to attempt performing in this fashion, but we will somehow get it to work."[19] Sperber would return to Chicago to conduct one of the two 1986 Do-It-Yourself concerts.

Following this series of events from 1984–1986, Margaret's relationship with Al Booth would be forever changed. Wisely, he was more careful in his future dealings with her after Hillis drew her line firmly in the sand. The matter of Sperber conducting a DIY *Messiah* would surface once again in 1988 with Booth suggesting Margaret consider bringing Sperber back to Chicago every other year to conduct these DIY concerts, though he wisely left the asking to Hillis, his artistic director of this program. Sperber would eventually take over the DIY concert series. Hillis's last DIY performances in 1991 were followed by Susan Davenny Wyner, who would initially share the series with Hillis and then continue on her own until 1995, after which Stanley Sperber assumed the appointment. It was Sperber's impression that Booth was promoting him so enthusiastically due to his outgoing approach, which contrasted to Margaret's more contained style, offering the audience only brief banter at the outset of each performance. It would be no match for Sperber's effusive manner throughout the program. Perhaps Booth did not have the heart to remove Hillis completely from these concerts, but he very much wanted to add variety to keep audiences coming back year after year. Margaret likely sensed that she was being edged out and reacted accordingly. This state of affairs became an added challenge in the 1986 fall season of many disappointments.

In Hillis's adept way, she refocused her energy, not dwelling on the challenges she was encountering in Chicago. She had an exciting role in the national spotlight that had begun in late 1984 on the National Endowment for the Arts (NEA) National Council, and she was determined to make the most of this extraordinary opportunity. However, it seemed like the issues she was encountering during that fall of 1986 had also infiltrated the NEA, taking the form of an old situation again rearing its ugly head. The dispute between professional versus amateur choruses was resurfacing and would require much time and energy to address. With Hillis in place on the National Council and also on the Board of the Association of Professional Vocal Ensembles (APVE), she was best positioned to exercise her influence on this complex matter.

Robert Shaw was stirring the pot again, revisiting a controversy he had started several years earlier while serving on the NEA National Council. In the *Choral Journal* of April 1986, the entire issue paying tribute to Robert Shaw's seventieth year, Shaw submitted a series of letters he had written to his Atlanta Symphony Chorus members over the years. One letter was titled "Second Thoughts on Amateurism in the Arts," originally written in September 1985.[20] Now that Shaw had stepped down from his official duties with the National Council, he undoubtedly felt freer to speak on a subject that had previously earned him much criticism among some of his fellow conductor colleagues. Shaw had initially backed down from his position regarding equal funding for amateur choruses after the Choral Panel members stated their serious objections. Now no longer part of the NEA, he returned to his original position. The April 1986 Shaw article indirectly endorsed increased NEA funding for volunteer choirs, such as his own in Atlanta, thereby lessening the amount that would be available to professional choruses. Shaw justified his thoughts, taking the position that greater dedication and love for choral singing was evident in volunteer choruses than in professional choruses and government funding should reward them accordingly.

> If it is decided that government has a role in the support of the arts, should that support go to the universally recognized establishments of the highest professional quality . . . or should it go also to the encouragement of grass-root folk-arts and/or amateur participation in the fine arts or both; and if to both, in what proportions?[21]

Shaw went on to compare the emotional commitment of an amateur versus a professional singer, challenging that the amateur is in it for the love of the art, implying for that reason alone there should be more equal financial support available for these amateur endeavors.

> The real problem for the professional musician is whether one's original commitment to the art and to collaborative effort can be maintained. That is a question of motivation, of what one values and ultimately loves. And *that*, friends, brings us right back to *amo-amare*: to love and to *amateurism*.[22]

Shaw's decision to include this letter in the *Choral Journal* sparked fury again within the ranks of the APVE. Bob Page would write an impassioned response, first to his APVE colleagues. In a memorandum initially sent to Janice Kestler, APVE's executive director, along with Paul Hill, Michael Korn, Margaret Hillis, and several other board members, Page sought approval for his planned formal response to Shaw. He would send it first to his APVE colleagues before sending it to the NEA on behalf of the APVE. In his message, Page explained his reasons for creating a public response to Shaw. Page wrote to his APVE colleagues:

> In the April 1986 issue of *The Choral Journal* there was a tribute to Robert Shaw. Included in the issue was an article by Mr. Shaw. . . . The article was filled with assumptions and partial truths, which were presented in the guise of Divine Doctrine. I was infuriated. . . . Several times I sat at the typewriter to write a positive open and evangelistic statement for APVE,

but just as many times I found myself writing a rebuttal to the Shaw article. Now, I think I have calmed down enough to write a statement which will in some ways be a rebuttal to the attitude expressed in the Shaw article, but more importantly a strong statement FOR rather than AGAINST [financial support that favors professional choirs].[23]

In Page's statement, he cleverly fashioned his response in the guise of a restatement of the Association of Professional Vocal Ensembles' mission, thereby indirectly enlisting continued support for professionals in the choral field.

Involving singers who are primarily engaged in other occupations and who choose to sing for inner enrichment, as well as singers who are professionally trained vocalists who bring to the ensemble the expertise of their schooling... These two constituencies do not compete: they complement and complete. To say that one segment is more committed or more loving of the art than the other is an unjust statement. . . . To imply that a singer is jaded or cynical or non-committed because he/she has chosen to be a professional musician is also unjust. . . . The word "professional" is in the title of the APVE for two reasons: to inspire the amateur to a higher degree of excellence, and to remind the professional conductor and singer of their true responsibility to the art of choral music.[24]

Once this response was approved by APVE colleagues, Page crafted his final version into an official position statement, which was presented in a keynote address at the Chorus America convention on June 4, 1987. It would become the official position of APVE, eventually shared with the NEA and the music community at large. At this same meeting, APVE would undergo the official name change from Association of Professional Vocal Ensembles to Chorus America. The impact of the controversy, begun anew with Shaw's very public statements regarding professional versus amateur choruses might well have influenced members of the NEA, as funding challenges for professional choruses would soon become evident. Margaret found herself in the middle of yet another conflict between APVE (now called Chorus America) and the NEA. It was only the beginning of a long, drawn-out controversy.

A Grave Error in Judgement

Margaret balanced her efforts between Chorus America and the National Council committees, along with her own organizations, including the American Choral Foundation (ACF) and the Hillis Fellowship Fund. Since the Services Division of the ACF had been recently transferred to Chorus America as of March 1985, she was finally able to regain control of the ACF expenses. She took further cost-cutting measures at that time, moving the Performance Division out of the expensive New York rental space and into her Chicago office. In January 1985, Hillis notified her New York ACF staff that they would be released as of March 1, leaving Hillis without a staff person to manage the Performance Division. This position, heretofore handled by New York staffer Bertha Bukas, involved oversight of all money coming into the Foundation from Hillis's conducting work and from donations and membership fees for the ACF. Hillis needed someone in Chicago to replace Bukas, someone who could be trusted to handle the Performance Division expenditures of the Foundation. She determined the best choice to replace Bukas would be her recently appointed administrative assistant, Chris Graves.

By 1985, Chris Graves had already been working for one year as Margaret's administrative assistant, appointed to that position after several years of managing her Hillis Fellowship Fund. By replacing Bertha Bukas in the ACF Performance Division, while continuing as the administrative assistant, Graves's role would become far more substantial, particularly as it related to Hillis's finances. He seemed a logical choice, given her satisfaction with him in the other roles he had assumed. Margaret trusted her judgement about Chris. Graves seemed a good fit for the position, considering how well she knew him by now, or so she thought—starting with his name—it was not really Christopher. His real name was Alan Graves.[25] But that is the least of what Margaret did not know about him. Hillis trusted people too easily. She had been lucky before, but in the fall of 1986, her luck would run out.

Graves followed a long line of successful assistants Hillis entrusted through the years. From the time Hillis appointed her first administrative assistant, former partner Elizabeth Burton, she was mindful of how much access they were given to her finances. Burton was a joint owner on one of Hillis's private checking accounts during the years they lived together. However, Burton never had any direct access to the Foundation funds. Her only involvement with the Foundation was in her communications with Bertha Bukas, who was managing all Foundation money. The Foundation covered Hillis's salary, along with her personal bills and expenses, and provided a central hub where all payments for Hillis's work would be sent. Hillis was essentially employed by the American Choral Foundation. Burton never handled Hillis's money directly. Instead, she would send bills that needed to be paid or expenses requiring reimbursement to Bertha Bukas, who processed the transactions.

When Elizabeth moved away, Hillis appointed a singer in the Chorus, Jerry Zachary, as her new administrative assistant. He had similar responsibilities to Burton's, however, unlike Elizabeth Burton, he had no access to Hillis's checking accounts. When Zachary was abruptly replaced in 1981 due to a mishandled matter with a disgruntled singer at a CSC audition, Douglas Asbury was hired as Hillis's next administrative assistant. Asbury had first become known to Hillis during her days at Northwestern University, where he was a graduate student in voice. He would again cross paths with Hillis while he was working at Orchestra Hall as an assistant in the Chorus library and as an administrative assistant with the Civic Orchestra. When he became aware of the administrative position for Hillis, he immediately applied and Hillis accepted him, knowing him as she did for a number of years.

The administrative assistant job, as Douglas recalled, entailed answering the phone in the beautiful glass-enclosed back porch of Hillis's home. Douglas would be charged with managing Margaret's schedule. He was tasked with pulling music from her home orchestra library and shipping it to her upcoming guest-conducting locations. He would also intercept any communications from Richard Carter, manager of the Chicago Symphony Chorus, and Robert Hanson, manager of the Elgin Symphony Orchestra and Margaret's assistant conductor. Douglas's other responsibilities included taking care of Margaret's animals, her car, and sometimes her garden. Douglas would take Margaret's Saab into the car dealership for a periodic oil change and tune-up. He cared for Hillis's cats and her dog O'Banshee, treating them with required medications, taking them to the vet, and walking O'Banshee when Hillis was away. Douglas recalled being paid extra for mulching her garden or doing other household chores beyond those Hillis deemed administrative duties. The only time he recalled handling any money was when he needed Margaret to sign a check for the vet or the car maintenance. Otherwise, he never handled money, never made deposits, and never wrote checks of any kind.[26] Asbury or Hillis herself went through Bertha Bukas for any financial requests.

Upon Douglas's departure in 1984, Hillis again found herself without an assistant and would turn to Chris Graves. From the beginning of Chris's work for Margaret, first on the Fellowship Fund committee in 1981 and then when he assisted her in arrangements for various catered events alongside his friend David Logan, Margaret was becoming increasingly impressed by Chris. Trusting her instincts, she appointed him as her administrative assistant, replacing Douglas Asbury in 1984.

Throughout their affiliation, Graves continually persuaded Hillis to increase his salary. He was always looking for opportunities to make more money, confiding in a few close friends that he was never satisfied with the salary Margaret paid him.[27] She frequently advocated for wage increases on his behalf with the Orchestral Association. After helping him obtain a salary for his work with the Foundation, she would again increase his salary when she hired him as her administrative assistant. At Graves's request, she helped him obtain the position of Chorus librarian when that position came open in February of 1985. In her recommendation letter to the Orchestral Association on his behalf, Hillis stated, "I have complete confidence in Chris."[28] He was subsequently hired to that position. By now, his Orchestra Hall salary included payments for his oversight of the Fellowship Fund, for his position as Chorus librarian, and for his position as a singer in the Chorus. A portion of the administrative assistant salary was also paid by the Orchestral Association with the other portion coming out of Hillis's personal funds. Hillis went even further, requesting that because of his increased earnings with the Orchestral Association, Chris should now be eligible for the standard benefit package offered to other employees.

In March 1985, once Hillis reorganized her American Choral Foundation, moving the Performance Division to Chicago, she appointed Graves to replace Bertha Bukas. In this position, he acquired check-signing authority for ACF accounts. He would also be given full access to all of Hillis's personal checking and savings accounts. Unlike any previous administrative assistant, Graves would now oversee the money exchanged in the Hillis Fellowship Fund, the American Choral Foundation, and in her personal bank accounts. In the history of administrative assistants, none had more access to Hillis's money than Chris Graves. Margaret considered herself fortunate to have someone so capable and reliable as Chris Graves. She could not have been more mistaken.

The convenience of having Chris Graves in all of these positions would change in an instant when Hillis received a phone call in November 1986, a call Chris would normally have intercepted. Since Graves was not yet in the office, Margaret picked up the call. The ensuing conversation rocked Hillis to the core. A credit card company was inquiring about an overdue payment. Hillis responded that she did not own a charge card from that company, to which the caller explained that indeed an account had been opened in her name. Realizing what had taken place, Hillis took swift action, immediately confronting and then firing Graves, also forcing his resignation from his duties as Chorus librarian and as a member of the Chicago Symphony Chorus. Hillis would be stunned to discover the extent of Graves's embezzlements taking place right under her nose in her home office over a period of several years.

Hillis discovered that only months after hiring Graves as her administrative assistant in 1984, the thefts began. Beginning in November 1984, he opened an unauthorized checking account under the name of the Hillis Fellowship Fund with himself as the sole signatory on the account. He diverted over $10,000 into this fraudulent account when it should have gone to the American Choral Foundation account. Another $12,000 belonging to the Orchestral Association and thousands more from Margaret's personal accounts was also deposited into the fraudulent checking account. Graves forged signatures on numerous checks and diverted a certificate of over $10,000 that was part of the endowment of the American Choral Foundation. All these funds were used to pay off Graves's personal bills, as he enjoyed a more extravagant lifestyle. One of Chris's friends recalled noticing that he seemed to have a good deal more cash on hand during this time in the mid-1980s, but he did not feel it appropriate to ask Chris how he had come into this money.[29]

Chris was able to hide these accounts from Hillis by renting a private post office box to which any mailings would be sent instead of going directly to Hillis's home address. As soon as Hillis confronted Graves, he immediately removed various accounting and banking records from the office computer before leaving, attempting to cover up additional illegal activity she had not yet discovered. He withdrew all but $1,000 from the fraudulent checking account, transferring that remaining sum into the ACF, thereby closing the forged Fellowship account in the hopes of not getting caught.

On May 19, 1988, Graves was convicted of grand theft, having diverted a total of $47,000 in funds for his personal use over a two-year period. Though Hillis and her attorneys had hoped for him to receive prison time, he was only given thirty months of probation and four hundred hours of community service. He was also ordered to pay restitution. On the day Graves was sentenced, Hillis was in court. After publicly apologizing to Hillis and the court, the judge intervened, stating that the best way to apologize to Hillis was to see that she gets her money returned along with the two associations (Orchestral Association and American Choral Foundation) from which he had additionally embezzled. Hillis would spend the next six years paying lawyers to chase Graves down, as he continually eluded the courts, hiding money he was earning by being paid only in cash and remaining completely dishonest in his dealings with her. Hillis would spend in excess of $30,000 in legal fees, accountants, and private investigators over the years, trying to hold Graves accountable, but little restitution was made by Graves. His dishonesty continued until his untimely death.

Though Graves had never before committed a crime, he acted in a way that suggested he was an experienced con man. He carefully groomed Hillis to trust him, and she was a perfect target for his financial schemes. Graves, with his charming and outgoing personality, had spent years in the catering business, serving as a *maître d'* at the University Club, where he was able to refine his skills for interacting with elite, highly educated clientele. David Logan and Chris Graves were able to take advantage of Hillis's generosity and fine taste in food, creating elaborate and expensive spreads for her lavish parties. What Hillis did not see was the darker side of both David Logan and Chris Graves. Hints of trouble surfaced in March 1985 when David Logan stopped attending rehearsals, resulting in Hillis dismissing him from the upcoming *St. Matthew Passion* performances and then placing him on probation with the Chorus. Logan would not return to the Chorus and just a few months later, in May 1985, he was found dead in his apartment. The cause of his death was mysterious; the autopsy revealed a combination of alcohol and drugs in his system. His naked body was bound in a chair, his apartment had been robbed, and his car was also taken. There was no forced sign of entry. Friends who knew David were aware of his drug and alcohol problems, but nothing was confirmed about the circumstances surrounding his death.

Nine years later, Chris Graves would also be found dead in his apartment, however his death was ruled a homicide. A friend described last seeing Chris the night he was killed, explaining that he and Chris had gone to dinner together, after which Chris hailed a cab, telling his friend that he was headed to a bar to pick up someone and bring him home for the night. Both Chris and his friend had agreed to meet the next day, where both would be traveling to the home of his friend's sister for Easter weekend. When Chris did not answer the phone the next morning, his friend assumed Chris had made other plans and left for the weekend without him. On Monday, when Chris was still not reachable, the friend decided to check on him in his apartment. The janitor of the building opened Chris's apartment door, where Chris was found dead, a butcher knife in his back.[30] The tragic ends to both Chris and David hold haunting similarities. One theory posited by friends was that, in both cases, they brought home the wrong guys. Neither case has ever been solved.

The fact that Hillis was now connected with two people of questionable pasts and ill intentions brought her great embarrassment. She was forced to confront the harm she inadvertently caused, impacting not only her personal reputation, but also the reputation of the Orchestral Association, the Hillis Fellowship Fund, and her American Choral Foundation. Henry Fogel would do damage control after an article in the *Chicago Tribune* appeared, stating that the CSO had lost $24,000 as a result of Graves's nefarious actions.[31] This information was factually incorrect, compelling Fogel to clarify matters for his CSO board of trustees and all CSO staff members. In his letter, Fogel stated,

> The Orchestral Association did not suffer any loss in this alleged theft. Mr. Graves was employed by Ms. Hillis as an administrative assistant. . . . The Hillis Fellowship Fund is a fund held by the Orchestral Association, acting as custodian for Ms. Hillis. These funds are not available for use by the Orchestral Association. . . . Please rest assured that no monies were taken from funds held by The Association. . . . Christopher Graves was employed by the Orchestral Association on a part-time basis, as the Chicago Symphony Orchestra Chorus librarian. In this position he had no access to cash held by the Association. . . . He resigned (from) the Association immediately, following the discovery of the alleged theft.[32]

Hillis was well aware that she alone had selected the wrong assistant and neglected to perform proper oversight of his work, particularly related to his handling of her finances. Her error in judgement was now on public display for all to see. It would be a humiliating episode that continued until Graves finally admitted guilt in May 1988. Hillis experienced similar embarrassment when facing the board of directors for her American Choral Foundation. Though sympathetic, ACF board members undoubtedly recognized a pattern resembling Hillis's previous mismanagement due to lack of oversight, forcing it to be reorganized once again and ultimately downsized to save it from financial demise. The disaster of Christopher Graves's egregious chicanery was finally exposed in that fateful fall of 1986.

RESILIENCY IN ACTION

In times of trial, resiliency is important. Of equal importance is having people who can be counted upon for support during difficult times. Fortunately for Margaret, she had a partner who had been in her life since 1979, someone truly there for her. Jane Samuelson met Margaret while interviewing her for a feature story she was writing for the popular *Chicago Magazine*, one of the many interviews Hillis granted during that active period shortly after her Carnegie Hall success. The interview was done over three dinners at Chez Paul, at that time one of the finest French restaurants in Chicago. It was the start of what became a lasting relationship.[33] Jane remained very much behind the scenes, avoiding the limelight of Margaret's world. This avoidance was Jane's choice, but it also came out of necessity for both of them. Jane's career as a successful writer for *Chicago Magazine*, along with other prominent writing positions and freelance work, and Margaret's conducting career would likely have been jeopardized if there had been any hint of the relationship between them, given society's prevailing attitudes at that time. Jane became the solid foundation for Margaret when her life became complicated. This period of 1986 was the first of others to come when Margaret would rely upon Jane's steadfast support.

Jane, with her warm personality and generous heart, attracted like-minded friends, who were regularly welcomed into Margaret's home, now shared by both. One of those friendships was a former work colleague, Dave Murray. Dave and Jane had known each other since their work together at Encyclopedia Britannica. Jane welcomed Dave and his family, including his two young sons, into their home on a regular basis. Margaret and Jane enjoyed the raucousness of Dave's two young sons playing with Jane's two young nephews of the same age, all frequent visitors, adding liveliness to their Wilmette home. Margaret greatly appreciated the relaxed, non-pretentious interactions with Dave's family, a welcome break from the formality of Margaret's professional life. It was all a breath of fresh air which Margaret embraced.

Not surprisingly, Hillis immediately thought of Dave for the vacant administrative assistant position. Hillis knew that Dave had recently been released from his position as vice president of communications at the National Association of Realtors, making him available for Hillis's offer to replace Chris Graves. However, he was hesitant to do so due to the drastically reduced salary she was offering, explaining that he needed to support his boys as a newly divorced dad. Hillis countered, offering generous arrangements beyond his salary, contributing to a college fund for both boys. Dave accepted the job. His substantial background in business and his gentle demeanor provided Hillis the perfect fit for this position. She trusted Dave, which turned out to be an accurate assessment of his character, a welcome change from his predecessor.

Dave recalled Chris Graves coming into the office to explain the responsibilities of the position. Dave described Chris as reeking of alcohol, eyes bloodshot, and subdued. After walking Dave through everything he needed to know, Hillis promptly appeared, sternly dismissing Graves and warning him never to return.[34] Dave's initial months on the job entailed meetings and phone calls "with lawyers and cops," and combing through accounts in preparation for the case against Graves.[35] Murray would come to be an important part of the insular family that Hillis would depend upon to see her through the difficulties of the Chris Graves debacle and in other challenges ahead. Applying the discipline she had developed over the years, Hillis found a way to compartmentalize the unpleasant reminders that continued to crop up in the fall of 1986. She was able to do so with her solid base of Dave Murray and Jane Samuelson supporting her, thereby freeing her to focus on more positive parts of her life.

The remainder of the 1986–1987 Chicago Symphony Orchestra season was less turbulent. Hillis enjoyed a welcome escape from the trauma of the previous months, beginning in December 1986, when she guest conducted the Puerto Rico Symphony Orchestra in a performance of *Messiah*. Returning home, she conducted her annual Hillis Fellowship Concert followed by a Do-It-Yourself *Messiah* concert. Several additional guest conducting appearances during the winter of 1987 included a performance of Bach's Mass in B Minor at the Boulder Bach Festival along with several workshops throughout the winter of 1987. Performing became a respite from the turmoil of recent weeks and months. The Chorus's thirtieth anniversary celebrations ahead also enabled Margaret an opportunity to shift her focus. Honoring her many achievements in Chicago and beyond, the first of many tributes was dedicated to

Margaret Hillis by Illinois Governor James R. Thompson, who declared April 29, 1987, Margaret Hillis Day in Illinois.

Always looking ahead, Hillis would shift away from negativity, inevitably finding a new project upon which to focus her energy. The project for this season entailed planning upcoming celebrations for the Chorus's thirtieth anniversary season. Events would begin in July 1987 with a Ravinia Festival performance of Mahler's Symphony No. 8 featuring the Chorus, followed by an elegant reception. A highlight of that event was the presentation of a Grammy Award, the second one for Margaret Hillis and James Levine collaborating, this time for their 1986 recording of Orff's *Carmina Burana* (Picture 65).

Picture 65.

Margaret Hillis and James Levine presented with Grammy Awards for Best Choral Performance (other than opera) for the 1983 RCA recording of Brahms's *A German Requiem*. The Grammy statuettes were presented following a performance of Haydn's *The Creation* at Ravinia on June 30, 1985. This was the Chorus's sixth Grammy Award and the first for Levine and Hillis collaboratively in a recording project. They would receive another Grammy Award for Orff's *Carmina Burana* in February of 1987. (Jim Steere, photographer) (Rosenthal Archives of the Chicago Symphony Orchestra Association)

The other highlight of that summer included Margaret's collaboration with Chorus America colleagues, leading a National Conductor Training Workshop along with conductors Andrew Davis, Bob Page, and Michael Korn. Hillis was able to pivot away from the difficulties of the past season by fully embracing time with treasured colleagues in the summer months, followed by the upcoming season that would bring honor to herself and to the Chorus she had founded thirty years ago.

In her planning of events for the coming season, Hillis engaged her Chorus Development Committee, formerly known as the Hillis Fellowship Fund Committee. Though this committee's main purpose was fundraising for the Fellowship Fund, the August 1987 meeting involved planning a reception following Hillis's conducting of the world premiere of Marvin David Levy's *Masada*. Featuring soloist Yaël Dayan, daughter of Israeli General Moshe Dayan, this new work was a perfect way to begin a season of CSC honors. Prior to this premiere, the Chorus would open their season performing in a star-studded concert honoring another momentous occasion, the seventy-fifth birthday of Sir Georg Solti. The gala event included opera luminaries Plácido Domingo and Kiri Te Kanawa performing with the Chicago Symphony Orchestra and Chorus. Hillis would be on the podium the following week to conduct *Masada*, accompanied by the Orchestra and Chorus.

Margaret was central to the planning of the post-concert festivities following the *Masada* opening night performance, hosted by private donors. In the August meeting of her development committee, Hillis proposed everything from an elegant menu of *hors d'oeuvres*, drinks, desserts, flowers, linens, and invitations for the occasion. She proposed the concert and reception be heavily promoted, suggesting press releases, radio spots, and significant signage throughout Orchestra Hall in honor of the Chorus's thirtieth year. Additionally, Hillis and the committee supervised the publication of a beautiful brochure in the Chorus's honor, "Chicago Symphony Chorus, Margaret Hillis, Director."[36] In that brochure commemorating the Chorus's history, there was acknowledgement of the more than 350 concerts, three dozen recordings, and over four hundred radio broadcasts of the Chorus in the United States and abroad. Also included was Hillis's vision for the Chorus's future, including a listing of objectives:

- An endowment fund to support the Chorus;
- Special projects including commissioning, performing, and recording new choral works;
- Development of a choral chamber and recital series; and
- A plan to make the CSC more accessible to high school and university educators and students through workshops, open rehearsals, and general education programs.

Hillis would return to the podium again during this season, conducting a "Special Concert: The Chicago Symphony Chorus's Thirtieth Anniversary" on March 13, 1988. The performance of Verdi's *Four Sacred Pieces* was paired with Mozart's Requiem, the piece the CSC had performed in their first appearance with the Chicago Symphony Orchestra on that same date thirty years earlier. However, this time the Chorus would be performing with the Civic Orchestra of Chicago instead of the Chicago Symphony Orchestra. The finale of this momentous season included Solti conducting performances and a recording of Bach's *St. Matthew Passion*.

There was yet another project on Hillis's mind during this anniversary season. The idea had been one she mulled over in previous years but would now become her primary focus. Hillis had long desired showcasing her Chicago Symphony Chorus to European audiences, and, true to form, she would approach this most daunting aspiration with determination and grit. Why now? After thirty years of spectacular accomplishments, what ignited the flame at this point in the Chorus's history? Quite simply, Margaret was beginning to plan her departure from the Chicago Symphony Chorus, and, in so doing, she wished for this remaining goal to be realized before passing the baton. In an interview for the *Kokomo Tribune* in March 1986, Ken Ford shared, "She plans to stay with the Chicago Symphony Chorus until 1991, the 100th anniversary of the [CSO]."[37] Hillis's self-imposed deadline was reiterated in John von Rhein's April 12, 1987, *Chicago Tribune* article in celebration of the Chorus's thirtieth year. "She says she would like to continue as chorus director at least through the orchestra's centennial, 1990–1991, which would coincide with Solti's retirement."[38] With a retirement date already in her mind and knowing that Solti too would retire after the centennial season of the CSO, Margaret realized that there would be no greater opportunity to launch a European tour than now.

The seed for this plan had been planted years earlier as revealed in a memo to Peter Jonas, artistic administrator of the CSO. Richard Carter, the chorus manager, sent Jonas a memo with the subject heading: "As per your request." The memo, dated May 9, 1979, contained details of estimated costs for the Chorus to join the Orchestra on a European tour, involving a maximum of two hundred singers. Carter estimated a fee of $295,000, and in his message he indicated that "should a trip hinge on some possible negotiations, the members would appreciate an opportunity to do so," implying there may be a willingness on the part of the singers to reduce their customary fees in order to make the trip possible.[39] The next Europe-related memo, dated January 8, 1985, contained a similar Chorus budget for a prospective tour September 3–13, 1986. This submission approximated costs for 170 singers, thirty fewer singers than in the first estimate, at a similar price tag of $292,194.04.

This September 1986 tour was given more serious consideration due to the fact that there was a concrete invitation for the Chicago Symphony Chorus to give five performances of Berlioz's *Damnation of Faust* and Beethoven's Symphony No. 9 at the Alte Oper in Frankfurt and at the Proms in London's Royal Albert Hall, with Solti conducting the performances. A flat fee was offered to the CSC for all performances, rehearsals, and warm-ups, as well as hotel, transportation, and a daily per diem to cover each singer's meals. The fee also covered any media rights. The stipulation with regard to media taping and broadcasting involved every singer waiving standard union payment from the BBC for the video, essentially giving up full rights for extra pay related to broadcast or rebroadcast of the concerts. Paul Chummers understood how difficult this would be for the Chorus to negotiate with their union, the American Guild of Musical Artists. Chummers conveyed his concern to Hillis in a memo sent to her on May 7, 1985, stating that he was generally enthusiastic about this performance opportunity, "but at the same time it is more complicated than it seems at first glance, particularly the issues of payment waivers by choristers and loss of broadcast rights to the Association."[40]

Seeing that she had an uphill climb, Hillis became all the more determined to overcome any obstacle in the way of making this tour a reality. After receiving the memo from Chummers, she received a fax on May 29, 1985, on which she was copied, containing a message sent by Chummers to Dr. Rudolf Sailer, the intermediary for the Frankfurt Opera. Chummers stated, "As I mentioned, the question of audiovisual rights to *Faust* is a serious union matter." He further went on to explain that he had reached out to the singers' union, the American Guild of Musical Artists (AGMA), and they made it clear they would not agree to any such waiver. Chummers appealed to Sailer to consider another source for payment of these very costly fees, set forth by the union for singers in a broadcast contract.[41] Upon seeing this fax, Hillis determined it was time to enlist Solti in this cause. On the same date of May 29, 1985, Hillis sent a letter to Solti, who was invited to conduct the Chorus on this tour, urging his support. In Solti's prompt response, dated June 4, 1985, he stated, "Thanks for your letter of May 29. . . . Please be sure I will have it high on the agenda for my discussions with Henry [Fogel] at the end of this month. You know I will do all I can to help."[42] Sailer faxed a reply to the Chummers message, which was received by all involved parties on May 31, indicating that the offer of $250,000 must include everything previously listed, including broadcasting rights. The offer was final, and he would need an answer to this offer by no later than June 23, 1985.[43]

Unfortunately, the deadline for the Alte Oper had come and gone, much to the disappointment of Hillis and her choristers, all of whom had been apprised of the prospective European tour. One of the members of the Chorus decided to take a bold step forward, pursuing the matter further with Dr. Sailer. Without permission from Hillis, longtime member Cathy Weingart-Ryan phoned Dr. Sailer on June 28, 1985, explaining the Chorus's great interest in this invitation, to which he responded that he would make this same offer for the following summer of 1987.[44] Weingart-Ryan then wrote a letter to Henry Fogel, now firmly in place as the CSO's new executive director. The letter, dated July 2, 1985, informed Fogel of this extended invitation for September 1987 and further enclosed a "Declaration of Intention," with ninety-four signatures of Chicago Symphony Chorus members enthusiastically in support for this tour.[45] The next day, Weingart-Ryan sent a letter to Mr. Gene Boucher and Mr. Herbert Noyer of the AGMA union explaining that it was the union's delayed response that caused the Chorus to lose the 1986 tour. She wrote, "Communications concerning the invitation between and among Alte Oper, . . . Chicago Symphony Chorus, and AGMA were insufficiently complete and the resultant delay . . . moved Alter Oper to invite the London Festival Chorus to perform in place of the Chicago Symphony Chorus."[46] She then shared that the invitation has been extended to the summer 1987 and referred AGMA to the enclosed "Declaration of Intention." Several days later, Weingart-Ryan distributed copies of letters recently sent to AGMA on their behalf, adding that singers who have not already done so should sign the "Declaration of Intention."

Margaret followed suit, sending a message to Solti on July 2, informing him of what had recently transpired between Cathy Weingart-Ryan and Dr. Sailer. In that mailing, Hillis enclosed the July 2 letter Weingart-Ryan had sent to Fogel.[47] Solti's secretary, Charles Kaye, responded for Solti on July 17, 1985, stating that neither he nor "Sir Georg" were aware of any extended invitation by Dr. Sailer and further he was not certain Sir Georg would be available to participate the following year.[48] Charles Kaye reminded Hillis, "The enthusiasm of your members, indicated by the signed declaration is most encouraging, but until such time as this is met by a similar spirit from the Union, I fail to see how we can begin to consider the Chorus participating in any project involving large-scale TV and Video distribution." Hillis responded on July 29, 1985, that she was frustrated with Chummers, who despite her pleas, denied her permission to take this matter to the Chorus. It was her hope to persuade members to override the union. Because it took Chummers most of the six weeks they were given to respond to the invitation, Hillis had only the last six days before the deadline to finally approach the Chorus. "Since this Chorus is the largest single contingent of AGMA other than the Metropolitan Opera Chorus, they could have gone against the union and demanded the waiver."[49] In closing, Hillis stated, "Needless to say, I am deeply sad about this whole mess, but optimist that I am, I'm hopeful about 1987 (the Chorus's thirtieth year) or 1989."[50]

A reply from the union on July 24, 1985, sealed the fate of any upcoming tour, making it clear that AGMA was unwilling to compromise despite the Chorus's enthusiasm to tour. In a response to Cathy Weingart-Ryan's July 3, 1985, letter, the national executive secretary stated: "AGMA is actively suspicious of 'lumpsum deals' that give no breakdown of monetary costs . . . it is our responsibility to see that the enthusiasm of performers does not lead them irrevocably into an agreement serving less than their best interest."[51] Additionally, they made note that one-fourth of the signatories on the declaration were not yet members of AGMA.

According to Weingart-Ryan, she approached Henry Fogel shortly after the latest tour was lost, suggesting to him that the Chorus would be willing to engage in fundraising efforts in support of a future European tour. Cathy believed that this conversation may have motivated him to form a committee, consisting of Margaret Hillis; Joe Fabbioli, the newly appointed manager of the Chorus; Martha Gilmer, artistic administrator; Russell Baird, a generous donor; and Cathy Weingart-Ryan, Chorus member. This committee may have provided the catalyst for more serious consideration of a European tour, perhaps for late August and early September 1988. Martha Gilmer requested Richard Carter to draw up a budget for a two-week tour to include four concerts with the Orchestra and possibly four concerts for the Chorus alone.[52] Costs were to be based upon travel to four different cities, three days each, including London, Vienna, Salzburg, and Frankfurt, with two days added at the end for a total of fourteen days. "Before we can even discuss the feasibility of a choir tour, we need to know what we are talking about in terms of dollars."

Carter's response after consulting with a respected tour agent was $471,925.00 for 170 singers. It was clear that no tour would be possible in 1987 given the expenses to be covered. The next hope for a tour was 1989.

Meanwhile, the Chicago Symphony Chorus embarked upon a fundraising campaign, offering their talents to perform in small groups for holiday parties and other private parties throughout the year. They again offered Vocal Valentine serenades, which had become very popular throughout the city as singers dispersed to downtown office buildings, hotels, stores, and restaurants to the prearranged location of their designated recipients. The Chorus would also put on an enormous jewelry and craft fair.

During the 1986–1987 season, Margaret was facing the possibility that they might lose a 1989 tour if something did not dramatically change. Though Chorus efforts in fundraising were heroic, income fell far short of the mark. The clock was ticking, as Solti's final years as the CSO music director approached. Hillis knew that this tour would likely not occur without him, nor did she want it to. A *Crain's Chicago Business* magazine article, appearing June 29, 1987, in tribute to the Chorus's thirtieth season, included statements from both Hillis and Fogel regarding the future of the Chicago Symphony Chorus. Hillis stated that her first goal for the near future was to raise enough money to take the group to Europe with the Orchestra during the 1988–1989 season. "Transporting and housing the chorus in Europe for ten days, for example, will cost a minimum of $400,000. No decision has been made on whether its members will accompany the symphony, but Mr. Fogel obviously is counting on Ms. Hillis to come up with most of the money. 'If the Chorus is able to raise a significant amount of the money, they will go to Europe.'"[53] Fogel had been in the process of eliminating a deficit in the Orchestra's endowment and was not in a position in his first seasons with the CSO to offer funding that would cover the Chorus.[54] The Chorus's difficulties in raising money were further complicated by Fogel's instructions that under no circumstances were Chorus members to approach any donor who had previously been a donor to the Chicago Symphony Orchestra. However, any donor was free to purchase small ensembles for events and valentines.

With time running out, Hillis was determined to lower the expenses of the proposed budget. Well aware that the most significant expense in the budget was in transporting the Chorus overseas, she took it upon herself to find a more cost-effective means of transportation. She first consulted Craig Jessop, at that time a captain in the United States Air Force and a fine choral conductor who was working overseas on assignment. He would later become the director of the famous Mormon Tabernacle Choir and then the head of Utah State University's Department of Music. Hillis had known Jessop for years, and she felt comfortable requesting his assistance in securing air support for the Chorus. In exchange for transportation, Hillis offered Chorus performances at several overseas airbases. Jessop responded that though he was not in a position to assist her, he recommended she contact the Illinois National Guard and the Illinois governor, as well as the commander-in-chief of the Military Airlift Command.[55] Hillis next decided to invite the president of the United States, the governor of Illinois, and the commander-in-chief of the Military Airlift Command to the CSC's March 13, 1988, thirtieth anniversary concert, which she was conducting. Hillis followed up with Vanessa Moss, CSO operations manager, in her letter of February 11, 1988, stating, "If we can get both the governor and the general on our side, we may have a good chance of getting free transportation for the Chorus."[56]

In the meantime, Hillis pursued other avenues of governmental support, including the U.S. Information Agency and Travel on Department of Defense aircrafts, but she was again turned down, told instead that the Armed Forces Professional Entertainment Office would have the authority to approve military sponsorship and airlift support. Hillis then reached out to Illinois Senator Paul Simon, enlisting his support in her quest for military transportation, stating, "Our being able to go to Europe may very well hinge on it."[57] She wrote a similar letter to Illinois Senator Alan Dixon, from whom she received the most disappointing response on December 6, 1988. Dixon had forwarded Hillis's request to Lt. Col. Stephen Sherwood. His response back to Dixon sent on November 5, 1988, stated, "While the Air Force does entertain civilian requests for airlift support, each request must meet established criteria and be in the best interest of the Air Force. This request does not meet the criteria and the Air Force support would place the Service in a position of competing with available commercial transportation companies."[58]

During the 1988 Ravinia Festival season and through the fall of 1988, it seemed as if hope was fading for the Chorus to join the Orchestra in any upcoming European tour. What Hillis did not know was that Solti had made very clear to Henry Fogel that before his final season as music director with the Orchestra, he wanted to take "his *Chor*" to Europe.[59] After Fogel became more public in acknowledging consideration of a European tour to include the Chorus, donors began to contribute to the cause, including a sizeable donation from Talman Federal Savings with whom Margaret had been affiliated for many years through their sponsorship of her Do-It-Yourself *Messiahs*. Other donations would follow, including a very generous donation from Dean and Rosemarie Buntrock. These significant contributions and others, along with the Chorus fundraising efforts, though short of the required amount, resulted in a successful outcome for Hillis and her singers.

In December 1988, Henry Fogel arrived during the dress rehearsal for the Hillis Fellowship Fund concert. His appearance was met with surprise by members of the Chorus who surmised something important must be brewing. In fact, they were correct. He had come to announce the exciting news to the Chorus in person. At the conclusion of the rehearsal, Fogel confirmed what the Chorus had hoped for. They would be joining the Chicago Symphony Orchestra in their upcoming European tour in August 1989. An exuberant Chicago Symphony Chorus cheerfully responded to Fogel's announcement, after which chorus manager Joe Fabbioli followed up with a notification to all members of the Chorus. "I am very pleased to share with you the news that the final decision regarding the Chorus's European tour has been made, and the Chorus will indeed be performing at the London Proms Festival and the Salzburg Festival in August." His memo went on to state Fogel's message to the Chorus, "Although all of the necessary funds have not yet been raised, the artistic merits of this tour are so great that the Chorus will participate in the tour."[60]

Margaret Finding Her Voice

The period between 1985–1989 would be perhaps the most tumultuous of Hillis's thirty-seven-year history with the Chicago Symphony Chorus. During these years, Margaret would find herself facing issues that had long been present; however, she was now at a point in her career where she was willing to confront them head on. Hillis, aware of the salary inequities throughout her career, was now willing to put her job on the line. Demanding more equitable treatment, she was finally calling attention to the discrepancies between her salary and the many accomplishments she had achieved over so many years. In addition to the inequities of salary, Hillis was willing to confront disloyalty, first in her treatment by the Elgin Symphony Orchestra, ultimately resulting in her resignation. Al Booth's disloyalty to Margaret Hillis in the form of offering up her performances of the DIY *Messiah* to other conductors after she had helped Booth get established in Chicago, she found untenable. Knowing she might possibly be removed from her position as artistic director for the Dame Myra Hess and Do-It-Yourself *Messiah* enterprises, she unabashedly confronted Booth, copying her dress-down letter to the stakeholders of these events. It was incredulous to Hillis that she would be treated this way after ten years of creating traditions that would last far beyond the lives of Booth and Hillis. In the most devastating act of betrayal coming from Chris Graves, whom Hillis had so greatly entrusted, she would experience not only the most egregious disloyalty but also public embarrassment for her part in allowing someone she had not judged nor supervised properly. Aware of her all too trusting manner and her unwillingness to properly oversee financial matters, Hillis boldly faced the situation, remaining stoic though shaken by this revealing episode. The Chris Graves matter would remain a nuisance for many years to come, always reminding her of her own flaws in judgement of character and her lack of managerial oversight.

Hillis's newly emboldened stance to advocate for herself had taken her over half of her lifetime to acquire. She was finally willing to demand the respect and loyalty she had earned throughout her impressive career. Through self-acknowledgement, Hillis was newly empowered to stand up for herself, unwilling to put up with the small indignities endured over a lifetime of being a woman in a man's field. Though she was not one to use this as an excuse for challenges she would encounter, she was able to see things for what they were, and for the first time she was willing to move beyond blindly accepting them as the status quo.

Hillis was able to remain steady through the adversities of the mid to late 1980s, in part with the support of her loyal companion Jane Samuelson, who would take on an even greater role in support of Margaret in the years to come. Having Jane to rely upon made the challenges of the recent years more tolerable. Jane and Margaret would travel in the summer months, enjoying treasured time away to reconnect without the constant stress of performances and politics. Their travels to France, Scotland, London, and Switzerland, along with periodic visits to Jane's summer home in Maine, grounded Hillis, enabling her to face the challenges that would come about with each new season.

Ever present in Hillis was her uncanny ability to forge ahead no matter the circumstances. Even as she would endure the disappointments of a reduced presence on the podium of the CSO and throughout many painful episodes culminating in the Chris Graves incident, Hillis compartmentalized her pain, refocusing her energy on her prestigious presidential NEA appointment and in new projects she would envision. Working tirelessly to get her Chorus to Europe, the seemingly impossible was made to happen in part because of Hillis's sheer determination to make it so. The upcoming European tour would become one of the greatest successes in the history of the Chicago Symphony Chorus. Hillis would hold on to the memories of that epic achievement as she confronted her greatest challenge yet to come.

ENDNOTES

1. Interview with Leonard Slatkin, August 8, 2012.
2. Ibid.
3. Ibid.
4. Leonard Slatkin, *Conducting Business: Unveiling the Mystery Behind the Maestro* (Milwaukee: Amadeus Press, 2012), p. 25.
5. Interview with Leonard Slatkin.
6. Author's recollection.
7. Interview of Henry Fogel, June 6, 2013.
8. Author's recollection.
9. Judith Neisser, "Hallelujah, Hallelujah: Singing the Praises of Al Booth and His Do-It-Yourself Messiah," *Chicago Magazine*, December 1982.
10. Interview with Stanley Sperber, October 24, 2020.
11. Letter from Al Booth to Margaret Hillis, August 13, 1984 (Margaret Hillis Collection, Rosenthal Archives of the Chicago Symphony Orchestra Association, Box 5).
12. Ibid.
13. Letter from Margaret Hillis to Al Booth, October 3, 1984 (Margaret Hillis Collection, Rosenthal Archives of the Chicago Symphony Orchestra Association, Box 5).
14. Letter from Al Booth to Margaret Hillis, September 16, 1986 (Margaret Hillis Collection, Rosenthal Archives of the Chicago Symphony Orchestra Association, Box 5).
15. Letter to Margaret Hillis from Al Booth, September 11, 1986 (Margaret Hillis Collection, Rosenthal Archives of the Chicago Symphony Orchestra Association, Box 5).
16. Letter from Al Booth to Margaret Hillis, September 16, 1986 (Margaret Hillis Collection, Rosenthal Archives of the Chicago Symphony Orchestra Association, Box 5).
17. Letter to Al Booth from Margaret Hillis, September 19, 1986 (Margaret Hillis Collection, Rosenthal Archives of the Chicago Symphony Orchestra Association, Box 5).
18. Letter from Margaret Hillis to Stanley Sperber, September 24, 1986 (Margaret Hillis Collection, Rosenthal Archives of the Chicago Symphony Orchestra Association, Box 5).
19. Letter to Stanley Sperber from Margaret Hillis, September 24, 1986 (Margaret Hillis Collection, Rosenthal Archives of the Chicago Symphony Orchestra Association, Box 5).
20. Robert Shaw, "Letters to a Symphony Chorus—Second Thoughts on Amateurism in the Arts (September 25, 1985)," *Choral Journal* (April 1986): pp. 9–10.
21. Ibid.
22. Ibid.
23. Letter written by Robert Page to members rebutting Robert Shaw's published article in the *Choral Journal* of April 1986. The memorandum was sent to select APVE board members on July 24, 1986 (Margaret Hillis Collection, Rosenthal Archives of the Chicago Symphony Orchestra Association, Box 8).
24. Ibid.

25. A friend of Chris Graves who has been interviewed and requests anonymity.

26. Interview of Douglas Asbury, October 10, 2020.

27. Interview with former friend of Graves, Jerry Goodman, October 2, 2020.

28. Letter to Paul Chummers, William Rahe, and Leonard Smith from Margaret Hillis, February 15, 1985 (Margaret Hillis Collection, Rosenthal Archives of the Chicago Symphony Orchestra Association, Box 5).

29. A friend of Chris Graves who has been interviewed and requests anonymity

30. Ibid.

31. Linnet Myers, "CSO Swindle Suspect Must Face the Music," *Chicago Tribune*, August 8, 1987.

32. Letter from Henry Fogel to the Orchestral Association Board of Trustees, August 18, 1987 (Margaret Hillis Collection, Rosenthal Archives of the Chicago Symphony Orchestra Association, Box 10).

33. Second interview with Jane Samuelson, October 8, 2020.

34. Interview with Dave Murray, November 4, 2012.

35. Ibid.

36. Author's personal collection.

37. Ken Ford, "Just Call Her 'Conductor,'" *Kokomo Tribune*, March 18, 1986, p. 9.

38. John von Rhein, "The Active Voice: Margaret Hillis' Perfectionism Keeps the CSO Singing Arm in Shape," *Chicago Tribune*, April 12, 1987, Section 13, p. 6.

39. Memo to Peter Jonas from Dick Carter, May 9, 1979 (Margaret Hillis Collection, Rosenthal Archives of the Chicago Symphony Orchestra Association, Box 6).

40. Letter from Paul Chummers to Margaret Hillis, May 7, 1985 (Margaret Hillis Collection, Rosenthal Archives of the Chicago Symphony Orchestra Association, Box 6).

41. Fax sent to Dr. Rudolf Sailer from Paul Chummers, May 29, 1985 (Margaret Hillis Collection, Rosenthal Archives of the Chicago Symphony Orchestra Association, Box 6).

42. Letter from Solti to Hillis, May 29, 1985 (Margaret Hillis Collection, Rosenthal Archives of the Chicago Symphony Orchestra Association, Box 6).

43. Fax from Dr. Rudolf Sailer to Paul Chummers, May 31, 1985 (Margaret Hillis Collection, Rosenthal Archives of the Chicago Symphony Orchestra Association, Box 6).

44. Interview with Cathy Weingart-Ryan, July 28, 2020.

45. Memo from Cathy Weingart-Ryan to Henry Fogel, July 2, 1985 (Margaret Hillis Collection, Rosenthal Archives of the Chicago Symphony Orchestra Association, Box 6).

46. Letter from Cathy Weingart-Ryan to AGMA, July 3, 1985 (Margaret Hillis Collection, Rosenthal Archives of the Chicago Symphony Orchestra Association, Box 6).

47. Letter to Solti from Hillis, July 2, 1985 (Margaret Hillis Collection, Rosenthal Archives of the Chicago Symphony Orchestra Association, Box 6).

48. Letter from Charles Kaye, secretary for Solti, to Hillis, July 17, 1985 (Margaret Hillis Collection, Rosenthal Archives of the Chicago Symphony Orchestra Association, Box 6).

49. Letter to Charles Kaye from Hillis, July 29, 1985 (Margaret Hillis Collection, Rosenthal Archives of the Chicago Symphony Orchestra Association, Box 6).

50. Ibid.

51. Letter to Cathy Weingart-Ryan from AGMA, July 24, 1985 (Margaret Hillis Collection, Rosenthal Archives of the Chicago Symphony Orchestra Association, Box 6).

52. Letter from Martha Gilmer to Dick Carter, February 7, 1986 (Margaret Hillis Collection, Rosenthal Archives of the Chicago Symphony Orchestra Association, Box 6).

53. Lewis Lazare, "At CSO: An Unsung Chorus is Raising Its Voice," *Crains Chicago Business*, June 29, 1987.

54. Interview with Henry Fogel, June 6, 2013.

55. Letter to Margaret Hillis from Craig Jessop, January 26, 1988 (Margaret Hillis Collection, Rosenthal Archives of the Chicago Symphony Orchestra Association, Box 6).

56. Letter from Hillis to Vanessa Moss, Manager of the CSO, February 11, 1988 (Margaret Hillis Collection, Rosenthal Archives of the Chicago Symphony Orchestra Association, Box 6).

57. Letter from Hillis to Senator Paul Simon, August 2, 1988 (Margaret Hillis Collection, Rosenthal Archives of the Chicago Symphony Orchestra Association, Box 6).

58. Letter to Hillis from Senator Alan Dixon, December 6, 1988.

59. Interview with Henry Fogel, June 6, 2013.

60. Memo to the Chicago Symphony Chorus from Joe Fabbioli, Chorus manager, December 21, 1988 (Margaret Hillis Collection, Rosenthal Archives of the Chicago Symphony Orchestra Association, Box 6).

PART IV

CHAPTER 19

THE AGE OF FULFILLMENT: 1989–1990

The exciting December 1988 announcement confirming the Chorus's European tour left only eight months for all necessary preparations. Chorus Manager Joe Fabbioli and a team of tour planners worked tirelessly to coordinate the hundreds of details required in moving this large group to Europe. The lighter performance schedule during the winter months offered some relief after a busy fall, allowing Hillis ample time for her meticulous preparation of Berlioz's *Damnation of Faust*, the tour piece chosen for performances in London and Salzburg.

Despite reduced concert commitments for the full Chorus, Hillis designed a rehearsal schedule that suggested otherwise. She needed to accommodate the unusually heavy summer season to come by scheduling Ravinia rehearsals alongside preparations for the remainder of the downtown season and upcoming tour. Rarely had there been a busier Ravinia summer. In just the month of June, the Chorus would be performing Verdi's Requiem, Holst's *The Planets*, Orff's *Carmina Burana*, and Stravinsky's *Symphony of Psalms*. Programming for July proved equally demanding, including Mahler's Symphony No. 3, Beethoven's Symphony No. 9, and selections from Strauss's *Die Fledermaus* and Lehár's *The Merry Widow*. Two Ravinia Pops concerts in August closed out the summer season just three weeks before the Chorus would depart for Europe. Hillis would need to carefully coordinate ample rehearsal time to ensure her Chorus's readiness for so many appearances in such close proximity.

Europe 1989

The Chicago Symphony Chorus (CSC) had performed *The Damnation of Faust* in the past, even winning a Grammy Award and a Grand Prix du Disque for their recording of the work, yet never were the stakes higher than in the upcoming tour. Hillis would demand the utmost of her choristers to ensure they made a lasting impression on European audiences. As Hillis told it, Solti initially wanted to perform Mahler's Symphony No. 8 on tour. Margaret objected, knowing the piece would require transporting three hundred singers along with finding a suitable children's chorus in Europe for both the London and Salzburg performances. "The logistics would have been a nightmare."[1] Hillis suggested instead that he consider *The Damnation of Faust*, telling Jon Bentz in an interview, "because nobody—but nobody can touch Solti with it."[2] Solti voiced concern, stating, "They don't like [*Damnation of Faust*] in Germany and Austria," to which Hillis argued, "But they'll LIKE this!"[3] Hillis eventually persuaded Solti, and it turned out to be the right choice after all!

The Chicago Symphony Orchestra (CSO) had an itinerary of fourteen concerts scheduled in eleven cities, of which the Chorus would participate in the first two performances. It would be the sixth appearance of Sir Georg Solti with his Chicago Symphony Orchestra in Europe and one of his last as music director, making this tour particularly significant for all who would partake. A total of 450 people would be traveling with the CSO, including 105 members of the Orchestra, 175 members of the Chorus, along with other essential personnel, spouses, and family members, and all the equipment required throughout the tour. Arrangements for visas, passports, hotels with convenient locations to and from the concert venues, a comprehensive tour book with hour-by-hour itineraries, locations of embassies, currency conversion, tipping customs, and useful expressions in foreign languages for countries they would be traveling to were provided. Doctors traveled with the Orchestra and Chorus, as did a special security detail, making this as safe as could be possible in such an undertaking for the performers. All arrangements were exponentially more complex in this 2.4-million-dollar operation now with the inclusion of the Chicago Symphony Chorus.[4]

The first official duties of the symphony choristers after arriving in London on Friday, August 26, 1989, were two rehearsals at the renowned BBC Studios. Choristers were thrilled as they entered the historic rehearsal space. Despite the excitement, Hillis recalled the first rehearsal with some dismay. "At the first piano rehearsal on the tour, they [CSC] were a little bit jet-lagged. I was standing around . . . sort of moping. . . . Moreover, on the Sunday rehearsal [the second piano rehearsal], they were still a little jet-lagged. . . . However, on Monday, when we entered the Royal Albert Hall . . . somehow magic took place . . . and when that rehearsal was over I thought—oh wow."[5] There was indeed something special about that Monday, August 28, rehearsal. In the largest performance space the Chicago Symphony Chorus had ever performed, choristers stepped onto that stage for the first time, awestruck by the magnitude of what was to come.[6] Henry Fogel recalled that rehearsal, as he sat listening with several London arts managers and administrators. When the rehearsal ended, one of the English managers remarked to Fogel, "Well, so much for the so-called vaunted British choral tradition."[7]

That evening, as the Chorus entered the stage, they were greeted with welcoming chants of "Chicago, Chicago!" Very different from the formality they were accustomed to back home, this crowd was more like one to be encountered at a major sporting event. For a brief moment, choristers became spectators to their audience, bearing witness to the colorful crowd chanting in perfect synchronicity comical phrases and words of welcome. Unknown to most on stage was that such behavior was typical before Proms concerts. It was a sight to behold! Thousands of people, as far as the eye could see, greeted the Chicago Symphony Chorus and Orchestra as they awaited the performance to come. Equally daunting were the BBC television cameras and lights enveloping the performers, a reminder of the thousands more who would be listening to the live broadcast of the evening's program (Picture 66).

From the moment Solti stepped on the podium there was an immediate shift in the crowd. Cheers and shouts were instantly transformed into an equally intense, disciplined silence. Hillis described her recollection of the evening:

I had a seat clear up on the side . . . there were seats all the way around— even behind the chorus . . . a thousand people [actually it was closer to six thousand] were there that night—When the performance began there was utter stillness and over a thousand people standing in the middle oval [a space on the floor in the center of the hall that is for standing room only]. They stood for three solid hours and DID NOT MOVE.

There was one person about ten minutes into the performance who fainted—and there was no scuffle, no flurry. Somebody just put a sweater under this woman's head and then they started listening again and that was it. If it were not for the fact that I just happened to turn around and see the person faint, I would not have even known that anyone had fainted. There were people leaning against the sort of a fence that was around them with that look of just utter love in their faces of the music.

In the back row there was a young man . . . standing with a miniature score—nodding his head—smiling as he turned the pages—and the LOVE at what they were hearing was so great that . . . we HAD to perform well. . . . Half of our performance [is] our own preparation. . . . The other half is what the audience gives back to you—and if that audience gives back to you, you can always surpass yourselves. . . . I have heard this chorus sing very well to an audience that was not receptive—especially one contemporary piece we did when the audience sat there cold and numb—the Chorus still would sing well. But to sing with that special spiritual value that makes a performance great, the audience has to contribute to that.

[After the performance] they [the audience] screamed and yelled. . . . Now, of course, the Chorus leaves the stage after the orchestra is off and the applause continued [until the Chorus left the stage]. At the end of the performance in London, there was not a dry eye in the Chorus—they were all so elated they were weeping. SO WAS I![8] It was just incredible! You have never seen a prouder group of people. The kind of magnificent pride, not arrogant pride that was on that stage.[9]

The thrill of that evening's successful performance did not end after the ten-minute ovation from a grateful audience. With audience shouts of "Arena to Chicago, come back soon!" ringing in their ears, the Chorus continued their celebration with a post-concert party at London's Windy City Chicago Bar and Grill. Solti spoke to the jubilant performers: "You know that I was always proud of you—all of you. But I have never been so proud of you as I am tonight."[10] The *Chicago Tribune*'s critic John von Rhein described the Chorus's performance, stating: "Without qualification . . . the one hundred seventy-five voices prepared by Margaret Hillis sang in a manner worthy of comparison with any of their greatest Chicago successes."[11] Summing up the night was a review in the *Manchester Guardian*.

I doubt there will be a better Prom this year than Georg Solti's with his stupendous Chicago Symphony Orchestra. . . . And what a chorus the Chicago Symphony has, to comply with Solti's needs, youthful, beautiful in tone and robust in attack, every word totally clear, understood and stylishly enunciated. Solti's chorus master is Margaret Hillis—simply the best. . . . This Berlioz was made even more special by such faultless and moving and witty chorus singing, fulfilling a crucial dimension of Berlioz's vision.[12]

Picture 66.
Berlioz's *Damnation of Faust* in London's Royal Albert Hall, August 28, 1989.
(Jim Steere, photographer) (Rosenthal Archives of Chicago Symphony Orchestra Association)

The tour continued as the Chorus and Orchestra next headed to Salzburg, Austria. During the morning rehearsal of Wednesday, August 30, at the Grosses Festspielhaus, the Chorus and Orchestra were greeted by a woman identifying herself as an official representative of the mayor's office. Ascending the stage at the conclusion of the dress rehearsal, she welcomed Solti and the performers, stating her excitement for their upcoming performance. After a brief rehearsal to acclimate everyone to the hall, choristers would return that night to a very different audience than the one that had greeted them in London. Chorus tenor Madison Bolt recalled the atmosphere as he ascended the stage, sensing a more reserved crowd. Unlike the enthusiastic audience of London's Proms concert, this audience, much more formally attired, was seemingly less welcoming, as if to be withholding judgement. Bolt recalled that the audience, which at first came across as "sitting on their hands," gradually warmed up shortly after the music began. It was as if they were suddenly aware of witnessing something very special.[13]

As intermission approached, something unusual caught the eyes of choristers and orchestra members who were able to see what was taking place in the concert hall. The woman who had greeted them earlier that day, supposedly representing Salzburg's mayor, was making her way down a side aisle of the hall on her hands and knees, moving slowly towards the stage. Each furtive move seemed to coincide with the music itself. She would periodically pause, briefly seating herself on the aisle floor, only to move again, gradually inching forward. Choristers had a clear view of what was taking place. Quietly advancing close behind the woman was a member of the CSO's security detail.[14] Maestro Solti, completely oblivious to what was transpiring, conducted the final minutes of Act One as the drama in the concert hall unfolded. Performers did their best to focus on the business at hand, though audience members and performers could not help but be distracted by the unusual situation transpiring. As Solti concluded the final chords of Act One, the audience erupted in applause, and only then did the security members tackle the woman, restraining her just moments before she reached the stage. She was quickly removed from the concert hall and the show would go on as planned following the intermission.[15]

At the conclusion of the concert, cheers and ovations replaced the audience's initial formality so much so that Solti had time to change into his street clothes during one of the many curtain calls that followed. Returning to the stage, Solti took one last bow, and then grabbed the hand of his concertmaster, Samuel Magad, leading him off the stage, thereby signaling the end of another glorious performance. Reviews for the Chorus were as complimentary in Salzburg as they had been in London. "Masterly . . . the CSO Chorus, prepared by Margaret Hillis, [was] in perfect control of everything from Rondo to Hell's language, and of all situations with ghosts, life, heaven, and hell. . . . No wonder the mounting ovation almost felt like a relief, equaling the ovation of a great opera premiere."[16]

Choristers enjoyed post-concert celebrations throughout the city on this last night of their European tour. One large group of choristers decided they would dine in style at one of Salzburg's most exclusive restaurants, Der Goldener Hirsch. Cathy Weingart-Ryan, who had been one of the primary forces in making this European tour a reality, organized dinner arrangements for eight of her Chorus colleagues.

Recalling that the restaurant had no room for her large party in the main dining room, they were instead seated at a spacious table reserved for them in the bar area of the restaurant. No sooner were they seated than Sir Georg Solti, Lady Valerie Solti, and their entourage entered the restaurant. Solti immediately spotted the singers and approached their table. He warmly congratulated them all, and then chided them for spending their hard-earned money at this expensive restaurant! He and his party then disappeared, heading into the main seating area of the restaurant. Solti would return to the singers' table a while later, accompanied by his younger daughter, Claudia. Solti was jovial, engaging in lively conversation, even posing for pictures with the group (Picture 67). He spoke of the Berlioz piece, encouraging the singers to read the prologue of *Damnation of Faust* in French to gain the greatest appreciation for the piece. After remaining for quite a while, Solti thanked the singers once more for a magnificent performance and then excused himself, apologetically stating that he must return to his party in the other room. Choristers reveled in the excitement of all that had taken place that evening, first with the successful concert they had performed, followed by their good fortune in a personal visit with their maestro. Following an elegant meal, choristers requested the bill, only to be told by their waiter that it had been "taken care of" by Solti. The singers were stunned, realizing that Solti had treated their party of eight to this extravagant meal.[17] It was a generous gesture for these singers, but the message was clear to all members of the Chicago Symphony Chorus. Solti was proud of his "Chor." He had won the hearts of the Chicago Symphony Chorus members on many occasions, but on this tour, after so many years of music making together, *they* had won *his* heart too.

Picture 67.
Sir Georg Solti and his daughter, Claudia, joining Chicago Symphony Chorus members at Goldener Hirsch restaurant in Salzburg, following the performance, August 30, 1989. Pictured here (*from left to right*) are CSC manager Joseph Fabbioli; singers Benita Wandel, Gail Friesema, Mary Ann Beatty, Cathy Weingart-Ryan; Sir Georg Solti; his daughter, Claudia; CSC associate conductor Richard Garrin; singer Sheri Owens; and her mother, Gigi Prunty. (Cathy Weingart-Ryan collection)

TURBULENCE BACK HOME

The flight home marked the end of an international success story and the beginning of an equally eventful concert season ahead, permitting choristers little time to dwell upon their achievements that would remain indelible memories for themselves and their newly cultivated European audiences. Memories of international success seemed less permanent for Hillis, as she soon faced an uncomfortable situation at the hand of the conductor who had so effusively praised her only weeks earlier. Though likely unintended, Solti made a move in their upcoming collaboration that would yet again cast a shadow upon Hillis's reputation as the leader of her Chorus. Solti invited a guest chorus master to "assist" Hillis in her preparation of the Chorus for the upcoming concerts and recording of Verdi's opera choruses in November 1989. One could not be sure how Hillis felt about this invitation based on her public persona. Her refined circumspection would not betray her as once again she was placed in an awkward situation. In light of all that had been recently accomplished in Europe, Solti's action left an uneasy feeling among some choristers who found this incident to be, at the very least, questionable, if not disrespectful.

As Solti planned for the important Verdi concert series and recording to follow, he invited English choral conductor Terry Edwards, with whom he had worked on numerous occasions in Europe, mostly at Covent Garden. Edwards was brought in to infuse a more dramatic flair to the Chorus, which Solti likely deemed Hillis's weakness. Solti may have also been thinking of Edwards as a possible Hillis replacement, knowing that she too had been considering retirement to coincide with his own. Edwards, an up-and-coming director of choruses in Europe and an equally accomplished opera chorus master, could be a good fit for Chicago's premier chorus. Having recently prepared a professional chorus for Solti in a BBC televised production of Beethoven's Ninth Symphony and already affiliated with major festivals and opera recording projects throughout Europe, Edwards convinced Solti of his expertise. The maestro would continue to play an important role in promoting Edwards with similar invitations, such as the one he extended for this Verdi project.

Hillis acknowledged her challenges in eliciting dramatic expression from her singers, particularly for opera performances.

> This Chorus is—I hate to use the term—but it is an 'oratorial' chorus. And, they are not used to having to act things out. In the *Damnation of Faust* I had an awful time getting the men to sound like a bunch of raucous students and still sing in tune. And they always want to sing it absolutely correctly— well correctly is not good enough. *Damnation of Faust* is in a sense an opera. They have an opening chorus—where they have to be peasants—and then there's this wonderful chorus of the sylphs and the gnomes who are the devil's crew where they have to sound absolutely seductive . . . then the soldier's chorus where they have to be a raucous bunch of kids . . . the expressions on their faces were so serious when they should be laughing. I never really did get them to smile.[18]

Verdi's choruses would feature the CSC in signature scenes from eleven operas and in the "Sanctus" from the Requiem. With such variety, the singers would be tasked to understand their role in each of these operas, conveying appropriate theatrical elements to execute convincing performances. Hillis likely knew by the time of her September 1989 interview with Jon Bentz that Edwards was to join her for the project. In that interview, Hillis readily admitted, "It is difficult with an oratorical chorus to get them to characterize in this particular way . . . which means they have to be actors and actresses . . . a little foreign to them. . . . They have to change character and change operas from one chorus to the next. . . . Plus having to have good Italian."[19]

Edwards was a lively personality. His energy and spirited way of "directing" the Chorus, along with his storytelling to contextualize each operatic scene, added energy and fun to the rehearsal process. Unlike the typical CSC routine of rehearsing seated in sections, Edwards had the Chorus up and moving around the room, encouraging them to sing with other sections rather than remaining confined to their own voice part. He coached them to "act out" each operatic scene. The rehearsals were enjoyable, yet it was not missed by some that the heavy lifting had already been done by Hillis before Edwards arrived at his first rehearsal. Getting the meticulous precision of each Verdi chorus, a signature feature of the Chicago Symphony Chorus, was strictly due to Hillis's expertise. Edwards provided the "icing on the cake," and though there may have been an added layer of interpretation, the sound of the Chorus did not significantly change, even after Edwards had "worked his magic." The *Chicago Tribune* critic felt otherwise, heaping praise on Edwards, crediting him for the great success of the November concert series and the recording that would follow: "Leaving nothing to chance, Solti had brought in a London opera coach, Terry Edwards, to work with the Chorus and this paid off handsomely in the extra whiff of theatricality one heard in their singing."[20] Though the singers appreciated Edwards's expertise, some felt uncomfortable about his shared duty with Hillis in the project. If Hillis experienced any discomfort with the situation, she never showed it, respectfully interacting with Edwards in every rehearsal. However, privately, Hillis felt very differently about the situation. Confiding to Bettie Buccheri, she conveyed her unhappiness with Edwards being brought in.[21]

Wisely, Hillis and Edwards prearranged how their shared duties would be organized, thusly avoiding any public disagreements that could ensue. Madison Bolt verified this in a conversation he and Edwards had on the matter. Bolt was reunited with Edwards sometime later when Edwards was a guest chorus master for the Chicago summer Grant Park Music Festival. It was then that Edwards revealed to Bolt how he and Hillis had come to an agreement about "who would handle what" during the rehearsals of the CSC.[22] They decided that Hillis would take charge of the technical elements of the Chorus's performance, including the intonation, precision, and tone quality. Edwards took charge of the theatrical elements.

At the end of the day, Hillis's first and only priority remained the same as it had always been. It was never about *her*. It was always about the *music*. Any resentment she may have harbored was simply put aside in service of the music. Her gracious manner with Edwards put choristers at ease. Thanks to Hillis putting her own ego aside, the resultant collaboration was a great success. Edwards would return to Chicago for another project, Verdi's *Otello*, in 1991. Solti created further discomfort for Hillis during that fall of 1989 when he decided to again scrutinize Hillis's selected singers as he had done several years earlier. He again auditioned CSC members individually for the January 1990 performances and recording of Bach's Mass in B Minor.

Hillis wisely turned away from any discomfort she may have suffered during the fall of 1989, instead shifting her focus to upcoming outside invitations, where her expertise was sought out, featured, and appreciated. She would return to conduct the Kenosha Symphony she had formerly led and then several upcoming *Messiah* performances, one in the standard concert version in Winston Salem and the others in the Do-It-Yourself version back in Chicago. Hillis would also be invited by a former Elgin Symphony Orchestra colleague to conduct an orchestra concert in Adrian, Michigan. It is noteworthy that even after Hillis severed ties with orchestras and colleagues, she must have done so in a way that caused no permanent animus. Both of her former orchestras would welcome her back periodically in the years that followed her departures.

Hillis accepted just enough guest conducting and workshop appearances for the 1989–1990 season to keep her conducting career active without interfering with her ability to remain present when needed at Orchestra Hall. This season's conducting engagements at Orchestra Hall were impressive, including her return appearance to lead the Civic Orchestra, along with a return to the podium for a CSO subscription series, conducting performances of Bartók's *Tri Dedinské scény (Three village scenes)* and *Cantata profana* and Haydn's *Lord Nelson Mass*. Hillis would make one additional appearance on the CSO podium during the 1989–1990 season, conducting a newly established "Choral Showcase," featuring members of the Chicago Symphony Chorus in a series of mostly a cappella works along with an Americana medley accompanied by members of the CSO. These impressive guest conducting appearances served to offset any negative situations Hillis was experiencing at the Hall.

FOCUSING ON SERVICE TO THE PROFESSION

When she was not performing as a guest artist, Hillis would further avoid ruminating over disrespectful encounters, focusing her energy instead on her prestigious presidential appointment with the National Council and on her important work as a board member of Chorus America. This particular period in both organizations would demand her utmost attention, given the tumultuous circumstances recently reignited on the topic of amateur versus professional choruses. The matter was now gravely impacting Hillis's treasured colleagues of many years, who were calling upon her for help. And help she did! Beginning in 1987, Margaret's colleagues counted on her to exercise her influence, given her position on the National Council. Even while inundated with arrangements to get her Chorus to Europe, Hillis began addressing the challenges faced by her colleagues, many of whom had been responsible for the establishment of the professional choral movement in the United States. These choral pioneers were suddenly finding themselves cut from the very funding they had cultivated. Whether or not Robert Shaw's position on funding professional versus amateur choruses was responsible for what was now occurring was no longer relevant. What mattered now was finding a way to save many of the established professional choruses, suddenly in peril, due to recent actions by the National Endowment for the Arts (NEA). As a member of the National Council, Hillis was perfectly positioned to be influential in resolving this situation on behalf of the industry she helped establish.

Hillis had been made aware of the crisis situation through messages she received from friends imploring her assistance. One such message was sent by Bob Page, copying Hillis on a letter he had written to NEA's Georgia Jones. In his letter, he stated concerns on behalf of Chorus America. "There have been many expressions of concern voiced by members of Chorus America regarding the NEA Choral Program recommendations of the current fiscal year."[23] He then went on to list those concerns:

1. The [Choral Program] panel members are mainly affiliated with academic institutions, "where they have little 'on the job' experience in dealing with the complexities of sustaining an independent operation";
2. Not enough attention is being given to the length of time [these choruses] have served the choral profession in supplying employment opportunities for the professional singer;
3. The weighting of artistic merit of an organization through the "anonymous listening" is felt to be out of proportion to other major factors in assaying an organization's excellence and inherent contribution;
4. The recent exclusion of submitting commercial recordings for the purpose of evaluation was his final concern.

By this time, the Los Angeles Master Chorale; the Philadelphia Singers; Vocal Arts of Cincinnati, Ohio; and the Robert Page Singers had all been "axed" from funding, some due to minor infractions of recently changed policies and procedures. Other premier choruses, including the Handel and Haydn Society, the Gregg Smith Singers, and Musica Sacra incurred severe reductions in NEA support. Soon, the Music of the Baroque and Paul Hills's National Chorale would endure a similar fate. In addition to Bob Page, others would follow suit, expressing their concerns to Hillis for what was happening. Richard Westenberg of Musica Sacra sent a letter to Margaret, stating, "Can you imagine a panel of administrators of community orchestras and conductors of small college orchestras having the ability, on the basis of two minutes' listening, to judge the BSO, the Philly, or the Chicago Symphony so negatively that their NEA funding would be wiped out entirely? It is a travesty."[24] Gregg Smith of the Gregg Smith Singers went even further in his communication with Hillis, questioning not only the membership of the Choral Program panelists but also appointments such as that of Georgia Jones, a controversial pick from the start, when she replaced Carleen Hardesty as the Choral Program specialist.[25] In an eight-page letter entitled "General letter to Margaret Hillis," Smith stated: "That you are with us in the battle is the greatest encouragement of all."[26]

Hillis acted upon all of these concerns, immediately addressing these issues directly with Georgia Jones. Questioning the reason for these cuts, Hillis requested a detailed response to the litany of inquiries she forwarded to Jones. By early January 1988, Hillis would again exercise her vast political influence, calling upon members of Congress whom she knew, hoping they would assist her in bringing pressure to bare upon NEA chairman Frank Hodsoll. Hodsoll had the power to reverse recent changes Choral Program panelists had made to the adjudication procedures. One congressional member Hillis contacted, the Honorable Sidney Yates, immediately acted upon Hillis's request, sending a letter to Frank Hodsoll in which he questioned the NEA panel evaluation procedures.

Hillis then reached out to Senator Claiborne Pell, chairman of the subcommittee on education, arts, and humanities, eliciting his support on behalf of her choral colleagues. Pell sent Hillis a copy of his letter sent to Frank Hodsoll, in which he stated:

> As you know I have always been keenly interested in preserving the integrity of peer panel review. . . . Over the years since I helped establish the agency you now chair, I have sought ways to strengthen this procedure. . . . It comes as something of a surprise to see the current controversy arise [referring to the number of objections Hodsoll was receiving from arts organizations with regard to procedures and panel personnel on the NEA]. In light of the critical nature of the issues . . . I urge you to delay further implementation of any change in the peer panel review system until you have completed a thorough re-examination.[27]

By the end of March 1988, Hillis began her own oversight of the Choral Program panelists, requesting all the tapes that they had adjudicated to assess them herself. Hillis requested the list of the 1988 panelists, which she then marked with numerous notations for herself, including a check mark next to members' names of whom she approved and comments next to panelists' names who she deemed questionable or unqualified for the appointment.[28]

By May 1988, pressure mounted further when Pennsylvania Senator Arlen Specter became involved in the matter, writing a letter to Frank Hodsoll, objecting to the Philadelphia Singers being denied NEA funding. By June 1988, Chorus America would present an official position statement to William Vickery (who replaced Frank Hodsoll) and Georgia Jones of the NEA, listing their concerns on behalf of Chorus America members. Included in their list was the questionable makeup of the Choral Program panel and the methodology recently enacted by them to judge choruses worthy of funding. In the strongest of terms, the position paper emphasized:

There is a concern about the entire funding process in regard to amateur choruses and the fact that they are actually taking money away from the funding of professional activity. Is it perhaps time once again, to consider the fact that this is the only Program [Choral versus other NEA Programs] that funds non-professional activity and time to re-evaluate?[29]

Included in the presentation of the position paper was a listing of recommended candidates as future panelists. Many on that list came from Hillis herself. Margaret was making headway, receiving a confirmation from William Vickery in August 1988 that panelists for the coming year would be taken directly from the recommended Chorus America list submitted to the NEA. Additionally, Vickery acknowledged that concerns over anonymous listening and other procedural matters related to the adjudication process would be taken up at a meeting in October 1988.[30] It looked like Hillis and her choral colleagues were on the right track, finally influencing necessary changes to create greater fairness and reliability for future funding of professional choruses.

By February 1989, however, Hillis would face another matter with potentially dire consequences for her choral community. Recent events in the art world ignited a movement that would put the NEA itself under fire. Losing this agency would threaten the survival of the Chicago Symphony Chorus, along with other professional choruses and numerous other arts organizations that had come to rely upon this national funding. Hillis would become invaluable to the NEA's survival, applying her well-practiced art of diplomacy by working all sides of the issue to protect the organization she had played such an important part in establishing. The survival of the arts in America was at stake, and Hillis would heed the call.

An art exhibit in the spring of 1989 opened a floodgate of controversy, placing the NEA squarely in the crosshairs. Longstanding debates regarding taxpayer monies to support the arts was suddenly brought to a head because of a divisive work by artist Andres Serrano. His 1987 photograph, entitled *Piss Christ*, depicted a crucifix submerged in the artist's urine. This controversial work was part of a traveling art exhibition, partially funded by the NEA. Among the first to protest was the American Family Association, releasing a statement on April 21, 1989, strongly objecting to the work of art. Claiming the photograph expressed anti-Christian sentiment, United Methodist minister Donald Wildmon vehemently objected to

NEA support of this art exhibit: "The fact that a government agency would spend tax dollars to help promote this piece . . . is deplorable. . . . The person at the NEA responsible for approving federal tax dollars for the promotion of the 'work of art' should be fired. . . . The government has no business spending tax dollars to support anti-Christian bigotry."[31]

In response to Wildmon, Hugh Southern, acting chairman of the NEA, stated, "The Endowment is expressly forbidden in its authorizing legislation from interfering with the artistic choices made by its grantees. . . . The NEA supports the right of grantee organizations to select . . . [awardees based upon] artistic criteria . . . even though sometimes the work may be deemed controversial and offensive."[32] Hillis and other National Council members were bombarded with letters from congressmen and countless stakeholders on both sides of the matter.

In the meantime, a new photo exhibit touring galleries throughout the country was adding fuel to this fire. The exhibit, titled *Robert Mapplethorpe: The Perfect Moment*, included "homoerotic images and nudes of children."[33] In an effort to avoid offending some of their patrons, gallery directors became proactive, canceling their commitments to host the Mapplethorpe exhibit. Such cancellations were stirring up heated debate, bringing even greater attention to the exhibit. By June 1989, Hillis began responding to congressmen who were challenging the NEA's support of this exhibit. In one response to a particularly angry senator, William Armstrong, Hillis's carefully crafted response is one of many examples when she became the voice of reason between two diametrically opposed sides of an issue.

> I am sorry so much distress was caused by Mr. Serrano's photograph. . . . At the May meeting during the Museum Application Review, the National Council discussed in detail the fellowship Mr. Serrano received from the Southeastern Center for Contemporary Art. We were appalled. As you know the Endowment is wisely mandated by Congress to refrain from interference with artistic content. This mandate has caused a daunting complexity in the grant-making procedures. Please be assured that these procedures will be carefully analyzed at the August meeting. . . . Though there have been very few mistakes in the 80,000 grant history of this remarkable institution we will make every effort to ensure it does not happen again.[34]

Though conciliatory in her tone, Hillis did not betray her loyalty to the NEA's position. Fiercely supportive of the NEA's right to protect artistic freedom, she would represent that position consistently while, at the same time, reaching across the aisle to demonstrate her understanding of conservative viewpoints on the matter. Hillis's upbringing in a Republican household back in her Kokomo, Indiana, days made her a valuable representative of the NEA during this difficult time. To that end, Chairman Hugh Southern made a point of thanking Hillis for her nuanced responses to many concerned congressmen, stating, "We appreciate your efforts on behalf of the agency and for all you do for the arts."[35]

By early August 1989, just prior to Hillis departing with her Chorus for Europe, she and the NEA National Council met in Washington, D.C., to discuss NEA talking points that would soon be sent to United States senators. Acknowledging both the Serrano and Mapplethorpe controversies as contributing factors of serious questions being raised about the role of government in the support of art, the NEA formed a statement emphasizing their position. "At stake is the ability of the Endowment to make determinations freely and independently on the basis of artistic merit."[36]

By October 1989, the new chair of the NEA, John Frohnmayer, instituted a policy whereby artists would be required to take an anti-obscenity pledge before money would be awarded to them. This act prompted numerous protests within the National Council and throughout the arts community at large. Included among those objecting to Frohnmayer's policy was conductor and composer Leonard Bernstein, who refused to accept the National Medal of Arts, NEA's highest honor bestowed to artists. By January 1990, the stakes got higher, as Congress began to debate the reauthorization of the NEA with its very survival now in question. Conservative politicians were seizing the moment, extrapolating isolated examples of NEA support for questionable artistic renderings to promote their stance for eliminating the NEA altogether.

By spring 1990, Hillis would actively campaign to protect the NEA from its demise. Hillis received support from politicians on both sides of the aisle. In a letter from Illinois Republican Senator John Porter, expressing his mixed feelings about the NEA supporting controversial art, he stated, "In my opinion the NEA does an excellent job providing small grants to hard working artists in a number of diverse fields. Only a handful of the thousands of grants and subgrants made by the NEA every year end up in the hands of artists who engage in intentionally offensive undertakings. . . . Please be assured that I will keep your thoughts in mind. . . . I appreciate you contacting me on this matter." Hillis received other encouraging responses, including those from Illinois Senators Paul Simon and Alan Dixon on the matter. She also received a response from President George H. W. Bush in June 1990. Though he did not approve of the NEA providing funding for what he defined as "inappropriate or obscene activities," he assured Hillis that Congress was still considering the reauthorization of the NEA and that he "will continue to work with Congress and its bipartisan commission on the NEA to find an appropriate policy balance that ensures that needed Federal support for the arts continues." Hillis's reach was vast and her efforts tireless to protect the NEA.

With Margaret's term nearing an end in the fall of 1990, she met one last time with the National Council, strongly weighing in against Frohnmayer's position regarding artists who would be forced to sign the anti-obscenity clause before receiving NEA funding (Picture 68).

THE NEW YORK TIMES **THE ARTS** SATURDAY, AUGUST 4, 1990

Council Opposes Making Artists Sign a Pledge

By WILLIAM H. HONAN
Special to The New York Times

WASHINGTON, Aug. 3 — The advisory council to the National Endowment for the Arts voted overwhelmingly today to recommend the elimination of an anti-obscenity pledge that artists and arts institutions have been asked to sign before they can receive grants from the endowment.

After an emotional debate, the National Council on the Arts voted 19 to 2 to ask the endowment's chairman, John E. Frohnmayer, to stop requiring recipients of endowment grants to agree in writing to comply with a Congressional directive banning the use of Federal money for work that might be deemed obscene or blasphemous.

The council vote is not binding on the endowment. Mr. Frohnmayer said, "I'm going to consider it and take my action in due course."

At Mr. Frohnmayer's urging, however, the council adopted an amendment saying that it was not recommending that the will of Congress be ignored. Without such a qualification, Mr. Frohnmayer said, the signal might be that the endowment could ignore Congress.

Objections to the Pledge

It was not clear what effect this action would have when Congress considers the future of the endowment in the fall. Nor was it clear what effect it would have on Mr. Frohnmayer's final consideration of controversial grant applications.

The requirement for the written pledge "got us into deep tapioca," said State Senator Roy Goodman of New York, who is on the 23-member panel appointed by the President to advise the endowment's chairman. Senator Goodman sponsored the motion to remove the anti-obscenity pledge, likening it to "the loyalty oath of the McCarthy era."

Mr. Goodman said the pledge insulted and alienated people involved in the arts and worsened the furor surrounding the endowment. "The artist knows what the law is," he said. "We don't have to rub his nose in it."

The two members of the panel who dissented were Jacob Neusner, a professor of religious studies at Florida State University at Tampa, and Bob Johnson, a state Senator from Florida.

How It Started

Mr. Frohnmayer instituted the pledge after Congress amended the endowment's $171 million budget last October to prohibit Federal support for obscene art.

The ban, prompted by protests about endowment support for a photographic exhibition of works by Robert Mapplethorpe, covers "depictions of sadomasochism, homoeroticism, the sexual exploitation of children or individuals engaged in sex acts."

Mr. Frohnmayer placed the text of the anti-obscenity ban in the regulations that govern awarding endowment grants. Of hundreds of agency grants approved by early July, about a dozen recipients have signed the pledge under protest, a half-dozen, including Joseph Papp and the New York Shakespeare Festival, have refused to sign and forfeited their grants, and challenges have been mounted in Federal courts.

Mr. Frohnmayer said his "sole intent" in requiring the written pledge was "to identify a portion of the law that applies to applicants which they may not be aware of." Earlier, he had expressed doubts about the constitutionality of the restriction.

Some Sharp Exchanges

Lloyd Richards, dean of the Yale School of Drama and a council member, said: "Possibly more was accomplished than was intended. Fear has been injected into the arts community and threatened to transform the N.E.A. into a 'National Endowment for the Agreeable.' "

Earlier in the day, some council members had sharp exchanges with Representative Ralph Regula, an Ohio Republican and the ranking minority member of the subcommittee that oversees the endowment's appropriation.

Mr. Regula, who said he had appeared before the council to explain the mood of Congress, said a vote last month was indicative of sentiment in the House of Representatives. In that case, Congressmen voted 297 to 133 to eliminate $1.6 million from an appropriation for the District of Columbia that would have allowed the University of the District of Columbia to exhibit art that many people found objectionable.

The installation, "The Dinner Party" by Judy Chicago, is an avowedly feminist work that includes an arrangement of objects to represent female sexual organs.

Harvey Lichtenstein, president of the Brooklyn Academy of Music and a council member, said he was stunned by the House's action, which he said was caused by "homophobia."

"You're characterizing 297 members of the Congress," Mr. Regula shot back.

"I don't think this country should stand for that kind of persecution," Mr. Lichtenstein said.

"You asked me to tell you about reality," Mr. Regula said. "That's it."

Changes Being Planned

Apparently in a move to gain favor among conservative members of the council and critics in Congress, Mr. Frohnmayer called on Randy McAusland, acting deputy chairman of the endowment, to report on procedural changes he said the endowment was planning.

This list included asking grant applicants to submit more letters of support; the addition of a lay person to grant-making panels; the arrangement of a wider geographical distribution of panel members, the opening to the public of meetings of the National Council on the Arts and strengthening the "conflict of interest" rules that apply to panel members.

The council unanimously supported these changes.

Representative Pat Williams, the Montana Democrat who is chairman of a House subcommittee that oversees the arts endowment, cautioned that there was "no chance" that Congress would authorize an extension of the endowment this year without some form of restrictions on obscenity.

Mr. Williams won applause from some council members and spectators crowding the hearing room in the Old Post Office Building when, speaking of Mr. Mapplethorpe, he assailed the "howling mob of people hurling verbal epithets at a dead male artist" and other artists whose works are controversial.

Today was the first of three days of council meetings to review grant applications in a public session. Previous meetings of the council have been conducted in private on the theory that applicants who are turned down deserve the protection of anonymity. But the endowment agreed on Tuesday to open its meetings after four newspapers — The New York Times, The Los Angeles Times, The Washington Post and The Philadelphia Inquirer — sought a court order to prevent a news blackout.

The council meets quarterly to review grant recommendations proposed by peer panels in various cultural fields. It also meets with the chairman of the endowment to advise him "with respect to policies, programs and procedures" and to "review applications for financial assistance" and "make recommendations thereon."

Mr. Frohnmayer is not bound by the recommendations, although he has consistently followed the council's lead since taking office last fall.

These are the members of the council:

David Baker, chairman of the department of jazz at Indiana University

Phyllis P. Berney, former member of the executive committee of the Wisconsin Arts Board

Sally Brayley Bliss, ballerina and artistic director of the Joffrey II Dancers

Nina Brock, former chairman of the Tennessee Arts Commission

Phyllis Curtin, opera singer

Joseph Epstein, professor of English at Northwestern University and editor of The American Scholar

Helen Frankenthaler, artist

Robert Garfias, ethnomusicologist and former dean of fine arts at the University of California at Irvine

Roy M. Goodman, New York State senator

Mel Harris, president of the Television Group of the Paramount Pictures Corporation

Margaret Hillis, director of the Chicago Symphony Chorus

Bob Johnson, Florida state senator

M. Ray Kingston, architect and former chairman of the Utah Arts Council

Ardis Krainik, general director of the Lyric Opera of Chicago

Harvey Lichtenstein, president of the Brooklyn Academy of Music

Wendy Luers, writer and lecturer

Talbot MacCarthy, former chairman of the Missouri Arts Council

Arthur Mitchell, founder and artistic director of the Dance Theater of Harlem

Carlos Moseley, former managing director, president and chairman of the board of the New York Philharmonic Society

Jacob Neusner, former member of the Institute for Advanced Study in Princeton

Lloyd Richards, director and dean of the Yale School of Drama

Jocelyn Levi Straus, former chairman of the Texas Commission on the Arts

James Wood, director of the Art Institute of Chicago

> A member says,
> 'The artist knows
> what the law is.'

Members of group that advises the chairman of the National Endowment for the Arts voting yesterday in Washington to approve a recommendation that the chairman, John E. Frohnmayer, stop asking grant recipients to sign a certification of compliance with an anti-obscenity provision.

Picture 68.

Margaret Hillis and members of the National Council vote to recommend John E. Frohnmayer rescind his policy of asking for grant recipient nominees to sign a letter with an anti-obscenity oath before accepting grant money. This *New York Times* article ran on August 4, 1990. (Paul Hosefros, photographer)[37] (Margaret Hillis Collection, Rosenthal Archives of Chicago Symphony Orchestra Association)

The NEA has historically endured similar challenges throughout its history. From President Ronald Reagan's initial attempt to eliminate the agency in 1981, challenges have continued. The 1989 controversies encountered by Hillis on the National Council would again emerge in the mid-1990s when House Speaker Newt Gingrich made another attempt to abolish the NEA. This fight would be continued into the twenty-first century with President Donald Trump making two more attempts to eliminate the agency, first in 2017 and again in 2018. These battles are likely to periodically recur as long as the agency exists. Fortunately, the NEA has weathered these challenges, in no small part due to the dedicated efforts of National Council members such as Margaret Hillis. Hillis and her council colleagues are owed much credit for protecting the agency early on, thereby sustaining professional choruses and other artists in the process. Hillis must be remembered for her willingness to take an unwavering stand for the freedom of artistic expression and for the agency protecting that freedom for artists in America today.

SEASON OF CHANGE

With the outset of the 1990–1991 season, great changes were on the horizon. This would be the final season for the Chicago Symphony Orchestra and Chorus with Sir Georg Solti serving as music director. Hillis would soon be answering to a new music director, Daniel Barenboim. This season would prove even more challenging for Hillis, as she would now, for the first time, encounter significantly reduced roles in her professional life. She was no longer given a concert series to conduct with the Chicago Symphony Orchestra. It would also be her final season conducting the Civic Orchestra. Added to these changes, Hillis's outside service activities were similarly reduced now that her National Council appointment had ended on September 3, 1990. With only her Chorus America and American Choral Foundation affiliations remaining, she would finally have time to build up her outside guest conducting, heretofore reduced to fulfill all the other commitments she had balanced. Such unprecedented circumstances of increased "downtime" allowed Hillis the opportunity to consider her next career move, one that might no longer include her at the helm of her beloved Chicago Symphony Chorus. Dreamer though she was, she had fulfilled her vision for the Chorus, creating a professional vocal ensemble equal to its orchestral counterpart. With the final goal of a successful European tour completed, added to her many Grammy Awards and a substantial history of superlative achievements, there were no more mountains to climb with the CSC. She accomplished all she had set out to do and significantly more than she originally envisioned. It seemed an appropriate time to step away from the organization she had spent half of her lifetime building. The decision seemed logical, though it would not be easy to leave her "musical family." This she would discover once her intentions became public. Her decision to retire from the Chicago Symphony Chorus would be the most difficult she would ever make.

ENDNOTES

1. Jon Bentz, "Interview of Margaret Hillis Director Chicago Symphony Orchestra, September 19, 1989, Archives Committee, Oral History Project, 1992," p. 36 (Margaret Hillis Collection, Rosenthal Archives of the Chicago Symphony Orchestra Association).
2. Ibid.
3. Ibid.
4. Clifford Terry, "Orchestrating the Logistics of the CSO's Trip to Europe," *Chicago Tribune*, August 27, 1989.
5. Bentz, "Interview of Margaret Hillis," p. 18.
6. Author's recollection of the event.
7. Interview with Henry Fogel, June 6, 2013.
8. Bentz, "Interview of Margaret Hillis," pp. 19–20.
9. Ibid., p. 18.
10. John von Rhein, "It's Knockout Night in London with 1-2 Punch of CSO, Chorus," *Chicago Tribune*, Overnight section, August 28, 1989.
11. Ibid.
12. Tom Sutcliffe, "The Devil Wins, Sublimely," *Manchester Guardian*, September 1, 1989.
13. Interview with Madison Bolt, November 2020.
14. Author's recollection of the event.
15. Author's recollection of the event.
16. Karl Harb, "Twenty Scenes from the Life of a Lonesome Man," *Salzburger Nachrichten*, September 1, 1989.
17. Interview with Cathy Weingart-Ryan, July 28, 2020.
18. Bentz, "Interview of Margaret Hillis," pp. 39–40.
19. Ibid., p. 40.
20. John von Rhein, "Georg Solti Begins His Final Two Years at the Helm of the CSO," *Chicago Tribune*, November 3, 1989.
21. Interview with Bettie Buccheri, November 21, 2020.
22. Interview with Madison Bolt, November 2020.
23. Letter to Georgia Jones from Robert Page, copied to Margaret Hillis, October 29, 1987 (Margaret Hillis Collection, Rosenthal Archives of the Chicago Symphony Orchestra Association, Box 8).
24. Letter from Richard Westenberg to Margaret Hillis, April 10, 1988 (Margaret Hillis Collection, Rosenthal Archives of the Chicago Symphony Orchestra Association, Box 8).
25. Interview with Carleen Hardesty.
26. Letter to Margaret Hillis from Gregg Smith, not dated but in a file from 1988 (Margaret Hillis Collection, Rosenthal Archives of the Chicago Symphony Orchestra Association, Box 8).

27. Letter to Frank Hodsoll from Senator Claiborne Pell, April 18, 1988, (Margaret Hillis Collection, Rosenthal Archives of the Chicago Symphony Orchestra Association, Box 8).

28. National Endowment for the Arts 1988 Chorus Update, with the names and positions of Choral Panelists who met in November 1987 and made recommendations for NEA Chorus grants (Margaret Hillis Collection, Rosenthal Archives of the Chicago Symphony Orchestra Association, Box 8).

29. Chorus America Association of Professional Vocal Ensembles board of directors position statement on the National Endowment for the Arts, presented Wednesday, June 1, 1988, to William Vickery and Georgia Jones (Margaret Hillis Collection, Rosenthal Archives of the Chicago Symphony Orchestra Association, Box 8).

30. Letter to Margaret Hillis from William Vickery, NEA director of music programs, August 15, 1988 (Margaret Hillis Collection, Rosenthal Archives of the Chicago Symphony Orchestra Association, Box 2).

31. Press release of Donald E. Wildmon, Executive Director of American Family Association, April 21, 1989 (Margaret Hillis Collection, Rosenthal Archives of the Chicago Symphony Orchestra Association, Box 8).

32. Statement by Hugh Southern, acting chairman of the NEA, April 25, 1989 (Margaret Hillis Collection, Rosenthal Archives of the Chicago Symphony Orchestra Association, Box 8).

33. Elizabeth Kastor, "Corcoran Decision Provokes Outcry Cancellation of Photo Exhibit Shocks Some in Arts Community," *Washington Post*, June 14, 1989, p. B1 and p. B9.

34. Letter from Margaret Hillis to Senator William L. Armstrong in response to his letter of concern regarding the NEA controversies, June 21, 1989 (Margaret Hillis Collection, Rosenthal Archives of the Chicago Symphony Orchestra Association, Box 8).

35. Letter to Margaret Hillis from NEA acting chairman High Southern, July 19, 1989 (Margaret Hillis Collection, Rosenthal Archives of the Chicago Symphony Orchestra Association, Box 8).

36. Sample letter focusing upon freedom of expression, for consideration of the NEA National Council, August 3, 1989.

37. William H. Honan, "Council Opposes Making Artists Sign a Pledge," *The New York Times*, August 4, 1990.

CHAPTER 20

THE FINAL YEARS: 1991–1998

The 1990–1991 season marked the centennial of the Chicago Symphony Orchestra (CSO). Solti chose this momentous season to be the last at the helm of "his" Orchestra and Chorus. Though the Chorus had fewer concerts than usual this season, Solti's "Chor" would be included in his climactic grand finale, scheduled in the spring at New York's Carnegie Hall. Two star-studded farewell performances of Verdi's *Otello* on a world-class stage provided a fitting backdrop for the man who substantially increased the world-class status of the Chicago Symphony Orchestra and Chorus. Other highlights of this centennial season included return appearances of Ned Rorem and Leonard Slatkin working together with Hillis for the world premiere of Rorem's *Goodbye My Fancy*. In Rorem's letter to Hillis anticipating the premiere in November 1990, he shared his excitement, stating, "It is an added security to know that the Chorus (which is actually three-fourths of the piece) is in your golden hands"[1] (Picture 69).

Picture 69.
Ned Rorem's *Goodbye My Fancy* premiere, Leonard Slatkin conducting. In the photograph (*from left to right*) are Margaret Hillis, Ned Rorem, John Cheek, and Wendy White, November 8, 1990. (Jim Steere, photographer) (Rosenthal Archives of the Chicago Symphony Orchestra Association)

The lighter Chorus schedule permitted Hillis the opportunity to accept several more guest appearances than usual. As per the norm, *Messiah* performances dominated her December schedule, including four concerts with the National Symphony Orchestra at the Kennedy Center. Reviews of Hillis's conducting were becoming less flattering, particularly when Hillis conducted in renowned venues, such as the Kennedy Center. Her National Symphony Orchestra reviews were, at best, mixed. Whereas the *Washington Post* reviewer characterized the performances as ones that Handel would have loved, the *Washington Times* review "NSO's *Messiah* Performance: Half Hallelujah, Half Humbug," was not nearly as positive:[2]

Margaret Hillis conducted as if with the assumption that we all know this score so well that we don't need to hear it done especially well. All the notes were there, but seldom did they add up to the inspired passages Handel intended. Her tempos tended towards the fast and metronomic, mechanical. . . . Hillis chopped the phrases well beyond baroque practice. Ornamentation was minimal and dull throughout . . . it took the magic of the violin obbligato to remind us how sublime this music really can be.[3]

Hillis's February 1991 appearance with the Civic Orchestra would yield similar mixed reviews. While the *Chicago Sun-Times* review was somewhat complimentary, it was becoming apparent that Hillis's clarity and precision would no longer suffice to earn her the stellar reviews of years past. In the Civic Orchestra review, Wynne Delacoma paired criticism of Hillis's interpretation with more positive remarks regarding her accuracy: "The players didn't transport us to Bruckner's unique universe, but their attention to detail and unflagging concentration resulted in a coherent clearly etched performance. . . . Hillis . . . set a clear resolute beat that kept the forward momentum firmly in hand."[4]

After viewing Hillis's performance of Bruckner's Symphony No. 8 performance, Henry Fogel determined that she would no longer be conducting the Civic Orchestra.[5] Martha Gilmer informed Margaret of this reduction in her conducting duties. In a letter sent to her the following summer of 1991, Gilmer, on behalf of Fogel, explained that Civic would be undergoing changes, which would no longer include her:

> Let me tell you the direction that Civic will be taking next year. In the current schedule there will be 5 actual performances. One concert will be conducted by Daniel Barenboim and we hope to have one concert conducted by James DePreist, who will be conducting a week of subscription concerts with us, and is well known as an orchestra trainer. . . . In addition, through our new collaboration with Northwestern University and through his reputation as a string pedagogue, we have also invited Victor Yampolsky to be a guest conductor. Michael Morgan will have a concert of music of black composers. . . . In addition, we are planning on having rehearsal sessions with Zubin Mehta, Pierre Boulez and hopefully Solti. We certainly do appreciate all you've done for the Civic in the past—your commitment to them has been exemplary.[6]

This latest demotion must have been demoralizing in light of her recent removal from any further conducting duties with the Chicago Symphony Orchestra. Her presence on the podium at Orchestra Hall going forward would be limited to conducting the Chorus in her Hillis Fellowship Concerts. She would no longer be invited to conduct the Chicago Symphony Orchestra nor the Civic Orchestra in concert.

April 1991 was a pivotal month for Margaret. Solti invited Terry Edwards back to Chicago to again team up with Hillis for the upcoming concert production of Verdi's *Otello*. In communications between Edwards and Hillis prior to his arrival, Hillis conveyed a gracious message, belying any ambivalence she had regarding his return: "I can't tell you how much the Chorus and I are looking forward to working with you again. I'm sure it will be another happy collaboration."[7] Edwards would join Hillis for a total of seven rehearsals, two Chicago concerts, and two final performances at Carnegie Hall, April 16 and 19, 1991.

There was great excitement about this production, nationally and internationally, particularly regarding the all-star cast, including soprano Kiri Te Kanawa and tenor Luciano Pavarotti. However, a harrowing rehearsal week would threaten this highly anticipated production, even before the opening night.

> The rumors couldn't have been more rampant if the topic had been a Beatles reunion. Luciano Pavarotti, scheduled to make his debut in the title role of Verdi's *Otello* Monday night . . . didn't know the part, according to the gossip mill. He was talking about canceling. . . . But the show did go on, even though Solti, entering his final set of concerts as the CSO's music director, was exhausted from the flu and conducted supported by a chair. This *Otello* is being performed [one more time] in Orchestra Hall and recorded live in Carnegie Hall concerts April 16 and 19. [Orchestra Hall concerts would also be used for the recording.] By the time Solti gets over the flu and Pavarotti becomes more familiar with the part, it should be memorable.[8]

After two very successful productions in Chicago, the Chorus and Orchestra headed to New York. Arriving for the dress rehearsal on Monday morning, April 15, performers witnessed yet another close call, threatening New York's opening night. Yet again, there were fears of Pavarotti canceling. This time, the cause was the stage setup in Carnegie Hall. A smaller stage space required a setup that located chorus members in closer proximity to the soloists than had been the case in Chicago. Before the rehearsal began, Pavarotti vehemently protested his position on the stage. Immediately approaching Henry Fogel, Pavarotti complained that he was "too far back" from the front of the stage.[9] Fogel went directly to William Hogan, CSO stage manager and the person responsible for all CSO setups both in Chicago and on tour. Hogan assured Fogel that Pavarotti was in fact the same distance "to the inch" that he had been in Chicago. Fogel then conveyed to Solti that [Pavarotti] was *his* problem to deal with, as he had tried initially talking Solti out of hiring Pavarotti, knowing how difficult he was to manage.[10]

As the rehearsal commenced, Pavarotti became increasingly angry, finally ranting, "I'm too far back! I'm too far back! They think I'm a member of the Chorus!"[11] Hillis, seated next to Fogel in the concert hall, leaned over, whispering, "He couldn't get *in* to *this* Chorus."[12] When it became apparent that Solti would not change the stage positioning, Pavarotti finally had had enough and stormed off the stage, leaving everyone onstage stunned about what had just taken place, wondering what was to become of the performance.[13] Solti remained calm, continuing the rehearsal without him. Pavarotti would return that evening and the next, performing to both sold-out, celebrity-filled Carnegie Hall audiences. Hillis's dear New York friends, "Red" and "Pick" Heller and Harriet Wingreen, were present to witness this final spectacular appearance of Solti and Hillis together one more time at Carnegie Hall. Interestingly, reviews both in Chicago and New York credited only Hillis for the Chorus's outstanding performance with no mention of Edwards. The *Chicago Tribune* reviewer stated: "The Chicago Symphony Chorus [was] superbly prepared by the redoubtable Margaret Hillis."[14] *The New York Times* review credited Hillis similarly. "Margaret Hillis's chorus unleashed every erg of sonic energy the hall could tolerate, vividly establishing the mood of violent events to come."[15] Terry Edwards would not return for any future collaborations with the Chicago Symphony Chorus (CSC).

Only a few weeks after the Carnegie Hall triumph, Hillis began her preparation of a very difficult program for her soon-to-be new music director, Daniel Barenboim. The women of the Chorus would be performing the U.S. premiere of four movements from a work by Pierre Boulez, *Le visage nuptial*. Barenboim was very different from Solti in his choice of repertoire and in his approach to preparations and performances. Solti was predictable. Hillis knew him well and could anticipate everything from his tempos to the tone quality he would expect. Hillis knew how to prepare a chorus for him, always able to rely upon his unwavering consistency. Unlike Solti, Barenboim was *not* predictable in any way. His tempos varied greatly from the norm, often taken to extremes. His rehearsals would not always reflect what he would do in performances. Though a great artist himself, Hillis knew that collaborating with him would be very difficult, particularly with her very disciplined style of preparation.

Henry Fogel recalled that once Daniel Barenboim was officially announced as Solti's replacement in February 1989, Hillis had likely made her decision to retire from the CSC shortly thereafter. Fogel shared that although she never stated Barenboim's appointment as the reason for her decision, he believed it to be so.[16] Hillis's decision had nothing to do with her personal feelings towards Barenboim. Fogel believed instead that it was Barenboim's "romantically flexible" approach to the music that was "utterly the opposite of Margaret's," which motivated her decision. As Fogel stated, Barenboim's artistry "was not how she saw music."[17] Daniel Barenboim was always respectful of Hillis and remained continually impressed by the superb quality of the Chorus. Yet, Fogel was convinced that Hillis did not want to spend her remaining years with the CSC working with a conductor "whose music making did not resonate with hers"[18] (Picture 70). In the first week of April during the final weeks of *Otello* preparations, Hillis would make her official announcement.

Picture 70.
During his first season as music director, Daniel Barenboim joined Margaret Hillis in cutting a cake for the celebration of her seventieth birthday, October 1, 1991. (Jim Steere, photographer) (Rosenthal Archives of the Chicago Symphony Orchestra Association)

The news of Hillis's retirement was met with mixed emotion by the choristers as they prepared for the *Otello* concert series. While being filled with anticipation for Maestro Solti's grand finale, they were now processing the news of yet another change in their musical family, one with far more impact on them directly: the departure of the only chorus master the Chicago Symphony Chorus had ever known. Solti's arrival in 1969 had been the last major change experienced by the CSC, and most of the Chorus members present for that transition had long since retired. For those choristers still remaining, Margaret Hillis had always been there, providing consistency in the wake of change. With impending retirements of both the music director of the Orchestra and the director of the Chorus, singers were in uncharted territory. Two great champions of their ensemble were departing in close proximity. With both Hillis and Solti leaving, singers for the first time would be going it alone, relying upon each other for moral support and musical consistency. It was difficult to imagine the future without these two giants leading the way.

Knowing when to leave is never easy, particularly for artists who dedicate their lives to something that is so much a part of who they are. Margaret knew, in theory, this was the right time to go, but she could not have anticipated the painful reality once it was upon her. Quoted in the *Chicago Tribune*, she acknowledged her age being a factor in her decision to step down. "The calendar tells me I am 70 years old, although I certainly don't feel it."[19] With other performance aspirations still in her purview, Hillis faced a difficult question—was she ready to walk away? Agreeing to remain long enough for the Orchestral Association to find her successor, Hillis committed to one more season, 1991–1992. This plan would allow Hillis to support her Chorus acclimating to a new director. A committee was formed in August 1991, and the search was underway.

The upcoming 1991–1992 season would be significant, not only as it was to be Hillis's last season as chorus director but also it was the thirty-fifth year of the Chicago Symphony Chorus. The season was scheduled to open with Beethoven's *Missa solemnis* and would be dedicated to Margaret Hillis. Instead, a labor dispute forced this plan to be postponed until the following season, which ultimately extended Hillis's stay. The closing of the CSO's 1991–1992 season ended fittingly as Hillis and Sir Georg Solti, now music director laureate, were reunited in May 1992 for performances and a recording of Haydn's *The Seasons*. As Hillis was acclimating herself to the idea of stepping down, she relinquished several concert preparations to her assistant conductors, focusing instead upon her conducting career outside of Orchestra Hall. It would take time to build up the guest conducting appearances she had previously reduced to accommodate her CSO commitments.

As Hillis continued to focus on her post-CSO career, she counted on continuing her recurring appearances, including the Do-It-Yourself *Messiah* productions. Having stated on numerous occasions how she planned on conducting these DIY concerts "for the rest of her life," they would unfortunately end sooner than she had anticipated.[20] When Hillis announced her CSC retirement in spring of 1991, Al Booth assumed it meant that she was planning to phase out her entire conducting career. In a letter he sent her shortly after the announcement, Booth stated:

> You might wish particularly at this time to reduce your workload of two performances each Christmas. . . . I thought this might be an ideal time for you to appoint Susan Davenny Wyner and Stanley Sperber your assistant conductors thus giving one of the two dates between you and the other each year.[21]

Hillis responded to Booth's suggestion, writing: "Thanks for your concern about my retirement, but as Mark Twain once remarked after reading his own obituary, 'The rumors of my death have been greatly exaggerated.'"[22] Hillis assured Booth that she was retiring from the Chorus, but she had no intention of retiring from music. As it turned out, her final collaboration with Booth would take place in December 1991. For various reasons, including Margaret's ill health, she would not return for the sing-along *Messiahs* she had lovingly procured. Although the relationship between Hillis and Booth had been at times contentious, Booth did make every effort through 1995 to bring Hillis back to the podium.

Hillis's imminent departure from the CSC became more real by the summer of 1992 when several guest conductors set the audition process into motion. Beginning with the Ravinia season, conductors selected by the search committee were brought in to prepare the Chicago Symphony Chorus for upcoming concerts. Hillis's reduced role caused contentious salary negotiations for her 1992–1993 contract. Though she was fully expected to keep the Chorus "on track" during the search process, the Association determined she would not be doing as much as she had in years past, and therefore her salary should be reduced. Once again, Hillis felt unfairly treated by this reduced offer and had no hesitation in making her frustration known. In a letter sent to Henry Fogel, Hillis stated her position. First, she pointed out that she had been dissatisfied with the salary reduction of the previous season, only signing that contract "because of my loyalty to the Chorus."[23] She then explained that two Ravinia concerts originally to have been hers were instead given to candidates for her replacement, further reducing her income. She then reminded Fogel that by no longer directing the Civic Orchestra, her salary had been reduced yet again. She totaled all reductions to her contracts, stating a figure of many thousands of dollars in lost income in recent years. Hillis reminded Fogel that the Orchestral Association had never incurred Social Security nor retirement benefits for her due to pay arrangements through the American Choral Foundation, providing the Association substantial savings. She then listed all her duties for the upcoming transitional year, emphasizing that the Chorus would require her daily attention, as it had in the past.

> Even when a job applicant is preparing the Chorus, I am needed to perform other duties; I must consult with the chorus manager regarding necessary personnel changes in small groups, assign assistants when needed, and most importantly calculate seating charts for sound. Seating charts alone often require ten hours of work. Even more than an orchestra, a chorus needs a sense of continuity. My presence at this time is their assurance of continued excellence. . . . When I was asked to be available this next season, I assumed compensation would include a small increase in recognition of my work. It is disappointing to realize that the Orchestral Association is showing its appreciation of my 35 years of service by reducing my income significantly.[24]

Hillis's message turned out to be effective, because she was able to successfully negotiate a better offer for the 1992–1993 season.

CELEBRATING THE PAST AND LOOKING TO THE FUTURE

Meanwhile, fitting tributes and celebrations for Margaret Hillis commenced with a Chicago Symphony Chorus reunion dinner on May 17, 1992. The event reunited singers of the past thirty-five years joining current members, all in celebration of shared accomplishments with their beloved director. Over six hundred concerts and eight Grammy Awards, numerous performances in New York, Washington, and a spectacular European tour were part of this storied legacy that was the Chicago Symphony Chorus. The afternoon was filled with laughter, reminiscences, and an opportunity to "roast" Hillis. Bettie Buccheri recreated a typical Chorus rehearsal, leading a group of choristers in a clever skit, lovingly poking fun at well-known "Hillis-isms" (see Appendix 8). Buccheri was fully garbed in one of Hillis's famous brocade gowns, smuggled from Hillis's home, complete with Margaret's iconic black Adidas sneakers and a wig Bettie borrowed from the nearby Lyric Opera's costume shop. Even the glasses Buccheri sported were almost identical to those of their director. With members of the Chicago Symphony Chorus neatly lined up to sing, Bettie began directing a "rehearsal," interjecting often-used Hillis sayings and mannerisms, eliciting rounds of laughter and applause with some of the loudest guffaws coming from Margaret herself. Bettie had been somewhat ambivalent about how Hillis might receive the satire, however Jane Samuelson reassured Bettie that Hillis had LOVED the show, watching the video of the performance several times after returning home that night! Bettie was further reassured upon receiving a thank-you letter from Margaret, in which she stated: "It was a riot to watch you impersonate me at the Chorus's thirty-fifth reunion dinner. From the sublime to the ridiculous—you handled both with great aplomb. I count myself lucky to have you as a personal friend and cherish our professional collaborations. Thank you for your thoughtfulness and your fine sense of humor—Fondly, Margaret."[25] Hillis's sense of humor was well-known to all who knew her best, which accounted for her good-natured attitude about the event. The reunion became a cherished memory as Chorus members past and present celebrated their tireless leader, whose vision had made so many shared successes possible.

More formal celebrations given by Margaret's "CSO family" took place in those final months of her tenure. A champagne reception hosted by the Women's Association in May 1992 was followed by a lavish event at Chicago's elegant Palmer House, including such prestigious guests as Itzhak Perlman, Daniel Barenboim, and others, praising Hillis for all the incredible achievements of her years with the Orchestral Association.

As it turned out, the thirty-sixth Chicago Symphony Chorus season would in fact become Hillis's final full season serving as chorus director. Having already committed to numerous outside conducting appearances for 1992–1993, as the original plan was for her to have already been retired, she fulfilled her CSO obligations as best she could. She would again delegate a portion of the season to her associate and assistant conductors while guest conducting in Canada, Utah, Montana, and Michigan, along with other scheduled appearances. Bookending this 1992–1993 CSO season were two major choral works Hillis would prepare, including Brahms's *A German Requiem* and Beethoven's *Missa solemnis*, originally scheduled for the fall of 1991 but postponed due to the Orchestra strike the previous fall. Hillis would assign the second concert of the season to her associate conductor. The third concert series of the season went to auditioning candidate Vance George, the conductor Hillis had helped position for the San Francisco Symphony Chorus position ten years earlier. Hillis remained involved throughout her final season, keeping a sense of order for the Chorus during a period of many directors coming and going.

Following the 1992–1993 season, rumbles of discontent for Barenboim's music making were beginning to surface among some Orchestra members, Chorus members, and, most unfortunately, in the press. John von Rhein's article preempting the 1993–1994 season's opener contained unflattering remarks regarding Barenboim performances of the 1992–1993 season, including several concerts with the Chorus.

The anticipation [of the new season] is mingled with a growing apprehension among a number of observers inside and outside the orchestra that, after two seasons, the marriage between music director Daniel Barenboim and the CSO is not working. . . . After two seasons of Barenboim as music director, some critics say the orchestra is slipping in its quality of sound, in its internal discipline, in its approach to making music. . . . Even those who routinely praise the music director's talent, versatility and capacity for work express puzzlement as to his overall artistic objectives; the seeming lack of focus in his myriad musical activities; his inconsistencies as an interpreter.

But the concerns are real. "Barenboim is the kind of conductor who, unlike Solti, does not have a fixed idea of what he wants at a given moment," says one CSO player. "I don't find his musicmaking so much inconsistent as I find it different in its application from one performance to the next." But some ears find his recent Bruckner symphony performances ponderous, an adjective one also would have to apply to both the Beethoven *Missa solemnis* and the Brahms *A German Requiem* he prepared here last season. The failure of his *Missa solemnis* was perhaps more explicable, given the fact that the performances had been delayed a year and a half because of the players' strike; also given the fact that Barenboim and CSO Chorus founder Margaret Hillis constantly disagreed about tempo during rehearsals, according to insiders.[26]

433

It appeared Margaret's instincts had been correct and must have reassured her that her decision to step down was indeed the right one.

By the fall of 1993, Hillis would prepare the Chorus for the season's opening concert, Verdi's Requiem. There was every expectation that a new director of the Chorus would likely be named soon, reducing Hillis's work to three of the five programs that season. Confronting yet another salary dispute, Hillis was again insistent that her salary remain the same for this final transitional season. Her request was justifiable, considering she was still expected to attend rehearsals of each candidate, including their dress rehearsal and final concert. Added to her other responsibilities of maintaining the Chorus, Hillis would go over and above what was asked of her, studying the music that the candidates were preparing in the event she might be needed to step in. The Association had assured Hillis otherwise, taking a "sink or swim" approach with the candidates. However, Hillis wisely remained vigilant, ready to save her Chorus if needed. Thankfully she had taken this approach, as she would replace one auditioning candidate, Donald Palumbo, who fell ill in February 1994, immediately stepping in his place to complete the preparation of Bruckner's Mass in E Minor. Hillis was the only person who could have taken over at a moment's notice, musically prepared and knowing her Chorus as she did. The Orchestral Association was fortunate to have had Hillis "on call" despite their initial sentiments to the contrary. Her insistence for a more respectable salary turned out to be appropriate. Though the Association would eventually acquiesce to Hillis's salary demands, she would harbor feelings of resentment for this "nickel and diming treatment," as she saw it. In her final months with the CSO, she deemed her value, yet again, to be underestimated.[27]

Her unexpected return to the podium to finish the Bruckner piece was greeted by a spirited ovation, welcoming Hillis "home," and she returned those sentiments with her warm smile. After a few words conveying her joy to be back, Hillis swiftly transitioned to the business at hand—Bruckner. The rehearsal was intense yet upbeat.[28] The steady stream of conductors auditioning in recent months was beginning to wear thin on the singers, some longing for a return to something familiar. Hillis's return after several months of being away provided them a sense of normalcy. Unbeknownst to all, these would be the last rehearsals Hillis and her Chorus would share. A new director would soon be named. There was never a final farewell nor any official closure to the era about to end. In an interview Hillis had given to *Chicago Tribune*'s John von Rhein, Hillis spoke of how she imagined her final rehearsal with the Chorus to be. "The last rehearsal I do with the Chorus, I'll probably break down and bawl, because I really do love each and every one of them."[29] Perhaps it was easier for everyone that the final rehearsal would come and go without any formal acknowledgment of its historic nature.

Coincidentally, the concert series of February 1994, in which Hillis replaced the ailing Donald Palumbo in the Bruckner program, would unite two conductors sharing more than a concert program together. Unbeknownst to all was that Hillis would be collaborating on this final concert series of her CSO career with her successor. Candidate Duain Wolfe was preparing the Chorus for the other half of the program with Schoenberg's *Friede auf Erden*. Neither Hillis nor Wolfe yet knew the symbolic nature of this event. Duain Wolfe had been recommended to the search committee by former assistant conductor of the Chicago Symphony Orchestra, Kenneth Jean, who had enjoyed the opportunity of working with Wolfe's Colorado Symphony Chorus in Denver on several occasions. Aware of the search taking place in Chicago, Jean sent his recommendation of Wolfe to the search committee. Hillis and another member of the search committee, James "Jim" Yarbrough, flew out to Denver on January 14, 1993, to meet Wolfe and to observe him in rehearsal. Dually impressed, they recommended Wolfe be invited to prepare the Chicago Symphony Chorus in an upcoming concert.

Wolfe had an extensive background as a conductor with Central City Opera beginning in 1974, and he established the Colorado Symphony Chorus in 1984. Also among his accolades, he founded the outstanding Colorado Children's Chorale in 1974. His impressively diverse background spanning all age groups and styles of music and his many years of successful symphonic concert work and opera productions established him as a more-than-qualified candidate for consideration. In August 1993, Wolfe would first prepare the CSC for a Ravinia program. His superb work in that program, a wide variety of opera choruses, earned him an invitation to return in February 1994.

As with the other candidates, Wolfe had almost no communication with Hillis during the audition process. After initially meeting her in Denver, they would see each other again when Hillis observed Wolfe a second time in Chicago. Hillis watched only thirty minutes of Wolfe's three-hour rehearsal with the CSC. To his recollection, there were no substantive conversations in those initial meetings aside from a brief exchange of pleasantries. His first conversation of any length occurred when Hillis provided Wolfe a ride to the artist's dinner following their shared February 1994 concert (Picture 71).

Picture 71.
Duain Wolfe, newly appointed director of the Chicago Symphony Chorus, ca. 1994.
(Rosenthal Archives of the Chicago Symphony Orchestra Association)

Perhaps there was another reason why Hillis would give so little time to her successor. An unexpected occurrence in the week or two following their shared concerts would dominate Hillis's time and attention in a way nothing had ever before. Margaret experienced "a visual disturbance" while driving home one afternoon, suddenly feeling as if a shade had come down over her eyes. She immediately phoned her doctor who instructed her to go directly to the emergency room, where she was ultimately admitted to the hospital, diagnosed with a carotid artery blockage. In the process of doing the tests to prepare her for her upcoming surgery to remove the blockage, doctors discovered a second serious problem—a tumor in her lung. Hillis was told that she would first need to undergo the carotid artery surgery, and after recovering, a second surgery would be arranged to deal with the tumor in her lung.

In mid-March 1994, shortly after Hillis's second surgery, her personal assistant, Dave Murray, received a frantic phone call from Margaret in the hospital. She had just been informed by her doctor that the tumor in her lung was malignant and, unfortunately, the cancer had spread. Murray and Hillis's partner, Jane Samuelson, headed immediately to her bedside, calming her down as she implored, "I cannot die. I have too much to do!"[30] Murray reassured Margaret, telling her that her entire life had been devoted to music and now it was time to devote herself to the task of getting well. That saying would become her mantra in the months ahead.

Margaret's calendar for the remainder of the spring and summer of 1994 was now substantially altered. Medical appointments and cancer treatments replaced guest conducting appearances in Flagstaff, Arizona; Washington, D.C.; Potsdam, New York; and San Antonio, Texas. In Margaret's adept way, she quickly pivoted from her briefly dismal outlook to the belief that she would tackle this greatest challenge. Convincing herself that her treatments would work, she was able to endure the difficult side effects of chemotherapy and radiation. Margaret was surrounded by her support team, including Dave Murray and Jane Samuelson, who would continue to be her lifeline throughout her illness. Always by her side, Jane kept Margaret's spirits high, though she privately felt less encouraged by the travails ravaging her partner's body and spirit. Jane would be a true companion, keeping Margaret company, providing her with whatever she needed, even coming up with a way she could eat when radiation had made it too difficult to do so. Jane invented a method of freezing Gatorade and Ensure, then chopping the frozen drinks into ice chips so that Margaret could manage to take in some nutrition despite the burns to her esophagus. The doctor predicted that if Margaret remained tumor-free for two years, she could likely survive the initially daunting prognosis. Ever an optimist, Margaret was convinced she would beat this disease despite the odds.

A New Era for the Chicago Symphony Chorus

As Margaret continued to convalesce, she and the Chorus would receive their ninth Grammy Award on March 1, 1994, for their recording of Bartók's *Cantata profana*, conducted by Pierre Boulez. Just two days later, the Chicago Symphony Chorus had their new director. Duain Wolfe would be officially named Hillis's successor on March 3, 1994. Wolfe would embark upon familiarizing himself with his new position but would do so with very little communication from Margaret Hillis. He was pretty much on his own, getting whatever support the conducting staff was able to provide. Wolfe kept the associate conductor, Cheryl Frazes Hill, and assistant conductors Don Horisberger and James Rogner from Hillis's staff, which created a degree of continuity for the Chorus while providing Wolfe guidance as to how things worked.

On several occasions as Hillis recovered, she invited Wolfe to her home, not to discuss the particulars of the Chorus but instead to show him her method of score marking, utilizing her intricate color-coding system. They shared dinner on several occasions, however those were purely social get-togethers. Wolfe wisely understood Hillis's avoidance to advise him in too much detail, realizing that in doing so, she would be fully acknowledging that the torch had been passed. Wolfe would venture forth on his own to carry forward the legacy that was before him.

With Wolfe firmly in place, he made his successful Ravinia Festival debut as the new director of the Chicago Symphony Chorus, preparing them for Beethoven's Symphony No. 9, conducted by Christoph Eschenbach. Following the Ravinia season, Wolfe began rehearsing the Chorus for the CSO's downtown season, preparing his first concert series as the new Chorus director for Daniel Barenboim. The concert series was to be dedicated to Margaret Hillis on the occasion of her official retirement (Picture 72). During the fall rehearsal period for this concert series, Wolfe would receive his own devastating news. He too was diagnosed with cancer and required immediate surgery. With Wolfe unavailable and Margaret Hillis not well enough to step in and prepare the Chorus, the concert was given to the associate conductor (Cheryl Frazes Hill) to complete. The Chorus was yet again in a state of limbo, holding out great concern for their music director, now ill and with no return date announced.

Picture 72.

Margaret Hillis receives Theodore Thomas Medallion for Distinguished Service on her retirement, September 17, 1994. She is acknowledged by Henry Fogel, Daniel Barenboim, and the Chicago Symphony Orchestra and Chorus. (Jim Steere, photographer) (Rosenthal Archives of the Chicago Symphony Orchestra Association)

Hillis attended the dedicated concert, which included Bruckner's *Psalm 150*, Wolf's *Der Feuerreiter*, and Beethoven's *Elegy* and *Choral Fantasy*. Wolfe, however, would miss this opening series and would remain unavailable to prepare the next work with rehearsals scheduled to begin directly following the opening performances. A conductor would be needed to prepare the women of the Chorus for Pierre Boulez's *Le visage nuptial*, scheduled for mid-December 1994. Hillis, now feeling stronger, was eagerly campaigning to step in again. The situation would become awkward. Unbeknownst to Hillis, Boulez had already selected Wolfe's replacement for this preparation, asking the Orchestral Association to hire Grant Gershon, who at the time was an assistant conductor for the Los Angeles Opera and was quite adept at managing the complexities of Boulez's contemporary work.

The Orchestral Association had several concerns about Margaret replacing Wolfe for the Boulez series. Though her health was slowly improving, Hillis's stamina was, as of yet, untested. There was already a plan for her to return to conduct her Fellowship Concert in early December, but those rehearsals would begin two months later, providing her more time to heal. After six months away from conducting, her

Fellowship Concert would be an easier project to manage. Another consideration was Hillis's comfort level with Boulez's complex contemporary piece. Though she had prepared several movements of this same work in May 1991, it remained an incredibly difficult undertaking, now increasingly so, as it would be performed in full. Returning after her six-month hiatus to the physical and musical demands of this work was simply not a good idea. Only Margaret did not see it that way.

Henry Fogel and Martha Gilmer were concerned about how to handle the situation. Beyond the other considerations, the Chorus was already transitioning in a new direction with a new Chorus director. Both Fogel and Gilmer thought it unwise to bring Hillis back again. Unwilling to directly confront her on the matter, they determined that Bettie Buccheri would best be suited to convince Hillis that a return was not a good idea. Buccheri agreed to break the news to Hillis in person, understanding she was the appropriate choice to speak with Margaret on this matter, not only as her revered colleague but also as one of her closest friends. Nonetheless, Buccheri was worried about the risk she might be taking upon their continued friendship. Buccheri recalled her extreme discomfort as she arrived at Hillis's home. Jane Samuelson and Dave Murray positioned themselves, unbeknownst to Margaret, in the kitchen to overhear what they knew would be a difficult conversation. In a very brief exchange, Bettie conveyed to Hillis, "Your legacy is amazing, but there comes a time when you have to let go, and I think the time is here." Bettie recalled seeing a look on Margaret's face that she had never seen before and would never see again. Obviously crestfallen, Hillis acknowledged Bettie's statement, replying that she understood and that Bettie was right. Though Margaret still planned to conduct the Chicago Symphony Chorus for her Fellowship Concert in December, it was now painfully clear to Margaret that the Orchestral Association had moved on. It was time for Margaret Hillis to do the same.

The choice to replace Wolfe with Grant Gershon instead of Margaret Hillis turned out to be a wise one. Margaret would not even be well enough to fulfill her return to Orchestra Hall for the December Fellowship Concert. She was to have been joined in that concert by Duain Wolfe along with several other conductors. With Wolfe no longer able to participate, this concert was now left for Margaret Hillis's associate conductor Cheryl Frazes Hill, and invited guest John P. Paynter, renowned wind ensemble conductor and head of conducting at Northwestern University. Hillis and Paynter had first become acquainted during Hillis's years at Northwestern, and they would come to share a good friendship built upon deep mutual respect. Just weeks prior to the first rehearsal for the Fellowship Concert, Hillis determined that she was not strong enough to participate, leaving the program to Frazes Hill, who would oversee the details and conduct the concert with John Paynter and several other guests.

Paynter joined Frazes Hill for a meeting at Margaret's home to discuss adjustments to the concert program, after which all three posed for newspaper photographs promoting the event (Picture 73). When Paynter and Frazes Hill departed, Paynter remarked his concern for Hillis's failing health, seeing the oxygen tanks and tubes that Hillis relied upon to breathe. Paynter had not seen Margaret in a number of years and her deterioration was unexpected. It would be the last time they would see one another.

Picture 73.
Margaret Hillis, John Paynter, and Cheryl Frazes Hill at Hillis's home to advertise the upcoming Hillis Fellowship Fund concert, November 1994. (Jerrold Howard, photographer)

A New Way of Life

Margaret continued to believe that her health would improve. Though housebound, Hillis became acclimated to a sedentary lifestyle, finally able to enjoy the simple pleasures she had long denied herself due to her relentless work schedule, which was now temporarily suspended. Hillis spent her days reading, watching her favorite Chicago sports teams, and occupying herself with crossword puzzles, word searches, and solitary card games, anything to challenge her mind. A loyal housekeeper of many years, Amanda would look after Hillis during the day while Jane was working. When Jane returned home, she would take over Margaret's care.

Dave Murray would leave Hillis in the fall of 1994, as little substantive administrative work was taking place. After finding a temporary replacement for Dave, Margaret hired Tina Laughlin in the spring of 1995 to be her new administrative assistant. Tina was an ideal choice for the position. The young percussionist had played under Hillis's direction with both the Civic Orchestra and the Elgin Symphony Orchestra. When Tina heard that Hillis was looking for an assistant, she requested an interview and was immediately hired. Laughlin confessed she knew nothing about administrative work but found Hillis to be a patient, supportive boss. Though there was little to do in the way of musical work, Tina would organize Hillis's scores, communicate with various people inquiring about hiring Hillis for future engagements, and she would keep track of the medical appointments, the bills, and other clerical work. Margaret continued to accept future conducting dates while recuperating, believing she would soon be well enough to fulfill them.

One commitment in particular Hillis hoped to continue was her conducting at a San Antonio music festival held in the San Fernando Cathedral. Since 1990, Margaret returned each summer to lead the San Antonio Master Singers with a festival orchestra. The invitation was made courtesy of the Bruni family. Donna Bruni had come to know Margaret Hillis during her years in Washington, D.C., working on Capitol Hill for Margaret's brother, Representative Bud Hillis. During those years, Donna would attend Margaret's concerts at the Kennedy Center. Recalling Bud's tremendous pride in his sister, Donna came to admire Margaret's talent, particularly as a woman in such a prestigious role.[31] Donna and her husband eventually moved to San Antonio, Texas, where Donna's mother-in-law, a great lover of the arts, sponsored a concert series every summer. When the duty was passed to Donna, replacing her mother-in-law in handling the concert series, she immediately thought of Margaret to conduct. Margaret quickly became a favorite with audiences and musicians, and she would return every year until she was forced to cancel in the summer of 1994, recuperating from her cancer surgery. The Brunis would invite Margaret to return in June 1995, and she accepted the invitation but would inevitably cancel again, not feeling ready to return.

By July of 1995, Hillis was willing to venture out. She believed she had regained strength enough to travel and desperately wanted to join her friends and colleagues at Chorus America's 1995 Saranac Lake Conducting Workshop. This workshop was the latest iteration of many others that had been based upon Hillis's prototype—the Choral Institute model she created so many years before. Through the years with the ongoing support of the Association of Professional Vocal Ensembles and Chorus America, these workshops continually raised the standards of conductors, thereby elevating the quality of choruses throughout the country. At Saranac Lake, the Gregg Smith Singers and a resident orchestra provided the "laboratory" for young conductors to refine their rehearsal and conducting techniques under the watchful eye of the country's most prestigious chorus masters. In the picturesque surroundings of upstate New York, the Saranac Lake Conducting Workshop first began in 1983. It existed for four years but was discontinued due to financial challenges. Dennis Keene, conductor and artistic director of Voices of Ascension, appreciated the benefits he had gained as a young conductor attending those sessions and advocated to the Chorus America board for its return. To his credit, the summer sessions were revived in 1993.

Keene was first made aware of the Saranac Lake program through Gregg Smith, with whom he had worked in the early 1980s. Smith encouraged Keene to attend the summer workshop, describing the extraordinary sessions being offered, urging him: "You just have to go!"[32] When Keene arrived, he was in awe of what was available to him. A first-rate roster of chorus masters provided expert coaching for selected student conductors. Keene described the thrill of so many notable directors, each given a day to teach on a variety of topics that were their specialty. "One day it was Margaret Hillis, the next day Roger Wagner, the next it was Gregg Smith, and the next day Bob Page."[33] He described each day's events with these master teachers. On the "Hillis day," she would lead three sessions on her elaborate score-marking technique and then an exploration of Handel's *Messiah*. Roger Wagner would oversee an in-depth study of a cappella Renaissance repertoire and then coach conductors on Fauré's Requiem. Each day, Gregg Smith would work with a different student conductor as they directed Smith's singers with orchestra. Keene was first involved as a staff accompanist, but eventually he would assist Gregg Smith in running these summer programs. There was simply no better workshop available to choral conductors at this time.

When Keene was able to persuade Chorus America to bring the program back to Saranac Lake in the 1990s, the master teachers also returned with the addition of renowned Canadian conductor Jon Washburn. Keene loved being around them all but cited Gregg Smith and Margaret Hillis as the most generous of the colleagues he encountered. As Keene described it, many people in the music business feel protective about what they know and are hesitant to reveal their "secrets." This was not the case with Smith and Hillis. They generously shared their scores and their knowledge, and they were always available to give advice.[34] Keene would keep in touch with Hillis, dining with her in New York when she was in town on business. She loved good food and wine, and together they explored many fine restaurants in the city. They would do the same when Keene visited Chicago. Keene recalled his pleasure in "tagging along with her," observing her rehearsals with the Civic Orchestra and then a performance of Solti conducting Bach's *St. Matthew Passion*. Keene believed it was Hillis who taught him his most important lessons as a young conductor:

> She talked about connecting with the sound. Getting into the sound. It means that there is a physical connection between your body and the sound coming out of the voices. . . . Thinking something and having the body do something changes the sound—you hear the sound before you conduct it and it impacts how the player plays and how the singers sing. And that is why you *must* know what you want from the score before you conduct—if the conductor doesn't know what they want, it is not organic. Margaret was the first one who talked about it. [It] changed everything. She also talked about not imposing yourself onto the music . . . to be a servant of the music. It was never about *her*.[35]

In 1993, Hillis returned with her colleagues to Saranac Lake once the workshops were reinstated. However, she would miss the summer of 1994, convalescing after surgery. Feeling up to traveling again in the summer of 1995, Hillis was anxious to return to work and to the colleagues she loved.

Getting Margaret to Saranac Lake was not easy under normal circumstances, but in her current medical condition it became exponentially more complex. This small town, nestled in the Adirondack Mountains had no direct flight. Tina arranged for Margaret to travel first to Jane's summer home in Harpswell, Maine, where Margaret could rest for the week prior to the Chorus America event. She then flew from Maine to Burlington, Vermont, where Tina arranged for conductor Andrea Goodman to pick her up and transport her to Saranac Lake. Tina coordinated all flights, ground transportation, hotel reservations, communications with anyone accompanying her to and from the airports, and all medical needs, including an oxygen compressor and tanks, tubing, nebulizer, and a wheelchair she would need at each destination.

Once she arrived at Saranac Lake, Hillis was given the royal treatment by her colleagues, who made sure the Hotel Saranac VIP suite went to her and no one else. Dennis recalled meeting her at the hotel one evening. He knocked on her hotel room door to which she responded, "Just a minute." He heard some rustling around, and then she greeted him at the door. To his astonishment, he could smell the cigarette smoke still present in the room.[36] Though Jane Samuelson and others were certain she had quit smoking by this time, Keene was certain of the event. Hillis quit smoking for good soon thereafter but apparently was still occasionally indulging that summer of 1995. Margaret's time at Saranac Lake became a precious memory for her and all those who were present during that summer. It would be Hillis's last visit to Saranac Lake.

Going forward, Hillis would continually make efforts to return to her conducting life, but each time she made progress, something would inevitably stand in the way. Margaret had hoped to conduct a massed choir in Texas scheduled for February 1996. However, as with all her other conducting commitments of this time period, Hillis would be forced to cancel. This time, it was not the cancer that interfered but instead an unfortunate accident at home. In October 1995, ambitiously trying to reach an item on an upper shelf of her closet, Hillis fell off a chair, shattering her ankle in a way that required surgery and two months of rehabilitation. Upon returning home from rehab in December 1995, she remained unable to walk. This accident also forced numerous additional cancellations, including her return to the Do-It-Yourself *Messiah* in December 1995.[37] In response to one of her cancellations, William Wyman, representing the ACDA North Central Division in Nebraska, sent a message pleading for her to reconsider fulfilling her commitment to conduct

Bach's *St. John's Passion* in March 1996. Hugh Kaylor, Hillis's manager, conveyed Wyman's correspondence: "[We] would accommodate her in any way necessary, i.e., with wheelchair access, conducting from a chair, etc., anything that might enable her to comfortably accommodate this engagement."[38]

Hillis would not return to her conducting career. No longer attending Chorus America workshops and no longer able to conduct performances, Hillis's only travel included summer trips to Maine, accompanied on some of these flights by her housekeeper Amanda, who had taken care of Margaret and her Wilmette home for many years. Amanda dearly loved Margaret, and the feeling was mutual. Amanda's presence in Maine was extremely helpful to Jane, who appreciated the extra assistance in caring for Margaret. Jane continued to be a remarkable companion to Margaret, keeping her active even as her health continued to decline. When in Maine, they would often go on scenic drives and enjoy dining out in the many wonderful restaurants throughout the town. If Jane wanted to go on a hike, Margaret was content to stay behind, reading or doing her puzzles. Jane was Margaret's lifeline, keeping her focused on what she *could* do, never dwelling on the limitations of their new normal.

Travel had been a staple throughout their relationship. Jane and Margaret traveled extensively together in the early years as time permitted with both of their work schedules. Once Margaret became ill and less mobile, their travel shifted to Maine and sometimes to Jane's sister's cabin in Wisconsin. Even when home in Chicago, Jane would drive Margaret around the lovely North Shore neighborhoods, enjoying the changing colors of the leaves during the fall and the colorful holiday lights at Christmastime. Jane was devoted to Margaret.

For a while it seemed hopeful that Margaret would survive. Though the tumors had not returned in two years, giving everyone hope for Margaret's recovery, the cancer did return shortly thereafter and would soon confine Margaret to her home, no longer able to travel nor dine out at the restaurants she so enjoyed. Jane continued to be at Margaret's side. Visitors were infrequent, however there was a group of Chicago Symphony Chorus members who would come by every so often, and this became a highlight for Margaret. Cathy Weingart-Ryan organized Sunday dinners, inviting several Chorus members to participate in the potluck meals. Everyone would contribute a course, which would be set up on Margaret's dining room table. The visits were always lively, and Margaret thoroughly enjoyed the company (Picture 74).

Picture 74.

Members of the Chicago Symphony Chorus enjoying a meal together at Margaret Hillis's home. Picture here (*from left to right*) are Kathye Kerchner Boyle, Don Bittner, Mary Ann Beatty, Margaret Hillis, Donald Horisberger, Cathy Weingart-Ryan, and Kip Snyder. (Cathy Weingart-Ryan collection)

Sometimes, Margaret would be asked to give a private conducting lesson or teach a session in score study. She was always happy to reengage in her musical life, albeit briefly. Despite all that Margaret was unable to do, she found a way to look on the bright side. Her positive attitude, along with Jane's support, no doubt extended her life from what was originally predicted as months to a survival of four years beyond the initial diagnosis. Some said it was Hillis's state of denial that kept her going. Others maintain it was Jane's unwillingness to let Margaret fade away, keeping her engaged in the outside world as long as it was possible to do so.

Just four months before Margaret's passing, on the occasion of the Chicago Symphony Chorus's fortieth anniversary, Margaret wrote her final "Dear People" letter to her beloved Chicago Symphony Chorus. In her message of October 6, 1997, she wrote:

Happy anniversary to us! I remember so clearly that first rehearsal forty years ago. Everyone in the Chorus was scared to death because they didn't know me or know what they'd sound like. As the rehearsal progressed, everyone began to smile and you've been smiling ever since!

When I first came here in the fall of 1957 to start a chorus for Reiner, I thought I'd be here for three or four years, get the chorus established and then turn it over to someone else. Each year was to be my last for the first six seasons. I realized that the challenge I had set for myself and you was to have a chorus that sang as well as the Chicago Symphony played, and I stayed thirty-seven years sustaining that ideal. I think we accomplished it as much because of you, as it was of me. Your loyalty and steadfastness made it possible.

May you continue this tradition of greatness in sound, phrasing, musicality, and just plain fun in making great music. I love you all and I miss you and so wish I could share this day with you in person.

Yours in Music
M. H.[39]

Margaret maintained her optimism until her final days, always believing she would get well. She lost her fight to cancer at age seventy-six on February 4, 1998. To those who had been around her during her four-year battle with the disease, it came as somewhat of a surprise when an outpouring of phone calls and attention followed the announcement of her death. Seldom had Margaret received phone calls from anyone outside of her "circle" during those final years of her life. Visitors were few, perhaps understandably so, because people did not want to invade her privacy. After all, Margaret *did* hold most people at arm's length. However, for those who were willing to take the chance, calling, visiting with her at her home, some even taking private lessons with her, they were witness to the enjoyment Margaret conveyed by their presence. Spending time with the grand lady in those final days was a special experience indeed.[40] For the first time in Margaret's life, she was not pressed for time because of work. Her time was now limited in other ways. There was a new sense of calm in Margaret. She had always been one to remain present with anyone fortunate enough to have time alone with her. No matter how busy her life had been in the past, she generously gave of her time unselfishly, teaching, guiding, and advising. Her assistants never felt rushed, nor was there ever any impatience on her part when they sought her advice or guidance in preparation for their next rehearsal. Nonetheless, Margaret's state of being in those final years revealed a new layer of calm in her demeanor. She did not seem in any way tortured, knowing in her heart, if not outwardly, that her career was likely at an end.

Her acquiescence to the situation is evident when viewing her advice to another giant-among-women in the arts world. When Ardis Krainik, general director of Chicago's Lyric Opera, announced her plans to step down from her position by April 1997, Margaret wrote a lovely note, revealing her own situation.

Dear Ardis,

It was with a sense of great loss that I read the article concerning your projected retirement. . . . Having been myself a partial invalid for the past two and a half years, I should advise you being a couch potato is not all bad. In addition to the above activities (teaching, being a consultant) if you need any good murder mysteries I have dozens I could forward on to you. I have hopes to return to the world of a conductor, although it looks doubtful. . . . My best love and admiration to you. If you need any further advice on retirement, please call me, I'm an old pro. Affectionately, Margaret.[41]

Picture 75.
Margaret Hillis and Ardis Krainik at CSC's thirty-fifth anniversary luncheon at Monastero's Ristorante, May 17, 1992. (Cathy Weingart-Ryan collection)

Krainik did not make it to her intended retirement date. Her ill-health forced her to step down in November 1996, and she would pass away just two months later. Margaret was likely aware of Ardis's serious health condition when she sent her message, conveying her understanding of how difficult it would be for her friend to accept the reality of bidding farewell to a career deeply loved and long enjoyed. It was a loss that Margaret had already faced and seemed to have reconciled.

Bidding Farewell

The memorials began shortly after Margaret's passing. A private funeral for family and friends was held in her beloved hometown of Kokomo where she was buried, not in the Hillis family plot but instead adjacent to it, next to her dear Aunt Esther.[42] A memorial service, given by the Chicago Symphony Orchestral Association, took place on March 14, 1998, at Orchestra Hall. Conductors Dale Warland, Dennis Keene, Robert Page, and Duain Wolfe each took their place on the conducting podium, leading members and alumni of the Chicago Symphony Chorus in some of Margaret's favorite choral music. Speakers included Margaret's brother Bud and others, addressing a fully packed concert hall. In Bettie Buccheri's remarks, she conveyed a symbolic moment in Kokomo several weeks earlier:

> At Margaret's burial on a lovely hillside in Kokomo, we sang "Amazin' Grace" and released large white helium balloons. . . . As we watched the balloons sail upward, we were dismayed that several got caught in a tall tree. But before we could utter our collective disappointment, those balloons twisted and struggled and freed themselves. For me, that was a symbolic re-enactment of Margaret's life. In many ways, she was "caught in the trees" of life's obstacles, both personal and professional. But—she always broke free and soared toward the heavens.[43]

Though Margaret Hillis would not live to fulfill all she had set out to do, she must have had a sense of fulfillment in all she had accomplished. Passing away almost exactly forty years after the first performance of the Chicago Symphony Chorus she founded, this ensemble proved to be the great love of her life. She could not have predicted her destiny all those years ago when her quest to conduct began. The circuitous paths taken led to achievements far greater than a successful conducting career may have yielded. Many famous conductors have come and gone, yet few leave a permanent imprint such as that rendered by Margaret Hillis.

Beyond her vast accomplishments apropos to the choral art, Margaret Hillis was beloved by those who knew her best. Admired as a leader in the field, Margaret was equally appreciated by those fortunate enough to experience the private side of her: warm, generous, personable, good-humored, compassionate, and kind. In Alfred Mann's "In Memoriam" of the *American Choral Review*, he paid tribute to his friend and colleague of so many years.

> [Margaret Hillis] was the first who made choral performance in this country a matter of public concern. . . . [Yet] the time has come to say that Margaret Hillis, the eminent artist and conductor, proved throughout her career invariably a wonderful friend. . . . The greatest honor bestowed upon her is the affection she earned from the entire world of her profession.[44]

Margaret Hillis would begin her life as a pioneer for those women who desired a conducting career. She would end her journey having blazed many trails, providing professional singers, choruses, and women who conduct greater dignity and opportunity than had existed when she began her quest. Throughout her life, she never sacrificed her personal nor her professional standards to achieve her goals. Her moral compass remained constant throughout her life. She set an example that continues today in new generations of conductors, singers, and professional choruses flourishing around the world. Through them all, her legacy lives on.

ENDNOTES

1. Letter from Ned Rorem to Margaret Hillis, March 9, 1990 (Margaret Hillis Collection, Rosenthal Archives of the Chicago Symphony Orchestra Association, Box 12).
2. Joan Reinthaler, "Margaret Hillis's Nonstop 'Messiah,'" *The Washington Post*, December 15, 1990, p. B3.
3. Octavia Roca, "NSO's 'Messiah' Performance: Part 'Hallelujah,' Part 'Humbug,'" *The Washington Times*, December 17, 1990, p. E3.
4. Wynne Delacoma, "Civic Orchestra's Concentration Tackles Bruckner," *Chicago Sun-Times*, February 3, 1991.
5. Interview with Henry Fogel.
6. Letter from artistic administrator Martha Gilmer to Margaret Hillis, July 22, 1991 (Margaret Hillis Collection, Rosenthal Archives of the Chicago Symphony Orchestra Association, Box 12).
7. Letter to Terry Edwards from Margaret Hillis, April 27, 1990 (Margaret Hillis Collection, Rosenthal Archives of the Chicago Symphony Orchestra Association, Box 7).
8. Wynne Delacoma, "Pavarotti Quiets Rumors, Warms Up Well to 'Otello,'" *Chicago Sun-Times*, April 9, 1991, p. 29.

9. Interview with Henry Fogel.

10. Ibid.

11. Author's recollection of the event.

12. Interview with Henry Fogel.

13. Author's recollection of the event.

14. John von Rhein, "Pavarotti, Solti Team Up in a Challenging 'Otello,'" *Chicago Tribune*, April 9, 1991, p. 116.

15. Donald Henahan, "Despite a Cold, Pavarotti Takes on Otello," *The New York Times*, April 18, 1991, Section 1, p. 10.

16. Interview with Henry Fogel.

17. Ibid.

18. Ibid.

19. John von Rhein, "Mama Chorus a Graceful Swan Song for the CSO's Margaret Hillis," *Chicago Tribune*, September 20, 1992.

20. Marilyn R. Abbey, "The Mass Appeal Messiah," *Discovery* (Winter 1985–1986): p. 40.

21. Letter from Al Booth to Margaret Hillis, May 23, 1991 (Margaret Hillis Collection, Rosenthal Archives of the Chicago Symphony Orchestra Association, Box 7).

22. Letter from Margaret Hillis to Al Booth, May 30, 1991 (Margaret Hillis Collection, Rosenthal Archives of the Chicago Symphony Orchestra Association, Box 7).

23. Letter to Henry Fogel from Margaret Hillis, July 2, 1992 (Margaret Hillis Collection, Rosenthal Archives of the Chicago Symphony Orchestra Association, Box 2).

24. Ibid.

25. Letter from Margaret Hillis to Bettie Buccheri, May 29, 1992 (Margaret Hillis Collection, Rosenthal Archives of the Chicago Symphony Orchestra Association, Box 7).

26. John von Rhein, "Sour Notes at Orchestra Hall," *Chicago Tribune*, September 12, 1993, https://www.chicagotribune.com/news/ct-xpm-1993-09-12-9309120068-story.html.

27. Author's conversation with Hillis, discussing representatives of the Association who disappointed her in the way she was treated in her final years with the organization.

28. Author's recollection.

29. von Rhein, "Mama Chorus."

30. Interview with Dave Murray.

31. Interview with Donna Bruni, June 2012.

32. Interview with Dennis Keene, June 24, 2014.

33. Ibid.

34. Ibid.

35. Ibid.

36. Ibid.

37. Letter from Tina Laughlin to Al Booth on behalf of Margaret Hillis, June 28, 1995 (Margaret Hillis Collection, Rosenthal Archives of the Chicago Symphony Orchestra Association).

38. Faxed message to Tina Laughlin from Hugh Kaylor Management, January 30, 1996 (Margaret Hillis Collection, Rosenthal Archives of the Chicago Symphony Orchestra Association).

39. "Dear People" letter, October 5, 1997, from author's personal collection.

40. Author's recollection

41. Letter to Ardis Krainik from Margaret Hillis, June 1996 (Margaret Hillis Collection, Rosenthal Archives of the Chicago Symphony Orchestra Association, Box 12).

42. Author's recollection.

43. Bettie Buccheri's speech memorializing Margaret Hillis during the public memorial service held at Orchestra Hall on March 14, 1998.

44. Mann, Alfred, "In Memoriam Margaret Hillis 1921–1998," *American Choral Review* XL, no. 2 (Summer–Fall 1998): p. 1.

EPILOGUE

Margaret Hillis did not embark upon a career in music to become an historic figure of the profession. Like so many others who dedicate their entire lives to a profession that demands no less, she followed a calling that unfolded in a direction she could never have imagined. She remained driven to the end to reach the unattainable level of perfection conceived by the great composers whose compositions she sought to realize. Her journey to fulfill this calling would be altered; what remains is a rich legacy that has transformed the choral landscape. And in its wake, opportunities for singers, for women conductors, and for audiences who appreciate the sound of a refined chorus have been forever changed.

Margaret Hillis's vision for a career in music began as a burning desire to become a conductor of orchestras. She claimed to have had that desire from her earliest recollections, and she never wavered from the calling. When choral conducting became the only option to fulfill her passion, she would become driven to raise the choral art in the likeness of orchestras she had initially hoped to direct. Transforming choruses from their amateur status to a professional entity required tireless work and dedication. Robert Shaw forged that path and Margaret Hillis assumed the mantle, further developing his techniques into her own and then making them accessible for others to replicate. Polished, refined choruses are no longer a rarity; they are plentiful in America and throughout the world, i.e., very much a part of the professional music scene. However, this status was not the case until Margaret Hillis and her predecessors exercised their influence. Margaret Hillis carried forward the ideas of Robert Shaw, who learned from his first mentor, Fred Waring. Each of these influencers added their own innovative brand, thereby advancing the choral art. Margaret Hillis's strategies produced a level of tone quality, precision, musicianship, and style in symphonic choirs heretofore unprecedented. These methods were made manifest in her exquisitely prepared Chicago Symphony Chorus, whose stellar performances can still be heard on recordings that remain a hallmark of choral artistry.

Margaret Hillis would foster an approach for reproducing her methods that continues to impact the work of the most respected choral conductors today. What began as a commitment to being thoroughly prepared for every rehearsal evolved into a desire for controlling every aspect of the process from the first rehearsal to the final concert. Margaret Hillis demonstrated respect for musicians through her own thorough preparation, never "winging it" or making it up as she went along. The result was a series of organizational strategies and procedures for all aspects of administrating and rehearsing a chorus, applicable to choruses of any size and ability. Her approach continues to be recognized as the gold standard.

Ms. Hillis would devote much of her life to spreading the gospel of her choral methods. Understanding the importance for conductors to have access to research materials, quality repertoire, and funding sources, all of which were sorely lacking when her career began, Margaret was compelled to invest much of her time and energy in service of educating conductors and giving them access to these necessities, knowing that only through well-trained conductors could choruses truly professionalize in the way that orchestras and opera companies already had. To this end, Ms. Hillis established the first choral organization, her American Choral Foundation, devoted to such support. She would also implement the first conducting institutes, which have continued to grow in number and quality, supporting the education of choral conductors under the discerning eye of distinguished mentors. Through her advocacy for conductors, Hillis continued in her quest for increasing the quality of choral ensembles.

Margaret Hillis did not pursue conducting to become the first woman to regularly conduct a major symphony orchestra in America. She was simply following her heart. She was raised to believe that all things were possible, which led her to believe she could become a conductor, despite the fact she was pursuing a field in which women were not welcome. Margaret remained undeterred, forging the way for women who shared her passion. As she advanced in her career, she willingly accepted the detour, conducting choirs, but all the while continuing to seek opportunities to direct orchestras. As her appearances with orchestras increased, she made this road easier for those women who would follow in her path.

HER WORK CONTINUES

Margaret Hillis was never satisfied that her work was completed. There was much she wanted to accomplish after retiring from the Chicago Symphony Chorus, but that was not to be. Though she achieved a great deal during her lifetime, her work remains unfinished. Professional choirs are still unable to sustain the needed funding to provide singers the potential for earning a respectable salary, akin to their orchestral colleagues, despite their artistic excellence. It was her hope that by raising the profile of choruses in quality and ingenuity, singers would be able to earn a more respectable wage. Thanks to the guidance of Margaret Hillis and her predecessors, their methods and standards have set a bar that must continue to be raised by future generations. The support of organizations such as Chorus America, the National Collegiate Choral Organization, and the American Choral Directors Association, inspired by the American Choral Foundation, remains critical for the continuing education of future choral artists.

As for women on the podium, that struggle still continues. In 2014, almost sixty years after Hillis's career began, Wynne Delacoma, a Chicago performing arts critic, shared her thoughts about the state of women on orchestra podiums. Delacoma cited that despite the inroads women have made, acquiring high visibility appointments in government and industry, there was much that still needed to be done for women desiring an orchestral conducting career. "In some quarters it seems, women who choose to become orchestral conductors—rather than singers, composers, teachers, violinists, flute players, or instrumentalists of any other stripe—are considered to be an exotic, if not seriously deficient species."[1] Her article went on to list situations women conductors have encountered through the years. Criticized for "making faces, sweating and fussing . . . being advised to stick with 'feminine music' [not Bruckner nor Stravinsky]," and scrutinized for their choice of apparel and overall appearance, women conductors have faced circumstances that their male counterparts would never encounter.

Issues remain in the way women are challenged when asserting their authority on the podium. They are still expected to "desexualize themselves," yet when doing so, they are criticized for being too masculine in their leadership style. Marin Alsop, a renowned conductor who has enjoyed an illustrious career as a music director and conductor of the world's major symphony orchestras, has spoken about this conundrum. "As women, we have a different approach to life and interpersonal relationships, so we must retrain ourselves in order to be the figure of authority."[2] Another female conductor speaks of "molding [her] behavior to fit into a leadership position saturated with masculine expectations."[3] A university conductor, Paula Holcomb observes, "If [a woman] adopts too much masculine authority, she is described as butch or a bitch, and if she reveals too much of her femininity, she is disparagingly labelled weak, or a pushover or peppy."[4] Margaret Hillis recalled, "When I started out, I felt like a two-headed calf. . . . I felt that people came to see the strange conductor on the podium."[5] She regularly endured questionable attitudes of both audiences and the musicians she conducted throughout her career. As the female musicians in orchestras continue to increase in number, so too does the support for women on the podium working to find their own style of leadership.[6] Though circumstances have improved, women continue to experience similar encounters conducting both orchestras and choruses.

Margaret never dwelled upon the limitations imposed upon her. She never used these challenges as an excuse for difficulties she encountered on the podium. She confessed that without a mentor she was on her own to parse the intricacies of bringing the choral score to artistic fruition. Confronted with this circumstance, she did her best. Even obtaining artistic management representation was a challenge for Hillis, who settled for lesser options because these were all that were available to her at the time. As a result, she was underpaid for most of her career. Even in the years that have followed, conductors such as Mei-Ann Chen, who was mentored by Marin Alsop and is now an accomplished international conductor, was unable to find a manager at the outset of her career. "When it comes to presenting women conductors, there are very few managers who feel female conductors are marketable. I couldn't get on people's radar. Before I started my tenure with the Atlanta Symphony Orchestra, the musicians and Robert Spano (the orchestra's music director) literally got on the phone with their colleagues across the country [to help promote her]."[7] Marin Alsop, JoAnn Falletta, Kate Tamarkin, Mei-Ann Chen, Mirga Gražinytė-Tyla, Karina Canellakis, Elim Chan, and Susanna Mälkki are a few of many who continue to overcome these hurdles for future generations of women conducting orchestras. However, there is still much to be done.

The Great Lessons to Be Learned from Margaret Hillis

Considering the work that still remains, it is worth reflecting upon more than Hillis's vast array of achievements. If the mantle is to be assumed by future generations, perhaps it is of even greater value to consider *how* Margaret Hillis was able to so greatly impact her profession despite all she was forced to overcome. Therein lies the value of her story. At a time in history when it was so difficult for women to be accepted in the music profession, Margaret Hillis's character traits provide a glimpse into how she was able to leave her indelible imprint. These personality traits are worth consideration for men and women alike. Though Margaret Hillis's life experiences cannot be duplicated, perhaps the way she comported herself *can* provide a path to be emulated by anyone pursuing the conducting field.

Margaret was a dreamer. From her first childhood vision of becoming a conductor and throughout her career, she was continually exploring new ideas for herself, her ensembles, and the choral profession.

Margaret was focused. From her earliest recollections, she wanted to become an orchestral conductor. Despite societal norms dictating otherwise, she found a way. When orchestral conducting was not an option, she remained focused on her ultimate goal, changing her course in pursuit of the choral field instead. Knowing that choruses were not viewed as professional ensembles, Hillis set her sights on changing that, creating an entire playbook to transform choirs into the equal of their orchestral counterparts. To that end, her expectations of her singers were no different from those she had of instrumentalists. She knew how orchestras functioned and imposed those same standards on her singers. For her sake as a conductor of choruses and for the level of singers she hoped to attract, she raised the profile of choral ensembles through her diligent approach.

Margaret was resourceful. Rarely taking "no" for an answer, Margaret was determined to make her ideas happen. When one door closed in pursuit of a dream, she simply found another way. She spent very little time focusing on disappointment. An eternal optimist to the end, she would always be looking forward, rarely dwelling upon the past.

Margaret was a generous and dedicated educator. As a descendant of a long line of Haynes/Hillis teachers, Margaret would continue that legacy, enthusiastically sharing her methods and organizational strategies with others. Beginning with her experiences instructing fighter pilots to fly during World War II, she learned how to present information with clarity and precision. She applied those teaching skills when rehearsing her choral ensembles, believing that effective teaching was at the heart of productive rehearsing. Breaking down the most complex concepts into accessible parts, she was able to clearly communicate her methods to her choirs and eventually to anyone who wanted to understand her techniques. She knew how to teach. Margaret's generosity in spreading her knowledge in rehearsal, in the classroom, and in her mentoring of individuals has enabled the continuation of her contributions to the choral art.

Margaret was an advocate. She was a champion for the profession and for the singers who contributed their talents to choral music. She was a great champion of singers, continuously advocating on their behalf. She was outspoken whenever she deemed them to be treated unfairly. From the time the Orchestral Association attempted to reduce the size of the Chicago Symphony Chorus for their 1971 Carnegie Hall performance of *Moses and Aaron*, Hillis stepped in, carefully plotting her strategy to resolve the matter. Taking her concerns about a reduced Chorus for this complex work directly to Georg Solti, he would ultimately intercede. Not only did she likely save that performance from potential failure, but she also protected the morale of her singers in the process. Cost-cutting measures impacting the Chorus continued to arise with the most difficult time occurring when Hillis was forced to drastically reduce the number of her paid singers. Always looking out for their best interests, she did not hesitate to speak out on their behalf. Hillis was never satisfied with the inequity of pay between singers and instrumentalists of orchestras, and she worked tirelessly to change this, knowing how important respectable pay for singers would be towards maintaining the quality of choral ensembles.

Hillis's advocacy went beyond her actions with the Chicago Symphony Chorus. She would continue her plight on behalf of singers as a founding member of the Association of Professional Vocal Ensembles (APVE), eventually renamed Chorus America. Her influence increased once she began her years of service on the National Endowment for the Arts. As Bob Page noted, "Without her, we would not have had the choral category of the National Endowment for the Arts."[8] Using her vast influence, reaching as far as the United States Congress and several U.S. presidents, Hillis would remain active in support of artists, eventually helping save the National Endowment itself when its very existence would become threatened. Hillis devoted her expertise, her time, and her money in support of professional singers and choruses in America through her extensive service work to the industry. She was never shy about using her connections to advocate on behalf of singers.

Margaret knew how to deal with people. She had a keen understanding of how to interact with people, particularly within the complex world of professional artists and administrators. As a result of her nuanced interactions, she had a remarkable ability to effect change. Coupled with her keen understanding of the political landscape, she was careful as to when she would step into the fray, only doing so when she deemed it absolutely necessary. She once advised that one should "keep their nose clean and avoid symphony politics," yet there was none wiser nor more effective than she when it came to navigating those "troubled waters."[9] Her ability to see both sides of an issue and to use her balanced approach enabled her to successfully negotiate with symphony orchestra managers, conductors, and with politicians. Her connections made her a valuable asset to APVE and Chorus America, particularly when speaking up on behalf of her treasured colleagues in their time of need. She could make things happen, and she did.

Margaret was a "pro" in every sense of the word. As a woman in a "man's profession," she understood what she could accomplish and how she needed to behave in order to remain influential among her peers and superiors. She knew how to operate within the limits of what was acceptable for her gender. Ruled by her standards and philosophy, her ethics were her professional and moral compass. She fought her battles strategically and respectfully, no matter how personally hurtful matters would become. Even when she left positions, as she did with Northwestern University and several symphony orchestras, she was careful to keep her personal feelings private. She preserved her dignity and was always in control, displaying respect for everyone she encountered even when disagreeable situations would arise.

Margaret was brave. Her advancement in the conducting field required continuous risk-taking and courage. As a conductor, she was always tasked with learning something new, never afforded the comfort of complacency. As she stated, "I find that if your life is music, you're constantly learning—day in, day out."[10] Nevertheless, learning new music, new methods of working, and constantly being put into new situations, she was always vulnerable to criticism and failure. She learned to deal with the risks and uncertainty from the earliest years of her career. Willingly shifting her focus to choral music, though her initial training had been in instrumental music, was just one of many examples of her courage. Once she embarked upon her career, she put herself and her New York chorus in venues where their performances would be on display for the discerning New York music critics. She willingly took the risk, exposing herself to reviews, both uplifting and critical. Instead of dismissing criticism, she took it to heart, saving all her reviews in scrapbooks and personal files. She wisely learned from the feedback, having no mentor to guide her way. In later years when her career was fairly set, she took another great risk, determining it necessary to learn a completely new way of conducting and score study. In Otto-Werner Mueller, she finally found someone to guide her, believing he had answers to questions that had plagued her throughout her career.

Margaret did not achieve the level of success as a conductor that she may have if a dedicated mentor had been available to her during the formative years of her career. Her willingness to step on a stage, knowing what she lacked, took tremendous courage. She embraced a philosophical approach when it came to reflecting on her conducting accomplishments. In an interview—as she was about to step down as director of the Chicago Symphony Chorus—she revealed a level of dissatisfaction with her conducting career. "I guess if I had another chance, I'd make the same damned fool mistakes all over again."[11] Yet she wonders, rather privately, what would have happened if women of her generation had had the same chance men had, where she and her friends would be now, if they'd had the opportunity to study with first-rate symphonic conductors, to build their own repertoire, and to get the all-important podium practice. "I learned to take a strong disadvantage and turn it to my advantage."[12]

Hillis's most memorable public display of bravery came about as she stepped onto the Carnegie Hall stage that fateful Halloween night in 1977. Margaret's courage was perhaps most poignantly displayed privately, as she dealt with her terminal illness, refusing to give in to the inevitable truth of her condition. Her strength in the face of this greatest challenge allowed her to live out her final days with dignity and grace. Bravery is a prerequisite of any conducting career, but even more so for women. Hillis was well practiced for the challenges she faced throughout her life. When speaking about her early years as a conductor, she reflected upon the sheer terror she had experienced. She likened it to being willing to "walk through the fire." In many ways, this was how Margaret Hillis led her entire life.

Margaret was self-aware. In a career filled with risk-taking, Margaret was very much attuned to her strengths and even more to her weaknesses. Hillis suffered from a level of insecurity, carefully masked but ever present. Underneath that stoic exterior was the recognition of her vulnerabilities professionally and personally. As with most musicians, self-awareness of faults can compel them to adapt a strong persona, lest their imperfections be revealed. Robert Shaw was plagued by his insecurities throughout his life. So too was Hillis. This insecurity would sometimes be revealed in her dealings with members of the Chicago Symphony Chorus. As Martha Gilmer observed, Margaret valued loyalty above all. If she perceived someone in the Chorus was being critical of her, she would become nervous.[13] Her main concern was being able to maintain discipline and a positive work environment so that she could make music. Though gossiping singers are endemic to a chorus culture, Margaret was one who often "looked over her shoulder." Referring to difficult personalities in the Chorus as "stinkers," such people caused Margaret to be always on her guard. As Gilmer saw it, "Margaret could never completely relax." In this competitive business, Margaret learned she could trust very few people. She was not alone in this. Hillis's effort to convey strength was a cover for the vulnerabilities she worked diligently to disguise.

Margaret was a realist. The fact remained that she lived at a time when the world was not ready to accept her professionally as a female conductor nor personally as a lesbian, compelling her to protect herself from hurtful encounters. For this reason, she revealed herself to a select few. That circumspect personality style, which she adopted to protect herself from "the real world," might also explain her difficulties as an expressive conductor. Perhaps a mentor early on in her career might have helped her overcome that barrier, guiding her to integrate the many endearing aspects of her personality that were only revealed to those who knew her best. The fortunate "inner circle" saw Margaret's humor, compassion, and kindness that others could only glimpse from afar.

Margaret had warmth. Albeit reserved for a select few, her closest friends and family were able to see that Margaret had another side to her beyond the professional persona she displayed to most. When she was completely comfortable around friends and companions or at home with her beloved pets, Margaret showed her capacity for conveying appreciation and affection. Though she tried, Margaret was not completely able to hide those endearing qualities in professional situations, which would account for the affection and admiration conveyed in tributes to her.

Margaret had a great sense of humor. Whether it was in the form of a quick-witted "wisecrack" she would deliver to lighten the mood during a particularly tense rehearsal or by other means, reserved for only her closest friends, Margaret could be very funny. That endearing quality was appreciated when she would reveal her clever wit, sometimes during a rehearsal when it would be least expected. Humorous "Hillis-isms" (see Appendix 8) would become legendary and would be affectionately recalled by musicians she rehearsed through the years.

Bettie Buccheri shared several lesser-known aspects of Margaret's endearing personality during the memorial service at Orchestra Hall on March 14, 1998:

> Margaret had a fabulous sense of humor. . . . I still have some of the rude birthday cards she sent me. And to this day, I can hear her infectious giggle when I opened them. She loved pranks and good jokes, clean and otherwise.
>
> Margaret was sentimental. She cried unashamedly at many of the movies she saw, and she even cried a few times when no one else would have. I took her to dress rehearsals at Lyric Opera after she retired and I wasn't surprised when she cried in the scene with Boris Godunov and his children. But *The Rake's Progress*??
>
> Margaret loved animals. There were Penelope, Menelaus, Big Red, and Morris, the cats, and, of course, Scotch and O'Banshee, the dogs. When any of them died she went into real mourning. They were important members of her family, and in some meaningful way they connected better with her than we did. When O'Banshee died . . . she stayed home in seclusion, missing Maestro Leinsdorf's *Meistersinger* orchestra rehearsals. Do you think he understood *that*?[14]

Bettie went on to describe how Margaret loved children, cars, and sports. She was also very passionate about fine food and traveling around the world.

Margaret was humble. One did not have to be a close confidant to see that side of her. Throughout her music making, it was always about the *music*, never about *her*. That humility towards others who participated in her life's work was always on display, often seen as she made a regular point of publicly acknowledging her pianists, her assistants, her diction coach, and her chorus managers, believing it was a team effort that made for so many of her great successes. Her most effusive gratitude was reserved for her Chicago Symphony Chorus. Martha Gilmer concurred that Margaret loved the Chorus and its members, who were in many ways like her extended family. Her devotion to them was always present when each concert would end, as she waited in the wings to thank her singers, each and every one. She sincerely appreciated the effort and the artistry in all who shared her success. Her profound respect for the art transcended all that she believed she had achieved. It was clear to everyone who worked with her that she saw her role as a facilitator to the great works of art she helped bring to life.

Margaret was kind. She had a tenderness that she fiercely protected from view. To exhibit that side was too difficult for Margaret, which would have made her more vulnerable to the slings and arrows in her position as a conductor. Bob Page relayed an incident that allowed him a rare glimpse into Hillis's incredible sensitivity. He recalled a meeting of Chorus America in Milwaukee when Michael Korn, conductor of the Philadelphia Singers, was suffering from AIDS. He did not want anyone to know he had this disease, although everyone was already aware of it. Given the prejudices against homosexuality at the time, Korn feared that if word were to come out that he had AIDS, he believed his life would be destroyed. Page recalled how he, along with Margaret Hawkins, conductor of the Milwaukee Symphony Chorus, and Doralene Davis, a founding member of Michael Korn's Philadelphia Singers and board member of Chorus America, would continually talk to Korn, supporting him through the difficulties of dealing with his failing health while trying to protect his reputation. Page became emotional as he recalled how it was Margaret who had the greatest impact on Korn. Page choked up, remembering, "Her tenderness with him showed me a Margaret Hillis that I knew had always been there. You never think of Margaret and the word 'tender,' [he chuckled], but she *was*."[15]

FINALE

Margaret Hillis was a private person who lived a very public life. Few knew her well, yet she touched many lives, and she is remembered fondly by those who were fortunate enough to learn from her teaching and share in her music making. Margaret believed she was not done with her journey when it was time for her to go. She was grateful for the path she chose, stating, "I cannot envision a more rewarding life's work than mine. Seeking out talented vocalists and drawing them together into a great musical instrument to interpret the magnificent choral repertoire."[16] Margaret

Hillis's life was dedicated to the choral art. Her journey continues through those whose lives she touched and through those who understand her teachings. Margaret Hillis was a legend of her time, a pioneer in music. She should never be forgotten.

ENDNOTES

1. Delacoma, Wynne, "It's About Time, Women Are Making Overdue Inroads on the Podium," *Ravinia Magazine* 8, no. 4, p. 23.
2. Brydie-Leigh Bartleet, "Female Conductors: The Incarnation of Power?" *Hecate: An Interdisciplinary Journal of Women's Liberation* 28, no. 2 (2003): pp. 220–221.
3. Ibid, p. 230.
4. Ibid, p. 230.
5. Virginia Gerst, "Conductor Takes the Direct Approach," *Evanston Life*, June 18, 1992, p. B2.
6. Marietta Nien-hwa-Cheng, "Women Conductors: Has the Train Left the Station?" *Harmony: Forum of the Symphony Orchestra Institute*, no. 6 (April 1998), www.soi.org.
7. Delacoma, "It's About Time," p. 28.
8. Alfred Mann, "A Giant Gone: Margaret Hillis Died, Wednesday, February 4, 1998," *The Voice of Chorus America* 21, no. 3 (Spring 1998): p. 21.
9. Advice given to the author.
10. Sue Bradle and Tom Wilson, "Music is My Life," *Accent* 6, no. 1 (September/October 1980): pp. 11–14.
11. Conversation with the author.
12. Karen Monson, "Musician of the Month: Margaret Hillis," *High Fidelity and Musical America* (October 1978): p. 7.
13. Interview with Martha Gilmer, July 10, 2012.
14. Speech given by Bettie Buccheri at Margaret Hillis's Memorial Service, Orchestra Hall, March 14, 1998 (personal copy provided by Bettie Buccheri to the author).
15. Interview with Robert Page, 2014.
16. Chicago Symphony Chorus, Margaret Hillis Director, brochure for the Thirtieth Anniversary of the Chorus.

APPENDIX 1
TIMELINE OF MARGARET HILLIS'S LIFE AND CAREER

October 1, 1921   Margaret Hillis is born in Kokomo, Indiana

1926   Begins piano lessons.

Spring 1937   Conducted her high school orchestra in the overture to Weber's *Der Freischütz*. She referred to this as her "first conducting job."

November 24, 1937   Hears Kirsten Flagstad for the first time in a performance of Wagner's *Tristan and Isolde* under the auspices of the Chicago City Opera Company at the Civic Opera House.

Fall 1938   Transfers from Kokomo High School to Tudor Hall for her junior and senior years of high school.

Margaret Hillis's high school graduation, ca. 1939. (Adams photograph)
(Margaret Hillis Collection, Rosenthal Archives of the Chicago Symphony Orchestra Association)

1940   Begins studies at Indiana University as a piano major.

Fall 1942–1945   Interrupts her studies at Indiana University to work for the United States Navy as a civilian flight instructor at the airfield in Muncie, Indiana.

Spring 1947   Graduates with a bachelor of arts degree in composition from Indiana University.

1947–1949   Attends the Juilliard School as a student of Robert Shaw.

1948   Begins working with the Metropolitan Youth Chorale in Brooklyn to fulfill a school requirement and continues to work with the ensemble after leaving Juilliard.

1950   Founds the Tanglewood Alumni Choir, soon renamed the New York Concert Choir and ultimately called the American Concert Choir.

Margaret Hillis in 1950. (J. Abresch, photographer)
(Margaret Hillis Collection, Rosenthal Archives of the Chicago Symphony Orchestra Association)

December 21, 1952   First collaborates with Igor Stravinsky, preparing his *Cantata on Elizabethan Songs*. He was so pleased with her preparation of the New York Concert Choir for this performance that it was the first of many future collaborations between Stravinsky and Hillis.

May 12, 1952   New York Concert Choir and Orchestra perform the first of two concerts at Carnegie Recital Hall. Hillis considers this performance to be her official professional conducting debut.

1950–1960   Serves as conductor and instructor at Union Theological Seminary in New York.

1950–1953   Serves as instructor and conductor at the Juilliard School, assisting Robert Hufstader (Robert Shaw's successor).

1952–1954   Serves as assistant conductor of Robert Shaw's Collegiate Chorale.

1952–1968   Serves as conductor of the American Opera Society.

January 16, 1953   With the generous support of her family, funds the first of five seasons of her Town Hall concert series, which she conducts. The only professional choral series to take place in Town Hall at that time, Hillis would conduct as many as five concerts in one season. This series concludes on February 19, 1958, with only one Town Hall performance in the 1957–1958 season. The Concert Choir appeared thereafter, performing only for other companies. Hillis prepared the chorus for others to conduct and would no longer conduct her chorus in concerts.

February 13, 1954   Fritz Reiner attends a rehearsal to audition the New York Concert Choir for a guest appearance with the Chicago Symphony Orchestra.

September 1954   New York Concert Choir and Orchestra is featured on a television series, "Concert Tonight." The series, on DuMont television network, is broadcast in New York City and the vicinity on September 15, 22, and 28, 1954.

1953–1954   Serves as director of the choral department at the Third Street Music School Settlement in New York.

1954   Founds and becomes the first music director of the American Choral Foundation (New York Concert Choir name is changed to the American Concert Choir to coincide with the name of the Foundation).

March 17–18, 1955	The New York Concert Choir, under the direction of Margaret Hillis, appears with the Chicago Symphony Orchestra in Barber's *Prayers of Kierkegaard* and Orff's *Carmina Burana*; Fritz Reiner conducts.
1956–1957	Serves as choral director of the New York City Opera.
1956–1960	Serves as founder and music director of the New York Chamber Soloists.
September 22, 1957	The Orchestral Association announces Margaret Hillis will organize and train a symphony chorus; Hillis begins auditions two weeks later.
November 30, 1957	The Chicago Symphony Chorus makes its informal debut at a private concert for guarantors and sustaining members. On the second half of the program, Margaret Hillis takes the podium—becoming the first woman to conduct the Chicago Symphony Orchestra—leading the Orchestra and Chorus in the final section of Purcell's *Ode for Saint Cecilia's Day*, Randall Thompson's *Alleluia* and William Billings's *Modern Music* (both a cappella), and the "Servants' Chorus" from Donizetti's *Don Pasquale*.
March 13–14, 1958	The Chicago Symphony Chorus makes its debut on subscription concerts in Mozart's Requiem; Bruno Walter conducts.
April 3–4, 1958	Fritz Reiner conducts the Chorus in performances of Verdi's Requiem.
April 1958	At the conclusion of the Chorus's first season, members of the ensemble establish the Margaret Hillis Fellowship Fund as a gift to Miss Hillis.
May 1958	The U.S. State Department invites the New York Concert Choir, Orchestra, and Margaret Hillis to represent the United States at the Brussels World's Fair.
1958–1959	Serves as conductor and choral director of the Santa Fe Opera Company.
December 26–27, 1958	Hillis becomes the first woman to conduct the Chicago Symphony Orchestra on subscription concerts, leading the Orchestra and Chorus in Honeggar's *Christmas Cantata*.

March 7, 1959   The Chorus makes its first commercial recording with the Orchestra—Prokofiev's *Alexander Nevsky* for RCA Records with Fritz Reiner conducting.

July 9, 1960   The Chorus first appears with the Chicago Symphony Orchestra at the Ravinia Festival in Mahler's Symphony No. 2 (*Resurrection*) under the direction of Walter Hendl.

January 28, 1961   Hillis conducts the Orchestra and Chorus in a special concert featuring Bach's *Jesu, meine Freude*; Poulenc's Mass in G Major; and Mendelssohn's *First Walpurgis Night* with Ellen Stuart, Walter Carringer, Sherrill Milnes, and Thomas Peck as soloists.

1961–1962   Serves as choral director of Chicago Musical College (now Chicago College of Performing Arts) at Roosevelt University.

1961–1968   Serves as music director and conductor of the Kenosha Symphony Orchestra.

1966   Becomes musical assistant to Jean Martinon, music director of the Chicago Symphony Orchestra.

1966–1970   Serves as artists' advisor to the National Federation of Music Clubs Youth Auditions.

1967–1991   Becomes resident conductor of the Civic Orchestra of Chicago.

Margaret Hillis in 1967. (Harry Johnson Studios)
(Margaret Hillis Collection, Rosenthal Archives of the Chicago Symphony Orchestra Association)

April 26, 1967	Receives an honorary doctor of music degree from Temple University.
November 12, 1967	The Chorus first appears with the Orchestra at Carnegie Hall in Henze's *The Sicilian Muses* and Ravel's *Daphnis and Chloe* under the direction of Jean Martinon.
December 17, 1967	Conducts the Orchestra and Chorus in a performance of Bach's Mass in B Minor, celebrating the tenth anniversary of the Chorus.
1968–1970	Serves as music director of the Choral Institute.
1968–1971	Serves on the Advisory Panel of the Illinois Arts Council.
September 1968–June 1977	Serves as director of choral activities at Northwestern University.
December 15, 1968	Conducts the Orchestra and Chorus in an Allied Arts Christmas concert featuring works by Britten, Costeley, Victoria, Stravinsky, and Sweelinck.
1969	Receives the Steinway Award in recognition of outstanding contributions in the field of music.

1969–1971	Serves as conductor and choral director of the Cleveland Orchestra Chorus.
April 3, 1969	Georg Solti first conducts the Chorus in a performance of Mahler's Symphony No. 2.
March 7, 1970	Receives the Outstanding Music Alumna Award for 1969 from the Indiana University School of Music Alumni Association.
June 2, 1970	Becomes a member of Pi Kappa Lambda, a national music fraternity.
April 15, 1971	The Orchestra and Chorus present the world premiere of Alan Stout's Fourth Symphony; Georg Solti conducts.
August 13, 1971	Begins her tenure as music director and conductor of the Elgin Symphony Orchestra.
1971	Selected to serve on the Visiting Committee of the Department of Music at the University of Chicago.
1972	Selected to serve on the Advisory Music Panel for the National Endowment for the Arts.
March 30, 31, and April 1, 1972	On short notice, Hillis replaces Rafael Kubelík, conducting three subscription concert performances of Handel's *Jephtha*.
April 16, 1972	Receives an honorary doctor of music degree from Indiana University.
May 15, 1972	The Chorus records with Sir Georg Solti and the Orchestra for the first time—Beethoven's Symphony No. 9.
June 17, 1972	Conducts the American premiere of Roberto Gerhard's *The Plague* at the Chorus's fifteenth anniversary concert.
January 18, 1973	Daniel Barenboim first conducts the Chorus in a performance of Brahms's *A German Requiem*.
April 15, 1976	The Chorus and Orchestra present the world premiere of Alan Stout's *Passion* for Soloists, Chorus, and Orchestra; Margaret Hillis conducts.

December 15, 1976	Leads the first Do-It-Yourself *Messiah* concert at Orchestra Hall.
October 1977	Becomes artistic director of the Dame Myra Hess Memorial Concerts series.
October 31, 1977	Replacing Sir Georg Solti on short notice, conducts the Chicago Symphony Orchestra, Chorus, and soloists in a performance of Mahler's Symphony No. 8 at Carnegie Hall.
December 22, 1977	Founded by Margaret Hillis, Walter Gould, Michael Korn, High Ross, Gregg Smith, and Roger Wagner, the Association of Professional Vocal Ensembles is incorporated (in 1988 the organization changed its name to Chorus America).
1978	Receives the Woman of the Year in Classical Music award from the *Ladies Home Journal*.
Fall 1978	Begins appointment as a visiting professor at Indiana University.
February 23, 1978	The recording of Verdi's Requiem wins the 1977 Grammy Award for Best Choral Performance—Classical.
May 4, 1978	Receives the Leadership for Freedom Award from the Women's Scholarship Association of Roosevelt University.
March 3, 1979	The Chorus records with Daniel Barenboim and the Orchestra for the first time—Bruckner's Psalm 150.
April 28, 1979	Conducts members of the Chorus in a performance for President Jimmy Carter at the annual White House Correspondents' Association dinner at the Washington Hilton Hotel in Washington, D.C.
May 1979	Receives honorary doctor of music degree from Carthage College.
May 10, 1980	Receives honorary doctor of fine arts degree from Lake Forest College.
June 1980	Receives the Michael Korn Founder's Award from Chorus America.

April 27, 1981	Receives a citation from the National Federation of Music Clubs in Birmingham, Alabama.
May 1981	Receives honorary doctor of music degree from Wartburg College.
December 19, 1981	The Chorus presents the first Margaret Hillis Fellowship Fund concert.
1982–1983	Serves as director of choral activities for San Francisco Symphony.
1981–1983	Serves as music director and conductor of Liberty Fremont Orchestra.
January 16, 1984	The Chorus appears with the Orchestra at the Kennedy Center in Washington, D.C., in Beethoven's *Missa solemnis* with Sir Georg Solti conducting.
March 22, 1984	The Orchestra and Chorus present the world premiere of Ezra Laderman's *A Mass for Cain*; Margaret Hillis conducts.
May 3, 1984	The YWCA of Elgin initiates the Annual Leader Luncheon Margaret Hillis Award for the Arts.
1984	Receives the Founders Award for Distinguished Achievement from Sigma Alpha Iota, an international music fraternity.
March 28– 29, 1984	Conducts the Baltimore Symphony Orchestra and Chorus in performances of Verdi's Overture to *La forza del destino* and *Four Sacred Pieces* and Dvořák's *New World Symphony*.
1985	Steps down as music director of the Elgin Symphony Orchestra.
September 13–15, 1985	Leads a choral workshop and conducts the Houston Symphony Orchestra.
December 7, 1985	Conducts the Fort Wayne Philharmonic.
March 16–18, 1986	Conducts performances with the Kokomo Symphonic Society.

July 20 and 23, 1986	Conducts performances at the Berkshire Choral Institute in Sheffield, Massachusetts.
December 6, 1986	Leads Handel's *Messiah* with the Puerto Rico Symphony.
March 1, 1987	Conducts Bach's Mass in B Minor at Boulder Bach Festival in Colorado.
April 29, 1987	Governor James R. Thompson declares Margaret Hillis Day in Illinois, celebrating the thirtieth anniversary of the Chorus.
October 15, 1987	The Chorus and Orchestra present the world premiere of Marvin David Levy's *Masada*; Margaret Hillis conducts.
December 10–11, 1987	Leads performances of Handel's *Messiah* with the Indianapolis Symphony Orchestra.
January 14, 1988	Conducts the United States Air Force Band in Washington, D.C.
March 13, 1988	Conducts the Chicago Symphony Chorus and Civic Orchestra in a performance of Mozart's Requiem and Verdi's *Four Sacred Pieces*, celebrating the thirtieth anniversary of the Chorus.
May 1, 1988	Conducts the Nebraska Choral Arts Society.
May 29, 1988	Receives an honorary doctor of humane letters degree from Saint Xavier University.
June 19, 1988	Leads a performance of Mozart's Requiem and Haydn's *Lord Nelson Mass* with the Ontario Choral Federation in Toronto.
July 11–14, 1988	Conducts concerts at Westminster Choir College in Princeton, New Jersey.
December 4, 1988	Leads a Do-It-Yourself *Messiah* with the Kokomo Symphonic Society.
April 22, 1989	Conducts a performance of Bloch's First Concerto Grosso and Sacred Service with the Seattle Symphony Orchestra.

August 28 and 30, 1989   The Chorus first appears with the Orchestra in Europe in Berlioz's *The Damnation of Faust* at Royal Albert Hall in London and the Grosses Festspielhaus in Salzburg; Sir Georg Solti conducts.

October 22, 1989   Conducts the Kenosha Symphony in Wisconsin.

December 3, 1989   Leads the Mozart Club of Winston-Salem, North Carolina, in Handel's *Messiah*.

October 21, 1990   Receives an honorary doctor of letters degree from Saint Mary of the Woods College.

November 8, 1990   The Chicago Symphony Chorus and Orchestra present the world premiere of Ned Rorem's *Goodbye My Fancy*, commissioned for the centennial of the Orchestra; Leonard Slatkin conducts.

December 14–17, 1990   Leads a performance of Handel's *Messiah* with the National Symphony Orchestra.

April 8 and 12, 1991   The Chorus appears with the Orchestra at Orchestra Hall and Carnegie Hall in Verdi's *Otello*, commemorating Sir Georg Solti's final concerts as music director.

June 9, 1991   Chorus America establishes the Margaret Hillis Achievement Award for Choral Excellence to be presented in a repeating three-year cycle of categories (volunteer choruses, professional choruses, and choruses with a professional core).

December 12, 1991   Pierre Boulez first conducts the Chicago Symphony Chorus in a performance of Bartók's *Cantata profana*.

February 21, 1992   Receives the Harold A. Decker Award from the Illinois chapter of the American Choral Directors Association.

May 17, 1992   Receives the Governor's Award of the Chicago chapter of the National Academy of Recording Arts and Sciences.

May 23, 1992   Receives an honorary doctor of fine arts degree from North Park College and Theological Seminary.

June 6, 1992   The Dale Warland Singers become the first recipient of Chorus America's Margaret Hillis Achievement Award for Choral Excellence.

November 23, 1992   Receives a national citation from Phi Mu Alpha, a
                     national music fraternity.

January 9, 1993   Margaret Hillis formally becomes one of the founding
                     directors of Chorus America.

March 1, 1993   Hillis and the Chicago Symphony Chorus win their ninth
                     Grammy Award: the 1993 award for Best Performance
                     of a Choral Work for the recording of Bartók's *Cantata
                     profana.*

Margaret Hillis's nine Grammy Awards. (Todd Rosenberg, photographer)
(Margaret Hillis Collection, Rosenthal Archives of the Chicago Symphony Orchestra Association)

June 1, 1994   Duain Wolfe becomes the second director of the Chicago
                     Symphony Chorus; Margaret Hillis becomes director
                     laureate.

June 1994   Receives the Distinguished Alumni Service Award for
                     musicianship and great strength of leadership from
                     Indiana University. (Miss Hillis and her brother Elwood,
                     former congressman from the fifth district in Indiana,
                     have been the only brother and sister who have both
                     received this award in IU history.)

September 17, 1994   Receives the Theodore Thomas Medallion for
                     Distinguished Service on her retirement after thirty-seven
                     years as director of the Chicago Symphony Chorus;
                     Mayor Daley proclaims September 20, 1994, Margaret
                     Hillis Day in Chicago.

June 3, 1995   Personally presents Chorus America's Margaret Hillis Achievement Award for Choral Excellence to Chanticleer (accepted by artistic director Louis Botto) at the annual conference in Seattle.

October 1995   Recognized as a distinguished alumna at the Park Tudor School in Indianapolis, Indiana.

May 1996   Receives an honorary doctor of music degree from the University of Missouri–Kansas City.

April 20, 1997   Receives the Legends in Teaching Award from Northwestern University.

February 4, 1998   Dies in Evanston, Illinois.

Appendix 2
Margaret Hillis Discography as Conductor

Margaret Hillis uses a megaphone to communicate with the Chorus, seated in a distant balcony of Medinah Temple, during a recording session of Wagner's *The Flying Dutchman*, May 1976. (Robert M. Lightfoot III, photographer) (Rosenthal Archives of the Chicago Symphony Orchestra Association)

As Director of the New York Concert Choir (American Concert Choir) with Margaret Hillis Conducting

Béla Bartók *Cantata profana* (1956)
Margaret Hillis, conductor
The New York Concert Choir and Orchestra
Bartok BR 312

Track Listing:
1. *Cantata profana*
2. Four Slovak Folk Songs
3. Eight Songs from 27 Choruses (Don't Leave Me, Hussar, Bread Breaking, Loafer, Enchanting Song, Teasing Song, Only Tell Me, The Wooing of a Girl [in English])

Contemporary Christmas Carols (1952)
Margaret Hillis, conductor
Members of the New York Concert Choir
Contemporary Records AP 122

Track Listing:
1. The Star Song (David Kraehenbuehl)
2. Ideo Gloria in Excelsis Deo (David Kraehenbuehl)
3. There is No Rose (David Kraehenbuehl)
4. A Song Against Bores (David Kraehenbuehl)
5. On the Morning of Christ's Nativity (Charles Jones)
6. The Shepherd's Carol (Charles Jones)
7. The Virgin's Lullaby (Manus Sasonkin)
8. Three Kings Went to Call (Manus Sasonkin)
9. Rejoice Greatly (Manus Sasonkin)
10. A King Is Born (Manus Sasonkin)
11. The Boar is Dead (Arthur Harris)
12. Rejoice (Arthur Harris)
13. The Christmas Chanters (Arthur Harris)

14. The Birds (John Gruen)
15. Sweet Was the Song (John Gruen)

Wilhelm Killmayer *Missa brevis and Lou Harrison Mass* (1957)
Margaret Hillis, conductor
New York Concert Choir and Orchestra
From Music Foundation "Twentieth Century Composers Series"
Epic LC 3307

Igor Stravinsky *Les noces*, *Mass*, *Pater noster*, and *Ave Maria* (1954)
Margaret Hillis, conductor
The New York Concert Choir and Orchestra
Adele Addison, soprano; Doris Okerson, mezzo-soprano; Robert Price, tenor;
    Arthur Burrows, baritone
Vox PS 8630

As Director of the American Concert Choir

Johann Sebastian Bach Cantata No. 198, BWV 198 (*Trauer Ode*) and Cantata No. 131 BWV 131 (*Aus der Tiefe*)
Robert Craft, conductor
    Columbia Symphony Orchestra
Margaret Hillis, director
    The American Concert Choir
Marni Nixon, soprano; Elaine Bonazzim contralto; Nico Castel, tenor; Loren Driscoll, tenor; Peter Binder, baritone; Robert Oliver, bass
Columbia ML 5577 (Date Unknown)

Franz Lehár *The Merry Widow* (1962)
Franz Allers, conductor
    American Opera Society Orchestra
Margaret Hillis, director
    American Opera Society Chorus
Laurel Hurley, soprano; John Reardon, baritone; Charles K. L. Davis, tenor; Paul Franke, tenor; Howard; Kahl, unknown; Paul Richards, unknown
Columbia ML OS 2280

Igor Stravinsky *Stravinsky Conducts Stravinsky* (1962)
Igor Stravinsky, conductor
The American Concert Choir
Margaret Hillis, director

Track Listing:
1. *Les noces* ("The Wedding")
2. *Renard* ("The Fox")
3. *Ragtime for Eleven Instruments*

Samuel Barber, piano; Aaron Copland, piano; Lukas Foss, piano; Roger Sessions, piano; Columbia Percussion Ensemble; Mildred Allen, soprano; Regina Sarfaty, mezzo-soprano; Loren Driscoll, tenor; Robert Oliver, bass
Columbia ML 5772

Igor Stravinsky Symphony in C* and Cantata** (1954)

Igor Stravinsky, conductor

*The Cleveland Orchestra

**Jennie Tourel, mezzo-soprano; **Hugues Cuenod, tenor; **Members of the
New York Concert Choir

**Margaret Hillis, director

**Philharmonic Chamber Ensemble

As Director of the Symphony of the Air Chorus

Ernest Bloch *America (An Epic Rhapsody)*
Leopold Stokowski, conductor
American Concert Choir
Margaret Hillis, director
Symphony of the Air
Vanguard- SRV 346 SD, 1960

The Sound of Stokowski and Wagner
Leopold Stokowski, conductor
Richard Wagner Ride of the Valkyries from *Die Walküre*
Richard Wagner Prelude to Act III from *Die Walküre*
Richard Wagner Entrance of the Gods into Valhalla from *Das Rheingold*
Richard Wagner Overture and Venusburg Music from *Tannhäuser*
Martina Arroyo, soprano
Carlotta Ordassy, soprano
Doris Yarick, soprano
Betty Allen, mezzo-soprano
Doris Okerson, mezzo-soprano
Louise Parker, contralto
American Concert Choir
Margaret Hillis, director
Symphony of the Air
RCA LM 2555, 1961

As Director of the Cleveland Orchestra Chorus

Maurice Ravel *Boulez Conducts Ravel*
Pierre Boulez conductor,
Daphnis and Chloe Suite No. 2
Pavane for a Dead Princess
Rhapsodie espagnole
Alborada del gracioso
Cleveland Orchestra Chorus
Margaret Hillis, director
Cleveland Orchestra
Columbia M 30651, 1971

As Director of a Children's Choir

Georges Bizet *Carmen*
Fritz Reiner, conductor
Risë Stevens, soprano (Carmen)
Jan Peerce, tenor (Don José)
Licia Albanese, soprano (*Micaëla)*
Robert Merrill, baritone (Escamillo)
Robert Shaw Chorale
Robert Shaw, director
L'Elysée Française Children's Chorus
Margaret Hillis, director (not credited)
RCA Victor Orchestra LM 6102, 1954

As Director of a Chamber Chorus for *Music from Ravinia*, Vol. 2

Igor Stravinsky *Les noces* and *L'histoire du soldat*
James Levine, conductor
Jann Jaffe, soprano
Isola Jones, mezzo-soprano
Philip Creech, tenor
Arnold Voketaitis, bass
Paul Schenly, piano
William Vendice, piano
André-Michel Schub, piano
Donald Koss, timpani
Gordon Peters, percussion
Sam Denov, percussion
Albert Payson, percussion
James Lane, percussion
Michael Green, percussion
Chamber Chorus
Margaret Hillis, director
Recorded in Medinah Temple in 1977
RCA Red Seal-RVC 2326

As Director of the Chicago Symphony Chorus

Johann Sebastian Bach Mass in B Minor, BWV 232
Sir Georg Solti, conductor
Felicity Lott, soprano
Anne Sofie von Otter, mezzo-soprano
Hans Peter Blochwitz, tenor
William Shimmell, baritone
Gwynne Howell, bass
Chicago Symphony Chorus
Margaret Hillis, director
Recorded in Orchestra Hall in January 1990 for London
1991 Grammy Award for Best Performance of a Choral Work

Johann Sebastian Bach *Nun ist das Heil und die Kraft,* BWV 50
Margaret Hillis, conductor
Chicago Symphony Chorus
Margaret Hillis, director
Recorded in Orchestra Hall in December 1984 by WFMT and released on *Chicago Symphony Chorus: A Fiftieth Anniversary Celebration* (*From the Archives*, Vol. 22) in 2008

Johann Sebastian Bach *Saint Matthew Passion,* BWV 244
Sir Georg Solti, conductor
Kiri Te Kanawa, soprano
Anne Sofie von Otter, mezzo-soprano
Thomas Moser, tenor
Tom Krause, bass
Hans Peter Blochwitz, tenor
Olaf Bär, baritone
Richard Cohn, baritone
Patrice Michaels, soprano
Debra Austin, mezzo-soprano
William Watson, tenor

Chicago Symphony Chorus
Margaret Hillis, director
Glen Ellyn Children's Chorus
Doreen Rao, director
Recorded in Orchestra Hall in March 1987 for London

Johann Sebastian Bach *Singet dem Herrn ein neues Lied,* BWV 225
Daniel Barenboim, conductor
Chicago Symphony Chorus
Margaret Hillis, director
Recorded in Orchestra Hall in May 1991 by WFMT and released on *Chicago Symphony Chorus: A Fortieth Anniversary Celebration* (*From the Archives,* Vol. 13) in 1998

Samuel Barber *The Lovers*
Andrew Schenk, conductor
Dale Duesing, baritone
Chicago Symphony Chorus
Margaret Hillis, director
Recorded in Orchestra Hall in October 1991 for Koch Classics
1992 Grammy Award for Best Contemporary Composition

Samuel Barber *Prayers of Kierkegaard*
Andrew Schenk, conductor
Sarah Reese, soprano
Chicago Symphony Chorus
Margaret Hillis, director
Recorded in Orchestra Hall in October 1991 for Koch Classics

Bartók Béla *Cantata profana*
Pierre Boulez, conductor
John Aler, tenor
John Tomlinson, bass
Chicago Symphony Chorus
Margaret Hillis, director
Recorded in Orchestra Hall in December 1991 for Deutsche Grammophon
1993 Grammy Awards for Best Classical Album, Best Performance of a Choral
    Work, and Best Engineered Album–Classical

Ludwig van Beethoven *Fidelio*, Op. 72
Sir Georg Solti, conductor
Hildegard Behrens, soprano (Leonore)
Sona Ghazarian, soprano (Marzelline)
Peter Hofmann, tenor (Florestan)
David Kübler, tenor (Jaquino)
Theo Adam, baritone (Don Pizarro)
Hans Sotin, bass (Rocco)
Gwynne Howell, bass (Don Fernando)
Robert Johnson, tenor (Prisoner)
Philip Kraus, baritone (Prisoner)
Chicago Symphony Chorus
Margaret Hillis, director
Recorded in Medinah Temple in May 1979 for London

Ludwig van Beethoven *Missa solemnis* in D Major, Op. 123
Sir Georg Solti, conductor
Victor Aitay, violin
Lucia Popp, soprano
Yvonne Minton, mezzo-soprano
Mallory Walker, tenor
Gwynne Howell, bass
Chicago Symphony Chorus
Margaret Hillis, director
Recorded in Medinah Temple in May 1977 for London
1978 Grammy Award for Best Choral Performance–Choral (other than opera)

Ludwig van Beethoven *Missa solemnis* in D Major, Op. 123
Daniel Barenboim, conductor
Tina Kiberg, soprano
Waltraud Meier, mezzo-soprano
John Aler, tenor
Robert Holl, bass
Chicago Symphony Chorus
Margaret Hillis, director
Recorded in Orchestra Hall in April and May 1993 for Erato

Ludwig van Beethoven Symphony No. 9 in D Minor, Op. 125
Fritz Reiner, conductor
Phyllis Curtin, soprano
Florence Kopleff, contralto
John McCollum, tenor
Donald Gramm, bass-baritone
Chicago Symphony Chorus
Margaret Hillis, director
Recorded in Orchestra Hall in May 1961 for RCA

Ludwig van Beethoven Symphony No. 9 in D Minor, Op. 125
Pilar Lorengar, soprano
Yvonne Minton, mezzo-soprano
René Kollo, tenor
Martti Talvela, bass
Chicago Symphony Chorus
Margaret Hillis, director
Recorded at the Krannert Center for the Performing Arts, University of Illinois at
Urbana-Champaign, in May 1972 for London

Ludwig van Beethoven Symphony No. 9 in D Minor, Op. 125
Sir Georg Solti, conductor
Jessye Norman, soprano
Reinhild Runkel, mezzo-soprano
Robert Schunk, tenor
Hans Sotin, bass
Chicago Symphony Chorus
Margaret Hillis, director
Recorded in Medinah Temple in September 1986 for London
1987 Grammy Award for Best Orchestral Recording

Hector Berlioz *La damnation de Faust*, Op. 24
Sir Georg Solti, conductor
Frederica von Stade, mezzo-soprano
Kenneth Riegel, tenor
José van Dam, bass-baritone
Malcolm King, bass
Chicago Symphony Chorus
Margaret Hillis, director
Glen Ellyn Children's Chorus
Doreen Rao, director
Recorded in Medinah Temple in May 1981 for London
1982 Grammy Award for Best Choral Performance (other than opera)
1982 Grand Prix du Disque for Choral Music

Hector Berlioz *La damnation de Faust*, Op. 24
Sir Georg Solti, conductor
Anne Sofie von Otter, mezzo-soprano
Keith Lewis, tenor
José van Dam, bass-baritone
Peter Rose, bass
Chicago Symphony Chorus
Margaret Hillis, director
Choristers of Westminster Cathedral
Rodney Greenberg, director
Recorded at the Royal Albert Hall in London in August 1989 for London (video)

Hector Berlioz Part 2 from *Romeo and Juliet*, Dramatic Symphony, Op. 17

James Levine, conductor

Men of the Chicago Symphony Chorus

Margaret Hillis, director

Recorded at the Ravinia Festival in July 1988 by WFMT and released on *A Tribute to James Levine* (*From the Archives*, Vol. 18) in 2004

Johannes Brahms *Ein deutsches Requiem,* Op. 45

Sir Georg Solti, conductor

Kiri Te Kanawa, soprano

Bernd Weikl, baritone

Chicago Symphony Chorus

Margaret Hillis, director

Recorded in Medinah Temple in May 1978 for London

1979 Grammy Award for Best Choral Performance–Classical (other than opera)

Johannes Brahms *Ein deutsches Requiem,* Op. 45

James Levine, conductor

Kathleen Battle, soprano

Håkan Hagegård, baritone

Chicago Symphony Chorus

Margaret Hillis, director

Recorded in Orchestra Hall in July 1983 for RCA

1984 Grammy Award for Best Choral Performance (other than opera)

Johannes Brahms *Ein deutsches Requiem,* Op. 45

Daniel Barenboim, conductor

Janet Williams, soprano

Thomas Hampson, baritone

Chicago Symphony Chorus

Margaret Hillis, director

Recorded in Orchestra Hall in September 1992 and January 1993 for Erato

Anton Bruckner *Helgoland*
Daniel Barenboim, conductor
Men of the Chicago Symphony Chorus
Margaret Hillis, director
Recorded in Orchestra Hall in March 1979 for Deutsche Grammophon

Anton Bruckner Psalm 150
Daniel Barenboim, conductor
Ruth Welting, soprano
Chicago Symphony Chorus
Margaret Hillis, director
Recorded in Orchestra Hall in March 1979 for Deutsche Grammophon

Anton Bruckner *Te Deum*
Daniel Barenboim, conductor
Jessye Norman, soprano
Yvonne Minton, mezzo-soprano
David Rendall, tenor
Samuel Ramey, bass
Chicago Symphony Chorus
Margaret Hillis, director
Recorded in Orchestra Hall in March 1981 for Deutsche Grammophon

Claude Debussy *Trois chansons de Charles d'Orléans*
Margaret Hillis, conductor
Laura Stanley, soprano
Kathleen Karnes-Ferrin, mezzo-soprano
Karen Zajac, mezzo-soprano
Thomas Dymit, tenor
Dale Prest, baritone
Chicago Symphony Chorus
Margaret Hillis, director
Recorded in Orchestra Hall in February 1982 by WFMT and released on
Chicago Symphony Chorus: A Fiftieth Anniversary Celebration (*From the Archives*, Vol. 22) in 2008

Claude Debussy Nocturnes
Sir Georg Solti, conductor
Women of the Chicago Symphony Chorus
Margaret Hillis, director
Recorded in Orchestra Hall in January 1990 for London

Jerry Downs *Bear Down, Chicago Bears*
Sir Georg Solti, conductor
Chicago Symphony Chorus
Margaret Hillis, director
Recorded in Orchestra Hall in January 1986 by WFMT and released on
    Chicago Symphony Chorus: A Fortieth Anniversary Celebration (*From the
    Archives,* Vol. 13) in 1998
(Jerry Downs was a pseudonym for Al Hoffman)

Jerry Downs *Bear Down, Chicago Bears*
Sir Georg Solti, conductor
Chicago Symphony Chorus
Margaret Hillis, drector
Recorded in Orchestra Hall in January 1986 for London
(Jerry Downs was a pseudonym for Al Hoffman)

Edward Elgar *Pomp and Circumstance* Marches Nos. 1, 2, 3, and 4 (arr. Peter
    Schickele)
James Levine, conductor
Kathleen Battle, soprano
Chicago Symphony Chorus
Margaret Hillis, director
Recorded in Medinah Temple in April 1994 for Disney

Gabriel Fauré Requiem in D Minor, Op. 48

Jean Martinon, conductor

Agnes Giebel, soprano

Gérard Souzay, baritone

Chicago Symphony Chorus

Margaret Hillis, director

Recorded in Orchestra Hall in April 1968 by WFMT and released on *Chicago Symphony Chorus: A Fortieth Anniversary Celebration* (*From the Archives*, Vol. 13) in 1998

Stephen Foster *Camptown Races* (arr. David Cullen)

James Levine, conductor

Marilyn Horne, mezzo-soprano

Chicago Symphony Chorus

Margaret Hillis, director

Cheryl Frazes Hill, assistant director

Recorded at the Ravinia Festival in July 1992 by WFMT and released on *Chicago Symphony Chorus: A Fiftieth Anniversary Celebration* (*From the Archives*, Vol. 22) in 2008

Giovanni Gabrieli Jubilate Deo and Miserere mei Deus from *Sacrae symphoniae*

Claudio Abbado, conductor

Chicago Symphony Chorus

Margaret Hillis, director

Recorded in Orchestra Hall in March 1983 by WFMT and released on *Chicago Symphony Chorus: A Fortieth Anniversary Celebration* (*From the Archives*, Vol. 13) in 1998

George Frideric Handel He rebuked the Red Sea, He led them through the deep,
But the waters overwhelmed their enemies, Moses and the children of Israel, and I
will sing to the Lord from *Israel in Egypt*
Margaret Hillis, conductor
Chicago Symphony Chorus
Margaret Hillis, director
Recorded in Orchestra Hall in December 1982 by WFMT and released on *Chicago
   Symphony Chorus: A Fortieth Anniversary Celebration (From the Archives,*
   Vol. 13) in 1998

George Frideric Handel *Messiah*
Sir Georg Solti, conductor
Kiri Te Kanawa, soprano
Anne Gjevang, contralto
Keith Lewis, tenor
Gwynne Howell, bass
Chicago Symphony Chorus
Margaret Hillis, director
Recorded in Orchestra Hall in October 1984 for London

Joseph Haydn *Die Jahreszeiten*
Sir Georg Solti, conductor
Ruth Ziesak, soprano
Uwe Heilmann, tenor
René Pape, bass
Chicago Symphony Chorus
Margaret Hillis, director
Recorded in Orchestra Hall in May 1992 for London

Joseph Haydn *Die Schöpfung*
Sir Georg Solti, conductor
Norma Burrowes, soprano
Sylvia Greenberg, soprano
Rüdiger Wohlers, tenor
James Morris, bass-baritone
Siegmund Nimsgern, bass-baritone
Chicago Symphony Chorus
Margaret Hillis, director
Recorded in Orchestra Hall in November 1981 for London
1983 Grammy Award for Best Choral Performance (other than opera)

Joseph Haydn *Die Schöpfung*
Sir Georg Solti, conductor
Ruth Ziesak, soprano
Herbert Lippert, tenor
Anton Scharinger, bass-baritone
René Pape, bass
Chicago Symphony Chorus
Margaret Hillis, director
Recorded in Orchestra Hall in October and November 1993 for London

Al Hoffman (see Jerry Downs)

Gustav Holst *The Planets*, Op. 32
James Levine, conductor
Women of the Chicago Symphony Chorus
Margaret Hillis, director
Recorded in Orchestra Hall in June 1989 for Deutsche Grammophon

Charles Ives Orchestral Set No. 2
Morton Gould, conductor
Members of the Chicago Symphony Chorus
Margaret Hillis, director
Robert Schweitzer, assistant director
Recorded in Medinah Temple in February 1967 for RCA

Charles Ives Symphony No. 4
Michael Tilson Thomas, conductor
Mary Sauer, piano
Members of the Chicago Symphony Chorus
Margaret Hillis, director
Richard Garrin, associate director
Recorded in Medinah Temple in April 1989 for Sony

Charles Ives A Symphony: *New England Holidays*
Michael Tilson Thomas, conductor
Fred Spector, jew's harp
Chicago Symphony Chorus
Margaret Hillis, director
Recorded in Medinah Temple in May 1986 for CBS

Zoltán Kodály *Psalmus Hungaricus*, Op. 13
Sir Georg Solti, conductor
Dennis Bailey, tenor
Chicago Symphony Chorus
Margaret Hillis, director
Glen Ellyn Children's Chorus
Doreen Rao, director
Recorded in Orchestra Hall in November 1982 by WFMT and released on
   Chicago Symphony Orchestra: The First 100 Years in 1990

Franz Liszt *Eine Faust-Symphonie in drei Charakterbildern*
Sir Georg Solti, conductor
Siegfried Jerusalem, tenor
Men of the Chicago Symphony Chorus
Margaret Hillis, director
Recorded in Orchestra Hall in January 1986 for London
1986 Grammy Award for Best Classical Orchestral Recording

Gustav Mahler Symphony No. 2 in C Minor *(Resurrection)*
Claudio Abbado, conductor
Carol Neblett, soprano
Marilyn Horne, mezzo-soprano
Chicago Symphony Chorus
Margaret Hillis, director
Recorded in Medinah Temple in February 1976 for Deutsche Grammophon

Gustav Mahler Symphony No. 2 in C Minor *(Resurrection)*
Sir Georg Solti, conductor
Isobel Buchanan, soprano
Mira Zakai, contralto
Chicago Symphony Chorus
Margaret Hillis, director
Recorded in Medinah Temple in May 1980 for London
1981 Grammy Awards for Best Classical Album and Best Classical Orchestral Recording

Gustav Mahler Symphony No. 3 in D Minor
Jean Martinon, conductor
Regina Resnik, mezzo-soprano
Women of the Chicago Symphony Chorus
Margaret Hillis, director
Chicago Children's Choir
Christopher Moore, director
Recorded in Orchestra Hall in March 1967 by WFMT and released on *Chicago
   Symphony Orchestra in the Twentieth Century: Collector's Choice* in 2000

Gustav Mahler Symphony No. 3 in D Minor
James Levine, conductor
Marilyn Horne, mezzo-soprano
Women of the Chicago Symphony Chorus
Margaret Hillis, director
Glen Ellyn Children's Chorus
Doreen Rao, director
Recorded in Medinah Temple in July 1975 for RCA

Gustav Mahler Symphony No. 3 in D Minor
Sir Georg Solti, conductor
Helga Dernesch, mezzo-soprano
Women of the Chicago Symphony Chorus
Margaret Hillis, director
James Winfield, associate director
Glen Ellyn Children's Chorus
Doreen Rao, director
Recorded in Orchestra Hall in November 1982 and March 1983 for London

Gustav Mahler Part 1: Hymnus: *Veni, creator spiritus* from Symphony No. 8 in
    E-flat Major
James Levine, conductor
Carol Neblett, soprano
Judith Blegen, soprano
Jann Jaffe, soprano
Isola Jones, contralto
Birgit Finnilae, contralto
Kenneth Riegel, tenor
Ryan Edwards, baritone
John Cheek, bass
Chicago Symphony Chorus
Margaret Hillis, director
Glen Ellyn Children's Chorus
Doreen Rao, director
Recorded at the Ravinia Festival in July 1979 by WFMT and and released on
    Chicago Symphony Orchestra: The First 100 Years in 1990

Simeon Butler Marsh *Jesus, Lover of My Soul*
Michael Tilson Thomas, conductor
Richard Webster, organ
Members of the Chicago Symphony Chorus
Margaret Hillis, director
Richard Garrin, associate director
Recorded in Medinah Temple in April 1989 for Sony

Lowell Mason *Nearer, My God, to Thee*
Michael Tilson Thomas, conductor
Richard Webster, organ
Members of the Chicago Symphony Chorus
Margaret Hillis, director
Richard Garrin, associate director
Recorded in Medinah Temple in April 1989 for Sony

Felix Mendelssohn *A Midsummer Night's Dream*, Opp. 21 and 61
James Levine, conductor
Judith Blegen, soprano
Florence Quivar, mezzo-soprano
Women of the Chicago Symphony Chorus
Margaret Hillis, director
Recorded in Deutsche Grammophon in July 1984 for Deutsche Grammophon

Wolfgang Mozart *Kyrie* in D Minor, K. 341
Claudio Abbado, conductor
Chicago Symphony Chorus
Margaret Hillis, director
James Winfield, associate director
Recorded in Orchestra Hall in March 1983 by WFMT and and released on
    *Chicago Symphony Chorus: A Fiftieth Anniversary Celebration (From the
    Archives*, Vol. 22) in 2008

Wolfgang Mozart Lacrymosa from Requiem in D Minor, K. 626
Bruno Walter, conductor
Chicago Symphony Chorus
Margaret Hillis, director
Recorded in Orchestra Hall in March 1958 by WBAI (New York) and released
    on *Chicago Symphony Chorus: A Fortieth Anniversary Celebration (From the
    Archives,* Vol. 13) in 1998

Wolfgang Mozart Mass in C Major, K. 317 *(Coronation)*
Rafael Kubelík, conductor
Lucia Popp, soprano
Mira Zakai, contralto
Alexander Oliver, tenor
Malcolm King, bass
Chicago Symphony Chorus
Margaret Hillis, director
Recorded in Orchestra Hall in March 1980 by WFMT and released on *Chicago Symphony Chorus: A Fortieth Anniversary Celebration* (*From the Archives*, Vol. 13) in 1998

Wolfgang Mozart Mass in C Minor, K. 427
Sir Georg Solti, conductor
Marvis Martin, soprano
Anne Sofie von Otter, mezzo-soprano
Jerry Hadley, tenor
Malcom King, bass
Chicago Symphony Chorus
Margaret Hillis, director
Recorded in Orchestra Hall in October 1985 (with orchestral inserts from December 1978) by WFMT and released on *The Solti Years* (*From the Archives*, Vol. 14) in 1999

Modest Mussorgsky Coronation Scene from *Boris Godunov*
Claudio Abbado, conductor
Philip Langridge, tenor
Ruggero Raimondi, bass
Chicago Symphony Chorus
Margaret Hillis, director
Recorded in Orchestra Hall in November 1984 by WFMT and released on *Chicago Symphony Orchestra: The First 100 Years* in 1990

Modest Mussorgsky *Joshua*
Lucia Valentini-Terrani, mezzo-soprano
Philip Kraus, baritone
Chicago Symphony Chorus
Margaret Hillis, director
Recorded in Orchestra Hall in March 1981 by WFMT and released on *Chicago Symphony Chorus: A Fiftieth Anniversary Celebration* (*From the Archives*, Vol. 22) in 2008

Modest Mussorgsky Chorus of Priestesses from *Salammbô*
Women of the Chicago Symphony Chorus
Margaret Hillis, director
Recorded in Orchestra Hall in March 1981 by WFMT and released on *Chicago Symphony Chorus: A Fiftieth Anniversary Celebration* (*From the Archives*, Vol. 22) in 2008

Carl Orff *Carmina burana*
James Levine, conductor
June Anderson, soprano
Philip Creech, tenor
Bernd Weikl, baritone
Chicago Symphony Chorus
Margaret Hillis, director
Glen Ellyn Children's Chorus
Doreen Rao, director
Recorded in Orchestra Hall in July 1984 for Deutsche Grammophon
1986 Grammy Award for Best Choral Performance (other than opera)

Sergei Prokofiev *Alexander Nevsky*
Fritz Reiner, conductor
Rosalind Elias, mezzo-soprano
Chicago Symphony Chorus
Margaret Hillis, director
Recorded in Orchestra Hall in March 1959 for RCA

Ned Rorem *An American Oratorio*

Margaret Hillis, director

Donald Kaasch, tenor

Chicago Symphony Chorus

Margaret Hillis, director

Recorded in Orchestra Hall in April 1986 by WFMT and released on *Chicago Symphony Chorus: A Fortieth Anniversary Celebration* (*From the Archives*, Vol. 13) in 1998

Arnold Schoenberg Seht die Sonne from *Gurrelieder*

James Levine, conductor

Chicago Symphony Chorus

Margaret Hillis, director

Recorded at the Ravinia Festival in June 1987 by WFMT and released on *Chicago Symphony Chorus: A Fiftieth Anniversary Celebration* (*From the Archives*, Vol. 22) in 2008

Arnold Schoenberg *Moses und Aron*

Sir Georg Solti, conductor

Franz Mazura, speaker (Moses)

Philip Langridge, tenor (Aron)

Barbara Bonney, soprano (A Young Girl)

Daniel Harper, tenor (A Young Man)

Kurt Link, baritone (Another Man)

Aage Haugland, bass (Priest)

Mira Zakai, contralto (An Invalid Woman)

Herbert Wittges, baritone (Ephraimite)

Thomas Dymit, tenor (A Naked Youth)

Jean Braham and Barbara Pearson, sopranos; Cynthia Anderson and Karen Zajac, contraltos (Four Naked Virgins)

Kurt Link and Richard Cohn, baritones; Paul Grizzell, bass (Three Elders)

Sally Schweikert, soprano; Elizabeth Gottlieb, mezzo-soprano; Karen Brunssen, contralto; Roald Henderson, tenor; Bradley Nystrom, baritone; William Kirkwood, bass (Six Solo Voices in the Orchestra)

Chicago Symphony Chorus
Margaret Hillis, director
Members of the Glen Ellyn Children's Chorus
Doreen Rao, director
1985 Grammy Award for Best Opera Recording

Arnold Schoenberg Six Pieces for Male Chorus, Op. 35
Robert Craft, conductor
Men of the Chicago Symphony Chorus
Margaret Hillis, director
Recorded in April 1965 for Columbia

Franz Schubert *Gesang der Geister über den Wassern*, D. 714
Daniel Barenboim, conductor
Men of the Chicago Symphony Chorus
Margaret Hillis, director
Recorded in Orchestra Hall in May 1991 by WFMT and released on *Chicago
    Symphony Chorus: A Fortieth Anniversary Celebration* (*From the Archives*,
    Vol. 13) in 1998

John Stafford Smith *Star-Spangled Banner* (arr. Frederick Stock)
Sir Georg Solti, conductor
Chicago Symphony Chorus
Margaret Hillis, director
Recorded in Orchestra Hall in January 1986 for London

Richard Strauss *Die Tageszeiten*, Op. 76
Erich Leinsdorf, conductor
Men of the Chicago Symphony Chorus
James Winfield, director
Recorded in Orchestra Hall in November 1979 by WFMT and released on
    Chicago Symphony Chorus: A Fiftieth Anniversary Celebration (*From the
    Archives*, Vol. 22) in 2008

Igor Stravinsky *Oedipus rex*

James Levine, conductor

Philip Langridge, tenor (Oedipus)

Florence Quivar, mezzo-soprano (Jocasta)

James Morris, bass-baritone (Creon)

Jan-Hendrik Rootering, bass (Tiresias)

Donald Kaasch, tenor (Shepherd)

Jules Bastin, narrator

Men of the Chicago Symphony Chorus

Margaret Hillis, director

Recorded in Medinah Temple in July 1991 for Deutsche Grammophon

Igor Stravinsky *Symphony of Psalms*

James Levine, conductor

Chicago Symphony Chorus

Margaret Hillis, director

Recorded at the Ravinia Festival in June 1989 by WFMT and released on *Chicago Symphony Orchestra: The First 100 Years* in 1990

Traditional *I've just Come from the Fountain* (arr. Carl Davis)

James Levine, conductor

Marilyn Horne, mezzo-soprano

Chicago Symphony Chorus

Margaret Hillis, director

Cheryl Frazes Hill, assistant director

Recorded at the Ravinia Festival in July 1992 by WFMT and released on *Chicago Symphony Chorus: A Fiftieth Anniversary Celebration* (*From the Archives*, Vol. 22) in 2008

Ralph Vaughan Williams Scherzo: The Waves from Symphony No. 1 *(A Sea Symphony)*
Raymond Leppard, conductor
Chicago Symphony Chorus
Margaret Hillis, director
Recorded in Orchestra Hall in May 1980 by WFMT and released on *Chicago Symphony Chorus: A Fiftieth Anniversary Celebration (From the Archives*, Vol. 22) in 2008

Giuseppe Verdi Opera Choruses
Gli arredi festivi giù cadano infranti from *Nabucco*
Va, pensiero, sull'ali dorate from *Nabucco*
Gerusalem! from *I lombardi alla prima crociata*
O Signore, dal tetto natio from *I lombardi alla prima crociata*
Tre volte miagola from *Macbeth*
Patria oppressa from *Macbeth*
Le rube, gli stupri from *I masnadieri*
Zitti zitti moviamo a vendetta from *Rigoletto*
Vedi! le fosche notturne spoglie from *Il trovatore*
Squilli, echeggi la tromba guerriera from *Il trovatore*
Noi siamo zingarelle . . . di Madride noi siam mattadori from *La traviata*
Posa in pace from *Un ballo in maschera*
Spuntato ecco il dì d'esultanza from *Don Carlo*
Gloria all'Egitto from *Aida*
Fuoco di gioia from *Otello*
Sanctus from *Messa da Requiem*
Sir Georg Solti, conductor
Marsha Waxman, mezzo-soprano
Richard Cohn, baritone
David Huneryager, bass
Chicago Symphony Chorus
Margaret Hillis, director
Terry Edwards, guest chorus master
Recorded in Orchestra Hall in November 1989 for London

Giuseppe Verdi *Otello*
Sir Georg Solti, conductor
Luciano Pavarotti, tenor (Otello)
Kiri Te Kanawa, soprano (Desdemona)
Leo Nucci, baritone (Iago)
Elzbieta Ardam, mezzo-soprano (Emilia)
Anthony Rolfe Johnson, tenor (Cassio)
John Keyes, tenor (Roderigo)
Alan Opie, baritone (Montano)
Dimitri Kavrakos, bass (Lodovico)
Richard Cohn, baritone (A Herald)
Chicago Symphony Chorus
Margaret Hillis, director
Terry Edwards, guest chorus master
Metropolitan Opera Children's Chorus
Elena Doria, director
Recorded in Orchestra Hall and Carnegie Hall in April 1991 for London

Giuseppe Verdi *Quattro pezzi sacri*
Sir Georg Solti, conductor
Jo Ann Pickens, soprano
Chicago Symphony Chorus
Margaret Hillis, director
Recorded in Medinah Temple in May 1977 and May 1978 for London

Giuseppe Verdi *Messa da Requiem*
Sir Georg Solti, conductor
Leontyne Price, soprano
Janet Baker, mezzo-soprano
Veriano Luchetti, tenor
José van Dam, bass-baritone
Chicago Symphony Chorus
Margaret Hillis, director
Recorded in Medinah Temple in June 1977 for RCA
1977 Grammy Award for Best Choral Performance (other than opera)

Giuseppe Verdi *Messa da Requiem*
Daniel Barenboim, conductor
Alessandra Marc, soprano
Waltraud Meier, mezzo-soprano
Plácido Domingo, tenor
Ferruccio Furlanetto, bass
Chicago Symphony Chorus
Margaret Hillis, director
Recorded in Orchestra Hall in September 1993 for Erato

Giuseppe Verdi Sanctus and Libera me from *Messa da Requiem*
Jean Martinon, conductor
Martina Arroyo, soprano
Chicago Symphony Chorus
Margaret Hillis, director
Recorded in Orchestra Hall in November 1968 by WFMT and released on
    Chicago Symphony Chorus: A Fiftieth Anniversary Celebration (*From the
    Archives*, Vol. 22) in 2008

Richard Wagner *Der fliegende Holländer*
Sir Georg Solti, conductor
Norman Bailey, bass-baritone (Dutchman)
Janis Martin, soprano (Senta)
Martti Talvela, bass (Daland)
René Kollo, tenor (Erik)
Werner Krenn, tenor (Steersman)
Isola Jones, mezzo-soprano (Mary)
Chicago Symphony Chorus
Margaret Hillis, director
Recorded in Medinah Temple in May 1976 for London

William Walton *Belshazzar's Feast*
Sir Georg Solti, conductor
David Ward, baritone
Chicago Symphony Chorus
Margaret Hillis, director
Recorded in Orchestra Hall in November 1976 by WFMT and released on
Chicago Symphony Chorus: A Fiftieth Anniversary Celebration (From the
Archives, Vol. 22) in 2008

Joseph Philbrick Webster *Sweet By and By*
Michael Tilson Thomas, conductor
Richard Webster, organ
Members of the Chicago Symphony Chorus
Margaret Hillis, director
Richard Garrin, associate director
Recorded in Medinah Temple in April 1989 for Sony

Heinrich Christopher Zeuner *Ye Christian Heralds*
Michael Tilson Thomas, conductor
Richard Webster, organ
Members of the Chicago Symphony Chorus
Margaret Hillis, director
Richard Garrin, associate director
Recorded in Medinah Temple in April 1989 for Sony

APPENDIX 3
LIST OF INTERVIEWS

I am extremely grateful to the people listed below. Participants include Hillis family members, dear friends, treasured conductor colleagues, symphony orchestra conductors, and many associated with Margaret Hillis through her years with the Chicago Symphony Orchestra, the American Concert Choir, the Collegiate Chorale, the Elgin Symphony Orchestra, the Kokomo Symphony Orchestra, Chorus America, the National Endowment for the Arts, Northwestern University, The Juilliard School, the International Music Foundation, and Hillis's American Choral Foundation. Their recollections, generously shared, added greatly to my understanding of Margaret Hillis's life and accomplishments.

Paul Aliapoulios

Douglas Asbury

Mary Anne Beatty

Madison Bolt

Donna Bruni

Karen Brunssen

Elizabeth Buccheri

William Robert Bucker

Diane Busko-Bryks

Charlotte Carlson (Boehm DeWindt)

Clark Chaffe

Frank Conlon

Joan Catoni Conlon

Katherine Connor

Ted Connor

Sir Andrew Davis

Joseph Fabbioli

JoAnne Falletta

Anne Feldman

Henry Fogel

Roberta Frazes Goldman

Vance George

Martha Gilmer

Andrea Goodman

Jerry Goodman

Gertrude Grisham

Kurt Hansen

Robert Hanson

Carleen Hardesty (Dixon Webb)

Connie Hillis

Carol Hillis

Elwood "Bud" Hillis

Gregory Hillis

Jeff Hillis

Joseph Hillis

Roldan Stephen Hillis

Donald Horisberger

Phillip Huscher

Isola Jones

Melvin Kaplan

Hugh Kaylor

Dennis Keene

Kathye Kerchner

Tina Laughlin

Kurt Link

Marsha Waxman Link

Sherrill Milnes

Rebecca Moan

David Murray

Brenda Nelson-Strauss

Frank Nemhauser

Robert Page

Alice Parker

Doreen Rao

Rosalind Rees

Mark Riggelman

James Sampson

Jane Samuelson

Jane Scharf

Leonard Slatkin

Gregg Smith

Sheldon Soffer

Stanley Sperber

Lee Anne Tuason

Susan Turbyfill

Frank Villella

Dale Warland

Ruth Warland

Jon Washburn

Eric Weimer

William Weinert

Cathy Weingart-Ryan

Harriet Wingreen

Duain Wolfe

John Wustman

James Yarbrough

APPENDIX 4
RESOURCES FOR MARGARET HILLIS'S METHODS OF SCORE STUDY, SCORE MARKING, REHEARSAL PLANNING, AND CONDUCTING GESTURES

Margaret Hillis marks her notes as she rehearses Mussorgsky's *Boris Godunov*, October 1984.
(Rosenthal Archives of the Chicago Symphony Orchestra Association)

Score Study and Score Marking
(See Appendix 5 for examples and guide to markings.)

Shrock, Dennis. "An Interview with Margaret Hillis on Score Study." *Choral Journal* 31, no. 7 (February 1, 1991): pp. 7–14.

Shrock engages Hillis in an interview about her score analysis procedures. Hillis describes her approach, from her initial overview of the score to the rehearsal planning phase. She addresses her score marking techniques in detail and describes all that she considers in the preparation of a score.

Conlon, Joan Catoni. *Wisdom, Wit, and Will: Women Choral Conductors on Their Art.* Chicago: GIA Publications, 2009.

Dr. Conlon's book provides a detailed exploration of Margaret Hillis's approach to the score. Included are examples of Hillis's charts, which helped her organize orchestra rehearsals. For example, she would identify which movements involved the largest numbers of instrumentalists and would rehearse those movements first. Also described is Hillis's "home study chart" system, which she would use to organize the entire series of Chorus rehearsals. These charts would also provide her singers useful information about what would be covered in each rehearsal, enabling them to prepare in advance of an upcoming rehearsal or practice what they missed when absent from a rehearsal. This information is covered in the chapter entitled "Margaret Hillis," written by Joan Whittemore, one of the contributing authors of Dr. Conlon's book.

Wagar, Jeannine. *Conductors in Conversation: Fifteen Contemporary Conductors Discuss Their Lives and Professions.* Boston: G.K. Hall and Co., 1991.

In this interview, Hillis describes her score analysis process, focusing on harmonic analysis. She talks at length about determining how chords function "as a tonic, subdominant, or dominant; whether a Neapolitan sixth is a substitute dominant or has a dominant function." She claims this helps her to determine where the leading tones are, always insisting that leading tones must be sung high. She also discusses her approach to a new score, first studying large sections, focusing next on smaller details within each section, and then returning again to the large sections of the piece. Hillis also describes her rehearsal techniques based upon her score study.

Developing Choral Tone—How Hillis Rehearses a Chorus

Keene, Dennis. "An Interview with Margaret Hillis." *The American Organist* 26 (January 1992): pp. 69–71.

Keene interviews Hillis on her approach to rehearsing a chorus. Hillis discusses her concepts of tone, including her ideas about vibrato, which she describes as a "color tool." "The two things you are really dealing with when you work with a chorus or an orchestra are the musicality of the people and their ears." Much of the article is spent on how Hillis approaches choral tone, including the way in which gesture influences sound.

Glenn, Carole J. "Choral Practices in the United States." Unpublished M.A. thesis, Occidental College, 1971.

Glenn interviews prominent choral conductors of the early 1970s, including Margaret Hillis, regarding their approach to developing choral tone, auditioning singers, communicating with the choir, and objectives for their chorus, along with discussions of their careers. Among other things, Hillis talks about how she handles blend within the chorus, particularly with solo singers.

Feldman, Ann. Host of *Noteworthy Women* radio series, a ten-program series celebrating Women's History Month. The first four programs were syndicated by WFMT Fine Arts network in 1995. A recording of this program is in the Margaret Hillis Collection, Rosenthal Archives of the Chicago Symphony Orchestra Association.

Dr. Feldman engages Margaret Hillis in detailed conversations as one musician to another. Dr. Feldman, an accomplished musician herself, inquires about Hillis's concept of choral tone. Hillis explains her process of determining the appropriate choral timbre of each work through analysis of the score. As Hillis explains, "Each great composer has his own voice [which she describes as the sound, the quality]. . . . I try to find that voice. "Bruckner had a different voice than Beethoven, Mozart very different from Verdi." Hillis also discusses how she prepares the Chicago Symphony Chorus for various conductors and how the sound changes very little despite the variety of conductors they work with. Hillis also discusses her rehearsal approach and how each piece dictates the way she organizes her sequence of rehearsals. She used Schoenberg's *Moses and Aaron* as an example.

The Gestural Legacy of Margaret Hillis

Greenlee, Robert. "The Gestural Legacy of Margaret Hillis." *Choral Journal* 48, no. 3 (2007): pp. 18–25.

The article covers Hillis's philosophy of gesture, created as a result of score study. Greenlee quotes Hillis, "There are gestures that get results, but I use them from the score out." Also discussed in this article is Hillis's conducting sound as a "physical phenomenon." Her understated gestures are dissected along with a detailed description of motion and body position in a variety of musical examples.

REHEARSAL TECHNIQUES APPLIED TO THE FIRST MOVEMENT OF BRAHMS'S *A GERMAN REQUIEM*

Frazes Hill, Cheryl. "The Rehearsal Techniques of Margaret Hillis: Their Development and Application to Brahms's *A German Requiem*." *Choral Journal* 43, no. 2 (October 2002): pp. 9–32.

The article provides an overview of how Margaret Hillis developed her methods of score study and rehearsal techniques following her early training at Juilliard with Robert Shaw and Julius Herford. Hillis became dedicated to achieving the same high level of musicianship in her chorus that she expected of an orchestra and developed rehearsal strategies to fulfill that mission. Using the first movement of Brahms's *A German Requiem* as an example, Frazes Hill describes Hillis's approach to color, intonation, dynamics, phrasing, text, and other details based upon her score analysis. Hillis's approach to every rehearsal was strategic. Though she rarely discussed analytical detail, Hillis always rehearsed structurally, giving the chorus an understanding of a work through a carefully planned series of rehearsals.

REHEARSAL TECHNIQUES APPLIED TO ANTON BRUCKNER'S MASS IN E MINOR

Hillis, Margaret, "Anton Bruckner's Mass in E minor: A Performer's Guide." *Journal of the Conductor's Guild* (Winter/Fall 2000): pp. 26–30.

Hillis provides a detailed approach to preparing a chorus and orchestra in the performance of Bruckner's Mass in E Minor. She talks about specific issues she addresses in each movement of the Mass, including her approach to phrasing, dynamics, balance, tuning, color, and articulation, as well as treatment of voices with consideration to the instrumentation throughout the work.

Diction

Dennen, Janel Jo. "Margaret Hillis and the Chicago Symphony Chorus: Perspective and Interview." *Choral Journal* (November 1982).

In this brief interview, Hillis discusses her approach to handling diction with a chorus, particularly in the early phase of a rehearsal series.

Choral Preparation and Her Overall Approach to Working with a Chorus She Prepares for Others to Conduct

Hillis, Margaret. Interview by Norman Pellegrini. Transcribed by Stanley Livengood. Margaret Hillis Collection, Rosenthal Archives of the Chicago Symphony Orchestra Association, October 6, 1997.

In this last interview Hillis gave five months prior to her passing, she discusses her approach to achieving color and balance, particularly within sections of heavily textured orchestration, and how she created the "Margaret Hillis sound" she was known for. Hillis discusses her approach to achieving good intonation, how she treats diction, and her method of creating ensemble with soloist-quality voices. Hillis also describes her approach to score study.

Bentz, Jon. "Interview of Margaret Hillis Director Chicago Symphony Orchestra, September 19, 1989, Archives Committee, Oral History Project, 1992." Margaret Hillis Collection, Rosenthal Archives of the Chicago Symphony Orchestra Association.

In this interview, Hillis describes how she rehearses a chorus structurally to help them internalize the form of a work. She also explains her approach to articulation and how it must be uniform, even when she is preparing the chorus for a conductor who may end up using a different articulation. Hillis emphasizes that a chorus already consistent in one method will be easier to modify into a different articulation. Hillis describes the collaborative process of preparing the Chorus for other conductors with specific details about how she prepared a chorus for Maestros Carlo Maria Giulini, Georg Solti, and James Levine.

General Principles in Margaret Hillis's Preparation of Choral Singers in the Chicago Symphony Chorus

Chicago Symphony Chorus Master Class Tape from Master Class Series (a
VHS tape that has been converted digitally entitled "The Art of Choral
Singing"). The script ("The Choral Singer," July 1984) of the video, the
VHS tape, and the digital version are in the Margaret Hillis Collection,
Rosenthal Archives of the Chicago Symphony Orchestra Association

On this video, Hillis demonstrates procedures for rehearsing a chorus using
a small ensemble from the Chicago Symphony Chorus. Hillis shows how
she approaches choral tone, diction, and demonstrates how she works with
professional singers to develop their rehearsal techniques, which she states
all singers must have. She also refers to a choral handbook she created for
the Chorus called "At Rehearsals" (see Appendix 9), which provides chorus
members with suggested ways to mark their scores along with other helpful
information for managing diction in multiple languages.

Application of Hillis's Score Study Method

Brahms's *A German Requiem* Master class in score analysis. Margaret Hillis
Collection, Rosenthal Archives of the Chicago Symphony Orchestra
Association.

On this video, Hillis goes through a measure-by-measure analysis and
rehearsal approach to Brahms's *A German Requiem*. The presentation is
direct, straightforward, and gives the viewer an in-depth exposure to Hillis's
analysis of a work and how she transforms her score study into a rehearsal
approach. The recording is found in the Margaret Hillis Collection, Rosenthal
Archives of the Chicago Symphony Orchestra Association.

Snow, Sandra. *Choral Conducting/Teaching: Real World Strategies for Success.* DVD. Chicago: GIA Publications, 2009.

Sandra Snow's DVD is illustrative of the way in which Margaret Hillis's score analysis informs substantive, interactive, and engaging rehearsal techniques. The video provides instruction in how a conductor transfers the discoveries from a "Hillis-style" score study and score marking regimen into rehearsal strategies. Snow recognizes the influence of Margaret Hillis and those who studied with her, acknowledging the DVD as "an extension of [Hillis's] potent ideas regarding score analysis and rehearsal technique."

APPENDIX 5
EXAMPLES OF MARGARET HILLIS'S BARLINE ANALYSIS AND SCORE MARKING TECHNIQUES

*To view these examples in full color, visit **www.giamusic.com/margarethillis***

WALTON: *BELSHAZZAR'S FEAST*
Publisher: Oxford University Press
p. 12

BACH: MASS IN B MINOR
Publisher: Barenreiter (1954)
pp. 34–35

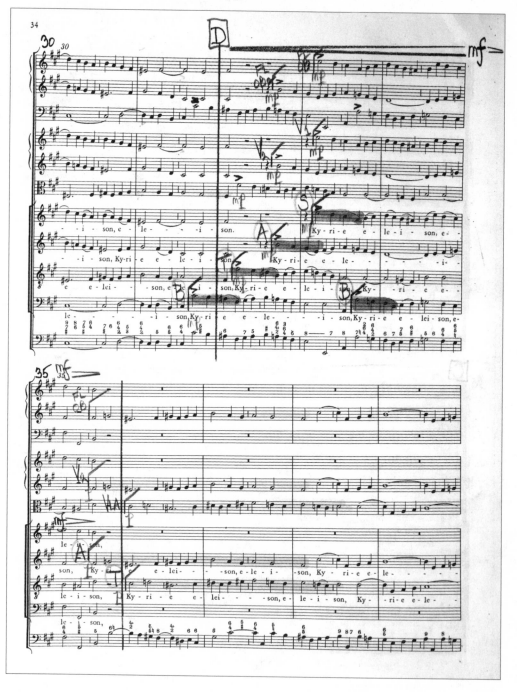

BACH: MASS IN B MINOR (CONT.)

Mahler: Symphony No. 8
Publisher: Universal (1911)
pp. 54–55

MAHLER: SYMPHONY NO. 8 (CONT.)

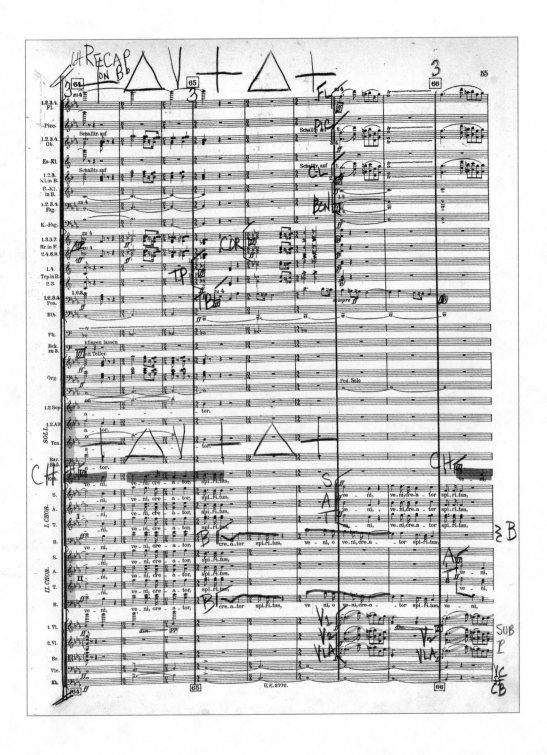

SIGNS AND SIGNALS

p. 2

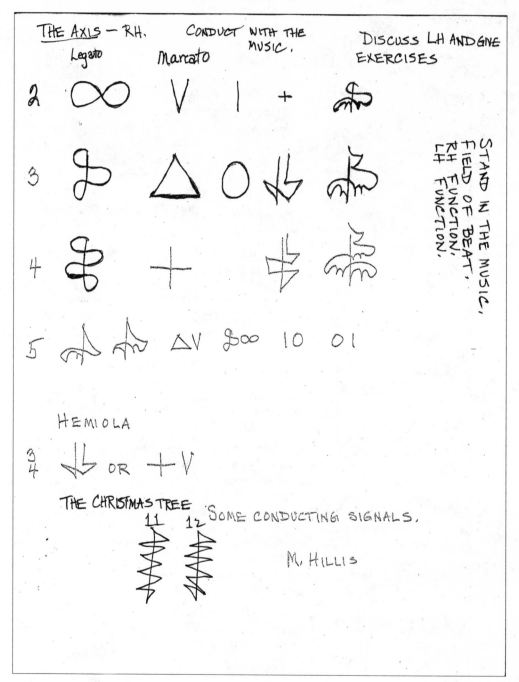

Igor Stravinsky: *Les noces*
Publisher: Edwin F. Kalmus

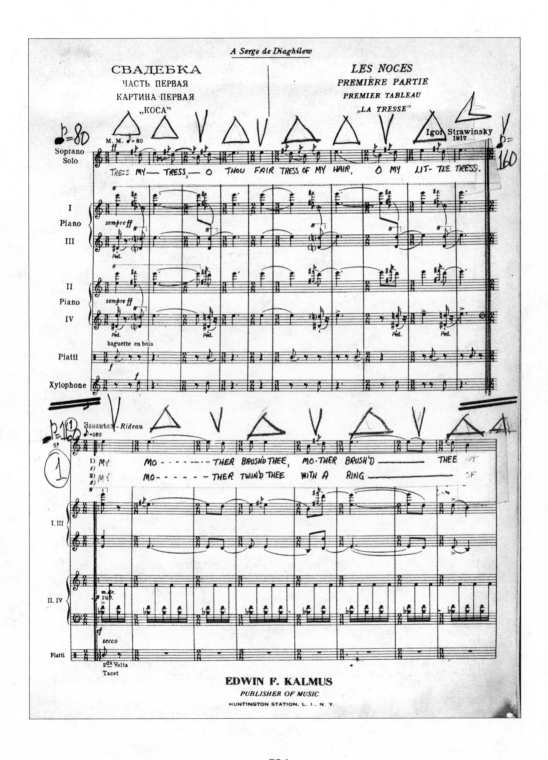

BEETHOVEN: *MISSA SOLEMNIS*
Publisher: G. Schirmer
pp. 132–134

Beethoven: *Missa solemnis* (Cont.)

BEETHOVEN: *MISSA SOLEMNIS* (CONT.)

Appendix 6
Hillis Charts for Home Study and Rehearsal Organization

*To view these examples in full color, visit **www.giamusic.com/margarethillis***

Home study chart of Bach's Mass in B Minor.
(Margaret Hillis Collection, Rosenthal Archives of the Chicago Symphony Orchestra Association)

Margaret Hillis created charts to help her determine the number of rehearsals she would need for each movement of a work. The chart indicates the divisi (number of sections) in each movement, the page number in the orchestra score, the page number in the chorus score, and her assessment of difficulty in each movement, indicated by the number of "x" markings. She determined "Confiteor" to be the most difficult movement of this piece. The more difficult the movement, the more rehearsals it received. Check marks indicate which movements she planned to cover in each rehearsal, with the scheduled rehearsal date listed at the top of the chart. As concert time drew nearer, more movements would be covered in one rehearsal.

Hillis used these charts to encourage her singers to study their music at home. She would also use these charts to organize her rehearsal time in such a way that she would make sure to cover a piece in a strategic way so as to have it prepared thoroughly. She also kept track of what she covered in a rehearsal. The red markings over a check mark indicate that in rehearsal the movement was covered. When a check mark was not given the red marking, it alerted her to make sure she covered it in the next rehearsal. This system kept Hillis and her singers organized and made rehearsals predictable so that if a singer missed a rehearsal, they knew what they missed and should review before returning the next week. Hillis would create her charts after doing a thorough score study, which helped her predict how much rehearsal time each section of a piece required. Her rehearsals were well planned and succeeded in the Chorus's thorough preparation for a concert series.

MESSIAH
G. F. Handel

No. / Movement	Keys	Vocal Reduction	Orchestra Score	Chorus	Soprano	Alto	Tenor	Bass	2 Oboes	2 Bassoons	2 Trumpets	Organ	Harpsichord	Timpani	6 Violin I	6 Violin II	4 Viola	3 Cello	2 Bass
PART THE FIRST																			
1. Overture	E mi	1	1						✓	✓		✓			6	6	4	3	2
2. Recit. Comfort ye	E	4	6				✓					✓							
3. Air Ev'ry valley	E	6	8				✓			1		✓			6	6	4	3	2
4. Chor. And the glory of the Lord	A	11	13	✓					✓	✓		✓	✓		6	6	4	3	2
5. Recit. Thus saith the Lord	D mi–A	19	23					✓				✓			1	1	1	1	1
6. Air But who may abide	D mi	21	25			✓				1		✓			1	1	1	1	1
7. Chor. And he shall purify	G mi	35	41	✓					✓	✓		✓	✓		6	6	4	3	2
8. Recit. Behold, a virgin shall conceive	D–A	41	48			✓						✓						1	
9. Air + Chor. O thou that tellest	D	41	48	✓		✓			✓	✓		✓	✓		6	6	4	3	2
10. Recit. For behold, darkness	B mi–F#	50	57					✓		1		✓			1	1	1	1	1
11. Air The people that walked	B mi	51	59					✓		1		✓			1	1	1	1	1
12. Chor. For unto us a child is born	G	55	62	✓					✓	✓		✓	✓		6	6	4	3	2
13. Pifa Pastorale Symphony	C	65	74							1		✓			6	6	4	3	2
14A. Recit. There were shepherds	C	66	75		✓							✓						1	
14B. Recit. And lo, the angel of the Lord	F–Bb	66	75		✓							✓			1	1	1	1	1
15. Recit. And the angel said	A6–F#	67	76		✓							✓						1	
16. Recit. And suddenly	D	67	76		✓							✓			1	1	1	1	1
17. Chor. Glory to God	D	68	77	✓					✓	✓	✓	✓	✓		6	6	4	3	2
18. Air Rejoice greatly	Bb	73	83		✓					1		✓			1	1		1	
19. Recit. Then shall the eyes	D6–A	79	88			✓						✓						1	
20. Air He shall feed his flock	F–Bb	81	89		✓	✓				1		✓			1	1	1	1	1
21. Chor. His yoke is easy	Bb	86	95	✓					✓	✓		✓	✓		6	6	4	3	2
PART THE SECOND																			
22. Chor. Behold the Lamb of God	G mi	91	101	✓					✓	✓		✓	✓		6	6	4	3	2
23. Air He was despised	Eb	94	105			✓				1		✓			1	1	1	1	1
24. Chor. Surely he hath borne	F mi	98	110	✓					✓	✓		✓	✓		6	6	4	3	2
25. Chor. And with his stripes	F mi–C	102	114	✓					✓	✓		✓	✓		6	6	4	3	2
26. Chor. All we like sheep	F–F mi	106	120	✓					✓	✓		✓	✓		6	6	4	3	2
27. Recit. All they that see him	Bb mi–Eb	114	131				✓					✓			1	1	1	1	1
28. Chor. He trusted in God	C mi	115	132	✓					✓	✓		✓	✓		6	6	4	3	2
29. Recit. Thy rebuke	Ab–Bb	122	140				✓					✓			1	1	1	1	
30. Air Behold and see	B mi–B	123	142				✓					✓			1	1	1	1	1
31. Recit. He was cut off	B mi–E	124	143				✓					✓			1	1	1	1	1
32. Air But thou didst not leave	A	124	143				✓			1		✓			1	1		1	1
33. Chor. Lift up your heads	F	127	145	✓					✓	✓		✓	✓		6	6	4	3	2
34. Recit. Unto which of the angels	A6–A	134	154				✓					✓						1	
35. Chor. Let all the angels of God	D	134	155	✓					✓	✓		✓	✓		6	6	4	3	2
36. Air Thou art gone up on high	D mi	238	265					✓		1		✓			1	1		1	
37. Chor. The Lord gave the word	Bb	146	168	✓					✓	✓		✓	✓		6	6	4	3	2
38. Air How beautiful are the feet	G mi	149	171		✓					1		✓			1	1		1	
39. Chor. Their sound is gone out	Eb	151	173	✓					✓	✓		✓	✓		6	6	4	3	2
40. Air Why do the nations	C–E mi	155	178					✓	✓	✓		✓			1	1	1	1	1
41. Chor. Let us break their bonds	C	161	186	✓					✓	✓		✓	✓		6	6	4	3	2
42. Recit. He that dwelleth in heaven	A6–E	167	194				✓					✓						1	
43. Air Thou shalt break them	A mi	167	194				✓			1		✓			1	1		1	1
44. Chor. Hallelujah	D	171	198	✓					✓	✓	✓	✓	✓	✓	6	6	4	3	2
PART THE THIRD																			
45. Air I know that my Redeemer	E	181	210		✓					1		✓			1	1		1	1
46. Chor. Since by man came death	C	186	215	✓					✓	✓		✓	✓		6	6	4	3	2
47. Recit. Behold, I tell you a mystery	D–A	189	218					✓				✓			6	6	4	3	2
48. Air The trumpet shall sound	D	189	219					✓		1	1	✓			6	6	4	3	2
49. Recit. Then shall be brought to pass	Bb	196	227			✓						✓						1	
50. Duet O death, where is thy sting	Eb	196	228			✓	✓			1		✓						1	1
51. Chor. But thanks be to God	Eb	199	229	✓					✓	✓		✓	✓		6	6	4	3	2
52. Air If God be for us	G mi	205	235		✓							✓			1	1		1	1
53. Chor. Worthy is the Lamb	D	217	244	✓					✓	✓	✓	✓	✓	✓	6	6	4	3	2

WATKINS SHAW EDITION

Instrumental chart of Handel's *Messiah*.

(Margaret Hillis Collection, Rosenthal Archives of the Chicago Symphony Orchestra Association)

This is an example of an instrumentation chart of Handel's *Messiah*. Included in this chart is the key of each movement, the instruments involved, and in what movements the instruments play. Hillis created these instrumental charts to determine the order in which she would rehearse movements, choosing to rehearse the movements with the greatest number of instruments first, then dismissing players when those movements were completed to avoid them sitting around and waiting for their movements to come up. This is done out of courtesy to instrumentalists, such as the trumpet players who perform fewer additional movements in this piece. In the instrumental chart, Hillis highlighted all choral movements in yellow.

W. A. MOZART
MISSA
C MINOR – KV 427 (417a)

INSTRUMENTATION CHART

Movement	Keys	Orchestra Score (Pages)	Piano-vocal Reduction (Pages)	Chorus	Soprano	Alto	Tenor	Bass	Flute	Oboe	Bassoon	Horns	Trumpets	Trombone	Organ	Timpani	Violin I	Violin II	Viola	Cello	Bass
Kyrie	C Mi	1	1	4	✓					2	2	2	2	3	✓	✓	✓	✓	✓	✓	✓
Gloria																					
Gloria	C	25	13	4		✓				2	2	2	2	3	✓	✓	✓	✓	✓	✓	✓
Laudamus	F	43	20	5		✓				2	2	2			✓		✓	✓	✓	✓	✓
Gratias	A Mi	61	28	8	✓					2	2	2	3	3	✓		✓	✓	✓	✓	✓
Domine	D Mi	66	30		✓	✓				2	2	2			✓		✓	✓	✓	✓	✓
Qui tollis	G Mi	77	36	4	✓	✓				2	2	2			✓		✓	✓	✓	✓	✓
Quoniam	E Mi	96	46	4	✓	✓	✓			2	2	2			✓		✓	✓	✓	✓	✓
Jesu Christe	C–Ga	113	56		✓	✓				2	2	2			✓		✓	✓	✓	✓	✓
Cum sancto	C	115	56	8						2	2	2	2	3	✓	✓	✓	✓	✓	✓	✓
Credo																					
Credo in unum Deum	C	150	72	5	✓					2	2	2			✓		✓	✓	✓	✓	✓
Et incarnatus	F	179	87		✓				1	1	1				✓		✓	✓	✓	✓	✓
Sanctus	C	195	96	8					2	2	2	2	3	3	✓	✓	✓	✓	✓	✓	✓
Osanna	C	202	99	8					2	2	2	2	3	3	✓	✓	✓	✓	✓	✓	✓
Benedictus	C	223	114		✓	✓	✓	✓	2	2	2	2	3	3	✓	✓	✓	✓	✓	✓	✓
Osanna	C	255	129	8					2	2	2	2	3	3	✓	✓	✓	✓	✓	✓	✓

Instrumental chart of Mozart's Mass in C Minor.
(Margaret Hillis Collection, Rosenthal Archives of the Chicago Symphony Orchestra Association)

In this instrumental chart, Hillis uses a combination of numbers for winds and brass with a check mark under each of the strings without indicating the quantity of each.

APPENDIX 7
A SALUTE TO MARGARET HILLIS BY ALICE PARKER

Alice Parker, Margaret, and board member Terry Knowles take a break during a conference

Alice Parker, Margaret Hillis, and Chorus America board member Terry Knowles during a
Chorus America conference. (*The Voice of Chorus America*, Summer 1997, p. 11)

Friends since their Juilliard days, Margaret Hillis and legendary composer, arranger,
and teacher Dr. Alice Parker would remain in touch throughout both of their
illustrious careers. Alice Parker and Margaret Hillis first met as choral conducting
students under Robert Shaw at Juilliard. Hillis would go on to pursue a professional
conducting career. Parker would continue her work with Robert Shaw, helping
him arrange choral music for his Robert Shaw Chorale. RCA Victor, the recording
company of Collegiate Chorale performances, required that for every classical album
they recorded, Shaw must produce a popular album, "one they could sell," as Parker
explained. Parker became a trusted collaborator for Shaw. She would go to the New
York Public Library, finding melodies from traditional songbooks and hymnals

541

that she and Shaw would then arrange for the albums. These arrangements became popular in choral ensembles from public schools to universities and churches. Dr. Parker would become an accomplished arranger and for years to come would become known for her brilliant teaching and mentoring of future composers, choral singers, and conductors, eventually founding her own non-profit organization, Melodious Accord, dedicated to performing and recording choral music. Dr. Parker is a beloved figure among choral musicians nationally and beyond. She wrote a beautiful tribute to Margaret Hillis after her dear friend's passing in 1998.

A Salute to Margaret Hillis by Alice Parker

Chorus America *Profiles*, 1999

(Reprinted with the permission of Alice Parker.)

This brief paragraph is not a formal summary of Maggie's life and achievements, no listing of her Grammys or awards or other signal honors—it is a loving remembrance of a dear friend and wonderful colleague. Our lives joined when she appeared at Juilliard to study with Robert Shaw. She was a figure of awe and mystery, but then— she trained Navy pilots during World War II! But she never spoke of that: her whole focus was on music, and there was no doubt of her serious commitment to her studies. Her outward dignity and reserve proved, with better acquaintance, to shield a delightful human being, full of humor and wit, with a broad range of interests and a true enjoyment of people.

She moved into several conducting assignments in New York City, many of which drew her into working with my husband, Tom Pyle, who served as her contractor. For several years they shared office space in a rambling apartment on West 79th St. Many great parties (as well as heavy conferences) took place in that space. Tom was contracting for several professional choruses at that time, and I remember well his admiration, affection, and respect for Margaret. "She ran the best-organized and most efficient rehearsals of all the conductors we sang under," he opined—and those others included some people far better-known than she.

We missed her when she returned to her native mid-west. I remember well the flurry of emptying that apartment when she finally gave it up. We inherited some huge music shelves and a prize cache of retired conducting gowns which were my girls' favorite dress-up articles for the next decade—typical thoughtfulness and generosity on Maggie's part.

Our paths began to cross more regularly after the establishment of the Association of Professional Vocal Ensembles—now Chorus America—took place. She was instrumental in its founding and growth, helping it to become a sturdy mission-oriented organization. She attended meetings faithfully, always with time to visit with old and new friends, full of ideas and enthusiasm, prodding us to take a larger view of our profession, to work together to establish a national presence for our art.

Maggie, your music will sing on in your recordings and the memories of all those thousands who worked with you. And your voice—oh that bass voice—will surely add a new resonance to the heavenly choir!

APPENDIX 8
MARGARET "HILLIS-ISMS"

As remembered by Kathye Kerchner and Cheryl Frazes Hill:

"You sing first with your ears, then your heart, mind, and voice."

"The eighth note has been lost since the beginning of time."

"Don't cheat the poor little eighth note."

"The eighth note is late, damn it."

"The music is not the page—only the notes."

"*Piano* doesn't mean passive."

"Enjoy the phrase, don't just be obedient."

"Match vibrato!"

"Listen like crazy!"

"Sorry to say, but, sopranos, those triplets are really constipated."

"Tenors you're lying very close to the ladies' parts, if you'll pardon the expression."

[On beginning sounds] "Make sure it's pitched; don't bring the garbage up from the basement."

"Go home and look for that note under the bed or somewhere."

"The bar line is like children, it should be seen and not heard."

"Voices are not made for music; music is made for voices. Serve the music!"

"Tenors, you sound like you're wearing neckties, and they're too tight!"

"Listen more, that is not a listened-to sound."

"Basses, don't swim, this is not a pool."

[To the altos in a *Damnation of Faust* sectional] "Don't sing in chest voice, angels don't have chests!"

"You sound like a German village band."

"That was not an E natural, that was a *demented* E."

"Don't breathe, breathe *after* the concert."

"Shape the silence."

"A musician's intelligence lies in his ears."

"A quarter note is twice as long as an eighth note, at least it was when I went to school."

"One of the GOOD things about your diction is that I can tell you're behind the beat!"

"I like your faces, not the tops of your heads."

"Anything that's HOLY should be in tune."

"You must be a good Presbyterian to sing Bach—have a strong sense of predestination."

"There's only one woman I know who could never be a symphony conductor, and that's Venus de Milo."

APPENDIX 9
"AT REHEARSALS" BOOKLET

This booklet was created by Margaret Hillis to support her singers in the Chorus with helpful tips on score marking, diction and pronunciation, and translations of terminology in a variety of languages. This is the original version created in 1969, and it was periodically updated through 1987.

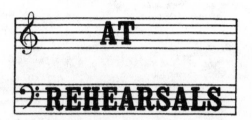

CHICAGO SYMPHONY CHORUS

The Chicago Symphony Chorus never sings a reading of a work: we sing a performance. There is a vast difference. At best, notation is an inexact blueprint of the composer's intentions. We try to sing these intentions even beyond the limits of our musical maturity (but not beyond the intelligent use of individual vocal resources).

The building of a great performance takes place in rehearsals. Choral singing demands intense awareness of the music itself, the conductor, the total sound, and each individual's contribution to the whole. Our rehearsals are oriented in two directions:

1. *Knowing everything on the page, thus becoming free to go beyond the surface of the notation into the inner life of the music.*

2. *Working the music into the minds, the ears, the voices, and the tongues so that the doing of it no longer imposes technical barriers to the musical imagination.*

This is known as discipline.

To achieve this discipline means frustration, disappointment in one's own feeble efforts when faced with a monumental task, intense concentration, and endless patience. It means an addiction to perfection in our service to music — an endless quest for more insight into the beauties of this great art.

My function is to serve you in this quest.

When you consulted your rehearsal schedule, you found sectional rehearsals listed. It is here that an important part of the technical mastery takes place. To miss **one** sectional rehearsal is equivalent to missing **four** full rehearsals. Rhythmic details and intonation are refined, and hearing is sharpened, and the all-important working-into-the-voice is achieved.

Mark your music! A pencil is a must at all rehearsals! Choral shorthand is an individual matter. Whatever method you have used, or care to use, is fine — so long as it is meaningful to you. Following are a few notations you might find helpful:

1

 Watch, or surprise entrance, tempo change, etc.

 Tempo control! Any problem of dragging, rushing or other time-related factor.

 Follow dynamics.

 Forte release, crescendo release; cutting short immediately, on direction, after a crescendo.

 Piano release.

 Circle any pitch where error has been made. Also, circle pitch in another part to help you.

 Listen! Arrow to another part for imitation, main theme, duet, etc.

 Cut-off on, for example, the 4th beat.

 Hold note and sustain intensity to the release.

 Placing a final consonant. Write the final consonant under the rest at the cut-off (or bar line).

kein | auge The perpendicular line indicates a glottal stroke before the vowel.

 Arrows indicate early consonants.

 No accent. Occurs, for instance, on a downbeat or at the top of an ascending scale where, for musical reasons, an accent is not to be made. *(Anacrusis)*

Stress. Used to highlight melodic and/or harmonic contour. Usually occurs on a stressed syllable of the text. *(Thesis)*

 Accent. Stronger than stress, indicating marcato. Usually separated.

2

Ben Marcato. Accents with no separation.

Super Accent.

Poco Detaché. Separate the notes. Used frequently when notes are repeated on the same pitch.

The following are standard markings:

Staccato.

Portato, or slurred *staccato* (called *Portamento* by instrumentalists).

Tenuto. Long note. Usually slightly separated when in a series (unless a slur occurs over them).

Crescendo (or *cres.* - - - - - -) Always draw the "hairpin" in all parts.

Diminuendo (or *dim.* - - - - - -) Always draw the "hairpin" in all parts.

Messa di voce, crescendo and *diminuendo* over one note.

Hold, or *fermata.*

Breathing marks. Also used to clear sound at overlapping cadences.

Helpful abbreviations: leg. *(legato),* esp. *(espressivo),* marc. *(marcato).*

During the course of rehearsals, you will find some harmonic analysis being done. This is for the sake of your ears, so make notations in your music (in lead pencil, **not in ink!**). A musician's **intelligence lies in the way he uses his ears.**

3

Study: Unless your music is marked, careful study during the week is impossible. This study must be done in the context of what happened at the last rehearsal. Make it a habit to spend at least twenty minutes a day on your music. Individual practice cannot be undertaken in full rehearsal. Iron out what technical problems you may have during the week.

Know the music: Become as familiar as possible with it. Complete memorization is not required, but well before concert time you should be so well acquainted with the music that a mere glance will recall a substantial phrase. The ideal is to spend 95% of the time watching the conductor, and only 5% glancing at the music (held high).

Listen! The essence of a musically intelligent ensemble lies in careful and critical listening. If a phrase comes to you from another section with a particular tone quality, shape, and articulation, it must be answered in kind. You must be aware of duets and trios as well. Intonation, appropriate sonority, phrasing, *crescendi,* and *diminuendi* depend entirely upon **how well you use your musical ears.**

Watch! Your conductor is with you in order to help you. Only by watching can you be helped.

At times fast pieces are rehearsed slowly and softly without text. This is done to accomplish three things:

1. Bring your ears into contact with the total score so that you know what is going on. Listen for duets, trios, and imitative materials, matching quality of sound, phrase contour, and detailed articulation.

2. It gives you a chance through your ears to make a unison in your section and to relate your intonation and vocal color to the total sound.

3. This is an opportunity to work the pitches into the voice, so make use of it by keeping a well-supported resonant tone.

Good Singing! Get inside the music. Always visualize and make a musical sonority appropriate to the score. The vowels must be in line, the attacks sung, not spoken (which makes

4

physical and mental preparation for an entrance of prime importance). The previsualization of the color of the required sound must be intense, and you must somehow make yourself capable of producing that required color anywhere in your vocal range. The need is for the vocal care of the best solo singing, wedded to the musical intelligence of an ensemble singer.

Count! The precise articulation of musical ideas cannot take place without clear organization of time. Care must be taken in the treatment of small note values; particularly the second of two eighth notes, the second and fourth of four sixteenth notes, and the short notes after dotted values. Counting, subdivision, length of vowel and vocal intensity on short notes will make those little notes live.

However, counting and subdivision, important as they are, are only tools. They must not be substituted for a conception of the phrase.

Be sure you are contributing your best vocalism at all times. This means:

1. An even register, with no pressing in the lower range and no pushing on top.

2. An even well-controlled vibrato throughout the whole dynamic range.

3. Clarity and consistence of vowels throughout the entire palette of possible vocal colors.

4. In *forte* singing, never going nearer than 10% of the loudest you can sing. Do not give in to the temptation to force if you are sitting next to a voice bigger than yours!

5. Keep the *piano* dynamic alive and intense.

6. Listen to the total sound. Be aware at all times of your own relationship to it.

This chorus does not have a "choral tone." To impose such inflexibility on a score is musically dishonest, even if superficially successful. Instead, we strive for a musical sonority appropriate to the expressive content of the particular composition to which we are committed. This is risky because of the vocal and musical demands it makes on all of us. We risk failure in an honest quest of true art.

5

Besides a basically good vocal technique, there are other devices which can be brought to the service of a score.

Generally, but not always, *piano* implies a covered tone and *forte* implies an open tone. Dynamics, particularly in romantic music, are often a color rather than only the number of decibels delivered.

Music is shaped sound, shaped by rhythm, harmony, color, dynamics, balances, and melodic contour. The alertness of your ears and musical intuition will make the difference between sheer "tone" and the shaped sound that is music.

Articulation: A useful definition of musical articulation is, "a way of grouping of two or more notes into a unit of musical, rhythmic, harmonic, and/or melodic thought." Besides a musically appropriate sound, sensitively wrought phrasing by means of detailed articulation is an essential expression of insight into the musical content of a score. Without this we have only a kind of electronic monster instead of musically participating human beings.

Good diction: The use of words is the main factor that distinguishes a chorus from all other wind instruments. Unless the consonants are precise and rhythmic, we have no articulation. Unless the vowels are well-formed, well-focused and maintain their shape throughout the full dynamic range as well as the full length of a note value (whether long or short), we have no sonority. In order to match the detailed articulation of the instruments in the orchestra, we often have to "cheat" in the handling of diction. This is particularly true in *THE CREATION* and the *MISSA SOLEMNIS*.

Consonants are to the singer what bow strokes are to the string player and tonguing is to the winds and brasses. They articulate the beginnings of sound. Vowels are the sustaining devices on which sound is carried.

Wherever possible, all vowels should be initiated, but not terminated, with a consonant. We in America speak wandering vowels, highly contaminated by their terminating consonants. In singing, this militates against clarity, vocal quality and intonation. All vowels must become clearer and more intense as they are sustained. This is particularly crucial in the sustaining of a legato line.

6

Consonants fall into two large categories, each with or without pitch:

With Duration		Without Duration	
Pitched	Unpitched	Pitched	Unpitched
v			
	f		
	h	b	p
l		g	c = k
m		d	t
n			ts
ng		j = dg	ch = tch
	s, c = s		q = k
z	ss	x = gs	x = ks

w (vowel)
y (vowel), i as in "it"
th (that)   th (think)
zz (azure, Fr. j)   sh (should)

It is the termination of the consonant (the arrival of the vowel) that delineates the beginning of a note. This being the case, all consonants with duration must rob some of the previous vowel's termination time (but not contaminate that vowel by so doing). When that consonant has pitch, it takes the pitch of the immediately preceding vowel.

When a durational consonant begins a phrase, it must anticipate the rhythmic unit sufficiently for the subsequent vowel to arrive precisely on its assigned schedule, and it must be vocalized on the pitch of the vowel.

The pitched consonants without duration always take the pitch of the subsequent vowel, and rob just enough time from the previous vowel to allow the subsequent vowel to arrive on schedule.

The l, the r, and the s are special cases: the l must be vocalized with the tip of the tongue in approximately the same position as the formation of a t. (The previous vowel may be somewhat contaminated with an i as in till, not with ɔ as in warm.)

The r is a special case in the English language, particularly in the Midwest. Its rules are as follow:

1. When followed by a consonant sound (not spelling), drop it. (Lord, where the)
2. Drop it at the end of a phrase.
3. Drop it when it is detached from the following note. (*Staccato* articulation)

7

4. When the r is dropped, substitute the neutral vowel (ə).
5. When followed by a vowel sound (except in detached articulation) flip it lightly off the end of the tongue. It is formed (and vocalized) with the tongue approximately in the position of a d.
6. Since the flipped r has the same tongue position as a t or a d, to flip it after either consonant would necessitate an awkward double stroke. Use an American r. (truth, dream)

The s is the only consonant multiplied by the number of people present. Vocalize the vowel to its scheduled termination, then place a short and light s exactly on its assigned rhythmic unit.

The g and k should be formed with the tongue approximately in the position it would have at the beginning of the word you. The farther forward these two consonants are enunciated, the more carrying power they will have and correspondingly less interference with the previous vowel.

These rules must be clearly understood, and the mastery of the doing of them must be secure before they can be broken for musical reasons, so read, study, and practice!

8

You may find the following reminder of terminology helpful:

Italian	German	French	Definition

1. For fast tempi the following terms are used:

Italian	German	French	Definition
allegro	*schnell*	*animé*	= quick
vivace	*lebhaft*	*vif*	= lively
presto	*eilig*	*vite, rapide*	= very fast, quicker than *allegro*

Qualifying terms:

Italian terms are made stronger by addition of the suffix *issimo;* they are made weaker by the suffix *ino* or *etto.*
Example: *prestissimo* — faster than *presto; allegretto* — not as fast as *allegro.*
Piu, (in German the suffix *er;* in French, the word *plus*) = more.
Example: *piu presto, schneller*

Italian	German	French	Definition
meno	*weniger*	*moins*	= less

Example: *meno allegro*

Italian	German	French	Definition
non troppo	*nicht zu*	*pas trop*	= not too

Example: *allegro non troppo* = not too fast

2. For slow and moderate tempi, the following terms are generally used:

Italian	German	French	Definition
adagio	*langsam, getragen*	*lent*	= slow
largo	*breit*	*large*	= broad
lento	*langsam*	*lent*	= slow
grave	*schwer*	*lourd*	= heavy
andante	*gehend*	*allant*	= moving
moderato	*mässig, gemässigt*	*modere*	= moderate

Qualifying terms:

The meaning of these terms can be intensified or reduced by adding:

Italian	German	French	Definition
molto, or *assai*	*sehr*	*très*	= very

Example: *molto adagio, très lent*

Italian	German	French	Definition
poco, un poco	*ein wenig, etwas*	*un peu*	= somewhat

3. Some indications for changing tempi:

Italian	German	French	Definition
accelerando (accel.)	*schneller werden*	*accelerer*	= to accelerate
stringendo (string.)	*dragend*	*en pressant*	= becoming faster and more intense
piu mosso	*bewegter*	*plus animé*	= faster
ritardando (rit.)	*langsamer werden*	*ralentissant*	= retard
rallentando (rall.)	*zurückhalten*	*ralentir,* or *ralentissant*	= retard or slacken
allargando	*verbreitern*	*enlargissant*	= broaden
meno moso	*weniger bewegt*	*moins vite*	= less fast
ritenuto (riten.)	*zurück gehalten*	*retenu*	= hold back

The gradation of a change of some length is marked, all with appropriate adjective:

Italian	German	French	Definition
poco a poco	*allmählich*	*peu a peu*	= little by little

The following terms mean a simultaneous reduction of tempo and loudness:

Italian	German	French	Definition
callando	*nachlassen*	*en diminuant*	= decrease
smorzando	*verloschen*	*en s'effacent*	= dying away
morendo	*ersterben*	*en mourant*	= dying down

Restoration of main tempo is marked: *a tempo* or *tempo primo*

LATIN ACCORDING TO ROMAN USAGE

A. VOWELS

Latin	IPA	English
a	[ɑ]	father
e	[ɛ]	wed (no diphthong)
i	[i]	me (never i as in it)
o	[ɔ]	warm.
u	[u]	moon (even rounder than in English)
ae	[eɪ]	day
oe	[eɪ]	day

B. CONSONANTS

Latin

b	=	b
c	=	tch, as in church, before e, i, ae, oe; otherwise c = k
d	=	d, a shade farther forward (more dentalized) than in English, and is lighter.
f	=	f
g	=	dg, as in just, before e, i, ae, oe; otherwise, g = hard g, as in go.
h	=	k in mihi, nihil and nihi only; otherwise, always silent.
j	=	y
k	=	k (appears only in Greek words, such as Kyrie).
l	=	l (always forward as described in the English rules).
m	=	m
n	=	n
gn	=	ny, as in canyon: agnus, magnam
p	=	p
ph	=	f
q	=	k
r	=	r, rolled lightly at beginning of word, less in the middle, flipped at the end.
s	=	ss always — never z: eleison, miserere.
sc	=	sh before e, i, ae, oe; otherwise, sk.
sch	=	sk always
t	=	t, a shade farther forward (more dentalized) than in English, and is lighter.
ti	=	tee, as in nati, except when followed by a second vowel, and it then becomes tsi, as in gratia, nationali.
v	=	v
w	=	Does not exist in Latin.
x	=	ks at end of word: pax.
y	=	i, as in me. Appears only in Greek words: Kyrie.
z	=	dz

11

ITALIAN LYRIC DICTION

A. VOWELS

Italian	IPA	English
a	[ɑ]	father
e (open)	[ɛ]	bet (no diphthong)
e (closed)	[e]	late
i	[i]	me
o (open)	[ɔ]	warm, naught (but darker; no diphthong)
o (closed)	[o]	obey
u	[u]	moon

B. CONSONANTS

b	=	b
c	=	ch before i and e (cielo); k before h, a, o, u (chiesa).
d	=	d in dental.
f	=	f
g	=	dg before i and e (giunio); gh before h, a, o, u (regali).
h	=	only to harden c, g, sc; otherwise never pronounced.
(j)	=	i or y (only in foreign words)
(k)	=	k (only in foreign words)
l	=	l in dental (forward)
m	=	m
n	=	n
p	=	p, with no escape of air; almost like b.
q	=	k, and is used only with u for kw sound.
r	=	r, but must be rolled.
s	=	z between two vowels or before a voiced consonant (rosa, sdegno); s at all other times (stella, rossa).
t	=	t in dental.
v	=	v
(w)	=	v or w (only in foreign words)
x	=	ks
(y)	=	i (only in foreign words)
z	=	dz or ts
gl	=	lli in million, billiards
gn	=	ny in canyon
sc	=	sh before i and e (scendere); sk before h, a, o, u (Gianni Schicchi).

Double consonant: implode the first, explode the second, always opens the preceding vowel.

All the dental consonants are contained in the word "dental."

"e" is closed before a single consonant, "è" is open; o, e as last syllable always open.

12

FRENCH PRONUNCIATION

A. VOWELS

	IPA	French	English
a	[a]	*lave*	father
a	[a]	*là, chat*	pat
au	[o]	*l'eau*	go
au+r	[ɔ]	*aurore*	not
e, è	[ɛ]	*père*	method
e, é	[e]	*marcher, été,* *chantez*	way
e	[ə]	*je, te, me*	earth (approx.)
eu	[φ]	*peu, Dieu*	does not exist in English
i	[i]	*bénisse*	piece
o	[ɔ]	*notre*	ought
oi	ωa	*soit*	swat
ou	[u]	*toujours*	foolish
u	[y]	*tu*	No such English sound. Round the lips as if to whistle, then pronounce the "e" of he.
ô	[o]	*nôtre*	rose

B. NASAL VOWELS

Generally speaking, when vowels are followed in the same syllable by m, or n, the vowel is nasalized and the m or n is not pronounced.

a	*quant*	taunt (without nt)
e	*temps*	" " "
i	*cinq*	sank
o	*bon*	bonbon (without the n's)
u	*un*	munch (without nch)

C. CONSONANTS

b	=	b, silent when final.
c	=	k before a, o, u, l or r; usually when final *(avec)*
ç	=	s and is used only before a, o, u *(Français)*
cc	=	k *(accorder)*
ch	=	sh *(chez)*
d	=	d in most cases. Place next to teeth.
	=	t, when linked *(quand il)*
f	=	f
g	=	g before a, o, u, l, or r *(grand)*
	=	zj before e, i, y *(gentil)*; see "j" below.
gn	=	nyuh *(campagne)*
gu	=	g *(orgueil)*
h	=	always silent *(l'homme)*
j	=	zj, as in *joli, Jesus;* (azure, in Eng.)
k	=	k
l	=	l, usually pronounced even when final; silent in *gentil.*

13

l	=	y when preceded by ai or ei *(le soleil)*
ll	=	yuh when preceded by i *(fille, billet)*
m	=	m at the beginning of a syllable *(calme);* when final in a syllable m causes preceding vowel to be nasalized but is not otherwise pronounced *(faim).*
mm	=	m *(l'homme).*
n	=	n *(nous);* when final, like rule above for m. Silent in *ent* verb endings.
nn	=	n *(bonne);* usually silent when final.
q	=	k
qu	=	k
r	=	r *(très, pour),* sung with slightly rolled English r; silent in infinitive endings *(er).*
s	=	s at beginning of a word or when preceded or followed by a consonant.
	=	z between vowels *(maison).*
	=	z when linked *(vous avez)*
	=	usually silent when final
	=	s in *fils, tous* (pronoun)
sc	=	sk before a, o, u, l or r
ss	=	s
t	=	t *(le temps)*
ti	=	s in -*tion* endings
v	=	v
w	=	in foreign words only; pronounce as in language borrowed from.
x	=	ks, excellent as in aches
	=	gs, exact as in eggs
	=	z when linked *(heureux epoux)* always silent when final.
y	=	in yes *(les yeux)*
z	=	z; silent in *ez* verb endings and in *chez,* except in linking.

The rules for the rhythmic placement of consonants are the same in any language as they are in English.

14

GERMAN DICTION

A. VOWELS

IPA	German	English
a [a]	Antwort, flach	man
a [a:]	Ader, Haar, Jahr	father, harbor
ä [æ]	hängen	pen
ä [ɛ:]	Fähre, Käse	fairy
e [ɛ]	Ente, besser	very, head
e [e:]	Ehre, Mehl, Ekel	male
e [ə]	Ehre, beantworten	perhaps, idea, mother
i [ɪ]	ich, nisten	bit, hymn
i [ɪ:]	ihre, liebe	be, beat, see, field
o [ɔ]	Rock	not
o [o:]	Hose, Sohn	tone
u [u]	Futter, Pult	foot, pull, could
u [u:]	Mut, Kuh	do, boot, soup
ü [y]	Hülte, füllen	(like i in miss but, when followed by two consonants, with lips protruded and rounded)
ü [y:]	Hüte, fühlen	(like ee in see, but with lips protruded and rounded as for whistling)
ö [φ]	Hölle	(like e in pen but, when followed by two consonants, with lips protruded and rounded)
ö [φ:]	Höhle	(like the a in male, but with lips protruded and rounded as for whistling)

B. DIPHTHONGS

ei, ai [aɪ]	mein, Mai	my, wife, high
eie, eihe [aɪə]	Feier, Reihe	fire, higher (with r silent)
au [au]	Haus	house, how
aue [auə]	Bauer	hour
eu, au [ɔɪ]	neu, Bäume	boy, noise
eue [ɔɪə]	Feuer	royal
ui [uɪ]	pfui	—

C. CONSONANTS

b=b [b]		Sounds as b at beginning of a syllable (Brod)
b=p [p]		Sounds as p at the end of a syllable (bleib)
c=k [k]		In isolation is used only in words of foreign origin (Café)
ch [ç]		Before e or i it is like the initial sound in the English word huge
ch [k]		Before other vowels or any consonants is pronounced as k (Charakter), except in words of French origin, when it sounds like sh in ship (Champagner)
ch [χ]		After the vowels a, o, u, au, it is pronounced like the ch in the Scottish word loch (Bach)
ch [ç]		After the vowels e, i, o, u, au, eu and after consonants it is pronounced like the initial sound in the English word huge (brechen, mancher, solcher)
ch= ks [ks]		The combination chs is pronounced like ks (Wachs, sechs) Exceptions: nächst, höchst)
d=d [d]		At the beginning of a syllable (der)
d=t [t]		At the end of a syllable (Rad)
dt=t [t]		The combination dt sounds as a t (Stadt)
f=f [f]		As in the English word father (frei, laufen)
g=g [g]		As in English word go (gut)
g=k [k]		At the end of a syllable after a, e, o, u (Tag)
g [ç]		At the end of a syllable after i it is pronounced like the initial sound in the English word huge (Honig)

h=h	[h]	At the beginning of a syllable *(Haus, Schön-heit)*
h	—	Is not pronounced after vowels nor after **t** *(Schuh, Theater)*
j	[j]	Represents the same sound as the y in **year** *(Jahr)*
k=k	[k]	As in English word **keep** *(Karte)*
l = l	[l]	Pronounced as in English. **Always forward**
m=m	[m]	As in English word **must** *(müssen, kommen)*
n=n	[n]	As in English work **night** *(Nacht, brennen)*
ng	[ŋ]	Same quality as in English word **singer** *(Finger)*
nk	[ŋk]	Same as in English word **sink** *(sinken)*
p=p	[p]	As in English word **post** *(Post, Suppe)*
pf=pf	[pf]	Is pronounced as written *(Pfund, Topf)*
ph=f	[f]	As in English word **phase** *(Photograph)*
qu=kv	[kv]	The **kv** is pronounced as spelled *(Quelle)*
r = r	[r]	As an English r, but **always rolled.**
s=z	[z]	At the beginning of a syllable before a vowel *(sein)*
s=s	[s]	Always like English s in **sing** at end of syllable *(das)*
ss=s	[s]	Always pronounced as **ss** in **hiss** *(Wasser, Fuss)*
sch	[ʃ]	As English **sh** in **shoe** *(Schuh)*
sp	[ʃp]	As **shp** at the beginning of a word *(Sprache)*. When a word beginning with **sp** takes a prefix or is combined with another word the sound remains the same *(Dichtersprache)*
sp=sp	[sp]	As in the English word **wasp** *(Wespe, wispern)*
st	[ʃt]	As **sht** at the beginning of a word *(stehen)*. When a word beginning with **st** takes a prefix or is combined with another word the sound remains the same. *(verstehen)*
st=st	[st]	As in the English word **first** *(barst, garstig)*
t = t	[t]	Same as the English **t** in **ten** *(Tat)*
v=f	[f]	Represents the same sound as **f** in **father** *(Vater)*
w=v	[v]	Represents the same sound as the English **v** in **very** *(Welt)*
x=ks	[ks]	Pronounced like English **x** in **fox** *(Axt)*
z=ts	[ts]	Pronounced like English **ts** in **cats** *(zehn)*

17

Margaret Hillis
September, 1969

Second printing January 1970
Third printing August 1972
Fourth printing 1974
Additional printing 1981
Additional printing 1983
Additional printing 1987

18

BIBLIOGRAPHY

A

"A Tradition Observed Collegiate Chorale Sings at Forum in Ninth Consecutive Appearance." *Herald Tribune*, October 26, 1952. In Scrapbook #1 of the Margaret Hillis Collection, Rosenthal Archives of the Chicago Symphony Orchestra Association.

A. B. "Concert Choir Town Hall February 12." *Musical America*, February 1953. In Scrapbook #1 of the Margaret Hillis Collection, Rosenthal Archives of the Chicago Symphony Orchestra Association.

A. B. "The Proms: Faust at Home." *The Daily Telegraph*, August 30, 1989.

Abbey, Marilyn R. "The Mass Appeal Messiah." *Discovery* (Winter 1985–1986).

Acocella, Joan. "Nights at the Opera." *The New Yorker*, January 8, 2007.

Ammer, Christine. *Unsung: A History of Women in American Music*. Westport, Connecticut: Greenwood Press, 1980.

B

Bartleet, Brydie-Leigh. "Female Conductors: The Incarnation of Power?" *Hecate: An Interdisciplinary Journal of Women's Liberation* 28, no. 2 (2003).

Baxter, Jeffrey. "An Interview with Robert Shaw: Reflections at Eighty." *Choral Journal* (April 1996).

Bentz, Jon. "Interview of Margaret Hillis Director Chicago Symphony Orchestra, September 19, 1989, Archives Committee, Oral History Project, 1992." Margaret Hillis Collection, Rosenthal Archives of the Chicago Symphony Orchestra Association.

Block, Adrienne Fried, and Carol Neuls-Bates. *Women in American Music: A Bibliography of Music and Literature*. Westport, Connecticut: Greenwood Press, 1979.

Bradle, Sue, and Tom Wilson. "Music Is My Life." *Accent* 6, no. 1 (September/ October 1980).

Breu, Giovanna, and Sally Moore. "For Margaret Hillis the Night to Remember Involved 395 Musicians, Mahler, and No Rehearsal." *People*, November 28, 1977.

Bucker, William Robert. "A History of Chorus America: Association of Professional Vocal Ensembles." DMA dissertation. University of Missouri– Kansas City, 1991.

Burris, Keith C. *Deep River*. Chicago: GIA Publications, 2013.

C

Campbell, Karen. "A Choired Excellence." *Symphony Magazine* (November/ December 1992).

Carroll, Margaret. "Hillis's Artful Compromise for a Passion." *Chicago Tribune*, April 11, 1976, ProQuest Historical Newspapers.

Cassidy, Claudia. "Bruno Walter and the Chicago Symphony in a Memorable Mozart Requiem." *Chicago Tribune*, March 14, 1958.

Cassidy, Claudia. "On the Aisle: 'Tusch' Standing Tribute Honor Walter in Orchestra Hall." *Chicago Tribune*, January 25, 1957.

C. B. "Concert Choir Town Hall January 16." *Musical America* (February 1953). In Scrapbook #1 of the Margaret Hillis Collection, Rosenthal Archives of the Chicago Symphony Orchestra Association.

C. B. "Russian Wedding." *Musical America* (February 1954). In Scrapbook #1 of the Margaret Hillis Collection, Rosenthal Archives of the Chicago Symphony Orchestra Association.

"Chicago Symphony Chorus 35th Reunion: Guest of Honor Margaret Hillis." Program Book, 1992.

"Chicago Symphony Orchestra Gala Centennial Concert." October 6, 1990. Commemorative book in celebration of the orchestra's centennial anniversary.

"Choral and Organ Guide." January 1953. Truncated clipping in Scrapbook #1 of the Margaret Hillis Collection, Rosenthal Archives of the Chicago Symphony Orchestra Association.

"Chorus Auditions Pay Off." *Chicago Sun-Times*, October 5, 1957.

"City of Cabots Views Its Dynamic New Leader." *Musical America* 45, January 22, 1927.

Colgrass, Ulla. "Conductor Hillis Reversed the Odds." *Music Management Magazine* (November/December 1981).

"Collegiate Chorale Premieres." *Musical Courier*, January 1, 1953. In Scrapbook #1 of the Margaret Hillis Collection, Rosenthal Archives of the Chicago Symphony Orchestra Association.

Collins, Gail. *America's Women: Four Hundred Years of Dolls, Drudges, Helpmates, and Heroines.* 1st ed. New York: William Morrow, 2003.

Collins, Walter S. "Presidents' Open Letter to the Membership." *Choral Journal* (September 1978).

"Concert Choir and Orchestra: Woman to Direct Guild Concert Here." *Pittsburgh Sun Telegraph*, September 30, 1955.

"Concert Choir Sings at Town Hall." *New York Herald Review*, February 1953.

"Concert Choir, Margaret Hillis Town Hall April 21." *Musical Courier*, May 15, 1954. In Scrapbook #1 of the Margaret Hillis Collection, Rosenthal Archies of the Chicago Symphony Orchestra Association.

Conlon, Joan Catoni. *Wisdom, Wit, and Will: Women Choral Conductors on Their Art.* Chicago: GIA Publications, 2009.

Cox, Meg. "Big Chicago Chorus Is Set to Show How It Handles 'Messiah.'" *Wall Street Journal*, December 17, 1979.

D

Davis, Ronald L. *Opera in Chicago.* 1st ed. New York: Appleton-Century, 1966.

Delacoma, Wynne. "A Vocal Leader: Chicago Symphony Chorus Founder Margaret Hillis Dies." *Chicago Sun-Times*, February 5, 1998.

Delacoma, Wynne. "Civic Orchestra's Concentration Tackles Bruckner." *Chicago Sun-Times*, February 3, 1991.

Delacoma, Wynne. "It's About Time, Women Are Making Overdue Inroads on the Podium." *Ravinia Magazine* 8, no. 4 (July 14–20, 2014).

Delacoma, Wynne. "Pavarotti Quiets Rumors, Warms Up Well to 'Otello.'" *Chicago Sun-Times*, April 9, 1991.

"Delphians Enjoy Guest Day Party at Hillis Home." *Kokomo Tribune*, April 30, 1934.

Dempsey, John. "Elwood's Innovation Known Universally: His Inventions Touch Our Everyday Lives." *Kokomo Tribune*, October 14, 2007.

Dempsey, John. "Grandchildren Keep Haynes' Prolific Spirit Alive." *Kokomo Tribune*, October 14, 2007.

Dennen, Janel Jo. "Margaret Hillis and the Chicago Symphony Chorus: Perspective and Interview." *Choral Journal* (November 1982).

Dettmer, Roger. "Extravaganza at Orchestra Hall." *Chicago American*, January 20, 1956.

Dettmer, Roger. "Spontaneous Ovation Greets Beloved Bruno Walter 81." *Chicago American*, March 14, 1958.

Downes, Olin. "Music Finds a Place in Metropolitan Museum as New Auditorium is Opened." *The New York Times*, May 16, 1954.

E

Early press book for The New York Concert Choir by David W. Rubin Artists Management, 1954, author's personal collection.

Elias, Albert J. "From Kokomo to Town Hall—Margaret Hillis Started as a Conductor at 14." *The New York Times,* March 1, 1953.

Ericson, Raymond. "Miss Hillis Carries Her Baton Lightly." *The New York Times*, November 2, 1977.

F

Feldman, Ann. Host of *Noteworthy Women* radio series, a ten-program series celebrating Women's History Month. The first four programs were syndicated by WFMT Fine Arts network in 1995. A recording of this program is part of the Margaret Hillis Collection, Rosenthal Archives of the Chicago Symphony Orchestra Association.

Ford, Barbara. "Margaret Hillis Unchanged by Fame." *Kokomo Tribune*, February 14, 1979.

Ford, Ken. "Just Call Her 'Conductor.'" *Kokomo Tribune*, March 18, 1986.

Furlong, William Barry. *Season with Solti: A Year in the Life of the Chicago Symphony*. New York: Macmillan Publishing, 1974.

G

George, Vance. "View from the Podium." *Cadenza* VI, no. 4, pp. 2–3.

Gerst, Virginia. "Conductor Takes the Direct Approach." *Evanston Life*, June 18, 1992.

"Glen R. Hillis." Obituary. *Kokomo Tribune,* October 20, 1965.

Glenn, Carole. *In Quest of Answers*. Chapel Hill, NC: Hinshaw Music, 1991.

"Going After Arbuckle for Having Booz." *Kokomo Tribune*, October 1, 1921.

Goldin, Milton. "The Foundation's Survey of Choral Groups." *Bulletin of the American Concert Choir and Choral Foundation, Inc.* 1, no. 1 (June 1958).

"G.O.P. Candidate for Governor." *Kokomo Tribune*, November 21, 1939.

Gray, Ralph D. *Alloys and Automobiles: The Life of Elwood Haynes*. Indianapolis: Indianapolis Historical Society, 1979.

Greenlee, Robert. "The Gestural Legacy of Margaret Hillis." *Choral Journal* 48, no. 3 (2007): pp. 18–25.

Groh, Jan Bell. *Evening the Score: Women in Music and the Legacy of Frédérique Petrides*. Fayetteville: University of Arkansas Press, 1991.

H

Haddon, Britton, and Henry Robinson. "Joyful Christmas Sounds and Sites." *Time*, December 29, 1980.

Harb, Karl. "Twenty Scenes from the Life of a Lonesome Man." *Salzburger Nachrichten*, September 1, 1989.

Harrington, Jan. "Memorial Resolution, Julius Herford." *Bloomington Faculty Council Minutes*, October 5, 1982. http://webapp1.dlib.indiana.edu/bfc/view?docId=B07-n.

Hart, Philip. *Fritz Reiner: A Biography*. Evanston: Northwestern University Press, 1994.

Haynes, Elwood. "How I Built My First Automobile." *The Haynes Pioneer*, July 1919.

Haynes, Elwood. "The Evolution of the Aeroplane." *The Haynes Pioneer*, October 1919.

H. C. S. "Concert Choir Sings in Unusual Program." *The New York Times*, March 12, 1954.

Henahan, Donal. "Chicagoans Play at Carnegie Hall." *The New York Times,* November 13, 1967.

Henahan, Donal. "Despite a Cold, Pavarotti Takes on Otello." *The New York Times*, April 18, 1991.

Henahan, Donal. "Woman Steps in for Solti, Wins Carnegie Hall Ovation." *The New York Times*, November 1, 1977.

Hill, Cheryl Frazes. "The Rehearsal Techniques of Margaret Hillis: Their Development and Application to Brahms's *A German Requiem*." *Choral Journal* 43, no. 2 (October 2002): pp. 9–31.

Hill, Paul. "Paul Hill Letter." *Association of Professional Vocal Ensembles Newsletter* 1, no.1 (October 1978).

Hill, Paul. "The Professional Choir in America: A History and a Report on Present Activity." *Choral Journal* (April 1980).

Hillis, Margaret. "Anton Bruckner's Mass in E minor: A Performer's Guide." *Journal of the Conductor's Guild* (Winter/Fall 2000): pp. 26–30.

Hillis, Margaret. *At Rehearsals*. Brochure. Barrington: Letter Shop, 1969.

Hillis, Margaret. Interview by Norman Pellegrini. Transcribed by Stanley Livengood. Margaret Hillis Collection, Rosenthal Archives of the Chicago Symphony Orchestra Association, October 6, 1997.

Hillis, Margaret. *Master Class Series: The Art of Choral Singing*. VHS. Chicago: Master Class Productions, U.S. Video Corporation.

Hillis, Margaret. Remarks in booklet, *Georg Solti, a City Remembers: Sir Georg Solti: the Chicago Years, 1969–1997* (Chicago: Chicago Symphony Orchestra).

Hillyer, Steven. "Podium Interview with Margaret Hillis." November 20, 1982. Transcription of the interview in the Margaret Hillis Collection, Rosenthal Archives of the Chicago Symphony Orchestra Association.

Hinley, Mary Brown. "The Uphill Climb of Women in American Music: Performers and Teachers." *Music Educators Journal* LXX/8 (April 1984).

Honan, William H. "Council Opposes Making Artists Sign a Pledge." *The New York Times*, August 4, 1990.

Huffman, W. Spencer. *Elwood Haynes, 1857–1925*. Howard County Historical Society, Kokomo, Indiana.

Hyer, Marjorie. "3,000 Sing 'Happy Birthday' to Reagan at Prayer Breakfast." *Washington Post*. February 6, 1981.

J

Jacobson, Bernard. "Civic Scores in Demanding Test." *Chicago Daily News*, May 8, 1972.

Jacobson, Bernard. "Symphony Chorus Gives Soft, Subtle Performance." *Chicago Daily News*, December 16, 1968.

Jagow, Shirley M. "Women Orchestral Conductors in America: The Struggle for Acceptance—An Historical View from the Nineteenth Century to the Present." *Chicago Music Symposium* 38 (October 1, 1998).

J. B. "Bach's B minor Mass Heard at Town Hall." *The New York Times*, April 22, 1953. In Scrapbook #1 of the Margaret Hillis Collection, Rosenthal Archies of the Chicago Symphony Orchestra Association.

Johnson, Harriett. "Rousseau Opera by New Friends." From Words and Music section, *New York Post*, November 10, 1952.

Johnson, Hope. "Smart Girls Tell How to Hit Jackpot." *New York World Telegram and Sun*, February 4, 1954.

Jones, Robert. "Walking into the Fire." *Opera News* XL/14 (February14, 1976).

K

Kastendieck, Miles. "Town Hall: Rameau Opera." *New York Journal America*, April 12, 1954.

Kastor, Elizabeth. "Corcoran Decision Provokes Outcry Cancellation of Photo Exhibit Shocks Some in Arts Community." *Washington Post*, June 14, 1989.

Keene, Dennis. "An Interview with Margaret Hillis." *The American Organist*, January 26, 1992.

Kozin, Allan. "Allen Sven Oxenburg, 64, Dead; American Opera Society Founder." From obituary of Allen Sven Oxenburg, *The New York Times*, late edition, July 7, 1992.

Kraglund, John. "From Choral Triumphs to Orchestral Mastery." *The Globe and Mail*, July 21, 1982.

L

Lanier, Sidney. *Music and Poetry*. New York: C. Scribner's Sons, 1914.

Lawson, Kay D. "Women Orchestral Conductors: Factors Affecting Career Development." Master's thesis. Michigan State University, 1983.

Lazare, Lewis. "At CSO: An Unsung Chorus is Raising Its Voice." *Crains Chicago Business*, June 29, 1987.

L. C. "New York Concert Choir." *Musical Courier*, April 6, 1956.

L. C. "The Concert Choir." *Musical Courier*, February 1, 1953. In Scrapbook #1 of the Margaret Hillis Collection, Rosenthal Archives of the Chicago Symphony Orchestra Association.

Ledger, Jonathan. "Menotti's The Unicorn, The Gorgon and the Manticore: A Study in Artistic Integrity and Sexual Identity." *Choral Journal* 60, no. 10 (May 2020): pp. 37–44.

Lepage, Jane Weiner. *Women Composers, Conductors, and Musicians of the Twentieth Century: Selected Biographies*. N.J. and London: The Scarecrow Press, 1980.

"Letter to the Readers." *Choral and Organ Guide* (February 1953).

Lilley, Helen. Notes from an interview of Margaret Hillis. Archival collection from the Helen Lilley Estate, Howard County Historical Museum.

Livengood, Stanley G. "A History of the Chicago Symphony Chorus, 1957-2000." DMA dissertation. University of Oklahoma, 2001.

Lowens, Irving. "Messiah Makes Season Official." *Washington Star*, December 10, 1976.

M

Macleod, Beth Abelson. *Women Performing Music: The Emergence of American Women as Classical Instrumentalists and Conductors*. Jefferson, NC: McFarland and Company, 1945.

Madrzyk, Anna. "Margaret Hillis, Maker of Music: The Road to Success Has Not Been Easy." *The Sunday Herald Tribune*, December 14, 1980.

"Maestro: P.E.O. Profile." *The P.E.O Record* (May 1983).

Malitz, Nancy. "For Hillis, Chorus Era Is Here." *The Cincinnati Enquirer*, March 30, 1980.

Mann, Alfred. "A Giant Gone: Margaret Hillis Died, Wednesday, February 4, 1998." *The Voice of Chorus America* 21, no. 3 (Spring 1998).

Mann, Alfred. "In Memoriam Margaret Hillis 1921–1998." *American Choral Review* XL, no. 2 (Summer–Fall 1998).

Marsh, Robert. "Austrian Crowds Go Wild as Solti, CSO Excel Again." *Chicago Sun-Times*, September 1, 1989.

Marsh, Robert. "'Do-It-Yourself Messiah' Wonderful, Naturally." *Chicago Sun-Times*, December 11, 1980.

Marsh, Robert. "'Moses and Aaron' a Triumph for Solti." *Chicago Sun-Times*, November 12, 1971.

Marsh, Robert. "Symphony's Chorus Excellent in Concert." *Chicago Sun-Times*, December 2, 1957.

Marsh, Robert. "Verdi Work Nobly Performed by Chicago Symphony, Soloists." *Chicago Sun-Times*, April 4, 1958.

Mathis, Russell. "ACDA's Forty-Year Journey." *The Choral Journal* 40, no. 4 (1999).

McElroy, George, and Jane W. Stedman. "The Chorus Lady." *Opera News*, February 16, 1974.

McLaughlin, Lillian. "Miss Hillis Busy with Choir Here," *Des Moines Tribune*, July 8, 1957.

M. D. L. "Hillis Conducts All-Contemporary Concert." No newspaper title or date in this clipping. In Scrapbook #2 of the Margaret Hillis Collection, Rosenthal Archives of the Chicago Symphony Orchestra Association.

Monson, Karen. "Musician of the Month: Margaret Hillis." *High Fidelity and Musical America* (October 1978).

Monson, Karen. "Sweet 'Brava!' for an Old Pro." *Chicago Daily News*, November 1, 1977.

"Mrs. Purdum To Head County's G.O.P. Women: Club Officers are Elected Thursday in Meeting at Hillis Home." *Kokomo Tribune*, February 2, 1934.

Mueller, Kate Hevner. *Twenty-Seven Major American Symphony Orchestras: A History and Analysis of Their Repertoires, Seasons 1842–43 through 1969–70.* Bloomington: Indiana University Press, 1973.

Mussulman, Joseph A. *Dear People . . . Robert Shaw.* Chapel Hill: Hinshaw Music, 1979.

Myers, Linnet. "CSO Swindle Suspect Must Face the Music." *Chicago Tribune*, August 8, 1987.

N

Nat. "The Concert Choir Town Hall." No information about the publication nor the date. Date would be between January and February 1954. In Scrapbook #1 of the Margaret Hillis Collection, Rosenthal Archives of the Chicago Symphony Orchestra Association.

National Endowment for the Arts, National Council on the Arts. "Annual Report." U.S. Government Printing Office, 1967.

Neisser, Judith. "Hallelujah, Hallelujah: Singing the Praises of Al Booth and His Do-It-Yourself Messiah." *Chicago Magazine*, December 1982.

Nien-hwa-Cheng, Marietta. "Women Conductors: Has the Train Left the Station?" *Harmony: Forum of the Symphony Orchestra Institute*, no. 6 (April 1998), www.soi.org.

O

O'Brian, Jack. "Serious Music." *New York Journal America*, September 16, 1954.

Ogasapian, John, and Lee N. Orr. *Music of the Gilded Age*. Westport, Connecticut: Greenwood Press, 2007.

P

Paige, Paul E. "Choral Institute '68." *Choral Journal* IX, no. 5 (March–April 1969): pp. 20–21.

Panetta, Gary. "Classic by Brahms in Award-Winning Hands." *Journal Star Peoria*, September 6, 1992.

"Passing Perfectly Tranquil, Example of Worthy Womanhood." Obituary. *Kokomo Tribune*, May 31, 1933.

Patner, Andrew. *A Portrait in Four Movements: The Chicago Symphony Under Barenboim, Boulez, Haitink, and Muti*. Chicago: University of Chicago Press, 2019.

Patner, Andrew. "Chorus Founder Remembered." *Chicago Sun-Times*, March 16, 1998.

Perkins, Francis D. "Concert and Recital Choral Music." *New York Herald Tribune*, January 17, 1953.

Perkins, Francis D. "Concert Choir at Town Hall with 'Vocal Chamber Music.'" *New York Herald Tribune*, April 2, 1955.

Petrides, Frédérique Joanne. "Women in Orchestras." *Etude* 56 (July 1938).

P. G. H. "Concert and Recital Margaret Hillis and Choir." *New York Herald Tribune*, March 13, 1953. In Scrapbook #1 of the Margaret Hillis Collection, Rosenthal Archives of the Chicago Symphony Orchestra Association.

P. G. H. "Concert Choir." *Herald Tribune*, May 27, 1952. In Scrapbook #1 of the Margaret Hillis Collection, Rosenthal Archives of the Chicago Symphony Orchestra Association.

P. G. H. "Margaret Hillis." *New York Herald Tribune*, February 21, 1955.

"Press Book for The New York Concert Choir, Margaret Hillis Musical Director and Conductor." David W. Rubin Artists Management.

"Proposal for an Institute for Choral Conductors, Divided into Quarterly Sections, Oriented to Work with Chorus and Orchestra, by Margaret Hillis." Proposal for the Choral Institutes, begun in 1968. (No date.) Perhaps this was an application for funds of the newly formed National Endowment for the Arts. In Margaret Hillis Collection, Rosenthal Archives of the Chicago Symphony Orchestra Association, Box 9.

R

Raven, Seymour. "Symphony to Carry Most of Schedule." *Chicago Daily Tribune*, November 22, 1953.

Reinthaler, Joan. "Margaret Hillis's Nonstop 'Messiah.'" *The Washington Post*, December 15, 1990.

Rice, Patricia. "Big Voice in Choral Singing." *St. Louis Dispatch*, May 19, 1981.

Riger, Rogert P. "Margaret Hillis, Admired Conductor, Spends a Holiday at Oak Bluffs." *Vineyard Gazette*, July 17, 1979.

Robinson, Hal. "An Appreciation of Margaret Hillis." *The Voice of Chorus America* 20 (Summer 1997): pp. 4–16.

Roca, Octavia. "NSO's 'Messiah' Performance: Part 'Hallelujah,' Part 'Humbug.'" *The Washington Times*, December 17, 1990.

Rogers, W. G. "Miss Margaret Hillis Conducts Concert Choir; Also Instructs Navy Fliers." *Newspaper title not available*, July 7, 1954. In Scrapbook #1 of the Margaret Hillis Collection, Rosenthal Archives of the Chicago Symphony Orchestra Association.

Rorem, Ned. *Knowing When to Stop: A Memoir*. New York: Simon and Schuster, 1994.

Rose. "'Concert Tonight,' with New York Concert Orchestra, Margaret Hillis, Conducting, Mitch Miller, Commentator." *Variety*, September 22, 1954. In Scrapbook #2 of the Margaret Hillis Collection, Rosenthal Archives of the Chicago Symphony Orchestra Association.

R. P. "Margaret Hillis Directs Concert Choir Here." *The New York Times*, May 13, 1952. In Scrapbook #1 of the Margaret Hillis Collection, Rosenthal Archives of the Chicago Symphony Orchestra Association.

R. P. "Miss Hillis Leads Opera by Rameau: Concert Choir Ends Season With 'Hippolyte et Aricie,' Said to Be U.S. Premiere." *The New York Times*, April 12, 1954.

R. S. "Concert Choir Town Hall March 12." *Musical America*, March 1953. In Scrapbook #1 of the Margaret Hillis Collection, Rosenthal Archives of the Chicago Symphony Orchestra Association.

S

Sablosky, Irving. "Reiner's Plans for Next Season." *Chicago Daily News*, March 11, 1954.

Sablosky, Irving. "Two Word Review, 'It's Fun' Sums Up Sprightly Orff Music." *Chicago Daily News*, March 18, 1955.

Samuelson, Jane. "For the Love of Music." *Chicago Magazine* (April 1980).

Schickel, Richard. *The World of Carnegie Hall*. New York: Julian Messner, 1960.

Schonberg, Harold C. "Opera: 'Moses and Aaron' in Concert." *The New York Times*, November 22, 1971.

Scott, Eleanor. *The First Twenty Years of the Santa Fe Opera*. Santa Fe: Sunstone Press, 1976.

Shannon, Lena. "Margaret Hillis Concert Well Received Here Saturday." No date or name of the paper indicated from the clipping. In Scrapbook #2 of the Margaret Hillis Collection, Rosenthal Archives of the Chicago Symphony Orchestra Association.

Shaw, Robert. *Dear People*. Chapel Hill: Hinshaw Music, 1979.

Shaw, Robert. "Letters to a Symphony Chorus: Second Thoughts on Amateurism in the Arts (September 25, 1985)." *Choral Journal* (April 1986): pp. 9–10.

Shrock, Dennis. "An Interview with Margaret Hillis on Score Study." *Choral Journal* 31, no. 7 (February 1, 1991).

Sigman, Matthew. "Alice Parker: The Belle of Hawley." *Voice* 35, no. 4 (Summer 2012).

"Sigma Alpha Iota Golden Anniversary Marked at Convention." *Musical Courier*, October 1, 1953. In Scrapbook #1of the Margaret Hillis Collection, Rosenthal Archives of the Chicago Symphony Orchestra Association.

Slade, Francis Fowler. "The Hillis Conducting Seminar: An Appreciation." *The Voice of Chorus America* 20, no. 4 (1997).

Slatkin, Leonard. *Conducting Business: Unveiling the Mystery Behind the Maestro.* Milwaukee: Amadeus Press, 2012.

Smaczny, Jan. "Proms/Jan Smaczny Reviews Berlioz: Polite Devilry." *The Independent*, August 30, 1989.

Solti, Sir Georg. *Memoirs*. New York: Alfred A. Knopf, 1997.

Staff Writer. "Margaret Hillis Unchanged by Fame." *Kokomo Tribune*, February 1, 1979.

Stern, Jonathan. "Music for the (American) People: The Concerts at Lewisohn Stadium, Volume 1, 1922–1964." PhD dissertation. The City University of New York, 2009. Accessed through https://academicworks.cuny.edu/cgi/viewcontent.cgi?article=3282&context=gc_etds.

Stickley, Gustav. "The MacDowell Chorus: A New Music Development in New York." *The Craftsman* 19 (October 1910–March 1911).

Stilwell, Robert Lee. "Concert Choir Program Described as 'Unsuccessful.'" No name of the paper in which it appears, nor the date. Concert took place at Indiana University, and this review is covering that concert. In Scrapbook #2 of the Margaret Hillis Collection, Rosenthal Archives of the Chicago Symphony Orchestra Association.

"Stravinsky: 'Les Noces,' Mass, and Two Motets." *Chicago Sun-Times*, June 27, 1954. In Scrapbook #1 of the Margaret Hillis Collection, Rosenthal Archives of the Chicago Symphony Orchestra Association.

"Stravinsky Les Noces: Mass; Two Motets—Pater Noster and Ave Maria." *Critique: A Monthly Review of Gramophone Records* 6, no. 9 (February 1955). In Scrapbook #2 of the Margaret Hillis, Rosenthal Archives of the Chicago Symphony Orchestra Association.

Sutcliffe, Tom. "The Devil Wins, Sublimely." *Manchester Guardian*, September 1, 1989.

T

Taubman, Howard. "Margaret Hillis Leads Collegiate Chorale in Its Annual Christmas Festival Concert." *The New York Times*, December 16, 1952.

Taubman, Howard. "Music: Mass by Mozart, Margaret Hillis Leads Choir in C-Minor Work." *The New York Times*, March 6, 1956.

Taubman, Howard. "Religion is Theme of Concert Choir: Poulenc's *Exultate Deo*, Bach's *Magnificat in D*, Schubert *Mass*, Sung in Town Hall." *The New York Times*, January 17, 1953.

Terry, Clifford. "Orchestrating the Logistics of the CSO's Trip to Europe." *Chicago Tribune*, August 27, 1989.

Thomson, Virgil. "Music: Concert Choir." *New York Herald Tribune*, January 13, 1954.

Thorpe, Day. "New York Choir's Concert Bridges Loss of 8th Voice." *The Evening Star*, March 5, 1955.

Tindall, Blair. "Call Me Madame Maestro." *The New York Times*, January 14, 2005.

Tuck, Jay Nelson. "On the Air, DuMont's Concert Tonight." *New York Post*, September 29, 1954.

V

Villella, Frank. *Chicago Symphony Orchestra: 125 Moments*. Chicago Symphony Orchestra Association, 2015.

Villella, Frank. "The Founding of the Chicago Symphony Chorus: 'A New Factor in the City's Musical Life.'" Featured in Chicago Symphony Presents, March 2018.

Villella, Frank. "The Making of a Symphony Chorus." *Notebook*, Chicago Symphony Orchestra Program Book, December 4, 5, and 6, 1997–1998.

von Rhein, John. "Georg Solti Begins His Final 2 Years at the Helm of the CSO." *Chicago Tribune*, November 3, 1989.

von Rhein, John. "Hillis Stands on Her Own as a Stand-in for Solti." *Chicago Tribune*, November 3, 1977.

von Rhein, John. "It's Knockout Night in London with 1-2 Punch of CSO, Chorus." *Chicago Tribune*, Overnight section, August 28, 1989.

von Rhein, John. "Mama Chorus a Graceful Swan Song for the CSO's Margaret Hillis." *Chicago Tribune*, September 20, 1992.

von Rhein, John. "Pavarotti, Solti Team Up in a Challenging 'Otello.'" *Chicago Tribune*, April 9, 1991.

von Rhein, John. "Sour Notes at Orchestra Hall," *Chicago Tribune*, September 12, 1993, https://www.chicagotribune.com/news/ct-xpm-1993-09-12-9309120068-story.html.

von Rhein, John. "The Active Voice: Margaret Hillis' Perfectionism Keeps the CSO Singing Arm in Shape." *Chicago Tribune*, April 12, 1987.

von Rhein, John. "Triumphal Tour: Solti's Sweep Through Europe Did CSO Proud." *Chicago Tribune*, September 21, 1989.

W

Wagar, Jeannine. *Conductors in Conversation: Fifteen Contemporary Conductors Discuss Their Lives and Professions*. Boston: G.K. Hall and Co., 1991.

Wakefield, Dan. *New York in the '50s*. New York: Houghton Mifflin Company, 1992.

Wakefield, Dan. *New York in the '50s*. New York: Open Road Integrated Media, 2016, Kindle.

Ward-Griffin, Danielle. "As Seen on TV: Putting the NBC Opera on Stage." *Journal of the American Musicological Society* 71, no. 3 (2018). Accessed April 3, 2021. link.gale.com/apps/doc/A568118601/ITOF?u=scha51546&sid=ITOF&xid=dedde978.

Weaver, Harriet. "Grandpa Haynes Invented Auto but Margaret Hillis Prefers 'Plane." *The World Telephone*, September 22, 1945.

Wilhelm, Imanuel. "Margaret Hillis Directs Group in Contemporary Arts Program." *Daily Illini*, March 15, 1955.

Williams, Donald. "As You See It: Margaret Hillis's Choir Deserves Praise." Editorial written by a graduate opera assistant, School of Music, Indiana University. No name of the paper in which it appears nor the date. Concert took place at Indiana University, and this is the contradictory viewpoint of Robert Stilwell's negative review of that concert. In Scrapbook #2 of the Margaret Hillis Collection, Rosenthal Archives of the Chicago Symphony Orchestra Association.

Williams, Lillian. "Realty Exec Orchestrates Free Concerts." *Chicago Sun-Times*, October 25, 1982.

"Woman Leader Opens Season for Music Guild: Margaret Hillis Brings Choir, Orchestra for Carnegie Hall Charter Concert." *Pittsburgh Post-Gazette*, October 1, 1955.

Z

Zuck, Barbara. "Hillis Conducts for Listeners, Not Lookers." *Columbus Dispatch Weekender*, January 21, 1982.

About the Author

D r. Cheryl Frazes Hill is the Conductor of the Milwaukee Symphony Chorus and the Associate Conductor of the Chicago Symphony Chorus (CSC). Beginning as a member of the CSC in 1976, Margaret Hillis appointed Frazes Hill to the CSC conducting staff in 1987. Frazes Hill has served as professor of music at Roosevelt University's Chicago College of Performing Arts since 2002. A frequent guest conductor, Frazes Hill is a published writer for national education and choral journals on topics of her research in music education and choral conducting. She is married to Dr. Gary Hill, and they have two children, Carlyn and Mitchell.

(Todd Rosenberg, photographer)

INDEX